The Structure of Scientific Articles

CSLI Studies in Computational Linguistics

This series covers all areas of computational linguistics and language technology, with a special emphasis on work which has direct relevance to practical applications, makes formal advances, and incorporates insights into natural language processing from other fields, especially linguistics and psychology. Books in this series describe groundbreaking research or provide an accessible and up-to-date overview of an area for nonspecialists. Also included are works documenting freely available resources for language processing, such as software, grammars, dictionaries, and corpora.

Series edited by Ann Copestake

CSLI Studies in
Computational Linguistics

The Structure of Scientific Articles

Applications to Citation Indexing and Summarization

Simone Teufel

Center for the Study of
Language and Information
Stanford, California

Center for the Study of Language and Information
Leland Stanford Junior University
Printed in the United States
14 13 12 11 10   1 2 3 4 5

Library of Congress Cataloging-in-Publication Data

Teufel, Simone.
The structure of scientific articles : applications to citation indexing and summarization / Simone Teufel.

p. cm. – (CSLI studies in computational linguistics)

Includes bibliographical references and index.

ISBN 978-1-57586-555-3 (cloth : alk. paper) –
ISBN 978-1-57586-556-0 (pbk. : alk. paper)

1. Information resources management–Abstracting and indexing.
2. Information technology–Abstracting and indexing.
3. Computational linguistics. 4. Abstracts. I. Title. II. Series.

T58.64.T43 2010
808′.062–dc22

2010002905

CIP

∞ The acid-free paper used in this book meets the minimum requirements of the American National Standard for Information Sciences—Permanence of Paper for Printed Library Materials, ANSI Z39.48-1984.

CSLI was founded in 1983 by researchers from Stanford University, SRI International, and Xerox PARC to further the research and development of integrated theories of language, information, and computation. CSLI headquarters and CSLI Publications are located on the campus of Stanford University.

CSLI Publications reports new developments in the study of language, information, and computation. Please visit our web site at
http://cslipublications.stanford.edu/
for comments on this and other titles, as well as for changes and corrections by the author and publisher.

Contents

Historical Overview and Acknowledgements

The ideas in this book evolved over more than 10 years and in collaboration with many people. Books don't follow the chronological course of events, so I will give a short overview of the timing of different versions of ideas, code, data and experiments, and of who helped me.

Argumentative Zoning (AZ) is the annotation scheme which was developed during my PhD at the University of Edinburgh between 1996 and 1999. This was the start of the research in this book. The original code of the AZ system was written during this time, the first version of the corpus now called CmpLG-D (see section 5.1) was compiled in the summer of 1996 in collaboration with Byron Georgantopolous, and the first AZ experiments (see sections 8.3 and 12.1) were performed then. My work during this time owes a huge amount to Marc Moens, who was an ideal supervisor. His sharp mind, good ideas and general enthusiasm helped me enormously throughout my PhD. I also profited very much from my unofficial second supervisor, Jean Carletta, who taught me about annotation methodology, rigorous scientific writing, and many other things. I want to thank my annotators, Vasilis Karaiskos and Anne Wilson, for their skilful and diligent work. The scientific atmosphere at the Center for Cognitive Science was stimulating and cooperative, and I had many great discussions with the staff there, especially Claire Grover, Chris Brew, Colin Mattheson and Jon Oberlander. During the final stages of the thesis, Paul Taylor and Andrei Mikheev helped me test and run the HMM and Maximum Entropy versions of AZ, respectively. Roughly around the same time Chris Paice, from the Computer Science department of the University of Lancaster, kindly gave me his corpus of agriculture articles (see section 5.3) which I often use for comparative purposes.

In 2000–1, I worked at the Computer Science Department at Columbia University in New York in Kathleen McKeown's group, mainly on things not directly related to the topic of this book: medical information extraction and multi-document summarisation. In project Parsival, the format of the original CmpLG corpus was reused to create a large medical corpus, in joint work with Noemie Elhadad (Teufel and Elhadad, 2002). This corpus format has since been further developed and applied to corpora in other disciplines, and is today called the SciXML format (Rupp et al., 2006). The freely available part of the Parsival corpus (cf. section 5.3) later served as one of the comparative corpora for the development of the discourse model of this book (KCDM). I also improved the AZ feature recognition module during that time, as reported in Teufel and Moens (2002), compiled the 352-article CmpLG corpus, and extrinsically evaluated the performance of extracts based on AZ in a search task (section 12.2; Teufel, 2001).

Since 2001 I have held a permanent position at the Computer Laboratory at Cambridge University. Our group, the Natural Language and Information Processing (NLIP) group, has been working on e-science and scientific information access in several disciplines, including chemistry and genetics. The CitRAZ project (GR/S27832/01) was an EPSRC-funded First Grant project running from February 2004 – January 2007, which resulted in an annotation scheme for citation function classification (CFC; Teufel et al., 2006b) and a machine classifier for it (Teufel et al., 2006a). This was joint work with Advaith Siddharthan and Dan Tidhar. A SciXML version of the entire ACL Anthology was also created during this time (see section 14.4). Bill Hollingsworth wrote the PDF-to-SciXML converter, Anna Ritchie developed a more sophisticated recogniser of citations and reference items, and Don Tennant rewrote the software for the linguistic preprocessing of the AZ corpus. AZ-related ideas are also used in the BBSRC-project FlySlip (BBS/B/16291), to support the scientific curation procedure of genetic information in the FlyBase Database.

Various other projects around AZ also took place in Cambridge: Valeria Feltrim, a PhD student from the University of Sao Paulo, visited our group during the summer of 2003 and ported the AZ feature recognition module to Portuguese. She used the AZ module for a writing tool which criticises students' writing style (Feltrim et al., 2005). Yoko Mizuta visited my group in Cambridge, and we discussed her AZ-type adaptation to biomedical text. And research with Rashid Abdalla, which originated as an MPhil project, lead to a recogniser module for scientific meta-discourse (Abdalla and Teufel, 2006). I would also like to thank Jochen Schwarze for the implementation of the first version of the XSLT/JSP-based annotation tool for CFC, which has served me very well since 2004 and has since also been used for AZ-II.

In the past few years, I have developed a discourse model which underlies both AZ and CFC, and which understands both of these as exemplars of a larger family of annotation schemes, which cover various phenomena centred around knowledge claims and argumentation. This book is the first attempt to explain the theoretical ideas behind this model, some of which already occur in embryonic form in my thesis.

Evidence is now mounting that AZ is applicable to other scientific disciplines, and this is where my current work lies. With my colleague Ann Copestake I am involved in the EPSRC project SciBorg (RG41794), which aims to extract different types of information from chemistry papers. An important aspect of SciBorg is the use of a general, semantic representation for all types of processing: RMRS (Copestake, 2003, 2009). Work with Colin Batchelor from the Royal Society of Chemistry (RSC) and Advaith Siddharthan on SciBorg has also been very productive and enjoyable. We developed AZ-II, another variant of the family of annotation schemes described here, for a wide range of chemistry papers (see section 13.1.2), demonstrated reliability, and are currently re-adapting the AZ-II guidelines to computational linguistics. Colin Batchelor has been indispensable as the expert for the "expert-trained non-expert" method, as one of his many roles on the project. In other work with Advaith Siddharthan on SciBorg, we showed how a form of anaphora resolution can help improve AZ (Siddharthan and Teufel, 2007).

Of my students' work, Anna Ritchie's PhD on citation-based IR is most closely connected to the research in this book. She studied how citation-based information can be combined with current IR techniques. Using a citation indexed version of the ACL Anthology she created, she showed that IR results improve if one indexes keywords extracted from the area around citations in a citing document, and associates them with the cited paper. Her experimental methodology involved the creation of a test collection with queries and relevance judgements, which were made by the authors of the conferences ACL-05 and HLT/NAACL-05.

I am also collaborating with Min-Yen Kan from the National University of Singapore. His group has built and is maintaining a digital library which incorporates several prototype information access methods based on natural language processing. In this larger framework, we are currently incorporating a robust form of AZ into the digital library, which can process texts that are in less informative formats than SciXML, e.g., the output of standard PDF-to-text converters.

The challenges here are how to adapt the features when the linguistic information available is imperfect.

In general, I would like to thank my co-workers in the NLIP group for many stimulating discussions over the years. The Computer Laboratory is an exceptionally free and productive research environment. I also thank the Human Communication Research Centre (HCRC) and the Institute for Communicating and Collaborative Systems (ICCS) at the University of Edinburgh, where I wrote the first draft of this book during my sabbatical leave in 2006, and Manabu Okumura, who hosted me for a sabbatical at Tokyo Institute of Technology, where it was finally finished.

With respect to the production of this book, my sincere thanks go to my excellent editor Ann Copestake. Many thanks also to Anna Ritchie for proofreading it so thoroughly.

1

Introduction

This book presents a discourse model for research articles, which describes the articles' structure in terms of scientific argumentation and rhetoric. It is theoretical in that it models and explains general linguistic phenomena, but it is also practical in that it is implemented and demonstrably improves performance in real-world information management applications. It robustly analyses naturally occurring text from two scientific disciplines, and should be relatively easily expandable to others.

I consider this work to contribute to the area of text understanding. However, this book does not contain any mention of ontologies or other representations of scientific content at all. No logical forms will be manipulated, and in fact, the science in the article will be left well alone. Instead, my approach tries to make sense of all the other, non-subject-matter information contained in the article, such as the physical and logical structure. It turns out that this is enough for some interesting tasks in the real world, so that full text understanding can be avoided.

This is certainly an unusual working hypothesis for something that calls itself a text understanding approach, so some explanation is in order. I will start by defining more clearly what I mean by "text understanding".

1.1 Text Understanding and Information Management

Text comprehension, i.e., the question of how to make machines "understand" what a text in natural language means, is one of the hardest and most exciting tasks of artificial intelligence (AI). My definition of full text comprehension is for an automatic process to read and represent all the contents of a text, in such a way that it can later manipulate this content, reason with it, and enter into a dialogue about it with another intelligent process. A solution to text comprehension would get us closer to the question of what the human mind does when it generates or understands language.

From a more practical viewpoint, text comprehension is also a prerequisite to building intelligent language agents. It has thus been a core interest in computational linguistics, artificial intelligence and cognitive science, and driven much research, particularly in the AI community in the 70s and early 80s. There is a large body of early, groundbreaking work in AI on text understanding (Winograd, 1972, Schank and Abelson, 1977, Lehnert, 1981), which presents several solutions to how knowledge could be recognised and represented.

However, this type of research used short and simple texts, many of which were artificially created. The solutions did not scale up when researchers ventured from heavily simplified micro-worlds (such as Winograd's *BlockWorld*) into the jungle of unrestricted arbitrary text: "real" language simply proved far too complex to be formalised in this way. Today, there is a consensus that a full analysis of the meaning of every individual statement in unrestricted text is impossible with current technology. The big advances in computational linguistics in the past 25 years, in terms of better parsers, large-scale distributional and robust semantics and many others, have still not been able to change this in principle. Not a single automatic process exists which is able to "understand" arbitrary text in that sense, and many breakthroughs in pragmatics, semantics and knowledge representation will be necessary before it will.

There are partial solutions to the text comprehension problem: for instance, Hahn et al. (1995), Schulz and Hahn (2005) augment traditional summarisation with domain knowledge from ontologies, and fact extraction methods can provide sophisticated representations of knowledge in a well-defined domain. There, the task is to filter huge amounts of previously unseen text to find entities of a particular, predefined semantic type, e.g., "perpetrator of terrorist attack". However, the texts treated, while unadulterated, are still from a narrow domain (such as reports of terrorist activity).

My approach, which aims at extracting information about discourse structure, i.e., logical and form-based phenomena, is an alternative method of partial text comprehension. For instance, consider Fig. 1, which shows a sketch of some steps of argumentation in a scientific article. This sketch does not contain the final language of the article, but is a possible intermediate step, a draft the author may have used during writing.

Any mention of the scientific content is removed from this sketch, but what is left is enough to gain a rough overview of the article.

Abstract

1. Introduction

S-0 *There has been a long-standing interest in the field of **F** in the problem of **Z**...*
S-2 *In particular, **X (1999)** tried to solve **Z** by ...* **S-4** ***Y (2002)** tried to expand that model but ran into huge problems with efficiency.* **S-5** *We will address their efficiency problem here.* **S-6** *In particular, we will investigate the use of **M** ...*
S-10 *Our method for **M** uses **Q**'s (1956) methodology.* **S-11** *Adaptations of this method include...*
S-20 *We then evaluate our system by ...,*

2. Q's methodology

3. A faster algorithm

S-64 *In this paper, we present an efficient method of addressing **Z**.*

4. Evaluation

5. Discussion

6. Conclusions

S-112 *We have shown that our system is more efficient than **Y's (2002)** on the problem of **Z**.* **S-113** *Our solution is based on **Q's (1956)** work and was tested on a corpus of...*

FIGURE 1 Structure of a Scientific Article.

For instance, we can see that the authors contribute a solution to the problem of Z (whatever Z may be), because we can guess that S-64 must be the main goal statement (S-64). We can also see how the article relates to previous work (it improves over Y's approach). Headlines, phrases such as *"in this paper, we present"*, and the location of citations and personal pronouns are stylistic, structural and argumentational information which are instantly recognisable to scientists reading an article, even in a discipline other than their own.

There are information management situations where understanding the article at this sketchy level is enough. For instance, a user who wants to read about further developments of Y's method should definitely find this article relevant. It would be even better if they were directly pointed to sections 2 and 3. In order to know that these sections are plausible locations for the information about Y in the article, we do not need to know what the problem Z is, nor do we need to understand any details of the authors' improvement.

The sketchy structural information could also be used to jump over certain textual segments that a user is currently *not* interested in – for instance, many segments are too detailed for a non-expert reader trying to gain an overview of a new scientific field. For instance, if a segment starts with *Our algorithm* and continues with only first-person pronouns, it can be safely omitted from reading in that situation. However, when we notice that this segment has come to an end – e.g., because the text resumes talking about general problems and solutions in the field – our user should start paying attention again, because such statements are likely to be of interest to her.

Another theme explored in this book is the connection between scientific argumentation and authors' affect towards citations. I will argue in chapter 2 that a search engine supporting relation-based searches would improve today's digital library environments. A user who searches for differences between an article and its rivals should be presented with sentence S-5 by such a search engine. Knowledge about the author's argumentation strategy can help predict where rival work is most likely to be found in the article; the search engine should thus take it into account. (Of course, to the user, the argumentation strategy in the article is not of any interest; they only care about their information need.)

In all these cases, what is being "understood" about the article is something about the status of statements in the rhetorical, stylistic, argumentational organisation of the text, not the statements themselves. As a result, the output of a system such as I am proposing here would not consist of any actual scientific knowledge, but only of a guide *towards* the scientific knowledge. This is similar to how a non-expert might approach this problem: they can take away high-level information from an article even if they do not understand its scientific details, and this information is usually more valuable to them than the details.

In fact, I propose that the processing of a text by a human non-expert is a meaningful model at an intermediate depth of text comprehension. The aim would then be to build a machine which "understands" something about all scientific articles (like a non-expert would), rather than a machine that understands all of the science contained in a small set of specialised articles (like an expert would). The shallower text understanding tool has the advantage that it is not limited to articles of a particular research type or discipline, and that its construction does not require the encoding of a large amount of scientific knowledge in some specialised format.

The price to pay is that the level of comprehension in such a purely structural analysis is rather modest. But the analysis would still accomplish a non-trivial abstraction over information coming from arbitrary texts with arbitrary scientific content and contributions. While it cannot tell us anything about higher-level human comprehension such as reasoning with scientific facts, it might tell us something about the *general* linguistic and logical processes that humans employ when writing and reading text.

The analysis would also be able to support practical information management tasks, because even without understanding the science, it can identify pieces of information which should be interesting to a human searcher. In a modern digital library setting, where the amount of text available to be searched is so large that humans cannot possibly inspect all of it, even imperfect system performance is often acceptable – as long as a system returns, amongst the errors, enough material of interest. Whether this point is reached cannot be judged by looking at the system output in isolation; an empirical evaluation in an information management situation is necessary. The system presented here will be tested in this way in chapter 12.

After this rough outline of how an intermediate-depth text comprehension system might generally approach its task, let us take a look at the linguistic phenomena that could provide guidance to it.

1.2 Discourse Structure and Scientific Argument

A core theoretical question for my approach concerns the right definition of discourse structure for scientific articles. Discourse structure refers to any type of structuring and ordering in a text above the sentence level. All coherent texts possess some kind of higher-level structuring, but there are differing views about what the most important factors are.

It is known that structuring principles differ from genre to genre.[1] For instance, in news and narrative text, the main structuring principle is the time-line, even if there may be counteracting devices such as stories within stories and flashbacks. In news stories, the structure is "pyramid-shaped", with the main events mentioned early and then further elaborated on in each layer, so that the reader can stop reading at any point in the story and still take away the main points.

The kind of discourse structure for scientific text that I am interested in here is rhetorical; it concerns which role each piece of text plays in the scientific argument. I will start with three general observations that can be linked to structure in this sense:

- **Observation 1:** Scientific discourse contains many descriptions of positive and negative states.

[1] I will use the terms *genre* and *text type* synonymously in this book.

- **Observation 2:** Scientific discourse contains many mentions of other researchers and their scientific contributions.
- **Observation 3:** Scientific discourse is the outcome of a rhetorical game, the goal of which is the promotion of one's own new research.

Let us start with Observation 1, the important role that positive and negative states play in scientific text. For instance, authors often express sentiment towards cited work:

> *For these reasons numerous Tröger's base derivatives have been prepared ...*(2,3,5).[2] *However, some of the above methodologies possess* ***tedious*** *work-up procedures or include relatively* ***strong reaction conditions*** *... with* ***poor to moderate yields****, as is the case for analogues* **4** *and* **5**.[3] (b200862a)

All example sentences used in this book come from real corpora, which are introduced in chapter 5. In the following, examples from the chemistry corpus (see section 5.2) are identified by the article number, which starts with "b", whereas examples from the computational linguistics corpus (see section 5.1) are characterised by the paper's CmpLG number and the sentence number according to my processing.

In the above example sentence, I have highlighted the negative indicators (some of which might sound somewhat unusual to a non-chemist, e.g., *tedious* or *strong conditions*); these make clear that the approach is being criticised. Such critical affect towards previous work often occurs in the motivation section of an article.

Let us now look at a positive context:

> *The OH BDE values of a series of alkyl- and alkoxy-substituted phenols have been* ***precisely*** *determined by Pedulli and coworkers ...*(24). *This method gives* ***accurate*** *BDE values relative to a reference compound, 2,4,6-tri-tert-butyl phenol. We have utilized this experimental data to evaluate the model for BDE determination ...* (b515712a)

Although the praise is not strong (*accurate, precisely*), the fact that the authors are using Pedulli et al.'s approach is an additional indication of positive stance.

---

[2] In many chemistry publications, footnote markers indicate references. In this book, in order to distinguish them from the real footnotes, I will place brackets around chemistry-style reference footnote markers.

[3] Chemical compound reference numbers are shown in bold face, following convention in chemistry publications. Such numbers point to a chemical compound defined elsewhere in the article.

The following examples of criticism and praise from computational linguistics show that Observation 1 holds across disciplines. Here, criticism is often expressed by subtle means; for instance, any hint at unclarity in a computational linguistics article is an unmistakable signal that something is amiss:

> *Previous parser comparisons . . . [Tom87, BL89, Sha89, BvN93, MK93]. It is* ***not clear*** *that these results scale up to reflect accurately the behaviour of parsers using realistic, complex unification-based grammars. . . .* (9405033, S-5/S-6)

> *The technical vehicle previously used to extract the specialized grammar is explanation-based generalization (EBG) [Mit86]. The EBG scheme has previously proved most* ***successful*** *for tuning a natural-language grammar to a specific application domain and thereby achieve* ***very much faster*** *parsing, at the cost of a small reduction in coverage.* (9405022, S-162/163)

Other positive and negative states that systematically and frequently occur in scientific discourse concern the situation in the research field as a whole, and in particular concepts such as problems and solutions, advantages and disadvantages of approaches, and the desirability or otherwise of situations. As far as their own work is concerned, the authors are of course biased and tend to describe positive aspects of their work, such as novelty and contributions to the field. Another interesting aspect is that good and bad states are often described in terms of successful and unsuccessful problem-solving processes.

The fact that negative and positive states areprevalent in scientific text should be of advantage, as automatic machinery for robustly recognising semantics at that level of abstraction exists, e.g., in the area of sentiment classification (e.g., Pang et al., 2002, Wilson et al., 2009). Another prominent type of statement in this category is the direct comparison to competitors which also has clear linguistic signals.

Observation 2 concerns the contributors of scientific ideas. A scientific article is a sequence of descriptions of ideas, as in the following:

> *Telomeres exist at the ends of eukaryotic chromosomes and can protect the chromosomes. . .*

> *Recently, many G-quadruplex stabilizers have been synthesized and studied . . . by many groups.*[(7a–c,8a–b,9a–b)] . . .

> *However, few reports of corroles in medicinal or biological applications have been published.*[(11a–d)]

> *In this paper, we shall report our synthesis of cationic corrole derivatives* ***3*** *and* ***5*** *. . .* (b704599a)

Concerning the scientific ideas, there is a progression from the more general to the more specific scientific area, finally leading to the specific research topic that the authors address. The first paragraph consists of background statements about telomeres. As these are (assumed to be) generally known, the authors do not associate anybody in particular with their contribution to the body of scientific knowledge. Citations 7a–9b, however, in the second paragraph, are associated with research that is quite similar to the authors'; the reference list at the end of the paper tells us who "owns" these ideas.

After citation 11d we reach the place in the article where the authors themselves come into appearance for the first time, and where they describe their own contribution. This place is often marked with a phrase such as "*in this paper...*". It is a special place in the article for several reasons, as we shall see.

I propose that it is possible to identify segments in the text which are defined by who owns the ideas being described. Other researchers are a prominent group of "idea owners", but it is clear who the most important group from the point of view of the authors is – they must style themselves as the owners of the new research ideas in the article, and will therefore dedicate large segments of the text to these. There are also segments that nobody in particular is associated with, as the ideas associated with them are in the common domain.

The question why other people's ideas are mentioned at all in an article ties in with Observation 3, which concerns the rhetorical game of defending the legitimacy of a new scientific claim. The authors need to show that their research leads to a more positive situation for science overall. What the authors will say is rather predictable: at a grossly oversimplified level, they will set up a competition between "us" (the authors) vs. "them" (other researchers). In doing so, they will portray other researchers in fixed roles, e.g., as rivals, as contributors to the solution, or as very dissimilar so that only a vague comparison is warranted. This will lead to mentions of other researchers (as per Observation 2), and in particular to rhetorical statements about negative and positive states (as per Observation 1).

The model I will develop describes how a scientific argument breaks down into rhetorical goals, each roughly corresponding to a speech act. One of the relevant observations in this respect is that certain sequences of such rhetorical goals are more likely than others. For instance, problem descriptions are often followed by a statement of the authors' research goal:

> *A problem not fully explored yet is how to arrive at an optimal choice of tree-cutting criteria. In the previous scheme, these must be specified manually, and the choice is left to the designer's intuitions. This article addresses the problem of automating this process and presents a method where the nodes to cut at are selected automatically using the information-theoretical concept of entropy.* (9405022, S-17/S-19)

> *However, some of the above methodologies possess tedious work-up procedures or include relatively strong reaction conditions . . . with poor to moderate yields, as is the case for analogues* **4** *and* **5**. *Considering these potential applications, we now report a simple synthetic method for the preparation of 5,12-dialkyl-3,10-diaryl-1,3,4,8,10,11-hexaazatetracyclo[6.6.1.0^{2,6}.0^{9,13}]pentadeca-2(6),4,9(13),11-tetraenes* **8a–e** *and 4,12-dimethoxy-1,3,5,9,11,13-hexaazatetracyclo[7.7.1.0^{2,7}.0^{10,15} heptadeca-2(7),3,10(15),11-tetraene-6,14-diones* **10a,b** *based on the reaction of 3-alkyl-5-amino-1-arylpyrazoles* **6** *and 6-amino-pyrimidin-4(3H)-ones* **9** *with formaldehyde in ethanol and catalytic amounts of acetic acid.* (b200862a)

In my approach, such indicators and regularities are modelled by features (see chapter 10), which are used for machine learning (see chapter 11). Citations are another important aspect, in particular the relationship between the cited work and the current article.

I restrict the analysis to scientific articles, and in particular to the experimental sciences. Two aspects of scientific discourse are of advantage for the automatic recognition of rhetorical structure: formulaic language and top-down rhetorical expectations. In terms of formulaic language, authors of scientific articles use recurrent headlines (e.g., "Methods") and fixed phrases (e.g., "*in this paper, we will show*", and "*an ANOVA revealed an interaction*"). Such phrases are called *meta-discourse*, and they will form an important theme of this book.

Secondly, there are strong *a priori* expectations and conventions in science about how the scientific content of the article should be "packaged up": for instance, one commonly sees statements that a given piece of research is novel and significant and urgently needed in its field. Both these aspects are used for recognition in my approach.

1.3 Outline of this Book

This book is an exploration of how much meaning can be automatically recovered from scientific articles using only structural and stylistic features. It will advocate a shallow kind of text comprehension which solves a practical search task, can be automated using current technology, but which avoids the complexities of full text comprehension.

A core concept of this book is discourse structure, which will be developed in chapter 6. My definition of discourse structure is closely connected to scientific argumentation, and I have already in this introduction touched upon some of the aspects that are central to it: scientific articles often contain affect and sentiment, both towards other people and towards the authors's own work, that who owns an idea is an important concept in the exposition, and that the writing of an article is akin to a rhetorical "game" where the existence of one's research needs to be justified.

The practical aim of this book is to support new and better types of information access, which succinctly point out similarities and differences between related scientific articles. The next three chapters are therefore dedicated to issues concerning information management in science. Chapter 2 reviews the foundations in the field of information retrieval and citation indexing; chapter 3 does the same for summarisation. In chapter 4, I will suggest two new kinds of information access, which rely on information about the rhetorical structure of the scientific argument. This information would be determined automatically and offline before search time.

Chapter 5 discusses the text corpora used in this book. The main scientific discipline I will be working with is computational linguistics, but some of my more recent research is on chemistry texts.

To define a discourse model that supports the tasks suggested in chapter 4 is the theoretical aim of this book. Chapter 6 develops such a discourse model, the *Knowledge Claim Discourse Model* (KCDM). An important motivation for it is Swales' (1990) theory of communicative acts in scientific writing. I additionally define other structuring principles in scientific discourse, including a segmentation according to the ownership of ideas, rhetorical moves about problem-solving, and the rhetorical function of citations. This results in a multi-layered discourse model.

Chapter 7 defines three annotation tasks based on the discourse model. The first, called *Knowledge Claim Attribution* (KCA), concerns the segmentation of the text according to who owns the knowledge claim for this segment. The second, called *Citation Function Classification* (CFC), determines the function that a citation plays in the scientific argumentation. The third, called *Argumentative Zoning* (AZ), combines several phenomena described in the KCDM. Chapter 8 empirically tests the three annotation schemes, by measuring the agreement between decisions arrived at independently by different human judges.

The schemes' categories are intricately connected to their surface indicators, which are described in chapter 10. The most important features are based on meta-discourse; chapter 9 describes this phenomenon in detail. Chapter 11 concerns the implementation of AZ, KCA and CFC. The features defined in chapter 10 are automatically determined for unknown text; on the basis of these features, supervised machine learning methods classify the sentence. The quality of the systems' output is evaluated in chapter 12. The first evaluation method is intrinsic: the automatically determined argumentative zones are compared with human-generated gold standard zones. The second is extrinsic: the usefulness of the rhetorical extracts is measured in an information management task with human subjects.

Chapter 13 discusses how far the model presented here requires changes when new disciplines are processed. This is an important question, because one of the claims of the discourse model is that its observations hold across scientific disciplines. The chapter also describes the adaptation of AZ to other languages and genres.

Any description of a larger research effort such as this one can only ever be a snapshot. Chapter 14 will discuss currently ongoing research projects in the framework of this research, including some new applications of the discourse model beyond summarisation and citation indexing. Chapter 15 will then summarise the contributions and limitations of this work.

Let us start now with the question of information access to the scientific literature, a problem faced by researchers on a daily basis.

2

Information Retrieval and Citation Indexes

The starting point of this book is scientific information management – how do scientists search the literature, and which tools are available to help them find what they need?

Information management is the science of organising information in such a way that users can efficiently access it. Anybody who is faced with enormous masses of information needs some form of information management. This certainly applies to scientists, and to anybody searching the scientific literature. Scientists must keep themselves up to date with new developments in their field. To do so, they regularly read articles in journals (and in some fields, in conferences as well) which report new developments in their field. In many disciplines the body of scientific knowledge is enormously large and growing very fast. For instance, the database PUBMED (`http://www.ncbi.nlm.nih.gov/pubmed/`) indexes over 18.6 million articles from the life sciences, currently covering a total of 21,253 journals. New conferences, journals and other publications spring into existence almost daily and expand the repository of scientific knowledge further.

These masses of information make it impossible for most scientists to read or even just skim-read all potentially relevant material. One way of dealing with this problem is to read *summary journals*. These are journals published by secondary publishers, which contain a large number of summaries of current articles in a range of journals in their area, rather than the full articles themselves. Another way is to use *keyword searches* on material which is indexed by an information retrieval engine. *Subject indexes* and subject headings (e.g., the US National Library's Medical Subject Headings (MeSH, `http://www.nlm.nih.gov/mesh/`) can also be used, which associate a manually-assigned semantic label with the document. Another tool one can use is the *citation index*. Citation indexes keep a record of who cites whom. They therefore allow for a type of search that does not require keywords, because related articles can be found by following citation links instead.

These are the main three ways of information management for the scientific literature commonly used today.

Searches in the scientific literature are not only done by experts, but also by non-scientists and inexperienced scientists. Non-scientists who need access to the scientific literature include industrial developers, funding agency employees, science reporters who turn to the primary literature for evidence to back up a story, and many others. Scientists, too, are non-expert at certain points in their career, i.e., in the early stages, or when moving sideways into a new field. I have a particular interest in non-expert users and how they are served in the information management landscape.

After looking at scientists' information needs in section 2.1, I will consider how well the information management tools currently available fulfil these needs: keyword-based search is examined in section 2.2, search by citation links in section 2.3, and summaries in chapter 3.

2.1 Information Needs in Science

All searches start with an *information need*. Information needs are preverbal constructs in the searcher's mind; for instance, a user may want to know how the Maximum Entropy algorithm works, or what the latest developments in active learning are. Searching the scientific literature is a special case of general search because scientists have different information needs from those of general users:

- Scientists require very deep and specialised knowledge of their field. This includes information which is hard to formalise, e.g., the information of which method is preferred by which research group.
- Their searches are often concerned with relationships between ideas.

Let us look at these aspects in turn. An experienced scientist has accumulated a large amount of knowledge about their speciality over the years. They know the main problems, evaluation methodologies, and influential approaches in a field, along with their strengths and weaknesses. It is also important for them to know about other scientists in their field: influential researchers, their specialities and methodologies, and which institutions or *schools of thought* they belong to. Bazerman (1985) coins the metaphor of a *research map* to describe the conceptual network of informal knowledge about a research field that experienced scientists have acquired. (He observed physicists; Charney

(1993) chronicles a similar situation for evolutionists.) Bazerman describes the acquisition of a research map by physicists as something that happens vicariously, effortlessly, and over a long time, by reading, through research, at conferences, and by discussions with colleagues.

Concerning the second point, the publication of research demands that scientists relate their own results and methods to the literature, and in particular to recent developments. Relationships are therefore extremely important to them (Shum, 1998, Mercer et al., 2004). At different stages of the research and writing process, different types of relationships need to be explored.

A particular statement or claim in a scientist's article might require *supportive* published evidence. The first thing they need to find out is if the claim has been made at all in print. If they use a search engine, it must either locate the source if it exists, so that they can cite it, or else convince the researcher that it really has not been published yet. Even if a particular article is already suspected to be the source of the claim, a check is often still necessary, because the original idea may go further back than the article the scientist knows about.

A scientist may also want to find out what impact a certain piece of published evidence had in the field (Shum, 1998). Several things could have happened to an (older) idea or claim – more recent work may still maintain it (possibly with additional evidence), or it may have produced some counter-evidence. Alternatively, and overall far more probable, the idea may also have died a quiet death.

Another important relationship-based search is for contrastive works. Scientists must know who cites their own work negatively, or more generally, how any approach in their field is criticised and what it is compared to. This could include searches for rival approaches, for contradictory evidence to some work, and for the particular aspect that constitutes the difference between similar approaches.

While we may imagine that experienced researchers, supported by their research map, can perform relationship-based searches more or less well, how about searchers with less expertise? According to Kircz (2001), such users are interested in the general aspects in the new field that might be of use for their own investigations. Specialist detail is not yet important to them, and jargon may still be largely unknown. The questions such searchers pose are often not precise (e.g., *"what are they doing in high-temperature super-conductivity?"*. Oddy et al. (1992) and Shum (1998) argue that partially-informed readers particularly need an embedding of the particular piece of work within a broader context and in relation to other works. The best information source is often an experienced colleague or a review article. In the many situations where neither is available, an automatic search tool should actively support novices during their learning process in the new field, in order to accelerate the acquisition of their mental research map. This is one of the motivations behind this book.

The rest of this chapter will look at what there is in terms of state-of-the-art information management tools for the scientific literature, be it for expert or novice scientists or non-scientists. The following section will start with an overview of information retrieval and introduce some of the concepts which we will require later on.

2.2 Keyword-Based Search

The task of an information retrieval (IR) engine is to find a good mapping between the user's query and the most relevant documents in the document set "known" to the IR engine, i.e., *indexed* by it. A key assumption behind keyword-based information retrieval is that all information needs can be adequately expressed in two formal languages, the *query language* and the *index language*, which consist of keywords and sometimes some other constructs.

Indexing is the process of associating the index language, which is an internal representation language, with a document, i.e., of describing the article using keywords. Likewise, the query is represented by the terms of the query language. The IR system then correlates the query (i.e., the representation of the information need) with terms of the index language (i.e., the representation of the documents), using one of a set of possible mathematical manipulations.

While manual indexing has been done for centuries,[4] automatic indexing as a method originates in the 1950s and 60s. Here, the system chooses keywords from the document, if it is electronically available, or from a *document surrogate* such as the title of an article or its summary otherwise. Document surrogates are shorter characterisations of the article which capture an important aspect of the meaning of the document and can therefore stand in for it during IR. A large IR literature on the relative usefulness of different document surrogates and indexing languages has accrued from the 1960s onwards (see the overview in Spärck Jones and Willett, 1997).

Which material a searcher can search over depends on the machine-readability of the document surrogate, rather than that of the document itself. Library catalogues tend to index only title, author and journal. When the full text is not available, as for most books and

[4]For instance, in the 17th century, Samuel Pepys devised a subject index covering the entire content of the 1000+ books in his private library.

dissertations, specialised search engines index the summaries instead (e.g., MEDLINE, http://medline.cos.com/, Bath Information and Data Services (BIDS, http://www.bids.ac.uk/), Inspec (http://www.theiet.org/publishing/inspec/), PsychInfo (http://www.apa.org/psycinfo/)). In scientific fields where most articles are made available on the world wide web, searchers can additionally use standard search engines such as Yahoo (http://uk.yahoo.com/) or Google (Brin and Page, 1998, www.google.com), or specialised search engines for the scientific literature such as CiteSeer (Giles et al., 1998, http://citeseerx.ist.psu.edu) or Google Scholar (http://www.googlescholar.com).

Most of today's query languages consist of keywords and operators (such as the Boolean operators), though more complex query languages exist, e.g., first-order-logic based query languages. Nevertheless, query languages are by necessity less expressive than natural language. Therefore, many information needs are too complex to be fully expressed in a formal query language, and query creation is often an imperfect process based on trial and error.

Due to the many complexities of natural language, IR matching is not normally error-free. Users must therefore inspect the results of an IR search and decide whether the system has returned irrelevant documents (which are called *false positives*). This process is called a *relevance decision*. In a search situation, irrelevant documents can be manually discarded from the search results, and the remainder, the supposedly relevant documents, can then be accessed, either physically (in the library or on inter-library loan), or electronically.

Whereas false positives (irrelevant documents which superficially look relevant to the IR engine) are noticed as a nuisance by the searcher, *false negatives* (relevant articles which the IR engine failed to find) will normally go unnoticed because the searcher cannot look through the entirety of the document collection. This is a real problem in those cases where one wants to find all relevant documents, e.g., in patent search and in legal searches.

Another problem is the definition of what should count as "relevant" to a particular information need. Relevance has been known to be cognitively problematic early on (Rees, 1966), and has attracted a vast experimental and theoretical literature in information science (Saracevic, 1975, Schamber et al., 1990, inter alia). The problem is that relevance is situational to a unique occasion (Spärck Jones, 1990): For the same query/document combination there can be large differences between two individuals' perception of relevance. Even the same individual's perception of the same data usually differs considerably over time. This is because there are many different reasons why a user would perceive a given document as relevant at a given point in time; to list just a few:

- because it exactly meets an information need, and the information has not been seen before;
- because it partially satisfies the information need;
- because it would have satisfied the information need if a similar document had not been seen earlier, which already fulfilled the information need;
- because it reminds the user of the real answer though it does not contain it.

Users have fundamentally different ideas about which of the cases above count as relevant and which do not, and they have different opinions as to the difference between the first two points, for instance. This poses a fundamental methodological problem for IR evaluation exercises: if the judges' perception of the relevance of documents is subject to unpredictable variation, this makes measurements of system success non-replicable.

2.2.1 Information Retrieval Methods

Let us now turn to what most research in information retrieval is concerned with, namely the mathematical matching algorithms between indexing and query language.

Most IR matching algorithms are associated with a particular query language. Boolean search, for instance, operates on a query language where keywords are combined with Boolean operators such as "AND", "OR" or "NOT". These operators are set-theoretically interpreted. This results in a binary relevance score: a document matches if and only if the Boolean set operations hold. The slightest violation of the Boolean conditions will therefore cause a non-match, irrespective of how many other parts of the query may match. Adding one wrong keyword can reduce the number of relevant documents to zero, whereas removing a good (i.e., restrictive) keyword can explode the number of irrelevant documents returned. Boolean search has nowadays been mostly superceded by relevance-weighted search, but until the 80s, it was the main literature search tool for scientists, often mediated by a specialised reference librarian. As Boolean searches were often run overnight in batch mode, it was crucial that queries were well-constructed: an error in the query would not be seen until the next day. Reference librarians acquired expertise in the black art of constructing queries which routinely contained as many as 50 keywords.

State-of the art IR systems are *relevance-weighted*, i.e., documents are considered relevant to a query to a certain degree, rather than absolutely as in Boolean search. The systems use models such as the vector space model (Salton, 1971), the probabilistic model (Robertson and Spärck-Jones, 1976), language modelling (Ponte and Croft, 1998), dimensionality reduction algorithms such as Latent Semantic Indexing (LSI, Deerwester et al., 1990), and many others. The degree of relevance depends on factors such as the number, relative importance and quality of match found for each query term, the relative distance between query terms in a document, and the length of the document. Such factors allow for a ranking of returned documents by their estimated relevance.

As a consequence of relevance weighting, and in contrast to Boolean search, there is no longer a guarantee that the returned documents contain all query terms. Instead, they represent the best compromise between query and indexed documents that the IR system could find. Relevance-weighted search also typically comes with more forgiving and intuitive query languages. For instance, most search engines interpret keyword lists as connected with an implicit "AND".

Modern search engines with relevance-weighted search have improved the situation for many searchers in several respects. The first concerns relevance decision. In Boolean return sets, where documents are more or less randomly ordered, there is no point in time at which the search can safely stop: particularly relevant documents are as likely to occur towards the end of the return list as towards the beginning. If the return set is large, the task of discarding irrelevant documents quickly becomes painstaking. If a return set is relevance-weighted, however, its size no longer matters: because documents deemed more relevant by the search engine can be inspected first, and one can stop scanning at any point in time.[5]

Relevance-weighted search also helps during the creation of queries. Because modern systems give an instant response, searchers can quickly revise queries on their own, and it has become easier for the average individual without much search experience to achieve reasonable results. This development, amongst other things, eliminated the need for reference librarians, who were so skilled at creating fine-tuned initial queries. It also arguably put inexperienced scientific searchers in a worse position than before: the one thing somebody searching the scientific literature nowadays cannot do without is solid knowledge of the scientific terminology in the respective field – but this is exactly the thing that these searchers lack.

[5] And indeed, the vast majority of web searches never go beyond the top 10 pages.

What is empirically known about how partially informed searchers experience keyword search? In the 1980s and 1990s, several user studies about IR search engines were performed (Bates, 1998, Borgman, 1996, Fidel, 1985, 1991, Saracevic et al., 1988, Ellis, 1992, Ingwersen, 1996). These studies examine factors such as search experience, task training, educational level, type of search questions and user goals. Not all studies include inexperienced users, but those that do agree that users with less well-defined queries and information needs are indeed put at a disadvantage by document retrieval systems (Clove and Walsh, 1988). Experts' information needs are often more precise than novices' information needs. Ellis (1989a,b) found that inexperienced searchers have particular problems with keyword searches, because their chosen search terms are often too unspecific and produce too many hits, hits where the term has another meaning, or no hits at all. It appears that keyword search can produce clean, relevant information best if searchers already know what they are looking for, a phenomenon which Kircz (1991) calls the "frustrating circularity of the Boolean search process".

2.2.2 Evaluation of Information Retrieval Systems

Let us now turn to how one can evaluate the performance of IR systems. Exercises such as TREC (the Text REtrieval Conference) have extensively and objectively tested such systems, e.g., TREC's core task, called "Adhoc", which was performed for thirteen years, between 1987 and 1999 and had dozens of participant systems each year. In that task, the assumption was that the user is an information analyst, who searches for objectively determinable information in a large corpus of newspaper articles.

The core evaluation metrics in information retrieval are directly related to the concepts of false positives and negatives mentioned above. *Precision* (P) refers to the percentage of true positives in the return set, whereas *recall* (R) refers to the percentage of true positives in the set of all relevant documents in the document collection. Precision measures how many false positives are erroneously found, whereas recall measures how many false negatives (that should have been found) are missed.

The aforementioned fact that an IR system's output does not show up false negatives has been referred to as the *recall problem*. In order to measure recall, one would have to inspect every single document in the entire corpus for relevance. To counteract this problem, relevance decisions are done on a large set of *potentially* relevant articles instead. The aim is to determine as many potentially relevant documents as possible before they are presented to the human judge. A common method for doing this is *pooling* (Spärck Jones and van Rijsbergen, 1976), which uses the union of the results of many different search engines. The pool can also be complemented by manual searches, a method that is known to substantially improve pool quality.

A commonly accepted combination of precision and recall is the F-measure (F; van Rijsbergen, 1979), the harmonic mean of precision and recall: $F = \frac{2PR}{P+R}$. There are also various summary measures for IR, such as the precision-recall cross-over point and 11-point precision, which estimate the area under the precision-recall curve, and *mean average precision* (MAP), which averages relative precision values each time a relevant document is found and thus rewards good performance in the top of the return list. Recall and precision are also often reported at various thresholds, e.g., within the top 30 documents. The best systems in the last year of the competition returned 40–50% relevant documents in the top 30 documents.

More recently, web search and many more specialised IR tasks (called *tracks* in TREC) are being evaluated. The task in the Genomics track (e.g., Hersh et al., 2004) is to retrieve documents about a particular gene, the name of which acts as the query. That this type of search appears to be typical of the search needs of many geneticists is a convenient fact for information access in genetics. It does however not generalise to all disciplines: it is hard to find universal concepts such as gene names that lend themselves as blueprints for a set of queries that a large set of people would find useful. Additionally, it is likely that relevance decision for gene-based queries is more objective and thus easier to decide than those for the relation-based queries that are part of the motivation of my work.

This overview has shown that there are several situations for which current keyword-based IR systems work provably well:

- General web searches, as examined in TREC's Web Search Track;
- Information-analyst style searches on news text, as examined in TREC's Adhoc Track;
- Specific fact-based scientific searches, e.g., in support of an experienced geneticist's information need about a particular gene, as examined in TREC's Genomics Track.

Many other information needs occur during a search of the scientific literature, which are more difficult and are less well served by keyword-based search. These include those of experienced scientists looking for information about relationships between articles, and those of inexperienced scientists and non-scientists looking for an overview of a new field.

2.3 Citation-Based Search

Citation indexes, either in printed or electronic form, record the fact that one article (the citing article) contains a formal citation to another article (the cited article). From the point of view of information management, the existence of citation links is extremely useful, as they provide an automatic mechanism for finding two sets of articles which are semantically related to an article of interest: those that are cited by that article (reaching into the past), and those that cite the article (reaching into the future). What makes these new types of connection particularly valuable for search is that they are orthogonal to keyword-based search. Thus, even if a related article does not share many keywords with the article of interest, it can still be found.

The main two uses of citations in information management are search and bibliometric assessment. Before we can look at these in detail, a short excursion into sociological territory will give us some background on the workings of the citation system.

2.3.1 The Citation System and Bibliometry

Science depends on the free exchange of ideas between researchers, but ideas are an ephemeral and essentially stealable good. A system for recording ideas is needed which ensures that the originators of the ideas are protected and rewarded, while simultaneously granting free access to the information (Luukkonen, 1992). This is the citation system, an informal societal contract, the rules of which have remained reasonably stable over decades.

The corresponding function in industrial research is fulfilled by the patent system. The patenting of ideas or inventions, i.e., the process of their registration with the patent organisation, marks them as belonging to the inventor. They can subsequently be made public and from then may only be used with permission of the patent holder. Non-acknowledgement of the ownership of the idea incurs the risk of a lawsuit.

In science, the institution at the core of the recording and reward system is the peer review, rather than the patent organisation. It is the main quality control mechanism for published scientific knowledge. Each publication must be sanctioned by it, a "credentialing process whereby knowledge claims are allowed into the scientific discipline's domain of shared putative knowledge" (Suppe, 1993). One of the peer review's functions is to enforce the publication rules for conferences and journals, which state that each article must contain original and previously unpublished research (Zuckerman and Merton, 1973).

Myers (1992) describes the publication process as the author staking a *knowledge claim*, i.e., a claim of intellectual ownership for that idea. From the moment of publication, if another author wants to "use" the knowledge claim in an article, this must be acknowledged by formal citation, roughly corresponding to the payment of a fee for a patented idea. Like in the patent system, failing to acknowledge a prior idea also incurs a risk: the lack of a directly relevant citation might be seen by the reviewers as a potentially fraudulent knowledge claim, or (more likely), as a sign of insufficient knowledge on behalf of the authors, both of which might lead to the rejection of the article. If the article is not outright rejected, the inclusion of the citation can be enforced.[6]

One of the practical uses of the citation system is as a formal measurement of a scientist's productivity and the impact of their ideas. Bibliometry is an established research field, which defines measures for the academic weight of publications (e.g., Garfield's (1979) *impact factor*), or for the quality of a researcher's output. Bibliometric measures can play an important role in university politics, affecting not only tenure decisions and promotions, but also university funding, via exercises such as the UK Research Excellence Framework (REF, CWTS, 2007).

There are two aspects to this. The originality criterion for publication ensures in principle that each citation corresponds to a new idea, because each knowledge claim can be staked only once. For this reason, the number of publications a scientist has published should be an indication of their productivity in terms of individual ideas. But because citations indicate the use of an idea, one can do even better than that: An scientist who is highly cited has produced ideas which have been taken up by other scientists, and which must therefore be of high quality.

In practice however, many articles never get cited at all: using the Web of Science (WoS), Vaughan and Shaw (2008) found the median number of citations in the field of library sciences to be zero for all types of publications except book chapters, and slightly higher (in the range of 1–3) for Google Scholar. For computer science and mathematics articles, Adler et al. (2008) estimated the modal number of citations to be around 0.8.

More advanced bibliometric measurements than raw citation counting exist. One of these is the *h-index* (Hirsch, 2005), which takes the shape of the distribution of an individual's citation counts across ar-

---

[6]Strictly speaking, publications with only one reviewing cycle (such as most conferences) cannot enforce, only strongly encourage the inclusion of the citation.

ticles into account. If a researcher has an h-index of h, they have at least h publications, each of which has at least h citations. In order to increase the h-index to $h + 1$, a new publication with $h + 1$ citations is needed, but also each of the existing h citations needs to be cited at least at least once more, i.e., $h + 1$ times. An advantage of the h-index over simple citation counts is that it penalises "one-hit wonder" publications and instead rewards sustained high citation records.

Bibliometric measures rely on the assumption that each citation is worth the same amount. This in turn assumes that a) each article contains the same "amount" of scientific contribution, and b) that each citation in an article expresses the same amount of acknowledgement. Critics of the purely frequency-based bibliometrics as a measurement of the quality and impact of scientific work have pointed out problems with these assumptions (e.g., Ziman, 1968, Bonzi, 1982).

Assumption a) is clearly an oversimplification. Research is typically a continuous activity carried out over decades by an individual and her co-workers (Latour and Woolgar, 1986). In fact, in the life sciences the infrastructure required often means that large problems are worked on by entire research groups for years or decades. The problem facing every researcher is that there is a pressure to publish, but new research results are a valuable resource, of which there is a limited supply. The amount of new research going into an article is therefore a strategic decision for every researcher. While the publication rules for conferences and journals require previously unpublished research, there are no hard and fast rules for *how much* of it is required for one article.

There is a temptation to boost one's publication count by publishing redundantly, i.e., by writing several articles about different aspects of one piece of research. Redundant publication, however, goes against the interest of the research community as a whole, because it wastes reviewers' and readers' time. The peer reviewing system therefore negotiates a minimum size of the so-called *smallest publishable unit* in a discipline, and polices against its shrinking.

Arguments against assumption b) include the observation that there are strong sociological motivations for citing. Ziman (1968), for instance, describes the motivations of "politeness" (towards powerful rival approaches), "policy" (by name-dropping and argument by authority) and "piety" (towards one's friends, collaborators and superiors). Others have voiced the intuition that not all citation types are equally valuable to a researcher's reputation. Bonzi (1982), for instance, argues that *negational* citations, while pointing to the fact that the work has been noticed, do not mean that it is received well.

The citation system is vulnerable to intentional manipulation, which could result in a distortion of the bibliometric measures. Such strategies include redundant publication (shrinking of the smallest publishable unit), failure to acknowledge rival prior ideas, and over-acknowledgement of one's own articles or those of one's scientific allies. Manipulation might even be subconscious: systematic bias in citation networks (in terms of gender, social status, and familiarity, amongst others) is a problem which has long been documented (e.g., Ferber, 1988, Boulton, 2002, Baldi, 1998). The peer review is the only line of defence against all these misdemeanors; overall, the citation system can only work as well as the peer review does.

After this excursion into the sociology of science, I will now turn to a strand of research within library science and the sociology of science that aims to improve standard bibliometric measures: the field of *citation content analysis*.

The goal of citation content analysis is to describe and classify semantic relationships between citing and cited works. Many classification schemes for relationships between citing and cited works have been devised over the years (Weinstock, 1971, Chubin and Moitra, 1975, Oppenheim and Renn, 1978, Frost, 1979, Swales, 1990, inter alia). Annotation schemes for *citation motivation* include judgements about sociological connections, e.g., the motivation of "paying homage to pioneers".

It is difficult to make decisions about citation motivation on the basis of the text alone, i.e., without access to the authors. For instance, Brooks' (1986) study included telephone interviews with the citing authors about the motivation for the 437 citations he investigated. Such sociological judgements are extremely dependent on the actual context of the citation event in time (and thus hard to replicate objectively); Swales (1986, p. 44) calls the field of citation content analysis "zealously interpretative".

Citation function, i.e., the "official" role a citation plays in the research context and argumentation, is a more objective property. Here, any political "hidden agenda" the authors may have had is ignored; the function of the citation is interpreted as literally as possible. Moravcsik and Murugesan (1975) contribute one of the earliest such studies. They divide citations into four dimensions: conceptual or operational use (i.e., use of theory vs. use of technical method); evolutionary or juxtapositional (i.e., own work is based on the cited work vs. own work is an alternative to it); organic or perfunctory (i.e., work is crucially needed for understanding of citing article or just a general acknowledgement); and negational vs. confirmatory (i.e., whether the correctness of the findings is disputed or not). They find, for example, that 40% of

1. Cited source is mentioned in the introduction or discussion as part of the history and state of the art of the research question under investigation.
2. Cited source is the specific point of departure for the research question investigated.
3. Cited source contains the concepts, definitions, interpretations used (and pertaining to the discipline of the citing article).
4. Cited source contains the data (pertaining to the discipline of the citing article) which are used sporadically in the article.
5. Cited source contains the data (pertaining to the discipline of the citing article) which are used for comparative purposes, in tables and statistics.
6. Cited source contains data and material (from other disciplines than citing article) which is used sporadically in the citing text, in tables or statistics.
7. Cited source contains the method used.
8. Cited source substantiated a statement or assumption, or points to further information.
9. Cited source is positively evaluated.
10. Cited source is negatively evaluated.
11. Results of citing article prove, verify, substantiate the data or interpretation of cited source.
12. Results of citing article disprove, put into question the data as interpretation of cited source.
13. Results of citing article furnish a new interpretation/explanation to the data of the cited source.

FIGURE 2 Spiegel-Rösing's (1977) Categories for Citation Motivations.

the citations are perfunctory, which casts further doubt on bibliometric measures based on raw citation counts.

Spiegel-Rösing's (1977) scheme is reproduced in Fig. 2 as a typical example of a citation function scheme. She examines the 2309 citations occurring in 66 articles of the journal *Science Studies*, a journal dealing with sociology, psychology and politics of science.

80% of Spiegel-Rösing's citations substantiate statements (category 8), 6% discuss history or state of the art of the research area (category 1), and only 5% cite comparative data (category 5). Note that both Spiegel-Rösing and Moravcsik and Murugesan distinguish between negatively evaluated citations and positively evaluated citations, i.e., they agree with each other that the phenomenon is noteworthy (i.e., frequent, explanatory or both).

Practitioners of citation content analyses do not normally envisage automatic annotation. The studies typically include one-off manual annotation by one annotator (often the inventor of the scheme); the categories' semantics are not confirmed by reliability studies with other humans, as modern corpus-linguistic methodology requires. However, even without formal reliability studies, these schemes are the result of much careful observation, and can thus inform later designs for similar tasks, particularly in the case of those categories which occur in several independent schemes.

2.3.2 Citation Indexes and Search

Let us now look at the technical aspects of citation indexing. Examples for traditional citation indexes are the Institute for Scientific Information (ISI)'s multidisciplinary citation indexes, ISI Web of Science (`http://www.thomsonisi.com/`) and BIDS (`http://www.bids.ac.uk/`). Such indexes typically do not cover all publications in a field but only a small percentage of journals. According to Garfield (1996), this is justified because the bulk of significant scientific results is accounted for by a relatively small number of journals.

Other examples of citation indexes are online proceedings of conferences which have been internally citation indexed, such as the computer science conference SIGMOD (SIGMOD, 1999).

Tools for autonomous, web-based citation indexing have emerged recently, e.g., CiteSeer (Giles et al., 1998) and Google Scholar (`http://www.scholar.google.com`). They build automatic citation indexes from scientific articles found on the web, using specialised web crawlers and a reference list parser. They also match superficially dissimilar, but logically identical citations from different documents to unique bibliographic entries. If a text search facility is to be supported, then parsing of the reference list is not enough: the location of a citation in running text must additionally be determined.

The simplest way to use a citation index is to search for related articles by following citation links in both directions, starting either from a known article or from a set of articles returned by a keyword-based search. Citation indexers list all citing articles for a given article (which together are responsible for the incoming citation count).

Given a citation index, one can also find articles which are similar to a source article. This can be particularly useful for search situations where keyword search might not be appropriate, e.g., if the user is uncertain about terminology (see section 2.2). Kessler's (1963) work on bibliographic coupling assumes that two articles with similar bibliographies must be similar. This principle can also be used to determine how close two scientific areas are to each other (e.g., White, 2004). In

1 **Lin (1998); Cited by 304 (12 self)**
...difficult problem. In (Hindle, 1990), a small set of sample results are presented. In (Smadja, 1993), automatically extracted collocations are judged by a lexicographer. In (Dagan et al., 1993) and **(Pereira et al., 1993)**, clusters of similar words are evaluated by how well they are able to recover data items that are removed from the input corpus one at a time. In (Alshawi and Carter, 1994), the collocations and the ...

3 **Hofmann (1999); Cited by 291 (7 self)**
...c regularization and is closely related to a method known as deterministic annealing [13]. Since a principled derivation of TEM is beyond the scope of this paper (the interested reader is referred to [**12, 7**]), we will present the necessary modification of standard EM in an ad hoc manner. Essentially, one introduces a control parametersfi (inverse computational temperature) and modifies the E-step in (5) ...

5 **Tishby, Pereira, Bialek (1999); Cited by 229 (27 self)**
...eparate (bifurcate) at somesnite (critical)s, through a second-order phase transition. These transitions form an hierarchy of relevant quantizations for dierent cardinalities of X, as described in [**6, 5**, 1]. Further work The most fascinating aspect of the information bottleneck principle is that it provides a unied framework for dierent information processing problems, including prediction,sltering an ...

8 **Hofmann (1999); Cited by 209 (5 self)**
...In clustering models for documents, one typically associates a latent class variable with each document in the collection. Most closely related to our approach is the distributional clustering model [**10, 7**] which can be thought of as an unsupervised version of a naive Bayes' classifier. It can be shown that the conditional word probability of a probabilistic clustering model is given by P (wjd) = X z2Z ...

9 **Resnik (1993); Cited by 178 (6 self)**
...oun cannot be modifiers on the same scale and therefore should not be grouped together. (For example, the phrase the tall, dark man provides evidence that tall and dark belong in different classes.) (**Pereira, Tishby, and Lee, 1993**) also use argument relationships to determine similarity, producing a clustering of nouns based on the verbs for which they appear as direct objects. Words and clusters are represented using the prob...

19 **Barzilay and McKeown (2001); Cited by 99 (4 self)**
...of particular applications; however, in general, the correspondence between paraphrasing and types of lexical relations is not clear. The same question arises with automatically constructed thesauri (**Pereira et al., 1993; Lin, 1998**). While the extracted pairs are indeed similar, they are not paraphrases. For example, while "dog" and "cat" are recognized as the most similar concepts by the method described in (Lin, 19...

20 **Slonim, Tishby, YI (2000); Cited by 98 (14 self)**
...nding a cluster hierarchy of the members of one set (e.g., documents), based on the similarity of their conditional distributions w.r.t the members of another set (e.g., words), was first introduced in [**17**] **and was** called "distributional clustering". The issue of selecting the 'right' distance measure between distributions remains, however, unresolved in that earlier work. Recently, Tishby, Pereira, an...

FIGURE 3 Highest-Ranking CiteSeer Contexts for *Pereira et al. (1993)*.

contrast, Small (1973) introduces the concept of co-citations: if two articles often co-occur in other articles' bibliographies then they must be similar. Additionally, both Elkiss et al. (2008) and Nanba et al. (2000) found that the physical distance between co-cited citations is also meaningful: articles co-cited in the same sentence, or in close proximity, are semantically more related than those which are co-cited further away in the same article.

Let us now look at some output from the citation indexer CiteSeer (Fig. 3). On July 12 2009, CiteSeer found 284 citations for article cmp_lg/9408011 from my corpus.[7] The citations are presented in their context in the running text of the citing article in the form of short extracts ("snippets"; 200 characters before and 200 characters after the citation). CiteSeer does not always detect the citation context for every citation it recognises; Fig. 3 shows the top 7 citations for which a citation context was found.[8] The ranking of the citing articles is determined by their incoming citation count, which is given after the authors' names and date, along with the number of self-citations amongst those. The incoming citation count might help inexperienced searchers find seminal articles in the field faster; at least this is true for those articles which have been around for long enough to attract citations.

However, CiteSeer's citation contexts cannot satisfy searchers who want to find out about the relationship between two articles, because the contexts are still not long enough for the user to judge in which respect one article cites another. For instance, if we were looking for articles which contrast themselves to or criticise *Pereira et al.*, we might guess that Fig. 3 contains two such cases: *Barzilay and McKeown (2001)* who state that *"the extracted pairs are similar but not paraphrases"*, and *Slonim et al (2000)*, who state that *"the issue of selecting the 'right' distance measure between distributions remains, however, unresolved in that earlier work"*. For the other articles, there is no indication as to how the citing article might relate to the cited article. All we learn from the other snippets is that *Pereira et al.*'s method is called "distributional clustering", a fact already known from the title of the article itself.

[7]Pereira, Tishby, Lee (1993). Distributional Clustering of English Words. In: *Proc. of the Annual Meeting of the Association for Computational Linguistics (ACL-93).*

[8]Highlighting in Fig. 3 is exactly as in the original CiteSeer display, but there are some minor differences in other aspects of the presentation. Some of the bibliographic information that CiteSeer displays is omitted, e.g., the titles of the citing articles. Also, CiteSeer does not show different citation contexts together in one listing; in order to create Fig. 3, each context had to be individually expanded. I also added in boxes the absolute rank of each citation context in the citation list.

One of the applications following from the ideas in this book is automatic citation classification (Teufel et al., 2006b,a). The first automatic citation function classification, to my knowledge, was performed by the citation-based search tool by Nanba et al. (Nanba and Okumura, 1999, Nanba et al., 2000) for Japanese scientific articles. They classify citations in running text into 3 types (*Type C* for contrasts, *Type B* for supportive relationship, and *Type O* for all others), using cue words. Citations are characterised by a context of three sentences around it. As a result of this analysis, documents which have the same kind of links with an article of interest can be displayed as a cluster.

The first fine-grained annotation scheme designed for automatic citation function classification is presented by Garzone and Mercer (2000), which has a total of 34 categories (the union of all categories from 11 historic annotation schemes from citation content analysis).

The ideas for citation-based search applications in this book, which will be introduced in section 4.2, differ from Nanba and Okumura's work (and also from autonomous citation indexing) in that they envisage a more sophisticated model of citation context and an explicit characterisation of the articles' contents, not just the relations between them. The overall characterisation of citation function in Teufel et al. (2006a) is not dissimilar to Garzone and Mercer's, but while our classification makes fewer distinctions, its reliability has been experimentally confirmed, using a much larger corpus.

Other Citation-Inspired Research

Citation sentences may not in themselves be enough to determine citation function, but they contain valuable information for several related bibliographic and natural language processing applications. For instance, Nakov et al. (2004) show that redundancy in citation sentences can be used to create a corpus of paraphrases. Elkiss et al. (2008) find that the union of all citation sentences has high lexical overlap with the author summary, using a citation network in bio-medicine with 2497 articles. However, the more citation sentences pointing to the same article one considers, the more lexically similar this set gets to itself. They conclude that citation sentences capture different aspects of the article which may not be mentioned in the author abstract. Qazvinian and Radev (2008) and Nakov et al. (2004) both inspect the factoids contained in the citation sentences for a smaller set in detail, using data sets from computational linguistics and the bio-sciences, respectively, and again find much overlap. This has been taken as motivation for a clustering approach to scientific multi-document summarisation, an idea I will discuss in section 14.3.

Bradshaw (2003) was the first to show that citation sentences can also improve ad-hoc document retrieval, using the observation that citation sentences are akin to anchor text in web retrieval. He compiled an index consisting of keywords from citation sentences, which he associated with the cited document, and showed that retrieval performance improved when compared to an index compiled by traditional techniques, i.e., keywords from the cited document. In my own group, this work was extended (Ritchie et al., 2008, Ritchie, 2008) by the use of a much larger data set (the ACL Anthology). Ritchie shows that a combined keyword-based and citation-sentence based index performs better than either of the individual indexes. In both cases, the improvements are small but significant, confirming Elkiss et al's claim that citation sentences must indeed contribute different information from the information contained in the article itself.

Shum et al.'s metadata scheme (Shum, 1998, Sumner and Shum, 1998, Shum et al., 1999) is an approach towards a manually created record of the relationships between articles, in particular the similarities and differences between scientific approaches. Their model is roughly comparable to citation function models, though the cited and classified entities are not documents, but 9 types of concepts relevant in the domain (e.g., THEORETICAL-PROBLEM, SOFTWARE or SCHOOL-OF-THOUGHT, as shown in the second column of Fig. 4).

REF: Smith, J. (1997) ATC Overload, Journal of ATC, 3 (4), 100-150		
ANALYSES	APPLIED-PROBLEM	*Air traffic controller cognitive overload*
USES/APPLIES	THEORY/FRAMEWORK	*use of video, undergraduate university physics, student ability*
PROBLEMATISES	SOFTWARE	*GOMS cognitive modelling tools*
MODIFIES/EXTENDS	LANGUAGE	*Knowledge Interchange Format (KIF)*
CHARACTERISES/RECASTS	TREND	*Electronic trading over the internet*
CHALLENGES	SCHOOL-OF-THOUGHT	*Postmodernism*
SUPPORTS	EVIDENCE	*multimedia, school chemistry teaching*

FIGURE 4 Shum's (1998) Document Representation by Cognitive Relations.

Shum distinguishes 10 cognitively defined relations between scientific works: ANALYSES, SOLVES, DESCRIBES-NEW, USES/APPLIES, MODIFIES/EXTENDS, CHARACTERISES/RECASTS, EVALUATES (SUPPORTS or PROBLEMATISES or CHALLENGES). An example of a representation of an article according to this meta-description is given in Fig. 4; for instance, the example article "problematises" a certain software (*"GOMS cognitive modelling tools"*). The model is used in the ClaiMaker project (Li et al., 2002, Uren et al., 2003, 2006, Shum et al., 2002, 2004), where sophisticated argumentation aspects such as conflicting research claims are modelled by a manually constructed graph of relationships.

Human experts (in the best case, the authors themselves) manually fill the slots with domain-specific material, e.g., while reading or writing an article. Shum is pessimistic about the prospect of automating the process, due to the high level of human cognitive analysis that is required.

I agree with Shum that in the long run, such metadata approaches optimally encode complex information about relations between articles: the information is taken "at source", at the time of production, from the people who know most about the article. It remains to be seen whether metadata-enabled annotation will become a routine part of writing and submitting articles in the near future. Until then, and for all legacy articles, an automatic extraction and analysis method is needed – even if its output is necessarily less sophisticated than human annotation.

Chapter Summary

In this chapter, I have asked how the scientific literature can be searched, in particular by novice searchers, by non-scientists, and by scientists who have just moved into a new area. With respect to existing information management tools we have seen that:

- *Subject indexes and information retrieval engines* support circumscribed, specific information needs well, but are not designed for the searches of less experienced searchers, who often lack the necessary knowledge of the terminology in the field.
- *Citation indexes* offer a way of finding related articles which is orthogonal to keywords, although they do not classify the links between articles. This is a problem, because for scientists, relationships are one of the most important pieces of information they seek from the literature.

In the next chapter, I will consider another aspect of information management, namely summaries, and the role they play in supporting the searches of less experienced users.

3

Summarisation

An important information management tool – apart from the information retrieval engines and citation indexes surveyed in the last chapter – is the summary.[9] So far, we have come across three functions of summaries in scientific information management:

- the user can read them in lieu of the source document, e.g., in summary journals;
- the user can read them to preview a source document that is not present, e.g., during relevance decision;
- IR indexing can use them as a document surrogate if the source document is not available in machine-readable form.

In order to see which properties of summaries are useful during scientific search, we will first take a close look at human-generated summaries in section 3.1. I will pay special attention to the structure of the summaries. Section 3.2 then reports on the main trends in automatic summarisation, as far as they are relevant to the approach described in this book.

3.1 Human Summarisation

Summarisation is a common day-to-day activity, and humans are generally very good at it – at least after childhood (Sherrard, 1985). Most of what we know about summaries does not come from these informal summaries though, but from summaries of scientific articles. These are practically the only kinds of summary with well-described properties which are commercially produced in large quantities.

[9] I will use the terms *abstract* and *summary* synonymously in this book.

3.1.1 Summary Journals and Professional Abstractors

Scientific summaries are published in the form of summary journals by information services (secondary publishers) like the *Institute for Science Information, Inc.*, *Physics Abstracts* or *Chemical Abstracts Service*, mostly in the life sciences and in medicine. Some primary publishers also produce summary journals, e.g., the *Royal Society of Chemistry* (RSC). The summaries are written by professional abstractors/indexers (also called information specialists). These are content experts who are additionally trained in the art of summarising and indexing articles and books.

Guidelines and recommendations exist which prescribe what professional summaries should look like (McGirr, 1973, Borko and Chatman, 1963, ANSI, 1979, ISO, 1976), e.g., in terms of maximum and minimum number of words. These guidelines are concerned with the informativeness and readability of the human-written summaries; they try to make sure that the summaries are general, long-lived and high-quality accounts of the information contained in a scientific article.

There is a well-known distinction between *indicative* and *informative* summaries (Rowley, 1982, Cremmins, 1996, Lancaster, 2003, Michaelson, 1990, Maizell et al., 1971, Mani, 2001). Indicative summaries contain an indication of the topic of the text (i.e., research purpose, scope or methodology), whereas informative summaries additionally mention the main findings and conclusions of the text.

Indicative summaries can be used in all situations where the full text is available alongside the summary, or where an indication of the general contents is enough. A prime example of such a function is the previewing function, where a summary is used much like a table of contents.

Informative summaries, on the other hand, are autonomous texts, which can be used as substitutes for the full texts. They are supposed to be self-contained (Lancaster, 2003): on the basis of reading an informative summary, the reader should be able to grasp the main goals and achievements of the work without needing to refer to the source document for clarification. This even means that if an informative summary contains a citation – which is rarely the case – then all bibliographic information of the citation should be listed in the summary (as well as in the bibliography at the end of the article).

Apart from the indicative–informative distinction, another commonly accepted summary distinction is that between *purpose-oriented* and *findings-oriented* summaries (Cremmins, 1996, ANSI, 1979). Both are subtypes of the informative summary, with the difference that findings-oriented summaries present results and conclusions first (which is potentially useful for the fast scanning of experimental results by experts), whereas purpose-oriented summaries present the goal and the methods first.

While there are no experimental studies with real users verifying which functions summaries play in an information management scenario, the informative-indicative and the purpose- or findings-oriented distinctions are generally assumed, and are motivated by certain hypotheses about summary functions. Lancaster (2003) lists five such functions, two for informative summaries (keeping abreast of new developments and refreshing the memory of a previously read article), and three for indicative summaries (relevance decision, previewing the structure of the article, and confirming that one has chosen the right database). This last function has become obsolete with modern library systems, which automatically combine many indexes.

But this fifth point is also an illustration of a larger phenomenon: namely that assumptions about how humans use summaries are grounded in a particular technological setting. Lancaster's functions, for instance, assume that information management is centred around printed documents. In such an environment, the outcome of one's relevance decisions cannot be seen for a long time, in the worst case not until an article arrives via inter-library loan. That has repercussions on what kinds of summaries are produced: to help guard against the risk of ordering the wrong article, professional summaries must be of particularly high quality and informativeness.

How do professionals write summaries? Cremmins (1996) states that most professional summaries are created by extracting sentences and subsequent rephrasing of the content. Abstractors are experts in the field, but they work under time pressure and do not attempt to understand all details of the science in the article.

This is confirmed by studies such as the ones by Endres-Niggemeyer and colleagues, who study the behaviour of professional abstractors in great detail (Endres-Niggemeyer et al., 1995, Endres-Niggemeyer, 1998), and by Jing (2000) and Saggion (2000), who catalogue the exact linguistic changes made by professional abstractors to a set of extracted sentences. Much of what the abstractors do is too complex to be simulated automatically, but observations of their work have inspired some of the importance measurements which will be surveyed in section 3.2.2.

Endres-Niggemeyer additionally finds that professional abstractors rely on discourse features such as overall text structure (e.g., as indicated by headings, key phrases and position in paragraphs) to organise summary and extract information. For instance, they prefer top-level segments of documents, consider beginnings and ends of units as relevant, examine passages and paragraphs before individual sentences, and determine the role of each section in the problem-solving process by reading the first and last sentence of each section or each paragraph. (Note that these observations fit well with the idea of a shallow text understander that aims to read like a non-expert, which I argued for in the introduction.)

3.1.2 Structure in Abstracts

Structuring is an important factor in the overall quality of a summary, and is of particular importance when summaries are used to preview the structure of the document. Before considering which content units are contained in summaries, we should first take a look at structure of full articles, as there are obvious parallels between the two.

The single most prominent property of experimental scientific articles is their structuring into *rhetorical sections* (or *rhetorical divisions*) and corresponding section headlines. The IMRD model assumes the divisions *Introduction, Method, Results, Discussion.* Depending on the discipline, a fifth typical section, *Conclusions*, may or may not be present. This model was first formally described by van Dijk (1980). He presents *text grammars*, i.e., conventionalised schematic forms, for many text types including narratives, newspaper articles, and scientific writing. The IMRD structure is also acknowledged in applied linguistics (Graetz, 1985, Swales, 1990) and in writing manuals (e.g., Day and Gastell, 2006, Alley, 1996, Farr, 1985, Houp et al., 2001, Lannon, 2008, Matthews and Matthews, 2007, Michaelson, 1990, van Emden and Easteal, 1996).

In the humanities, the IMRD section heading is practically non-existent. The article structure there is typically internal to the argument and thus far more "hidden" from superficial observation than in the sciences.

Several researchers study linguistic correlates of IMRD structure in articles (Milas-Bracovic, 1987, Biber et al., 1998, Salager-Meyer, 1994, Riley, 1991). For instance, Biber et al. (1998) consider correlation between IMRD structure and tense, and Salager-Meyer (1994) between rhetorical moves similar to IMRD structure and hedging. Hedging is a frequent pragmatic construct in scientific writing, which occurs when authors distance themselves from a scientific statement. Therefore, it is associated with speculative statements, which tend to occur in *Discussion* sections.

That-nominals such as *"the observation that..."* often indicate fact-stating sentences (Biber and Finegan, 1994, West, 1980), and are also correlated to IMRD structure. West (1980) finds them more likely to occur in the *Introduction* and *Discussion* sections than in the *Results* section, and least likely of all in the *Method* section.

Within a single experimental discipline, division structure is often much finer-grained than IMRD; for instance, a *Method* section in an experimental psychology article can be subdivided into *Subjects, Materials* and *Procedure*. Suppe (1998), Kando (1997) and Kircz (1991) present such finer-grained discipline-specific models, where the categories contain "hard-wired", discipline-specific domain knowledge. For instance, consider Kircz' model for experimental physics in Fig. 5. Some categories, e.g., *Presentation of Smoothed Experimental Results* and *Error Analysis*, encode particular methodologies specific to experimental physics and could therefore not be applied to other disciplines.

There are various theories about where section structuring comes from. Mullins et al. (1988) and Hyland (1998b) argue that all texts which serve a common purpose among a community of users eventually take on a predictable structure of presentation. Section structuring in experimental sciences is an example of this general principle, as it helps scientists understand the contents of an article and search for information in it. A psycholinguist, for instance, looking for the number of experimental subjects in a particular study, will usually find this information with high speed and accuracy.

Let us now turn to the structure of abstracts. The following content units, the so-called *ANSI categories*, are defined for abstracts in the experimental sciences (ANSI, 1979, ISO, 1976, Rowley, 1982, Cremmins, 1996):

- *Purpose/Problem*
- *Scope/Methodology*
- *Results*
- *Conclusions/Recommendations*

The ANSI structure therefore closely mirrors the IMRD structure.

Guidelines agree on the applicability of the ANSI categories, but often disagree with respect to more peripheral content units such as related work, background, incidental findings and future work. According to Alley (1996, p. 22), background is a useful content unit in a summary if it is restricted to being the first sentence of the summary, whereas other authors (Rowley, 1982, Cremmins, 1996) recommend against the inclusion of any background information. Abstractors are also discouraged from mentioning related work (Weil et al., 1963), unless the cited studies are replications or evaluations of earlier work (Cremmins, 1996).

1. Definition of the research subject in broad terms
    (a) Redefinition of the problem in the actual research context
2. Experimental setup
    (a) Experimental constraints
    (b) Experimental assumptions
    (c) Experimental ambiguities
    (d) Relation of experimental setup with other experiments
3. Data collection
    (a) Data handling methods
    (b) Data handling criteria
    (c) Error analysis
4. Presentation of raw experimental data
    (a) Presentation of smoothed experimental data
    (b) Pointers to pictorial or tabular presentation
    (c) Comparison of own data with other results
5. Theoretical model
    (a) Theoretical constraints
    (b) Theoretical assumptions
    (c) Theoretical ambiguities
    (d) Relation of theoretical elaboration with other works
6. Theoretical/mathematical elaboration
7. Presentation of theoretical results/predictions
    (a) Comparison with other theoretical results
    (b) Pointers to pictorial or tabular presentation
8. Comparison of experimental results with own theoretical results
    (a) Comparison of experimental results with other theoretical results
    (b) Pointers to pictorial or tabular presentation
9. Conclusions
    (a) Experimental conclusions
    (b) Theoretical conclusions
10. Reference to own previous published work
    (a) Reference to own work in progress
11. Reference to other people's published work
    (a) Reference to other people's work in progress

FIGURE 5 Kircz' (1991) Argumentative Taxonomy.

In many fields *structured abstracts* have become compulsory instead of prose summaries without a formal structure, e.g., in medicine, where compliance to the prescribed headings is a condition of publication in most journals (Adhoc, 1987, Arndt, 1992, Rennie and Glass, 1991). Rules for the preparation of structured abstracts are elaborate (Haynes, 1990), and differ by journal and article type. For instance, in the *Annals of Internal Medicine*, the structure of summaries for clinical trial reports is as follows: *Background, Objective, Design, Setting, Patients, Interventions, Measurements, Results* and *Conclusions*, whereas for reviews, headings include *Objective Data Sources* and *Study Selection.*

There is empirical evidence that structured abstracts are easier to read and overall more efficient than prose summaries (Hartley et al., 1996, Hartley and Sydes, 1997) and that they are more likely to contain more complete information than prose ones (Taddio et al., 1994). This does not mean that all published structured abstracts are indeed fully correctly structured: Froom and Froom (1993) found that many structured abstracts in *Annals of Internal Medicine* do not contain all of the information requested in the guidelines, even when this information was present in the article itself.

Recently, automatic approaches to detecting rhetorical ANSI-type structure in summaries have been developed for biomedical articles (McKnight and Arinivasan, 2003, Lin et al., 2006, Hirohata et al., 2008). These typically use a corpus with structured as well as unstructured abstracts (only 9% of MEDLINE abstracts are structured) to learn a statistical model of abstract structure, which can then be applied to the unstructured abstracts in their collection.

But structure in abstracts exists even in disciplines where there is no formal requirement for it.

Liddy (1991) empirically studies the rhetorical structure of summaries written by professional abstractors. Based on a corpus of summaries and interviews with the abstractors, she finds summaries written by different abstractors to be similar to each other in terms of their structure (i.e., the content units and the type of sentences), even if not in terms of the actual sentences chosen. Fig. 6 shows the seven most important components of Liddy's building plan (*prototypical components*) in boldface capitals, the next level of importance (*typical components*) in capitals, and the least important ones in lowercase. The components cover short text spans (parts of sentences rather than sentences), which can be recursively embedded into each other.

In other disciplines, less well-structured abstracts have been found. Similar to Froom and Froom's (1993) findings for structured abstracts, Salager-Meyer's (1992) examination of 77 medical abstracts finds that only 52% contain the rhetorical categories she expects in the right order.[10] Buxton and Meadows (1978) find summaries in physics do not report material from the *Method* section.

Tibbo (1992) compares chemistry, psychology and history with respect to six content categories: the four ANSI categories (*Purpose, Scope/Methodology, Results, Conclusions*), plus *Background* and *Hypotheses*, and finds that in history, fewer than 40% of the summary sentences fall into one of the ANSI categories, although the ANSI stan-

[10] She used Swales's (1990) scheme, which I will discuss in section 6.3.

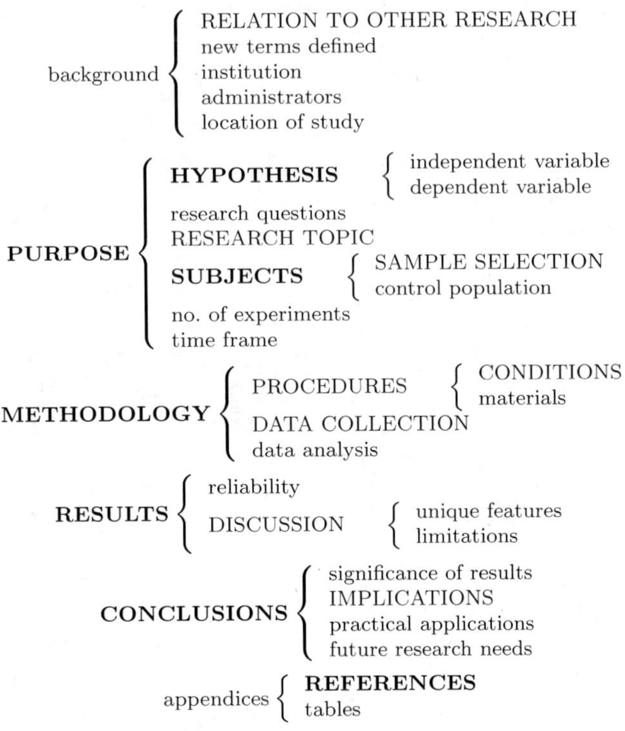

FIGURE 6 Liddy's (1991) Empirical Summary Components.

dard claims applicability to the social sciences and humanities. Milas-Bracovic (1987) studies sociological and humanities summaries with similar results.

What about computational linguistics, the discipline chosen for much of the experimentation in this book? Structured abstracts are not in use in CL, and with respect to empirically observed structure, we will find in section 5.1.2 that the full texts in my corpus do not follow the IMRD structure, and in section 8.6 that the abstracts do not comply to the ANSI model either.

Let us now turn back to the aim of this book, namely scientific information management for less experienced searchers. The guidelines for professional summaries recommend that summaries should be aimed at a particular kind of reader, a semi-expert: somebody who knows enough about the field to understand basic methodology and general goals but who would not understand all specialised detail. Kircz (2001) states that such users read articles particularly for the general approaches described, the relation to other work, and the conclusions. Therefore, generic manual summaries should be ideal for them.

For other kinds of users, however, such summaries are far less suitable. Inexperienced users have more generic information needs: they read introductions and conclusions, overview figures/graphs if present, and the list of references. Much of this material is not present in a summary written for a semi-expert, and much of what is there is too detailed for them (Kircz, 2001). On the other hand, informed readers, who want quick, direct access to the specific description of the experiments or theory and the specific results, are not interested in the general parts contained in generic summaries. Expertise-tailored summaries are therefore attractive, but the manual summarisation industry cannot provide them (Herner, 1959, Lancaster, 2003), due to the high production cost of consistently high-quality, stand-alone summaries.[11]

This implies that it would be best if summaries were automatically created and tailored to the expertise of their users. User-tailoring is a task well-known from language generation (Spärck Jones, 1988, Paris, 1988, 1994). In the medical informatics community there have been efforts to tailor extracts as well (Wellons and Purcell, 1999), as section 4.1 will describe in more detail.

Automatic summarisation techniques are the natural starting point for the creation and tailoring of such summaries. In the following section, I will concentrate on content selection, the subtask of summarisation where the best material for a summary is collected from the source document. The section will not discuss developments in the presentation of linguistic material for summaries, such as sentence compression (Knight and Marcu, 2000, Clarke and Lapata, 2008), sentence re-generation (Barzilay and McKeown, 2005) and models of summary cohesion (Barzilay and Lapata, 2004).

3.2 Automatic Summarisation

The traditional text comprehension-based model for summarisation is shown schematically in Fig. 7. It has three stages: a) linguistic analysis of the text (syntactic, semantic, pragmatic), which results in the reconstruction of the document semantics in a semantic representation language, b) compression of the contents, by some kind of manipulation of the representation language and finally c) generation of the summary text from the reduced representation.

---

[11]Note that neither the indicative vs. informative distinction nor the findings-oriented vs. purpose-oriented distinction would particularly help expert or uninformed readers, even if these different version of the summary were available.

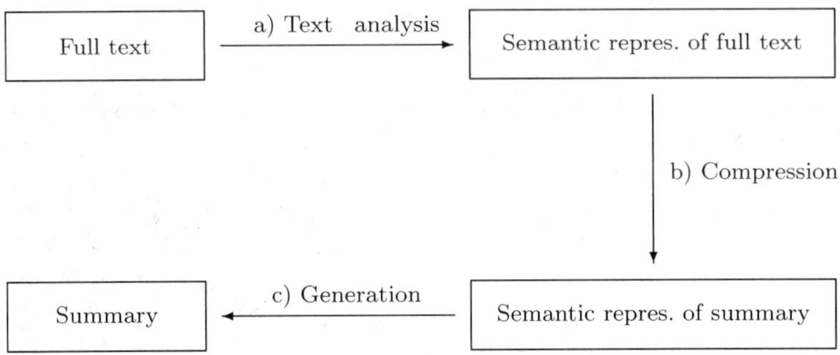

FIGURE 7 Summarisation by Text Comprehension.

In the introduction, I have already dismissed Step a) as unrealistic: it is not possible yet to construct a suitable semantic representation reliably and robustly from unrestricted text. This state of affairs makes the model irreconcilable with the goal of robust summarisation. This is regrettable, as plausible and interesting solutions for the other steps of the model exist (e.g., Kintsch and van Dijk, 1978, Alterman, 1985, Brown and Day, 1983, Sherrard, 1985, for Step b).

The *fact extraction* approach (which I will discuss in section 3.2.1) can be seen as a shortcut to the deep model. This approach was named by Spärck Jones (1994), to replace the term *information extraction* with a more precise description of what kind of information is being extracted. In this approach, a semantic representation of the document is derived by filling fixed templates with snippets of text. The text snippets are carefully chosen from the text so that they represent facts and core participants in events.

The use of such fixed templates vastly simplifies the knowledge representation problem. Step a) then consists only of the fact extraction step, in which the slots in the template are filled. The fact that the semantics of the template is known *a priori* also simplifies Step c). This, therefore, is a plausible route for an accurate summarisation system, which uses reasonably deep processing. However, its big restriction is that it only works for predefined, limited domains, as we will see.

Text extraction (to be discussed in section 3.2.2) is an even more radically simplified version of the deep model. Here, Step a) is performed by condensing each textual segment to a minimal representation, namely a set of features associated with it. An example for one such feature is whether or not the sentence contains the cue phrase *"to summarize"*. Step b), compression, is performed by selecting a set of these segments, for instance the n highest-ranking ones, whereas Step c) is omitted completely: the textual segments whose scores were chosen in Step b) directly constitute the output.

Let us now consider the two alternatives in detail.

3.2.1 Fact Extraction Methods

Summarisation by fact extraction relies on domain-specific templates which represent core aspects of the meaning of the document. Summarisation consists of filling the slots of these templates with extracted textual material, followed by a possible template compression step. Text generation methods are then used to create a new textual summary from the compressed template or templates.

Fact extraction templates (or information extraction templates) are shallow knowledge representation schemes which encode information about entities and their relations. The templates are an instance of the frames well-known from symbolic text comprehension and memory organisation theories (Minsky, 1975, Schank and Abelson, 1977, DeJong, 1982).

Fig. 8 shows a filled template describing a terrorist attack. The template contains information such as location and time of a bombing. The slots are associated with particular semantics (e.g., "*perpetrator*" and "*human target*"), and are filled with material extracted from the text. Fig. 9 contains the source text which gave rise to the filled template in Fig. 8.

MESSAGE: ID	
SECSOURCE: SOURCE	Reuters
SECSOURCE: DATE	March 3, 1996 11:30
PRIMSOURCE: SOURCE	
INCIDENT: DATE	March 3, 1996
INCIDENT: LOCATION	Jerusalem
INCIDENT: TYPE	Bombing
HUM TGT: NUMBER	"killed: 18" "wounded: 10"
PERP: ORGANIZATION ID	

FIGURE 8 MUC-4-Style Template (Domain: Terrorist Attacks).

The first formal definition of the task of filling such templates was provided in the late 1980s by the first Message Understanding Conference (MUC), a large-scale competitive evaluation, where participant systems perform fact extraction from real-world newspaper text. A

TST-REU-0001
JERUSALEM - A Muslim suicide bomber blew apart 18 people on a Jerusalem bus and wounded 10 in a mirror-image of an attack one week ago. The carnage by Hamas could rob Israel's Prime Minister Shimon Peres of the May 29 election victory he needs to pursue Middle East peacemaking. Peres declared all-out war on Hamas but his tough talk did little to impress stunned residents of Jerusalem who said the election would turn on the issue of personal security.

FIGURE 9 Source Text for Template in Fig. 8.

series of MUCs with gradually more sophisticated templates followed until 1998 (e.g., Grishman and Sundheim, 1995). Different domains were chosen each year: naval sightings and engagements (MUC-1 and MUC-2), terrorist attacks in Central and South America (MUC-3 and MUC-4), international joint ventures and electronic circuit fabrication (MUC-5), changes in company management (MUC-6) and telecommunications satellite launches (MUC-7). Since the end of the MUC conferences, the tradition of fact extraction evaluations has continued in the form of conferences such as CoNNL-03 (Daelemans and Osbourne, 2003), BioCreative (`http://biocreative.sourceforge.net/`), the ACM KDD cup (`http://www.sigkdd.org/kddcup`), JNLBPA (Kim et al., 2004), LLL (Nedellec, 2005), and the BioNLP-09 Shared Task (Kim et al., 2009). Many of these shared tasks concentrate on biomedical text, and in particular on the extraction of genes and gene–protein interaction.

A staple method used in fact extraction are *lexico-semantic patterns*. These are regular expressions combining actual text ("lexico") with the slot type associated with the text ("semantic"). These patterns express domain-specific information and the corresponding linguistic realisation in text. If they are written manually – which is typically the case – a large knowledge engineering effort is required. Learning approaches for fact extraction patterns exist (Riloff, 1993, Agichtein and Gravano, 2000, Culotta and Sorensen, 2004) and have somewhat alleviated this problem, but they are either specialised to certain relations or require training material in the form of manually filled templates.

Paice and Jones' (1993) approach to the summarisation of scientific articles in the field of crop husbandry uses a domain-specific template with slots such as SPECIES, CULTIVAR and PEST, as illustrated in Fig. 10. Fact extraction (i.e., slot filling) is performed by a heuristic pattern matching procedure and a weighting scheme on the basis of the frequency and the contexts of the slot fillers.

SPECIES:	*winter wheat*
CULTIVAR:	
HIGH LEVEL PROPERTY:	*each field a grid*
LOW LEVEL PROPERTY:	
PEST:	*Brent Geese Branta*
AGENT:	
INFLUENCE:	
LOCATION:	*Deepsdale Marsh, Burnham, Deepdale*
TIME:	*1985, 1986*
SOIL:	
CLIMATE:	
TREATMENT:	
PROCESS:	
NUTRIENT:	

FIGURE 10 Paice and Jones' (1993) Template for Agricultural Articles.

Title: The effect on winter wheat of grazing by Brent Geese Branta Bernicla

Journal of Applied Ecology, 1990, 27:821-833

This paper studies the effect of Brent Geese Branta on the each field a grid of winter wheat [sic]. *The experiment took place at Deepdale Marsh, Burnham, Deepdale. The fact that ear density increased due to grazing in one yield indicates that there is probably little value in the farmer sowing seed at a higher density in an attempt to compensate for geese grazing.*

FIGURE 11 Paice and Jones' (1993) Summary for the Template in Fig. 10.

The summary in Fig. 11 is generated by slotting the best candidate strings from Fig. 10 into a fixed natural language template. Note that the identification of an erroneous string (such as *"each field a grid"* in the example) can lead to ungrammatical output. The third sentence is added by traditional text extraction, using indicator strings such as "*results indicate that*" (underlined in Fig. 11); this should in principle turn the result into an informative summary.

A similar principle is followed in the SUMMONS system (Radev and McKeown, 1998, McKeown and Radev, 1995), which compresses several descriptions about the same event from multiple news stories and uses a set of MUC-style templates such as Fig. 12 as input. The compression strategy is specific both to the domain (terrorist activity) and to the text type and situation (newspaper texts about the same event, published in a narrow time window). Examples for the template compression rules used are: a) if two or more messages reflect similar patterns over time, these can be reported in one statement (e.g., three

consecutive bombings at the same location) and b) prefer more specific information over more general, e.g., the name of a terrorist group rather than the fact that it is Palestinian.

Message: ID	**TST-REU-0001**
Secsource: Source	Reuters
Secsource: Date	March 3, 1996 11:30
Primsource: Source	
Incident: Date	March 3, 1996
Incident: Location	Jerusalem
Incident: Type	Bombing
Hum Tgt: Number	"killed: 18" "wounded: 10"
Perp: Organization ID	

Message: ID	**TST-REU-0002**
Secsource: Source	Reuters
Secsource: Date	March 4, 1996 07:20
Primsource: Source	Israel Radio
Incident: Date	March 4, 1996
Incident: Location	Tel Aviv
Incident: Type	Bombing
Hum Tgt: Number	"killed: at least 10" "wounded: 30"
Perp: Organization ID	

Message: ID	**TST-REU-0003**
Secsource: Source	Reuters
Secsource: Date	March 4, 1996 14:20
Primsource: Source	
Incident: Date	March 4, 1996
Incident: Location	Tel Aviv
Incident: Type	Bombing
Hum Tgt: Number	"killed: at least 13" "wounded: more than 100"
Perp: Organization ID	"Hamas"

Message: ID	**TST-REU-0004**
Secsource: Source	Reuters
Secsource: Date	March 4, 1996 14:30
Primsource: Source	
Incident: Date	March 4, 1996
Incident: Location	Tel Aviv
Incident: Type	Bombing
Hum Tgt: Number	"killed: at least 12" "wounded: 105"
Perp: Organization ID	"Hamas"

FIGURE 12 Examples of MUC-4-Style Templates.

Summary generation in SUMMONS is far more sophisticated than in Paice and Jones' approach: the summary is deep-generated by a generation component which chooses connectives, tense and voice, satisfies anaphora constraints and avoids repetition of constituents, resulting in the following multi-document summary for the templates from Fig. 12:

> *Reuters reported that 18 people were killed in a Jerusalem bombing Sunday. The next day, a bomb in Tel Aviv killed at least 10 people and wounded 30 according to Israel Radio. Reuters reported that the radical Muslim group Hamas had claimed responsibility for the act.*

The fact that this summary is deep-generated is illustrated by the many changes in comparison to its source texts. During the combination and surface realisation phase, SUMMONS changed voice and tense in the first and third sentence of the summary respectively, and replaced the phrase *"the Islamic fundamentalist group Hamas"* with *"the radical Muslim group Hamas"*. It also added the phrase "*the next day*", which did not appear in the original text.

The depth of representation and the additional knowledge about semantic relationships between slots has clear advantages: summaries generated on the basis of domain-specific templates and generation techniques often read well and are logically well-structured. But the high summary quality comes at the price of robustness: fact extraction summarisation is restricted to narrow domains, such as the MUC domains listed above.

Spärck Jones (1999) calls fact extraction methods "what you know is what you get" techniques. What is meant by this is that world knowledge is hard-wired into the slot definitions of the templates, e.g., the causal relationship between the bombing event and the killing or wounding of the HUMAN TARGETS. This means that only text segments that fit the constraints expressed by the slots and catered for by specialised recognition machinery can be handled; in our case, these are only the physical effects of the attack. Any unexpected facts are necessarily ignored in the final summary. In the case of text TST-REU-0001 (Fig. 9), this includes information about Mr. Peres' prospects in the election and the future of the peace process, which is an important topic in that text. This is a clear disadvantage of this approach.

I have said in the introduction that my approach to text understanding is less ambitious than full text comprehension. Its ambitions, however, go beyond those in fact extraction in one respect; the entities it seeks to extract and encode are general, domain-independent and are not known beforehand, unlike in fact extraction.

3.2.2 Text Extraction Methods

A diametrically opposed approach is text extraction. It was historically the first summarisation method ever used (by Luhn, 1958), and it is still popular, even ubiquitous, nowadays.

Text extraction relies on the identification of a small number of "meaningful" sentences or other text pieces from a source text. Each textual segment is represented by a number of features associated with it, e.g., whether or not the segment contains words with particular frequency properties, or cue phrases such as *"to summarise"*.

The output of the text extraction process is called an *extract*: the set of extracted units, reproduced verbatim and presented to the user, typically in the order in which they appeared in the source text. In the simplest case, the selection method just chooses the n units with the highest scores. A more sophisticated method, Maximum Marginal Relevance (MMR, Carbonell and Goldstein, 1998) chooses the optimum from the set of next-most relevant sentences, which is minimally similar to the sentences already in the extract. This avoids redundancy in the summary, which is a particular problem in multi-document summarisation.

The idea of text extraction might sound rather crude, but recall from section 3.1.1 that it is also the method of choice of professional summarisers during the initial stages of summary creation. Most of today's summarisation systems use text extraction in some form, including many commercially available ones, e.g., Microsoft's AutoSummarize (Microsoft, 1997), Sinope (`http://www.sinope.info`), Copernic (`http://www.copernic.com`), SSSummarizer (`http://www.kryltech.com`), InXight (`http://www.inxightfedsys.com`), TextAnalyst (`http://www.scienceplus.nl/textanalyst`) and Pertinence Summarizer (`http://www.pertinence.com`). Even research systems for automatic summarisation often use text extraction as a first step before additional linguistic processing is applied, such as sentence ordering or compression.

The big advantage of text extraction is its robustness. Due to the low level of analysis performed, it is possible to process texts of all kinds, independently of writing style, text type and subject matter. This means that unexpected turns in a story, sudden changes in topic and other difficult phenomena can be treated in a shallow way – the output will, to a certain degree, reflect such textual particularities.

As an example of an extract, I created a 10-sentence extract of the example article from the last chapter, *Pereira et al. (1993)* using the commercial software AutoSummarize (Fig. 13, Microsoft, 1997). Boldfaced entries are titles or subtitles; item j) is a part of a bibliography item, all other items are sentences.[12] The AutoSummarize extract gives the general topic of the article ("*clustering*"), and also suggests that it is written in a technical style, uses statistical techniques, and probably contains an algorithm of some kind. All of this is useful information for a rough-and-ready relevance indication, particularly in a document retrieval environment where no human-written indicative summary is available.

Experiments show that extracts are useful for reading comprehension (Morris et al., 1992) and for rapid relevance assessment (Mani et al., 2002). For reading comprehension, Morris et al. (1992) found no

[12]Discontinuities in sentences e) and f) are not AutoSummarize's "fault"; they are due to my representation for sentences containing equations in separate paragraphs, as will be explained in section 5.4.

a)	***Distributional Clustering of English Sentences***
b)	***Distributional Similarity*** *To cluster nouns n according to their conditional verb distributions pn, we need a measure of similarity between distributions.*
c)	*We will take (1) as our basic clustering model.*
d)	*In particular, the model we use in our experiments has noun clusters with cluster memberships determined by p(njc) and centroid distributions determined by p(vjc).*
e)	*Given any similarity measure d(n;c) between nouns and cluster centroids, the average cluster distortion is*
f)	*If we maximize the cluster membership entropy*
g)	***Clustering Examples***
h)	*Figure 1 shows the five words most similar to the each [sic] cluster centroid for the four clusters resulting from the first two cluster splits.*
i)	***Model Evaluation***
j)	*1990. Statistical mechanics and phrase transitions in clustering.*

FIGURE 13 AutoSummarize Extract for *Pereira et al. (1993).*

performance difference between subjects using the full text, subjects using indicative human-written summaries and subjects using extracts whose length was 20% and 30% of the original texts.[13] Mani et al. (2002) found in the SUMMAC evaluation that extracts of 17% length enabled subjects to perform relevance decision in half the time, with roughly the same precison and recall as a control group of subjects using the full documents.

Method

The first step in text extraction is to segment the text into units of extraction. In most cases these are sentences (e.g., Brandow et al., 1995, Kupiec et al., 1995), but they can also be paragraphs (e.g., Strzalkowski et al., 1999, Abracos and Lopes, 1997, Salton et al., 1994b). The segments are then scored according to some algorithmically determined measurement of their importance. Paice (1990) presents an early overview of commonly used extraction features. These include frequency of key words (Luhn, 1958, Baxendale, 1958), location of the sentence in the source text (Baxendale, 1958), connections with other sentences (Skorochod'ko, 1972, Salton et al., 1994a), lexical cohesion (Morris and Hirst, 1991, Barzilay and Elhadad, 1997), co-reference information (Baldwin and Morton, 1998), sentence length (Kupiec et al., 1995), presence of bonus/malus words (Luhn, 1958, Pollock and Zamora, 1975), title words (Edmundson, 1969), proper nouns (Kupiec

[13]In this book, I will express the level of summary compression in terms of the length of the original text. This is because I want to avoid the term *compression rate*, which is inherently confusing.

et al., 1995) and indicator phrases (Paice, 1981, Johnson et al., 1993). Some of these will be used in my approach and discussed in chapters 9 and 10.

There are also context- and similarity-based properties that could be taken into account when deciding what should be extracted. For instance, Radev et al. (2004) choose sentences which are most similar in vector space to the overall vector of the document, whereas Mihalcea and Tarau (2004) and Erkan and Radev (2004) choose sentences which scored high according to a variant of the PageRank (Brin and Page, 1998) algorithm.

Single heuristics tend to work well on document collections where documents resemble each other in style and content. For the more robust creation of extracts from texts with a high degree of variation in style, it is advantageous to combine these heuristics, by weighting their relative usefulness. While Edmundson (1969) assigns the weights manually, the weights of the features in Kupiec et al. (1995) are automatically adjusted according to corpus data. Their method requires as a prerequisite positive training examples, i.e., a definition of the "right answer". This is commonly called a *gold standard.*

Kupiec et al.'s (1995) define their gold standard as the set of sentences in the document which are maximally similar (aligned) to a sentence in the summary. They use a corpus of 188 engineering articles and align the sentences in a semi-automatic way: candidate sentences are initially automatically identified by edit-distance and then inspected by a human. Minor modifications between sentences are allowed, and partial matches are also recorded. In their dataset, 79% of the summary sentences are aligned with sentences in the source text.

Kupiec et al. redefine sentence extraction as a statistical classification task. The Naive Bayes (NB) Classifier in Fig. 14 is used to estimate the probability of a sentence to be contained in the summary, given its feature values, $P(F_j|s \in S)$. Probabilities for the occurrence of each individual feature ($P(F_j)$) are derived by maximum likelihood estimation from the corpus; the corresponding conditional probabilities in the abstract $P(F_j|s \in S)$ are likewise calculated.

Kupiec et al.'s best result is a co-selection of $P = R = 0.44$ (see next section). When they train their system on gold standards gained by uncorrected alignment, they find them almost as good as the manually corrected ones. Subsequently, the idea of using the summary as a gold standard has found a number of followers, including myself (Teufel and Moens, 1997, Mani and Bloedorn, 1998, Marcu, 1999a, Aone et al., 1999, Grover et al., 2003).

$$P(s \in S|F_1, \ldots, F_k) = \frac{P(F_1,\ldots,F_k|s\in S)P(s\in S)}{P(F_1,\ldots,F_k)} \approx \frac{P(s\in S)\prod_{j=1}^{k} P(F_j|s\in S)}{\prod_{j=1}^{k} P(F_j)}$$

$P(s \in S\|F_1, \ldots, F_k)$:	Probability that sentence s in the source text is included in summary S, given its feature values;
$P(s \in S)$:	Probability that a sentence s in the source text is included in summary S unconditionally; compression rate of the task (constant);
$P(F_j\| s \in S)$:	Probability of feature-value pair occurring in a sentence which is in the summary;
$P(F_j)$:	Probability that the feature-value pair occurs unconditionally;
k:	Number of feature-value pairs;
F_j:	j-th feature-value pair.

FIGURE 14 Kupiec et al.'s (1995) Naive Bayes Classifier.

Evaluation

Let us now turn to the question how the quality of an extract can be determined. Evaluation is usually performed by comparison to a gold standard; in the case of extraction, the gold standard is called the *target extract.* Agreement measures are then based on *co-selected* sentences, i.e., those sentences that are both chosen by the system and the target extract. One can then report *co-selection overlap*, i.e., the proportion of sentences in the document which are co-selected over all document sentences, *co-selection precision*, i.e., the proportion of co-selected sentences in the system extract, or *co-selection recall*, i.e., the proportion of co-selected sentences in the target extract. *Co-selection F-measure* can be calculated in the obvious manner as the harmonic mean of co-selection precision and co-selection recall. *Co-selection accuracy* exists as well; it considers sentence selection as a classification task and gives the proportion of sentences correctly classified as extracted or non-extracted, over total number of sentences in a document. What is unintuitive about this metric, however, is that it treats non-extracted sentences as equally important as extracted sentences, even though there are normally far more non-extracted sentences in a document. This means that co-selection accuracy is also dependent on document length, which further complicates matters.

Different definitions of target extracts exist. In early summarisation efforts, researchers often defined their own target extracts, relying only on their own intuitions (e.g., Luhn, 1958, Edmundson, 1969). A more objective approach is to use subjects who are not involved in the creation of the summarisation algorithm. Subjectivity and bias may be a problem even if the subjects have no part in the development of the summariser: Paice and Jones (1993) decide against evaluation by target extract, because they found a strong bias towards the subjects' individual research interests when they asked them to extract "important" sentences. Some researchers collate the target extracts from more than one human to create a majority opinion-based target extract. Even better methods of evaluation define the gold standard by some historic decision (e.g., of an information specialist). As such gold standards are outside the system developers' control at evaluation time, they are guaranteed to be unbiased.

Earl (1970) pioneered the use of historic relevance decisions as a gold standard. Her target extracts of book chapters are defined on the basis of a back-of-the-book index: for each index term, all sentences on the indexed page containing that indexed term are declared to belong to the target extract. Kupiec et al.'s definition of a gold standard as those document sentences which are maximally similar to summary sentences is in a similar vein: it uses the historic relevance decision of the person who produced the summary (the author or professional abstractor). In their case, there is still a human in the loop at evaluation time, namely the person who decides whether a document and a summary sentence are aligned or not. However, the decision whether two sentences mean the same thing is much more straightforward than the decision how important a sentence is within the document and should thus result in a more objective gold standard.

Most extraction experiments, including my own (Teufel and Moens, 1997), assume that the creation of target extracts by humans is a well-defined task, and do not measure human agreement. However, in the few cases where agreement was formally measured, it turned out to be problematically low.

Rath et al. (1961) asked six subjects to select 20 sentences out of *Scientific American* texts ranging from 78 to 171 sentences. Co-selection overlap was 8% between all six subjects, and 32% between five. Rath et al. also found that if they asked annotators after six weeks to choose sentences from the same texts again,[14] co-selection overlap was 55%. Salton et al. (1997) found 47% co-selection overlap between 2 subjects. Edmundson (1961) reports similarly low agreement.

Some researchers have reported higher agreement figures, but they use a different agreement metric, namely co-selection accuracy with re-

[14] This kind of agreement is called *intra-annotator* agreement; see chapter 8.

spect to the majority target extract defined by several subjects. Marcu (1997b) reports 71% co-selection accuracy with the majority target extract between 13 judges asked to select sentences from 5 *Scientific American* texts. In a different domain, Jing et al. (1998) report 96% agreement between 5 subjects, who were asked to produce 10% extracts of 40 news articles. These numbers have to be interpreted carefully, however: comparisons to majority opinion are always numerically inflated because the lowest possible value is 50% (see section 7.1). Another disadvantage is the above-mentioned sensitivity of co-selection accuracy to the number of non-selected sentences in a document, which can lead to artificially raised values in long documents.

Many summarisation researchers do not believe in comparisons to target extracts. There is a general consensus that "the" best sentence extract for a document does not exist (e.g., Jing et al., 1998, Boguraev et al., 1998, Mani, 2001). Rath et al. (1961) state that:

> "[the] lack of inter- and intra subject reliability seems to imply that a single set of representative sentences does not exist for an article. It may be that there are many equally representative sets of sentences which exist for any given article." (Rath et al., 1961, p. 141)

Sentence extraction seems to be another instance of the problem of situational relevance perception, which was discussed in section 2.2.1: Two human extracts might both be equally "good", but very different, so measuring a system against only one of them is potentially inaccurate.

Additionally, co-selection can only provide a binary measure of sentence identity. A system is penalised for selecting any sentence other than the ones extracted in the human gold standard, even if the system-selected sentence shares propositional content with one of the gold standard sentences. What one would want is a continuous measure of the similarity in meaning between sentences, so that a graded score can be given to such matches between sentences.

There are sub-sentential metrics which address this dilemma: Radev et al. (2003) discuss many string-based evaluation metrics. The Document Understanding Conference[15] DUC (e.g., 2001) used sentence co-selection as a measure in its early runs, but replaced it by two sub-sentential evaluation methods – ROUGE (Lin, 2004) and SCUs/pyramids (Nenkova and Passonneau, 2004), which are based on semantic units called factoids (van Halteren and Teufel, 2003). Semantic similarity is currently a hot research area, which is also examined to the RTE textual entailment task (Dagan et al., 2006).

[15]Later installations of this conference are called Text Analysis Conference (TAC).

There are baselines which extractive summaries are standardly compared against. One of these is the random baseline, i.e., a selection of n randomly extracted sentences. Another is the *leading* baseline, i.e., the n first sentences in the text. Brandow et al. (1995) were the first to report the disturbing fact that for news text, the leading baseline can be so high that most automatic sentence extraction systems, even reasonably sophisticated ones, will actually perform *below* it. However, the very concept of a "baseline" implies comparison to a mechanistic, simple algorithm rather than to human intelligence. This is not the case for the leading baseline in journalistic writing: as journalists are trained to place the most relevant information first, the leading baseline is in a way already the optimal human summary (and automatic systems are normally "sophisticated" enough to choose at least one sentence from somewhere else but the beginning). This would argue against the use of a leading baseline for news texts. In scientific articles, on the other hand, leading baselines have been found to do far less well; Kupiec et al.'s leading baseline achieves only (co-selection) $F = 0.24$ against their gold standard, in comparison to their best single feature (cue phrases) which achieved $F = 0.33$. This is due to the fact that introduction sections in scientific articles do not serve as a summary of the full text, unlike the initial sections in news text.

Problems

The summarisation literature agrees that extracts are generally texts of low readability and low text quality (Mani, 2001, Brandow et al., 1995, Cremmins, 1996, Boguraev and Kennedy, 1999). This impression is corroborated by findings that extracts are read much slower than comparable coherent text. In the SUMMAC evaluation (Mani et al., 2002), the extracts' average length was 17% of the full texts', but their average reading time was 50% of the full texts'. That means that proportionally, extracts were read three times slower than full texts. Long reading time is indicative of higher cognitive load during reading, which in turn is usually associated with low textual quality. However, it is possible that summaries, even human-written ones, are generally read slower than their source-texts, as King (1967) found in her experiments, possibly due to their higher information density.

Extracts often suffer from syntactic unconnectedness. They can contain uninterpretable ellipsis, references, or conjunctions. In particular, dangling anaphora are a common problem in extracts. There are suggestions in the literature how this particular problem could be remedied, e.g., by automatic anaphora resolution, by rejection of sentences with potential dangling anaphora (Paice and Husk, 1987) or by the additional inclusion of the previous sentence if it is likely to contain the referent (Johnson et al., 1993). Incidentally, the example extract in Fig. 13 (p. 49) does not contain any dangling anaphora, and each individual sentence can be interpreted in isolation.

But that still does not guarantee that the extract as a whole will be semantically interpretable and truth-preserving. Possible problems include repetition, logical jumps and unexpected topic shifts. An extract can contain non-introduced discourse participants and events as well as statements which will be interpreted in a truth-conditionally wrong way. For instance, sentence d) in Fig. 13, which starts with *"In particular"*, gives the impression that it elaborates on its predecessor sentence c), but this is unlikely: in the document context, the two sentences are separated by 24 sentences. In the best case, such cases are spotted by a reader; in the worst case, the reader will draw the wrong conclusions about the meaning of the original text, without even noticing that there is a problem.

The external form of how an extract is presented to the user can also matter: if a text looks like prose, readers will automatically try to construct a coherent interpretation of it (Kintsch and van Dijk, 1978). In order to visually signal that the output is not coherent prose, Kupiec et al. (1995) show their extract as an itemised list, whereas AutoSummarize displays the extracted material highlighted in its document context.

The problem of disconnectedness gets worse with longer and more complex input texts such as scientific texts. Morris' results show that readers need summaries of at least 30% of the original text in order to answer reading comprehension questions well. For newspaper text, extracts of that length would still be short enough to be read as an indicative "summary", even if its component sentences do not form a coherent text. A long scientific article of 20 pages, however, would have to be reduced to a 6-page collection of semantically unconnected sentences, which is not something that is fit for human consumption. Even if there was a tailoring post-processing step, it is not clear what it could do with such a collection of sentences. There is no way around the fact that the extracted material has lost something essential through the extraction process, which no later processing can restore.

Chapter Summary

In this chapter, I have described how summaries can help during scientific information management. We have seen that human-written summaries are high-quality texts produced at high cost. This is perfectly justified in a paper-based library environment, where the cycle of search–and–access is slow. High production cost is also one of the reasons why there is typically only one version of such summaries, which caters to an intermediate expertise level. This is a compromise, which often makes the resulting summaries too terse for non-experts and too verbose for informed readers. The automatic creation of user-tailored summaries is therefore an attractive goal.

With respect to which methods one might use for this task, this chapter has surveyed fact extraction and text extraction methods. While text extraction has the desirable property of robustness, it also has the problem that the extracted material is so semantically disconnected as to be unusable for direct post-processing.

Another problem is that traditional human-created summaries are designed with the needs of the slow-paced paper-based library world in mind. Today's electronic search environment puts us in a very different situation, where a new, fast-paced information workflow needs to be supported. Due to the electronic availability of the full document, the time span between search and access is now negligible. We do not know much about such environments and what kinds of document surrogates are most suitable for them; the little we know about how users actually use summaries stems from paper-based search environments and does not fully apply here. Also, the document surrogates we want to build are probably not going to be traditional summaries, but should also include some of the functionality from citation indexing, as discussed in chapter 2.

For these reasons, the design of adequate dynamic document surrogates will involve some experimentation. I believe that one should start the quest with a preliminary task and a simple, plausible prototype, which can be tested by users and subsequently improved. The proposals in the next chapter should be seen as initial designs of dynamic document surrogates in this spirit.

4

New Types of Information Access

Previous chapters have found that scientists' search needs often involve relations between articles, and that their search experience is affected by their level of expertise. These needs are not specifically catered for by today's information management tools, e.g., summaries, information retrieval engines and citation indexes. The current chapter starts with the observation that better searches in the scientific literature would be possible if the rhetorical context of the extracted material was known. This will lead to two proposals for new information access methods, one of which improves on sentence extraction, the other on citation indexing.

Both methods rely on an automatic analysis of the rhetorical structure of an article, which is performed in an offline fashion prior to the creation of the document surrogates. The rhetorical analysis, which is described in chapter 6, is the core contribution of this book. The information access methods presented here play an important role in the design of the rhetorical analysis, because they define the kinds of information that the analysis must deliver.

4.1 Rhetorical Extracts

We saw in the previous chapter that sentence extraction has various flaws, all of which have to do with the fact that contextual information is lost during the extraction process. Sentences are simply not stand-alone entities – as their meaning is strongly influenced by neighbouring sentences and by the logical and rhetorical organisation of the entire text, they often cannot be interpreted out of context. I am interested in the sentence's *rhetorical context*, i.e., its communicative function in the context of the article, such as "describe the research goal", "give conclusions", or "criticise previous research".

While there is a clear correlation between the propositional content of a sentence and its rhetorical function, the rhetorical function of a sentence cannot always be predicted from the propositional content alone. To see this, consider the following sentence from *Pereira et al. (1993)*, the example article well-known from chapters 2 and 3. It states that some approach works successfully:

> *The resulting clusters are intuitively informative, and can be used to construct class-based word coocurrence* [sic] *models with substantial predictive power.* (9408011, S-165)

This sentence could well describe the authors' reasons for using somebody else's approach as part of their solution. The same sentence in a different context could conversely be a statement of the authors' own success. (It happens to be the latter, but one needs to look at the context to make this distinction; the propositional content is not enough.)

Importantly, there is a connection between the rhetorical function and whether or not the sentence is relevant to a given information need (in addition to the well-known connection between a sentence's relevance and its propositional content). For instance, if we are interested in positive aspects of the authors' solution, the above sentence will be relevant in the second context and not in the first. This is not an isolated effect. Something similar happens with the very next sentence in the article:

> *While the clusters derived by the proposed method seem in many cases semantically significant, this intuition needs to be grounded in a more rigorous assessment.* (9408011, S-166)

This sentence, if it appeared in the motivation section, could well describe a limitation of somebody else's work. In that case the current article is likely to provide the promised rigorous assessment, and this might just meet somebody's information need. If, however, the sentence describes a limitation of the approach presented in the *current* article (as indeed it does), the rigorous assessment is, on the contrary, quite unlikely to be forthcoming in the article. This example also shows that the rhetorical function of a sentence can be influenced by its neighbours: if we already know that S-165 refers to the authors' own work, we are much more inclined to accept S-166 as a statement of limitations, rather than a motivation.

My first proposal for a new information access method exploits this observation. Simple tailored sentence extracts, which I call *rhetorical extracts*, are produced on the basis of a rhetorical analysis. This is

	Informed Reader	**Uninformed Reader**
General Purpose, Short	2 AIM	1 BACKGR. (AIM) 1 BACKGR. (PROBL.) 2 AIM
General Purpose, Long	2 AIM 2 SOLUTION	1 BACKGR. (AIM) 1 BACKGR. (PROBL.) 2 AIM 2 SOLUTION
Similarity/ Difference, Short	2 AIM 1–2 CONTRAST 1–2 BASIS	1 BACKGR. (AIM) 1 BACKGR. (PROBL.) 2 AIM 1–2 CONTRAST + DESCR. 1–2 BASIS + DESCR.
Similarity/ Difference, Long	2 AIM 2–3 CONTRAST 2–3 BASIS	1 BACKGR. (AIM) 1 BACKGR. (PROBL.) 2 AIM 2–3 CONTRAST + DESCR. 2–3 BASIS + DESCR.

FIGURE 15 Building Plans for Rhetorically Tailored Extracts.

performed prior to extraction and tags each sentence with its rhetorical function in the overall text.

Fig. 15 shows building plans for rhetorical extracts which are varied according to user expertise, task and length. Each label ("AIM", "BASIS") corresponds to one sentence of the respective rhetorical status. In contrast, "normal" sentence extracts cannot be tailored because their rhetorical information was lost during extraction (see section 3.2.2).

Uninformed readers require more background material in comparison to informed readers (Kircz, 1991, Paris, 1994); here, background information is provided by sentences of type "BACKGROUND (AIM/PROBL.)". As far as previous approaches are concerned, a citation might not be enough for uninformed readers to characterise an approach. The building plans therefore add a short description of the approaches ("DESCR."). As a result, extracts for uninformed readers are generally longer than those for informed readers.

The extracts can also be tailored to the task that is to be performed with them. I differentiate *general purpose* extracts from *similarity-and-*

difference extracts. The general purpose extracts are designed as decision aids in the "standard" task of relevance decision. For this task, we are looking for the most general, "vanilla" description of an article. Central to this is of course the main scientific goal of the article (the content unit "Aim"). Short general purpose extracts should consist of the best specific research goal sentence and nothing else; for their longer counterpart, one or more high-level sentences describing the method or results could be added ("Solution"). This simulates informative summaries.

In contrast, similarity-and-difference extracts have a more specific task: they characterise contrasts with similar articles, and describe intellectual ancestry between articles. Similarity-and-difference extracts distinguish the most relevant rival approaches ("Contrast") and the most relevant positively mentioned work ("Basis"). Behind this is the idea that an article is best characterised by its relation to similar articles, and by its overall position in a field. Therefore, relationships to published work are central in this type of extract.

The idea of rhetorical extracts is illustrated in Figs. 16 and 17. Fig. 16 gives a long general purpose extract for uninformed readers, whereas the extract in Fig. 17 is aimed at informed readers performing a similarity-and-difference task. They read reasonably well (with the possible exception of the first sentence in Fig. 17, which contains the dangling anaphor "similar"). Because the extract in Fig. 17 is created for an expert, previous approaches are characterised by citation alone. If the sentence that expresses the relationship happens not to contain the corresponding citation, as is the case in sentences S-9 and S-14, I attached the citation in parentheses.

One can vary the length of rhetorical extracts in a simple and obvious manner, e.g., by increasing or decreasing the number of previous approaches mentioned in similarity-and-difference extracts. In general, such extracts have the advantage of being generally highly compressed at around 5% of the length of the originals. Summary length in automatic summarisation is more typically in the 15–20% range (e.g., Mani et al., 2002, Tombros et al., 1998).

The extracts in Figs. 16 and 17 were created manually by selecting candidate sentences of the correct rhetorical type from the example article when more than one sentence of an information type is available, as is usually the case. However, for the experiment in section 12.2, where the concept of rhetorical extracts is tested, automatic extracts were needed. A simple implementation of the selection process is used, which makes a random choice. An example of such a rhetorical extract is given in Fig. 121 (p. 334).

BACKGR./AIM:
S-1 *Methods for automatically classifying words according to their contexts of use have both scientific and practical interest.*
BACKGR./PROBL.:
S-4 *The problem is that for large enough corpora the number of possible joint events is much larger than the number of event occurrences in the corpus, so many events are seen rarely or never, making their frequency counts unreliable estimates of their probabilities.*
AIM:
S-164 *We have demonstrated that a general divisive clustering procedure for probability distributions can be used to group words according to their participation in particular grammatical relations with other words.*
AIM:
S-22 *We will consider here only the problem of classifying nouns according to their distribution as direct objects of verbs; the converse problem is formally similar.*
SOLUTION:
S-26 *Our classification method will construct a set EQN of clusters and cluster membership probabilities EQN.*

FIGURE 16 Rhetorical Extract: General Purpose, Uninformed, Long.

More sophisticated methods for extract creation are possible. One could take into account the level of technicality of the terms contained in the sentences, for example. For the extract in Fig 16, which is targeted at uninformed readers, I chose AIM sentence S-164 because it contains relatively general terms (e.g., *to group, words, grammatical relations*). Contrast this to the comparable AIM sentence S-10 in the extract for informed readers (Fig. 17), which contains more technical terms (e.g., *to factor, word association tendencies*). A method for estimating the level of technicality of terms is suggested by Caraballo and Charniak (1999). Another option for improving the extracts is to maximise the (lexical) coherence of the resulting extract, by methods such as Siddharthan's (2003), who simplifies news text using coherence constraints, or Barzilay and Lapata's (2004), who use lexical coherence for sentence ordering in summaries.

It is generally thought that document surrogates such as extracts should not only be evaluated by what they *look* like and other intrinsic properties, but by how they perform in a real search task (Spärck Jones and Galliers, 1996, Teufel, 2001, Dorr et al., 2005). In such extrinsic evaluations, the quality of an extract is measured in terms of subjects' task performance. I will test rhetorical extracts in this way in section 12.2. I use a newly defined search task and my automatically

AIM:

S-10 *Our research addresses some of the same questions and uses similar data, but we investigate how to factor word association tendencies into associations of words to certain hidden senses classes and associations between the classes themselves.*

AIM:

S-22 *We will consider here only the problem of classifying nouns according to their distribution as direct objects of verbs; the converse problem is formally similar.*

CONTRAST:

S-9 *His notion of similarity seems to agree with our intuitions in many cases, but it is not clear how it can be used directly to construct word classes and corresponding models of association. (Citation in **S-5**: (Hindle 1990))*

CONTRAST:

S-14 *Class construction is then combinatorially very demanding and depends on frequency counts for joint events involving particular words, a potentially unreliable source of information as we noted above. (Citation in **S-13**: (Brown et al. 1992))*

BASIS:

S-113 *The analogy with statistical mechanics suggests a deterministic annealing procedure for clustering (Rose et al. 1990), in which the number of clusters is determined through a sequence of phase transitions by continuously increasing the parameter EQN following an annealing schedule.*

BASIS:

S-65 *The combined entropy maximization entropy and distortion minimization is carried out by a two-stage iterative process similar to the EM method (Dempster et al. 1977).*

FIGURE 17 Rhetorical Extract: Similarity–Difference, Informed, Short.

constructed rhetorical extracts are compared against competing document surrogates such as a list of keywords and the author's abstract.

Task- and expertise-tailoring of extracts is still a mainly unexplored area. The only other approach known to me which explicitly tailors extracts to tasks is manual and comes from the medical informatics community: Wellons and Purcell (1999) create a range of different extracts, which are modelled on structured abstracts (see section 3.1.2). The assumption behind this is that different kinds of content unit are needed for different types of professional work. There are five recurring medical tasks which they assume to be relevant for the readers of the *Annals of Internal Medicine*, namely (a) browsing the literature, (b) evaluating clinical studies, (c) matching patients with clinical studies, (d) treating/counselling patients, and (e) planning clinical research. An example for a content unit they use is *Experimental Setting.*

My approach is modelled on Wellons and Purcell's (1999) work, and also bears some similarities to fact extraction approaches (see section 3.2.1) as it too fills pre-existing slots with extracted material, as the building plans in Fig. 15 show. The main difference to both types of approach is the rhetorical nature of my slots: because of my decision to avoid modelling domain knowledge, the slots cannot be defined by constraints in the task domain (like in fact extraction), nor by medical task considerations (like in Wellon and Purcell's approach). As a result, my slot types are of a more general kind, e.g., SOLUTION, and should generalise to all kinds of experimental work.

I will now turn to the other information access method proposed here, which takes citation indexes rather than extracts as its starting point.

4.2 Citation Maps

My second proposal aims to support users' information gathering during the search process in a more dynamic manner. It is a new document surrogate called a *citation map*, which is designed for the interactive exploration of a set of related articles, by visualising an article's place in its field through its relation to related articles.

One aspect of information management that I have not discussed so far is the how the medium of reading interacts with the rest of the information access environment. With the move from printed to electronic articles, new display mechanisms evolved: previewers such as Ghostview or Adobe Acrobat can display the text in high quality and provide textual links (e.g., to references and section headings). However, studies of readers in electronic environments confirm that these cannot yet fully compensate for the loss of the physical properties of paper (Dillon et al., 2006, Hornbaek and Frokjaer, 2003, Qayyum, 2008, Obendorf and Weinreich, 2003, Dillon, 1992, Levy, 1997, Adler et al., 1998, O'Hara et al., 1998).

One of the strategies most affected by current display technology is the *non-linear* reading strategy (Samuels et al., 1987, Dillon et al., 1989, Hoey, 1991), which experienced scientists employ routinely. Non-linear reading involves scanning the table of contents, the conclusion and the section headers in order to build a model of the text's structure. The reader then extracts the main concepts of the article by jumping between the relevant points (Pinelli et al., 1984, Bazerman, 1988). This works well with printed articles, but O'Hara and Sellen (1997) found that non-linear reading is disrupted in electronic environments. They recommend that reading tools for electronic articles should retain the possibility for non-linear reading, possibly even actively encourage it. Recent function-augmented hypertext systems replace some of the functionality of paper and add new ways of interaction (Bradshaw and Light, 2007, Macinino and Scott, 2006, Couto and Minel, 2006).

What I suggest here is a type of information access that allows users to experience the processes of skim-reading, within-article navigation and search as parallel and interleaved activities. Some aspects of this are rather mundane: users should not have to download citing articles or find the relevant citation context in running text, as these are tasks which are easily automatable. Also, and this is a more involved task, intelligent document surrogates should be dynamically compiled in the background so that they are ready when needed.

As far as navigation within the article is concerned, the tool should provide the best possible description of which material can be found in which section. This might take the form of enriching an existing table of contents with extracted text pieces. I believe the main disincentive against non-linear reading in current electronic environments is that readers are not shown enough information about what they will find at the other end of a non-linear jump. Given how easily one can still get lost in an electronic article, they might decide against the risk of losing their current position in the article, and just page through it instead.

A search tool could counteract this tendency. If it detected a match between some piece of structural information (e.g., a headline), and the author's linguistic description of the contents of that section, it could convey this fact to the user, which should increase their confidence that what they will find at the end of a link is what they expect. (With respect to which linguistic descriptions might be useful for this task, I will later return to the concept of a "sign-post" sentence). The tool should also allow for the kind of finer-grained within-article navigation that I suggested in the introduction, e.g., it should allow a user to jump over detailed algorithm descriptions, or hide them from view.

As far as navigation between articles is concerned, an important aspect is the availability of summary-style information (the most salient points of an article) in parallel with relation-style information (relatedness between articles). None of the common document surrogates supplies both: manual summaries rarely contain reference to other work, as we saw in section 3.1.2, and citation indexers in turn do not make summary information available. But both types of information are needed simultaneously during a new-style search, where users can follow links, do keyword searches, and skim-read relevant passages. There is no fixed workflow in this type of search; text pieces displayed by the tool may either satisfy the user's information need or spark off a new search in a new direction. My design of a citation map illustrates which form an interleaved search environment could take.

Before we look at a citation map in detail, I should mention that it is a rather involved way of using rhetorical status for search. Other designs are possible. Kando (1997) and Kircz (1991) explore rhetorical indexing in information retrieval, i.e., they index different information types differently. Rhetorical indexing would allow a user to query for approaches criticising a particular approach or theory, for instance. At a much simpler level, Tbahriti et al. (2006) show experimentally that performance of their information retrieval engine increases if more weight is given to purpose- and conclusion-style sentences.

Fig. 18 shows a citation map. Citation relations between a set of articles from CmpLG-D[16] are graphically displayed, centred around the example article *Pereira et al. (1993)*, which is shown as a grey box in the middle. Articles are represented by their bibliographic details (authors and year of publication); boxed articles are those whose full text is contained in CmpLG, i.e., for which the reference list is available; non-boxed articles are those outside CmpLG, so only their bibliographic information is known.

All articles cited by the central article are shown here, as are the articles cited by these articles. Additionally, the six CmpLG-D articles which cite the central article are also shown. Given a citation index and an appropriate visualisation strategy, a graphical representation like this is already technically feasible. Everything I will describe from now onwards, however, is specific to my design.

The articles in Fig. 18 are further characterised by sentences describing their specific research goals (shaded circles above the article boxes). The sentences were extracted from the article's text and can be shown to the user on request. For the example article, this includes the following sentence (which we have already come across in the rhetorical extract in Fig. 16):

> *We have demonstrated that a general divisive clustering procedure for probability distributions can be used to group words according to their participation in particular grammatical relations with other words.*
> (9408011, S-164)

If one wants to explore relationships between articles, citation links are the method of choice. My proposal is to classify (or type) citation links, i.e., to augment them with a characterisation of their rhetorical

[16]CmpLG-D is a subset of CmpLG, the main corpus used in this book; see section 5.1.

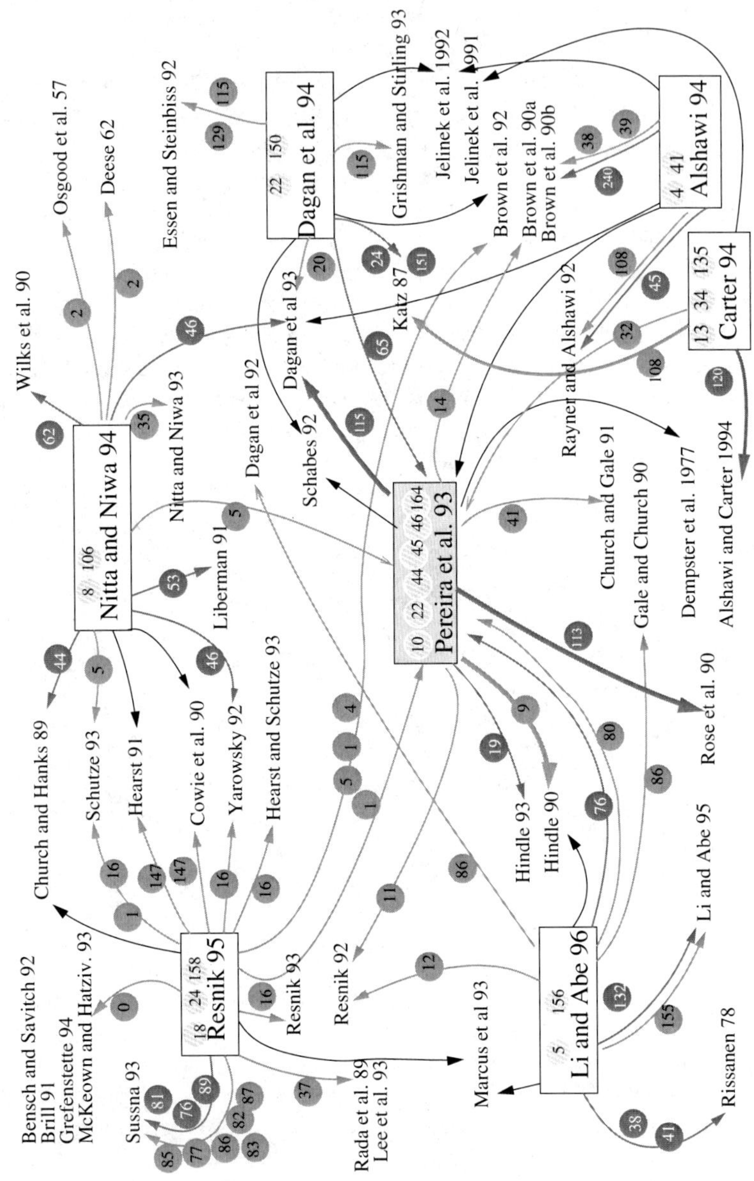

FIGURE 18 A Citation Map.

or sentiment type. The links shown in Fig. 18 are either *contrastive* (light grey arrows), *continuative* (darker grey arrows), or neutral (black arrows).

I have mentioned contrastive and continuative relationships before: while contrastive links include criticism, contrast or comparison, continuative links mark intellectual ancestry (where some prior work gives the intellectual basis for an article), use of an approach by another, supportive evidence, and positive review. In the field of computational linguistics, the use of the same grammar formalism or statistical framework can constitute a strong continuative link, whereas the use of (merely) somebody else's tool or data is a weaker continuative link.

Typed citation networks contain topological information which can be read off at a glance, i.e., without requiring access to the text. We can guess from the citation map that, of the articles which cite the central article, three must be quite similar because they all cite the example article contrastively (*Nitta and Niwa (1994)*, *Resnik (1995)* and *Carter (1994)*); the first two of these also contrastively co-cite a cluster of four other articles in the corpus (e.g., *Schütze (1993)* and *Hirst (1991)*). Two other articles (*Dagan et al. (1994)* and *Alshawi (1994)*) form another natural sub-cluster in that they cite the central article positively or neutrally.

When deciding which links to follow, one might also want to know how important a citation is to the citing article. Thicker arrows in the citation map correspond to more important citations. For instance, arrow thickness tells us that *Pereira et al.'s* use of *Hindle (1993)*'s work seems to be just a small part of the solution, whereas *Rose et al.*'s method is far more central. The estimation of local citation importance is another outcome of the rhetorical analysis proposed in this book. The analysis identifies the textual segment in an article which describes a particular cited approach. Under the assumption that important cited approaches are discussed at greater length, the citation arrow's thickness is determined by the size of its corresponding segment in the article.

The biggest technical and practical contribution of citation maps is that they enrich the topological information with textual information of the right rhetorical status. Link classification tells us that there is a criticism link between two articles, but in order to know in which aspect the work is criticised, we need to see text which describes the relationship to the cited article. For instance, the example article contains the following characterisation of its relationship to *Hindle (1990)*:

His notion of similarity seems to agree with our intuitions in many cases, but it is not clear how it can be used directly to construct word classes and corresponding models of association. (9408011, S-9)

In the citation map, the sentence number 9 appears in a circle next to the citation link arrow, which can be expanded upon request. As my definition of contrastive link includes neutral differences as well as criticism, the following mention of *Resnik (1992)* also qualifies:

While it may be worthwhile to base such a model on preexisting word classes (Resnik 1992), in the work described here we look at how to derive the classes directly from distributional data. (9408011, S-11)

There are also two continuative links in *Pereira et al. (1993)*:

The analogy with statistical mechanics suggests a deterministic annealing procedure for clustering (Rose et al. 1990). (9408011, S-113)

The corpus used in our first experiment was derived from newswire text automatically parsed with Hindle's (1993) parser Fidditch. (9408011, S-19)

These sentences confirm the relative importance of the citations estimated by segment length earlier, namely that the use of *Rose et al.*'s *(1990)* knowledge claim (which concerns a statistical method) is indeed more involved than that of *Hindle*'s *(1993)* knowledge claim (which concerns the mere use of a tool).

If some time has elapsed since the article was published, it may even have attracted some citations itself. The citation map can then also provide evidence about how it was received in its research community. In the case of *Pereira et al. (1993)*, incoming citation links appear soon after its publication. It is indeed the article that attracted most CmpLG-D-internal citations overall.[17]

We have already seen a contemporary list of incoming citations to *Pereira et al. (1993)*, namely the CiteSeer output in Fig. 3, which is from July 2009. The articles in CmpLG-D, however, were deposited between 1994 and 1996. Of the CmpLG-D articles that cite *Pereira et al. (1993)*, *Resnik (1993)* is most highly ranked in the 2009 list, and the only CmpLG-D article that made it into the top 7 shown in Fig. 3.

[17]Raw incoming citation counts should always be interpreted against the time frame in which an article could potentially have collected citations. *Pereira et al. (1993)* is one of the oldest articles in the corpus (only 6 out of the 80 CmpLG articles are from 1993 or earlier), and CmpLG covers only 28 months of deposit time (1994–1996), so the bulk of other articles had had less time to collect citations.

The citations to *Pereira et al.* are often located early in the citing articles' introduction sections (visible by the low sentence numbers next to the incoming arrows). This indicates that the article was perceived as an important approach within a relatively short time.

Three articles have continuative links to *Pereira et al.*, i.e., have taken up methods from it, namely *Resnik (1995)*, *Nitta and Niwa (1994)*, and *Li and Abe (1996)*, but it also incurred some contrastive citations, such as the following example from *Nitta and Niwa (1994)*:

> *However, using the co-occurrence statistics requires a huge corpus that covers even most rare words.* (9503025, S-5)

This example also shows that an article can have both contrastive and continuative links to another. Consider the continuative link from *Nitta and Niwa (1994)* to our example article:

> *Since then, there have been some promising results from using co-occurrence vectors, such as word sense disambiguation (Schütze 1993), and word clustering (Pereira et al. 1993).* (9503025, S-4)

Inexperienced users might be the ones that benefit most from citation maps. As they they still lack the terminology in the field, citation-based search is often generally a better option for them than keyword-based search, at least initially. If their search engine allows them to skim-read relevant parts of articles in a natural and interactive way, the population of their internal research map (Bazerman, 1985) can go hand in hand with the vicarious acquisition of relevant keywords.

Let us now consider where the rhetorical information needed for citation maps might be found in an article. In the examples given above, citation links are characterised by exactly one sentence. In general, however, it is not clear how much context is needed to convey the citation relationship. Nanba and Okumura (1999) display three sentences around the physical citation, whereas CiteSeer, which until recently used to display a sentence-like context of 100 characters around the citation, has now changed this to 400 characters, as shown in Fig 3.

Shorter, non-redundant characterisations are of course preferable, as they are more economical with screen space and users' reading time, but they run a higher risk of missing the relevant context. Wider contexts, such as the ones used by Nanba and Okumura and by the current incarnation of CiteSeer, have a better chance of finding the right context, but often still fail to do so. A CiteSeer-style context would represent the contrastive link with *Hindle (1990)* as follows:

> ... *ible joint events is much larger than the number of event occurrences in the corpus, so many events are seen rarely or never, making their frequency counts unreliable estimates of their probabilities.* **Hindle (1990)** *proposed dealing with the sparseness problem by estimating the likelihood of unseen events from that of "similar" events that have been seen. For instance, one may estimate the likelihood of a particular....*
> (9408011, S-4/S-6)

S-4 describes some of the general problems motivating *Pereira et al.*'s work, and S-5 and S-6 give a high-level summary of Hindle's approach. None of this characterises the authors' opinion of Hindle's work, repeating the effect from Fig. 3, where only 2 out of the top 7 citation contexts gave us a hint about the relationship to the cited article, despite the large amount of screen space their display occupies.

For the robust classification of citation links, it is obviously not enough to look at a fixed window around the citation, no matter how wide the window is. Results from section 8.6 confirm that textual separation between a citation and the expression of sentiment towards it is frequent. Moreover, because more important citations have more space allocated to their description, and evaluative sentences often occur at the end of their discussion, those citations tend to be particularly far removed from their evaluative sentence.

For these reasons, the automatic detection of the rhetorically "best" sentence such as sentence S-9 above, attractive as it is, is a hard task – certainly much harder than simply finding the physical citation, which is typographically marked. My solution, presented from chapter 6 onwards, is to use generalisations about the typical discourse structure in scientific articles for their detection.

The selection of the most informative sentence that expresses a citation relation also has a subjective element to it. While I opted for S-9 in the situation above, somebody else might have chosen a different sentence. It is therefore necessary to study to which degree humans agree in their selection of evaluative sentences, as I will do in chapter 8.

Note that the concept of similarity between articles I have developed here differs from the one used in much NLP work today, e.g., in latent semantic indexing, the vector space model or language modelling. Their type of similarity is *implicit*, in that it derives from a statistical analysis of the words used by the authors during the creation of their text. Such implicit lexical similarity exists whether or not the authors are aware of the other text. In contrast, similarity between articles in my approach is *explicit* in that it is derived from the authors' statements in the text.

Explicit similarity exploits the fact that authors were aware of the the relation to other works and tell us about it, using the medium of natural language. This task of interpreting this type of similarity is closer to artificial intelligence than the statistical approaches, and relatively under-explored.

Similarity by citation behaviour, as has been used for information management for a long time (Small, 1973, Kessler, 1963), has an intermediate status somewhere between explicit and implicit similarity: while the authors are obviously aware of the work they directly cite, important aspects of citation-based similarity arise in a distributed manner from the entirety of the citation network, and therefore could not be predicted by the authors at the time of writing.

As explicit and implicit similarity are complementary, one can expect that their combination should be beneficial.

Chapter Summary

In this chapter, I have suggested two new methods for information access to the scientific literature:

- Rhetorical extracts, which are tailored to the expertise of the user reading them, and to the task they are performing;
- Citation maps, which allow for the interactive exploration of citation links.

What is common between these two methods is that they both characterise an article by its relation to other articles. A second commonality is the methods' reliance on rhetorically defined content units such as "criticism of an article" and "goal statement". I have argued that the same rhetorical analysis could support both methods, and could additionally be used for non-linear navigation within an article and for estimations of citation importance.

The rhetorical analysis that stands behind these applications will be a core theme from now on – how it can be defined and automated, and to what degree humans agree on its phenomena. It will be introduced in chapter 6, where I describe my discourse model and the phenomenology of rhetoric and argumentation in science which lead to it. Chapter 7 operationalises the model so that it can be directly annotated in text, and chapter 8 measures to what degree humans can reliably annotate it in naturally occurring text. Later chapters will be concerned with automation.

The next chapter will pave the way for these practical experiments by describing the corpora that I collected and used for this work.

5

Experimental Corpora

The practical approach in this book is corpus-linguistic; the aim is to develop a robust and practical discourse analysis for unrestricted scientific text. Corpus-based or empirical natural language research advocates the study of examples of real life language use, whereby a large sample of naturally occurring (and thus unpredictable) language is used, rather than invented or artificially simplified examples. As a general methodology, corpus linguistics has come back into fashion in the past two decades, and is now used for many research questions and tasks in theoretical linguistics and natural language processing, e.g., lexicography, word sense disambiguation and lexical semantics (Manning and Schütze, 1999). While the aim in such research is to describe as much of the data as possible, it not normally possible to account for 100% of the data.

It is nowadays generally accepted that corpora are a reliable source of frequency-based data. The use of corpora is also a more powerful scientific methodology than introspection as it is open to verification of results (Leech, 1992), and as it will turn up "real examples" – with all the unexpected turns of real language use which even a talented linguist's introspection alone cannot predict. Additionally, new formulations due to language change can only be detected by a corpus-based method.

I believe that corpus-based studies are a particularly good idea for discourse linguistics. As discourse theories cannot be directly validated, one of the most convincing ways to substantiate such claims is to show that they can be applied to many different arbitrary real-world texts of the kind the theory claims to cover. The texts should be naturally-occurring and non-edited.

The current chapter describes the experimental corpora used in this book for experimentation and model development. The corpora cover five scientific disciplines and consist of 581 articles, totalling 2.5 million words. Illustrative examples from those corpora will be used throughout the book.

The most important corpus, CmpLG, is in the discipline of computational linguistics. Its 352 conference articles were taken from the Computation and Language E-Print Archive (`http://xxx.lanl.gov/cmp-lg`) and cover the years 1994-2001.

A subpart of this corpus was the main corpus for the experiments reported in chapters 8 and 12. It contains 80 articles from 1994-1996 and is now called CmpLG-D. CmpLG and CmpLG-D are described in section 5.1, along with many of their properties which play a role for discourse structure, such as to what degree their authors follow the IMRD section structure (see section 3.1.2), and how similar their summary sentences are to sentences in the body of the text (see section 3.2.2).

Section 5.2 describes the corpus in the second discipline I experimented with, namely chemistry. The other corpora are from genetics, cardiology and agriculture; they will be discussed in section 5.3.

All texts are encoded in an XML vocabulary called SciXML, which records the physical structure of the articles. SciXML originated in my PhD work, and has been used and reworked in several projects I was involved with at Columbia University (Teufel and Elhadad, 2002) and at the Cambridge University Computer Laboratory (Rupp et al., 2008, Lewin, 2007). In section 5.4, I will give a brief description of the SciXML format and explain how the various corpora were converted into this format.

5.1 Computational Linguistics (CmpLG)

Computational Linguistics (CL) is a nascent, highly interdisciplinary field, which incorporates experimental sciences (psychology, neuroscience), engineering (language engineering, software engineering), humanities (linguistics, philosophy of science), applied sciences (discourse analysis, English for Special Purposes), artificial intelligence and theoretical computer science. Articles often combine research methodologies from more than one discipline, e.g., a psychological experiment of some language phenomenon might be accompanied by a computer simulation. The interdisciplinary nature of the field was one of the reasons why I chose it as the first discipline to work on. It provides a challenging mix of methodologies and presentation and writing traditions, and can thus arguably serve as a stand-in for a corpus covering various different disciplines. There is also a practical reason for the choice of CL: if one is working in one's own field, then the annotation and assessment of system output does not necessarily require any outside experts.

Moreover, the field of computational linguistics is compact: the currently 16,000 articles in the ACL Anthology cover the most important computational linguistics publications from 1962 to now.[18] If an entire field is encapsulated in tens of thousands of articles rather than millions of articles, this is useful for the study of sociological developments, such as the development of schools of thought. It is also of advantage in studies of citation behaviour, because collections in compact fields often have a higher proportion of collection-internal citations.[19]

5.1.1 Source

The source of the CmpLG corpus is the Computation and Language Archive (CMP_LG, 1994), a preprint archive which is part of the CoRR (Computing Research Repository).[20] If a preprint archive is mediated, as CMPLG is, then a mediator makes sure that only appropriate and relevant material is deposited. Most of the articles deposited on the CMPLG archive are conference or workshop articles.

The function of preprint archives is twofold: to allow for rapid dissemination of research results by making articles available to the research community after peer review, but before formal publication, and to archive the articles in a field for later use. Preprint archives were more prevalent in the 1990s than they are now. It is now more common for researchers to put camera-ready articles on their websites (Goodrum et al., 2001), where search engines can index them. This takes care of the function of making articles available, but has an undesirable side-effect for practical corpus collection.

Articles on personal webpages typically use the portable document format (PDF), a visual and printer format which does not guarantee that the text is fully machine-readable. For processing which requires the full text as well as the structural properties of an article, e.g., the parsing of the reference list, PDF is therefore problematic. In contrast, articles on preprint archives are deposited in their source text (often LaTeX), which makes it more feasible to automatically extract structuring information as well as clean text, without the need to use optical character recognition (OCR). This was initially my main reason for choosing CMPLG as my source.

[18] I will describe the ACL Anthology corpus in section 14.4.

[19] Ritchie (2008) finds this to be true for the ACL Anthology; results in section 14.4.

[20] To distinguish the archive from the corpus, I will refer to the archive as CMPLG and to the corpus I collected from it as CmpLG.

For computational linguistics, the ACL Anthology has now mostly taken over the second function that was traditionally performed by CMPLG, namely the backward archiving of historic material.

If a preprint archive is chosen as a corpus source, one may have to filter the articles, as the deposition of articles there is voluntary and unsystematic; researchers may choose to deposit many or none of their articles. Filtering is necessary for reasons of representativeness. Representativeness is an important property for any corpus: corpora are supposed to be a "random sample" of the larger universe of texts they represent. What should be avoided is the selection of a subset of texts with special properties which do not apply to the entirety of texts. To counteract this, one should define formal and replicable selection criteria before starting the data collection.

A small corpus taken from a preprint archive can never be as representative of a discipline as a large repository such as the ACL Anthology, which contains most of the high-quality texts published in the entire field of computational linguistics (and only these). However, there should be no systematic difference between the articles in the CmpLG corpus and any selection of new articles from the CMPLG archive.

CmpLG consists of 352 articles deposited between the beginning of the preprint archive in 1994 and the end of the second data collection phase in December 2001. Each article on the CMPLG archive is uniquely identified by its CMPLG number: a 7-digit string, where the first two digits are reserved for the year, the next two for the month, and the last three are a running number of articles deposited that month starting at "001" (i.e., allowing for a maximum of 999 articles per month).[21] CmpLG mostly contains conference articles, but also three very long journal articles.[22]

These 352 articles are a subset of the 968 articles which had been deposited during this time frame. Any article which fulfilled the following selection criteria was included in CmpLG:

- It had to be peer reviewed in a CL-relevant conference or journal, which means that all PhD theses were excluded.
- Its LaTeX source had to be available.
- It had to have an abstract.
- It had to pass through my automatic LaTeX to SciXML conversion pipeline.[23]

[21]The example article used throughout this book, *Pereira et al. (1993)*, which has CMPLG number 9408011, is thus the 11th article deposited in August 1994.

[22]9404008, 9503008, 9504003.

[23]About 20% did not pass or showed too many errors for manual correction.

CmpLG-D is an 80-article subset of CmpLG. It was compiled in 1996 in collaboration with Byron Georgantopolous. At that time, no publicly available full-text corpus of scientific articles existed; many other sources of articles, e.g., the US National Library of Medicine's bibliographic database MEDLINE, distributed only abstracts. The "D" in the corpus name stands for "development", as it was used to develop the earliest prototype of the systems described in chapter 11.

In order to be part of CmpLG-D, a CmpLG article had to be deposited between 04/94 and 05/96 and published in one of the following conferences or workshops (including student sessions):

- ACL, the *Annual Meeting of the Association for Computational Linguistics*;
- EACL, the *Meeting of the European Chapter of the Association for Computational Linguistics*;
- any ACL-sponsored or EACL-sponsored workshop;
- ANLP, the *Conference on Applied Natural Language Processing*;
- COLING, the *International Conference on Computational Linguistics*.

The length of the articles was restricted by the publication rules of the corresponding conference or workshop proceedings. Most articles are between 6 and 8 pages; minimum and maximum values are 3 and 10 pages. A list of all CmpLG-D articles with their statistics is given in appendix A. A version of CmpLG-D has been distributed by the TIPSTER initiative as part of the SUMMAC program (Tipster SUMMAC, 1999).

Fig. 19 gives the profile of publication years in CmpLG and CmpLG-D. Note that the year of publication can be different from the year of deposit, which is marked in the article's ID number. Only 11 CmpLG articles were published before the start of the archive in 1994.

Fig. 20 gives the statistics for CmpLG and CmpLG-D, in terms of words, sentences, abstract sentences and paragraphs. CmpLG consists of roughly 1.5 million words, with an average of 165 sentences per article.

Year	**87**	**88**	**89**	**90**	**91**	**92**	**93**	**94**	**95**	**96**	**97**	**98**	**99**	**00**	**01**
CmpLG	1	2	1	3	0	1	3	54	78	57	63	37	15	36	1
CmpLG-D	1	1	1	1	0	1	1	33	35	6	0	0	0	0	0

FIGURE 19 Frequency of Publication Years in CmpLG and CmpLG-D.

Articles in CmpLG-D and CmpLG are encoded in SCIXML format (see section 5.4). The text and XML markup is very clean, considering

	CmpLG	CmpLG-D
Articles	352	80
Words	1,587,908	337,522
avg/article	4,511	4,219
min/max	1,332/15,842	1,332/7,726
Sentences (in body of text)	58,156	12,471
avg/article	165	156
min/max	45/669	45/322
Abstract Sentences	1,602	356
avg/article	4.6	4.5
min/max	1/13	2/13
Paragraphs	17,211	3,842
avg/article	48	48

FIGURE 20 Corpus Statistics for CmpLG and CmpLG-D.

that they were imported through an information-lossy process. Their initial processing was automatic, but I have manually corrected them with respect to most aspects of the markup over the years. For instance, CmpLG-D no longer contains any sentence boundary errors; CmpLG may still contain some such errors, but they get repaired whenever a problem is noticed, e.g., during annotation work.[24] The most recent checks were for correctness of references (i.e., items in the reference list), and for correctness of citations in running text.

CmpLG consists almost exclusively of conference articles, rather than journal articles, and there is a question as to whether this might constrain the research done with it in any way. But with respect to the phenomena that matter to me (e.g., the scientific argumentation), journal and conference articles are very similar, and my discourse model should in principle describe journal articles as well as conference articles. Some informal experiments with articles from the journal *Computational Linguistics* have confirmed this.

As far as the scientific quality of the articles is concerned, we should not see much of a difference, as conferences are important in CL.[25]

[24]This means that over time, slightly different versions of CmpLG or CmpLG-D have been used for experiments. For instance, the contingency table on p. 278, which was compiled from the 1999 version of CmpLG-D, report a total of 12,422 sentences. The 2002 version of the CmpLG-D, which is used in Teufel and Moens (2002), has 12,188 sentences. The 2007 version of the CmpLG-D, which was used in the experiments in chapter 12, has 12,464 sentences, whereas the current, "final" CmpLG-D version (Fig. 20) has 12,471 sentences.

[25]However, Goodrum et al.'s (2001) study of citation behaviour in computer science (which is very similar to CL as a discipline) found that the most highly cited articles are journal articles and books, not conference articles.

Working with relatively shorter texts is also of advantage if one wants to sample as many different writing and argumentation styles as possible, given that the time available for annotation is always limited.

There are nevertheless factors which would make the analysis of journal articles attractive. Journal articles should be of a generally higher text quality than conference articles, because they are more rigorously edited. They also have more space to cite a greater number of previous approaches, which is of advantage to citation function classification, one of the annotation schemes introduced in chapter 7, for which there are never enough data points (citations) in an article. My approach to rhetorical relations would also profit from the fact that cited approaches are discussed in more detail in journal articles: the approach depends heavily on the explicit mention of previous work, as will become clear in chapter 6.

The greater length of journal articles also presents a challenge for summarisation. It has been suggested that summarisation approaches which take large-scale discourse structure into account, such as mine, should be able to deal with longer articles better than approaches which do not (Spärck Jones, 1994).

Let us now look at CmpLG-D in more detail, in particular at its structural properties.

5.1.2 Properties

Most CmpLG articles are concerned with logic programming, statistical language modelling, theoretical semantics and computational psycholinguistics. I estimate that most of the articles (about 45%) concern implementational work, 25% theoretical linguistic work, 20% experimental work (corpus studies or psycholinguistic experiments) and 10% evaluation (i.e., no new methodology is introduced in these articles; instead, known systems or theories are compared and evaluatively measured).

In terms of text quality, the CmpLG articles contain typographical errors and some instances of not fully grammatical English, although the majority of the articles are acceptable; they seem to be either written by or at least proofread by native speakers. However, there is a large variability in terms of register, as the following sentence pair illustrates:

> *While these techniques can yield significant improvements in performance, the generality of unification-based grammar formalisms means that there are still cases where expensive processing is unavoidable.*
> (9502021, S-7)

> *This paper represents a step toward getting as much leverage as possible*

out of work within that paradigm, and then using it to help determine relationships among word senses, which is really where the action is.
(9511006, S-158)

Computational linguistics is a young discipline, and informal descriptions of the research are often accepted at conferences.

The use of passive voice to refer to the author's own work is another common aspect of scientific writing style, particularly in the life sciences. This phenomenon is not prevalent in CmpLG-D; although I found some examples of such use of the passive voice, the majority of the authors use active constructions to refer to themselves.

To what extent is the IMRD section structure present in CmpLG-D? Fig. 21 lists the most frequent CmpLG-D headlines in comparison to corpora in cardiology, chemistry and genetics (these corpora will be described later in this chapter). Only 29 articles in the chemistry corpus could be used, as the other 21 did not contain any headlines.

CmpLG-D (80 articles)		**Cardiology** (66 articles)	
Introduction	79% (63)	Introduction	100% (66)
Conclusion(s)	59% (47)	Results	98% (65)
Acknowledg(e)ment(s)	31% (18)	Discussion	98% (65)
Discussion	16% (13)	Methods	96% (64)
Example	13% (10)	Conclusion(s)	46% (31)
Experimental Results	10% (8)	Statistics	43% (29)
Results	10% (8)	Limitations	33% (22)
Evaluation	9% (8)	Statistical Analysis	25% (17)
Background	9% (7)	Patients	25% (17)
Implementation	8% (7)	Patient Characteristics	15% (10)
Chemistry (29 articles)		**Genetics** (69 articles)	
Introduction	100% (29)	Discussion	68% (47)
Results and discussion(s)	68% (20)	Result(s)	62% (43)
Conclusion(s)	68% (20)	Introduction	57% (39)
Experimental	62% (18)	Conclusion(s)	48% (33)
Discussion	27% (8)	Materials and Methods	43% (30)
Results	24% (7)	Background	41% (28)
Materials and methods	13% (4)	Method(s/ology)	33% (23)
Materials	10% (3)	Supporting Information	30% (21)
Experimental section	10% (3)	Competing Interests	30% (21)
Experimental set-up	6% (2)	Authors' Contributions	29% (20)

FIGURE 21 Most Frequent Headlines in CmpLG, Cardiology, Chemistry and Genetics Corpora.

As was expected, the cardiology corpus is largely compliant with the IMRD structure: I (100%), M (96%), R (98%), D (98%), C (46%). The low frequency of *Conclusion* sections is as per van Dijk's (1980) prediction. After rank 5, there are lower-level headlines which roughly correspond to Kircz's (1991) categories. In chemistry, a similar picture emerges, although there are variations in terms of headlines: "Methods" is typically replaced by "Experimental", and some combination of the result and discussion sections can be observed. If these are normalised, the numbers are: I (100%), M (95%), R (92%), D (92%), C (68%).

Even more normalisation was necessary in the genetics corpus, which superficially does not look as if it complies to IMRD well. Lexical variations include "Background" for "Introduction", "Materials and methods" and "Experimental" for "Methods". 14 articles have a joined "Results and Discussion" sections, which I split. This leads to an IMRD compliance of I (95%), M (84%), R (83%), D (88%) and C (56%).

In contrast, CmpLG-D is far less well-described by the IMRD model. After headline normalisation (e.g., "Implementation" for "Methods", and "Evaluation" for "Results"), the numbers are: I (88%), M (10%), R (22%), D (16%), C (59%). That means that the only two common IMRD sections in CmpLG-D are introductions and conclusions. While clearly marked discussion sections are rare, most deviation from IMRD occurs with respect to the presentation of methodology: in the entire corpus there were only two headlines called "Method" or "Methods" (the others were variations such as "Implementation"). As CL is nevertheless largely an experimental science, authors must be packaging up the corresponding textual material idiosyncractically, i.e., under non-prototypical headlines (e.g., "Multiple Adjunction"). Later experiments in chapter 11 will confirm that more than 45% of all sentences in CmpLG-D are covered by non-prototypical section headings.

We might have expected a small part of CmpLG-D to be non-IMRD compliant, namely the theoretical linguistic articles. These consist mainly of interpretative arguments and narrative supporting those arguments, as is typical in the humanities (see section 3.1.2). However, the numbers in Fig. 21 indicate some other anti-IMRD influence, which probably comes from computer science, the other strong tradition in computational linguistics. Orasan's (2000) results point in this direction: he analyses 67 journal and conference articles in computer science and finds that only 58% contain the content units he expects (namely *Introduction, Problem, Solution, Evaluation* and *Conclusion*) in that order. There are some life-science style experimental articles in CL, but obviously not enough to counteract this tendency. This means that a discourse model that sets out to model the structure in CmpLG articles cannot simply rely on the IMRD structure, but will need a more flexible means of description.

Another property of interest is whether CmpLG's abstract sentences align with its document sentences. I therefore replicated the first step of Kupiec et al.'s (1995) extraction method (Teufel and Moens, 1997). The similarity measure used is based on the longest common subsequence (LCS) of non-stop-list words.[26] The length of the longest common subsequence between two strings X and Y can be calculated as follows:

$$LCS(X,Y) = \frac{length(X) + length(Y) - edit(X,Y)}{2}$$

where $edit(X,Y)$ is the minimum number of deletions and insertions necessary to transform X into Y. Normalisation by the average lengths of the two input strings (sentences) turns the length of the longest common substring into a similarity score which ranges between 0 and 1:

$$LCS_{\text{norm}}(X,Y) = \frac{2 \cdot LCS(X,Y)}{length(X) + length(Y)}$$

LCS-similarity disagrees with semantic similarity often enough to make manual post-correction necessary. If a sentence pair displays a very high LCS_{norm} score (≥ 0.8), it was automatically marked as aligned. Those pairs with medium LCS_{norm} scores (between 0.5 and 0.8) were manually checked. Here is an example of a human-confirmed match of two sentences:

> **Summary:** *In understanding a reference, an agent determines his confidence in its adequacy as a means of identifying the referent.* (9405013, A-3)
>
> **Document:** *An agent understands a reference once he is confident in the adequacy of its (inferred) plan as a means of identifying the referent.* (9405013, S-131)

Here is an example of a non-match despite a reasonably high LCS score:

> **Summary:** *Recent studies in computational linguistics proposed computationally feasible methods for measuring word distance.* (9601007, S-2)
>
> **Document:** *The paper proposes a computationally feasible method for measuring context-sensitive semantic distance between words.* (9601007, A-0)

[26] My implemention follows the Hirschberg (1975) algorithm.

In this example, one sentence refers to previous work and the other to the new work introduced in the article; the human judge therefore decided against the match.

The resulting alignment rate was only 31%, as opposed to the 79% alignment rate measured by Kupiec et al. for a corpus of engineering articles. The drastic difference in alignment rates is probably mainly due to the fact that the CmpLG abstracts, as conference articles, are written by the authors, whereas the abstracts in Kupiec et al.'s journal articles were written or at least checked by professional abstractors. The summarisation literature agrees however that author abstracts are of a lower text quality in comparison to professional abstracts (Lancaster, 1998, Cremmins, 1996, Rowley, 1982, Borko and Bernier, 1975, Dillon et al., 1989).

Fig. 22 illustrates the alignment phenomenon using the example article. The human judge rejected most of the LCS-suggested alignments (these are shown greyed out; LCS_{norm} scores are given in parentheses), and only accepted the alignment between abstract sentence A-0 and document sentences S-0 and S-164. But the quality of this match is low: Firstly, its component matches are *partial*, i.e., only parts of sentences S-0 and S-164 overlap with abstract sentence A-0. Secondly, the match is *additive*: the matching parts of sentences S-0 and S-164 align with A-0 only if taken together.

I manually searched all CmpLG-D articles for possible alignments overlooked by LCS (Teufel and Moens, 1997), which uncovered some new alignments. However, for many abstract sentences, no match was found; often the material in the abstracts was at a higher level of abstraction than that of the closest document matches. Not much is known about how non-information specialists create their abstracts, but a possible explanation is that many CmpLG authors wrote their abstracts from scratch, rather than reuse textual material from the body of the text as professional abstractors do (see section 3.1). Unfortunately, such cases systematically undermine the assumption behind the surface-similarity alignment approach.

The author-written abstracts are also less systematically structured in rhetorical terms; there are large individual differences and few shared rhetorical patterns (see results in section 8.6), quite unlike the nicely structured abstracts that trained abstractors tend to produce (Liddy, 1991). Another problem concerns the rule that abstracts are supposed to be self-contained, i.e., that they should be understandable without reference to the full article. Several CmpLG abstracts are not. In five cases, the abstracts even contain information which is not repeated anywhere else in the main article. This means that not even the *article*

Abstract sentences	Aligned document sentences
A-0 *We describe and experimentally evaluate a method for automatically clustering words according to their distribution in particular syntactic contexts.*	**S-0** `(partial match)`: *Methods for automatically classifying words according to their contexts of use have both scientific and practical interest.* (0.421) **S-164** `(partial match)` *We have demonstrated that a general divisive clustering procedure for probability distributions can be used to group words according to their participation in particular grammatical relations with other words.* (0.287)
A-1: *Deterministic annealing is used to find lowest distortion sets of clusters.*	**S-113** `(match rejected)`: *The analogy with statistical mechanics suggests a deterministic annealing procedure for clustering [Rose et al. 1990], in which the number of clusters is determined through a sequence of phase transitions by continuously increasing the parameter EQN following an annealing schedule.* (0.296)
A-2: *As the annealing parameter increases, existing clusters become unstable and subdivide, yielding a hierarchical "soft" clustering of the data.*	**S-49** `(match rejected)`: *As in unsupervised learning. the goal is to learn the underlying distribution of the data.* (0.308)
A-3: *Clusters are used as the basis for class models of word coocurrence,* [sic] *and the models evaluated with respect to held-out test data.*	**S-165**: `(match rejected)` *The resulting clusters are intuitively informative, and can be used to construct class-based word coocurrence models with substantial predictive power.* (0.304)

FIGURE 22 Alignment between Abstract and Document Sentences in *Pereira et al. (1993).*

is self-contained. The authors must have assumed that the abstract would always be read before the main document, and "misused" it as an introduction, possibly to save space. Again, in such a situation, any alignment between abstract and the full article is by definition impossible.

This concludes the (informal) description of CmpLG-D properties in terms of size, research types covered, linguistic quality, register, IMRD compliance, abstract quality, and alignment. We will now turn to the corpus' citation behaviour.

5.1.3 Citation Behaviour

CmpLG markup recognises both references and citations. What is meant by a *reference* is an item in the bibliography list at the end of an article, whereas a *citation* (or a *citation instance*) refers to the occurrence of such a reference in running text. Marking up references is common in modern digital libraries, but it is still unusual to also mark up citations, as it requires a more involved processing of both the reference list and the entire running text. (How this is done in detail will be described in section 11.1.) This is particularly the case for the citation style common in CmpLG.

Citations in computational linguistics follow almost exclusively the Harvard citation style, where both the author and the date are given in running text. The bracketing style distinguishes between cases where the citation is *authorial*, i.e., where it forms a syntactic part of a sentence, often as the subject, and those where it is *parenthetical*, i.e., where it does not constitute a syntactic part of the sentence. In authorial citations only the year appears in parentheses, in parenthetical citations both the authors' names and the year.

	CmpLG	**CmpLG-D**
References, total (token)	6,027	1,260
total (type)	3,655	977
occurring only once	2,649	789
avg/article	17.2	15.8
min/max	4/53	4/37
Self-references	833 (14%)	138 (9%)
Citation Instances, total	8,260	1,714
avg/article	23.6	21.4
min/max	2/77	2/50
Self-citations	1,325 (16%)	323 (5%)
Cited Authors, total	2,568	483
avg/article	7.3	6.0
min/max	0/79	0/79

FIGURE 23 Citation Statistics for CmpLG and CmpLG-D.

Fig. 23 lists the numbers of references, citations, and cited author names found in CmpLG and CmpLG-D. The difference between *token* and *type* counts in the figure refers to whether repetition of the same item is taken into account (token) or not (type). Overall, the numbers show that CmpLG-D and CmpLG are similar: an article contains on average roughly 16 references, 22 citation instances and 6 cited authors. The proportion of self-citations differs between CmpLG-D and CmpLG, from 5% to 16%. The proportion of self-references shows a similar, but less strong tendency. This is somewhat surprising, but it could possibly be explained by the difference in publication types between the two corpora.

In order to compile the numbers in Fig. 23, formal citations had to be identified in running text and linked to their corresponding reference items. All references within CmpLG are globally disambiguated, so that citation and reference identifiers uniquely point to the same articles. I also disambiguated author names (including first names); this is a pre-requisite to recognising and marking self-citations and self-references.

Let us now see how this processing can be applied to bibliometric measures. Fig. 24 contrasts the most referenced with the most cited articles in CmpLG. Articles which are themselves contained in CmpLG are shown in boldface. 160 CmpLG articles are cited at least once within CmpLG (46%), whereas only 15 CmpLG-D articles (19%) are cited at least once within CmpLG-D (including *Pereira et al. (1993)*). The difference between Cmplg-D and CmpLG is probably due to the fact that the core of CmpLG-D covers only 28 months (between March 1994 and June 1996). In the citation life-span of a typical CmpLG article, this is not long enough to collect a representative number of citations.

The left-hand side of Fig. 24 shows reference numbers, as used in traditional bibliometric measures. We can see that within CmpLG, *Marcus et al. (1993)* is the most-referenced article.[27]

The right-hand side of Fig. 24 shows the frequencies of citation instances in running text. Traditional bibliometric metrics assume that all citations are equal in importance, but we have heard arguments against this assumption in section 2.3.1. Citation instance counts which are not commonly used by bibliometric measures or citation indexers, but I believe they could be of benefit to them. Citation instances can be used to estimate the local importance of a reference within its citing article. They also allow us to differentiate between references which are mentioned only once in most articles ("ticked off"), from those which are debated and discussed in detail in a scientific field.

In the citation instance list, *Marcus et al. (1993)* is demoted to third rank. This may have to do with the fact that it describes a widely-used corpus resource, something that people use but do not focus their own research on. In contrast, the highest-ranked citation instance, *Grosz and Sidner (1986)*, is indeed discussed in far more detail in the articles that cite it, even though there are fewer such articles (21) than those that use *Marcus et al.*'s corpus (43).

[27]We can see from the lack of boldfacing that it is not itself contained in CmpLG.

References		Citation Instances	
42	Marcus et al. 1993	47	Grosz and Sidner 1986
23	Church 1988	42	**Ramshaw and Marcus 1995**
21	Grosz and Sidner 1986	42	Marcus et al. 1993
18	Pollard and Sag 1994	34	Alshawi 1992
18	Alshawi 1992	28	Grosz et al. 1986
16	**Pereira et al. 1993**	28	Brown et al. 1992
16	Cutting et al. 1992	27	Church 1988
16	Brown et al. 1992	26	Ferro et al. 1999
13	Yarowsky 1992	24	Hindle and Rooth 1993
13	Katz 1987	23	Pollard and Sag 1994
12	Resnik 1993	22	**Pereira et al. 1993**
12	Kaplan and Bresnan 1982	22	Brill and Resnik 1994
12	Gazdar et al. 1985	22	Brill 1995
12	Dempster et al. 1977	21	Katz 1987
12	Carpenter 1992	21	Carpenter 1992
11	Pollard and Sag 1987	20	Cutting et al. 1992
11	Miller 1990	20	**Collins and Brooks 1995**
11	Hindle and Rooth 1993	20	Collins 1996
11	Grosz et al. 1986	19	Resnik 1992
11	Dagan et al. 1993	19	Ratnaparkhi et al. 1994
11	Brill 1992	19	**Collins 1997**

FIGURE 24 Most Frequent Formal References (in Bibliography List) vs. Citation Instances (in Text) in CmpLG.

Raw citation instance numbers, however, are susceptible to bias, particularly in a small sample like CmpLG. A reference might accrue its high citation instance count from relatively few articles, if they together cite the reference disproportionately frequently. This effect is of course aggravated if the reference in question is a self-reference. Consider Fig. 25, which lists the top-scoring citations *within* CmpLG, with frequencies of references and citation instances (the information in Fig. 25 is a subpart of that in Fig. 24, as the former contains only the boldfaced entries in the latter). Frequencies of self-references and self-citations are given in brackets.

If references are considered, *Pereira et al. (1993)* is the highest-ranked article in CmpLG-D, which was the original reason for choosing it as the example article for this book. If citation instances are considered, it is overtaken by *Ramshaw and Marcus (1995)*, whose 42 citation instances come from only 6 articles. None of these are self-citations, but 16 citation instances occur in one single article.[28] How should this compare to the much flatter citation instance distribution for *Pereira et al.*

[28]This is an unusually high number of citation instances to one reference item in a computational linguistics article, which may be due to my decision to expanded citation abbreviations, see below.

References		Citation Instances	
16 (2)	Pereira et al. 1993	42 (0)	Ramshaw and Marcus 1995
9 (0)	Magerman 1995	22 (4)	Pereira et al. 1993
9 (0)	Collins 1997	20 (0)	Collins and Brooks 1995
8 (0)	Collins and Brooks 1995	19 (0)	Collins 1997
8 (2)	Brennan et al. 1987	18 (0)	Magerman 1995
7 (2)	Rayner and Carter 1996	17 (6)	van Halteren et al. 1998
7 (1)	Elworthy 1994	17 (2)	Brennan et al. 1987
6 (3)	Walker and Whittaker 1990	12 (4)	Whittaker and Stenton 1988
6 (1)	Ratnaparkhi 1997	12 (0)	Buchholz et al. 1999
6 (0)	Ramshaw and Marcus 1995	11 (2)	Rayner and Carter 1996
6 (6)	Alshawi and Carter 1994	11 (8)	Murata and Nagao 1993
5 (3)	Walker 1992	11(10)	Johnson et al. 1999
5 (1)	van Halteren et al. 1998	9 (9)	Roth 1998
5 (4)	Rayner et al. 1996	8 (0)	Di Eugenio 1990
5 (2)	Murata and Nagao 1993	8 (3)	Chanod and Tapanainen 1995
5 (0)	Chanod and Tapanainen 1995a	7 (1)	Kozima 1993
4 (1)	Whittaker and Stenton 1988	7 (1)	Elworthy 1994
4 (4)	Roth 1998	7 (0)	Carroll et al. 1999
4 (1)	Resnik 1995b	7 (7)	Bird and Liberman 1999
4 (4)	Rayner et al. 1994b	7 (7)	Alshawi and Carter 1994
4 (1)	Litman and Passonneau 1995	6 (3)	Walker and Whittaker 1990

FIGURE 25 CmpLG-Internal References and Citation Instances.

(1993)? There, 22 citation instances are contributed by 16 different citing articles, with the highest contribution of 3 from any one article. It seems possible but not trivial to design informative bibliometric measures that take citation instances into account and avoid various kinds of bias. When designing such a measure, one should consider carefully how much value should be assigned to the different aspects of the citation distribution.

Finding mentions of author names in running text would allows us to go one step further. When author names occur without a date, i.e., in a context without a formal citation, in many cases there is nevertheless an unambiguous association with a particular citation.[29] The corpus encoding format SciXML reserves an XML element for non-formal mentions of cited authors, and makes provisions for logically linking the author names to their corresponding reference. In CmpLG, author names are identified but not yet linked to their reference item; numbers of cited author are given in Fig. 23.

Texts sometimes contain idiosyncratic abbreviations for citations, which the authors designed for reasons of convenience, such as the following:

[29] Some obscure cases of ambiguous association of author names to reference item exist, but are rare.

The formalism is that of Carroll and Rooth (1998), henceforth C+R...
(9905009, S-17)

The placeholder "*C+R*" logically corresponds to a citation from now on in the text, and this has been accounted for in CmpLG. I have manually marked all such citations in the same way as formal citation instances.

Such kinds of normalisation can lead to an even more informative picture of citation behaviour. Another example is Giles and Councill's (2004) work, who parse acknowledgement sections and argue that such informal mentions should be considered in bibliometric metrics, because they constitute a registration of intellectual contribution akin to citations.[30] As will be discussed later, Kim and Webber (2006) and Kaplan et al. (2009) present approaches based on reference to citations, which could be part of a sophisticated model of the linguistic nature of citation context that could also include other accounts of coherence.

5.2 Chemistry

In more recent experiments in the SCIBORG project, I used a corpus of 50 journal articles published in 2004 by the Royal Society of Chemistry. The articles were random-sampled from a larger corpus used in project SCIBORG (see section 13.1) and cover all areas of chemistry and some areas close to chemistry, including climate modelling, process engineering, and a double-blind medical trial. Corpus statistics in comparison to CmpLG are given in Fig. 26.

The chemistry articles are overall shorter than the CmpLG articles (3650 vs. 4511 words), although the former contains journal articles and the latter conference articles. The average number of abstract sentences is comparable (4.2 vs. 4.6). There are more references per article in chemistry than in computational linguistics (28.2 vs. 17.2), but the proportion of self-references is almost the same (11% vs. 14%). There are also on average more citation instances per article (43.9 vs. 23.6), again with a near-identical ratio of self-citations.

There are differences in citation style between chemistry (where citations are typeset as numerical footnotes, with the number acting as an identifier into the reference list), and CL, which uses the Harvard style.[31] The citation style in chemistry via footnotes means that all citations are logically in parenthetical form, i.e., they cannot form a

[30] Citations of "personal communications" have somewhat non-official status which is similar to that of acknowledgements.

[31] SCIXML, the encoding used for all corpora in this book, generalises over citation styles and represents all citations as the same XML element (further detail in section 5.4).

	Chemistry	CmpLG
Articles	50	352
Words	182,514	1,587,908
avg/article	3,650	4,511
min/max	1,129/8,251	1,332/15,842
Sentences (in body of text)	5,156	58,156
avg/article	103	165
Abstract Sentences	210	1,602
avg/article	4.2	4.6
References, total (token)	1411	6,027
avg/article	28.2	17.2
min/max	3/63	4/53
Self-references	150 (11%)	833 (14%)
Citation Instances, total	2,196	8,260
avg/article	43.9	23.6
min/max	6/243	2/77
Self-citations	333 (15%)	1,325 (16%)
Cited Authors, total	157	2,568
avg/article	3.1	7.3

FIGURE 26 Statistics of Chemistry Corpus, in Comparison to CmpLG.

syntactic part of the sentence. The only way that a citation can be made authorial in chemistry is by explicitly mentioning the authors' names. Such cases are however rarer in chemistry than in computational linguistics (3.1 vs. 7.3).

My informal observation of the written language in chemistry is that there is much less overt argumentation than in computational linguistics. In chapter 13, where I discuss the porting of my theory and recognition machinery from computational linguistics to chemistry, I will speculate as to why this might be so.

5.3 Genetics, Cardiology, Agriculture

Three corpora in other disciplines were used: genetics, cardiology and agriculture. Fig. 27 gives the statistics. It is important for the work in this book to have access to corpus examples from a range of different research styles. For instance, while the task in synthetic chemistry is to build a new compound according to specifications (a task which resembles engineering and computer science), in other disciplines such as genetics or crystallography, the task is to *discover* something about a natural process, e.g., a pathway or the crystal structure of a substance. This could well have an impact on the argumentative structure.

	Genetics	Cardiology	Agriculture
Articles	72	66	41
Words	421,184	236,245	109,943
avg/article	5,849	3,579	2,681
min/max	645/22,424	1,890/5,317	674/5,614
Sentences	—	9,381	—
avg/article	—	142	—
Abstract sent.	—	672	—
avg/article	—	10.2	—
References	3157	—	—
avg/article	43	—	—
min/max	4/145	—	—
Cited Authors	533	—	—
avg/article	7.4		

FIGURE 27 Statistics for Corpora in Genetics, Cardiology, and Agriculture.

The FLYSLIP project at the University of Cambridge[32] processed journal articles about the genome of the fruit fly *Drosophila*. The genetics corpus I used consists of the 72 SCIXML articles which are distributed as examples of SciXML-CB.[33]

The average number of references per article is very similar to that of the chemistry corpus, although the inclusion of some very long articles shifts the average number of words far beyond that in chemistry and CmpLG. The occurrence of cited authors is as common in genetics as it is in computational linguistics (7 per article on average) and far more common than in chemistry.

Not all annotation types are available for this corpus: while references and cited authors have been identified, citations in running text have not, and sentences are also not separated.

The Persival project at Columbia University (McKeown et al., 2001) produced a corpus of over 80,000 articles in cardiology, which are encoded in SCIXML (Teufel and Elhadad, 2002). However, not all of this data is freely available. Of the freely available journals, I randomly selected 66 articles for closer study.

The clearest point of divergence from CmpLG and chemistry is the fact that the abstracts are very long (10 sentences on average). This may well have something to do with the prevalence of structured abstracts in medicine, which may have influenced the abstract writers'

[32] `http://www.wiki.cl.cam.ac.uk/rowiki/NaturalLanguage/FlySlip`

[33] `http://www.wiki.cl.cam.ac.uk/rowiki/NaturalLanguage/FlySlip/Flyslip-resources`.

behaviour, although the abstracts in the Persival corpus themselves are not structured (in the sense that the status of sentences is not formally marked in any way).

41 articles in crop husbandry were given to me in 1998 by Chris Paice from Lancaster University. The data has been typed in by hand. The texts only contain the title and the full text of the main body of the article. The following are missing: abstract, reference list, author names and publication data. There are nevertheless many questions (e.g., about the typical meta-discourse in the discipline), for which such a corpus is still useful.

5.4 SciXML

SciXML is an XML vocabulary[34] which encodes scientific articles, both their textual content and their non-textual document semantics. In a printed article, non-textual information is encoded in conventionalised typesetting, which humans can easily recognise (e.g., the fact that headlines are often bold-faced and appear together with the section number, whereas running text is set in a smaller font and left and right flushed). SciXML explicitly abstracts over the typographic conventions of the source document, e.g., the layout style of a particular journal, and encodes non-textual information logically rather than via its manifestations on paper.

If the native document format does not encode document semantics but only layout information, as PDF and HTML formats tend to do, the document semantics must be painstakingly reverse-engineered from the layout when the data is transformed into SciXML; this is an information-lossy process. In contrast to PDF and HTML, XML and LaTeX tend to encode document semantics as logical elements, which makes the transformation process cleaner. Transformation pipelines into SciXML exist for the following input formats: LaTeX, PDF, publisher-specific XML and publisher-specific HTML. These will be described in section 5.4.2.

Fig. 28 shows the beginning of *Pereira et al. (1993)* in SciXML. SciXML's *Document Type Description* (DTD) is given in appendix B.[35]

[34] "Vocabulary" is XML-terminology for a meta-data scheme. Examples for other XML vocabularies are Docbook (a markup language for books), MathML (Mathematical Markup Language) and CML (Chemical Markup Language).

[35] A DTD is a BNF-style description of the logical structure of an XML instance file, using XML's two main encoding constructs *elements* and *attributes*. The DTD (and the transformation scripts) for SciXML can be downloaded from `sourceforge` (`https://sourceforge.net/projects/scixml/`).

```
<?xml version="1.0"?>
<!DOCTYPE PAPER SYSTEM "paper-structure-annotation.dtd">
<PAPER>
<CURRENT_TITLE>Distributional Clustering of English Words</CURRENT_TITLE>
<CURRENT_AUTHORLIST> <CURRENT_AUTHOR>Fernando
<CURRENT_SURNAME>Pereira</CURRENT_SURNAME></CURRENT_AUTHOR>
<CURRENT_AUTHOR>Naftali <CURRENT_SURNAME>Tishby</CURRENT_SURNAME>
</CURRENT_AUTHOR> <CURRENT_AUTHOR>Lillian <CURRENT_SURNAME>Lee
</CURRENT_SURNAME></CURRENT_AUTHOR></CURRENT_AUTHORLIST>
<METADATA><FILENO>0408011</FILENO>
<CURRENT_REFLABEL>Pereira et al. 1993</CURRENT_REFLABEL>
<APPEARED><CONFERENCE TYPE="MAIN">ACL</CONFERENCE><YEAR>1993</YEAR>
</APPEARED> </METADATA>
<ABSTRACT>
<A-S ID="A-0" DOCUMENTC="S-0;S-164">We describe and experimentally
evaluate a method for automatically clustering words according to their
distribution in particular syntactic contexts.</A-S>
<A-S ID="A-1">Deterministic annealing is used to find lowest distortion
sets of clusters.</A-S>
<A-S ID="A-2">As the annealing parameter increases, existing clusters
become unstable and subdivide, yielding a hierarchical ``soft''
clustering of the data.</A-S>
<A-S ID="A-3">Clusters are used as the basis for class models of word
coocurrence, and the models evaluated with respect to held-out test data.
</A-S></ABSTRACT>
<BODY> <DIV DEPTH="1">
<HEADER ID="H-0"> Introduction </HEADER>
<P>
<S ID="S-0" ABSTRACTC="A-0">Methods for automatically classifying
words according to their contexts of use have both scientific and
practical interest.</S>
<S ID="S-1">The scientific questions arise in connection to
distributional views of linguistic (particularly lexical) structure
and also in relation to the question of lexical acquisition both from
psychological and computational learning perspectives.</S>
<S ID="S-2">From the practical point of view, word classification
addresses questions of data sparseness and generalization in statistical
language models, particularly models for deciding among alternative
analyses proposed by a grammar.</S>
</P> <P>
<S ID="S-3">It is well known that a simple tabulation of frequencies
of certain words participating in certain configurations, for example of
frequencies of pairs of a transitive main verb and the head noun of its
direct object, cannot be reliably used for comparing the likelihoods of
different alternative configurations.</S>
<S ID="S-4" >The problem is that for large enough corpora the number of
possible joint events is much larger than the number of event occurrences
in the corpus, so many events are seen rarely or never, making their
frequency counts unreliable estimates of their probabilities.</S>
</P> <P>
<S ID="S-5"><REF REFID="R-7" ID="C-0">Hindle 1990</REF> proposed
dealing with the sparseness problem by estimating the likelihood of
unseen events from that of ``similar'' events that have been seen.</S>
<S ID="S-6" TYPE="TXT"> For instance, one may estimate the likelihood
of a particular direct object for a verb from the likelihoods\dots
```

FIGURE 28 *Pereira et al. (1993)* in SciXML Encoding (Excerpt).

5.4.1 Description

The following is an overview of the main structural information in the version of SciXML that I have been using for human annotation and automatic processing.[36]

- There is a logical separation of an article into title, authors, meta-data, abstract, body, reference list, and additional appendix-like elements such as document-final lists of footnotes, figures and captions. Meta-data is information which is associated with the article, e.g., its publication information, but which does not itself appear in textual form anywhere in the article. The article's title is marked by the XML element `CURRENT_TITLE`, and surnames of authors as `CURRENT_SURNAME`.
- The abstract is marked as such (`ABSTRACT`) and contains only abstract sentences (`A-S`). These are numbered, and attributes can be assigned to each of these, e.g., the sentence's rhetorical status. If a similarity between a sentence in the abstract and a sentence in the document was detected (e.g., by the process described in section 5.1.2), then both sentences are marked by a double link: attributes `DOCUMENTC` in abstract sentences, and `ABSTRACTC` in document sentences list the respective aligned sentence numbers.
- The division structure of the main body of the text (`BODY`) is captured by the element `DIV`, whose first element is a headline element (`HEADER`). Divisions can recursively contain other divisions. The depth of embedding of a division can be explicitly encoded with the optional `DEPTH` attribute. Divisions may also contain the following other elements: paragraphs, figures, equations, and lists of example sentences (`EX-S`).
- Paragraphs are marked by element `P`. They can contain sentences (`S`), bullet lists, and lists of example sentences (`EX-S`).
- Sentences, abstract sentences, citations, reference items, footnotes and headlines have a document-wide unique identifier (attribute `ID`). As well as raw text, sentences can contain all the XML elements that occur directly in running text, such as equations (`EQN`), cross-references (`XREF`), citation instances (`REF`), cited authors' names (`REFAUTHOR`), and footnotes (`FOOTNOTE`). (The `sourceforge` version of SciXML additionally includes typographical markers coming from publisher-specific formats, such as italicisation (element `IT`).)

[36]Several other versions of SciXML exist, which differ in various small aspects. For instance, some versions of SciXML, including the `sourceforge` version of SciXML, assume that raw data is contained in paragraphs rather than sentences, whereas in other versions, sentences are already marked up.

- The reference list (REFERENCELIST) contains only reference items (REFERENCE). Fig. 29 shows the first reference item in the example article. Reference items carry a document-wide unique identifier (ID), and the date of publication (DATE) and all authors' surnames (SURNAME) are marked. Depending on the success of the transformation into SCIXML, various other bibliographic information such as the TITLE of the publication, and the journal (element JOURNAL) can be marked as well. A reference item can additionally be characterised by the element REFLABEL.

```
<REFERENCE ID="R-0">
<REFLABEL SELF="NO">Brown et al. 1990</REFLABEL> Peter F.
  <SURNAME>Brown</SURNAME>, Vincent J. <SURNAME>DellaPietra
  </SURNAME>, Peter V. <SURNAME>deSouza</SURNAME>, Jenifer C.
  <SURNAME>Lai</SURNAME>, and Robert L. <SURNAME>Mercer</SURNAME>.
  <DATE>1990</DATE>.
  Class-based n-gram models of natural language. In Proceedings
  of the IBM Natural Language ITL, pages 283-298, Paris, France,
  March.
</REFERENCE>
```

FIGURE 29 A Reference Item Encoded in SCIXML.

- Citation instances in running text (element REF) have a document-wide identifier (attribute ID) and a REFID attribute which links them to their corresponding reference in the reference list. Fig. 30 gives a citation instance in the example article, which cites the reference item from Fig. 29.

```
<S ID="S-13">Most other class-based modeling techniques for natural
language rely instead on "hard" Boolean classes <REF REFID="R-0"
ID="C-2" STYPE="P">Brown et al. 1990</REF>.</S>
```

FIGURE 30 A Citation Instance Encoded in SCIXML.

Citation instances with attribute SELF="YES" are self-citations; this means that at least one of the articles' authors is mentioned in the author list of the reference item. If a citation style such as the Harvard style was used in the original document, then it is possible to differentiate parenthetical citations (STYLE="P") from authorial citations (STYLE="A"). The REFID attribute links the citation instance to its corresponding reference item; in principle, REF items could therefore be empty. For convenience, the REF element in CmpLG contains an additional corpus-unique label consisting of name and date (and optional letter) in the form of PCDATA, e.g., "*Brown et al 1990*" in Fig. 29. These labels have been automatically constructed and manually checked.

- If names of cited authors occur without a date context, they are marked as `REFAUTHOR`.
- `FOOTNOTELIST` contains footnote elements (`FOOTNOTE`) which are linked to their place of occurrence with a unique identifier (`ID`).
- Figures and tables can contain captions. Blocks of linguistic example sentences (marked as `EXAMPLE`) can contain separate example sentences, each marked as `EX-S`. For discourse studies, it is important to distinguish these from the main text of the article, because one is only interested in the main text, which should be coherent, i.e., neighbouring sentences should occur next to each other, no matter where they appeared in the original layout.
- Appendices do not receive special treatment. If an article contains an appendix, it is placed under a `DIV` heading directly before the reference list.

When designing a vocabulary such as SciXML, one would in principle want to encode *all* of the article's textual and non-textual information as exactly as possible. However, this may be in conflict with the aim of a conceptually simple hierarchy, or even with the rules imposed by XML. For instance, certain typographic constructs observed in the real world are irreconcilable with parts of the hierarchy just introduced.

In particular the rule that sentences may occur only under paragraphs can be problematic in some circumstances. For instance, equations are often syntactically part of a sentence, yet long enough to warrant their own paragraph. In the pattern "*On the basis of* * `EQN`, * *we see that* * `EQN`", the asterisks mark possible paragraph breaks. One syntactic sentence then spans across more than one paragraph.

My decision that sentences (`S`) should always occur under paragraphs (`P`) means that meta-sentences such as the one described above have to be broken into syntactically incomplete sentence fragments, each of which occupies its own paragraph. This is suboptimal, a) because structual/logical information is lost and b) because we now have some incomplete (i.e., unparsable) sentences in our corpus.[37] However, it avoids the many technical problems associated with the only other possible solution, namely making paragraphs recursive.

Similar problems come from the fact that the items in a bulleted list can have different syntactic status. If they are noun phrases or single

[37]Incidentally, one of these fragments was chosen by AutoSummarize on page 49.

words, the entire bullet list can be treated as a sentence. But a single bullet item can also encompass large pieces of text, e.g., a paragraph or even more than one paragraph. This makes it impossible to incorporate bulleted lists systematically into the hierarchy of paragraphs and sentences; my solution is therefore to make all bullet items sentences (`S`) by default. Bullet item sentences are marked with the (optional) attribute (`TYPE="ITEM"`). Paragraphs which occur as elements in a bullet list can also carry this attribute.

5.4.2 Transformation from Source Formats

Four different kinds formats can be automatically converted into SciXML; I am listing these along with the year when work on the conversion began:

1996: From LaTeX (CmpLG; Teufel, 2000)
2000: From publisher-specific HTML (Cardiology; Teufel and Elhadad, 2002)
2003: From PDF (Genetics, ACL Anth; Hollingsworth et al., 2005, Lewin, 2007, Karamanis et al., 2007)
2006: From publisher-specific XML (Chemistry; Rupp et al., 2006)

Of these, publisher-specific XML is the cleanest source, because document semantics needed for SciXML is already present in a logical form. PDF, as a printer-oriented format, is the most information-lossy.

In the case of the LaTeX source deposited at CMPLG, all the information needed to reconstruct the SciXML-type document semantics is in principle present. The core of the LaTeX to SciXML pipeline is a program called Latex2HTML(Drakos, 1994, Latex2Html, 1999). Several `perl` scripts then transform the resulting HTML format into SciXML, as far as this is possible. However, LaTeX is a very powerful language which offers authors a wide range of syntactic constructs. In particular the interpretation of many LaTeX macros is beyond the capability of Latex2HTML. It is therefore almost impossible to retrieve all the information without reconstructing a LaTeX compiler.

SciXML also encodes some information which no automatic processing can perform yet, unless it comes natively from a publisher-specific format. An example of this is the determination of (linguistic) example sentences in text, and the separation of text belonging to tables and figures from running text when the LaTeX `verbatim` environment was used. In the case of CmpLG, all text has been manually screened for such problems, and repaired if necessary.

The second transformation pipeline, from several publisher-specific HTML formats, follows a similar route as the first. In project PARSIVAL, publishers provided us with the electronic HTML versions of cardiology journals from their electronic publishing website. Scripts similar to the ones interpreting the Latex2HTML output were created, one for each publisher. Some problems occurred because HTML is not a logical format: its elements are designed to express how something will look in the browser, not what its document semantics is. Nevertheless, this process, which did not involve any manual intervention, produced reasonably clean output.

A better method is the direct import of information from the publisher's pre-print or pre-electronic internal XML format, if such a format exists. In project SciBorg, three publishers (*Royal Society of Chemistry (RSC), Nature Publishing* and *the International Union of Crystallography (IuC)*) provided us with XML versions of their publications. While the three formats agree in principle which elements should be encoded, with each other and with SciXML, there were still divergences in the information types and coverage used. Rupp et al. (2006) describes the XSLT-based architecture of this XML-to-SciXML transformation.

The noisiest transformation route is from PDF. PDF encodes layout information in a low-level style, e.g., the indentation of a line is expressed in number of pixels. Such layout features need to be translated into the structural elements that are "meant" by them. The challenge is to do this in a way which is independent of the particular typographic conventions used by one particular publisher. Bill Hollingsworth wrote the PDF-to-XML conversion software which resulted in the ACL Anthology SciXML corpus, which will be described in section 14.4.[38] The genetics corpus used for this book was also transformed from PDF. It was the outcome of the FlySlip project, which uses similar software (Lewin, 2007, Karamanis et al., 2007).

Chapter Summary

This chapter has described the five corpora which are used for two main purposes in this book:

- to inform the definition of the discourse model in chapter 6;
- in the case of CmpLG, to provide the data for the reliability studies (chapter 8) and the automatic experiments (chapter 11).

[38]The ACL Anthology corpus is attractive for the work in this book due to its large size, but it is not yet cleaned up enough to serve as input for the automatic AZ or CFC in chapter 11. There is an ongoing effort to bring it into full SciXML format (see chapter 14).

The scientific disciplines covered are computational linguistics, chemistry, genetics, cardiology and agriculture. The computational linguistics corpus (CmpLG) is the central corpus for this book. It contains 352 articles with meticulous markup in terms of text, citations, references, and general structure.

I discussed properties of this corpus, in terms of structure and citation behaviour. For instance, I found that the articles in CmpLG do not comply to the IMRD section structure, and that the sentences in its abstracts do not align as well with document sentences as those in the engineering articles in Kupiec et al.'s (1995) experiment did. In terms of citation behaviour, computational linguistics articles contain relatively few citations in comparison to chemistry, but the proportion of self-citations is comparable.

SciXML is a format which captures logical and structural aspects of scientific articles along with their textual content. Such logical and structural aspects include division structure, meta-information, linking of references and citation instances in running text, and sentence boundaries, amongst others. Format conversions into SciXML exist from LaTeX, PDF, publisher-specific HTML and publisher-specific XML.

This concludes the description of the data that my discourse model is meant to cover, and we can now proceed to the model itself.

6

The Knowledge Claim Discourse Model (KCDM)

Central to the two information access methods introduced in chapter 4 (rhetorically tailored extracts and citation maps) was the idea that an article is best characterised by its logical position in its scientific field, and by its relation to similar articles. Both methods rely heavily on a rhetorical analysis, i.e., a process that can analyse pieces of text according to their rhetorical status. This process has so far remained hypothetical, but the present chapter will define the discourse model that underlies it.

The rhetorical analysis was presented in chapter 4 as a fundamental "service task", which also supports other information management applications, such as within-article navigation, estimation of citation importance and improved bibliometric measures. To fit in with such a wide range of tasks, the discourse model should aim for categories and phenomena which are as general as possible. This is of course a sensible aim for independent reasons too.

Discourse models attempt to build structure from text by generalising over the contents of the text. The variant presented here, which I named the *Knowledge Claim Discourse Model* (KCDM), uses scientific argumentation as its core mechanism, and is limited to scientific discourse. My claim is that in this context, discourse structure can be meaningfully defined without requiring any representation of, or reasoning about, real world relationships. In this respect the KCDM differs from traditional discourse models, which typically assume that some domain knowledge is available during recognition (e.g., Mann and Thompson, 1987, Grosz and Sidner, 1986, Cohen, 1987). What I suggest doing instead is to trace statements about knowledge claims in a fairly shallow way.

6.1 Overview of the Model

My discourse model is centred around the concept of a *knowledge claim* (short: KC). Knowledge claims were introduced in section 2.3.1 as the scientific contributions associated with an article. The KCDM explains how structure arises from argumentation about knowledge claims, and in particular from the relationship between the new knowledge claim being staked in the article and other knowledge claims, which are already established in the field. Another concept which plays an important role in the model is the *research space* (Swales, 1990), a model of how shared knowledge is accumulated in a field over the years.

The KCDM consists of several levels, which describe different types of communicative acts. The higher levels of the model are defined by the authors' intentions and are therefore rather abstract, whereas the lowest level is closely linked to the physical presentation of the textual material.

The top level, called Level 0, formalises the authors' high-level rhetorical goals, which serve to defend the new knowledge claim of an article against possibly hostile peer review (section 6.2). For instance, authors must argue that their new knowledge claim is novel and significant, and sufficiently different from already existing knowledge claims to warrant publication. Level 0 goals are not directly textually expressed and to recognise them, the reader often has to do inference. It is nevertheless possible to formalise these goals because the rhetorical tasks behind them are standardised and thus predictable.

Level 1 breaks the abstract high-level goals down into lower-level rhetorical goals (section 6.3), which can be correlated with textual statements called *rhetorical moves*. An example of a rhetorical move is the statement that the problem addressed has received a lot of attention in the literature. The rhetorical moves can be seen as specialised author intentions. They often contain scientific meta-discourse phrases such as *"In contrast to traditional approaches"*.

Level 2 is concerned with other people's published knowledge claims: how they are described, and in particular, who they are attributed to. A core function of Level 2 is to record where in the text descriptions of knowledge claims begin and end. This task is called *Knowledge Claim Attribution*; section 6.4 describes it in detail.

Level 3 concerns how existing knowledge claims fit into the authors' overall scientific argument. It formalises the different functions that existing knowledge claims can play: as a rival, as a neutral contrast or as part of the new solution. My description of these relationships in section 6.5 is informed by the citation functions from citation content analysis (see section 2.3.1). However, the relationships in Level 3 operate between knowledge claim segments, rather than between articles/citations. I call the phenomenon of connections between new and existing knowledge claims *hinging*, because the connections act like a hinge between two (block-like) knowledge claims.

Relationships to existing knowledge claims are crucial in my approach: on the one hand, they are the very mechanism which logically "locates" the new knowledge claim in a particular niche of its scientific field; on the other hand, they can be identified in the text and tied to a particular location in the article. This makes them the linchpin between the information access applications, which require a logical description of the article in relation to similar articles, and the discourse model, which connects its logical descriptive components to their place in the article structure.

Level 4 concerns the presentational conventions followed for linearising the textual material. During the writing of an article, complex facts and relationships need to be pressed into the linear medium of language. Level 4 describes the elements in the text which signal how this is done. One such element is the IMRD section structure that we already came across in section 5.1.2. Another consists of explicit statements that inform the reader about the structure, such as article overviews, section summaries and other so-called "sign-post" sentences. Different disciplines use different presentational conventions; therefore Level 4 is the only part of the model that is not discipline-independent.

Let us now consider each level in turn.

6.2 Level 0: Goals in Argumentation

Chapter 2 described the influence that the publication process, the reward system of science and peer review have on the way that articles are written. Because there is competition between articles for publication, authors are expected to promote their potential new knowledge claim by justifying its validity. Myers (1992) describes a research article as one complex rhetorical speech act, where the high-level communicative goal is to persuade the scientific community of the relevance, reliability, quality and importance of the work. As a result, the use of rhetoric is prevalent in scientific prose. This is the case even in those disciplines where overt argumentation is not part of the presentational tradition, i.e., in the life sciences. (Scientific prose in these disciplines is made to *appear* emotionally detached, disinterested and thus objective, e.g., by the recommendation in prescriptive guidelines to avoid the active voice when referring to own work (Josselson and Lieblich, 1996).)

My claim is that all scientific disciplines impose roughly the same high-level rhetorical goals on authors. They are a consequence of scientific methodology in general, and of the publication rules in particular. The KCDM formalises them as the following Level 0 goals:

HLG-1: Show: Knowledge claim is significant
HLG-2: Show: Knowledge claim is novel
HLG-3: Show: Authors are knowledgeable
HLG-4: Show: Research is methodologically sound

Most of the high-level goals are *private* goals in the sense of Grosz and Sidner (1986) – they will never be explicitly expressed in text (with the slight exception of HLG-2, see below). Instead, such goals are at a high abstraction level. They cannot always be directly be mapped to textual units, and sometimes some inference may be required for the reader to recognise them.

In order to do something interesting with the high-level goals, we next need the concept of the *research space*, which is an idealised model of the entirety of knowledge in a field. The idea of scientific work being situated in a logical research space derives from research in the philosophy of science. Gopnik (1972) identified three basic types of scientific article: the "controlled experiment", the "hypothesis testing" and the "technique description". Each type has its own structure, but according to Hutchins (1977) they can be reduced, either by degradation or by amelioration, to a problem-solution structure. The view of science as a problem-solving activity is common (Hoey, 1979, Jordan, 1984, Zappen, 1983, Trawinski, 1989, Solov'ev, 1981), but the research space itself has in my opinion most clearly been described by Swales (1990).

If the peer review accepts the authors' argument, then the knowledge claim (which corresponds to one problem-solving act) is incorporated into the research space via the process of publication. The addition of each new legitimate knowledge claim increases the overall amount of knowledge in the research space, leading to a "better" situation. The new article then occupies its own little niche in the research space, and has connections to the articles that played a part in its justification. Over time, new connections with newly published articles are added. As a result of this process, the entire research space consists of a network of individual problems (some solved, others semi-solved) and solutions addressing them.

This also leads to a definition of the "leading edge" or "outer margin" of a field as the newly evolving problems at the periphery of this space. Each knowledge claim can introduce new problems or have limitations, which provides an opportunity for future knowledge claims to attach themselves to the leading edge of this research space (in the same way as an existing knowledge claims' limitations motivate the current knowledge claim).

The research space is central to the KCDM for two reasons:

- In terms of the envisaged information access applications, it provides the model for how the article's new knowledge claim is to be characterised (namely by its relations to its similar articles).
- In terms of the discourse model, the entities and relationships associated with the research space help us interpret the scientific argument; for instance, there are rules about what kinds of things normally happen in the research space.

What is new in my use of the research space is that I provide explicit rules for where in this space a new knowledge claim can be attached, and under which conditions: knowledge claims are justified if they address open scientific questions or remaining problems in existing knowledge claims, or if they provide a better solution to an already solved problem, in comparison to some already existing solution. Scientists have a strong sense of what needs to be present for a scientific argument to be complete. For instance, some sub-argument must be present to explain why the work is significant. A possible set of rules and some necessary subgoals are given in Fig. 31. If put together correctly, the subgoals should constitute a sound justification for the new knowledge claim.

The model is an idealisation in several ways. For instance, it assumes that one knowledge claim corresponds to exactly one article. Some of the problems with that particular assumption were already discussed in section 2.3.1 in the context of bibliometric measures. There are also some uncertainties about the exact definition of a knowledge claim.

The goal of the KCDM is to describe knowledge claims in the sciences, but what counts as an acceptable knowledge claim differs from one research type to the next. In the theoretical sciences, the researchers' task is to find an adequate and explanatory *model* that accounts for the evidence obtained from observations of the real world, whereas in the experimental sciences, the task is to find *evidence* for some theory about how the world works, or to explore objects within the framework of a particular theory – the problem might be "*what is the structure of this crystal?*". In engineering, physical or theoretical *artifacts* are designed, such as computer programs, which fulfil a certain predefined function. Therefore, we may need to broaden our definition of a problem-solving process if we want to describe knowledge claims

Increase in Knowledge: The inclusion of the new knowledge claim should increase the total knowledge contained in the research space, i.e., the article's problem-solving act should result in a positive sum for science. If there are problems or limitations associated with the new knowledge claim, these should be "smaller" than the main problem the knowledge claim addresses. This provides support for HLG-1 (significance).
Importance of Problem: Claims of the importance of the problem addressed also support HLG-1, as a solution to an important problem should advance science more than that to a marginal problem.
Novelty: There must be at least one new aspect to a knowledge claim to warrant publication; most often this is the solution presented. This constitutes HLG-2 (novelty).
Superiority: In case the problem/task addressed is well-known, the justification for the new knowledge claim requires proof of superiority over existing knowledge claims in at least one respect. This is an alternative way of supporting HLG-2.
Other's Flaws: Statements of flaws in (potential) competitors' solutions can constitute a proof of superiority of the new knowledge claim for well-known problems, and thus support HLG-2.
Difference: If the problem is new, there cannot logically be an existing solution to it which the authors' solution could be superior to. Instead, the authors' argument for HLG-2 must argue for the novelty of the *problem*, e.g., by stating the lack of a solution to it, or by stressing that existing knowledge claims are different to the new knowledge claim, e.g., in terms of their goals.
Comparison: All comparisons to existing knowledge claims will in principle contribute to HLG-3 (demonstration of authors' knowledge). In particular, the peer review expects to see citations of the most relevant, the earliest, and the most salient articles.
Agreement: Statements of agreement with existing knowledge claims additionally support HLG-4 (methodological soundness). In contrast, statements of disagreement with existing knowledge claims additionally support HLG-1 (significance).
Praise: When the authors use existing knowledge claims in their solution, these KCs are "incorporated" into the new knowledge claim; the validity of the new knowledge claim now partially depends on their validity. Any argument in favour of the quality of the existing knowledge claim then strengthens the new knowledge claim, supporting HLG-4.
Sound Methodology: The rest of the description of the new knowledge claim should reassure the reviewers that it is based on methodologically sound principles in science (HLG-4), e.g., replicability and sound evaluation, particularly in the case of null results.

FIGURE 31 Rules Relating High-Level Goals to Subgoals.

across several research styles and disciplines.

The KCDM requires each article to have at least one tangible knowledge claim. An example of a technical, and thus tangible knowledge claim is an experiment, an observation, a theory, a tool or experimental data. That means that review and position articles are excluded from KCDM analysis. In such articles, the authors' intellectual contribution is not technical, but interpretative or secondary: other pieces of work are analysed, described and compared, and it is this that constitutes the knowledge claim.

The definition of tangibility of a knowledge claim is however flexible enough to include some cases where the contribution is not straightforwardly technical. So-called *evaluation articles* are of this type: a particular approach (typically, one's own) is formally evaluated on a given task, possibly against other approaches. In some evaluation articles, the suitability of several approaches (none of which are the authors' own) is experimentally established for a task the authors are interested in. In evaluation articles, the knowledge claim is the evaluation experiment itself, which the KCDM treats as a special case.[39]

It is also not clear how concrete an idea has to be to count as a knowledge claim. The status of authors' suggestions for future work is an example. On the one hand, the formulation of future research tasks is an intellectual contribution by the authors. On the other hand, the research suggested has not yet been performed or evaluated by peer review, and it might never be.

Another question is whether null results should count as knowledge claims; the practical answer differs somewhat from discipline to discipline. (Null results are cases where a method employed by a researcher was found not to work.) On the one hand, they increase the total knowledge available to the research community. In practice it is harder for null results to pass the peer review, as the failure of the method could also have been due to problems with the authors' research method.

I will now turn to the subgoals from Fig. 31, which constitute the building blocks for the high-level goals.

6.3 Level 1: Rhetorical Moves

There is a general intuition in discourse linguistics that atomic textual units exist which correspond to author intentions (Webber, 2004). Swales (1990) was the first to apply this principle to scientific text. He

[39] If one of the evaluated approaches is the authors' own, it might already have been published in a previous article, or it might form part of the knowledge claim of the current article.

Move 1: Establishing a Territory	
1.1	Claiming Centrality
1.2 (1.2A OR 1.2B	Making Topic Generalisations Background Knowledge Description of Phenomena)
1.3	Reviewing Previous Research
Move 2: Establishing a Niche	
2A OR 2B OR 2C OR 2D	Counter-claiming Indicating a Gap Question-Raising Continuing a Tradition
Move 3: Occupying a Niche	
3.1A OR 3.1B	Outlining Purpose Announcing Present Research
3.2	Announcing Principle Findings
3.3	Indicating Article Structure

FIGURE 32 Rhetorical Moves in Swales' (1990) CARS Model.

defines a rhetorical move as a clause or a sequence of clauses which together fulfil one particular rhetorical function in the framework of the overall text. Swales' CREATING A RESEARCH SPACE model (CARS; see Fig. 32) gives a writing plan for an introduction section in science. It is based on his analysis of two corpora, one consisting of several hundred research articles in the physical sciences, the other of a mix of research articles from several science and engineering fields.

The model works as follows: authors must first establish a "territory" (Move 1). This can be done by describing the larger problem or motivating why a methodology is desirable. Move 2 describes the creation of a "niche", e.g., by justifying why the author chose their specific research goal. Several types of justification are possible. Move 3 corresponds to the occupation of that niche, e.g., by giving details of the new research, such as results, and by giving an overview of the rest of the article. Linguistic variations for the expression of each rhetorical move are allowed; for instance, humans can recognise the underlying rhetorical move of a research gap whether it is expressed as lack of a solution or as failure of a previous method.

Swales (1990) assumes that the moves are recognisable by linguistic cues and gives lists of fixed phrases co-occurring with each move (p.144; pp. 154–158; pp. 160–161). These cues belong to a set of phrases called *scientific meta-discourse*, the topic of chapter 9.

Another relevant aspect of CARS is that it imposes an ordering on the moves, which sometimes allows for replacement by alternative moves. For instance, three alternative methods for motivating a piece of research exist: as criticism of a previous approach (Move 2A), as lack of a solution (Move 2B), or as continuation of a tradition (Move 2D).

Swales' model has been used extensively by discourse analysts and researchers in the field of ESP (English for Special Purposes), and for tasks as varied as teaching English as a foreign language (EFL), human translation and citation analysis (Myers, 1992, Thompson and Yiyun, 1991, Duszak, 1994). Salager-Meyer (1990, 1991, 1992) establishes Swales-style moves for medical abstracts.

Like Swales, I believe that it is possible to list the most common rhetorical moves, the ones that are typically required in the argumentation, but mine are at a finer level of granularity. Level 1 of the KCDM contains 12 rhetorical moves, which talk about properties of the authors' new knowledge claim and its relationship to the state of the research space. These are listed in Fig. 33 (the mnemonic "R-" stands for "rhetorical move").

Properties of the Research Space:	
R-1	PROBLEM ADDRESSED EXISTS
R-2	NEW GOAL/PROBLEM IS NEW
R-3	NEW GOAL/PROBLEM IS HARD
R-4	NEW GOAL/PROBLEM IS IMPORTANT/INTERESTING
R-5	SOLUTION TO NEW PROBLEM IS DESIRABLE
R-6	NO SOLUTION TO NEW PROBLEM EXISTS
Properties of the new KC:	
R-7	NEW SOLUTION SOLVES PROBLEM
R-8	NEW SOLUTION AVOIDS PROBLEMS
R-9	NEW SOLUTION NECESSARY TO ACHIEVE OWN GOAL
R-10	NEW SOLUTION IS ADVANTAGEOUS
R-11	NEW SOLUTION HAS LIMITATIONS
R-12	FUTURE WORK FOLLOWS FROM NEW SOLUTION

FIGURE 33 Rhetorical Moves R-1 to R-12 (Level 1).

Other types of rhetorical moves exist in the KCDM, but at different levels: Level 3 moves are concerned with how the new KC relates to existing knowledge claims (section 6.5), whereas Level 4 moves concern the physical structure of the article (section 6.6).

Let us now look at the 12 rhetorical moves in turn. Articles typically start with a portrayal of the research space *before* the inclusion of the new knowledge claim. It is in the authors' interest to describe this situation as undesirable; the central motivation of the article is then to improve an unbearable situation. One can do this by stating that the problem addressed really is a problem (R-1), that it is new (R-2) or that it is hard (R-3).

> **R-1:** *The problem is that for large enough corpora the number of possible joint events is much larger than the number of event occurrences in the corpus, so many events are seen rarely or never, making their frequency counts unreliable estimates of their probabilities.* (9408011, S-4)
>
> **R-1:** *It is generally considered synthetically prohibitive to develop receptors for analytes in a complex mixture.* (b505518k)
>
> **R-2:** *We report here what is, to our knowledge, the first example of Cl^- transport in mouse trachea epithelial cells that is stimulated by a completely synthetic amphiphilic peptide ionophore.* (b513940f)
>
> **R-3:** *Correctly determining number is a difficult problem when translating from Japanese to English.* (9511001, S-0)

We also find many statements of how interesting and popular a task or problem is (R-4):

> **R-4:** *Both principle-based parsing and probabilistic methods for the analysis of natural language have become popular in the last decade.* (9408004, S-0)
>
> **R-4:** *Recently, the use of imines as starting materials in the synthesis of nitrogen-containing compounds has attracted a lot of interest from synthetic chemists.*[(1)] (b200198e)

However, the problem could equally well be portrayed as shamefully neglected:

> **R-4:** *Despite the importance of this question to the applied NLG community, however, it has not been discussed much in the research NLG community, which I think is a pity.* (9504013, A-1)
>
> **R-4:** *The study of discovery in linguistics is not fashionable today.* (9506023, S-7)
>
> **R-4:** *In this paper, we focus on the application of the developed techniques in the context of the comparatively neglected area of HPSG generation.* (9502005, S-4)
>
> **R-4:** *While the chemical effects of acoustic cavitation generated by the action of pressure waves on a fluid have been extensively investigated, surprisingly scarce attention has been paid to the chemical consequences of hydrodynamic cavitation which occurs during turbulent flow of liquids.* (b503848k)

The amount of interest a problem encounters is always at the extremes of the scale; I never found a statement of "medium" interest for a problem. This points to the fact that the main rhetorical function of move R-4 is to highlight the true importance of the authors' problem, whether or not the scientific field agrees.

The research space should overall be a better place after the new knowledge claim was added. Statements about the desirability of the solution (R-5) fit well into this sub-argument:

> **R-5:** *The knowledge of such dependencies is useful in various tasks in natural language processing, especially in analysis of sentences involving multiple prepositional phrases, such as: ...* (9605013, S-10)

> **R-5:** *The selection and management of forage species in different environments will be improved through a greater understanding of their individual responses to temperature.* (A031)[40]

> **R-5:** *Therefore it is important to find some new surfactants which are able to polymerize under much milder conditions.* (b600498a)

R-6 is the gap statement. When a solution to a problem is simply missing, then certainly something is at fault in the research space:

> **R-6:** *Benzotelluretes have to the best of our knowledge never been synthesized.* (b515712a)

> **R-6:** *To our knowledge the question, whether the Lambek calculus itself or its associated parsing problem are* [sic] *NP-hard, are still open.* (9605016, S-125)

> **R-6:** *Details of the response in barnyard millets and sorghum, however, have not been established.* (A031)

> **R-6:** *To the best of our knowledge, there has been no systematic study of pulmonary pressure in patients with thalassemia major.* (C109, S-98)[41]

Move R-6 fulfils the high-level goal HLG-2 (novelty) explicitly. HLG-2 can also be fulfilled implicitly, e.g., by listing the closest similar work to the new KC. In that case, the novelty of the research goal has to be inferred by the reader from the fact that these approaches are still quite different from the new KC.

[40] Corpus examples from the agriculture corpus (see section 5.3) are identified by article number (starting with "A").

[41] Corpus examples from the cardiology corpus are identified by the article number (starting with "C"), followed by the sentence number.

Note that R-6 is also closely related to R-2, which explicitly states that something has been done for the first time. R-6 is less informative than R-2 in that it only pragmatically implies, and does not state, that the authors will indeed do the thing that hasn't been done before.

The same function as expressing non-desirability of the original situation (R-1, R-3) and desirability of resulting situation (R-5) can also be fulfilled by portraying the new knowledge claim as a successful problem-solving act, e.g., by stating its general success (R-7), its avoidance of problems (R-8), or the necessity of the chosen solution for the problem (R-9).

> **R-7:** *This account also explains similar differences in felicity for other coordinating conjunctions as discussed in Kehler (1994) ...* (9405010, S-100)

> **R-8:** *This paper presents a treatment of ellipsis which avoids these difficulties, while having essentially the same coverage as Dalrymple et al.* (9502014, S-9)

> **R-9:** *We have argued that obligations play an important role in accounting for the interactions in dialog.* (9407011, S-217)

One could also simply list its advantages (R-10):

> **R-10:** *Other than the economic factor, an important advantage of combining morphological analysis and error detection/correction is the way the lexical tree associated with the analysis can be used to determine correction possibilities.* (9504024, S-138)

> **R-10:** *Moreover, the simplicity and ease of application of the electrochemical method ... should also be emphasised and makes it an interesting and valuable synthetic tool.* (b513402a)

More than one move of type R-7 through R-10 can occur in a scientific argument, but for the argument to be complete at least one of them must be present. The most likely place in the argumentation for moves R-7 to R-9 is after the approach has been introduced and evaluated; this is in contrast to moves R-1, R-3 and R-5, which are more likely to occur before the introduction and evaluation of the approach. The authors could claim that the original motivation behind the research was to find a better method, i.e., one with exactly the positive properties that the new solution has. This is equivalent to a strategy of motivating the research in some other way, and listing those advantages at a later state in the article – as if they had only been "noticed" by the authors upon inspection, after the research was already completed. We will see later on in this section that it is typical for scientific writing that such "stories" are constructed post-hoc.

Mentioning the limitations of one's approach is a move which often concludes a scientific article. The limitations could be new problems introduced by the new knowledge claim, or they could be new research questions which only came to light during the current problem-solving process. They could also be parts of the original problem which are left unsolved.[42]

> **R-11**: *Nonetheless, some remaining problematic cases call for yet more flexibility in the definition; the isomorphism requirement may have to be relaxed.* (9404003, S-211)

> **R-11**: *Satisfactory correspondence to the experimentally determined energy distributions was however not obtained, most likely due to shortcomings in the representation of the phonon bath in our simulation code (TACO).* (b105514n)

> **R-11**: *However, as the experiment was terminated before the maximum number of spikes had been produced the effect of ozone on the total number of seeds produced per plant cannot be assessed, so longer term experiments are needed.* (A033)

> **R-11**: *Although this study provides important information about the long-term impact of the stent on HRQOL, it has several important limitations. Our sample represents only a subset of the entire STRESS trial...* (C049, S-132/S-133)

Stating limitations is one way of making sure that one's claims are not too strong, which increases the article's chances of passing peer review. It can also preempt negative follow-on work by others.

However, on the surface, limitations might seem to work against HLG-1. As one needs to end up with a positive sum for the entirety of scientific knowledge, additional argumentation might be required to show that the limitations are less severe than the problems which motivated the research. Consider the following examples, which all include an attempt to downplay the limitations:

> **R-11**: *The only limitation of this search technique is that, for sentences which are modeled poorly, the search might exhaust the available memory before completing both phases.* (9504030, S-140)

> **R-11**: *However, this is not a serious limitation: most linguistically significant rules are binary, and those which are not can be easily converted in binary rules.* (9601002, S-83)

---

[42] *Partial solution-hood* may be lexically signalled by the statement that a problem has been "*addressed*", rather than "*solved*".

> **R-11**: *The logic we have described comes with 2 limitations which at first glance appears to be somewhat severe, namely: NO atomic values; NO precedence as a feature.* (9502017, S-99)

Note also that without context, several of the R-11 moves above, which describe limitations of the *new* knowledge claim, are indistinguishable from H-1 moves, which describe limitations of an *existing* knowledge claim (see also the ambiguous example in section 4.1). Given the different roles that moves H-1 and R-11 play for information access applications, the fact that their surface forms are so similar is an argument for a discourse-context aware approach such as the one advocated here.

Limitations are often followed by (and sometimes hard to distinguish from) suggestions for future work, the R-12 move. Future work sections foreshadow the publication of new research following from the current article, whether by the authors or by somebody else, as in the following examples:

> **R-12**: *As yet, we have not implemented moves that enable the construction of arbitrary context-free grammars; this belongs to future work.* (9504034, S-88)

> **R-12**: *One or more of these features may be linked to SERRS activity but it is clear that many more cases must be studied in order to pinpoint spectral features that are unique to SERRS active particles.* (b506644a)

> **R-12**: *A future article will discuss the profitability of irrigating sugar beet and how it can be improved by careful scheduling.* (A008)

> **R-12**: *Given the high prevalence of preserved systolic function, future research should include definition of optimal drug therapy for patients who have heart failure associated with preserved systolic function.* (C019, S-169)

Future work sections can be used to mark territory that the authors intend to work on in the future, and to "time-stamp" ideas which are not in a state to be published yet (these are then described as "current" or "ongoing" work). The existence of future work can also form part of an argument for HLG-1 (significance): only small problems can be solved in a single article once and for all. It can even be the case that an entire new research direction is launched by a particular partial solution presented in an article.

From an application viewpoint, the entirety of future work suggestions in a field can be thought of as the outer margin of the research field, i.e., as the hot topics that researchers are currently working on. Knowing about this outer margin, or being able to search in it, should be attractive for several target groups, e.g., PhD students looking for a topic, or research councils planning future funding strategies.

The 12 rhetorical moves I have just described are not the only possible choice of moves one could have made. More or fewer moves are possible; for instance, a separate class could have been given to some moves which often occur in combination (e.g., moves R-3 and R-4). The set of 12 is a compromise between opposing demands: the moves are roughly of equal "size" in that they can all be expressed in one sentence; each of them was observed at least a few times in text; and they form a complete set in the sense that they together cover the entire scientific argument.

Comparison to Prior Work

As already mentioned, Level 1 of the KCDM, my model of rhetorical moves in scientific prose, takes its main inspiration from Swales's (1990) CARS model. CARS was a good starting point because it defines a finite set of rhetorical labels and assumes that the argumentative structure is close to the textual form. Some of my rhetorical moves directly correspond to his: for instance, my moves R-1, R-2, R-3 and R-4 are like his Move 1.1 ("Claiming Centrality"), and my move R-6 is like his Move 2B ("Indicating a Gap").

There are however differences in remit between CARS and the KCDM: CARS only covers introduction sections, whereas the KCDM covers the entirety of the article. CARS has been mainly informed by engineering articles, whereas I aim for a model of all experimental sciences. And finally, CARS was designed to assist in the teaching of scientific prose, rather than for automatic recognition.

Unlike CARS, the KCDM does not model order directly. Formally, the only constraint on rhetorical moves in the KCDM is that they need to occur *somewhere* in the article, if they are required by the high-level goals of Level 0. In particular, no special status is given to the knowledge claim that occurs in the motivation. The reason for this is the observation that CmpLG contains many unexpected sequences of moves, so that a CARS-style fixed order would not describe them well. Consider Fig. 34, the introduction of the CmpLG article 9407011, which contains parallel strands of motivation:

- **S-0–S-4**: Introduction of *Cohen and Perrault (1979), Allen and Perrault (1980), Grosz and Sidner (1986)*; rebuttal.
- **S-11**: Part of authors' knowledge claim described (contrastively).
- **S-13–S-15**: Introduction of *Litman and Allen (1987); Cohen and Levesque (1991), Grosz and Sidner (1990)*; rebuttal.

- **S-21**: Part of authors' knowledge claim described (contrastively).
- **S-23–S-26**: Introduction of *Mann (1988)*, *Kowtko et al. (1991)*; rebuttal.
- **S-28/S-30**: Introduction of *Airenti et al. (1993)*, *Litman and Allen (1987)*; rebuttal.
- **S-32**: Beginning of the full description of authors' knowledge claim.

S-0 *Most computational models of discourse are based primarily on an analysis of the intentions of the speakers* **(Cohen and Perrault 1979, Allen and Perrault 1980, Grosz and Sidner 1986)**.
...
S-4 *This approach has many strong points, but does not provide a very satisfactory account of the adherence to discourse conventions in dialogue.*
...
(Example)
S-11 *As a result, it does not explain why A says anything when she does not know the answer or when she is not predisposed to adopting B's goals.*
S-12 *Several approaches have been suggested to account for this behavior.*
S-13 **Litman and Allen (1987)** *introduced ...*
S-14 *Others have tried to account for this kind of behavior using social intentional constructs ... (*__Cohen and Levesque 1991, Grosz and Sidner 1990__*).*
S-15 *While these accounts do help explain some discourse phenomena more satisfactorily, they still require a strong degree of co-operativity to account for dialogue coherence, and do not provide easy explanations of why an agent might act in cases that do not support high-level mutual goals.*
(Examples)
S-21 *As these examples illustrate, an account of question answering must go beyond recognition of speaker intentions.*
...
S-23 *Some researchers, e.g.,* **Mann (1988), Kowtko et al. (1991)**, *assume a library of discourse level actions, sometimes called dialogue games, which encode common communicative interactions.*
...
S-26 *Games provide a better explanation of coherence, but still require the agents to recognize each other's intentions to perform the dialogue game.*
...
S-28 *An interesting model is described by* **Airenti et al. (1993)**, *which separates out the conversational games from the task-related games in a way similar way to* **Litman and Allen (1987)**.
...
S-30 *It is left unexplained what goals motivate conversational co-operation.*
S-32 *We are developing an alternate approach that takes a step back from the strong plan-based approach.*

FIGURE 34 Part of the Motivation Section of CmpLG Article 9407011.

The motivation occurs in the form of cycles of type "prior approach – rebuttal". In two places in this cyclic structure (S-11, S-21), a part of the authors' new knowledge claim is delivered, interleaved with the motivation. It is this construction in particular which is in conflict with CARS' Move 2, even if we modified CARS to allow for iterative repetition of Move 2.

The fixed order of moves has also been found problematic by several discourse analysts who employed the model with non-engineering domains (Crookes, 1986, Duszak, 1994). Busch-Lauer (1995) similarly found that many of Swales' moves were missing from the abstracts of the German medical articles she analysed.

Empirically, a certain degree of order amongst the moves is observable, and the order predicted by CARS tended to be the most frequent one for several patterns I studied (see quantitative results in section 8.6). Even though I decided not to formalise order in my model, any actual order observed in the data can still be exploited by an automatic recogniser (section 10.7 describes how this is done in my implementation).

There is also a problem concerning the interchangeability of argumentation strategies. Scientific rhetoric demands that at least one justification for the new knowledge claim must be given in the introduction. Depending on the strategy for Move 2 (namely continuation (Move 2D) or comparison/competition (Move 2A)), one knowledge claim is elevated into a central position – or the lack of one, in the case of the research gap (Move 2B), when no existing knowledge claim is close enough to the new work. The problem is that there is usually ample choice as to which approach could be put into this central position. Even if the research is in a relatively unexplored area, there will be some relatively "similar" approaches the authors need to distance themselves from. The choice of a motivation for an article is part of the construction of the scientific story and largely arbitrary, as research in the philosophy of science confirms.

According to Medawar (1963), the argumentative structure of an article is not a reconstruction of the authors' thought processes that gave rise to the results presented in the article. Only in rare cases is the stated motivation for the research the "real" one at research time. Garvey and Griffith (1971) and Gilbert and Mulkay (1984) confirm the constructive aspect of scientific writing by comparing "shop talk" among scientists with their published scientific prose and conclude that sequences of procedures reported differ dramatically from the actual sequences of procedures.

The KCDM therefore does not specifically record which approach is portrayed as the motivation. Instead, it recognises the type of underlying relationships with the existing knowledge claim. It does so for all existing knowledge claims, independently of their position in the argumentation. For instance, the KCDM defines rival approaches as those that already occupy the niche in research space that the new knowledge claim wants to occupy. Rivalry is a functionally important property, which is practically relevant for search applications. In contrast, it is relatively unimportant how the rivalry is linguistically conveyed – as the motivating problem for the article or as a mere contrast in the result section. The KCDM abstracts over the place in the argumentation and also identifies moves with equivalent article–article relationships, as will be described in section 6.5.

Let us now turn to Level 2, which is concerned with all knowledge claims appearing in an article: already existing knowledge claims owned by other researchers as well as the authors' new knowledge claim.

6.4 Level 2: Knowledge Claim Attribution

Who owns the knowledge claim of an idea described in an article is a core organisation principle in the KCDM, which I call *Knowledge Claim Attribution* (KCA).

We have just seen that the authors' main rhetorical goal is to advance their new knowledge claim; the previous section has listed several explicit rhetorical moves that can be used for that purpose. But authors also reserve a substantial amount of space in their article to talk about other people's existing knowledge claims. This behaviour follows from the high-level goals and rules (Fig. 31): for instance, by acknowledging all relevant knowledge claims, authors try to convince reviewers that they are knowledgeable in their field, while the argument for the novelty of the current knowledge claim may require a comparison against similar established works.

Whereas moves are associated with particular propositions in the text, knowledge claims are attributed to *segments*. Consecutive statements often have the same knowledge claim status as their neighbours, whereas attribution of knowledge claim status tends to happen at the beginnings and ends of segments.

I define the KCA task as a linear segmentation of a scientific article into non-overlapping segments of the same KCA status. KCA is a *full-coverage* segmentation, i.e., all KCA segments together cover the entire article. Four different types of knowledge claim attribution are differentiated (see Fig. 35): No-KC, Ex-KC, ExO-KC and New-KC. I will now describe the segments in turn, starting with No-KC, the non-existent KC.

NO-KC	No knowledge claim is associated with the segment.
EX-KC	Knowledge claim is existing and attributed to somebody else.
EXO-KC	Knowledge claim is existing and attributed to the authors.
NEW-KC	Knowledge claim is new and attributed to the authors.

FIGURE 35 Knowledge Claim Attribution Status (Level 2).

NO-KC segments do not have a specific knowledge claim associated with them. They might describe general ideas or well-known facts which the authors consider as generally accepted, e.g., because they come from a text book. Such segments are often background material, and roughly correspond to Swales' Moves 1A and 1B.

> **No-KC**: *The traditional approach has been to plot isoglosses, delineating regions where the same word is used for the same concept.* (9503002, S-3)
>
> **No-KC:** *It has often been stated that discourse is an inherently collaborative process ...* (9504007, S-171)
>
> **No-KC:** *A wide range of organosulfur compounds are biologically active and some find commercial application as fungicides and bactericides*(1-4). (b514441h)

NO-KC segments are often general observations about the world. Such observations often occur at the beginning of the article, but this is not always the case. For example, articles in linguistics may contain descriptions of linguistic phenomena towards the middle of the article, as in the following cases:

> **No-KC:** *In the Japanese language, the causative and the change of voice are realized by agglutinations of those auxiliary verbs at the tail of current verbs.* (9411021, S-56)
>
> **No-KC**: *Downdrift is the automatic lowering of the second of two H tones when an L intervenes ... Bamileke Dschang has downstep but not downdrift while Igbo has downdrift but only very limited downstep.* (9410022, S-69/70)

In the following example, an explanatory NO-KC segment (S-20–S-43) explaining entropy and perplexity occurs at the beginning of a section, between a goal statement (S-19) and a more detailed description of the solution (from S-44 onwards), i.e., between two NEW-KC segments:

> **New-KC: S-19** *This article addresses the problem of automating this process and presents a method where the nodes to cut at are selected automatically using the information-theoretical concept of entropy.* **No-KC: S-20** *Entropy is well-known from physics, but the concept of perplexity is perhaps better known in the speech-recognition and natural-language communities.* **No-KC: S-21** *For this reason, we will review the concept of entropy at this point, and discuss its relation to perplexity.*
>
> *4.2.5. Entropy*
>
> **No-KC: S-22** *Entropy is a measure of disorder.*
> **No-KC: S-23** *Assume for example that a physical system can be in any of N states ...*
>
> **New-KC: S-44** *We now turn to the task of calculating the entropy of a node in a parse tree.* (9405022)

It is typical for No-KC statements not to contain any citations. If an author makes a statement without citing anybody for it, it can only mean one of two things: they either claim intellectual ownership for the statement themselves, or they feel the statement is so commonly known that nobody in particular can be cited for it.[43] (Had they described somebody else's specific knowledge claim, then the reward system of science would have demanded that they cite it.) It is the latter case which is covered by No-KC.

Some No-KC segments do contain citations, e.g., historical accounts of a particular problem area. Ziman (1969) calls the function of such citations "paying tribute to pioneers". Although a knowledge claim is associated with the segment, it is likely to be of little importance to the citing article overall. Indirect rhetorical goals associated with such accounts exist: they signal that the problem is indeed hard, and that it has apparently already been worth other researchers' time. In my model, KCs with only a vague connection to the current KC are considered No-KC, even if they contain a citation.

Let us now turn to the segment type called Ex-KC, which covers descriptions of specific existing knowledge claims owned by other researchers. These knowledge claims are called *existing* because they are already part of the research space (unlike the new KC); they were included in it through the process of their publication. Normally, such segments are introduced by formal citation.

[43] A general observation at this point: there seem to be considerable differences in people's intuitions about which ideas are specific enough to deserve a citation.

Ex-KC: *Conte and Castelfranchi (1993) present several strategies of moving from obligations to actions, including...* (9407011, S-89)

Ex-KC: *Hung et al.*[(195)] *found that ultraviolet light did not affect bacterial density in biofilms but did decrease the percentage of respiring bacterial cells as the dose of UV light increased.* (b404735b)

While the article is sure to contain a statement somewhere in the text which attributes the segment to the existing knowledge claim (such as the examples above), most of the sentences in Ex-KC zones are rhetorically neutral and simply describe details about the knowledge claim:

Ex-KC: *Cooccurrence probabilities of words are then modeled by averaged cooccurrence probabilities of word clusters.* (9405001, S-15)

Ex-KC: *This means, as desired, that for each choice of an event* **EQN** *of Mary's telephoning, and reference time* **EQN** *'just after' it, there is a state of Sam's being asleep, that surrounds* **EQN**. (9502023, S-59)

ExO-KC is a special case of an existing knowledge claim, namely one which has been made at an earlier point in time by the authors themselves. That means that citations associated with ExO-KC are self-citations.

ExO-KC: *...it also holds for 2) if we want to interpret a sentence like a man stole a bike as* **EQN** *where the quantifier introduced by the subject does not in fact have maximal scope (an analysis I have argued for elsewhere (Ramsay 1992a)).* (9411019, S-23/24)

ExO-KC: *Our group has also reported the synthesis of InS and InSe nanoparticles capped with TOPO and nanoparticles of InSe capped with 4-ethylpyridine by a single-source route using tris(diethyldithiocarbamato)-indium (iii) or tris(diethyldiselenocarbamato)indium(iii) as precursors*[(47)] *(Fig. 5).* (b512182e)

ExO-KC: *In a previous study at our institution, Salcedo et al. showed that LV mass had an effect on thallium stress test sensitivity.*(C149, S-86)

Many articles in chemistry and some in CmpLG use impersonal constructions to refer to their own previous work, either the passive voice (chemistry) or third person pronouns (CL):

ExO-KC: *Gafos and Brent (1994) demonstrate that phonotactics can be learned with high accuracy from the same unsegmented utterances we used in our simulations.* (9412005, S-158)

> **ExO-KC:** *A number of reactions of imines, such as aziridination* [(2)] *alkylation, aldol reaction, hetero-Diels-Alder reaction, have been well documented* [(2)]. (b200198e)

There are also many cases where the fact that the authors talk about previous work is not explicitly stated, but follows logically from the content of the sentences (shared infrastructure, articles planned in the future by the authors, etc.):

> **ExO-KC:** *More detail both on the dialogue manager and its operation on this example can be found in Traum (1994).* (9407011, S-174)

> **ExO-KC:** *...precludes illustrating the substitutional approach through further examples, though more are discussed in Alshawi et al. (1992) and Cooper et al. (1994b).* (9502014, S-147)

> **ExO-KC:** *The syntactic generator VM-GEN is a further development of TAG-GEN (Kilger, 1994) within the framework of VERBMOBIL, a speech-to-speech translation system.* (9410033, S-113)

> **ExO-KC:** *A recent Article* [sic] **[6]** *surveyed the extent of irrigation up to 1986. A future article will discuss the profitability of irrigating sugar beet and how it can be improved by careful scheduling.* (A008)

> **ExO-KC:** *We used a modified test for stimulation of thoracic bristles (Vandervorst and Ghysen, 1980) that is described in detail elsewhere (Melzig et al., 1996).* (FBrf0104486)[44]

What plays into this inference is that authors are likely to reuse infrastructure or materials resulting from their own previous work, rather than use those resulting from somebody else's work, simply for the practical reasons of feasibility or lower effort involved in reuse.

Let us now consider the fourth segment type, New-KC, which describes the authors' new problem-solving process. Most material in an article will typically be of this type, including descriptions of the method used, results and future work sections[45]). Some New-KC examples:

> **New-KC:** *We first show that the minimization of the relative entropy yields the natural expression for cluster centroids.* (9408011, S-101)

[44]Corpus examples from the genetics corpus (see section 5.3) are identified by FlyBase Reference number, which starts with "FBr", followed by a 8-character string.

[45]As has been mentioned before, the knowledge claim status of future work is unclear. An argument could be made that it should be No-KC, and this is a decision which has been taken in later work on a new annotation scheme, see Fig. 127 (p. 358) in section 13.1.2.

New-KC: *If our input 'sentence' now is the definition of trans/3 as given above, we obtain the following parse forest grammar (where the start symbol is* **EQN***).* (9504026, S-51)

New-KC: *To indicate species specific patterns of germination rate and spread, we determined the period to reach 25% and 75% of the total germination recorded.* (A009)

New-KC: *Before and after 1 hour of deslunoside infusion, we performed blood sampling for the measurements of plasma levels of neurohumoral factors and measured the hemodynamic parameters.* (C009, S-28)

In the life sciences, impersonal constructions such as passive voice or nominalisations are commonly used to describe *new* knowledge claims (as well as *existing own* knowledge claims, which can happen for CL too, as we have just seen):

New-KC: *After stirring for 24 hours at room temperature the reaction was stopped and separation of products* **18** *and* **19** *from the receptor could be accomplished by flash chromatography.* (b110865b)

New-KC: *Subsequent hydroboration with 9-BBN and accompanying oxidation afforded the diol* **7** *in 88%; ...* (b110865b)

New-KC: *The percentage of transheterozygous flies is defined as the ratio of transheterozygous to total flies and was determined for each day and over the 5-day period (Fig. 3N).* (FBrf0125151)

Most sentences in a NEW-KC segments are rhetorically neutral. The following examples show that this is a normal state of affairs for NEW-KC segments:

New-KC: *The extent to which these (Markovian) assumptions hold depend on the extent to which relation edges represent all the relevant information for translation.* (9408014, S-157)

New-KC: *Enantiomeric excesses of up to 30% were obtained in one case for the major regioisomer.* (b110865b)

New-KC: *Two 50-cm rows per plot were used for observation of heading, anthesis, and yield.* (A027)

New-KC: *Patients with obesity and a history or clinical evidence of heart disease were excluded.* (C043, S-11)

Overt marking of KCA tends to occur at the segment *boundaries*, i.e., those places in text where knowledge claim attribution changes.[46]

[46] The observation that it is the *change* of knowledge claims which is likely to be explicitly signalled, rather than the *continuation* of a knowledge claim, will also have consequences in my design of automatic features for KCA: in chapter 10, most

This means that it is quite normal that there are large segments of a particular knowledge claim status which are relatively unmarked.

New-KC segments can be very long, and one may therefore consider modelling their internal structure. For instance, a subdivision into the different stages of the scientific problem-solving process, possibly corresponding to the IMRD sections, is quite intuitive. However, the KCDM does not recognise internal structure of knowledge claim segments as a central principle.[47] From a theoretical viewpoint, my core analytic interest lies in explaining how different knowledge claims are interwoven into a coherent scientific argument, rather than what the internal structure of the knowledge claim is. From a practical viewpoint, it is also less important for the information access applications in chapter 4 to know about a knowledge claim segment's internal structure, than to know where it starts and ends.

The segments types, as I defined them here, share various properties. For instance, ExO-KC, previous knowledge claims by the authors, is situated somewhere between Ex-KC and New-KC: Both ExO-KC and Ex-KC deal with already published, specific knowledge claims, which means they probably both contain a formal citation and use the past tense. In another aspect, ExO-KC is more similar to New-KC, the new knowledge claim put forward in the current article: the research done by the authors before and currently is probably similar, and authors are probably as positive towards their old work as they are towards their new work (and generally more positive than they are towards other researchers' work).

Despite, or rather because of, the similarities between New-KC and ExO-KC, it is crucial that these two categories be kept apart, whatever else we do in the classification scheme. This follows from the design of the applications in chapter 4, which gives an article's unique knowledge claim a special status. It is the very thing that differentiates this article from similar ones (in particular, from similar ones by the same author). Therefore, a separation between New-KC and ExO-KC is indispensable if we want to enable the user to choose which one out of a set of articles written by the same authors they should read for a particular information need.

Having introduced the four KCA types, let us now look at how knowledge claim status is transmitted from the author to the reader. Authors have an interest in clearly expressing their knowledge claim: there should be no trace of unclarity left in a reviewer's mind about

features relevant to KCA are associated with segment boundaries, whereas fewer features model the continuation of knowledge claim attribution.

[47] Although it is explored in the annotation scheme in section 13.1.2.

the exact nature of the knowledge claim. It is the reviewers' job to judge whether a knowledge claim is enough to warrant publication. The chances of rejection increase if the authors did not do their part of their job, namely to state the claim clearly. A clear indication of KCA status is therefore one aspect of overall textual quality of a scientific article, even if experts write for experts.

Authors differ in their intuitions about how explicitly attribution should be signalled. A common error by novice writers is not to convey whether a particular statement is established fact or their own new knowledge claim.[48] In my experience, this problem often goes beyond mere textual signalling: novice writers often do not actually conceptually make the distinction between established and new KC, because they have not yet understood the mechanics of knowledge claim staking in scientific writing. Additionally, they may not have the knowledge of the literature to decide whether their idea is an established one or not.

Let us now look at what effects this has on the reader. My assumption in the following is that when humans read an article, they automatically and subconsciously interpret and track ownership of claims. When a reader is faced with long segments without attribution, the normal procedure is to assume one is still in the same segment, unless a change of knowledge claim status is noticed. Overt signals are best, but in many texts domain knowledge and inference is required to interpret the KCA structure. This is why expert readers typically have no problem reading text with only few KCA signals (like much expert-directed text), whereas non-experts find such texts hard to understand.

In particular, readers are sometimes left wondering whether or not some piece of work described in an article has already been published elsewhere by the authors (EXO-KC) or whether it is described for the first time in the present article (NEW-KC). Knowledge claims by the same author (existing and new) share linguistic features, so there is a danger that their descriptions in the text "bleed" into each other. In the worst case, such ambiguities can span across many paragraphs in an article. This phenomenon (I call it *zone bleeding*) is exacerbated when the external section structure of an article is ambiguous and when clear markers such as *"in this paper"* are missing. While such situations are normally due to carelessness on the part of the authors, they could be a deliberate attempt at publishing several similar articles based on the same results under the radar of the peer review.

[48]Manning (1990) reports a parallel problem that novices have with writing informative summaries, because these require that one contrasts the findings of the text with already-established findings in the field.

Zone bleeding is sometimes noticed by readers, through an inconsistency between their assumption of who owns a particular knowledge claim and certain text signals; e.g., a pronoun might be in the wrong person or a verb in the wrong tense. When this happens, the reader may have to mentally re-analyse, possibly using non-linear jumps back to earlier text segments. They may never find out who – according to the author – owns a given knowledge claim, or worse, they may get the wrong impression because they never even notice the conflict. Human annotation of KCA is studied in section 8.2, and we will see there that zone bleeding and unmarked knowledge claim segments are indeed a likely source of disagreement.

The double-blind review process, together with the short turnaround in conference publications, might inadvertently be a contributor to zone bleeding effects. It requires that authors' identities are anonymised in article submissions. The rules state that self-citations can be either non-anonymous (i.e., one's name remains in the citation) or anonymous (i.e., the citation is explicitly marked as "anonymous"). The former option requires that the discussion of the previous work must not "give away" the author's identity, whereas in the anonymous case, no such requirement applies. As a result, non-anonymous descriptions of previous own work should look more like Ex-KC segments than like ExO-KC segments: the authors' previous KC must be presented as if there was no special connection to the new KC, beyond one that any other previous KC could have.

Knowledge claim attribution is a central part of the KCDM; other levels of the model use KCA segmentation as a basis for defining moves. The KCDM levels form a cross-classification: a textual piece can belong to more than one level. It may be of type R-10 and also be part of a New-KC KCA segment. Several of the rhetorical moves in section 6.3, namely those which argue in favour of the new knowledge claim, would normally be part of a New-KC segment, whereas the moves which describe the research space tend to occur in No-KC segments. In fact, rhetorical moves often appear in characteristic positions within knowledge claim segments, e.g., at their start, a fact the recognition mechanism can exploit.

But KCA is also a useful exercise in its own right, because its recognition directly enables various information access methods. For document retrieval, one may decide to weight keywords occurring in New-KC segments higher than other keywords, somewhat similar to the experiments by Tbahriti et al. (2006), who successfully used different weights for different IMRD sections. KCA information should allow us to dampen the contribution of keywords associated with other knowledge claims, which happen to be in the article for rhetorical reasons but which do not specifically characterise the article's knowledge claim. Beyond indexing, there are various other misrepresentation errors a KCA-informed information management system can avoid: we definitely do not want an article to be characterised on the basis of the Ex-KC or ExO-KC segments it contains.

Another application of KCA concerns bibliometry and citation support. I have assumed in chapter 4 that there is a correlation between the length of an Ex-KC or ExO-KC segment and the relative importance of the approach described in it. This assumption is based on the observation that all writing in conference or journal articles works against space limitations. Therefore, authors should only reserve space for those approaches which are central to their purpose. The length of Ex-KC and ExO-KC segments could be used to rescale traditional bibliographic measurements (as I have suggested in chapter 5), or to determine the thickness of links in a citation map (as I have done in Fig. 18).

I will now turn to Level 3, which concerns the mechanism by which knowledge claim segments are combined into a coherent argument.

6.5 Level 3: Hinging

Level 2 serves to identify the descriptions of previous knowledge claims that authors have chosen to include in their article. Level 3 provides an explanation for why those segments are included, and in particular, what they have to do with authors' new knowledge claim. The connection between knowledge claim segments is called a *hinge function* (or *hinge* for short); the imagery is that of two KCA blocks held together by a hinge. Statements expressing the hinge function are called *hinge moves*.

Hinge function is closely related to citation function, a concept studied in detail in the field of context of citation content analysis (see section 2.3.1). The main difference is that hinge function operates between two knowledge claim segments, one of which must be the new knowledge claim, whereas citation function holds between a citing article and a formal citation.

There are a multitude of ways that previous work can relate to a particular new knowledge claim, but a certain set of connection types occur over and over again. We have already implicitly come across these moves in the rhetorical rules in Fig. 31; in terms of the KCDM and the goal of explaining scientific argumentation, they are the last missing piece in the puzzle.

The hinge moves I distinguish (see Fig. 36) can be subdivided into statements about properties of existing knowledge claims (H-1 to H-5), statements about the relationships between existing knowledge claims and the new knowledge claim (H-6 to H-16), and indirect hinge moves (H-17 and H-18).

Properties of Existing KCs:

H-1	Existing Solution is Flawed
H-2	Existing Solution does not Solve Problem/Achieve Goal
H-3	Existing Solution Introduces New Problem
H-4	Existing Solution Solves Problem
H-5	Existing Solution is Advantageous

Relationships between Existing and New KC:

H-6	New Solution is Better than Existing Solution
H-7	New Solution Avoids Problems (When Existing Does Not)
H-8	New Goal/Problem/Solution is Different from Existing Goal /Problem/Solution
H-9	New Goal/Problem is Harder than Existing Goal/Problem
H-10	New Result is Different from Existing Result
H-11	New Claim is Different from/Clashes with Existing Claim
H-12	Agreement/Support between Existing and New Claim
H-13	Existing Solution Provides Basis for New Solution
H-14	Existing Solution Provides Part of New Solution
H-15	Existing Solution Provides Part of New Solution, After Adaptation
H-16	Existing Solution is Similar to New Solution

Indirect Hinges:

H-17	Existing KC Provides Evidence that (Other) Existing Solution Used is Promising
H-18	Existing KC Provides Evidence that New Problem Exists/is Hard/is Worth Solving

FIGURE 36 Hinge Moves H-1 to H-18 (Level 3)

The authors' ulterior motives for citing somebody may well involve political and sociological considerations (such as "to placate one's rivals" or "to signal loyalty to one's school of thought"). While these are treated in some works in citation content analysis, I only recognise those hinge functions which directly and transparently support the argument in favour of the current knowledge claim. (This concerns the difference between citation motivation and citation function discussed in section 2.3.1.) I assume that under the pressures of space limitation, it is against the authors' interest to cite somebody else's work which does not have a substantial subject-matter relation to their own knowledge claim. I will next discuss the hinges one by one.

Hinge Moves Expressing Properties

If the problem addressed in the article is well-known, a common way to motivate the new knowledge claim is to state a weakness of an existing knowledge claim that has addressed it in the past (Hinge move H-1). This is a simple and obvious move; I chose it in the introduction to motivate affect towards citations. It is also recognised by Swales (p. 108; Move 2A) and by Spiegel-Rösing (p. 26; categories 10, 12, possibly 13).

In particular, a weakness can be stated by listing undesirable properties of the criticised previous work (H-1):

> **H-1:** *Here, we will produce experimental evidence suggesting that this simple model leads to serious overestimates of system error rates...* (9407009, S-7)

> **H-1:** *Goal-freezing ... is equally unappealing: goal-freezing is computationally expensive, it demands the procedural annotation of an otherwise declarative grammar specification, and it presupposes that a grammar writer possesses substantial computational processing expertise.* (9502005, S-59)

> **H-1:** *The disiloxane* $(Me_3)_2CH(SiMe_2)_2O$ *(**1**) has been synthesised previously via dehydration of ... in air over three days* (5)*. However, this reaction appears to be somewhat capricious, frequently giving very low yields of* **1** *and/or samples of widely differing purity, and so we sought a more reliable route to this species.* (b510692c)

> **H-1:** *The structures of (2) and (5) have been reported briefly in a proof of constitution study (Chatterjee et al. 1998) but very few details were given. In particular, the numbers of data and of refined parameters were not specified, so any evaluation of the reported R factors is precluded; the twofold rotational symmetry of the bipyridyl unit in (2) and the inversion symmetry of the acid unit in (5) were not mentioned, nor was there any indication of how the H atoms had been located; and more important in the present context, the earlier report contained no description or analysis of the supramolecular aggregation patterns.* (b030100)

> **H-1:** *Roth (1985) and Cother and Cullis (1985) also used an individual plant sampling procedure to study the effects of R. solani infections on yield. However, because they did not disinfect their seed tubers, their R. solani stem and stolon infections could have been caused by soil-bourne and/or tuber-bourne inoculum.* (A042)

Another way of declaring a weakness of a previous KC is by indicating a flaw in the associated problem-solving act, either by stating that the solution does not solve a problem (H-2), or that it introduces a new problem (H-3):

> **H-2:** *Computational approaches fail to account for the cancellation of pragmatic inferences: once presuppositions or implicatures are generated, they can never be cancelled.* (9504017, S-20)

> **H-2:** *Unfortunately, however, these studies were hampered by the experimental difficulties encountered in determining the surface tensions and densities of high melting salts (e.g., NaCl; mp 803* deg *C)*$^{(25)}$ *and no related investigations followed.* (b513453f)

Several studies in content citation analysis found that clear negational citations are rare (e.g., Moravcsik and Murugesan, 1975, Spiegel-Rösing, 1977). MacRoberts and MacRoberts (1984) propose that the reason for this is the fact that negational citations are potentially politically dangerous, and must therefore be made more acceptable by "dissembling". Negative points are therefore softened by initial praise.[49] Their hypothesis is confirmed by Brooks' (1986) interviews of scholars.

In my analysis of the CmpLG corpus, I also found a recurring pattern of a positive statement about an existing KC followed by a negative one, as in the following examples:

> **H-1:** *Even though these approaches often accomplish considerable improvements with respect to efficiency or termination behavior, it remains unclear how these optimisations relate to each other and what comprises the logic behind these specialized forms of filtering.* (9604019, S-21)

> **H-2:** *This account makes reasonably good empirical predictions, though it does fail for the following examples: ...* (9503014, S-75)

> **H-1:** *Hidden Markov Models (HMMs) (Huang et al. 1990) offer a powerful statistical approach to this problem, though it is unclear how they could be used to recognise the units of interest to phonologists.* (9410022, S-24)

It seems safe to assume that the real intention in these examples was to criticise, as it is almost always the negative sentiment which comes last. This is important to know in situations where one is forced to make a choice between the interpretation of praise or criticism for these sentences (e.g., in sentence-based annotation schemes such as the ones I will introduce in chapter 7).

It is rare that authors point out a weakness in their own earlier work, but it sometimes happens, as in the following article by Schütze:

[49] Hyland (1998a) makes a similar case for hedging: in order for a researcher to protect their position in their research community, controversial and challenging statements must be "packaged up" so that they are less conspicuous.

H-3: *In a previous paper (Schütze 1993), we trained a neural network ... This scheme fails for cases like "The soldiers rarely come home" vs. "The soldiers will come home" where the context is identical and information about the lexical item in question ("rarely" vs. "will") is needed in combination with context for correct classification.* (9503009, S-24/25)

I will now turn to the positive moves H-4 and H-5. Here, the existing knowledge claim is portrayed as participating in some successful problem-solving act (H-4) or as being otherwise advantageous (H-5). H-5 is also known from the introduction to this book, and corresponds to Spiegel-Rösing's category 9:

H-4: *The Direct Inversion Approach (DIA) of Minnen et al. (1995) overcomes these problems by making the reordering process more goal-directed and developing a reformulation technique that allows the successful treatment of rules which exhibit head-recursion.* (9502005, S-15)

H-5: *Since head-driven generation in general has its merits, we simply return to a syntactic definition of "head" and demonstrate the feasibility of syntactic head-driven generation.* (9405004, A-2)

H-5: *This method is known to be inexpensive and remarkably accurate from the prediction of harmonic force fields(31).* (b510675c)

Moves H-1 to H-5 describe *properties* of existing knowledge claims, rather than relationships between the existing knowledge claim and the authors's new knowledge claim. They are classified as hinge moves here nevertheless, because there is an implicit relationship between the existing KCs and the new KC which motivates the positive or negative portrayal of the existing KC.

Hinge Moves Expressing Relationships

Let us now look at more direct expressions of relationships between knowledge claims. Paramount amongst these is the wish to show that one's own problem-solving process is more successful than a competing existing knowledge claim. The most direct way to do this is to simply assert that one's new solution is better:

H-6: *We found that the MDL-based method performs better than the MLE-based method.* (9605014, S-11)

H-6: *We see several advantages of this approach over that of Lascarides and Asher ...* (9405002, S-56)

This move is semantically close to move R-10 from Level 1 (advantageousness of own solution). The difference is that H-6 discusses both the new and the existing knowledge claim, i.e., makes the comparison explicitly, whereas R-10 talks about the new knowledge claim in isolation. This is the theory, anyway; in practice, there are ambiguous cases between R-10 and H-6, which are hard to decide.

Authors do not always explicitly state that the problem they address is well-known. In the following case, this can nevertheless be inferred from the existence of previous approaches to the same problem:

> **H-6:** *We present an unsupervised algorithm for prepositional phrase attachment in English that requires only an part-of-speech tagger and a morphology database, and is therefore less resource-intensive and more portable than previous approaches, which have all required either treebanks or partial parsers.* (9807011, S-14)

The sentence expresses both the semantics of H-6 (superiority of new knowledge over existing one) and of H-1 (existing knowledge claim is flawed). As a general principle, the more informative move is chosen in a conflict; between H-1 and H-6, this is H-6.

Avoiding a problem that others have run into is another way of ending up with a better solution:

> *This is not captured by the Lascarides and Asher account because sentences containing the past perfect are treated as sententially equivalent to those containing the simple past.* ... **H-7:** *All of these facts are explained by the account given here.* (9405002, S-70/72)

> **H-7:** *Although most previous studies have added auxiliary redox agents to facilitate electron transfer, our results show that these redox agents are not necessary when using AC methods instead of DC methods and operating at the open circuit potential.* (b307591e)

H-7 is a combined move, in that its semantics consists of the fact that the existing KC has a problem (H-1 or H-2), which the new KC does not have (R-7 or R-8). A specialised move is warranted because the combination occurred surprisingly often in the corpus.

The rules in Fig. 31 decree that a different argumentation route must be taken when the problem addressed is *new*. Showing that the problem really is new is now the most important task. This can be done with hinge moves H-8 and H-9, which state that an existing knowledge claim (which might be considered similar to the new knowledge claim) is in fact sufficiently different from it to warrant publication. Therefore, contrast moves can promote the new knowledge claim, although they express neutral author stance towards existing work. Such contrast statements correspond to Spiegel-Rösing's category 5:

H-8: *Unlike most research in pragmatics that focuses on certain types of presuppositions or implicatures, we provide a global framework in which one can express all these types of pragmatic inferences.* (9504017, S-124)

H-8: *This type of reference is different from the type that has been studied traditionally by researchers who have usually assumed that the agents have mutual knowledge of the referent (Appelt 1985a, Appelt and Kronfeld 1987, Clark and Wilkes-Gibbs 1986, Heeman and Hirst 1992, Searle 1969), are copresent with the referent (Heeman and Hirst 1992, Cohen 1981), or have the referent in their focus of attention (Reiter and Dale 1992).* (9405013, S-12)

Statements of the new goal being *harder* than those of the existing knowledge claim (H-9) are sometimes used as an alternative to H-8:

H-9: ... *disambiguating word senses to the level of fine-grainedness found in WordNet is quite a bit more difficult than disambiguation to the level of homographs (Hearst 1991; Cowie et al. 1992).* (9511006, S-147)

Rhetorically, H-8 and H-9 are equivalent, as both moves mainly function to assert that there is enough difference between the two knowledge claims. H-9 is also similar to R-3 (the statement that the own goal is hard), but R-3 does not involve any comparison with previous KCs.

If the relationship with the existing knowledge claim concerns a disagreement with respect to its results (H-10) or claims or conclusions (H-11), rather than a contrast in methods or goals, the situation is somewhat different. An article containing H-10 or H-11 describes a new examination of a research problem already addressed by some existing KC, and hinges H-10 and H-11 tend to occur in the result or discussion section, whereas H-8 and H-9 are often part of the declaration of research goals. H-10 and H-11 serve to support HLG-1 (significance), rather than HLG-2 (novelty); H-11 does so to a higher degree.

H-10: *Although purification of* **8b** *to a de* [sic] *of 95 percent has been reported elsewhere*[31]*, in our hands it was always obtained as a mixture of the two [EQN]-diastereomers.* (b310767a)

H-10: *There is no obvious match between our product spectrum and the reported spectrum of chloral (CCl3CHO)*[32,33]. (b310495h)

H-10: *This is opposite to findings by Trolldenier and von Rheinbaben (1981a) for wheat and Trolldenier (1973) for rice who observed that with NH4+-nutrition, bacterial abundances on roots were higher than with NO3-nutrition in hydroponic culture.* (A020)

> **H-11:** *Despite the hypothesis that the free word order of German leads to poor performance of low order HMM taggers when compared with a language like English, we have shown that the overall results for German are very much along the lines of comparable implementations for English, if not better.* (9502038, S-117)

H-11 moves are covered by Spiegel-Rösing's categories 12 and 13 ("disproval or new interpretation of claims in cited literature"). Lisacek et al. (2005) make the observation that such sentences (they call them "paradigm shift" sentences) tend to mark articles which make large contributions and which often have a particular impact in the scientific community; more about this in section 9.5.

The statement that the claims of the new and an existing knowledge claim mutually support each other (H-12) serves to reassure reviewers of the likely validity of the research and of the authors' knowledge of the literature. Spiegel-Rösing distinguishes according to the direction the support takes: her category 8 means that a claim in the literature supports the authors' argument; her category 11 means the opposite. As the directionality of support is often unclear in CL, and as I observed many statements of mere *compatibility* between approaches, my move H-12 applies to support in both directions, as long as it involves an existing and the new KC:

> **H-12:** *Work similar to that described here has been carried out by Merialdo (1994), with broadly similar conclusions.* (9410012, S-36)

> **H-12:** *Notice that Hobbs' (1985) remark that "the more deeply the pronoun is embedded and the more elaborate the construction it occurs in, the more acceptable the non-reflexive" is consistent with our assumption.* (9605007, S-114)

> **H-12:** *This is in line with the findings of Martin and Illas for inorganic solids* [(84,85)]. (b515732c)

> **H-12:** *Greater survival of tillers under irrigated conditions agrees with other reports in barley [4,28] and wheat [10,13,26].* (A027)

> **H-12:** *In addition, on Doppler echocardiography, E, A, E/A ratio, and deceleration time have also been shown to relate most strongly to initial left ventricular filling pressure, which changes minimally in patients without heart failure during dobutamine-induced ischemia. The hemodynamic results of our study support these findings.* (C001, S-104/S-105)

Let us now turn to the case where existing knowledge claims are presented as contributing part of the solution (like in the *continuation* links in the citation map in section 4.2). Most inventions described in articles are not entirely new; instead research builds on prior work, e.g., by the same authors, or by the same school of thought. In those cases, some previously published methodology or idea is taken as the basis for the reported research and applied, either with or without adaptation.

The strongest such relationships with an existing KC is continuation of a tradition (H-13): the authors state that the existing KC provides the intellectual basis for their new KC. This corresponds to Spiegel-Rösing's category 2:

H-13: *We present a different method that takes as starting point the back-off scheme of Katz (1987).* (9405001, S-24)

H-13: *Our study builds on prior work by Floudas, Klok and coworkers who have investigated phase transitions in the solid state of these copolymers using differential scanning calorimetry (DSC), polarized optical microscopy (POM), Fourier transform infra-red (FTIR) spectroscopy and SAXS/WAXS*[(4,5)]. (b508772b)

H-13: *As a program aimed at the applications of imines*[(2,5)] *we have studied the formation of carbanions from imines and their subsequent reactions.* (b200198e)

Swales' Move 2D (CONTINUING A TRADITION) marks continuation links in introduction sections, but I often found that H-13 moves also frequently occurred in other places in the article.

Simple *use* of an existing knowledge claim (H-14) is a "weaker" way of incorporating somebody else's work into one's own knowledge claim. Which aspect of an existing KC is used and how it is used often depends on the particular discipline; it may be a theory, data, software, definitions or other entities. My move H-14 does not distinguish between these different aspects of use, but many citation function annotation schemes, including Spiegel-Rösing's, do. This is probably motivated by a possible application of the schemes to bibliometrics, with the intuition that a researcher should get more credit for use of their theory than for the use of their data.

H-14: *We use the framework for the allocation and transfer of control of Whittaker and Stenton (1988).* (9504007, S-36)

H-14: *We use as a corpus the 1987 Wall Street Journal in the CD-ROM I (Liberman 1991), which has a total of 20 M words.* (9503025, S-53)

H-14: *The diamine* **10** *was prepared following a previously published procedure*[(4d)]. (b110865b)

H-14: *We have utilized this experimental data to evaluate the model for BDE determination (Fig. 2, ESI).* (b515712a)

The existing knowledge claim can sometimes only be used after it has been adapted in some form. I differentiate use with adaptation (H-15) from unchanged use (H-14):

> **H-15:** *We adopt Resnik's approach... However, we adapt it taking into account the syntactic position of the relationship.* (9409004, S-82/S-83)

> **H-15:** *We therefore revise the earlier framework to model what we will term occurrences of f-structures as resources explicitly in the logic.* (9502015, S-67)

> **H-15:** *The reaction pathway used by us can be considered as a slight modification of the one previously described*[(21)] *to prepare compounds* $[Pt(S\text{-}C_5H_4SN)_2(dppe)]$ *(**2**) ...* (b508438e)

Moves H-13 to H-15 are often accompanied by moves H-4 and H-5 (praise of existing knowledge claim). Because use logically "incorporates" an existing KC into the new KC, the quality of the existing KC now becomes important for the quality of the new KC. Praise of the existing KC therefore indirectly promotes the new KC.

An existing knowledge claim can be a contributor to the new knowledge claim and at the same time the object of (implicit) criticism: authors chose an existing approach, which is sound enough to be used, but nevertheless lacking in some respect, necessitating some adaptation. Statements of adaptation (H-15) often combine both aspects of this complex relationship. It can therefore be hard in practice to demarcate the rhetorical expressions of adaptation, criticism and use.

Statement of similarity (H-16) is also a positive hinge, but its function in the overall argument is minor. Spiegel-Rösing's scheme, for instance, does not provide a category for similarity. H-16 moves however do contribute somewhat to HLG-3 (knowledge of the literature):

> **H-16:** *In some respects this is similar to Dagan and Itai's (1994) approach to word sense disambiguation using statistical associations in a second language.* (9408014, S-240)

H-16 moves often occur in combination with other hinge moves. A typical pattern is similarity–contrast:

> **H-11:** *Resnik (1992) performed a similar learning process, but while he was only looking for the preferred class of object nouns, we are interested in all the possible classes.* (9409004, S-100)

In analogy with the praise–criticism pattern, it is again the contrast which comes last. Contrast is considered the more informative category, which is why the sentence above is classified as H-11: as one typically only compares things which are already similar in at least one respect, a statement of similarity is redundant if it occurs in combination with a contrast. In fact, H-16 often gets "overwritten" by more informative moves because it is rhetorically so bland.

If H-16 occurs without a more informative hinge move in the vicinity ("lone" H-16 move), this is sometimes an indication of an unclear argumentation strategy. As no specific relationship to an existing KC is stated, the reader may be left wondering why its similarity should matter for the new knowledge claim contributed in the article.

Indirect Hinge Moves

We now come to the hinges H-17 and H-18, which have a more indirect connection to the argumentation than moves H-1 to H-5 (properties of existing KCs) and moves H-6 to H-16 (relationships between existing KC and new KC). They concern existing knowledge claims which are used as motivation for the new KC, but where there is neither a comparison nor a use relationship.

H-17 applies when the authors cite evidence which makes them think that a particular approach will work in their research situation:

> **H-17:** *Charniak (1995) and Carroll and Rooth (1998) present head-lexicalized probabilistic context free grammar formalisms, and show that they can effectively be applied in inside-outside estimation of syntactic language models for English, the parameterization of which encodes lexicalized rule probabilities and syntactically conditioned word-word bigram collocates.* (9905009, S-0)

> **H-17:** *It has also been shown that the combined accuracy of an ensemble of multiple classifiers is often significantly greater than that of any of the individual classifiers that make up the ensemble (e.g., Dietterich 1997).* (0005006, S-9)

The connection between the existing KC and the new KC that H-17 expresses is vague: the new KC builds on the *information* given in the existing KC (i.e., that hard-lexicalised probabilistic context free grammar formalisms or ensembles of multiple classifiers are a good idea). Two different sets of authors can in principle be involved, the one contributing the idea, and the one which makes the statement that the idea is useful; often, these are one and the same.

The definition of H-17 additionally requires that the motivated approach is actually used in the article. Thus, the fact that S-9 is considered an H-17 implies that article 0005006 must indeed use ensembles of classifiers.

H-18 moves also do not directly include the new KC. Instead, they involve an existing KC which gives evidence for the fact that the authors' chosen problem really is a problem (R-1), that it is hard (R-3) or worth solving (R-4):

> **H-18**: *These unseen events generally make up a substantial portion of novel data; for example, Essen and Steinbiss (1992) report that 12% of the test-set bigrams in a 75% - 25% split of one million words did not occur in the training partition.* (0001012, S-2)

> **H-18**: *Another problem that affects the corpus-based WSD methods is the sparseness of data: these methods typically rely on the statistics of co-occurrences of words, while many of the possible co-occurrences are not observed even in a very large corpus (Church and Mercer 1993). (We address this problem in several ways.)* (J98-1002, S-12/S-13)[50]

> **H-18**: *When mapping into the surface form, the selection of appropriate forms for anaphora is very important to make the generated text a cohesive unit (McDonald 1980; Dale 1992). (In this paper, our goal is the computer generation of anaphora in Chinese.)* (J97-1007, S-2/S-3)

Again, it is essential that the problem thus discussed is indeed addressed by the new KC (note that the goal of article 0001012 is to estimate unseen events).

Rhetorical and hinge moves are normally independent of their place in the argumentation, but H-17 and H-18 are not, which is another reason why they are unusual. As they both serve to motivate the new KC, they must occur before the "meat" of the article, where the authors' novel KC is discussed in detail.

We have now seen all 18 types of hinge moves defined in the KCDM. Let us next look at the process of hinging itself: how do Level 3 hinge moves connect to Level 2 KCA segments in detail, and what is the interplay of textual citations with this process?

Citation Blocks

I use the name *citation block* to describe the local context around a physical citation. A citation block is normally a KCA segment, but there are many KCA segments which do not contain citations and are thus not citation blocks.

The idea of identifying an area around a citation which logically belongs to that citation is not new. O'Connor (1982) defines a *citation*

[50] This and the next example was taken from the ACL Anthology corpus, which I will describe in section 14.4.

statement as one or more sentences following the physical citation and expressing ideas attributed to that work. He manually identifies such contexts and proposes rules for automatically marking them. He reports that the exact starting and end points of citation block can be hard to find, because they are often linguistically unmarked.

Fig. 37 shows a contrastive citation block from the example article *Pereira et al. (1993)*. We have already come across it in section 4.2: it is an Ex-KC segment which stretches from S-5 to S-9. The formal citation *Hindle (1990)* occurs in sentence S-5, and the subsequent sentences continue to neutrally describe Hindle's approach. S-9 is the hinge move,[51] i.e., the sentence which describes how and why Hindle's work matters to the new knowledge claim. The first half of S-9 states the authors' agreement with Hindle (H-12). The criticism (H-1) occurs in the second half: Hindle does not directly construct word classes and models of association. The sentence is formulated in a rather neutral way, which is why it could have been alternative classified as H-8 (contrast). The example also demonstrates the meek criticism effect described by MacRoberts and MacRoberts: a statement of praise softens the criticism that something is missing in Hindle's approach.

In terms of the argumentation, the criticism is used as a motivation for the new knowledge claim. Swales' model predicts a goal statement next, which is indeed the case. (S-10 is not part of the citation block, as its main topic is no longer the cited work, but the authors' own work. It is therefore not contained in Fig. 37, but it can be found on p. 62.)

S-5 **Hindle (1990)** *proposed dealing with the sparseness problem by estimating the likelihood of unseen events from that of "similar" events that have been seen.* **S-6** *For instance, one may estimate the likelihood of a particular direct object for a verb from the likelihoods of that direct object for similar verbs.* **S-7** *This requires a reasonable definition of verb similarity and a similarity estimation method.* **S-8** *In* **Hindle***'s proposal, words are similar if we have strong statistical evidence that they tend to participate in the same events.* **S-9** **His** *notion of similarity seems to agree with our intuitions in many cases, but it is not clear how it can be used directly to construct word classes and corresponding models of association.* (9408011)

FIGURE 37 Citation Context with Contrastive Hinge.

[51] In section 4.2 I called this an *evaluative sentence*.

Different linguistic expressions are used to refer to the discourse referent *Hindle* in the citation block; these are shown in bold face in Fig. 37. In S-5, there is a full citation, signified by a box around the citation. Later reference to the cited authors or the cited work is often made using a *referring expression*, i.e., a shorter linguistic form which refers to the same discourse referent. In S-8, Hindle's name occurs without a date; in S-9, he is referred to by personal pronoun.

The referent of the pronoun is clear in this particular case, but this is not always so. Kim and Webber (2006) study the referential behaviour of the plural pronoun *they* in the vicinity of citations in astrophysics articles, which could refer to citations ("*Lambrecht et al.*") as well as to object level referents ("*the stars*"). They present a disambiguation algorithm based on machine learning and sentential features. Studies like these provide important insights into the linguistic principles which are in operation inside citation blocks. In a similar line, Kaplan et al. (2009) use co-reference chains to identify citation blocks.

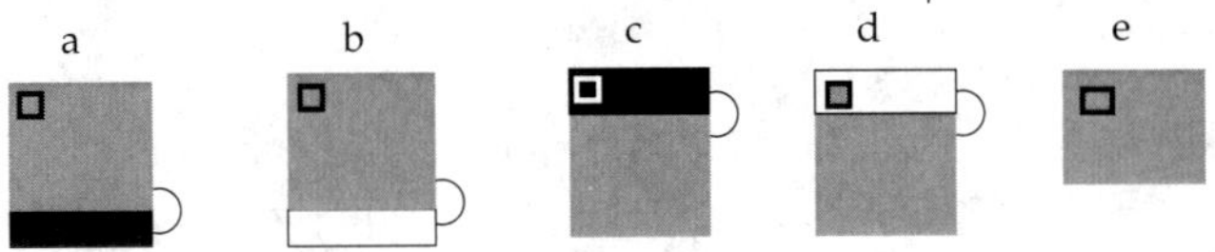

FIGURE 38 Citation Blocks in Ex-KC Segments (Grey); with Contrastive (Black) and Continuative (White) Hinge Moves.

Certain rhetorical patterns tend to recur in citation blocks. Consider Fig. 38, where grey areas correspond to (the neutral part of) Ex-KC or ExO-KC segments, black areas to contrastive hinge moves, and white areas to continuative hinge moves. Hinge function is graphically expressed by a little arch between the two KCA segments that the hinge connects. Small black boxes signify citations.

For citations with a contrastive stance, such as the one in Fig. 37, a typical pattern is **a**, where the existing knowledge claim is first identified by citation and then neutrally described. The hinging statement follows. The parallel situation with continuative citation function is shown in **b**. It can also be the case that the same sentence contains identification, description and hinge all in one. In that case, no neutral Ex-KC block exists; the hinge sentence makes up the entire citation block. Such approaches have been afforded little "article real estate", and according to my assumption about length of KCA segments and importance, the approach should be less important for the overall argumentation. Other variations are possible too: in cases **c** and **d**, the hinge move precedes the neutral description (EX-KC or EXO-KC segment).

In situation **e**, a citation and a neutral description of it are present, but no stance towards the existing KC is expressed. This is similar to the "lone H-16" (similarity statement) discussed before. Such citation blocks do not actively advance the scientific argument, although they might serve to promote HLG-3 (demonstration of authors' knowledge) to a certain degree. Surprisingly many such patterns occur in CmpLG, as we will see in section 8.6. One possible explanation for the existence of such citation blocks is that they are the result of a post hoc (and possibly reluctant) inclusion of a citation in response to a request by the peer review.

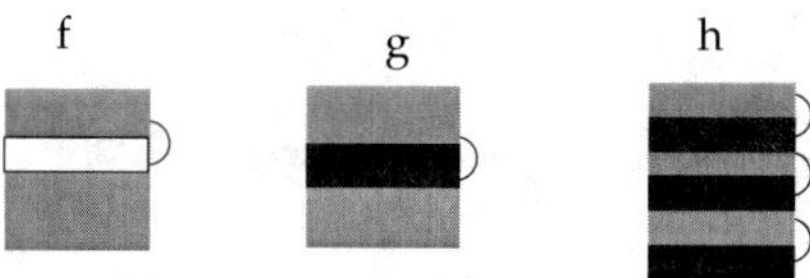

FIGURE 39 Citation Blocks in NEW-KC Segments (Grey); with Contrastive (Black) and Continuative (White) Hinge Moves.

Citation blocks can also be contained in NEW-KC segments, as is illustrated in Fig. 39 – here, the grey areas correspond to NEW-KC segments, rather than EX-KC or EXO-KC cases. Case **f** describes a continuative hinge inside a method section: this could be an acknowledgement of the use of an existing knowledge claim (H-13, H-14 or H-15). Contrastive statements which occur within NEW-KC segments (**g**) are often comparisons between the own KC and existing ones, e.g., in terms of numerical results (H-6 and H-7 and H-10 and H-11). Such comparisons are frequent in the results, conclusion and discussion sections. They typically occur *after* the authors' solution has been introduced. If more than one existing KC is contrasted to the new KC (or if different aspects of a KC are contrasted), pattern **h** emerges. As we will see later in section 8.6, by and large continuative descriptions within own work are shorter than contrastive ones.

Observations about Hinging and Sentiment

There are clear parallels between the knowledge-claim based hinge moves and sentiment classification, as I have argued in Teufel (2005). The task of automatic sentiment classification (Pang et al., 2002, Turney, 2002, Yu and Hatzivassiloglou, 2003) has gained considerable prominence in natural language processing. As the overview by Pang and Lee (2008) relates, this strand of research started with data-driven

Subjective	*At several different levels, it's a fascinating tale.*
Objective	*Bell Industries Inc. increased its quarterly to 10 cents from seven cents a share.*
Subjective Speech Act	*The South African Broadcasting Corp. said the song "Freedom now" was "undesirable for broadcasting".*
Objective Speech Act	*Northwest Airlines settled the remaining lawsuits filed on behalf of 156 people killed in a 1987 crash, but claims against the jetliner's maker are being pursued, a federal judge said.*

FIGURE 40 Wiebe's (1994) Subjectivity Categories.

work on automatically predicting the polarity of an adjective (Hatzivassiloglou and McKeown, 1997, Turney, 2002), and was extended to the task of classifying entire documents, e.g., movie reviews, according to their sentiment into positive or negative, in Pang et al. (2002). The task has also been expanded to classifying sentences rather than documents or single words (Pang and Lee, 2004). Recently, work has moved to adaptive (e.g., Blitzer et al., 2007) and unsupervised (e.g., Wan, 2008) sentiment classification and to sentiment detection of word senses (e.g., Wiebe and Mihalcea, 2006).

In most later work on sentiment classification, a neutral category has been added, and it has been a general observation that one of the most difficult subtasks in sentiment classification is the distinction between sentences with sentiment and objective sentences, which bear no sentiment. This has been foreshadowed in Wiebe's (1994) work, whose analysis is aimed at the rhetorical feature of *evidentiality* or point of view in narrative. The source of information in text is classified as either subjective or objective. In news reporting and narrative, this distinction is important, as coherent segments presenting opinions and verbal reactions are mixed with segments presenting objective fact. Wiebe's four categories are given in Fig. 40 (examples taken from Wiebe et al. 1999, p. 247).

The distinction between positive and negative is also grounded in the literature: All the citation schemes from citation content analysis I surveyed, and also Shum's (1998) and Nanba and Okumura's (1999) work, make this distinction, although each scheme adds other distinctions. As a result, sentiment detection around citations should provide a plausible feature for the recognition of citation function (see section 10.3).

How do subjectivity and sentiment relate to Level 3 of the KCDM? The citation map from section 4.2 (Fig. 18) distinguishes the function of citations in a similar manner to classic sentiment classification, namely into neutral, positive (continuative) and negative (contrastive) ones. Fig. 41 shows how the 16 direct hinge functions can be mapped to those three citation functions.

Continuative/Positive:	H-4, H-5, H-12 to H-16
Contrastive/Negative:	H-1, H-2, H-3, H-6, H-7, H-9, H-11
Neutral:	H-8, H-10

FIGURE 41 Division of Hinge Moves into Continuative and Contrastive.

There is another reason why the positive–negative distinction is important: it might help recognise statements about problem-solving activities. Several Level 1 and 3 rhetorical moves are concerned with problem-solving, e.g., H-1 to H-4 and H-7. Some problem-solving moves are positive/successful (e.g., *manages to*), others are negative/unsuccessful (*fails*). Similarly, situations in the research space are either desirable or not. Whether a putative problem-solving statement or situation description is positive or negative is constrained by its position in the argumentation, and by which rhetorical statements are still missing from a full, valid argument. These factors should aid in recognition.

I believe that the negative–positive distinction of problem-solving processes in science is one of the most interesting and potentially most explanatory aspects of discourse structure and argumentation in scientific texts. The high-level goals are most straightforwardly fulfilled if the authors' problem-solving activities – and those of incorporated knowledge claims – have positive properties. The problem-solving activities of rival approaches, in contrast, would be expected to be assigned negative properties (although there are some exceptions to this, particularly in chemistry, as we will see in chapter 13).

In many cases it is not even clear whether a certain state of affairs is indeed a problem, and how much of a problem it is. It is part of the rhetorical act of an article to convince the reader of the authors' view in that respect. For instance, we have seen during the discussion of rhetorical move H-11 ("New solution has limitations") that authors must portray their own solution's limitations as a smaller problem than the original problem of the article.

I want to illustrate this with some examples from the chemistry corpus, in the field of organic synthesis. In the experiments conducted in that field, it is quite common that one gains only small amounts of a substance. If such a low yield result occurs, it can be described as more or less catastrophic, depending on the argumentation and the rest of the experiment. The following examples are presented in increasing order of severity of the problem:

> *Although a transformation took place, product isolation in the presence of* **3***, even in small quantities, caused problems since the amine adducts partially decomposed during workup. In this case, the reaction could be efficiently performed using the xanthate* **13** *(11 equiv. with respect to* **12***) (Scheme 3).* (b600220j)

> *The inferior yields with phosphine ligands were due to the poor percentage of conversion and also the concurrent formation of biphenyl through the homocoupling of PhB(OH)2, which was negligible with dm-phen ligand.* (b311492a)

> *Unfortunately, the observed low yields of the crystalline samples have prevented the use of NMR measurements.* (b514105m)

Some problems are deal-breakers, necessitating a return to some earlier subgoal, whereas smaller problems are mentioned, but have no further effect on the overall strategy. Note the phenomenon of recovery, e.g., in the first example above, which allows the authors to proceed normally after a minor problem has been encountered.

Due to their sentiment aspect, scientific texts can even be seen as special kinds of "plots", along the lines of Lehnert's (1981) theory of *plot units.* On the basis of transitions from positive to negative mental states, her model explains the structure of narratives using positive–negative or negative–positive transitions in mental states as the atomic units.

The 3-way distinction in Fig. 18 and in Fig. 41 is simple and intuitive, and it reiterates the importance of negative/positive affect in science. When I used it in Fig. 18, it allowed me to keep the argument simple and the figure visually uncluttered. But although there is definitely a sentiment aspect to Level 3 hinge functions, this is not the whole story.

Many of the "positive" categories in Level 3 are less concerned with positiveness and more with the different ways in which the cited work is *useful* to the current work (e.g., is it used lightly or as a starting point; is it used as is or with changes?). Many of the contrastive categories have no negative connotation at all and simply state a (sentiment-free) difference between approaches. It is this comparative/neutral aspect in particular which the KCDM gives much weight to. For instance, the annotation scheme in section 7.3 distinguishes at its highest level between positive, negative, comparative and entirely neutral hinge function.

Note also that the instructions for human annotation of Level 3 moves (to be discussed in section 7.3 and 7.4) do not specifically mention sentiment, but instead use concepts which are only indirectly related to sentiment, such as *problem*, *advantage*, and *superiority*.

This concludes the discussion of Level 3 of the discourse model. We are now moving to Level 4, which is concerned with how authors linearise a scientific experiment into a textual description, and how they signal this linearisation.

6.6 Level 4: Linearisation and Presentation

The structure of scientific articles is not based on the procession of time. This is different from many other textual genres, such as news stories and narrative text, which are mainly structured around a chronological skeleton – although there may be occasional flashbacks and other text parts which are not linearly structured by time alone. What makes scientific articles different? After all, at some point the intellectual work that gave rise to the scientific article must have taken place in linear time.

Latour and Woolgar (1986) describe the creation of a scientific article as a complex process, with many interacting levels of actions, presentational as well as scientific, all of which have an impact on the structure of articles. Ziman (1969) states that researchers' writing aims to give the impression that their work is simple, efficient and objective, that one step followed logically on the next, and that the conclusions derived are inevitable. False starts, mistakes, unnecessary complications, difficulties and hesitations which happened in real time are deliberately omitted. This also serves the purpose of creating the semblance of an emotional "distance" between scientists and their observations, which is further cultivated by the textual avoidance of reference to the authors, e.g., by the use of the passive voice. Mulkay (1984) points out the distinction between the private and public phases of scientific work, where only the public phase is subject to rigorous policing.

The results and findings generated by research in the real world are a non-linear complex network of relationships between facts, causal and otherwise. All this material about the new knowledge claim must be somehow linearised into running scientific prose. In the KCDM, two ways of linearising facts are recognised: explicit section structure, and specialised rhetorical moves.

Rhetorical section structure (or IMRD structure; see section 3.1.2) is an external, typographic way of structuring scientific prose which can help users find information fast. While it is in principle possible to base a discourse model for science mainly on this structure, such a model would not describe the structure in CmpLG well, as its articles do not adhere to the IMRD section structure much (see section 5.1.2). Not being able to fallback on simple IMRD makes the definition of discourse structure "harder" than the task of finding rhetorical sections in medical articles or summaries (as do McKnight and Arinivasan, 2003, Lin et al., 2006, Hirohata et al., 2008). From a discourse–theoretical point of view, using section structure as a main structuring principle is also dispreferred. It is discipline-dependent, was caused by arbitrary historical facts which have become fossilised over time (Gilbert and Mulkay, 1984, Myers, 1992) and has therefore little explanatory power.

In those cases where it does exist, section structuring can nevertheless contribute valuable information to a model of scientific discourse. For instance, the status of an unmarked fact is easier to interpret if we know that it occurs in the introduction section: it is then more likely to be background material and not the authors' new knowledge claim. Section structuring will therefore provide one of the features for the recognition of discourse structure in chapter 10.

The alternative explicit linearisation device which serves to orient the reader is the presentational move. Such moves help the reader assimilate the new knowledge claim by summarising it, or by pointing to particular pieces of content in the description of that new knowledge claim (*sign-post* function). I have described in section 4.2 which form within-article navigation support could take; e.g., the section structure could be augmented with additional information extracted from the text. Presentational moves are prime candidates for providing this information.

IMRD and presentational moves fulfil the same function and have a complementary relationship. In computational linguistics, where there is not much adherence to the IMRD model, presentational moves are frequent; in chemistry, where the IMRD section structuring is strong, presentational moves are rarer. It is also generally the case that in longer articles, the need for presentational moves is greater.

P-1	Goal Statement (Summary of New Knowledge Claim)
P-2	Structure of Rest of Article
P-3	Preview of Section Contents
P-4	Summary of Section Contents

FIGURE 42 Presentational Moves P-1 to P-4 (Level 4).

Fig. 42 introduces the presentational moves in Level 4 of the KCDM. The goal statement, P-1, has already been described as an important move. P-1 statements can be seen as summaries of the authors' new knowledge claim (Moves 3A or 3B in Swales' model). We have seen in chapter 4 that they are instrumental in locating an article in research space. Myers (1992) describes such sentences in detail in his article entitled "In this Paper we Report... – Speech Acts and Scientific Facts", along with the linguistic phrases that often accompany them (e.g., *"our aim"* or *"in this paper, we present"*). Myers also notes that the goal statement is often the first reference in the article to the authors themselves, or to the present time and place ("here and now"):

> **P-1:** *The aim of this paper is to examine the role that training plays in the tagging process ...* (9410012, S-32)

> **P-1:** *We now describe in this paper a synthetic route for the functionalisation of the framework of mesoporous organosilica by free phosphine oxide ligands, which can act as a template for the introduction of lanthanide ions.* (b514878b)

> **P-1:** *Our aim was to quantify the response of this forage to temperature, particularly its response to low temperatures.* (A031)

> **P-1:** *Our objective in this study was to determine the relationship of hemostatic variables to atherosclerotic narrowing and other vascular risk factors with the ABI used as an indicator of lower limb arterial stenosis.* (C003, S-10)

P-1 moves can also be direct research questions which are addressed in the new KC:

> **P-1:** *How do children combine the information they perceive from different sources?* (9412005, S-15)

The description of the new knowledge claim (NEW-KC) is typically a long stretch of text, which has to be "served up" in a linear form. Moves P-2 through P-4 help the reader understand the logical structure of such segments. Explicit statements of textual structure act as a "sign-post" indicating to the reader where they can expect what content.

The first of these moves (P-2) is identical to Swales' Move 3.3 (Indication of article structure):

> **P-2:** *The rest of this document is organized as follows: We begin in Section 2 by examining ...* (9601006, S-9)

> **P-2:** *This article is structured as follows: in section 2 we describe the experimental details of this study while in section 3 the observed rotational spectrum is discussed together with ab initio calculations ...* (b600682e)

Moves P-3 and P-4 are section summaries: P-3 summarises the contents of a section in a forward-looking way, whereas P-4 does so in a backward-looking way. Such moves do not occur in introduction sections and are therefore not included in Swales' scheme.

> **P-3:** *In this section, we are going to motivate the reasons which lead us to choose grammatical words as discriminant.* (9502039, S-21)
>
> **P-4:** *In this section, we have tried to increase the lifetime of the conventional electrolyte by the addition of THA+ to the conventional electrolyte without compromising its functions.* (b517588g)
>
> **P-4:** *The previous section provided illustrative examples, demonstrating the performance of the algorithm on some interesting cases.* (9511006, S-125)

In the KCDM, the section structure provides a *linearisation frame*, into which the rest of the material is slotted. That material consists of KCA segments, which are joined together with Level 3 hinge moves. There are rules about how to slot KCA segments into the linearisation frame: Introduction sections typically start with background material (i.e., NO-KC segments), whereas Method sections, for instance, are mainly filled with NEW-KC segments. The EX-KC or EXO-KC segments in such sections typically describe those existing knowledge claims which form part of the authors' solution. At least one existing knowledge claim is normally used in a motivation section (unless there is an argument for a research gap).

Rhetorical moves are incorporated into the KCA segments in strategic places, so that the four high-level goals are fulfilled. The positioning of "sign-post" sentences are the last step in this process: they make the reading of this complex material easier by previewing what is still to come, or by summarising what has just been discussed.

Now that I have discussed all four levels of the discourse model suggested here, I can illustrate it with a prototypical article (Fig. 43), in which elements of all four levels have been highlighted. The KCDM's four levels are situated on top of the "object level" of science (to be explained in section 9.3), which is outside the model's remit.

On Level 4, we see the physical section structure and the presentation moves P-1 to P-4 in strategic places. As we just saw, their function is to announce and repeat the main contributions or research goal of the article (P-1), to provide an overview of the article's structure (P-2), and to summarise or foreshadow section content (P-3 and P-4).

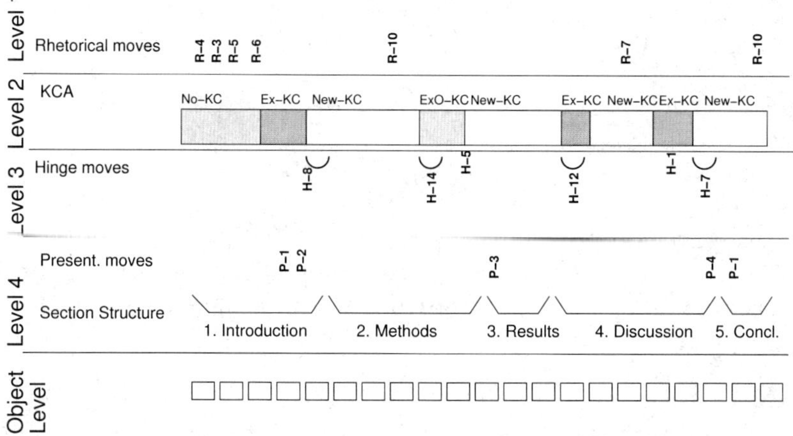

FIGURE 43 Example of Multi-Level Annotation in the Knowledge Claim Discourse Model.

On Level 3, the hinges between knowledge claim segments are identified. In this example, there is a difference from an existing knowledge claim (H-8), a use of the authors' own existing KC (H-14), and a statement about the quality of that existing KC (H-5). There is also a statement of support for or by an existing knowledge claim (H-12), a weakness of somebody else's existing KC (H-1), and a solution to a problem which is left unsolved by an existing knowledge claim (H-7).

Level 2 shows knowledge claim attribution. In the example, all four segment types are present (NO-KC, EX-KC, NEW-KC and EXO-KC).

Level 1 is represented by rhetorical moves stating that the problem addressed is interesting (R-4) and hard (R-3), that a solution to it would be desirable (R-5), but is not yet existing (R-6). Twice we hear that the authors' solution is advantageous (R-10), and once that it manages to solve the problem (R-7).

The high-level goals of Level 0 are omitted from Fig. 43 because they are non-textual, i.e., they are too abstract to be directly related to the text. In this example, significance (HLG-1) is fulfilled by the Level 1 and 3 moves R-4, R-5, R-7 and R-12, whereas novelty (HLG-2) is fulfilled by R-6 and H-8. Authors' knowledge (HLG-3) is fulfilled by the Level 2 segments EX-KC as well as by H-7, and in order to fulfil soundness (HLG-4), the methodology in NEW-KC as well as moves H-12, R-10, R-7, H-7, H-4 are used.

Let us now consider how the KCDM compares to other discourse models in the literature which, like mine, give author intentions a special status. What particularly interests me is the models' attitude towards world knowledge.

6.7 Traditional Intention-Based Discourse Models

The recognition of author intentions has a long-standing history in AI, and there is a clear connection to text understanding and discourse structure. Author intentions (e.g., "to convince a reader", "to provide an example" or "to recapitulate") are an intuitively informative way of structuring language, both monologue and dialogue. General intention recognition is a prerequisite to true text comprehension (Pollack, 1986) and therefore attractive, but it is too hard to be done in the general case. The models discussed here all attempt to make intention-based recognition of discourse structure feasible, by identifying general, i.e., non-domain-specific, principles which relate authors' intentions to document structure. These principles are defined by something more general than world knowledge, although some models assume access to world knowledge in addition to the general principle. The main differences between the models concern which generalisations are chosen: which intentions and relationships between those intentions are defined, and how much world knowledge is assumed to be recognised by other processes.

There are theories which explain argumentation in scientific discourse from a theoretical and logic point of view (Toulmin, 1972, Perelman and Olbrechts-Tyteca, 1969, Horsella and Sindermann, 1992, Sillince, 1992, Reed and Grasso, 2007), but argumentation in these approaches is concerned with facts about the world, and it is assumed that the relation between these facts will be obvious to a human reader. These models are not intended for automatic recognition, as they would require full text comprehension.

Cohen's (1987) general framework of argumentation is computationally-minded and intended for all text types, but it still assumes that world knowledge is available. The model constructs claim-evidence trees from argumentative text (see Fig. 44, taken from Cohen 1987, p. 15). Processing uses the linear order of facts and surface meta-discourse ("clues"), e.g., the phrase "*returning to city problems*". Rules express where in the tree incoming propositions can be attached. This model requires knowledge of whether a certain incoming proposition is evidence for another statement already in the discourse tree. This problem is sidestepped by the assumption of an *evidence oracle*, which can provide the right answer. This makes the model non-implementable.

Rhetorical Structure Theory (RST; Mann and Thompson 1987,

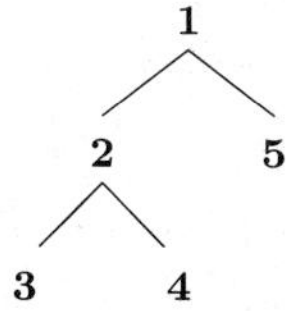

1 The city is a disaster area
2 The parks are a mess
3 The park benches are broken
4 The grassy areas are parched
5 Returning to city problems, the highways are bad too

FIGURE 44 Cohen's (1987) Evidence-Claim Trees.

1988) also uses author intentions. In RST, these are encoded as relations operating between two adjacent text pieces. Clauses (or rather *edus*, elementary discourse units) are the atomic text units, but relations can also hold between conglomerates of clauses. This relies on the notion that intentional structure is hierarchical, a frequent assumption in intention-based theories.

RST uses a fixed set of rhetorical relations, which are typically asymmetric and include CIRCUMSTANCE, SOLUTION-HOOD, ELABORATION, BACKGROUND, ENABLEMENT, MOTIVATION, EVIDENCE, JUSTIFICATION, CAUSE (VOLITIONAL AND NON-VOLITIONAL), RESULT (VOLITIONAL AND NON-VOLITIONAL), PURPOSE, ANTITHESIS, CONCESSION, CONDITION, INTERPRETATION, EVALUATION, RESTATEMENT, SUMMARY, SEQUENCE and CONTRAST. Relations can connect two or more text segments, one of which is the dominant part in the relationship (*nucleus*), whereas the other is the less important part (*satellite*). Some relations contain two nuclei with equal status, e.g., JOIN.

The definitions of the rhetorical relations are kept general on purpose, as illustrated by the one for JUSTIFY:

> JUSTIFY: a JUSTIFY satellite is intended to increase the reader's readiness to accept the writer's right to present the nuclear material.
> (Mann and Thompson, 1987, p. 9)

An RST analysis consists of the most plausible connection of intentions the analyst can find. For each part of the discourse, the analyst interprets which reason the writer might have had for its inclusion; see Fig. 45, taken from Mann and Thompson (1987, p. 13–14).

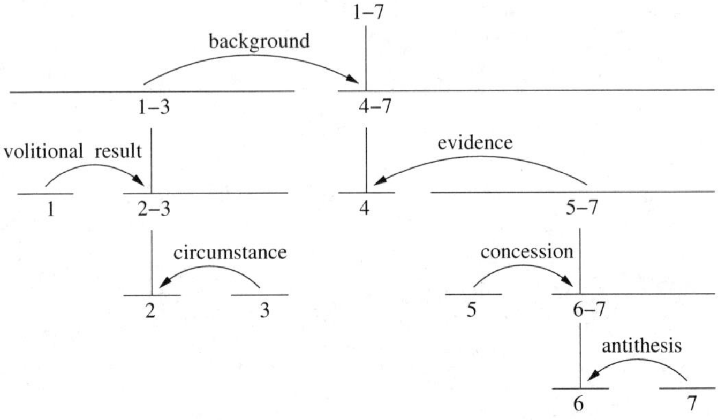

1 Farmington police had to help control traffic today
2 when hundreds of people lined up to be among the first applying for jobs at the yet-to-open Marriott Hotel.
3 The hotel's help-wanted announcement – for 300 openings – was a rare opportunity for many unemployed.
4 The people waiting in line carried a message, a refutation, of claims that the jobless could be employed if only they showed enough moxie.
5 Every rule has its exceptions,
6 but the tragic and too-common tableaux of hundreds or even thousands of people snake-lining up for any task with a paycheck illustrates a lack of jobs,
7 not laziness.

FIGURE 45 Sample RST Analysis.

The relations are split into intentional and informational ones. Justify is an intentional relation, because it exists only in the authors' and the readers' minds. It is defined by the authors' intentions of bringing their message across. Cause is an example of an informational relation: it is defined by a real relationship in the world. Often, more than one RST relation can apply for a particular text. Moser and Moore (1996) notice that there is a systematic tendency for certain informational and intentional relations to occur simultaneously. Sometimes, this ambiguity even leads to non-isomorphic RST trees.

RST has been extensively and successfully used for text generation, e.g., of tutor responses (Moore and Paris, 1993), and of texts describing ship movements and air traffic control procedures (Hovy, 1993).

Approaches for the automatic recognition of RST exist as well (Ono et al., 1994, Marcu, 1997b). They have to deal with two main problems: most rhetorical relationships are not explicitly marked by connectives, and it is not clear at which level in the tree a given unit should connect. Marcu's (1997a, 1999b, 1999c) automatic recogniser for RST structure in popular science text derives an RST structure for a text, relying on punctuation, occurrence of cue phrases, empirical observations about the cue phrases connection preferences, and heuristics for tree-attachment.

Like RST, I also use atomic, enumerable author intentions, but there are important differences between the KCDM and RST:

- **Text type specificity**: The KCDM is text-type specific. It only covers the text type of scientific articles and can therefore concentrate on a few select rhetorical relations that occur there. What one can potentially gain from text-type specificity are text-type-specific expectations, which can help in the recognition of rhetorical structure. In contrast, RST's remit is all text types.
- **No world knowledge**: The KCDM intentions operate only in the research space; they do not concern themselves with scientific domain knowledge. In contrast, the definition of RST relations is based on world knowledge. The defining principles of informational relations rely entirely on relationships in the world, and those of the intentional relations partially do, e.g., the analyst has to decide whether hearing statement X would make hearer H more likely to accept statement Y.
- **Global, not local relations**: The rhetorical moves in the KCDM, in as far as they are relations at all, hold between the rhetorical act of the article and individual text pieces, not between two text pieces. This means they are text-global. In contrast, the rhetorical relationships in RST are local, and apply in a bottom-up fashion between adjacent text pieces.
- **Non-hierarchical**: As a consequence of the previous point, the elements in the KCDM are defined in a non-hierarchical manner; e.g., the internal structure of a segment of type NEW-KC is not represented. At a certain level of abstraction, text *is* undoubtedly hierarchically structured, but for many information access applications such as summarisation and navigation this does not necessarily matter; all we need to know is the start and end point of a segment and its overall rhetorical function. In contrast, RST assumes that text is hierarchically structured.

Let us consider these last two points in more detail. The KCDM describes global rhetorical relationships, i.e., those holding between one rhetorical act and the entirety of the article. I am far less interested in local rhetorical relationships, i.e., those which operate between two adjacent text pieces. The global/local distinction is related to van Dijk's (1980) distinction of *micro-discourse* and *macro-discourse*. Coherence relations at micro-level hold between sentences or propositions which immediately follow each other in discourse. The meaning relationships between these units, e.g., specification or generalisation relations, are constrained by micro-level coherence conditions.

It is recognition at this level that RST specialises in. The cue phrases used in RST approaches (e.g., Knott, 1996, Marcu, 1997c) tend to be connectives, i.e., they operate between clauses. RST analyses also typically concern short texts: Marcu's (1997c) texts have an average length of 14.5 sentences, and Mann and Thompson (1987) describe a text of 15 utterances as a "larger text" (p. 22).

But micro-level structure is less informative about the forces that hold larger segments together. RST analysts find it harder to annotate higher-up links than the more local ones, and many of the higher-up links end up being annotated as the semantically empty category Join. In a scientific article, the principles which connect the larger segments are the overall argument and text-type specific expectations, which are instances of macro-level relations.

Macro-level analysis concerns the meaning of discourse as a whole. It is concerned with global topics in discourse, and with the rhetorical status of a textual unit with respect to the overall discourse function. Macro-level relationships are inherently less hierarchical than micro-level relationships. Schank and Abelson (1977) argue that the macro-level, i.e., global expectations, can guide text comprehension. It is this type of relation my approach concentrates on.

Let us now look at a discourse model which emphasises the top-down intention component more than RST does. Grosz and Sidner (1986) present a model which is based on the interplay between three types of information: hierarchical intentions associated with text spans, linguistic constraints operating over these text spans, and an attentional model of the salient objects in the reader's mind at each stage of processing the text.

Intentional structure is defined by those intentions that the writer or speaker intended the hearer to recognise (in contrast to private intentions like the wish to impress). Each intention is associated with a discourse segment on the linguistic level. There are two kinds of structural relation that hold between intentions: dominance and satisfaction-precedence. The structural relationships between intentions control the nesting and ordering of discourse segments, leading to a hierarchy and partial ordering amongst the intentions.

The attentional level explains which objects can be the focus of attention at which point in the conversation. A stack data structure (called the *focus space*) contains focus blocks, each of which is associated with exactly one discourse segment and contains all objects, relations and properties mentioned in the segment. As the discourse is processed, the precedence and dominance relationships between the corresponding discourse blocks cause focus blocks to be pushed or popped off the stack. The assumption is that at any point in the conversation, the objects that are mentally available to the speakers are those of the focus blocks currently on the stack. The focus space is therefore a model of salience which can be used to constrain the search space for interpreting certain linguistic expressions in the discourse blocks, such as referring expressions. The model also supports the reverse assumption, namely that intention recognition could be supported by knowledge about linguistic phenomena.

Grosz and Sidner place no formal restrictions on the types of intentions modelled, and certainly do not offer a fixed list such as RST. In their example dialogues between apprentices and experts, there is a clear structure imposed by a joint task, which hierarchically splits into smaller, well-defined sub-tasks. It is the context of the task which supplies restrictions about the possible states that the intentions can operate over. Task-structure therefore acts as a special case of the intentional structure posited, and also provides common knowledge about the task.[52]

The Grosz and Sidner model has had a strong impact on the discourse community and is generally recognised as both elegant and explanatory. However, task-structure can only be of help where it is present and as clearly expressed as in the example texts. The problem of general intention recognition remains.

The KCDM aims towards an intermediate goal in intention recognition, but lowers the bar drastically by restricting which kinds of intentions can be described. The intentions it models are twofold: textual incarnations of certain rhetorical intentions (Level 1) and higher-level "private" intentions (Level 0):

- Level 0 intentions are not associated with actual text pieces – this would be a seriously hard task, for which the technology (in terms of

[52]A similar type of task-structuring is used in Iwanska's (1985) analysis of procedural texts.

knowledge representation, inference machinery etc.) is not available.

- Even on Level 1, the model only recognises a fixed set of intentions (like RST), not an open-ended set like Grosz and Sidner. No intentions which directly rely on domain knowledge are allowed, in contrast to RST. The intentions are furthermore specialised to the global macro-structure of scientific text. The only intentions recognised are those necessary to promote the argument for the new knowledge claim. This restricts the applicability of the discourse model to scientific discourse, but makes recognition easier in comparison to that of *general* author intentions (e.g., Pollack, 1986), which is known to be an AI-hard task.
- Intentions on Level 1 are not associated with segments, not even non-hierarchical ones. They just mark a point in the text where it is likely that the intention is expressed. A *segmentation* by intentions, like in Gross and Sidner's model, would be much harder: decisions would have to be made about hierarchical nesting and about which text part gives evidence for which other part (like in Cohen's model). Such a task would almost certainly require domain knowledge, so no attempt is made to go beyond move-based intention recognition.
- The discourse model does have a segmentation stage on Level 2, which is however based on a much simpler principle than intentions. It concerns the attribution to (or ownership of) knowledge claims, i.e., who contributed the ideas described in the segment.

These constraints make the Knowledge Claim Discourse Model more realistic for automatic recognition, but they also make its remit more modest. Nevertheless, my hope is that the KCDM could be a possible "stepping stone" towards the ultimate goal of more general intention recognition.

Chapter Summary

This chapter has introduced the Knowledge Claim Discourse Model (KCDM), a model which captures several aspects of the structure of scientific articles. The knowledge claim is a central concept in this model because it links the information access methods from chapter 4 with text structure, and thus discourse theory. In terms of information access, knowledge claims are important because they characterise an article by the position of its central knowledge claim in the logical research space. One of the practical outcomes of a KCDM analysis is the acquisition of knowledge about the relationships between the new knowledge claim and similar, already published knowledge claims by others.

The KCDM defines discourse structure in scientific writing in terms of segments and moves, both of which are defined by author intentions. These concern the defense of the authors' new knowledge claim, using well-known rhetorical moves, and often arguing about other people's knowledge claims. In comparison with intention-based discourse theories for general text, the kinds of intentions modelled here (which I called *rhetorical moves*) are limited: a fixed set of author intentions centred around relationships and properties in the abstract research space. However, this setup makes it possible to perform some automatic processing of intention without requiring any truth-conditional representation of the scientific content of the text.

The KCDM consists of five levels of structure: Level 4 (Linearisation and Presentation) contains four presentational moves. It is concerned only with the physical structure of the article. Section structuring can often be typographically determined (e.g., by headlines), but this level also recognises four presentational moves (P-1 to P-4). The presentation and linearisation of an article often follows discipline-dependent conventions, but the core of the discourse model (Levels 0–3) is designed to be generally discipline-independent. In comparison to the other levels, the status of Level 4 in the model is less central.

Level 3 (Hinging) contains 18 hinge moves (section 6.5), which model how the new knowledge claim relates to already existing knowledge claims in the research space.

Level 2 (Knowledge Claim Attribution) is concerned with who owns the knowledge claim associated with a given textual segment (section 6.4). This results in the segmentation of an entire article into four knowledge claim attribution types (NO-KC, EX-KC, EXO-KC and NEW-KC).

Level 1 contains 12 rhetorical moves, which describe properties of the authors' new knowledge claim and its position in the research space (section 6.3). The moves borrow from Swales' (1990) CARS model. They mostly occur in NO-KC and NEW-KC zones, and many of them describe successful or unsuccessful problem-solving activities.

Level 0 models the four high-level goals, which form the skeleton of the authors' argument in favour of the new knowledge claim. The moves and segments of Levels 1, 2 and 3, taken together and assembled according to the rules in Fig. 31, should fulfil all high-level goals, namely novelty and significance of the new KC, propriety of the methodology used, and sufficient knowledge of the authors.

The analytic elements in all levels bar Level 0 are designed in such a way that they can be directly associated with text. This has methodological reasons; it allows me to verify the discourse theory using annotation methodology, where an interpretative label is attached to a piece of text. This is a generally accepted way of addressing the problem that the aspects of language described by discourse theories are inherently interpretative and subjective. If humans can independently annotate text according to a description of the model, with good agreement, then some truth must be contained in the description.

The questions that dominate the rest of this book are how intuitive the phenomena covered by the discourse model are to humans, and whether automatic processes can simulate a human's interpretation of these phenomena. In order to study these questions, one needs a clearer definition of the task: what exactly does it mean to analyse a text with the KCDM? The discourse model is sufficiently complicated that not all of its aspects can be annotated at once.

Chapter 7 will therefore operationalise Levels 1–4 of the model. Three annotation schemes will be defined: Level 2 annotation (Knowledge Claim Attribution) and Level 3 annotation (Citation Function/ Hinging) can be studied in independent experiments. The third annotation scheme covers the most important phenomena from all four levels at once, i.e., knowledge claim attribution, hinging, rhetorical moves and presentational moves.

These annotation schemes will be tested with humans in formal reliability studies in chapter 8, and will eventually provide the training material for the supervised machine learning in chapter 11.

7

Annotation Scheme Design

In this chapter, I will operationalise the Knowledge Claim Discourse Model, which was introduced in the last chapter. This will result in three annotation schemes. The schemes are conceptually simple: they consist of flat, mutually exclusive labels, which are applied to sentences or citations. Chapter 8 will present reliability studies for human annotation with these schemes.

Annotation methodology, originally employed in the field of content analysis (Krippendorff, 1980), offers the possibility to collect objective evidence for subjective theories. Discourse theories have a methodological problem: how can one show that the phenomena described in a discourse model "exist", or are at least intuitive or learnable? The human perception of a particular rhetorical structure that is predicted by a theory is an internal process which is not easily observable. To counter this problem, there has been a general trend towards corpus-based annotation work in higher-level linguistic theory such as pragmatics and discourse. This has raised the standards of what it means to substantiate a discourse theory's claims of truth and applicability. Similar validations to the one I will present here have been brought forward for lower-level discourse phenomena, such as pronouns (Poesio, 2004, Poesio et al., 2004), metonymies (Markert and Nissim, 2005), noun compounds (Girju et al., 2005, O'Seaghdha and Copestake, 2008), but also for rhetorical and discourse properties of text (Carlson et al., 2003, Miltsakaki et al., 2004).

Annotators are given an (informal) description of the model and are asked to associate a piece of text with a possible interpretation offered by the model. If several annotators independently assign the same category to a piece of text, they must have arrived at this analysis by perceiving the same phenomenon (Krippendorff, 1980, Craggs and Wood, 2005). High agreement in reliability studies therefore shows that the phenomena concerned are intuitive or at least learnable, i.e., that they can be transferred from one human brain to another by means of description. Even more compelling evidence is provided if naturally occurring text is used, and large amounts of it, rather than text which is artificially created or simplified.

There are two properties of an annotation scheme which can be confirmed in reliability studies: *reliability* (also called *reproducibility*) and *stability* (Krippendorff, 1980). Reliability or *inter-annotator agreement* is the extent to which different annotators will produce the same classifications. Reliability thus measures the consistency of shared understandings held by more than one annotator. *Stability* or *intra-annotator agreement* is the extent to which one annotator will produce the same classifications at different times. There is a third property of annotation schemes, *validity*, which is much harder to prove: namely, that it captures some "truth" of the phenomenon being studied. While there is no formal proof of validity, most people would be inclined to believe in the validity of a stable and reliable scheme if agreement can be reached with relatively simple instructions by naive annotators, i.e., people who were not involved in the design of the scheme.

Annotation schemes need to be carefully designed, because for most interesting phenomena, high intra- and inter-annotator agreement is generally hard to reach. Human annotators have cognitive restrictions, in particular concerning the number of categories they are able to work with. During annotation, they must keep all categories in mind – not only the descriptions of each category, but crucially the rules for distinguishing between categories. Only the distinctions between *similar* categories matter in practice, but even these will soon become too many, as the number of category distinctions grows quadratically with the number of categories. Therefore, if an annotation scheme has too many categories, it will almost invariably result in low agreement. A rule of thumb in annotation studies is that classification schemes should have at most 20 categories, preferably fewer than 10.[53]

An additional and rather obvious requirement for annotation schemes, apart from reliability and stability, is informativeness. Human annotation exercises should make non-trivial distinctions, i.e., those which are useful for a realistic application and hard enough to actually require human judgement in the first place. An example of a non-informative task is the annotation of words with the number of vowels they contain. Even perfect agreement between many judges on this task is meaning-

[53]Another consideration, although not one that should drive our decision making here, is the question of what a machine learner is able to acquire. Current machine learning models, for instance, work best with a small, finite set of target categories.

less: there is nothing we can learn from a corpus of human-annotated numbers of vowels; it would never be useful for supervised machine learning, because automatic vowel-counting already produces a perfect result.

This means that the distinctions made by an annotation scheme must not be too "easy" (otherwise the scheme is not informative, even if it is reliable), and they must not be too "hard" (otherwise the scheme is not reliable, even if it is informative). Annotation schemes which are both reliable and informative often have a long development cycle. The proof of reliability of a new scheme requires considerable development before the formal measurement of reliability and stability, e.g., a description of the categories and their distinctions must be written. Both the preparation and the measurement itself are time-consuming, and one might have to bring several variants of a scheme to the point of measurability, until acceptable agreement is achieved. Additionally, if a scheme is novel, then the proof of informativeness may require a demonstration of the scheme's usefulness in a real-world application.

The three KCDM-based annotation schemes presented here are a case at hand:

- Knowledge Claim Attribution (Level 2) – section 7.2
- Citation Function Classification (a task closely related to the hinging functions of Level 3) – section 7.3
- Argumentative Zoning, which covers both Knowledge Claim Attribution and moves from Levels 1, 3 and 4 – section 7.4.

Several similar but unworkable annotation schemes had to be discarded before the reliability and informativeness of the schemes could be confirmed. Reliability is demonstrated in chapter 8, whereas informativeness for one task is demonstrated in chapter 12, and follows more generally from the the design of the information access tools presented in chapters 4 and 15.

Historically, Knowledge Claim Attribution (KCA) and Argumentative Zoning (AZ) were the first schemes I worked with. KCA is conceptually simple, whereas the attraction of AZ lies in the fact that it is a simplified version of the entire discourse model. Work with Citation Function Classification (CFC), which explores the model's hinging aspect (Level 2), followed later. The model could have given rise to different annotation schemes beyond KCA, AZ and CFC; section 7.4 will give a recipe for how to create such schemes.

As soon as we look at the KCDM as a possible target for annotation, we notice how complicated it is. The model contains 12 rhetorical moves, 18 hinge moves, 4 presentational moves, and 4 knowledge claim segments. Furthermore, the phenomena it describes are logically at different levels; a piece of text can be a move and part of a knowledge claim segment at the same time. While it would be theoretically attractive if the entire model could be annotated and validated in a single scheme, such a scheme is likely to be too complex for direct human annotation.

Practical annotation with the KCDM therefore requires an operationalisation of the model, i.e., a modularisation and simplification, which is the topic of this chapter. In the following section, I will describe the methodology behind the annotation of KCDM-related discourse effects.

The first step in the operationalisation is the choice of the most appropriate *type* of annotation task. The general type of annotation used here is *categorial classification*, i.e., the attachment of a semantic label to a particular piece of text with a known start and end point (here: a sentence). In principle, more complex types of annotation could have been used to capture the KCDM's phenomena. One could for instance have asked a human to segment a text according to KCA, then to annotate the fact that a sentence or a clause contains a Level 1 or 3 move, and then to annotate hinging function on the Ex-KC segments or possibly on citations. Instead, the schemes presented here describe the KCDM's phenomena using flat category labels from a fixed set of labels. (The alternatives, and why I did not choose them, are discussed in section 7.5.) The resulting schemes are drastically simplified, but they have the advantage that they are demonstrably reliable and informative.

The next operationalisation step is the selection and description of a set of categories such that annotators are likely to be able to distinguish them. I will introduce the details of the KCA, CFC and AZ annotation schemes in sections 7.2 through 7.4. All of this will put us in a position, by the end of the current chapter, to appreciate the reliability studies presented in chapter 8.

7.1 Fundamental Concepts

There are different practical and theoretical reasons for performing annotation experiments, and these influence some important methodological questions, e.g., how annotators' disagreement should be interpreted, and how to decide if a system has reached acceptable performance. These questions are rather independent from how the categories are defined or how agreement is measured in detail. In fact, the resolution of the fundamental questions has repercussions for the organisation of the practical annotation exercise, and therefore constitutes the first phase of annotation scheme design. For instance, before setting out on any annotation experiment, one should establish what will count as the ground truth. I have therefore kept the methodological considerations (the current section) apart from the detailed definition of the schemes' categories (which will follow later in this chapter), and from the definition of agreement metrics (which will follow in section 8.1).

Annotation of Properties or of Category Membership

Categorial assignment is the task of attaching a semantic label to a particular piece of text; that text piece is called an *item*. There are different ways in which label assignment can be interpreted theoretically: as assignment of one or more independent properties to that item, or classification of the item as a member of a class. Whichever mathematical model of label assignment is used, it should result in easily interpretable agreement figures. For instance, if label assignment is *exhaustive* (i.e., if there are no items that do not receive one of the possible labels), then all other counts which the assignment model produces can be compared to the total number of possible item–label assignments.

Let us first consider the case of properties. In the simplest case, each item has p properties, which are independent of each other. Each property has v values. An example of the binary case (v=2) is Moravcsik and Murugesan's (1975) classification of citations, where 4 binary categories define a space of a maximum of 2^4 individual label combinations that an item can receive. If each property is applicable to each item, then label assignment is exhaustive. In that case, there are v^d possible individual label combinations, with each item being assigned to exactly one of these. With N items and k annotators, there are v^dNk possible assignment events, and a contingency table with all relevant marginal distributions can be derived for all properties, leading to easily interpretable agreement figures. If label assignment is non-exhaustive, the distribution table can still be produced by adding an additional value "undefined" for each partial property. Thus, the interpretation of item–label assignments as a set of independent properties generally leads to well-defined statistics.

Let us now consider the case of annotation as the assignment of the item's membership to a given category. One can conceptualise a category as a "bundle" of properties which co-occur so often that they have been given a categorial name. As a general rule, all members of a category should be similar to each other, because they share the defining characteristics of the category. If the categories are defined exhaustively, then the interpretation of categorial assignment or *classification* is akin to partitional clustering. For instance, the category

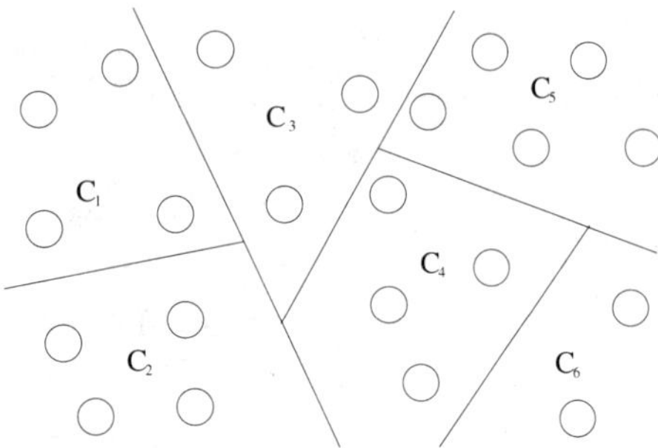

FIGURE 46 Categorial Assignment with Mutually Exclusive Categories.

assignment in Fig. 46 contains 6 categories C_1 to C_6. An item can be assigned to exactly one of the m possible categories; with N items and k annotators, our universe consists of exactly Nmk possible assignment events. For each category $C_1 \dots C_m$, the number of items assigned to category C_l, which is given as $N(C_l)$, is calculated as follows:

$$N(C_l) = \frac{\sum_{i=1}^{N} \sum_{j=1}^{m} m_{ij}}{Nmk}$$

where m_{ij} is the number of annotators which assigned item i to category j. The numbers add up to Nmk in the obvious way. Therefore, the assumption that each item can only be member of one category makes the space of possible events easily interpretable. Krippendorff (1980) indeed recommends the use of exhaustive categories for all content analyses.

In many realistic annotation tasks, there are two effects which complicate matters:

- There are usually some items whose membership to a category is weaker than that of others.
- There are usually some items which could belong to more than one category.

A "soft clustering" annotation model would deal with both these problems. There, the membership of an item to a category is not absolute but graded, i.e., it is modelled by a probability distribution. No annotation model based on soft clustering exists; to create one which is mathematically and cognitively well-founded would be a considerable enterprise. It would for instance require a replicable method of how to elicit intuitions about graded memberships from annotators, and

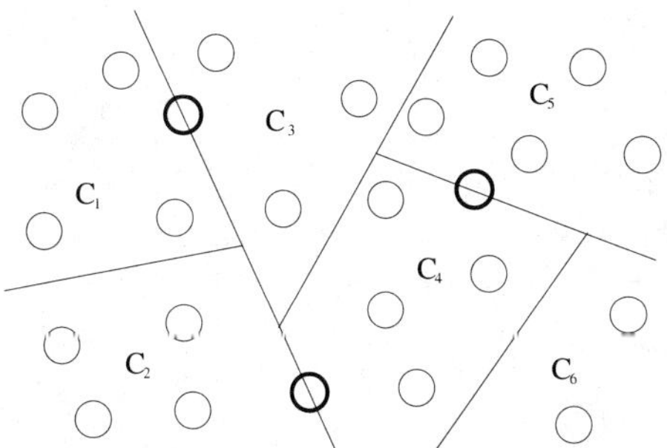

FIGURE 47 Multiple Assignment to Categories.

a suitable metric working over probability distributions (such as the Kuhlback-Leibler distance) that agrees with this intuition.

Allowing for multiple annotation is a simpler way to address the second of the problems mentioned above. This is illustrated in Fig. 47, where three items are multiply assigned, one to categories C_1 and C_3, one to C_2 and C_4, and one to C_4 and C_5. However, as soon as multiple annotation is allowed, it is difficult to find an overall agreement metric, because the event space of joint events has now become extremely large and sparsely populated. The number of possible label combinations is $2^m - 1$, the cardinality of the power set of all categories, minus the empty set, which is not an allowable label.

Practical annotation exercises often allow for multiple assignment, but this can pose difficulties with how to report and interpret the results. Raw numbers (as reported in, e.g., Garzone and Mercer, 2000) are hard to interpret because they do not add up to the Nmk event space. (Di Eugenio et al., 1998, Core and Allen, 1997) report agreement per category, i.e., they interpret each category as a binary property in our parlance from above. This avoids the $2^m - 1$ event space, but there still is no summary measure expressing the overall agreement.

Others have experimented with hierarchical annotation schemes, where annotators can use categories higher up in the hierarchy as a "back-off" in cases where they are not sure if a lower-level distinction applies (Shriberg et al., 2004, Geertzen and Bunt, 2006). In such schemes, it is possible to report agreement at various depths of the hierarchy, e.g., by simply collapsing all categories below a specified depth into larger pseudo-categories, and then measuring agreement. Geertzen and Bunt (2006) present a partial agreement measure for hierarchical schemes, using a special case of a weighted agreement metric. However, it is important to realise that even in weighted or hierarchical schemes systematic measurement of agreement requires label assignment to be exhaustive, i.e., operating in an event space with Nmk annotation events.

Let us now turn to the first of the two real-world complications mentioned above: the fact that some items are bad representatives of their category. One way of keeping those badly-fitting items out of the respective category is to assign them to a specially-designed *garbage category*, which collects badly-matching items from all categories. Such categories often have names such as "Other" or "None of the above". This however means that the items which are assigned to the garbage category cannot possibly be similar to each other, and this in turn is in conflict with an important assumption about category assignment. If one cares about the principle that all members in a category should be similar, one may decide against a garbage category, and tolerate the fact that categories can contain some not-very-typical items. (A separate issue is that garbage categories cannot be well-recognised by supervised machine learning either).

Most annotation tasks in computational linguistics therefore use mutually exclusive category assignment with flat annotation schemes without a garbage category. As an example, consider the annotation of *dialogue acts* in conversational speech. Dialogue acts are speech-act-like units, where categories have types such as STATEMENT, QUESTION, BACKCHANNEL, AGREEMENT, DISAGREEMENT, and APOLOGY. An example of an annotated dialogue from Stolcke et al.'s (2000) Switchboard corpus is given in Fig. 48. The unit of annotation is the utterance; unit boundaries are fixed before annotation begins.

Dialogue act recognition is a prerequisite for automatic dialogue systems. Manual dialogue act annotation provides the large annotated corpora necessary for standard supervised learning techniques. The CL community has had extensive experience with this type of annotation (Alexandersson et al., 1995, Carletta et al., 1997, Jurafsky et al., 1997, Stolcke et al., 2000, Shriberg et al., 2004).

Such annotated corpora are often very large: 1,155 annotated conversations, 205,000 utterances, 1.4 million words in Stolcke et al.'s case. They are long-term resources, which are often collaboratively generated, at different institutions, and at different points in time. Under these circumstances, high agreement is paramount because it ensures that an annotator, working independently, can create an annotated text which fits in with the already existing annotation. Several of the schemes cited above report high inter-annotator agreement ($\kappa > 0.8$);[54]

[54]The agreement metric κ (kappa) will be explained in section 8.1; for now, it

Dialogue Act	Utterance
YES-NO-QUESTION	**A:** So do you go to college right now?
ABANDONED	**A:** Are yo-,
YES-ANSWER	**B:** *Yeah,*
STATEMENT	**B:** *it's my last year* [laughter].
DECLARATIVE-QUESTION	**A:** You're a, so you're a senior now.
YES-ANSWER	**B:** *Yeah,*
STATEMENT	**B:** *I'm working on my projects trying to graduate* [laughter].
APPRECIATION	**A:** Oh, good for you.
BACKCHANNEL	**B:** *Yeah.*
APPRECIATION	**A:** That's great,
YES-NO-QUESTION	**A:** um, is, is N C University is that, uh, State,
STATEMENT	**B:** *N C State.*
SIGNAL-NON-UNDERST.	**A:** What did you say?
STATEMENT	**B:** *N C State.*

FIGURE 48 Example of Dialogue Act Annotation (from Stolcke et al. (2000)).

to achieve this, annotators are extensively trained, and annotation guidelines are used to describe the task and the semantics of the categories.

The style of annotation used in my work is closely modelled on these exercises, but the goals behind my annotation exercise are somewhat different. Neither the rhetorical task proposed here, nor the applications based on it, are anywhere near as well-researched as the creation of automatic dialogue systems. Therefore, my main motivation is not the creation of a practical corpus resource in its own right; I am more interested in the cognitive properties of the new task. While reliability is not as absolutely crucial to me as it is in dialogue act coding, it is still desirable: if the KCDM-based schemes prove to be learnable, some of the intuition behind the discourse model would be automatically validated.

The Definition of the Truth

Annotation of discourse theories requires annotators to make interpretative judgements, and is thus subjective. KCDM annotation, for instance, includes judgements about which intentions the author might have had when writing the text. This unfortunately means that annotator disagreement is part and parcel of discourse annotation: if one

suffices to know that while perfect agreement is reached at $\kappa = 1$, $\kappa = 0.8$ already represents very high quality agreement.

asks several subjects to annotate discourse structure, one should not be surprised if they frequently disagree. This does not turn annotation into a futile exercise. It does however mean that what is seen as the underlying truth becomes an important decision.

I am interested in finding out if my generalisations about scientific discourse structure which are expressed in the KCDM are intuitive and natural to humans. In order for any annotation scheme to be cognitively real, there first needs to be a *private* understanding of the categories in one annotator's mind (initially, the guideline developer). This should enable the annotator to apply the scheme consistently, within her own understanding. If a scheme is not stable, it is doomed: the definition of the categories must be consistent within one person's mind before it can be communicated to others.

Research in the field of citation content analysis (section 2.3.1) often uses only one annotator, frequently the developer of the annotation scheme, without reporting intra-annotator agreement (e.g., Weinstock, 1971, Garzone and Mercer, 2000). However, it is then difficult to defend a truth defined by only one annotator against the argument that the same person might have annotated very differently at some other time.

In many cases stability can be reached even without written category definitions. However, the claim of cognitive reality of a scheme becomes much more convincing if it can be shown that the private understanding of the categories can be communicated to others, to form a *shared* understanding of the categories. This requires a reliability study.[55]

There has been some disagreement in the literature as to whether reliability or stability is the more important property of a scheme. Since consistent shared understanding requires consistent private understanding, an unstable annotation can never be reliable; it is thus commonly assumed that a proof of the reliability of a scheme implies its stability. Many experimenters therefore only measure and report reliability (e.g., the MUC conferences). In contrast to this, some researchers in document retrieval and summarisation have argued against the use of reliability, because there is not normally only one acceptable gold standard (see section 3.2.2). If several different gold standards would have satisfied a user, measuring agreement against just one of these does not make sense. According to this argument, stability is a more appropriate measurement, because it at least operates only within one person's understanding. If this person changes their mind about the right answer after some time, then the corresponding concept is not

[55] As most content citation analyses use only one annotator, the measurement of reliability is not possible, unlike the measurement of stability, which can be done with only one annotator).

well-defined. I consider both stability and reliability important, and will report both, whenever possible.

Communicating the categories to other annotators could in principle take the form of informal discussions, but if the training process is to be replicable, then written annotation guidelines (also called *coding manuals*) are crucial. If one is interested in the psychological reality of an annotation scheme, then a scheme is a scheme only to the degree that it can be written down and that this written material causes others to independently annotate similarly. If, on the other hand, the private understanding cannot be communicated to others via written guidelines, then something is wrong with the scheme or the guidelines (which is the same for our purposes). Guidelines which result in consistent agreement when given to new, unbiased annotators are therefore arguably the most valuable and durable outcome of an annotation experiment. I consider them the only repository of truth. Krippendorff (2004, p.127) even goes so far as to say that if the guidelines that belong to an annotated corpus were ever lost, the corpus itself would become meaningless.

In the literature, there have been various alternative definitions of truth for annotation schemes:

- Expert Annotator
- Majority Opinion or Adjudicator
- Annotator Discussion

My decision to place that much importance on the guidelines, in the tradition of Krippendorff (1980) and Carletta (1996), cannot be well reconciled with these other definitions of truth, as I will now discuss, repeating Carletta's (1996) argument.

Some annotation tasks declare an "expert" judge (e.g., Kowkto et al., 1992). This could be the initial developer of the annotation scheme, or it could be somebody who has access to more knowledge than the other annotators, e.g., because she is a domain expert. However, defining truth through one designated expert has the obvious practical disadvantage that experiments are not replicable without this individual, and that the cognitive realities of the other annotators are ignored in cases of disagreement. In my annotation experiments, no annotator is by definition considered to know the truth any more than any other (with the exception of the trainer during the training phase). However, in annotation tasks which are more factual than the ones considered here, expert opinion can be a good way of reaching agreements fast.

Truth can also be defined by majority opinion: with an odd number of judges, a majority opinion exists in most cases,[56] and annotators can then be compared to this definition of truth (Passonneau and Litman, 1993, Hearst, 1997). From an annotation engineering point, this is a clear, if somewhat expensive solution. However, this solution has the fundamental flaw that it does not in general correspond to one annotator's consistent solution, but consists of a mix of many people's decisions. This becomes particularly problematic when there are logical dependencies between individual annotated items within one person's work, as these don't necessarily get copied into a majority gold standard. Arguably, such a gold standard then cannot capture the cognitive reality of the categories. Carletta (1996) points out that this definition of truth has the additional negative side-effect that the statistic is numerically inflated, in that it is necessarily above 50% (as illustrated by the high agreement numbers for sentence selection reached by majority opinion in section 3.2.2).

Agreement can also be reached by post-annotation negotiation between the annotators, or by asking an adjudicator to decide in the case of disagreement (thus practically making her the expert judge, with the difference that she judges only in some cases). In certain tasks, such as lexicography, the annotated material itself is the end result of the work: it has high value and is kept for a long time. The high agreement needed in such situations can be reached by negotiation (e.g., see Kilgarriff's (1999) high agreement figures for word sense disambiguation, which was achieved that way). However, negotiation often obliterates the cognitive phenomena behind the annotation, namely the question of whether a certain category was intuitive to an annotator or not.[57] In contrast, the final outcome of my annotation work are the guidelines, if they result in reliable annotation. The error-free production of annotated material, although of course desirable for several reasons, is not the driving force behind my annotation experiment. I therefore measure agreement of independent annotation *before* discussions.

In terms of who is "right" in a disagreement, the first instance is the guidelines. In the second instance, all annotators are equally right. In order to see how this works, I will now discuss the practical annotation procedure I used.

---

[56] A majority opinion cannot be guaranteed if there are more categories than annotators as it is then possible for annotators to each choose a different category.

[57] There is another, practical problem with allowing pre-measurement discussions, pointed out to me by Jean Carletta: there is a danger that the annotator with the strongest personality decides the outcome of unclear cases, which is neither objective nor replicable.

Guideline Development

Guideline development is the process of writing guidelines in such a way as to enable new annotators to annotate consistently. The development and testing of an annotation scheme breaks down into the phases of guideline development, annotator training and formal reliability study. During the guideline development phase, one or more guideline developers write and adapt rules for the guidelines, normally in response to annotation performed on a development corpus. Once a rule (or rule change) is decided, it is noted down in the guidelines. Verbal agreements between the scheme developers beyond what is written down should be avoided, because such agreements (whether or not they have a positive effect on the scheme developers' performance) have no chance of being communicated to the final annotators. Krippendorff (2004, p.135) also recommends the use of decision trees as a tool for defining category semantics, because they linearise the questions an annotator has to answer.

During day-to-day guideline development, disagreements are discovered and discussed (to a certain degree this can also still happen during annotator training, as discussed below). The guidelines are always right, but they are subject to the annotators' interpretation; it is therefore the annotators' responsibility to keep themselves aware of all the material in the guidelines, and to annotate carefully. If the annotators disagree on a case which is already described in the guidelines, then the continued disagreement is either due to an annotator overlooking a rule (in which case they should try to be less sloppy in the future), or to different interpretations of the guidelines (in which case the guidelines are ambiguous and should be changed). If a point of disagreement is *not* discussed in the guidelines, as is normally the case, all developers are equally right by definition. If the case is deemed to be generalisable, i.e., if it is expected to occur again in some form in the future, a new rule should be added to the guidelines. This way, the guidelines represent a snapshot of the current consensus between guideline developers. This snapshot must be fixed at the point in time when the reliability studies begin, i.e., when agreement is formally measured.

My earlier annotation studies (section 8.2 and 8.3) used pencil-on-paper annotation, which I manually edited into XML versions of the documents. In the more recent work (sections 8.5 and 13.1.2), a custom-written annotation tool was used to record the annotation directly. The tool has two modes: an annotation mode and a comparison mode. The annotation mode, which is used during guideline development and annotation, allows annotators to select a category for each item and to type in a comment for each item. Formal rules about what this comment should look like can enforce more compliance to the guidelines (see section 13.1.1).

The comparison mode is used during guideline development, in order to structure the discussion of disagreements. The tool can either show disagreements in the relevant textual context, including annotators' comments and section numbers, or show the judgements in an anonymised form, so that guideline developers cannot see which category they originally chose. As will be reported in section 13.1.1, we found that this makes the discussion more objective and thus more productive.

It is often not obvious when the guideline development phase should be brought to an end. On the one hand, guideline development is long-winded and therefore expensive, so one wants to conduct formal agreement studies as early as possible. On the other hand, due to the need to hire annotators, formal agreement studies are even more expensive, so one does not want to risk measuring agreement formally until until the guidelines are mature enough, because this might result in low agreement. Looking at the guidelines themselves is not enough to find out if this point has been reached: considering more development text steadily increases guideline quality and continues to do so for a long time. Nevertheless, guidelines will never be perfect, so guideline development simply has to be brought to an end at some stage, otherwise it would continue *ad infinitum.*

In my experience, a good time to end the guideline development and start annotation is when the guideline developers achieve acceptable intra- and inter-annotator agreement on a representative sample. This annotated material can then also be used as reference material for annotator training.[58]

Annotator Training

For the reliability studies, one ideally hires new annotators who were not involved in guideline development. In my training phase, the annotators read the guidelines, then went through a training routine which consisted of several sessions where walk-through annotation examples were presented and the trainee annotators' initial annotation work was critiqued. The annotation itself was done independently outside the training sessions.

[58] Krippendorff however finds the practice of guideline developers annotating questionable, because "it is not possible to distinguish whether the data generated under these conditions are the products of the written instructions of or the analysts' conceptual expertise ..." Krippendorff (2004, p.131).

Meetings should concentrate on teaching the annotators to apply the guidelines. During the training phase, the scheme developers exceptionally take on the role of expert annotators, i.e., they (with their superior knowledge of the guidelines) define the truth. They point out in which cases the annotators' deviated from the truth and explain the reasons for assigning the correct categories, with reference to the guidelines.

All information the annotators are exposed to during the training phase should be grounded in the guidelines and in examples, and in as little else as possible. If further explanation is necessary, it too should go into the guidelines. One should also make sure that all annotators are exposed to the same information: joint sessions with a slide presentation are better than separate meetings with each annotator, because this controls the amount of additional information they are given.

While it is clear that the guidelines must remain fixed during the reliability study, Krippendorff (2004) debates whether minor changes to the guidelines should be allowed in the training phase. On the one hand, new annotated text encountered during training is bound to reveal new cases, necessitating guideline change. As long as formal measurement is taken after the last of these changes, the agreement numbers will be untainted. On the other hand, guideline changes will invalidate some of the annotated reference material the annotators have used for training, and might also invalidate any prior measured agreement results reached between the scheme developers. In either case, Krippendorff advises against involving the annotators in the guideline development phase.

Annotation Phase

After the training phase, the reliability study begins with the assignment of the material to the annotators and ends when agreement is measured. During this time, the annotators work absolutely independently and do not communicate with each other. The annotation tool used should make their job as easy as possible, but not too easy.

There are practical considerations about whether annotation speed and agreement could be increased by asking annotators to *correct* somebody else's output, e.g., a machine's, rather than them having to decide on each category from scratch. Such correction methods have been shown to increase agreement as well as throughput, e.g., in manual parts-of-speech (POS) tagging. However, there is a danger that annotators accept the suggestions they are presented with too easily, particularly when tired. When annotating from scratch, as in the experiments done here, annotators are forced to hypothesise potential candidate categories for the item themselves. This is less likely to result in an artificially consistent, "default" annotation.

Apart from the annotation performed during the reliability studies, *production mode* annotation is a different type of annotation. While reliability studies are performed as one-off exercises in order to prove certain desirable properties of the scheme and the guidelines, they are too expensive to produce the large amounts of training material required for supervised learning. When an annotation project goes into production mode, only one version of each text is annotated. Either the entire material is annotated by a single annotator, or it is split into parts, each of which is annotated by a different annotator. Large-scale annotation projects often use a small overlap between different annotators' materials, e.g., 5%. This means that inter-annotator agreement can be measured throughout the production phase for quality assurance.

This ends my discussion of general annotation methodology. I will now turn to the main part of this chapter, the design of the three KCDM-based annotation schemes.

7.2 The KCA Scheme (Knowledge Claim Attribution)

The ideas behind knowledge claim attribution were discussed in detail in section 6.4. The annotation scheme based on it is given in Fig. 49; it is the simplest of the three schemes in this chapter. The categories are the segment labels from section 6.4, with ExO-KCbeing incorporated into the Ex-KC category.

No-KC	No knowledge claim is associated with the segment.
Ex-KC	A knowledge claim exists, which is held by somebody specific.
New-KC	A new knowledge claim is staked by the authors.

FIGURE 49 Annotation Scheme for Knowledge Claim Attribution (KCA).

The task is a categorial classification task with mutually exclusive categories. As a result, a KCA-annotated scientific article is covered by a contiguous, non-overlapping sequence of categories assigned to sentences. Many of these categories will be identical to their neighbours.

The KCA annotation scheme was developed using 26 CmpLG articles, and it resulted in minimal guidelines (5 pages, see appendix C.1, including the decision tree in Fig. 50). This mirrors the assumption that the task is basic and rather intuitive. The trivial KCA decision tree shows that annotators only have to answer one question, which con-

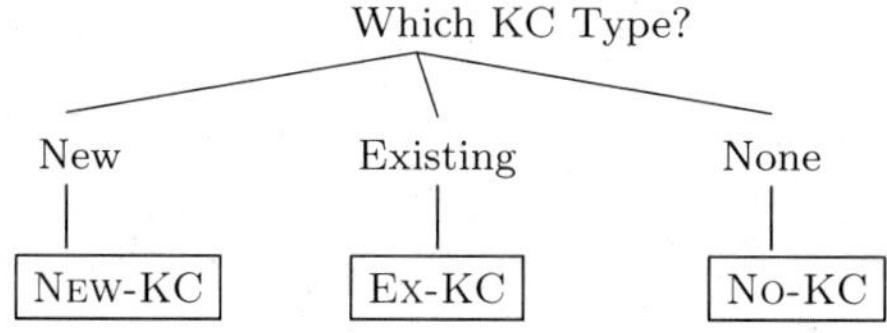

FIGURE 50 Decision Tree for KCA.

cerns the type of knowledge claim in the annotated sentence.[59] Human annotation performance with this annotation scheme will be studied in section 8.2.

In annotation scheme design, practical and theoretical priorities are often pitched against each other. The reasons for collapsing EXO-KC and EX-KC are a good illustration of this.

EXO-KC is a category of in-between status; collapsing it with one of its semantically "neighbouring" categories (NEW-KC or EX-KC) might well lead to higher agreement, as fewer categories generally lower the cognitive load of the annotators, but the distinctions in the annotation scheme still need to be informative enough for downstream tasks to do something interesting with them. So if EXO-KC is collapsed with anything, which category should it be?

From the viewpoint of the applications in chapter 4, an article's most important property is the new knowledge claim it introduces. Therefore, the distinction between EXO-KC and NEW-KC matters more than that between EXO-KC and EX-KC. (The reader has already heard this argument in section 6.4.) Operationally, the distinction between EX-KC and EXO-KC may not be worthy of human annotation effort anyway, as much of it can be automatically decided via the recognition of self-citations. This will however not solve some of the harder cases, such as the EXO-KC examples on p. 122.

An annotation example may help the reader develop some intuition about practical KCA annotation, before we turn to the next annotation scheme. Fig. 51 shows the first page of the example article *Pereira et al. (1993)*, annotated with the KCA scheme. The abstract in its entirety is a NEW-KC segment. The article itself starts, quite traditionally, with a NO-KC segment, where the general research area is described (*"distributional classification of words"*), along with a general problem in that area (*"data sparseness"*). A trivial solution (*"tabulating raw frequencies"*) is discredited. All of this is still part of the initial NO-KC

[59]In decision trees, a category is arrived at by answering the questions at branching points and then following them to the branches of the tree.

No–KC
Ex–KC
New–KC

Distributional Clustering of English Words

Fernando Pereira Naftali Tishby Lillian Lee

Abstract

We describe and experimentally evaluate a method for automatically clustering words according to their distribution in particular syntactic contexts. Deterministic annealing is used to find lowest distortion sets of clusters. As the annealing parameter increases, existing clusters become unstable and subdivide, yielding a hierarchical "soft" clustering of the data. Clusters are used as the basis for class models of word occurrence, and the models evaluated with respect to held–out data.

Introduction

Methods for automatically classifying words according to their contexts of use have both scientific and practial interest. The scientific questions arise in connection to distributional views of linguistic (particularly lexical) structure and also in relation to the question of lexical acquisition both from psychological and computational learning perspectives. From the practical point of view, word classification addresses questions of data sparseness and generalization in statistical language models, particularly models for deciding among alternative analyses proposed by a grammar.

It is well known that a simple tabulation of frequencies of certain words participating in certain configurations, for example the frequencies of pairs of transitive main verb and the head of its direct object, cannot be reliably used for comparing the likelihoods of different alternative configurations. The problem is that in large enough corpora, the number of possible joint events is much larger than the number of event occurrences in the corpus, so many events are seen rarely or never, making their frequency counts unreliable estimates of their probabilities.

Hindle (1990) proposed dealing with the sparseness problem by estimating the likelihood of unseen events from that of "similar" events that have been seen. For instance, one may estimate the likelihood of a particular direct object for a verb from the likelihoods of that direct object for similar verbs. This requires a reasonable definition of verb similarity and a similarity estimation method. In Hindle's proposal, words are similar if we have strong statistical evidence that they tend to participate in the same events. His notion of similarity seems to agree with our intuitions in many cases, but it is not clear how it can be used directly to construct classes and corresponding models of association.

Our research addresses some of the same questions and uses similar raw data, but we investigate how to factor word association tendencies into associations of words to certain hidden senses classes and associations between the classes themselves. While it may be worthwhile to base such a model on preexisting sense classes (Resnik, 1992), in the work described here we look at how to derive the classes directly from distributional data. More specifically, we model senses as probabilistic concepts or clusters c with corresponding cluster membership probabilities EQN for each word w. Most other class–based modeling techniques for natural language rely instead on "hard" Boolean classes (Brown et al., 1990). Class construction is then combinatorically very demanding and depends on frequency counts for joint events involving particular words, a potentially unreliable source of information, as we noted above. Our approach avoids both problems.

Problem Setting

In what follows, we will consider two major word classes, <EQN/> and <EQN/>, for the verbs and nouns in our experiments, and a single relation between a transitive main verb and the head noun of its direct object. Our raw knowledge about the relation consists of the frequencies <EQN/> of occurrence of particular pairs <EQN/> in the required configuration in a training corpus. Some form of text analysis is required to collect such a collection of pairs. The corpus used in our first experiment was derived from newswire text automatically parsed by Hindle's parser Fidditch (Hindle, 1993). More recently, we have constructed similar tables with the help of a statistical part–of–speech tagger (Church, 1988) and of tools for regular expression pattern matching on tagged corpora (Yarowsky, p.c.). We have not yet compared the accuracy and coverage of the two methods, or what systematic biases they might introduce, although we took care to filter out certain systematic errors, for instance the misparsing of the subject of a complement clause as the direct object of a main verb for report verbs like "say".

We will consider here only the problem of classifying nouns according to their distribution as direct objects of verbs; the converse problem is formally similar. More generally, the theoretical basis for our method supports the use of clustering to build models for any n–ary relation in terms of associations between elements in each coordinate and appropriate hidden units (cluster controids) and associations between these hidden units.

FIGURE 51 First Page of *Pereira et al. (1993)* with KCA Annotation.

segment. Then a specific KC (EX-KC) is described – it is owned by Hindle, who is formally cited.

The annotator recognises seven existing knowledge claims on the first page: by *Hindle (1990)*, *Resnik (1992)*, *Brown et al. (1990)*, *Hindle (1993)*, *Church (1988)*, and *Yarowsky (p.c.)*. The short description of Resnik's work, which is presented in contrast to the authors' own work, is included in the NEW-KC segment. Alternatively, if the annotator had decided that the segment was more "about" Resnik's KC than about the new KC, a separate EX-KC label would have been possible. The description of the author's new KC is split into several parts, the first of which occurs after the description of Hindle's KC. Most sentences in the second section (*"Problem Setting"*) are classified as NEW-KC, but inside this long NEW-KC segment, a text piece describing the use of various other KCs is identified as EX-KC.

7.3 The CFC Scheme (Citation Function Classification)

The second operationalisation of the KCDM explores human and automatic recognition of the different hinge functions of Level 3, which were defined in section 6.5, and are listed in Fig. 36 (p. 128). Hinges connect knowledge claim segments, and they encode functions such as "existing knowledge claim has a flaw" (H-1) or "new knowledge claim uses existing knowledge claim after adaptation" (H-15).

The scheme, which I designed in 2005 together with Advaith Siddharthan and Dan Tidhar in the framework of the CITRAZ project, is given in Fig. 52. It is called Citation Function Classification (CFC for short) and contains 12 categories. The names for the categories are mnemonics with prefix P- for positive and CO- for comparative semantics. Some categories consist of a single hinge function from Fig. 36, namely COCOGM (H-8), COCOR0 (H-10), PSUP (H-12), PBAS (H-13), PUSE (H-14), PMODI (H-15) and PSIM (H-16). Others are defined as the union of several hinges. For instance, COCO- is assigned to either of the various ways in which the new KC can be better than an existing KC; PMOT encodes various ways in which a citation can be positive about the authors' chosen method or problem addressed, and WEAK is the label for various flawed problem-solving processes an existing KC can be involved in. A neutral category (NEUT) was also added. Category COCOXY is unusual in various respects and will be explained below.

Hinges are defined as relationships which hold between KCA segments, but the units of annotation used in CFC are citations (includ-

Category	Hinge Function	Description
WEAK	H-1, H-2, H-3	Weakness of existing KC
CoCo-	H-6, H-7, H-9, H-11	Unfavourable contrast/comparison (new KC is better than existing KC)
CoCoGM	H-8	Contrast/comparison in goals or methods (neutral)
CoCoR0	H-10	Contrast/comparison in results (neutral)
CoCoXY	–	Contrast between two existing KCs
PSUP	H-12	New KC and existing KC are compatible or provide support for each other
PBAS	H-13	New KC uses existing KC as starting point
PUSE	H-14	New KC uses tools, algorithms or data of existing KC
PMODI	H-15	New KC adapts or modifies tools, algorithms or data in existing KC
PSIM	H-16	New KC and existing KC are similar
PMOT	H-17, H-18	Existing KC is positive about approach used by the authors or problem addressed (motivation for new KC)
NEUT	–	Neutral description of existing KC; or unlisted hinge function; or not enough evidence for known hinge function

FIGURE 52 Annotation Scheme for Citation Function Classification (CFC).

ing idiosyncratic abbreviations) and cited authors.[60] The reason for this is that units of annotation should be trivially automatically definable, which is the case for citations but not for KCA segments. KCA segments can be linguistically signalled in so many different ways,that human annotation is required to determine them – or alternatively statistical annotation by an automatic process. It is good practice to design an annotation scheme independently of the outcome of a prior statistical classification or human annotation, so that the units of annotation are guaranteed to stay the same across experiments.

The definition of units in the CFC scheme is therefore different from that in classic citation classification, where only formal citations are used (see section 2.3.1). The two definitions are nevertheless close enough that the results of the analyses remain comparable.

[60] As discussed in chapter 5, these are marked in SciXML as `REF` and `REFAUTHOR`, respectively.

The development of the scheme used 30 articles from CmpLG and resulted in guidelines of roughly 25 pages with around 150 rules. The guidelines contain many examples, a decision tree and a list of decision aids for systematically ambiguous cases. The categories are defined in terms of certain objective types of statements. For instance, PMOT is broken down into 7 cases, one of which is "Citation makes the statements that problem Y is hard, or presents facts that can support the statement that this is so". To illustrate the level of detail in the guidelines, appendix C.3 (p.433) reproduces the 41 rules covering the contrastive categories CoCoGM, CoCoXY, CoCoR0 and CoCo-.

Fig. 53 describes the categories as a decision tree. The questions in the tree are as follows:

Q0: Is there evidence in the text that there is a hinge for this citation?

Q1: What is the general sentiment toward the existing KC?

Q2: Is the existing KC criticised (rather than being compared)?

Q3: Does the new KC praise the existing KC, or claim support from or for it?

Q4: Does the existing KC provide the motivation for the new KC?

Q5: Does the new KC use the existing KC in some form (as opposed to being merely similar)?

Q6: Does the existing KC form the basis of the new KC (as opposed to being merely used)?

Q7: Is the existing KC used with or without changes?

Q8: Is the new KC involved in the comparison with the existing KC, or are two or more existing KCs compared to each other?

Q9: Does the comparison concern goals or methods (as opposed to results)?

Most of these questions have been directly or indirectly discussed in section 6.5. For instance, question **Q1**, which distinguishes citations by their main sentiment, into negative (or contrastive), positive (or continuative, support and use) and comparative functions, corresponds to the split discussed in section. 6.5. Note that CoCo- ("Superiority of own knowledge claim") is both a comparison and has a negative stance towards an existing KC. Its mnemonic expresses the comparative aspect, whereas its position in the tree expresses the negative stance.

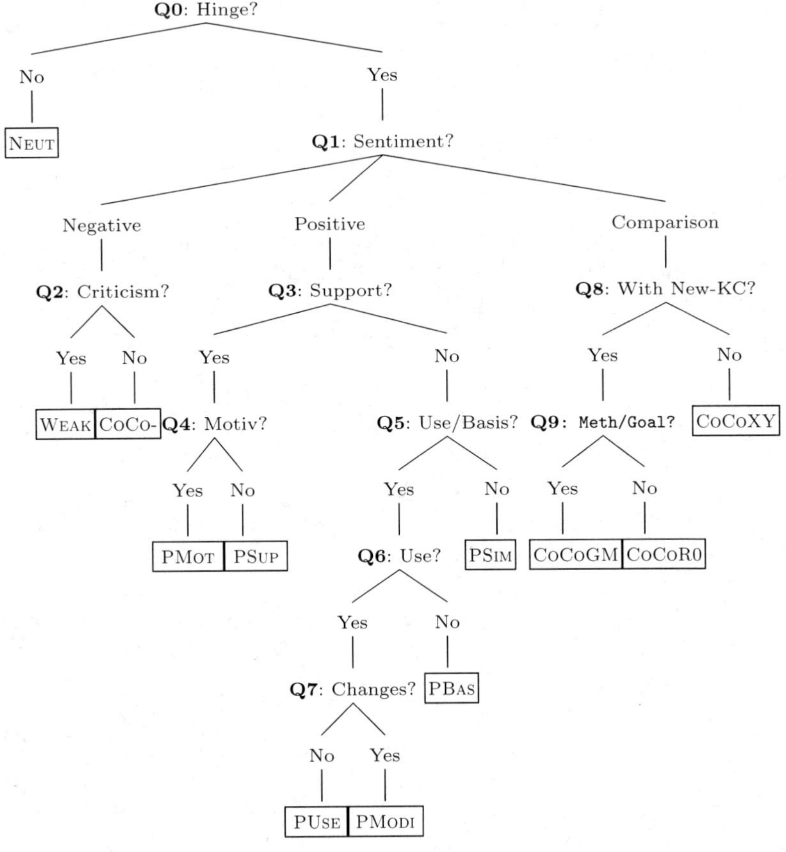

FIGURE 53 Decision Tree for CFC.

A fourth top-level category is formed by NEUT (neutral), which is split off at the top of the tree (question **Q0**). This category includes situations where

- some hinge is felt to be present, but the scheme does not provide a fitting classification, i.e., the connection is indirect and vague;
- a hinge function recognised by the scheme is present, but it is not strong enough, or not explicitly enough expressed;
- the citation is truly neutral in the argumentation; no hinge function is recognisable.

PMOT covers the indirect hinge moves H-17 and H-18. As stated in section 6.5, H-17 is unusual in that it might involve two existing KCs, the KC which is being praised and the KC which makes the statement of praise, as in the following example:

> *For example, a Naive Bayesian classifier (Duda and Hart 1973* [**Neut**]*) is based on a blanket assumption about the interactions among features in a sense tagged corpus and does not learn a representative model.* **H-17:** *Despite making such an assumption, this proves to be among the most accurate techniques in comparative studies of corpus-based word sense disambiguation methodologies (e.g., Leacock et al. 1993* [**PMot**]*).* (0005006, S-5/S-6)

The category PMOT is always applied to the existing KC which makes the statement of praise (here: *Leacock et al.*). The praised KC (here: *Duda and Hart*) is the one that is being used, but the use hinge function is not expressed here and is therefore not annotated (it will probably be expressed later in the text).[61] With respect to H-18, there is no such ambiguity, because there is only one existing KC involved (the one that makes the statement about the problem).

There is one other new category, COCOXY, which also expresses a relationship that does not involve the new KC. However, unlike PMOT, COCOXY does not directly correspond to a hinge function from Fig. 36; it marks explicit comparisons between two existing KCs, neither of which is the authors' new KC. Consider the following examples:

> *Unlike previous approaches (Ellison 1994* [**CoCoXY**], *Walther 1996* [**CoCoXY**]*), Karttunen* [**CoCoXY**] *'s approach is encoded entirely in the finite state calculus, with no extra-logical procedures for counting constraint violations.* (0006038, S-5)

> *Cardie and Pierce (1998* [**CoCoXY**]*) store POS tag sequences that make up complete chunks and use these sequences as rules for classifying unseen data. This approach performs worse than the method of Argamon et al.* [**CoCoXY**] *(F=90.9).* (0005015, S-128/129)

> *This paper reports on a comparison between the transformation-based error-driven learner described in Ferro et al. (1999* [**CoCoXY**]*) and the memory-based learner for GRs described in Buchholz et al. (1999* [**CoCoXY**]*) on finding GRs to verbs by retraining the memory-based learner with the data used in Ferro et al. (1999* [**PUse**]*).* (0008004, S-12)

[61] If the authors who make the statement of praise also contribute the solution that is being used, the corresponding citation will be annotated as PMOT in this context, and additionally as PUSE in the context where the use is stated, if such a context exists.

If comparisons between existing KCs advance the argumentation for the new knowledge claim, they do so very indirectly. They therefore do not belong to the KCDM; instead, one might argue that they are part of the "object world", the "science" of the article, which is generally ignored by the KCDM. There are reasons for recognising them nevertheless, which provide another illustration that both theoretical and practical considerations influence annotation scheme design.

From a theoretical viewpoint, the most important role that the CoCoXY citation function plays is in evaluation articles, such as article 0008004 (third example above). In such articles, the comparison between two or more existing approaches constitutes the authors' knowledge claim; they do not have to lay claim to the invention of the approaches (see section 6.2). From a practical viewpoint, the linguistic signalling of the CoCoXY citation function is similar to that of the other comparison-type citation functions (CoCo-, CoCoGM and CoCoR0). Humans have no problem with this distinction, but supervised learning algorithms are in danger of wrong associations. If there was no CoCoXY class, such instances would be left unannotated (or rather: annotated as Neut), which would likely lead to their misclassification as CoCo-, CoCoGM or CoCoR0 in many cases. Defining a new class for CoCoXY forces the statistical classifiers to look out for features which distinguish the CoCoXY cases from the other comparative categories, which are of much more interest in most articles.[62]

One of the major developments in the CFC guidelines is the requirement that only linguistically signalled citation functions can be annotated with anything other than Neut. (The guidelines for KCA and AZ annotation, which were written much earlier, also discouraged annotators from using reasoning on the basis of their domain knowledge when assigning a particular category, but did not formalise this requirement as much as the CFC guidelines did.) Annotators must be able to point to textual evidence for assigning a particular function. In-depth knowledge of the field or of the authors does not count as evidence; a lexical phrase such as "*better*" or "*used by us*" must be found, or general text interpretation principles applied, such as the resolution of anaphora and ellipsis. For each non-Neut citation, the textual evidence must be typed into the annotation tool. These rules were the first step in a more general move in my work towards keeping the annotation as domain knowledge-free as possible, as I will discuss in more detail in chapter 13. This make the definition of citation function more

[62]This argument is somewhat weak, because annotation scheme design should really only be guided by the underlying "truth" and not by considerations about automatic recognition.

objective, and makes it more feasible for a domain knowledge-poor automatic recogniser to recognise it.

The need for textual evidence cuts down the space of hypotheses, but CFC is nevertheless a difficult task which often requires subjective judgement. Authors do not always state their purpose clearly; for instance, we have seen that negational citations are rare (Moravcsik and Murugesan, 1975, Spiegel-Rösing, 1977, MacRoberts and MacRoberts, 1984). This makes it more difficult to judge whether or not a hinge is present or strong enough.

It can also be hard to distinguish similarity with a method (PSIM) from use of the method (PUSE), in cases where authors do not want to admit (or stress) that they are using somebody else's method:

> *This is done, in the spirit of the Dependency Model of Lauer (1995* **[PUse]***), by selecting the noun to its right in the compound with the highest probability of occuring with the word in question when occurring in a noun compound.* (0008026, S-99)
>
> *Unification of indices proceeds in the same manner as unification of all other typed feature structures (Carpenter 1992* **[PUse]***)* (0008023, S-87)

Another difficult distinction concerns the judgement of whether the authors continue somebody's intellectual ancestry (i.e., PBAS), or whether they merely *use* the work (i.e., PUSE).

If a piece of text contains one unit of annotation but more than one hinge (e.g., when an approach is praised then criticised), annotators need to decide which hinge function is stronger; that function takes precedence over the others, and the annotation unit is annotated with it.

If the citation and the hinge statement are textually separated, the citation function is annotated on the nearest appropriate annotation unit. The allowable context for the interpretation of citation function is by default constrained to the same paragraph. In rare cases, when the semantics of a category requires information which is not normally local to the paragraph, annotators are allowed to find the evidence elsewhere in the article. For instance, in order to tag a praised approach as PMOT, it must be used by the authors. Annotators are therefore asked to skim-read the article before annotation.

To my knowledge, the only other comparably fine-grained citation function scheme designed for automatic use is Garzone and Mercer's (2000). This scheme has 34 categories, which are the union of those from 11 historic annotation schemes from content citation analysis. Garzone and Mercer's scheme contains 7 negational categories (differing in type and strength of the challenge posed); 5 affirmational categories (differing in strength of support or confirmation); 7 use categories (differing according to which aspect of a work is used); 2 contrastive categories (differing in whether the citing article is involved in the comparison or not); 4 "reader alert" categories which correspond to weak support; and 5 other categories concerning interpretation of results, future work and tentative results. This scheme makes distinctions far subtler than ours, but without reliability studies, there is some doubt as to whether humans can reliably make that many distinctions.

Fig. 54 shows the first page of *Pereira et al. (1993)* with CFC annotation. Two citations are annotated as Weak, one as Neut, one as CoCoGM, and four as Use. The example also illustrates the fact that articles typically have far fewer CFC data points (citations) than KCA or AZ data points (sentences). CFC annotation will therefore always involve a higher effort than KCA or AZ annotation, as the annotation of each individual article includes a fixed time for non-annotation tasks, such as skim-reading and familiarisation with the article's main points.

7.4 The AZ Scheme (Argumentative Zoning)

Argumentative Zoning (AZ) is historically the first task in the framework of the KCDM, and it is the one that most experiments in this book concentrate on. AZ describes selected phenomena from Levels 1–4 of the KCDM in one annotation scheme.

Argumentative Zoning derives its name from the fact that its zones are defined by argumentation steps, and that it results in sequences or zones of sentences of differing length.[63] The guidelines are 16 pages long and are given in appendix C.2. Human annotation experiments with the AZ scheme are reported in sections 8.3 and 8.4.

Fig. 55 shows that AZ categories are defined either by KCA segmentation (categories Background and Other and Own) or by rhetorical, presentational, and hinge moves (categories Aim, Contrast, Basis and Textual).[64] AZ categories can correspond to more than one move. Parentheses around moves in Fig. 55 indicate that a particular move is not a clear-cut example of the category; it might however receive the given AZ category, if the context in an article is right.

[63] With hindsight, "argumentational" rather than "argumentative" would have been a better choice of name, but the damage is done.

[64] For space reasons, I will sometimes use obvious abbreviations for the category names, namely: Bkg for Background; Bas for Basis; Oth for Other; Txt for Textual; and Ctr for Contrast.

Distributional Clustering of English Words

Fernando Pereira Naftali Tishby Lillian Lee

Abstract

We describe and experimentally evaluate a method for automatically clustering words according to their distribution in particular syntactic contexts. Deterministic annealing is used to find lowest distortion sets of clusters. As the annealing parameter increases, existing clusters become unstable and subdivide, yielding a hierarchical "soft" clustering of the data. Clusters are used as the basis for class models of word occurrence, and the models evaluated with respect to held–out data.

Introduction

Methods for automatically classifying words according to their contexts of use have both scientific and practial interest. The scientific questions arise in connection to distributional views of linguistic (particularly lexical) structure and also in relation to the question of lexical acquisition both from psychological and computational learning perspectives. From the practical point of view, word classification addresses questions of data sparseness and generalization in statistical language models, particularly models for deciding among alternative analyses proposed by a grammar.

It is well known that a simple tabulation of frequencies of certain words participating in certain configurations, for example the frequencies of pairs of transitive main verb and the head of its direct object, cannot be reliably used for comparing the likelihoods of different alternative configurations. The problem is that in large enough corpora, the number of possible joint events is much larger than the number of event occurrences in the corpus, so many events are seen rarely or never, making their frequency counts unreliable estimates of their probabilities.

NEUT Hindle (1990) proposed dealing with the sparseness problem by estimating the likelihood of unseen events from that of "similar" events that have been seen. For instance, one may estimate the likelihood of a particular direct object for a verb from the likelihoods of that direct object for similar verbs. This requires a reasonable definition of verb
WEAK similarity and a similarity estimation method. In Hindle's proposal, words are similar if we have strong statistical evidence that they tend to participate in the same events. His notion of similarity seems to agree with our intuitions in many cases, but it is not clear how it can be used directly to construct classes and corresponding models of association.

Our research addresses some of the same questions and uses similar raw data, but we investigate how to factor word association tendencies into associations of words to certain hidden senses classes and associations between the classes themselves. While it may be worthwhile to base such a model on preexisting sense classes (Resnik, 1992), in the work de– CoCoGM
scribed here we look at how to derive the classes directly from distributional data. More specifically, we model senses as probabilistic concepts or clusters c with corresponding cluster membership probabilities EQN for each word w. Most other class–based modeling techniques for natural language rely instead on "hard" Boolean classes (Brown et al., 1990). WEAK
Class construction is then combinatorically very demanding and depends on frequency counts for joint events involving particular words, a potentially unreliable source of information, as we noted above. Our approach avoids both problems.

Problem Setting

In what follows, we will consider two major word classes, <EQN/> and <EQN/>, for the verbs and nouns in our experiments, and a single relation between a transitive main verb and the head noun of its direct object. Our raw knowledge about the relation consists of the frequencies <EQN/> of occurrence of particular pairs <EQN/> in the required configuration in a training corpus. Some form of text analysis is required to collect such a collection of pairs. The corpus used in our first experiment was derived from newswire text automatically parsed by Hindle's parser Fiddltch USE
(Hindle 1993). More recently, we have constructed similar USE
tables with the help of a statistical part–of–speech tagger
(Church 1988) and of tools for regular expression pattern USE
matching on tagged corpora (Yarowsky, p.c.). We have not USE
yet compared the accuracy and coverage of the two methods, or what systematic biases they might introduce, although we took care to filter out certain systematic errors, for instance the misparsing of the subject of a complement clause as the direct object of a main verb for report verbs like "say".

We will consider here only the problem of classifying nouns according to their distribution as direct objects of verbs; the converse problem is formally similar. More generally, the theoretical basis for our method supports the use of clustering to build models for any n–ary relation in terms of associations between elements in each coordinate and appropriate hidden units (cluster controids) and associations between these hidden units.

FIGURE 54 First Page of *Pereira et al. (1993)* with CFC Annotation.

I will in the following introduce the move-based AZ categories AIM, CONTRAST, BASIS and TEXTUAL. The segment-based categories (BACKGROUND, OTHER, OWN) correspond to the KCA segments NO-KC, EX-KC and NEW-KCand therefore require no further introduction.

The AIM category is assigned to sentences which give a direct description of the specific research goal of the article. These have a central status in the information management tasks described in chapter 4. Rhetorically, such sentences are often of type P-1 (direct goal descrip-

Category	Move	KCA Segment	Description
Move-Based Categories:			
Aim	P-1, (R-7), (R-10)		Statement of research goal
Contrast	R-6,H-1 to H-3, H-6 to H-11		Existing KC is presented as weak or compared/contrasted to the new KC
Basis	H-12 to H-16, (H-4), (H-5)		Existing KC provides basis for new KC
Textual	P-2 to P-4		Indication of article's textual structure
Segment-Based Categories:			
Background		No-KC	Description of generally accepted background knowledge
Other		Ex-KC, ExO-KC	Description of existing KC
Own		New-KC	Description of any aspect of new KC not covered by Aim or Textual

FIGURE 55 Annotation Scheme for Argumentative Zoning.

tion), but they could also be positive statements about the new KC's problem-solving activity, e.g., R-7 (solution-hood of the new KC) or R-10 (advantages of the new KC). In some rare cases, Aim sentences are extremely indirectly expressed, e.g., as an R-8 move (avoidance of problems by new KC) or as an R-9 move (necessity of new KC).

Basis, which we first encountered in the citation map in chapter 4 as a *continuation link*, is a category which collects several hinge moves with a generally positive connection between existing KC and new KC, e.g., when the existing KC is incorporated into the new KC, either in the form of intellectual continuation (H-13) or of use (H-14 and H-15). Basis hinges can also express similarity of an existing KC with the new KC (H-16), support for or by an existing KC (H-12), or praise (H-4 and H-5).

Contrast statements are critical or contrastive mentions of (potential) competitors' knowledge claims, including direct criticism of the existing KC (H-1, H-2, H-3), superiority of the new KC over the existing KC (H-6, H-7, H-9), contradiction (H-11) or neutral difference (H-8, H-10). R-6 moves (absence of a competing knowledge claim) are also included in this category, even though strictly speaking no hinge can be present, because no existing KC is involved. However, a hypothetical KC of this type would be a rival, as it would occupy the same niche in the research space as the new KC. Therefore, R-6 moves count as CONTRAST.

The TEXTUAL category applies to "sign-post" sentences: those which give an indication of the article structure (P-2), preview content (P-3) or summarise it (P-4). Linearisation is, as we have seen, not directly linked to scientific argumentation per se: its realisation is also more discipline-specific than the other levels of the discourse model. What makes TEXTUAL sentences nevertheless worthy of their own category is their potential to support navigation applications such as dynamic, non-linear skim-reading (see section 4.2).

An important design criterion for the AZ categories is the need to provide information for the information access tasks in chapter 4:

- AIM, BASIS and CONTRAST are needed for citation maps and for rhetorical extracts.
- TEXTUAL can provide support for within-article navigation, e.g., by augmenting a table of contents dynamically.
- OTHER segments can be used to weight the importance of citations in a citation map and to determine which citations correspond to an existing KC.
- BACKGROUND segments can be used for rhetorical extracts for non-experts.

The misclassification of an AIM or CONTRAST sentence would lead to extracts or citation maps of a drastically lower quality, whereas classification performance inside a larger segment (e.g., OWN, OTHER, BACKGROUND) matters considerably less; such segments only form the "search ground" or "backdrop material" for secondary tasks, such as the identification of a citation associated with a contrastive hinge move. Therefore, the rare and short move-based categories AIM, CONTRAST,

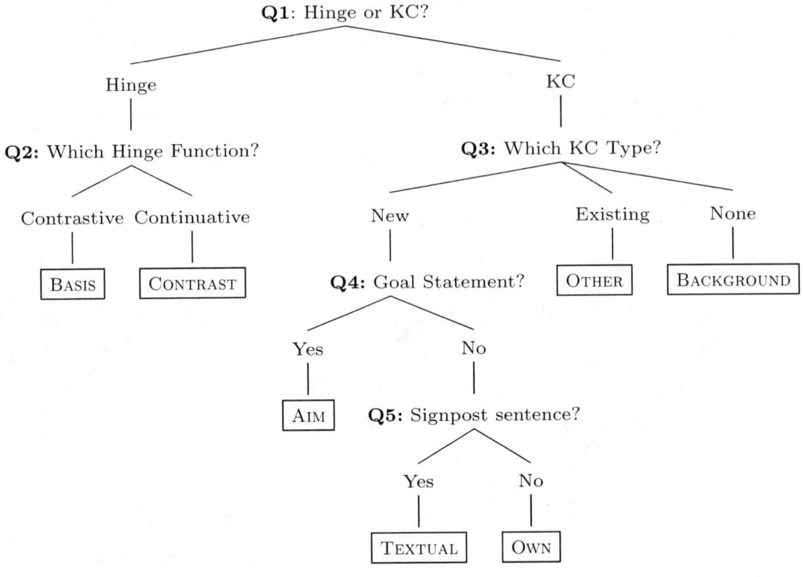

FIGURE 56 Decision Tree for AZ.

Basis and Textual are very important for the downstream applications, whereas the segment-based categories Own, Other and Background, which cover large areas of the article, matter far less.

It is often the case that the downstream tasks drive the design of categories. For instance, Wellons and Purcell's (1999) rhetorical scheme for medical literature snugly fits the respective search tasks (see section 4.1, page 62).

The semantics of the seven AZ categories can be described by the decision tree in Fig. 56, with the following five questions:

Q1: Is this sentence a hinge move or part of a knowledge claim segment?

Q2: Which hinge function is described?

Q3: Which KC type is described?

Q4: Does the sentence describe the research goal?

Q5: Is it a sign-post sentence?

Notice that there is a family resemblance between the decision trees we have encountered in this chapter. The right-hand side of the AZ decision tree (the sub-tree under **Q3**) looks similar to the decision tree for KCA (Fig. 50), and the left side (the sub-tree under **Q2**) looks similar to the decision tree for CFC (Fig. 53). In fact, many similar

AZ-annotation schemes could be built by replacing parts of the tree with more or less detailed distinctions. The AZ scheme explores certain moves with specialised categories (TEXTUAL and AIM) and corresponding questions (**Q4** and **Q5**), mainly because these pieces of information are needed for the envisaged information management applications. A variant scheme could follow the same general drift, but choose some other moves of particular interest, or make finer distinction with respect to hinge function or to KCA. In fact, I have recently started, together with my colleagues Colin Batchelor and Advaith Siddharthan, to experiment with a finer-grained version of AZ, called AZ-II, which will be introduced in section 13.1.2.

A scheme like AZ which covers more than one KCDM level must decide what to do if a text piece belongs to more than one KCDM level, i.e., it must define which category should have preference in this case. In AZ, the general rule is that moves are always treated preferentially to segments: if one of the moves associated with an AZ category is present in the text, the sentence receives the move-based AZ category; otherwise (by default) it receives a category corresponding to its KCA segment. This mechanism allows for several aspects of the model to be annotated at the same time, while prioritising the more important ones.

Moves have preference over KCA segments for two reasons:

- Moves often carry sentiment or importance statements. Knowing if a sentence is a move is therefore in general more informative than knowing that it belongs to a particular KCA segment, which is rhetorically unmarked and neutral.
- Moves often start or end KCA segments; therefore, their explicit annotation may help in the identification of start and end points of KCA segments.

The preference of move assignment over segment assignment is shown in Fig. 57 using the hypothetical article from chapter 6 (Fig. 43; p. 149). Black arrows denote the assignment of a move-based AZ category, grey arrows the assignment of a segment-based AZ category. For instance, sentences S-6 and S-10 are both annotated as CONTRAST, because the moves expressed in those sentences (R-6 and H-8) are recognised in AZ and associated with CONTRAST. Moves that are not recognised by the annotation scheme are shown greyed-out; such sentences (e.g., S-0, with move R-4) receive a segment-based category. Sentences without any rhetorical moves (e.g., S-4) are also annotated according to their KCA segment.

The important principle of what makes an annotation scheme belong

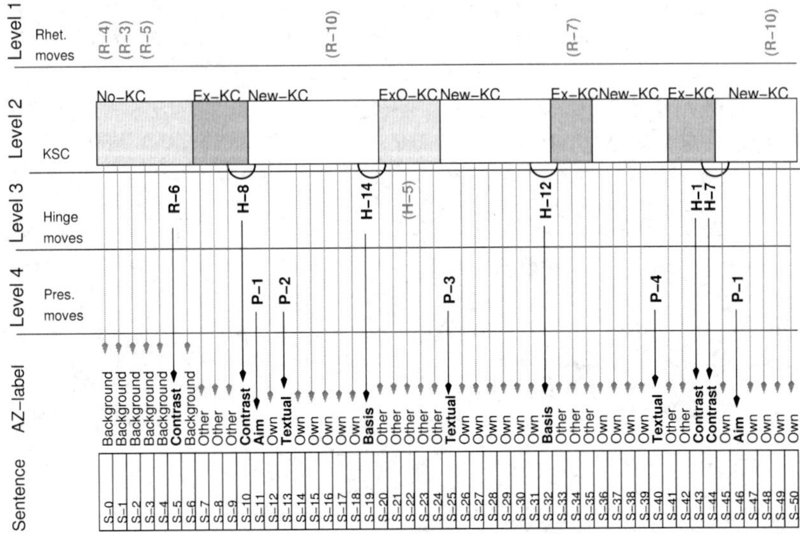

FIGURE 57 Example AZ Annotation: How Moves and Segments are Combined.

to the AZ family is that its distinctions are defined by the Knowledge Claim Discourse Model. Any such KCDM-based annotation scheme should in principle be informative, as long as it feeds into applications similar to the one tested in chapter 12. Whether it is also reliable would have to be tested with separate reliability studies (as will be done for AZ-II in section 13.1.2).

AZ was historically the first workable incarnation of the KCDM, and the experimental part of this book focuses on AZ. However, it should be clear from what has been said above that there is nothing magical about AZ's seven categories: experiments with other AZ-variants, such as AZ-II, could equally well validate the ideas in the KCDM. Nevertheless, AZ represents a good balance between simplicity and informativeness. With only seven categories, it is a compact annotation scheme, which simplifies both human annotation and statistical machine learning. While AZ is far less detailed and explanatory than the full discourse model, its categories are still informative enough to support the information access tasks in chapter 4, and explanatory enough to distinguish several of the theoretically interesting phenomena covered in the discourse model.

Let us move to the – by now traditional – example annotation of the first page of *Pereira et al (1993)*, given in Fig. 58. This annotation, like the one in Fig. 51, was done by me in 1998, whereas the one in Fig. 54 was done by me in 2005. AZ annotations by two other annotators are also shown, in Figs. 59 and 60. On the text piece shown, annotation between Annotators A and C is near perfect (only three sentences are annotated differently), whereas Annotator B disagrees to a higher degree with both A and C.

The example article starts with a NO-KC and an EX-KC segment (*Hindle (1990)*), as we already know from the KCA annotation in Fig. 51. These segments are annotated as BACKGROUND and OTHER in the AZ scheme. However, Annotator B saw a knowledge claim in the general solution of tabulating frequencies, and annotated an OTHER zone followed by a CONTRAST. This is almost certainly a misinterpretation, as there is nobody who such a knowledge claim could be attributed to. What is agreed by all three annotators is that there is a problem with Hindle's approach (the fact that his method cannot be directly used to construct word classes) – this creates a short, one-sentence CONTRAST zone.

This is followed by a comparison of the new KC's research goals with Hindle's ("*Our research addresses some of the same questions, but we investigate ...*"). I annotated this sentence as CONTRAST (and so did Annotator B). AIM is another possibility, as was Annotator A's choice. Next, there is a contrastive statement of the authors' research goal, involving *Resnik (1992)*.

Annotator C opted for the CONTRAST category (as did Annotator B, whereas Annotator A saw no particular contrast or goalhood and just annotated the sentence as OWN). The next sentence ("*More specifically...*") describes part of the authors' method; it is thus annotated as OWN by all three annotators. The sentence after that – a description of a weakness of *Brown et al's (1990)* method – is annotated as a CONTRAST. The last sentence in that section talks about an advantage of the authors' own work, and so is annotated as OWN (both other annotators decided against this and remained in the CONTRAST zone). The fact that there is no introduction-final TEXTUAL zone is atypical for CmpLG articles.

In the second section, most sentences are classified as OWN, a common effect in many articles without a "Previous Work" section. As occasionally happens this late in an article, the example article contains other explicit goal statements, e.g., the AIM sentence starting "*We will consider here...*". In most articles, OWN sentences are predominant after this point in the article. On the first page shown here, one statement was seen as BASIS by two annotators, namely the sentence starting "*The corpus used...*".

Background
Other
Own
Basis
Aim
Contrast

Distributional Clustering of English Words

Fernando Pereira   Naftali Tishby   Lillian Lee

Abstract

We describe and experimentally evaluate a method fo automatically clustering words according to their distri bution in particular syntactic conte Deterministic annealing is used to find lowest distortion sets of cluste As the annealing parameter increases, existing clusters become unstable and subdivide, yielding a hierarchical "soft" clustering of the data. Clusters are used as the basis for class models of word occurrence, and the models evaluated with respect to held-out data.

Introduction

Methods for automatically classifying words according to their contexts of use have both scientific and practial interest. The scientific questions arise in connection to distributional views of linguistic (particularly lexical) structure and also in relation to the question of lexical acquisition both from psychological and computational learning perspectives. From the practical point of view, word classification addresses questions of data sparseness and generalization in statistical language models, particularly models for deciding among alternative analyses proposed by a grammar.

It is well known that a simple tabulation of frequencies of certain words participating in certain configurations, for example the frequencies of pairs of transitive main verb and the head of its direct object, cannot be reliably used for comparing the likelihoods of different alternative configurations. The problem is that in large enough corpora, the number of possible joint events is much larger than the number of event occurrences in the corpus, so many events are seen rarely or never, making their frequency counts unreliable estimates of their probabilties.

Hindle (1990) proposed dealing with the sparseness problem by estimating the likelihood of unseen events from that of "similar" events that have been seen. For instance, one may estimate the likelihood of a particular direct object for a verb from the likelihoods of that direct object for similar verbs. This requires a reasonable definition of verb similarity and a similarity estimation method. In Hindle's proposal, words are similar if we have strong statistical evidence that they tend to participate in the same events. His notion of similarity seems to agree with our intuitio in many cases, but it is not clear how it can be used dire ly to construct classes and corresponding models of ass ation.

Our research addresses some of the same questions an uses similar raw data, but we investigate how to factor wo association tendencies into associations of words to certa hidden senses classes and associations between the classe themselves. While it may be worthwhile to base such a m on preexisting sense classes (Resnik, 1992), in the work d bed here we look at how to derive the classes directly fro distributional dat More specifically, we model senses as probabilistic concepts or clusters c with corresponding cluster membership probabilities <EQN/> for each word Most other class-based modeling techniques for natural langu rely instead on "hard" Boolean classes (Brown et al., 199 Class construction is then combinatorically very demand and depends on frequency counts for joint events involvi particular words, a potentially unreliable source of inforr ation, as we noted above Our approach avoids both problems.

Problem Setting

In what follows, we will consider two major word classes, <EQN/> and <EQN/>, for the verbs and nouns in our experiments, and a single relation between a transitive main verb and the head noun of its direct object. Our raw knowledge about the relation consists of the frequencies <EQN/> of occurrence of particular pairs <EQN/> in the required configuration in a training corpus. Some form of text analysis is required to collect such a collection of pairs. The corpus used in our first experiment was derived from newswire text automatically parsed by Hindle's parser Fidditch (Hindle, 1993). More recently, we have constructed similar tables with the help of a statistical part-of-speech tagger (Church, 1988) and of tools for regular expression pattern matching on tagged corpora (Yarowsky, p.c.). We have not yet compared the accuracy and coverage of the two methods, or what systematic biases they might introduce, although we took care to filter out certain systematic errors, for instance the misparsing of the subject of a complement clause as the direct object of a main verb for report verbs like "say". We will consider here only the problem of clas fying nouns according to their distribution as direct ob of verbs; the converse problem is formally simi More generally, the theoretical basis for our method supports the use of clustering to build models for any n-ary relation in terms of associations between elements in each coordinate and appropriate hidden units (cluster controids) and associations between these hidden units.

FIGURE 58 First Page of *Pereira et al. (1993)* with AZ Annotation, Annotator C.

Background
Other
Own
Basis
Aim
Contrast

Distributional Clustering of English Words

Fernando Pereira Naftali Tishby Lillian Lee

Abstract

We describe and experimentally evaluate a method fo automatically clustering words according to their distri bution in particular syntactic conte Deterministic annealing is used to find lowest distortion sets of cluste As the annealing parameter increases, existing clusters become unstable and subdivide, yielding a hierarchical "soft" clustering of the data. Clusters are used as the basis for class models of word occurrence, and the models evaluated with respect to held–out data.

Introduction

Methods for automatically classifying words according to their contexts of use have both scientific and practial interest. The scientific questions arise in connection to distributional views of linguistic (particularly lexical) structure and also in relation to the question of lexical acquisition both from psychological and computational learning perspectives. From the practical point of view, word classification addresses questions of data sparseness and generalization in statistical language models, particularly models for deciding among alternative analyses proposed by a grammar.

It is well known that a simple tabulation of frequencies of certain words participating in certain configurations, for example the frequencies of pairs of transitive main verb and the head of its direct object, cannot be reliably used for comparing the likelihoods of different alternative configurations. The problem is that in large enough corpora, the number of possible joint events is much larger than the number of event occurrences in the corpus, so many events are seen rarely or never, making their frequency counts unreliable estimates of their probabilties.

Hindle (1990) proposed dealing with the sparseness problem by estimating the likelihood of unseen events from that of "similar" events that have been seen. For instance, one may estimate the likelihood of a particular direct object for a verb from the likelihoods of that direct object for similar verbs. This requires a reasonable definition of verb similarity and a similarity estimation method. In Hindle's proposal, words are similar if we have strong statistical evidence that they tend to participate in the same events. His notion of similarity seems to agree with our intuitio in many cases, but it is not clear how it can be used dire ly to construct classes and corresponding models of ass ation.

Our research addresses some of the same questions ar uses similar raw data, but we investigate how to factor wo association tendencies into associations of words to certa hidden senses classes and associations between the classe themselves. While it may be worthwhile to base such a model on preexisting sense classes (Resnik, 1992), in the work described here we look at how to derive the classes directly from distributional data. More specifically, we model senses as probabilistic concepts or clusters c with corresponding cluster membership probabilities <EQN/> for each word Most other class–based modeling techniques for natural langua rely instead on "hard" Boolean classes (Brown et al., 199 Class construction is then combinatorically very demandi and depends on frequency counts for joint events involvi particular words, a potentially unreliable source of inform ation, as we noted above Our approach avoids both problem

Problem Setting

In what follows, we will consider two major word classes, <EQN/> and <EQN/>, for the verbs and nouns in our experiments, and a single relation between a transitive main verb and the head noun of its direct object. Our raw knowledge about the relation consists of the frequencies <EQN/> of occurrence of particular pairs <EQN/> in the required configuration in a training corpus. Some form of text analysis is required to collect such a collection of pairs. The corpus used in our first experiment was derived from newswire text automatically parsed by Hindle's parser Fidditch (Hindle, 1993). More recently, we have constructed similar tables with the help of a statistical part–of–speech tagger (Church, 1988) and of tools for regular expression pattern matching on tagged corpora (Yarowsky, p.c.). We have not yet compared the accuracy and coverage of the two methods, or what systematic biases they might introduce, although we took care to filter out certain systematic errors, for instance the misparsing of the subject of a complement clause as the direct object of a main verb for report verbs like "say".

We will consider here only the problem of clas fying nouns according to their distribution as direct ob of verbs; the converse problem is formally simi More generally, the theoretical basis for our method supports the use of clustering to build models for any n–ary relation in terms of associations between elements in each coordinate and appropriate hidden units (cluster controids) and associations between these hidden units.

FIGURE 59 First Page of *Pereira et al. (1993)*, with AZ Annotation, Annotator A.

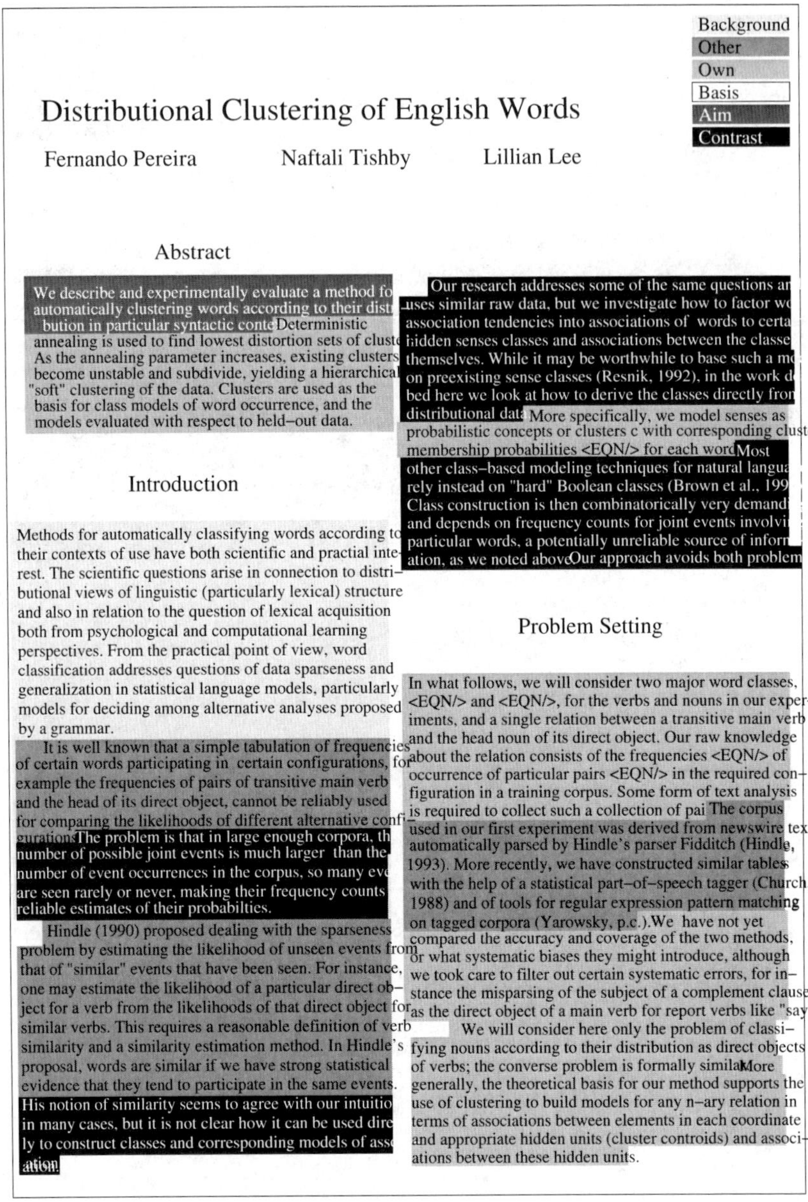

Background
Other
Own
Basis
Aim
Contrast

Distributional Clustering of English Words

Fernando Pereira Naftali Tishby Lillian Lee

Abstract

We describe and experimentally evaluate a method fo automatically clustering words according to their disti bution in particular syntactic conte Deterministic annealing is used to find lowest distortion sets of clust As the annealing parameter increases, existing clusters become unstable and subdivide, yielding a hierarchical "soft" clustering of the data. Clusters are used as the basis for class models of word occurrence, and the models evaluated with respect to held–out data.

Introduction

Methods for automatically classifying words according to their contexts of use have both scientific and practial inte-rest. The scientific questions arise in connection to distri–butional views of linguistic (particularly lexical) structure and also in relation to the question of lexical acquisition both from psychological and computational learning perspectives. From the practical point of view, word classification addresses questions of data sparseness and generalization in statistical language models, particularly models for deciding among alternative analyses proposed by a grammar.

It is well known that a simple tabulation of frequencies of certain words participating in certain configurations, for example the frequencies of pairs of transitive main verb and the head of its direct object, cannot be reliably used for comparing the likelihoods of different alternative confi-gurationsThe problem is that in large enough corpora, th number of possible joint events is much larger than the number of event occurrences in the corpus, so many eve are seen rarely or never, making their frequency counts reliable estimates of their probabilties.

Hindle (1990) proposed dealing with the sparseness problem by estimating the likelihood of unseen events from that of "similar" events that have been seen. For instance, one may estimate the likelihood of a particular direct ob–ject for a verb from the likelihoods of that direct object for similar verbs. This requires a reasonable definition of verb similarity and a similarity estimation method. In Hindle's proposal, words are similar if we have strong statistical evidence that they tend to participate in the same events. His notion of similarity seems to agree with our intuitio in many cases, but it is not clear how it can be used dire ly to construct classes and corresponding models of ass ation.

Our research addresses some of the same questions ar uses similar raw data, but we investigate how to factor wo association tendencies into associations of words to certa hidden senses classes and associations between the classe themselves. While it may be worthwhile to base such a mo on preexisting sense classes (Resnik, 1992), in the work de bed here we look at how to derive the classes directly fron distributional data More specifically, we model senses as probabilistic concepts or clusters c with corresponding cluster membership probabilities <EQN/> for each wordMost other class–based modeling techniques for natural langua rely instead on "hard" Boolean classes (Brown et al., 199 Class construction is then combinatorically very demandi and depends on frequency counts for joint events involvi particular words, a potentially unreliable source of inforn ation, as we noted aboveOur approach avoids both problem

Problem Setting

In what follows, we will consider two major word classes, <EQN/> and <EQN/>, for the verbs and nouns in our exper–iments, and a single relation between a transitive main verb and the head noun of its direct object. Our raw knowledge about the relation consists of the frequencies <EQN/> of occurrence of particular pairs <EQN/> in the required con–figuration in a training corpus. Some form of text analysis is required to collect such a collection of pai The corpus used in our first experiment was derived from newswire text automatically parsed by Hindle's parser Fidditch (Hindle, 1993). More recently, we have constructed similar tables with the help of a statistical part–of–speech tagger (Church, 1988) and of tools for regular expression pattern matching on tagged corpora (Yarowsky, p.c.).We have not yet compared the accuracy and coverage of the two methods, or what systematic biases they might introduce, although we took care to filter out certain systematic errors, for in–stance the misparsing of the subject of a complement clause as the direct object of a main verb for report verbs like "say".

We will consider here only the problem of classi–fying nouns according to their distribution as direct objects of verbs; the converse problem is formally similaMore generally, the theoretical basis for our method supports the use of clustering to build models for any n–ary relation in terms of associations between elements in each coordinate and appropriate hidden units (cluster controids) and associ–ations between these hidden units.

FIGURE 60 First Page of *Pereira et al. (1993)*, with AZ Annotation, Annotator B.

In general, most of the remaining non-OWN AZ zones are found in the *Related Work* section, if it exists, and in the *Conclusion* section. BASIS statements will also appear in the *Method* section (see section 6.5), and CONTRAST in the *Result* section. As only the first page of *Pereira et al. (1993)* is shown in Fig. 58, we cannot see those sentences, but I will list all BASIS sentences I found:

> BASIS: *The corpus used in our first experiment was derived from newswire text automatically parsed by Hindle's (1993) parser Fidditch.* (9408011, S-19)

> BASIS: *More recently, we have constructed similar tables with the help of a statistical part-of-speech tagger (Church 1988) and of tools for regular expression pattern matching on tagged corpora (Yarowsky 1992).* (9408011, S-20)

> BASIS: *The analogy with statistical mechanics suggests a deterministic annealing procedure for clustering (Rose et al. 1990).* (9408011,S-113)

> BASIS: *The data for this test was built from the training data for the previous one in the following way, based on a suggestion by Dagan et al. (1993).* (9408011, S-155)

The CONTRAST sentences are:

> *Hindle (1990) proposed dealing with the sparseness problem by estimating the likelihood of unseen events from that of "similar" events that have been seen. ...* CONTRAST: *His notion of similarity seems to agree with our intuitions in many cases, but it is not clear how it can be used directly to construct word classes and corresponding models of association.* (9408011, S-5/S-9)

> CONTRAST: *While it may be worthwhile to base such a model on preexisting word classes (Resnik 1992), in the work described here we look at how to derive the classes directly from distributional data.* (9408011, S-11)

> *Most other class-based modeling techniques for natural language rely instead on "hard" Boolean classes (Brown et al. 1990).* CONTRAST: *Class construction is then combinatorially very demanding and depends on frequency counts for joint events involving particular words, a potentially unreliable source of information as we noted above.* (9408011, S-13/S-14)

> *We could sidestep this problem (as we did initially) by smoothing zero frequencies appropriately (Church and Gale 1991).* CONTRAST: *However, this is not very satisfactory because one of the goals of our work is precisely to avoid the problems of data sparseness by grouping words into classes.* (9408011, S-40/S-41)

Comparing the example article's KCA and AZ annotations in Figs. 51

and 58, we see that the move-based AZ categories (Aim, Textual, Basis, Contrast) do indeed tend to occur at the beginnings or the ends of KCA segments. The extent of the Background/No-KC segment is exactly the same in AZ and KCA, but there are differences between AZ and KCA which involve the Other/Ex-KC segments. The criticism of Hindle at the end of the first Ex-KC segment has been reclassified as Contrast in AZ; the rest of the Ex-KC segment remains as Other. The sentence after that, which expresses a contrast between Hindle's approach and the new KC, is annotated as New-KC in KCA, but as Contrast in AZ. The comparison with *Brown et al.*, which in KCA is analysed as Ex-KC, now becomes a Contrast in AZ (rather than being part of the neutral Other zone, which would have been the other possibility). The last sentence in the introduction, which is New-KC in KCA, is now Own in AZ. The mention of continuative aspects with existing KCs ("*The corpus used in*") was Ex-KC in KCA and is now Basis in AZ. In general, we see that hinges and rhetorical moves "eat into" the KCA segments at whose margins they are located: New-KC becomes Own minus hinges and rhetorical moves; New-KC turns into Other minus hinges and rhetorical moves.

This ends the description of the three annotation schemes. I will now reconsider some of the decisions I took during annotation scheme design: the annotations are defined as a classification rather than as a segmentation task, the units of annotation are sentences and citations, and the entire article is annotated. Alternatives to these decisions exist, and I will in the following defend my choices in those three questions.

7.5 Alternative Scheme Definitions

The most fundamentally different way that the annotation task could have been defined would be as labelled segmentation, i.e., by asking the annotators to insert boundaries into text, and then asking them to classify their units. This is in contrast to using readily identified units as in categorial classification.

Labelled segmentation is not possible for CFC, which is not a text-covering annotation. Citations are single, clearly identifyable units surrounded by non-citation material, so categorial classification is the only possible type of annotation. However, as KCA is a segment-based task, labelled segmentation is a possibility. This may even be so for AZ, too, although the move-based AZ categories do not have any segmental interpretation.

Type of Annotation

Mutually exclusive category assignment, as used in the annotation schemes presented here, is also practised in dialogue act coding, as we have seen in section 7.1. In contrast, in segmentation tasks, subjects are given only raw text with no indication what the classifiable units are, and are asked to decide where units start and end. Krippendorff (2004) and Artstein and Poesio (2008) call this task "unitizing". This is exemplified by unlabelled annotation tasks such as topic segmentation (e.g., Hearst, 1994) or named entity recognition, or by labelled ones such as discourse segmentation (e.g., Passonneau and Litman, 1993). For instance, Passonneau and Litman (1993) asked seven subjects to insert boundaries where they perceive a change of speaker intention; Fig. 61 shows how many subjects placed a boundary at the various possible locations.

and he u-h puts his pears into the basket.

6 Subjects

U-hi a number of people are going by, one is [um/you know/I don't know], I can't remember the first... the first person that goes by.

1 Subject

Oh

1 Subject

A u-m.. a man with a goat comes by.

2 Subjects

It see it seems to be a busy place. You know, fairly busy,

1 Subject

it's out in the country, maybe in u-m u-h the valley or something.

7 Subjects

A-nd u m he goes up the ladder

FIGURE 61 Human Segmentation of a Monologue (Simplified, from Passonneau and Litman (1993)).

AZ and KCA annotators could have been asked to insert boundaries wherever a move or zone ends, and then to classify it according to its rhetorical type. If segmentation boundaries are allowed only between sentences, then the two task definitions produce equivalent output, a fact that allows us to re-interpret the classification-based annotation post-hoc as a segmentation. This would have created objects of variable length, as opposed to the sequences of objects of roughly the same length (i.e., one sentence long), which result from categorial classification. However, as with all post-hoc re-definitions, we need to keep in mind that the two tasks are likely to seem conceptually different to a human: humans might have annotated differently if we had actually asked them to segment rather than to classify.

KCA annotation can be quite straightforwardly reinterpreted as labelled segmentation. Although I will still primarily consider it a categorial classification task in what follows, KCA performance will also be given using (labelled) segmentation metrics, which I will introduce in section 8.1.

In contrast, for AZ annotation a reinterpretation as labelled segmentation would be more problematic, because the AZ categories differ greatly amongst themselves in terms of length, frequency and relative importance. The move-based AZ categories are typically short and infrequent, but important for the downstream task, whereas the segment-based AZ categories result in long segments which are less task-relevant. It is hard to define what good labelled segmentation annotation would mean under those conditions: On the one hand, the length of a segment should matter. Within segments of the same type, agreement on long segments should be rewarded more than agreement on short segments. On the other, the type of a segment should also matter: due to the importance of the move-based categories, the same amount of text should count relatively more in a short segment than it would in a long segment.

It is not clear how to weigh these two requirements against each other. For instance, in many segmentation tasks it has been observed that humans agree about the presence of a boundary in some general area, but not about its exact placement. In the case of AZ, whether or not we care about where the exact boundary lies between two segments depends on which segments are concerned. If two long, unimportant segments meet (e.g., an ExO-KC and a New-KC segment), we do not care much if a segment boundary is one sentence removed from where it should be. However, if a short but important segment is involved, which may only be a sentence long, being one sentence off is a grave error.

In contrast, defining AZ as a categorial classification task allows for an intuitive and conceptually simple interpretation of agreement, so this is what I will do in the rest of this book.

Unit of Annotation

KCA and AZ use sentences as the unit of annotation. That was not an obvious decision: rhetorical moves are propositions, i.e., semantic objects which express one state or event. Propositions do not directly map to syntactic sentences, and this can cause problems. Consider the following cases, where two rhetorical moves occur in the same sentence:

> *However, this is not very satisfactory because one of the goals of our work is precisely to avoid the problems of data sparseness by grouping words into classes.* (9408011, S-41)
>
> *While we know of previous work which associates scores with feature structures (Kim, 1994)* [sic] *are not aware of any previous treatment which makes explicit the link to classical probability theory.* (0502022, S-9)

The first sentence contains both an H-1 and a P-1 move, the second both an Ex-KC segment and an R-6 move. Such cases are infrequent, but they frustrate annotators and confuse automatic recognisers. As only one of the two moves or segments contained in such a sentence can be annotated, some part of the sentence ends up with an incorrect annotation. This means that the features coming from that part of the sentence are associated with a wrong target category, leading to degraded performance of a machine learner.

Of the possible alternative annotation units, *clauses* are the most obvious. It seems likely that current statistical parsers would be robust and accurate enough for the automatic identification of clauses, given a human-directed but formal definition of a clause. But this is the crux: No theoretical model of a clause exists, and defining what a clause is is difficult, syntactically and semantically. For instance, nominalisations of verbs often represent an event, particularly if they include syntactic arguments, so one might consider them clauses on semantic grounds, although they are syntactically not clause-like and might be embedded in another clause. It is hard to draw the line. Guidelines for manual identification of clauses or *elementary discourse units* (*edus*), as used in discourse theories such as RST, exist, but are often lengthy and involved (e.g., Carlson et al., 2003).

Second, while clause-level annotation could potentially lead to more accurate annotation, this effect would be restricted to the rare cases where a sentence does contain more than one move. This has to be weighed against the much larger number of cases where one move or segment covers the sentence. The introduction of a large number of smaller classification objects will likely translate into decreased automatic annotation performance as well as increased effort during manual annotation. For instance, it is known from text classification that shorter classification entities result in overall worse performance; for instance, it is much easier to classify documents according to sentiment than it is to classify sentences (e.g., Pang and Lee, 2004).

Sentences are roughly at the right granularity for the majority of cases, and their boundaries are typographically marked,[65] so I made them the annotation units in KCA and AZ. The cases where more than one move appears in a sentence are then tolerated as a rare problem. Nevertheless, whether or not clauses would make better annotation units for KCA and AZ is an empirical question, which should be tested at some point.

Areas of Annotation

Annotating entire articles is costly, both during the reliability study and production mode annotation. Supervised machine learning requires much annotated material, and results will typically improve with more material; but annotation of texts with my schemes is expensive enough that simply building larger data sets is not an attractive option. If the annotation of parts of the source text instead of the entire text would result in acceptable training material with less effort, then the corresponding annotation time could be invested in covering more articles and different disciplines. This section therefore considers cheaper methods of producing the required training material. The discussion is phrased in terms of AZ annotation, but similar arguments apply to the other annotation schemes.

Due to the difference in importance between the segment-based and the move-based categories, there are two possible annotation shortcuts.

Firstly, one could consider annotating only special areas in the article, namely those where move-based categories occur more frequently than in the rest of the article. The abstract, conclusion and introduction sections are prime candidates, because according to general writing guidelines these should be "condensed versions" of the entire article (Swales, 1990, Manning, 1990). In the case of the abstract, there is even reason to believe that it would be *easier* for humans to determine rhetorical status in comparison to the rest of the article, as abstracts should deliver the rhetorical message of the article particularly clearly.

This proposal can be empirically tested, once we have access to the annotation for the entire article (which the experiments in chapter 8 will deliver). One can then measure how much degradation in agreement each of these shortcut strategies brings with it. I will report the results of this post-analysis in section 8.6.

A second proposal relies on the alignment of document and abstract sentences, as discussed in section 5.1.2. The method assumes that KCA

[65] However, the automatic identification of sentence boundaries is not entirely trivial, see section 11.1.

and AZ status is conserved under alignment. If that is the case, an annotation of the abstract would produce additional AZ-annotated material for free, namely the aligned document sentences. This material could then even be used directly to create rhetorical extracts.

The second proposal requires good alignment between document and abstract sentences, and we already know from section 5.1.2 that CmpLG displays a low rate of alignment. Let us nevertheless consider how alignment would work, using the example paper. Out of *Pereira et al. (1993)*'s four abstract sentences (Fig. 22; page 84), only one is aligned:

> AIM: *We describe and experimentally evaluate a method for automatically clustering words according to their distribution in particular syntactic contexts.* (9408011, A-0)

LCS, the longest common substring measure, aligns this sentence (weakly) with the following two document sentences:

> BACKGROUND: *Methods for automatically classifying words according to their contexts of use have both scientific and practical interest.* (9408011, S-0)
>
> AIM: *We have demonstrated that a general divisive clustering procedure for probability distributions can be used to group words according to their participation in particular grammatical relations with other words.* (9408011, S-164)

For one of these half-aligned sentences (S-164), A-0's goal statement status is preserved under alignment, but not for the other (S-0). In the case of S-0, which is a BACKGROUND sentence, the superficial alignment found a spurious match with the description of the authors' goal in A-0 (*"methods for automatically classifying words"*).

This example is somewhat inconclusive, but it does not provide an optimistic outlook for the possibility of inferring the rhetorical status of document sentences from annotated abstracts. It could however be worthwhile to investigate this question with a corpus that shows a higher alignment rate.

However, there is a general argument against annotating only part of an article: some areas might not contain all rhetorical categories required for the downstream task, or they might not contain enough instances for a machine learner to classify them accurately. For instance, in section 3.1.2 we have already encountered at least three AZ categories which are not normally included in abstracts, namely descriptions of existing knowledge claims (OTHER), as well as contrastive or continuative mentions of previous work (CONTRAST and BASIS). All of these are crucial for the information access methods which motivate this analysis.

In section 8.6, I will use the annotated material to determine the distribution of AZ categories in different areas of the article, in order to answer this question.

Chapter Summary

Chapter 6 introduced the KCDM and discussed various rhetorical phenomena in scientific text. But there are many ways in which one could practically annotate these phenomena. What I have done in this chapter is to radically simplify the discourse model, so that aspects of it can be captured by three flat-label annotation schemes.

I started the chapter with some general points about annotation methodology, about which types of annotation schemes exist (flat, hierarchical, mutually exclusive categories or property-based) and how ground truth should be defined. I also described how the practical annotation exercises in this book were performed.

The core of this chapter introduced the three annotation schemes, which explore different aspects of the KCDM discourse model:

- The **KCA** annotation scheme considers knowledge claim attribution (Level 2);
- The **CFC** annotation scheme considers citation function classification, which is very similar to the hinge moves from Level 3;
- The **AZ** annotation scheme (Argumentative Zoning) combines Knowledge Claim Attribution (Level 2) and certain moves from Levels 1, 3 and 4 in one scheme.

I have also explained why categorial classification of sentences is used instead of labelled segmentation or clause-based classification, why annotation is sentence-based, and which subparts of the article could be annotated in case the annotation of the entire article is too expensive.

An obvious question now is how consistently humans can annotate text with these three schemes. Chapter 8 will give the answer in the form of reliability studies for the three schemes.

8

Reliability Studies

I have introduced three annotation schemes in chapter 7, which encode various aspects of the Knowledge Claim Discourse Model from chapter 6. The current chapter describes the reliability studies that I performed for the three schemes. Reliability studies are formal annotation experiments with human annotators, which assess to which degree the humans agree with each other (and with themselves after some time has passed) when annotating with a particular scheme. If agreement is high, this will count as partial proof of the intuitiveness of the annotation scheme (and in this particular case, the discourse model behind it).

I performed four reliability studies: annotation of KCA (Study I; section 8.2), AZ (Studies II and III; sections 8.3 and 8.4), and CFC (Study IV; section 8.5). As already mentioned in chapter 7, AZ has a special status amongst the three schemes because it is a small version of the entire KCDM, and because its labels can directly support several information management tasks. The AZ experiments (Studies II and III) are therefore the core of the human-based evidence, and are discussed more extensively than the other experiments.

Study II uses task-trained annotators. A positive outcome of Study II would mean that AZ categories can be explained to other humans in written form, and must therefore be psychologically real to a certain degree. In contrast, Study III uses annotators without any training. A positive outcome of Study III would not only reduce the training effort in comparison to Study II, it would also allow for stronger claims about the validity (the psychological reality) of the AZ scheme.

Beyond validating a theory, human annotation can also provide the training material for supervised machine learning. After the reliability studies had confirmed certain properties of the annotation scheme, I assumed that the annotated material could in principle be used as training data for machine learning experiments in chapter 11.[66] As explained in chapter 7, training material produced in "production mode" is typically annotated by one person only, whereas several annotators are required for the reliability studies, which are normally performed as a one-off exercise.

Annotated material can also be used for post-hoc analyses, which allow for quantitative statements about the schemes and the corpus. For instance, I have hypothesised in chapter 6 that ease of KCA, CFC or AZ annotation may be a sign of writing quality. I do not have access to an independent judgement of writing quality for the articles in CmpLG, but the annotated data allows me to correlate ease of annotation with other, more objective properties of the article that are likely to be related to writing quality, such as alignability, ratio of self-citations, article and average sentence length, and publication type (workshop, conference or student session). Such analyses are presented in section 8.6.

I will begin this chapter with a discussion of possible agreement metrics, ceilings and baselines.

8.1 Agreement Metrics, Ceilings and Baselines

While there are metrics that measure specific aspects of similarity, e.g., the degree of similarity concerning one particular category, one is typically first and foremost interested in a *summary metric*, i.e., one metric that gives an assessment of the overall similarity of annotation. When choosing an evaluation metric for the questions addressed in this book, we have to keep in mind that the annotation we intend to perform places particular demands on the summary metric (other than that its general assessment of "overall annotation similarity" should agree with ours):

- AZ is likely to result in a skewed distribution, as move-based categories are rare and KCA segment-based categories are common. CFC is likely to result in a skewed distribution too, because the Neut category threatens to be the dominant category. The metric should thus be tolerant of skewed distributions.
- Performance on some of the categories is inherently more important to us, because of the needs of the downstream applications (see section 7.4). Hence, the metric should reward agreement on rare categories more than it rewards agreement on frequent categories. (If this is not possible, the evaluation strategy should at least include metrics which measure performance per category.)

[66] However, see the discussion about this point on p. 237.

- We will want to compare annotations created by different pools of annotators. Agreement in the reliability studies in this chapter is measured between three or more human annotators. The metric will also be used to assess automatic annotations and trivial baselines in chapter 12, where comparison is with a single human. My definition of a ceiling (see below) also requires comparisons of annotator pools of different strengths. The agreement metric should therefore produce numerically comparable results for annotation situations with different numbers of annotators.

I will discuss categorial agreement measures which can fulfil at least some of these requirements. Because it is possible to re-interpret KCA as a labelled segmentation task, I will also define the metrics used for that task. I will then discuss baselines and ceilings for the task.

Agreement Metrics

The annotation tasks we consider here are categorial classification tasks, and the classic metric for classification tasks is *accuracy* $P(A)$.[67] It is defined as the proportion of items which are correctly classified, over all items.

Accuracy poses at least two problems for empirical agreement studies of the kind presented here. First, it does not allow for numerical comparison of annotations between different numbers of annotators. This is illustrated by the separate accuracy numbers reported by Rath et al. (1961) for sets of 2, 3 and 5 annotators (see p. 52). Even more serious is the problem that accuracy has with skewed distributions: it overestimates the contribution of the frequent categories in such distributions, which is particularly problematic if it is the performance of the *rare* categories that one is really interested in.

The overestimation problem is best explained with the situation in information retrieval. What matters for the quality of an IR system is the system's performance on the relevant documents; how many of the irrelevant documents it does or does not retrieve is largely immaterial. Because accuracy averages over individual items (here: documents), and because in modern document collections, the number of irrelevant documents is orders of magnitude larger than that of the relevant ones, the contribution of the large set of irrelevant documents by far overshadows that of the few relevant documents. Accuracy is therefore unrealistically high for *all* systems in almost all situations, so that it becomes practically unusable for distinguishing them. Instead, precision (P), recall (R), and F-measure (F) are used (they were defined in section 2.2.2).

[67] Also called *percentage agreement* or *raw agreement* in the literature.

For classifications with more than two categories, P, R and F are reported for each category separately. I will do so routinely, as the performance on individual categories matters in my task. (In IR, where the classification is binary, the convention is to report only the P, R and F values of the relevant documents).

However, P, R and F are not summary metrics. A summary metric which is a good alternative to accuracy is *Macro-F*, the average of the F-measures of all categories. It is commonly used in text classification (Lewis, 1991). Macro-F is a *macro-averaged* metric, i.e., the average of the F values is calculated over *categories*. In contrast, *micro-averaging* metrics such as accuracy always average over each individual classified *item*. As Macro-F is independent of the number of items in a given category, it gives relatively more importance to rare categories. This counteracts the tendency of micro-averaging techniques to overestimate the contribution of frequent categories, but might sometimes go too far.

For instance, it is well-known that macro-averaged measures can underestimate a supervised machine learner's results. This is due to the fact that rare categories generally perform worse, as there are less training cases available for them. Therefore, macro-averaged automatic classification results are generally numerically lower than the respective micro-averaged counterparts (Yang and Liu, 1999).

Note that all of the measures discussed up to this point are only comparable across a constant number of annotators. Carletta (1996) argues against accuracy and similar measures for yet another reason: they do not take chance agreement into account. Chance agreement is the spurious, meaningless agreement that would occur if annotators randomly assigned categories. A metric that reports only the amount of agreement that goes beyond what can be expected to occur by chance is therefore preferable, as the numbers it produces are comparable across experiments.

Chance agreement varies according to the number of categories used, the distribution of the categories, and the number of annotators. For instance, in skewed distributions, chance agreement is always higher than in uniform ones with the same number of categories.

An agreement measure that corrects for chance agreement is the Kappa coefficient κ (Fleiss, 1971, Siegel and Castellan, 1988), which is a multi-annotator generalisation of Scott's (1955) π. This is the agreement measure predominantly used for annotation experiments in natural language processing. κ corrects raw agreement $P(A)$ for agreement by chance $P(E)$:

$$K = \frac{P(A)-P(E)}{1-P(E)}$$

Chance agreement $P(E)$ is defined as the level of agreement which would be reached by random annotation using the same distribution of categories as the real annotators:[68]

$$P(E) = \sum_{j=1}^{n} p_j^2$$

$$p_j = \frac{C_j}{Nk}$$

$$C_j = \sum_{i=1}^{N} m_{ij}$$

N is the number of items used, n the number of categories and k the number of annotators. m_{ij} is the number of annotators which have assigned item i to category j. C_j is the number of times category j was selected overall. p_j is the overall frequency of category j.

$P(A)$ is defined as the average number of pairwise agreements achieved in the entire dataset, divided by the number of pairwise agreements possible:

$$P(A) = \frac{1}{N}\sum_{i=1}^{N} S_i$$

S_i is the proportion of observed pairwise agreements for item i, compared to the possible pairwise agreements ($k(k-1)$):

$$S_i = \frac{\sum_{j=1}^{n} m_{ij}(m_{ij}-1)}{k(k-1)}$$

κ factors out chance agreement: no matter how many items or annotators, or how the categories are distributed, $\kappa = 0$ when there is no agreement other than what would be expected by chance, and $\kappa = 1$ when agreement is perfect. The lower bound on κ is $-\frac{P(E)}{1-P(E)}$. Negative values of κ indicate that two annotators agree *less* than expected by

[68]The notation I use here is Siegel and Castellan's (1988).

chance. κ is stricter than accuracy $P(A)$ in that its numerical value is lower in all cases other than perfect agreement.

κ is also designed to abstract over the number of annotators as it defines $P(A)$ as the proportion of expected vs. observed *pairwise* agreements possible. That is, κ for k annotators will be an average of the values of κ taking all possible m-tuples of annotators from the annotator pool (with $m < k$).[69]

Artstein and Poesio (2005), in their thorough review of the use of agreement metrics in CL, observe that there are several versions of κ which differ in how many annotators can be compared, and in how $P(E)$ is calculated. In particular, Fleiss' (1971) κ above differs from Cohen's (1960) κ.[70] in that Fleiss' κ calculates $P(E)$ by single distribution, i.e., as the average observed distribution of all annotators, whereas Cohen's κ calculates $P(E)$ by individual distributions. This means that the different versions of κ are not numerically comparable,[71] although the differences are not large in practice, with Fleiss' κ being equal to or smaller than Cohen's κ.

There are different scales for the interpretation of κ. The strictest of these is Krippendorff's (1980): $\kappa \geq 0.8$ indicates *reliable* annotation, $0.67 \leq \kappa < 0.8$ *marginally reliable* annotation and $\kappa < 0.67$ *unreliable* annotation. On Landis and Koch's (1977) more forgiving scale, agreement of $0 \leq \kappa \leq 0.2$ is considered as showing *slight* correlation, $0.2 < \kappa \leq 0.4$ as *fair*, $0.4 < \kappa \leq 0.6$ as *moderate*, $0.6 < \kappa \leq 0.8$ as *substantial*, and $\kappa > 0.8$ as *almost perfect*. Practical work with κ shows that it is difficult to achieve κ values above 0.67 (Krippendorff's *marginally reliable* criterion) on many informative annotation schemes in CL, so that many researchers accept this value as another meaningful cut-off point apart from $\kappa = 0.8$.

Different ways of calculating the variance of κ exist, which can be used for computing confidence intervals around the measured κ values, or for performing significance tests. However, as Krenn et al. (2004) point out, it is unfortunately not yet common in CL to report confidence intervals for κ.

---

[69] Despite the fact that κ corrects error over the number of categories and number of annotators, it is nevertheless good practice to report the numerical κ value always in combination with N (the number of items used), n (the number of categories) and k (the number of annotators).

[70] Artstein and Poesio (2005) argue that Fleiss' (1971) κ should really be called "multi-π". While I agree with this statement, I will continue to call it κ, for reasons of consistency with the CL literature.

[71] It is worth noting that the κ implemented in the much-used WEKA classification package (Witten and Frank, 2005) is Cohen's, rather than Fleiss'.

Fleiss et al. (1969) give a formula for the variance of κ which can be used for arbitrary number n of categories, but which is restricted to the case of two annotators. It is based on the *confusion matrix* between two annotators, which has n^2 cells (the columns being associated with one annotator, the rows with the other). The cells are filled by p_{ij}, the proportion of items placed in the i, jth cell. Let

$$pi. = \sum_{j=1}^{n} pij$$

the proportion of items placed in the ith row and

$$p.j = \sum_{i=1}^{n} pij$$

the proportion of items placed in the jth column. Then $\sigma^2_{binary}(\kappa)$, the variance of κ between two annotators, is given by

$$\sigma^2_{binary}(\kappa) = \frac{1}{N(1-P(E))^4}[\sum_{i=1}^{n} p_{ii} \cdot [(1-P(E)) - (p_{.i}+p_{i.})(1-P(A))]^2$$

$$+(1-P(A))^2 \sum_{i=1}^{n} \sum_{j=1;j\neq i}^{n} p_{ij}(p_{.i}+p_{j.})^2 - (P(E) \cdot P(A) - 2P(E) + P(A))^2]$$

Note that the original formula by Fleiss et al. is for the general case of n categories, whereas adapted the formula given by Krenn et al. (2004) is for the special case of two categories.

Fleiss (1971) proposes a different formula for the variance of κ, which relaxes the assumption that the k annotators are the same individuals for each annotated item. An example for an appropriate situation is one where different sets of doctors diagnose a group of patients with similar diseases. In contrast, in CL it is usually the same team of annotators that annotate all items, which means that Fleiss' formula might be too general for our purposes. Nevertheless, if one wants to calculate the variance of κ for more than two annotators, this is the only formula that I am aware of.

$$\sigma^2_{many}(\kappa) = \frac{2}{Nk(k-1)} \cdot \frac{\sum p_j^2 - (2k-3)(\sum p_j^2)^2 + 2(k-2)\sum_j p_j^3}{(1-\sum_j p_j^2)^2}$$

The standard error $se(\kappa) = \sqrt{\sigma^2(\kappa)}$ can then be used for significance testing and for the calculation of error bars (confidence intervals). For instance, the 95% level confidence interval stretches between $[\kappa - 1.96 \cdot se(\kappa), \kappa + 1.96 \cdot se(\kappa)]$.

There are two significance tests which can be performed: against the hypothesis that κ is any other value $\hat{\kappa}$ except 0, or against the null hypothesis that $\kappa = 0$.

- To test against the hypothesis that $\kappa = \hat{\kappa}$:

$$z = \frac{\hat{\kappa} - \kappa}{se(\kappa)}$$

  The hypothesis that κ is $\hat{\kappa}$ would be rejected if the critical ratio z were found to be significantly large for tables of the normal distribution.

- For testing the hypothesis that the underlying value of κ is 0, Fleiss et al. (1969) show that the appropriate standard error of κ is estimated by

$$se_0(\kappa) = \frac{1}{(1 - P(E))\sqrt{N}} \sqrt{P(E) + P(E)^2 - \sum_{i=1}^{n} p_{i.}p_{.i}(p_{i.} + p_{.i}}$$

  The hypothesis may be tested by referring the quantity

$$z = \frac{\kappa}{se_o(\kappa)}$$

  to tables of the standard normal distribution and rejecting the hypothesis if z is sufficiently large (a one-sided test is more appropriate here than a two-sided test).

However, this latter test is not often applied by practitioners because it is trivially easy to pass for any annotation with a reasonably high number of items. It can however be used to test if the number of items in an experiment is high enough.

Troubleshooting is a common part of scheme design; for instance Bayerl and Paul (2007) discuss methods for determining which factors (schema changes, coding team changes, etc.) were involved in causing poor annotation quality. An important instrument for troubleshooting are the following two κ-based tests, which allow for a category-specific measurement of agreement.

The first is Krippendorff's (1980) diagnostics for *category definition*, which measures how well an individual category is defined. Agreement is measured for a binary distinction over the data, where the first category is the category of interest, and the other is a pseudo-category made up of all other categories collapsed together. If κ increases when compared to the overall agreement result, that means that the category is better distinguished than average.

The second is Krippendorff's (1980) diagnostics for *category distinction*, which tests how well two categories of interest are distinguished from each other, by creating a new distinction where the two categories are collapsed into an artificial one. If the new κ increases in comparison to the old κ, then the distinction was harder to make than average.

There are various criticisms of κ in the CL literature. For instance, one complaint is that κ can be very low in skewed distributions, even though $P(A)$ is high (DiEugenio and Glass, 2004). Krenn et al.'s (2004) criticism is that the null assumption is implausible that inter-annotator agreement is only due to chance. Their suggestion is a measure which estimates "true agreement" and "chance agreement" between annotators as two homogeneous distributions, the sum of which corresponds to surface agreement, which is what we can observe. This metric contributes κ-like values, but with confidence intervals and arguably a more well-founded interpretation. It is to be hoped that the CL community will experiment and gather more experience with such new chance-corrected agreement metrics.

However, the metrics discussed so far treat all disagreements equally. This contradicts the intuition that disagreements between certain categories are more serious than others. There is a range of weighted agreement metrics to choose from, which can be applied in these cases, e.g., Cohen's (1968) weighted κ_w or Krippendorff's (1980) α, as championed by Passonneau for anaphora resolution, word-sense tagging and summarisation (Passonneau, 2006, 2004, Passonneau et al., 2006, Nenkova and Passonneau, 2004). Geertzen and Bunt's (2006) weighted κ for hierarchical tagging schemes also falls into this category.

Although some of the categories in my three schemes are similar to each other (particularly so in the CFC scheme), I do not use weighted measures in this book. I agree with Artstein and Poesio (2008) that it is not obvious that disagreements between similar categories should be weighed less – after all, distinguishing between similar categories is harder, not easier, than distinguishing between dissimilar ones.[72]

In the rest of this book, I will use Fleiss' κ as my preferred chance-corrected agreement metric to report agreement in human and automatic annotation. Despite its disadvantages, κ is the metric that the CL community has most experience with. I will also demonstrate the use of Fleiss's (1971) and Fleiss et al.'s (1969) error bars on κ in some of

[72]In more recent work, (e.g., Siddharthan and Teufel, 2007), we do however report Krippendorff's α for AZ performance, using a similar intuition to Geertzen and Bunt's (2006).

the situations where they are appropriate, although not in all of them (e.g., I will not calculate them when it is clear from the limited amount of data that the error bars will be very large). Confidence intervals will be calculated with σ^2_{many} (Fleiss, 1971) in situations with more than two annotators, and with σ^2_{binary} (Fleiss et al., 1969) if only two annotators are compared. For the main experimental values, I will also report Cohen's κ, but only for comparison and to convince the reader that the differences are indeed negligible. According to Artstein and Poesio (2008), a small difference between Fleiss' and Cohen's κ is an indication for low annotator bias.

κ is not directly sensitive to agreement on rare categories, so in order to report performance on each individual category, I will use Krippendorff's (1980) diagnostics and R, P and F. Macro-F is the other main summary measure used here; it is directly sensitive to agreement on rare categories, but it is not chance-corrected and can only be used to measure pairwise agreement. My use of $P(A)$, R, P, F and Macro-F implies a situation where only two annotators are compared, be they human or automatic. (When I will use averages of these metrics, I will explicitly say so.) Where accuracy $P(A)$ is reported at all, it is only to provide comparability to the literature.

I now turn to the evaluation metrics for unlabelled segmentation. This is for the sake of KCA, which can be reinterpreted as a segmentation task, as we saw in section 7.5. Segmentation metrics which do not take segment length into account are calculated by comparing the number of annotators' boundaries with gold standard boundaries (often arrived at by majority opinion); they are all based on precision and recall. Such metrics were developed for topic segmentation, where segments are assumed to be roughly of equal size, so that segment size is not an issue. For the requirements of KCA, such metrics are not appropriate.

There are segmentation metrics which do take segment length into account, such as p_k (Beeferman et al., 1999) and *win-diff* (Pevzner and Hearst, 2002). These metrics work with a window-based probe that steps through two aligned annotations (one the gold standard annotation (ref for "reference") and the other the annotators' (*hyp*)), from each possible boundary to the next possible boundary (e.g., sentence boundary or paragraph boundary), taking a measurement at each step, and recording if the two ends of the probe are covered by the same respective segment, as illustrated in Fig. 62 (taken from Pevzner and Hearst (2002)). k, the window size, is set to half the average true segment size. Overall performance is then recorded as the number of different measurement points, divided by all measurement points. This means that *win-diff* is an error measurement where lower numbers are better. In order to eliminate a principal problem that p_k has, *win-diff* imposes the additional requirement that for a measurement to pass, the number of boundaries between the probes must be the same.

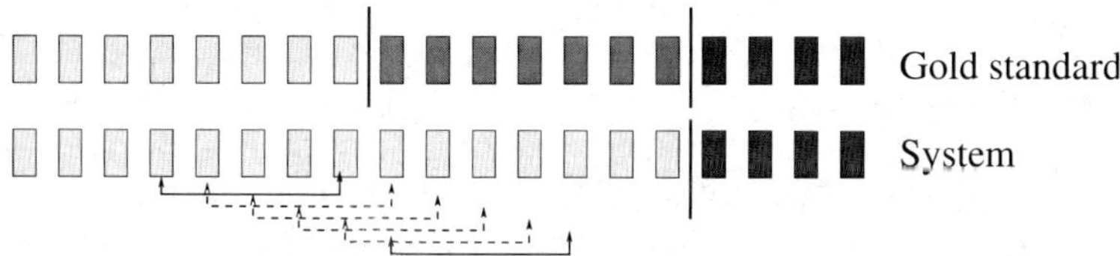

FIGURE 62 Probe-based Measurement in *win-diff* (from Pevzner and Hearst (2002)).

I use *win-diff* as an additional metric for recording performance on KCA annotation. The standard definition is:

$$\textit{win-diff}\,(ref, hyp) = \frac{1}{N-k}\sum_{i=1}^{N-k}(|b(ref_i, ref_{i+k}) - b(hyp_i, hyp_{i+k})| > 0),$$

where w is the window size, $b(i,j)$ is the number of boundaries between positions i and j in the text and N is the number of sentences in the text. I adapt this for the labelled case by additionally requiring that $cat(ref_i) = cat(hyp_i)$ and $cat(ref_{i+k}) = cat(hyp_{i+k})$, i.e., that the labels assigned by gold standard and annotator at both ends of the probe must agree. This metric is called *win-diff$_{label}$* in the following.

We should however keep in mind that *win-diff$_{label}$* is still not perfect, as it has no mechanism for recording the differing importance of segment types, and also treats long and short segments equally, e.g., concerning disagreements at their boundaries.

There is not always an obvious comparison between AZ and KCA on the one hand, and other tasks in the literature, with segmentation of dialogue into coherent units maybe being the closest existing task. Multi-party topic segmentation produces (unlabelled) *win-diff* scores which consistently fall into the 0.25 range, e.g., Galley et al. (2003) at 0.254, Hsueh et al. (2006) at 0.284 and Purver et al. (2006) at 0.284. Midgley (2009) uses many volunteer annotators to segment dialogue, and achieves a majority-based *win-diff* of 0.108 against one human gold standard, whereas the best single annotator achieved 0.245.

Baselines

Baselines are trivial algorithms that give a lower bound on the performance of a more complex automatic system. In this book, they are needed in chapter 12, when the performance of the automatic AZ, CFC and KCA classifiers from chapter 11 is to be interpreted. Reliability studies do not normally report baselines, as one would expect humans to beat all baselines easily. The reason that the baselines are discussed here nevertheless is that the choice of evaluation metric can affect how good or bad a baseline looks, and vice versa. This interaction between evaluation metric and baseline illustrates some of the properties of the metrics just discussed.

Classification tasks often use the Most-Frequent-Category (MFC) baseline, which classifies each item as the most frequent category. However, if the most frequent category is also the category of least interest, an annotation that results in all items being classified as the most frequent category would produce unattractive output, because none of the rare, but more desirable categories would ever be chosen. This effect is particularly noticable for highly skewed distributions, as in information retrieval and in all of my annotation schemes.

One can also define random choice as a baseline for classification. There are different possible models of randomness: a *uniform-random* baseline means that a random generator chooses the category for each item with the same probability for each category. In a *random-by-observed-distribution* baseline, the probability of a category being chosen is determined by the observed category distribution, which should be known from an earlier annotation experiment. Note that the definition of random choice by observed observation corresponds to $P(E)$ in the definition of κ. If this baseline is compared against any other annotation, κ should therefore theoretically be 0.

The automatic systems for AZ, CFC and KCA, which will be introduced in chapter 11, use relatively sophisticated features for classification. We therefore need to compare these systems against simpler classification methods, such as the bag-of-word models commonly used in text classification, in order to see if the additional effort is justified.

Bag-of-word models rely on binomial classification over words.[73] One of the baselines used in chapter 12 is the bag-of-word text classification package LIBBOW (McCallum, 1996), which uses a multinomial Naive Bayes unigram model.[74] To make this model applicable

[73]This is also the classification method used in Nanba and Okumura (1999).

[74]As an alternative to this, I also tested a Maximum Entropy model on unigrams and bigrams, but it performed worse than LIBBOW and is thus not reported.

to sentence-based classification, each sentence had to be treated as a pseudo-document.

My intuition about the relative quality of these baselines is as follows: The LIBBOW baseline should perform best, because unlike the other baselines it has access to some form of linguistic information from the classified items. The MFC baseline is the least useful baseline, and any sensible metric should report low agreement between it and a real annotator. As far as the random baselines are concerned, a random model that uses the observed distribution should do better than an uninformed random model.

Let us now consider which of the evaluation metrics ($P(A)$, κ or Macro-F) accommodates these intuitions best. Fig. 63 shows agreement figures between the baselines and one human annotator, as well as between two human annotators. These figures are previews of results that will be reported in sections 8.3 and 12.1.

Baseline	$P(A)$	Macro-F	κ	$P(E)$
MFC	0.71	0.12	-0.12±0.06	0.74
Random, uniform distrib.	0.17	0.08	-0.11±0.02	0.25
Random, observed distrib.	0.54	0.14	0.00±0.04	0.54
LIBBOW	0.72	0.30	0.30±0.03	0.60
Annotator B vs. C	0.87	0.70	0.71±0.04	0.55

FIGURE 63 AZ: Human and Baseline Performance.

All metrics correctly predict that LIBBOW is the baseline which is hardest to beat, and that random by uniform distribution is worse than random by observed distribution. However, $P(A)$ seriously overestimates the quality of MFC, predicting that it is practically equivalent to LIBBOW, that it beats random baselines, and that LIBBOW and MFC are quite close to human performance. This makes $P(A)$ the least suitable evaluation metric for this task.

κ makes the opposite predictions to $P(A)$, namely that MFC is far worse than random by observed distribution[75] (κ = -0.12 vs. 0; difference statistically significant at 95%). This is because chance agreement $P(E)$ for MFC is high (0.74), in comparison to random by uniform (0.25) and to random by observed distribution (0.54). According to κ, random by uniform distribution fares no better than MFC (statistically indistinguishable). κ also shows that LIBBOW, the hardest-to-beat baseline, is still quite far removed from human performance. What

[75]The agreement for random by observed distribution, measured at $\kappa = 0$, empirically confirms the theoretically predicted value.

makes human agreement stand out is that its $P(E)$ is relatively low at 0.55, whereas $P(A)$ is high at 0.87.

Macro-F occupies second place amongst the metrics. It overall agrees quite well with the intuitions, apart from the fact that it places MFC between the random and observed random baselines.

Ceiling

A related question is how one should define the *upper bound* (also called *ceiling*) for an annotation task. An upper bound is the theoretically best measurement that an automatic procedure can reach. The upper bound I use is the human reliability level: when well-trained humans systematically do not agree beyond a certain degree, then no machine can perform any better than this level of agreement.

That idea can in principle be turned into a test for automatic procedures as follows: if the performance of a pool of independently annotating human annotators stays the same when an automatic approach is added to the pool, then the automatic approach has reached the theoretically best possible performance. This requires a metric that can make a direct numerical comparison between annotator pools of different cardinalities. (In practice however, the results of this test can be hard to interpret, as they depend on the number of annotators in the pool.)

Annotation metrics, baselines and ceiling discussed, we can now turn to the reliability studies proper.

8.2 Study I: Knowledge Claim Attribution (KCA)

Study I measures to which degree three task-trained annotators can independently distinguish the three categories of the KCA annotation scheme (Fig. 49 on p. 174). To recapitulate, the scheme establishes which knowledge claim segment a current sentence is in: if it discusses the authors's own KC, it is classified as New-KC. If it discusses an already existing KC, it is classified as Ex-KC. If it is not associated with a KC, it is classified as No-KC. The scientific discipline chosen for this experiment was computational linguistics. The study took place in the framework of my PhD studies (Teufel, 2000) in spring 1998.

Study I: Method

Three annotators participated in Study I: Annotator A holds a Master degree in Cognitive Science; Annotator B was a student of Speech Therapy at Queen Margaret's College, Edinburgh at the time of the study, and Annotator C is myself. Annotators A and B were paid for their work at the standard academic student rate of the University of

Edinburgh. In terms of expertise, Annotators A and C have at least overview knowledge in most of the subfields represented in the corpus, whereas Annotator B was not an expert in CL or in CS, but did have some knowledge in phonology and phonetics, and to a lesser degree in theoretical linguistics.

The materials consist of 25 articles from the CmpLG-D corpus, as listed in Fig. 64. The total number of sentences is also given. The first four articles in CmpLG-D were used for training. Another 21 articles constitute the annotation set; they are the chronologically next articles, with the exclusion of those articles whose first author is already represented in the set. Author repetition is undesirable because I aim to cover as much variety in writing style as possible. Article 9410005 was excluded on these grounds, leaving 21 articles as annotation material. Out of these, four were chosen at random for the stability (intra-annotation) study.[76]

Type of Material	Articles	Sent.
Training	9405001 9405002 9405004 9405010	532
Annotation	9405013 9405022 9405023 9405028 9405033 9405035 9407011 9408003 9408004 9408006 9408011 9408014 9409004 9410001 9410006 9410008 9410009 9410012 9410022 9410032 9410033	3643
Intra-annotation	9405028 9407011 9410022 9410032	948

FIGURE 64 Study I: Materials.

The task definition states that each sentence in the article is to be annotated, including those in the abstract, but excluding those in acknowledgement sections. As discussed in section 7.2, the guidelines consist of 5 pages and are given in appendix C.1. They define the categories of the annotation scheme, using corpus examples and the simple decision tree in Fig. 50. For practical annotation, the KCA categories are associated with a mnemonic colour: yellow for NO-KC, orange for EX-KC, and blue for NEW-KC. No special instructions about the use of meta-discourse phrases (such as *"we present here"*) are given, although some of the example sentences contain meta-discourse.

[76]Teufel (2000) reports *five* files used for the stability study. The file concerned is 9405001, which had also been used during training and should therefore not have been included in the stability study, but this was only noticed after submission of the thesis. The numbers reported here exclude this file and are therefore slightly different from those in Teufel (2000).

The training procedure described in section 7.1 was followed. Annotators marked up the 21 training articles, 5–6 articles per week. All annotation was done pencil-on-paper and then manually edited into an XML version of the documents. Reading and annotating an article took the annotators 20–30 minutes on average. During annotation, no communication took place between the annotators, and no changes were made to the guidelines. Agreement is only reported on independently annotated material, not on training material.

6 weeks after the end of the first annotation phase, stability was measured by an intra-annotation experiment, where annotators were asked to re-annotate the four randomly chosen articles.

Study I: Results and Discussion

The results show that the KCA annotation scheme is stable ($\kappa = 0.82$, 0.78, 0.85; N=948; k=2 for Annotators A, B and C respectively) and reliable ($\kappa = 0.78$, N=3643, k=3).[77] This confirms that trained annotators are capable of making the KCA distinction between the new knowledge claim, existing specific knowledge claims, and sections without a clear knowledge claim. The average Macro-F was 0.80.

According to Fleiss's (1971) estimate of standard error, $se(\kappa) = 0.0174$ for the reliability result, placing κ in the interval [0.747 – 0.815].

The intuition that these numbers indicate high agreement is corroborated by the low average $\textit{win-diff}_{label}$ value of 0.123 achieved if KCA is reinterpreted as a labelled segmentation task. This result is far better than those typically observed for unlabelled discourse segmentation, which tend to be in the 0.25 range, as discussed on p. 213.

As expected, the category distribution for KCA is very skewed, with relative frequencies of 80.4% (New-KC), 12.8% (Ex-KC) and 6.8% (No-KC).

One of the questions to be asked is if all annotators agree with each other to the same degree. In particular, it is important to see what happens to the results when the main developer of the annotation scheme (Annotator C) is left out of the annotator pool. Fig. 65 shows pairwise annotator agreement. There is variation across annotators (κ from 0.74 to 0.82, Macro-F from 0.76 to 0.84, and $\textit{win-diff}_{label}$ from 0.143 to 0.109, and Annotator C is involved in the highest agreement.[78] Annotation between Annotators A and C was closest, as confirmed by

[77]Calculating κ using Cohen's (1960) assumptions of different distributions for $P(E)$ would have resulted in virtually identical numbers: $\kappa_{Cohen} = 0.78114$ vs. $\kappa_{Fleiss} = 0.78111$ (reliability).

[78]However, the differences are not statistically different at the 95% confidence interval.

	A–B	A–C	B–C
κ	0.74± 0.052	0.82 ± 0.067	0.78 ± 0.059
Macro-F	0.76	0.84	0.80
$\textit{win-diff}_{label}$	0.117	0.109	0.143

FIGURE 65 Study I: Pairwise Agreement between Annotators.

all three metrics, i.e., highest Macro-F (0.84), highest κ (0.82) and lowest $\textit{win-diff}_{label}$ (0.109). This may indicate that despite the high agreement overall, the guidelines could still be improved. Overall, the pairwise comparison of annotators nevertheless shows that there is no "rogue annotator".

In order to see which category distinctions are relatively harder to make, I use Krippendorff's (1980) category diagnostics, where increases in reliability, when compared to the overall reliability, indicate a difficult distinction (see section 8.1). Fig. 66 shows that the hardest distinction in the KCA annotation scheme is the one between Ex-KC and No-KC ($\kappa_{\text{New-KC}}$ = 0.83). This distinction concerns whether a knowledge claim is hinged or not; it also concerns the degree of specificity of previous work. Such distinctions are known to be hard: Swales (1990) reports similar difficulties with a distinction between his two related moves 1.2 (making topic generalisations; background knowledge) and 1.3 (reviewing previous research). With respect to significance, the difference between $\kappa_{\text{No-KC}}$ and the overall κ is significant at the 95% level, as is the difference between $\kappa_{\text{New-KC}}$ and the overall κ.

Categories		κ
New-KC + Ex-KC 93.2%	No-KC 6.8%	$\kappa_{\text{No-KC}}$ = 0.58 ± 0.0649
New-KC 80.4 %	Ex-KC + No-KC 19.6%	$\kappa_{\text{New-KC}}$ = 0.83 ± 0.0339
New-KC + No-KC 87.2%	Ex-KC 12.8%	$\kappa_{\text{Ex-KC}}$ = 0.79 ± 0.0459

FIGURE 66 Study I: Krippendorff's Diagnostics for Category Distinction.

Although one could analyse the KCA data further, I will end the discussion of Study I results here, so that we can move on to Studies II and III. AZ is the annotation scheme of central interest in this book, and it is in connection with it that the most extensive analysis will be performed.

8.3 Study II: Argumentative Zoning (AZ)

The following two studies test the reliability and stability of the AZ annotation scheme, which was introduced in section 7.4. Categories are listed in Fig. 55 (p. 186). To recapitulate, AZ contains seven categories (AIM, TEXTUAL, CONTRAST, BASIS, OWN, OTHER and BACKGROUND), out of which three (OWN, OTHER and BACKGROUND) are variants of the KCA categories, whereas AIM describes goal statement, TEXTUAL "sign-post" sentences, BASIS positive mentions of cited work and CONTRAST contrastive mentions. Both studies were performed in the framework of my PhD studies (Teufel, 2000) in spring 1998; Study II is also reported in Teufel et al. (1999).

The scheme will be tested under two conditions: Study II uses task-trained annotators, and Study III uses untrained annotators. Study II is the more important study, in that it represents a "standard" case for much annotation work in CL. Most high-level interpretative tasks require some degree of training for humans to perform them reliably. A positive outcome of Study II confirms that the most important aspects of the discourse model in chapter 6 can be explained to humans in a fairly objective way. In contrast, Study III is more speculative. AZ annotation is a complex task, and we cannot necessarily expect unprepared annotators to immediately grasp the distinctions on the basis of a one-page description of the scheme, and then successfully apply them in all difficult cases encountered in the wild. However, if there was a positive outcome of Study III, this would allow for strong claims about the validity of the scheme, apart from bringing practical benefits in terms of the training necessary.

Study II: Method

Study II uses the same annotators as Study I. The materials for Study II consist of the CmpLG-D articles listed in Fig. 67. The initial set of 32 articles (articles 9405013, 9408011, and 9502021–9504030) includes two articles which were also used in Study I (articles 9405013 and 9408011).[79] Out of this set, three articles (9503014, 9503015, and 9503018) were excluded because their authors were already represented in the annotation set, and one article (9503013) was excluded because it was found to be a review article, an article type AZ is not designed to deal with. Five of the remaining articles were chosen as training material. From the remaining 23 articles, which are the material for the main annotation experiment, 7 were randomly chosen for the stability (intra-annotation) experiment.

[79] Note that article 9408011 is the example article used throughout this book.

Type of Material	**Articles**	**Sent.**
Training	9502021 9502022 9503005 9503007 9504007	784
Annotation	9405013 9408011 9502023 9502024 9502031 9502033 9502035 9502037 9502038 9502039 9503002 9503004 9503009 9503017 9503023 9503025 9504002 9504006 9504017 9504024 9504026 9504027 9504030	3420
Intra-annotation	9408011 9502024 9502033 9502035 9503009 9503023 9504026	1092

FIGURE 67 Study II: Materials.

Essentially the same training and annotation procedure as in Study I was used for Study II, with the only difference that this time the AZ scheme was used (Fig. 55; decision tree in Fig. 56). The AZ-guidelines are 16 pages long (see appendix C.2). Once the annotation phase started, no communication between the annotators took place, and the guidelines remained unchanged. Agreement is only reported on independently annotated material, not on training material. Annotation was done pencil-on-paper, and categories were associated with a mnemonic colour: yellow for BACKGROUND, orange for OTHER, blue for OWN, green for CONTRAST, magenta for AIM, red for TEXTUAL, and purple for BASIS. Annotation times similar to those in Study I were observed. As in Study I, stability was also measured after 6 weeks.

As Study II chronologically followed Study I and as the same annotators were used, the annotators already knew the semantics of the three segment-based AZ categories (OWN, which is very similar to NEW-KC; OTHER, which is very similar to EX-KC; and BACKGROUND, which corresponds to NO-KC) when they began the AZ annotation. This might have sped up the learning process in comparison to entirely untrained annotators; however there was a gap of several weeks between the two experiments so it is unlikely that this effect was substantial.

Study II: Results and Discussion

The results show that the AZ annotation scheme is stable ($\kappa = 0.81$, 0.81, 0.74 for Annotators A, B and C, respectively; N=1092, n=7, k=2) and reliable ($\kappa = 0.71$, N=3420, n=7, k=3). This corresponds to $P(A) = 0.92$ (stability) and $P(A) = 0.87$ (reliability), and an average Macro-F of 0.707. Again, calculation of κ using Cohen's (1960) formula resulted in near-identical values: $\kappa_{Cohen} = 0.70603$ vs. $\kappa_{Fleiss} = 0.70582$ (reliability).

According to Krippendorff's (1980) scale, reliability is *marginally significant*, whereas two out of the three stability measurements are *significant*. According to Landis and Koch's scale, reliability is *substantial* and stability *almost perfect*. This is the single most important result for Argumentative Zoning, as it confirms its intuitiveness and learnability: the distinction between the seven AZ categories can consistently be applied by trained annotators.

The reliability values for Argumentative Zoning measured here do not quite reach the levels found for the best dialogue act coding schemes, where κ values of 0.8 are typically reached or exceeded (e.g., $\kappa = 0.83$ for the 14-tag MapTask coding scheme (Carletta et al., 1997), $\kappa = 0.80$ for the 42-tag Switchboard DAMSL scheme (Stolcke et al., 2000) and $\kappa = 0.90$ for the 20-tag subset of the CSTAR scheme (Doran et al., 2001)). The AZ annotation requires more subjective judgements and is likely to be cognitively more complex. I therefore find the agreement acceptable. A reliability around the observed value of $\kappa = 0.71$ is probably a realistic upper bound for automatic AZ.

Pairwise annotation between annotators varies only minimally according to κ (between 0.70 and 0.71), as Fig. 68 shows; the results are statistically indistinguishable at the 95% confidence interval. Macro-F values are more varied (between 0.69 and 0.73), and Macro-F predicts that A and C are most similar to each other. (Compare this to the fact that Annotator C's stability is statistically significantly lower than that of the two other annotators, with C's κ interval [0.6652 – 0.8103], but A's [0.7364 – 0.8927] and B's [0.7441 – 0.8829].)

	A–B	**A–C**	**B–C**
κ	0.70± 0.038	0.70 ± 0.038	0.71 ± 0.038
Macro-F	0.69	0.73	0.70

FIGURE 68 Study II: Pairwise Comparisons between Annotators.

Although I have argued in section 7.5 that a reinterpretation of AZ into a labelled segmentation task is probably not sensible, I will give the pairwise *win-diff*$_{label}$ values nevertheless, so that we can compare them to other segmentation tasks. I measured *win-diff*$_{label}$ values of 0.213 (A–B), 0.224 (B–C), and 0.202 (A–C). These values are more in line with those observed in dialogue segmentation, but are much worse than those measured for KCA segmentation. This mirrors my intuition that AZ is a harder task, with more segment changes and higher variation in segment size, and also that overall KCA annotation is more reliable than AZ annotation.

Note that in either metric, the results do not change dramatically when the main developer of the annotation scheme (Annotator C) is left out of the annotator pool,. This is a positive result, in that it shows that the guidelines and training conveyed the semantics of the categories fairly well to the two annotators who were not involved in annotation scheme development.

Fig. 69 gives the absolute and relative frequencies of the seven categories, averaged over all three annotators. Note that as each item is annotated 3-ways, the number of annotated sentences sums to $3 \times 3420 = 10260$. The distribution is skewed, with the most frequent category (OWN) at 71.4% and the least frequent one (TEXTUAL) at 1.1%. However, there is no sharp contrast in frequency between the move-based and the segment-based categories: the difference between the most frequent move-based category (CONTRAST at 4.2%) and the least frequent KCA category (BACKGROUND at 5.2%) is not large.

Category	**Sentences**	
OWN	7328	(71.4%)
OTHER	1490	(14.5%)
BACKGROUND	533	(5.2%)
CONTRAST	434	(4.2%)
AIM	231	(2.3%)
BASIS	136	(1.3%)
TEXTUAL	108	(1.1%)
	10260	(100.0%)

FIGURE 69 Study II: Frequencies of AZ Categories.

We can now also test whether we have enough annotated material. Krippendorff's (2004) rule of thumb says that this point is reached if each category occurs at lease 5 times by chance. According to this test, Study II does not use enough data by at least a factor of 10: TEXTUAL would occur only $0.011 \cdot 0.011 \cdot 3420 = 0.41$ times by chance in the 3420 examples. This, in my opinion, illustrates the stringent requirements in traditional content analysis, where precise annotation is seen as a means to an end, which is a very different situation from the one in annotation studies for cognitive purposes in CL.

How Annotators A, B and C annotated the first page of *Pereira et al.* was shown in Figs. 58 through 60, where the disagreement in this small sample was also discussed. It turns out that the example article's reliability was slightly below average at $\kappa = 0.67$ (N=170, n=7, k=3).

Although the annotation of the 23 articles was overall reliable, weaknesses in annotation schemes and in the procedure can in general be detected by asking the following questions:

- Which category distinctions are hard(er) to make?
- Which articles are hard(er) to annotate?

Confusion matrices can show which categories tend to be confused with which other ones. The confusion matrix in Fig. 70 compares annotations by Annotators A and C. The diagonal shows the number of items they agree on, all other cells the number of items they disagree on.[80] From looking at the two different marginal distributions created by the annotators, we can see that they are very similar, but that Annotator C, for instance, uses CONTRAST more often than Annotator A does. One can use the χ^2 test, which tests the strength of deviation of a distribution from the marginal distribution. Wiebe et al. (1999) suggest looking at differences between the marginal distributions from different annotators to find indications of whether disagreements are caused by systematic bias (as opposed to random noise) and in which categories they occur.

		C							
		AIM	CTR	TXT	OWN	BKG	BAS	OTH	**Total**
	AIM	**65**	3		7				**75**
	CTR	1	**82**	1	10	5		12	**111**
	TXT			**26**	3			3	**32**
A	OWN	17	34	11	**2302**	26	15	124	**2529**
	BKG	2	4		27	**124**		25	**182**
	BAS				18	1	**32**	7	**58**
	OTH		23		56	18	8	**328**	**433**
	Total	**85**	**146**	**38**	**2423**	**174**	**55**	**499**	**3420**

FIGURE 70 Study II: Confusion Matrix between Annotators A and C.

[80]Accuracy is thus the ratio of diagonal cells by all cells.

There is only one category that the category AIM is confused with considerably, and that is OWN. What these two categories have in common is that they refer to the new KC. The decision of whether or not to assign an AIM label to a sentence in an OWN segment is principally a relevance judgement. CONTRAST sentences are often confused with OWN sentences, which again is natural, as such sentences often compare own and other work. In this case, annotators have to judge which aspect of a comparison (own or other) is more dominant, another highly subjective decision. BACKGROUND sentences are confused with OTHER and OWN sentences, because annotators do not always agree on whether statements are associated with knowledge claims or not.

Much of the confusion of BACKGROUND and CONTRAST sentences may be due to cases where a failure of some general method in the field is discussed. Disagreement between OTHER and CONTRAST is often due to the question whether a sentence describes an existing KC neutrally, or whether author stance is present. The most likely disagreement involving the BASIS category is with OWN (the question is if an aspect of the own work has indeed been contributed by an existing KC, or is part of the new KC), and with OTHER (which concerns neutrality vs. author stance).

	AIM	CTR	TXT	OWN	BKG	BAS	OTH
P	0.76	0.56	0.68	0.95	0.71	0.58	0.66
R	0.87	0.74	0.81	0.91	0.68	0.55	0.76
F	0.81	0.64	0.74	0.93	0.70	0.57	0.70

FIGURE 71 Study II: P, R and F per Category (Annotators A and C).

Fig. 71 gives precision, recall and F-measure per category between Annotators A and C (corresponding Macro-F is 0.73, as Fig. 68 showed). AIM displays high agreement ($P = 0.76$; $R = 0.87$; $F = 0.81$). Due to the role that AIM sentences play in the characterisation of articles for information management tasks, AIM annotation performance is particularly important. The task of extracting AIM sentences can be roughly compared to that of human sentence selection, where subjects identify "most relevant" sentences from an article. Numerically, AIM classification performance is much higher than the sentence selection results typically reported in the literature (e.g., Rath et al. (1961)). This may be an indication that the selection of AIM sentences is indeed easier and more well-defined than the selection of globally relevant sentences, at least if done in the confines of an AZ annotation experiment (e.g., with detailed guidelines).

Another test that tells us about category distinctiveness is Krippendorff's (1980) diagnostics for category definition, where one measures agreement between a category of interest and all other categories collapsed together (see section 8.1). Fig. 72 shows the diagnostic for the four move-based AZ categories.

TXT (vs. rest)	AIM (vs. rest)	CTR (vs. rest)	BAS (vs. rest)
$\kappa = 0.77 \pm 0.126$	$\kappa = 0.75 \pm 0.187$	$\kappa = 0.56 \pm 0.090$	$\kappa = 0.48 \pm 0.166$

FIGURE 72 Study II: Krippendorff's Diagnostics for Category Definition.

In contrast to the precision/recall results from Fig. 71, Fig. 72 predicts the highest distinguishability for TEXTUAL ($\kappa = 0.77$), although AIM also fares well ($\kappa = 0.75$). Anecdotally, all annotators reported that they perceived TEXTUAL as the category which was easiest to annotate. (At the the 95% interval level, however, neither category shows a significant difference to the overall reliability of 0.71, due to the relative rarity of these categories.)

The annotators were worse at determining BASIS and CONTRAST; this is discernible from the precision/recall values in Fig. 71, where $F = 0.41$ (BASIS) and $F = 0.53$ (CONTRAST), and from Krippendorff's diagnostic in Fig. 72, where both kappas are statistically significantly below the overall reliability of 0.71 at the 95% confidence interval. Worryingly, recall on BASIS sentences is only 0.29.

There could be many reasons for these difficulties. It seems that neutral descriptions of existing KCs (OTHER) are hard to distinguish from similar descriptions which express author stance (CONTRAST and BASIS). Empirical research in sentiment classification confirms that most annotator agreement concerns the distinction between objective sentences and those with polarity Andreevskaia and Bergler (2006). This is particularly so in the case of contrastive stance, which is rarely openly expressed. The BASIS category, in turn, may be harder to find due to the wide variability of its associated meta-discourse expressions (discussed in chapter 9). The recognition of BASIS and CONTRAST could also be more prone to lapses of attention during annotation. They are not always marked by formal citations (which are typographically immediately detectable), and their location is often "hidden", interspersed within longer OWN zones. In contrast, AIM and TEXTUAL sentences are often found at prototypical locations (e.g., at the beginning or end of the introduction section), and on top of this they are lexically marked.

Note however that not all annotators perform equally well in each category, as we can see if the category distinctions are applied to the intra-annotation study (Fig. 73). Disagreements in the intra-annotation study are an absolute indication of low-quality annotation, which cannot be put down to subjective judgement across humans. The results presented here are extremely preliminary, due to the sparsity of data which makes the standard error very high. Nevertheless, it is surprising to see that different annotators had problems with very different categories: TEXTUAL in the case of Annotator A ($\kappa = 0.44$) and BASIS in the case of Annotator B ($\kappa = 0.44$). Annotator C, whose overall stability is lower, performs more uniformly, but is only really good at annotating TEXTUAL ($\kappa = 0.80$). If such annotation problems are noticed during the training phase, one should try to improve the annotators' understanding of the categories, but the intra-annotation study is often performed only after the end of the reliability studies.

	AIM	BASIS	CONTRAST	TEXTUAL
Annotator A	0.84	0.65	0.66	**0.44**
Annotator B	0.88	**0.44**	0.73	0.92
Annotator C	0.68	0.67	0.64	0.80

FIGURE 73 Study II: Annotators' Stability Per Category (in κ).

If high reliability was my absolute priority, the reliability of the scheme could be boosted to $\kappa = 0.74 \pm 0.03$ by collapsing CONTRAST, OTHER and BACKGROUND into one category. For some AZ-related task, this may be an acceptable compromise: such a scheme would maintain most of the distinctions concerning KCA, while also providing separate categories for AIM, TEXTUAL and BASIS sentences. However, in terms of the discourse model a category consisting of EX-KC, NO-KC and a contrastive move is not immediately intuitive; I do not therefore consider this collapsed scheme (or similar ones).

So far in this analysis, I have considered what influence annotators and categories have on the agreement. I will now discuss the influence of the annotation materials. The single most surprising result in this experiment is the large variation in reliability between articles: Fig. 74, which plots how many articles fall into certain reliability intervals, shows something like a bimodal distribution. There is a cluster of articles with high reliability (κ in the range of 0.85), and another cluster of articles with medium reliability (κ in the range of 0.6). Different factors could explain this variation.

The first of these I looked at was conference type: out of the 23 articles, 4 were presented in student sessions, 4 came from workshops and the remaining 15 were main conference articles. Although this is too

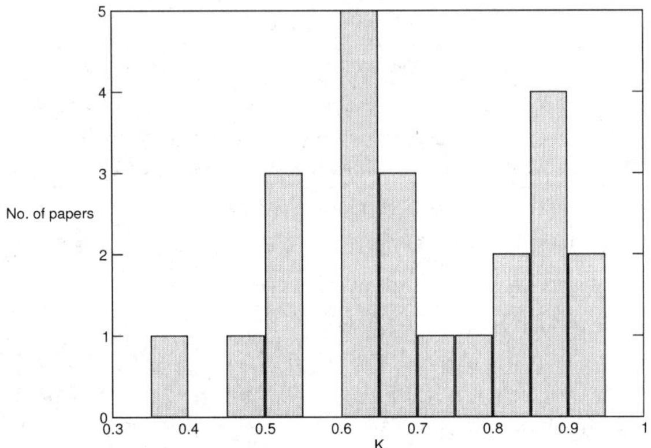

FIGURE 74 Study II: Distribution of Reliability Values.

small a sample to base any firm claims on, the following reliabilities were observed: $\kappa = 0.78$ for student articles, $\kappa = 0.71$ for conference articles, and $\kappa = 0.66$ for workshop articles. Student session articles are shorter and have a simpler structure, with fewer mentions of previous research; this should make them easier to annotate. Main conference articles dedicate more space to describing and criticising other people's work than student or workshop articles do (on average about one quarter of the article). The reason why they are easier to annotate than workshop articles may have to do with the fact that conference articles are prepared more carefully and contain clearer explanations than workshop articles, as they report finished work to a wider audience.

One frequent problem the annotators reported was a difficulty in distinguishing the categories OTHER and OWN. This may be due to an unclear distinction in the text between the new KC and an existing KC by the same authors (a problem I called "zone bleeding" in section 6.4). I hypothesised that articles where self-citations play an important part are more prone to zone bleeding. I therefore split the articles into three groups according to the ratio of self-citations to all citations in the article and measured reliability in each group. Five articles had a ratio of 0 (no self-citations); the remaining articles were divided into two equally sized groups according to their self-citation ratio (the borderline ended up at 18% self-citation ratio).

The results confirm that self-citation ratio is a predictor of overall reliability: reliability in articles without self-citations was $\kappa = 0.74$, in articles with low self-citation rate it was $\kappa = 0.76$, and in articles with high self-citation rate $\kappa = 0.63$. A complete lack of self-citations may well mark the work of less experienced scientists at the beginning of their career, whereas *too many* self-citations might signal zone bleeding. It is clear that articles which cite their own previous work frequently are the most difficult to annotate. At least part of this effect can be attributed to a difficulty in distinguishing the categories OWN and OTHER: Krippendorff's category distinction test between OWN and OTHER showed a higher increase in reliability in the high self-citation group, when compared to the lower self-citation groups. However, there may be other reasons why articles in the low self-citation group are simplest to annotate: they might report on some more isolated piece of research, or be more simply structured for some other reason.

Another persistent problem in some articles was the distinction between OWN and BACKGROUND. This could be a sign that the authors aimed their writing at an expert audience, and thus thought it unnecessary to signal clearly which statements are commonly agreed in the field, as opposed to their own new claims. If an article is written in such a way, understanding it requires a considerable amount of domain knowledge, which the annotators did not necessarily have.

Intuitively, the reasons behind the large variation in reliability between articles are qualitative differences in individual writing style, i.e., how well articles are structured and how clearly they are written. This quality difference was also perceived by the annotators, who commented that writing quality substantially influenced ease of annotation. An interesting experiment for the future would be to compare the reliability results with independent judgements of the writing quality of the articles. Positive results would support the claim that ease of AZ annotation is an indicator of the clarity of scientific argumentation and thus writing quality.

8.4 Study III: Argumentative Zoning, Untrained

Study III is more speculative than Study II, as it uses untrained annotators. It tests whether the semantics of the categories can be conveyed with extremely short guidelines of one page, and without the training phase described in section 7.1. A positive outcome would be a convincing demonstration of the intuitiveness of the categories.

Study III: Method

A different annotator pool from Studies I and II was used, namely 18 subjects without any prior AZ-specific training. All of them have a postgraduate degree in Cognitive Science, with two exceptions: one was a postgraduate student in Sociology of Science, and one holds a Masters degree in English and Spanish Literature. It can be assumed that due to their daily work or studies all subjects were accustomed to reading academic articles.

Three articles (articles 9405013, 9408011 and 9503009) were randomly chosen from the pool of those articles for which the trained annotators had achieved reasonable agreement in Study II ($\kappa \geq 0.65$). Particularly difficult articles were excluded from annotation because the absence of training already makes Study III very speculative, without the added difficulty of using harder articles. One of the three randomly sampled articles had a substantially lower reliability than the other two (article 9405013: $\kappa = 0.85$, N=192, n=7, k=3; article 9408011: $\kappa = 0.67$, N=205, n=7, k=3; article 9503009: $\kappa = 0.87$, N=144, n=7, k=3).

Each annotator was randomly assigned to one of three groups. Each member of a group independently annotated the same single article: Group I annotated article 9405013, Group II article 9408011 and Group III article 9503009. Subjects were given the decision tree in Fig. 56 (p. 188) and the minimal instructions reproduced in Fig. 75.

Study III: Results and Discussion

The results show that reliability varies considerably between groups ($\kappa = 0.49$, N=192, n=7, k=6 for Group I; $\kappa = 0.35$, N=205, n=7, k=6 for Group II; $\kappa = 0.72$, N=144, n=7, k=6 for Group III). As κ is designed to factor out the number of annotators, lower reliability in Study III in comparison to Studies I and II is not an artifact of how κ was calculated.

These results are disappointing, in two respects. With respect to the psychological reality of the AZ categories, the results indicate that the intended semantics of the categories were not intuitive to all naive subjects, at least not on the basis of the very short guidelines. With respect to practical annotation, the results show that a drastic shortening of the training procedure is not a realistic way to reduce the annotation effort.

It is likely that the low reliability is at least partially due to the materials: Group III, which annotated the article found to be most reliable in Study II, performed as well as the trained annotators; Group II, which performed worst, also happened to be assigned to the article with the lowest reliability according to Study II.

However, even in the groups with lower performance, there are pockets of higher agreement. Fig. 76 shows reliability for the most similar three annotators in each group, successively adding the next similar annotator to the pool. The performance between subjects varies

This coding scheme is about the ownership of ideas in scientific articles and about author's stance towards other work. Your intuitions about the structure of this article will be useful input to help build better tools for information extraction from scientific articles, which in turn will improve automatic bibliographic search.

Read the complete article first to get a sense of what it is about. You do not have to understand the details of the article. Then, working from the beginning, annotate each

- sentence in the main body
- sentence in the abstract
- caption of a figure or a table
- figure, table, equation in running text
- example sentence (in linguistics articles)

as one and only one of the seven categories, using the decision tree to make your choice. Try not to leave anything unannotated. If you feel that more than one category applies to one entity, then choose the first one you come to in the decision tree. You should look at the surrounding context when making your choice. Try to annotate from the author's perspective, even if you do not agree with their portrayal of the situation.

When you are done with coding, please put a star next to the one single sentence in the main body of the text (not in the abstract!) that best expresses what the article was about.

Some rules of thumb for assigning the categories:

- Not all articles have all categories.
- OWN, OTHER, BACKGROUND often come in chunks; there are many of them.
- CONTRAST, BASIS, AIM, TEXTUAL often come singly and they are rarer.

FIGURE 75 Study III: Guidelines for Naive Annotators.

much more in Groups I and II than in Group III, where all annotators performed more or less similarly well. Within each group, there is a subgroup of "more similar" annotators. Even in Groups I and II, the three most similar annotators reached respectable reliability ($\kappa = 0.63$, N=192, n=7, k=3 for Group I; $\kappa = 0.5$, N=205, n=7 k=3 for Group II). This result, in combination with the good performance of Group III, seems to point to the fact that the annotators shared at least some understanding of the meaning of the categories.

I found out after the experiment that some part of the low reliability results in Group I and Group II was due to a superficial misunderstanding: several subjects had misinterpreted the semantics of the TEXTUAL category as including sentences that refer to figures and tables in the text. This could easily be rectified in future experiments by more explicit instructions.

The two non-computational linguists in the subject pool performed reasonably well: while neither was in the cluster of most similar anno-

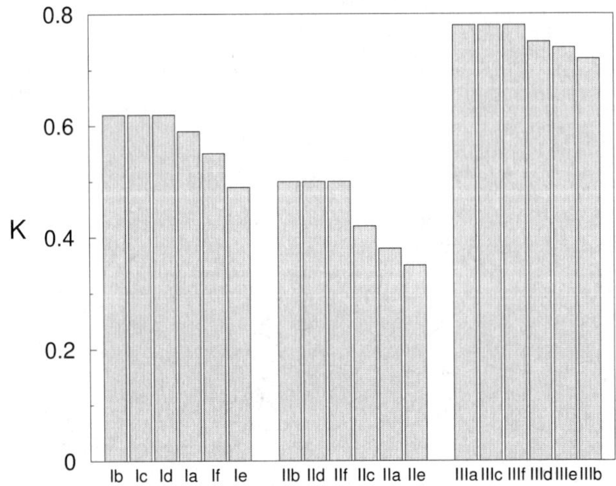

FIGURE 76 Study III: Reliability per Group and per Subject.

tators in their group, neither of them was the least similar annotator of their group either. This is remarkable as the strategy they must have used for Argumentative Zoning could not have involved much discipline-specific knowledge. Their alternative strategies must have been based on factors such as the physical layout, meta-discourse, and possibly the relative order of the individual argumentative moves instead, i.e., at least some of the features discussed in chapter 10. This is of much interest given the hypothesis that shallow features can help both non-experts and systems in the detection of interesting phenomena about structure argumentation, without requiring full text understanding. The possibility of systematic annotation by non-experts is discussed in more detail in chapter 13.

8.5 Study IV: Citation Function Classification (CFC)

The purpose of Study IV is to measure the reliability of the CFC annotation scheme given in Fig. 52, and thus to confirm whether humans can make the distinctions hypothesised in Level 3 of the KCDM. Study IV was performed in early 2006, and results are reported in Teufel et al. (2006b).

To recapitulate, the CFC scheme has 12 categories: one neutral category (NEUT), two categories for neutral comparisons of cited work to the own KC (COCOGM and COCORO), four categories for use, support and intellectual ancestry (PMODI, PSUP, PBAS and PUSE), a category for statements of similarity (PSIM), two categories for criticism and statements of superiority (WEAK and COCO-), a category for the statement that current work is well-motivated (PMOT), and a category for comparisons of two citations with each other (COCOXY).

Study IV: Method

Guideline development used 42 articles chosen at random from the part of CmpLG which is not CmpLG-D (Fig. 8.5). Annotation was performed on 27 different articles, which were chosen at random from the non-CmpLG-D articles deposited between 1995 and 1998. Citations and author names in running text had been previously automatically identified and manually checked; therefore, all units of annotation were correct. The 27 annotation articles contain a total of 100,568 words and 548 citation instances and author names (avg. of 26.8 per article). Stability was not measured.

Type of Material	Articles
Development	9405001 9503015 9504002 9504026 9405002 9503017 9504006 9504027 9405004 9503018 9504007 9504030 9407001 9503023 9504017 9504033 9503014 9503025 9504024 9905008 9905009 9907010 9907013 0001012 0003055 0007035 0008016 0008017 0008020 0008021 0008022 0008023 0008024 0008026 0008029 0008034 0008035 0009027 0010020 0011007 0011020 0102019
Annotation	9505011 9505024 9506017 9508005 9605023 9606028 9606031 9607001 9607019 9702002 9703002 9704002 9704008 9706013 9707009 9711010 9806001 9806019 9807001 9808008 9808009 9808012 9809027 9809106 9809112 9810015 9811009

FIGURE 77 Study IV: Materials.

The three annotators used are the co-developers of the CFC scheme (Advaith Siddharthan as Annotator A, Dan Tidhar as Annotator B and myself as Annotator C). All three are domain experts.

Guidelines of 50 pages were used during annotation. Annotation was entirely independent, as described in section 7.1. A specially developed annotation tool based on XML/XSLT technology was used,[81] which supports the assignment of categories to each citation and uses a standard web browser and dynamic HTML to write the annotator's chosen

[81] This tool was originally written by Jochen Schwarze.

category and an optional comment back into the XML copy of the article. Categories are presented as a pull-down list; mnemonic colours are used which mimic those of the original AZ.

This procedure means that annotators work directly with the SciXML version, which does not encode equations, tables and figures, and so have access to exactly the same document information as will be available to the automatic procedure in chapter 11. This is in contrast to earlier annotation experiments, where annotators had access to more information than the automatic process, because they were working with a printed version of the article.

Study IV: Results and Discussion

The results show that the CFC scheme is reliable (κ = 0.717±0.047, N=548, n=12, k=3).[82] This corresponds to an average Macro-F of 0.62. The fact that reliability for CFC is roughly as high as for AZ is surprising, considering the higher number of categories and the additional difficulties of the task, for instance, the non-local dependencies. However, CFC guideline development was much longer than in earlier studies, resulting in more detailed guidelines. Also, in this study, the guideline developers are the annotators, which might result in higher agreement than if naive subjects had been used.

Pairwise reliability is given in Fig. 78 (left-hand side). The highest agreement occurs between Annotators A and C, and Annotator B seems to annotate noticeably differently from A and C.[83] Therefore, it might be possible to increase the upper bound even beyond the $\kappa = 0.72$ measured here, by detecting specific disagreements of individual annotators and annotator pairs, and by further changes to the guidelines.

	CFC (12 cat.)		**Collapsed CFC (4 cat.)**	
	κ	Macro-F	κ	Macro-F
A–B	0.70±0.07	0.61	0.71±0.08	0.71
A–C	0.76±0.08	0.66	0.79±0.10	0.78
B–C	0.69±0.08	0.58	0.74±0.09	0.72

FIGURE 78 Study IV: Pairwise Agreement between Annotators.

The relative frequency of each category is listed in Fig. 79. As expected, the distribution is very skewed, with 60% of the citations categorised as NEUT. What is interesting is the relatively high fre-

[82] Cohen's κ is 0.7174, whereas Fleiss' κ is 0.7173.

[83] Although there is not enough data to show a statistical difference.

quency of use categories (PUSE, PMODI, PBAS) with a total of 20.9%. Clearly negative citations (WEAK and CCM) are rare at a total of 2.8%, whereas the neutrally–comparative categories (COCOR0, COCOXY, COCOGM) are more frequent at 7.5%. This result is in agreement with earlier annotation experiments (Moravcsik and Murugesan, 1975, Spiegel-Rösing, 1977). For instance, the category in Spiegel-Rösing's scheme most closely corresponding to NEUT (category 8; "substantiating statements") was even more frequent in her corpus (80%). Nevertheless, the fact that six categories have a frequency of around or lower than 1% can be expected to create difficulties for machine learning.

Category	%	Category	%	Category	%
NEUT	60.0	PMOT	3.0	COCO-	0.9
PUSE	19.2	WEAK	1.9	PSUP	0.7
COCOGM	5.5	COCOR0	1.5	PMODI	0.5
PSIM	5.1	PBAS	1.2	COCOXY	0.5

FIGURE 79 Study IV: Frequencies of CFC Categories.

The hierarchical nature of the CFC annotation scheme (see the decision tree in Fig. 53 on p. 180) allows for alternative coarser-grained distinctions between categories. We can for instance use sentiment (question **Q1** in the tree) to distinguish four categories: NEUTRAL, POSITIVE, COMPARATIVE and NEGATIVE. This coarser (collapsed) scheme has a reliability of $\kappa = 0.746 \pm 0.05$ (N=548, n=4, k=3) and an average pairwise Macro-F of 0.74. The increase in reliability could however not be shown to be significant: there is still not enough annotated data because there are so few CFC data points per article. The right-hand side of Fig. 78 shows pairwise reliability results for the collapsed scheme. Fig. 80 gives the confusion matrix between Annotators A and C for the collapsed scheme.

		A				
		NEG.	POS.	COMPAR.	NEUTRAL	**Total**
C	NEGATIVE	**9**	1	7	5	**22**
	POSITIVE	0	**140**	1	12	**153**
	COMPAR.	0	3	**38**	0	**41**
	NEUTRAL	4	27	5	**296**	**332**
	Total	**13**	**171**	**51**	**313**	**548**

FIGURE 80 Study IV: Confusion Matrix for Annotators A and C, Collapsed Scheme.

I also performed Krippendorff's diagnostic for category distinction, first for the full scheme. The results are given in Fig. 81 (all are κ with N=548, n=2, k=3); they show that five categories have reliability greater than the overall reliability and are thus well distinguished: Neut, PMot, CoCoGM, PUse and CoCoR0. It is advantageous that Neut is one of these, because this shows that the annotators agree whether a hinge was associated with a citation (and thus, indirectly, with a knowledge claim). The determination of citation function is a core aspect of the discourse model in chapter 6. It is also similar in spirit to the detection of sentiment around a category, and for this task we have seen in section 6.5 that the detection of subjectivity vs. objectivity (i.e., whether or not sentiment is present) is often harder than the decision which sentiment is present.

Category	κ	**Category**	κ	**Category**	κ
PMot	0.79	Neut	0.74	Weak	0.52
CoCoGM	0.77	PSim	0.65	CoCo-	0.46
PUse	0.76	PModi	0.55	PBas	0.41
CoCoR0	0.75	CoCoXY	0.55	PSup	0.27

FIGURE 81 Study IV: Krippendorff's Diagnostics for Category Distinction.

Out of the other categories which are easily distinguished, the most important is PUse, due to its relatively high frequency. For the characterisation of an article in an information management scenario, the detection of comparative citation function (CoCoGM, CoCoR0) is also highly relevant.

Confidence intervals are not shown in Fig. 81 because they are large for most categories. PUse and Neut are an exception in that they are significantly above Krippendorff's cutoff for marginally reliable annotation ($\kappa = 0.67$), although not significantly above the overall reliability value ($\kappa = 0.72$).

Let us now look at the categories which fall below the average of $\kappa = 0.72$. The first observation is that all of these are rare categories (Weak with 1.9% is the most frequent of these). PSup is the least distinctive category, with a reliability which is close to random at $\kappa = 0.27$. This category should be defined further in the future, because its semantics should in principle be quite intuitive. Also, although it is rare, it can provide valuable information for information management. The other categories below average distinctiveness are PModi ($\kappa = 0.55$) and PBas ($\kappa = 0.41$). These are obviously harder categories than PUse, i.e., simple unchanged use. The semantics of PModi has an aspect of criticism, which makes annotation more ambiguous. The semantics of PBAS might require sociological judgement from the annotator, because it concerns statements of intellectual ancestry with published work. To increase agreement, these categories could straightforwardly be merged into PUSE (and this has happened in the AZ-II annotation scheme to be presented in section 13.1.2).

The negative categories WEAK and COCO- are amongst the least distinctive categories. This is an effect we have also seen in connection with the AZ category CONTRAST. There are sociological reasons that speak against clearly negative citations; MacRoberts and MacRoberts (1984) discuss the measures authors might take to mask such cases and give an explanation for this phenomenon (see section 6.5).

Another concept which seems difficult to distinguish is COCOXY. Here, two knowledge claims are compared, neither of which is the article's new one. I have discussed possible practical applications which exploit COCOXY in section 7.3, most of which have to do with the special case of evaluation articles. But as the semantics of COCOXY is peripheral to the KCDM and the message of this book, it could easily be given up if problems with its definition persist.

For the collapsed scheme, Krippendorff's diagnostics result in the following reliabilities for the four categories: $\kappa = 0.74 \pm 0.05$ (NEUTRAL); $\kappa = 0.74 \pm 0.16$ (COMPARATIVE); $\kappa = 0.50 \pm 0.28$ (NEGATIVE); and $\kappa = 0.79 \pm 0.06$ (POSITIVE). This means that the NEGATIVE category remains problematic, whereas the POSITIVE category is now well distinguishable.

In sum, we have seen that CFC annotation is overall acceptably reliable and shows good reliability on some categories. The annotated material is probably still too small to perform as extensive an analysis as for Study II. Nevertheless, what the four reliability studies taken together show is that key elements of the KCDM can be taught to human annotators, who can then demonstrate their understanding of the categories in terms of practical annotation.

After positive reliability results, an annotation project typically goes into single-annotation production mode. This has happened here too, following the common assumption in the field that acceptable reliability implies usability as training material for supervised learning. This assumption has however recently been challenged by Reidsma and Carletta (2008). Using different artificially generated types of noise in the disagreements between annotators (random vs. systematic), they showed that systematic divergence of one annotator from the truth will be picked up by machine learners, which is problematic. This can happen even if κ is as high as 0.8.

However, Reidsma and Carletta admit that it is difficult to assess whether there is a systematic divergence from the truth. Their suggestion is to run an association test between the labels of two annotators, using only the items where there is disagreement. Neither Bayerl and Paul's (2007), Wiebe et al.'s (1999) nor Krippendorff's (1980) techniques for troubleshooting disagreements is designed to detect systematic annotation bias. These papers recommend the development of additional diagnostics for patterns in annotator disagreements to be used by the CL community.

The near-identical values of Cohen's κ and Fleiss' κ in the studies just reported can be interpreted as an indication that the difference in annotator bias in our data is not strong (Artstein and Poesio, 2008), but this still does not preclude one annotator's systematic deviations from the truth.

Production mode annotation for KCA and AZ resulted in annotation of the entire CmpLG-D corpus (80 articles), done by one annotator (myself). Production mode annotation for CFC resulted in annotation of a subpart of CmpLG (116 articles, 2829 citations), shared between 3 annotators (the three guideline developers Advaith Siddharthan, Dan Tidhar and myself). This material was randomly drawn from the part of CmpLG which was not used for CFC human annotation, for CFC guideline development or CFC cue phrase development.

While the main purpose of the production mode annotation is to provide the training material for the system in chapter 11, it also enables the exploration of corpus characteristics. I will do this in the next section, using Argumentative Zoning as the test case.

8.6 Post-Hoc Analyses of Study II Data

The purpose of the post-analyses is to investigate the AZ-structure of the annotated articles quantitatively, and to verify or disprove various hypotheses I made about rhetorical structure in chapter 6. While I mostly use the 80 singly-annotated articles of CmpLG-D, some questions require a comparison of reliability values. In those cases, the 23 three-way-annotated articles from Study II are used.

Full Texts

Fig. 82 reports the frequency distribution over categories in CmpLG-D (80 articles), as found by one annotator (left-hand side of figure), in comparison to the one derived in Study II by three annotators on 23 articles (repeated from Fig. 69). The distributions are overall similar, but the frequencies of the rare categories Textual, Aim and Basis have changed ranks.

	Study II (k=3)		Prod. (k=1)	
	Sentences		Sentences	
OWN	7614	73.6%	8433	67.8%
OTHER	1426	13.8%	2013	16.2%
BACKGROUND	484	4.7%	720	5.7%
CONTRAST	414	4.0%	597	4.8%
AIM	205	2.0%	209	1.6%
BASIS	112	1.1%	223	1.7%
TEXTUAL	92	0.9%	227	1.8%
	12422	100.0%	10347	100.0%

FIGURE 82 AZ Category Frequencies: Study II vs. Production Mode.

Let us now look at AZ zones. The 80 articles contain 2184 AZ zones, an average of 27.3 per article. Fig. 83 shows how the number of zones is distributed across articles. Most articles contain between 15 and 39 zones, but there are extremes: two articles contain 9 zones or fewer, and one contains over 60.

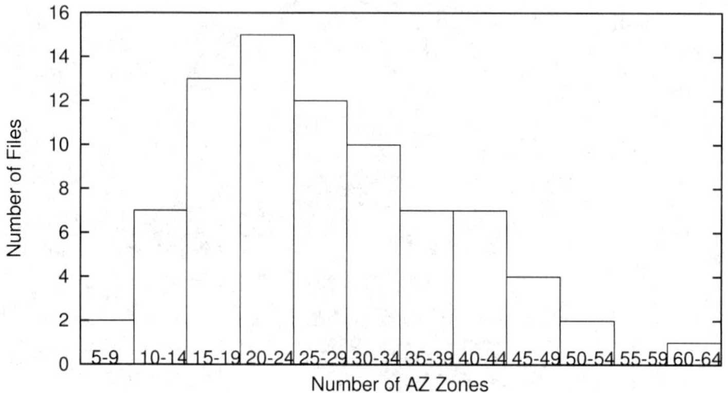

FIGURE 83 Number of Argumentative Zones per Article (CmpLG-D).

Fig. 84 shows how zone number and zone length are distributed across categories. The average AZ zone is 5.7 sentences long. As expected, move-based zones (AIM, TEXTUAL, CONTRAST and BASIS) are shorter than segment-based zones (OWN, OTHER and BACKGROUND). The longest zones on average are OWN zones (12.8 sentences), whereas the shortest ones are BASIS zones (1.12 sentences).

Number of zones does not separate move- and segment-based AZ categories, as frequency did: there are more BASIS and CONTRAST zones

	No. of Zones		Zone Length
	Total	Avg. per article	Avg., in sentences
Own	660 (30.2%)	8.24	12.80
Other	440 (20.1%)	5.50	4.54
Contrast	349 (15.9%)	4.36	1.65
Basis	215 (9.8%)	2.68	1.12
Background	187 (8.5%)	2.37	4.07
Aim	186 (8.5%)	2.33	1.28
Textual	147 (6.7%)	1.83	1.63
Total	**2184 (100.0%)**	**27.30**	**5.70**

FIGURE 84 Number of Zones and Zone Length, per AZ Category.

than there are Background zones. This of course is related to the fact that each individual Background zone is relatively long. Analogously, only 30% of all zones in the corpus are Own, as can be seen from Fig. 84; but Fig. 82 tells us that these contain 68% of all sentences in the corpus.

The least frequent zone is Textual (6.7%). In fact, only 59 documents contain any Textual zones at all. This may be due to the relative shortness of the articles, which makes presentational aids such as sign-post sentences less necessary. Similarly, 20% of all documents do not contain any Basis sentences. While the lack of Textual may be a matter of personal writing style, the lack of Basis is probably more to do with the type of research performed. Other categories have better coverage: every document, apart from three documents, contains at least one Contrast sentence, and every document contains at least one Aim sentence (but note that the guidelines explicitly require this).

Let us now turn to various hypotheses I have raised so far in this book, and see if the AZ-annotated data can help us validate or disprove them:

1. Most articles start with background material (CARS and section 6.4).
2. Many Textual segments are article overviews (section 6.6).
3. The pattern Contrast–Aim is a frequent motivation strategy (CARS and section 6.3).
4. Textual separation of citations and hinges is a frequent phenomenon (sections 4.2 and 6.5).
5. In section 6.5 I speculated that Contrast zones should be longer than Basis zones, as many Basis zones only acknowledge the use of somebody's data or method.

6. Contrast and Basis behave similarly in citation blocks (cases **a** and **b** in Fig. 38).
7. Isolated neutral citations, i.e., those where no hinge is expressed at all (case **e** in Fig. 38), should be rare, and they should be less important in the context of the article.
8. Authors often dissemble: in order to soften criticism, they also praise, with the criticism usually coming last (MacRoberts and MacRoberts, 1984, and my observations in section 6.5).
9. Basis sentences and Contrast sentences can both occur in Own segments, but Basis sentences occur in the *Method* section, whereas Contrast sentences occur in the *Result* section (Fig. 39).

I will now address these hypotheses in turn.

1: The most likely first zone in an article should be a Background. Overall, this is true: 56 articles start with a Background zone (71%), 13 with an Other zone (16%), 9 with an Aim (11%), and one with Own and Basis respectively (1%). There are 131 Background zones which do not occur as the first zone in the article, but these are on average shorter (3.7 sentences) than the ones that do start the article (4.9 sentences).

I also predicted that in a typical document, Other will often follow after article-initial Background. This is the case in 30 out of the 56 cases of article-initial Background (54%). This proportion falls to 40% (74 out of 187) if we consider all Background zones, not just article-initial ones.

2: How many of the Textual zones are section overviews (P-2), as opposed to section summaries (P-4) or previews (P-3)? 83 (37%) of the 227 Textual sentences occur in the *first* Textual zone in the document. Out of the 49 articles which contain both a section entitled *Introduction* and a Textual zone, 36 (73%) have a Textual zone in the introduction. This Textual zone is on average longer than the overall average Textual zone (2.03 vs. 1.63 sentences). The position at the end of the introduction seems prominent: out of the 36 documents with a Textual zone in the introduction, in 23 (64%) it occurs as the last zone in the introduction, i.e., is likely to be of type P-2.

3: Both the cars model (Swales, 1990) and the KCDM (chapter 6) predict that the pattern Contrast–Aim (contrastive introduction of specific research goal) should be frequent in introduction sections. But out of the 63 sections titled *Introduction*, 14 (22%) do not even contain an Aim zone at all, i.e., cars would not describe them well. Of the ones that do, only 28 out of 79 (35%) first Aim zones are directly preceded by a CONTRAST zone, and only 28 of the 75 first CONTRAST zones (38%) are directly followed by AIM. These numbers show that the CONTRAST–AIM pattern is less likely than expected, at least in direct succession.

4: In section 6.5 I also made several predictions with respect to textual separation in citation blocks. For instance, separation should occur more frequently between a contrastive statement and its corresponding citation, than between a continuation statement and its citation. Indeed, I found that BASIS statements co-occur far more often in the same sentence as their citation than CONTRAST statements do: 69% of BASIS sentences contain the corresponding citation, but only 21% of CONTRAST sentences. One would additionally like to compare the distance between CONTRAST sentences and their citations, to that between BASIS sentences and theirs, but this would require an annotation of the association between each citation and its corresponding hinge (if any), which does not yet exist.

5: The data in Fig. 84 straightforwardly confirms that X CONTRAST zones are indeed overall longer than BASIS zones (1.12 vs. 1.65 sentences). Their communicative function is very different, and the function of BASIS zones is often to succinctly state whose methods have been used, which can be in many cases be done in a sentence or less. CONTRAST zones often include a more complicated description of a contrast or a problem.

6: My model of a citation block expects hinge statements to occur adjacent to neutral descriptions of the knowledge claim (OTHER zones). There are 440 OTHER zones, and 199 of these are followed by a CONTRAST zone. This creates pattern **a** from Fig. 38 (p. 140), the most frequently observed citation context. There are only 108 cases of pattern **c**, where the evaluation precedes an OTHER zone. I suspect however that this number might be an overestimation due to unrelated citations in the vicinity.

OTHER zones are less frequently followed by a BASIS zone (39 times) than they are followed by a CONTRAST zone (199 times). Unexpectedly, in the case of BASIS, the pattern BASIS–OTHER is more frequent that the OTHER–BASIS pattern (49 times vs. 39 times). This could have to do with the fact that BASIS zones are generally shorter and often contain their relative citation in the same sentence, thus not requiring a neighbouring OTHER zone at all. Therefore, many of the OTHER zones in the vicinity may not be related to the statement in the BASIS sentence.

The existence of unrelated citations makes all of these estimates approximate. More definitive answers would again require a case-by-case annotation of the association between a hinge and its corresponding citation.

7: OTHER zones can also occur without a hinge, i.e., the existing KC is mentioned without any statement about how it relates to the article's new KC. This corresponds to case **e** in Fig. 39 on p. 141. Out of the 440 OTHER cases, 131 (30%) were neither preceded nor followed by either a BASIS or a CONTRAST zone. The first observation is therefore that such cases are not really rare.

I have also posited that unconnected OTHER zones should overall be less important for the argumentation of an article. If my other speculation is true, namely that there is a correlation between the length of a citation context and its importance, then stand-alone OTHER zones should be shorter than other OTHER zones. However, this is not the case: at 5.5 sentences they are *longer* than the average OTHER zone length of 4.5 sentences, counter to hypothesis. Several things could be at fault: the estimation uses only direct zone neighbourhood and does not allow for the possibility that the evaluation statement belonging to a (seemingly stand–alone) OTHER zone is nearby, but not directly adjacent. It could also be that OTHER zone importance and zone length are not correlated. More analysis of this is clearly required, e.g., in the form of the annotation of association between hinges and citations.

8:. If we are looking for evidence for MacRoberts' and MacRoberts' (1984) hypothesis that authors dissemble ("meek criticism" effect; see section 6.5), we might search for BASIS–CONTRAST patterns. There are 10 BASIS–CONTRAST patterns in the corpus, which are however offset by 11 CONTRAST–BASIS patterns. Although it cannot be empirically confirmed by direct zone adjacency, the annotators informally confirmed that they noticed the BASIS–CONTRAST pattern during annotation.

The granularity of AZ-annotation seems too coarse to show up this pattern. In the cases where both CONTRAST and BASIS occur in the same sentence, the BASIS aspect would not have been annotated because it is "overwritten" by CONTRAST. The granularity of CFC annotation, which only has one annotatable item per citation mention, is even coarser. However, the current annotation is a good starting point for a finer-grained re-annotation of the meek criticism effect, because annotation could start from CONTRAST contexts.

9: I have predicted in section 6.5 that hinges embedded in OWN zones are more likely to be of type BASIS than CONTRAST. Indeed, 89 OWN–BASIS–OWN patterns were found, as opposed to 68 OWN–CONTRAST–OWN patterns. This holds even though the overall number of CONTRAST zones is much higher than the number of BASIS zones

(349 as opposed to 215), pointing strongly to the fact that comparisons within Own segments are less typical than statements of use/import of other solutions (pattern **f** versus **g** in Fig. 39).

In sum, the structural evidence reported here could confirm some of the predictions of the KCDM from chapter 6. More informative evidence could be provided if associations between citations and their hinge statements were annotated.

Abstracts

The annotated material also allows us to examine the structure of the author abstracts in CmpLG-D in terms of AZ zones. Section 5.1.2 has described how the author abstracts were created (by authors rather than by professional abstractors), which has a negative impact on their structuring, as I informally observed. Empirically, I found 40 different patterns of AZ zones in the 80 articles. 28 of these were unique; Fig. 85 lists all non-unique sequences. Only one pattern is frequent (Aim–Own; the main goal of the article, followed by more detailed information about the solution), which occurs 23 times. All other sequences occur 3 times or less. This is in contrast to Liddy's (1991) observations with professional abstractors reported in section 3.1.2, and more in line with the findings of Salager-Meyer (1992), Froom and Froom (1993) and Orasan (2000), who all found deviation from the ANSI model in abstracts.

Zone Sequence	**Freq.**
Aim – Own	23
Background – Aim – Own	6
Other – Aim– Own	3
Aim – Contrast – Own	3
Other – Contrast – Aim	3
Other – Aim	2
Aim – Own – Contrast	2
Aim – Own – Aim	2
Aim – Own – Basis – Own	2
Background – Contrast – Aim – Own	2
Own – Aim – Own	2
Background – Aim	2

FIGURE 85 Most Frequent Sequences of AZ Categories in Abstracts.

All but one abstract contain at least one AIM sentence. As for the combination AIM–OWN, 29% of the abstracts in CmpLG-D consist entirely of this pattern, and 73% contain it in direct sequence. The success of a scientific article depends on a clear establishment of the knowledge claim at the earliest point of contact with the reader, and this is exactly what the sequence AIM–OWN does. The abstract's communicative function might also explain the low frequency of zones referring to other researchers' work.

Another interesting phenomenon is the number of zones contained in abstracts, see Fig. 86. The average is 2.95 zones per abstract; most abstracts contain only 2 or 3 argumentative zones. This is another reason against the alignment-based shortcut discussed in section 7.5, i.e., the idea to build rhetorical extracts by alignment of abstract sentences in the style of Kupiec et al. (1995). As the abstracts are short and their category distribution is strongly skewed, the method is unlikely to produce enough training material for all categories. In addition, alignment in CmpLG is low (see section 5.1.2).

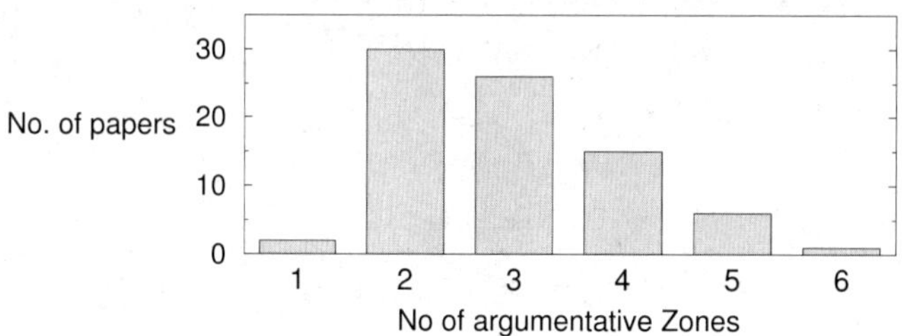

FIGURE 86 Distribution of Number of AZ Categories in Abstracts.

To summarise, even though the information contained in author abstracts is most certainly *relevant* in some sense, there are large individual differences and preference with respect to what kind of rhetorical information the CmpLG abstracts contain. What we know is that the abstracts will contain at least one AIM sentence, which is most likely followed by OWN material. This is reminiscent of the 60% non-classifiable material that Tibbo (1992) found in history abstracts.

Other article divisions

I have argued in section 8.6 that one might want to restrict AZ-annotation to the abstract, the introduction and the conclusions, or a combination of these, in order to try to reduce the cost of annotation. As any selective annotation will reduce the number of annotated sentences per article in the training material, there is a danger that this would result in too few training examples for some AZ categories, something that is known to affect supervised machine learning performance negatively. I will therefore first look at the distribution of all categories over special areas in the entire CmpLG-D, in order to assess whether enough examples of the rare categories would be found for machine learning. For this, I will use the 80 singly annotated articles. I will then assess how reduction of annotation effort to these special areas would affect reliability, for which I will use the 23 three-way-annotated articles.

The special areas considered are introduction sections, conclusion sections, abstracts, the set of abstract-aligned document sentences, and the first $\frac{1}{5}$ and $\frac{1}{10}$ and the last $\frac{1}{10}$ and $\frac{1}{20}$ of sentences in the document. The fixed cutoffs (such as the first $\frac{1}{10}$ of sentences) approximate introduction and conclusion sections for those articles which do not contain explicit rhetorical sections. In the following figures, sections entitled *Motivation*, *Background* or *Summary* are treated as if they were called *Introduction* or *Conclusions*, respectively.[84]

	Textual	Basis	Contrast	Aim	**Total**
Document	207	230	622	286	**1345**
Introduction	89	45	181	88	**403**
First 1/10	46	33	153	70	**302**
First 1/5	100	68	251	102	**521**
Middle	101	118	258	24	**501**
Conclusion	3	13	38	57	**111**
Last 1/10	6	37	85	59	**187**
Last 1/20	3	23	54	54	**134**
Abstract	0	7	28	101	**136**
Abstract-Aligned	3	11	15	51	**80**
Total	**558**	**585**	**1685**	**892**	**3720**

FIGURE 87 Frequency of AZ Categories in Various Article Divisions.

Fig. 87 lists the distribution of AZ categories in various special areas in the document. On the basis of this data, Fig. 88 shows the proportion of AZ categories found in each area, whereas Fig. 89 conversely shows for each category which areas it is likely to come from.

[84] In the absence of a marked *Conclusion* section, *Discussion* sections are still not treated as conclusion sections, as discussion sections contain more speculative material.

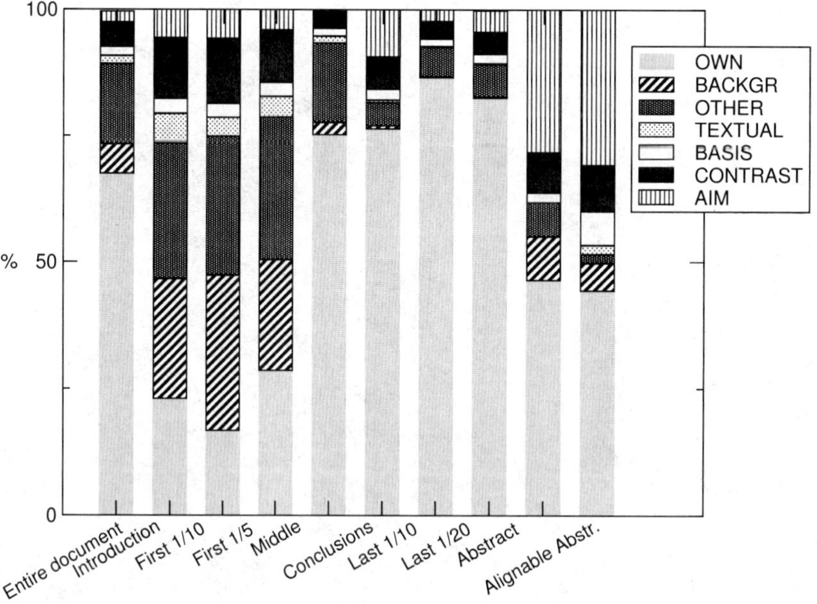

FIGURE 88 Areas by AZ Categories.

We see that some areas do not even contain all categories. For instance, conclusions mainly consist of OWN sentences, with occasional AIM and CONTRAST sentences. This is due to the fact that this section does not provide information about the method (which is assumed to be known by now), but serves to highlight own contribution, relevance of results, limitations, future work, and advantages over rival approaches. This mixture of categories might be enough for some tasks, but probably not for the ones introduced in chapter 4.

As far as abstracts are concerned, the percentage of BACKGROUND, BASIS and TEXTUAL sentences is low, although the relatively high proportion of AIM sentences found in abstracts would be advantageous for some aspects of the downstream tasks. However, even if one considered annotating conclusions and abstract together, BACKGROUND, BASIS and TEXTUAL would still end up being very infrequent. The introduction section, in contrast, contains a good distribution of all four move-based categories, making it a prime candidate for annotation reduction.

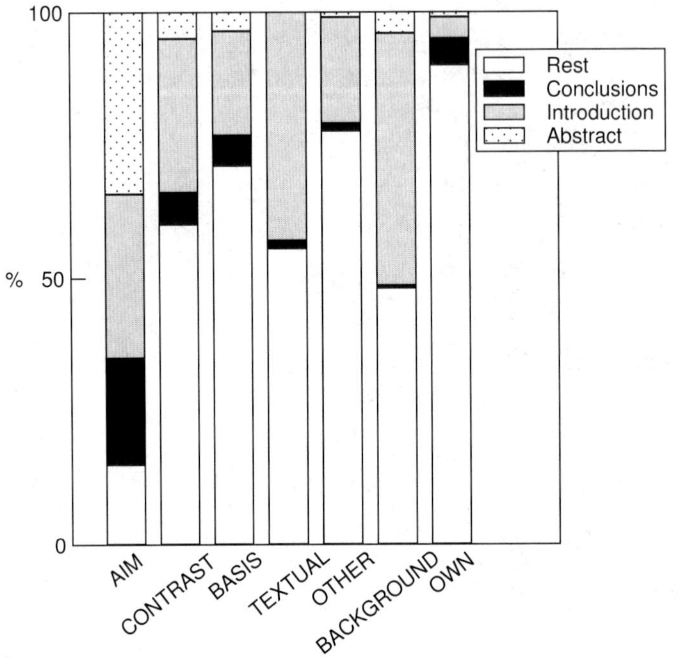

FIGURE 89 AZ Categories by Areas.

Let us now see how the different strategies of annotation reduction affect reliability. Higher than average reliability in an area is likely to also correspond to higher annotation speed, and should thus recommend the area for annotation reduction. Fig. 90 shows that annotation reliability is increased in conclusion sections ($\kappa = 0.85$) and in abstracts ($\kappa = 0.80$). Those two sections have the clearest summarisation function of the article, and in general, authors seem to manage to make their own contributions clear in these sections.

All other areas show reduced or average reliability when compared to the average reliability in the entire article. Disappointingly, the introduction section (which shows the best variety in terms of argumentative categories) also shows a slight decrease in reliability. Location approximations, both at the beginning and the end of the article, perform particularly badly, e.g., the last $\frac{1}{10}$ has a reliability of only $\kappa = 0.61$. This means that the last few lines in articles that are not explicitly

Area	κ
Document	0.71
Introduction	0.69
First 1/10	0.66
First 1/5	0.70
Conclusion	0.85
Last 1/10	0.61
Last 1/20	0.63
Abstract	0.80
Abstract-Aligned	0.68

FIGURE 90 Reliability by Areas.

marked as a conclusion section do not normally contain conclusion-type material and should be avoided as an approximation.

A compromise between efficiency and annotation quality might be to annotate abstracts, introductions and conclusions where available, and first and last paragraphs only as a fallback option. The price to be paid for the increase in annotation speed is the loss of all annotated material occurring in the large area marked "Middle" or "Rest" (white zones in Fig. 89). BASIS is the category that would be most badly affected by this, losing almost two thirds of its sentences, closely followed by CONTRAST and TEXTUAL. Only the AIM category would retain most of its sentences.

When deciding whether or not to use an annotation shortcut, one consideration should be whether the articles in one's corpus display enough textual redundancy with respect to the important AZ categories. Good writing style and professional editing will mean that the important material from the middle of the document is reiterated in the periphery; if this is consistently the case, one might be able to use annotation shortcuts without much loss of information at all. In the CmpLG, however, there are known anomalies with respect to textual redundancy, e.g., the tendency to "misuse" the abstract as an introduction (see section 5.1.2). This means that shortcuts would be a risky strategy.

In summary, it is possible to reduce the annotation effort by restricting the annotation to certain areas within an article, at the price of somewhat reduced quality of the training material. One could restrict the annotation to sentences appearing in the introduction section, even though annotators will find them harder to classify, or to the conclusion section, even though this will restrict the range of AZ categories covered. It is in the context of a practical application that the advantages and disadvantages of such a strategy have to be weighed against each other.

Chapter Summary

This chapter reports how reliably humans can perform annotation with the three annotation schemes from chapter 7. Section 8.1 introduces metrics, ceilings and baselines for measuring and comparing human agreement. In sections 8.2 to 8.5, four reliability studies are reported. Study I shows that the KCA annotation scheme, which distinguishes sentences on the basis of knowledge claim attribution, is particularly reliable, both between annotators ($\kappa = 0.78$) and at different points in time with the same annotators ($\kappa = 0.82$, 0.78, 0.85). This confirms a high level of "truth" or "learnability" behind the idea of knowledge claim attribution. As KCA is an integral part of the discourse model, this is an important result.

Studies II and III concern Argumentative Zoning. Study II demonstrates that the AZ annotation scheme can indeed be learned by trained annotators and subsequently applied in a consistent way, across annotators and across time ($\kappa = 0.71$ reliability; $\kappa = 0.81, 0.81, 0.74$ stability). AIM and TEXTUAL are overall annotated more reliably than BASIS and CONTRAST. While Study III tentatively confirms some element of intuitiveness of the scheme by employing untrained annotators, it shows that Argumentative Zoning is too complex a task to be performed consistently without any training. In particular, Study III shows that very short annotation instructions do not provide enough information for reliable AZ annotation.

Study IV is concerned with citation function classification (CFC), for which a reliability of $\kappa = 0.72$ is achieved. The negative categories are found to be the hardest to annotate. However, CFC is possibly more complex than AZ; for instance, the guidelines for CFC are far more elaborate than those for KCA and AZ.

Section 8.6 then reports the results of post-hoc analyses of a corpus of 80 AZ-annotated articles. Properties of AZ zones are examined in different article sections: in the entire article, in the abstract and in various other article sections. Several predictions about shallow order effects in AZ-based discourse structure from chapter 6 are empirically confirmed, e.g., that BASIS sentences are more likely to contain their corresponding citation than CONTRAST sentences, and that the abstracts in CmpLG-D are particularly heterogeneously structured.

Section 8.6 also discusses some alternative annotation strategies for cases when full annotation is too costly. There are only two areas in the article where the reliability of annotation is higher than average reliability for the entire article: the abstract and the conclusion section.

In sum, this chapter has provided the first part of the justification for the KCDM, the discourse model introduced in chapter 6. Using the three annotation schemes described in chapter 7, I have shown that independent human annotators agree on the occurrence of many of the phenomena described by the discourse model in naturally occurring texts.

Let us now turn to the second piece of evidence for the KCDM: can the analysis be simulated automatically, and can the result be used for information management? Chapters 11 and 12 will address these questions, respectively. Supervised machine learning is used for the recognition of the KCDM. But before we turn to these experiments, we must talk about features, superficial textual cues which are associated with various aspects of the discourse model and which will be used in the automatic classification. The automatic determination of these features is a prerequisite for the supervised machine learning experiments. How the features are defined is the topic of chapter 10.

The most sophisticated features used in this book are those that model meta-discourse. Meta-discourse is an important enough concept in the framework of this book to deserve its own chapter, the following chapter 9. After a description of how meta-discourse is used for recognition in my approach, chapter 10 will describe the practical implementation of all features.

9

Meta-Discourse

Chapter 8 has presented evidence that the KCDM-based annotation schemes are intuitive and learnable. Automation of the annotation is the other experimental goal of this work, which we turn to now.

The current chapter is concerned with *meta-discourse*, which is one of the most important features for the recognition of KCA, CFC and AZ. It is a pragmatic concept well-studied in applied linguistics (Hyland, 1998b, Myers, 1992). Meta-discourse is generally defined as those pieces of text which do not convey pure propositional content, but have other functions, for instance to signal the author's communicative or presentational intention. Scientific meta-discourse mostly occurs in the form of highly conventionalised expressions, e.g., "*we present original work...*", or "*An ANOVA analysis revealed a marginal interaction/a main effect of...*". The name meta-discourse captures the fact that the statements concern the discourse between the author and the reader, rather than about the science contained in the article, i.e., what I have earlier called the *object level.*

Looking at the linguistic form of the various rhetorical moves introduced in chapter 6, we see that they often contain phrases such as the following bold faced ones:

> **P-1:** ***We have demonstrated*** *that a general divisive clustering procedure for probability distributions can be used to group words according to their participation in particular grammatical relations with other words.* (9408011, S-164)

> **P-1:** ***In this study we report*** *the synthesis of a new class of biomolecular probe called a SERRS Beacon, which uses the detection technique of surface enhanced resonance Raman scattering, SERRS.* (b506219e)

> **P-1:** ***Here we propose*** *surface enhanced resonance Raman scattering (SERRS) as an alternative spectroscopy for detection.* (b311589e)

Such meta-discourse phrases are the topic of this chapter.

Category	Function	Examples
	Textual meta-discourse	
Logical connectives	express semantic relation between main clauses	*in addition; but; therefore; thus*
Code glosses	help readers grasp meanings of ideational material	*namely; eg; in other words*
Endophoric markers	refer to information in other parts of the text	*noted above; see Fig 1; below*
Frame markers	refer to discourse acts or text stages	*to repeat; our aim here; finally*
Evidentials	refer to source of information from other texts	*according to X; Y (1990)*
	Interpersonal meta-discourse	
Hedges	withhold author's full commitment to statements	*might; perhaps; it is possible*
Emphatics	emphasize force or author's certainty in message	*in fact; definitely; it is clear; obvious*
Relational markers	explicitly refer to or build relationship with reader	*frankly; note that; you can see*
Attitude markers	express author's attitude to propositional content	*surprisingly; I agree; X claims*
Person markers	explicit reference to author(s)	*I; we; my; mine; our*

FIGURE 91 Hyland's (1998b) Meta-Discourse Categories.

Hyland (1998b) classifies scientific meta-discourse (see Fig. 91) on the basis of a study in four disciplines (biology, astrophysics, marketing and applied linguistics). He mainly distinguishes between textual meta-discourse (where the communicative goal is to organise and convey the text structure to the reader) and interpersonal discourse (where the communicative goal is to signal the author's viewpoint to the reader).

Textual meta-discourse is concerned with rather "low-level" phenomena, such as logical connectives (*"but"*, *"thus"*), code glosses ("*in other words*"), endophoric markers ("*see Fig. 1*"), frame markers ("*our aim here*") and evidentials ("*according to Chomsky*"). Interpersonal meta-discourse is split into hedges (*"possible"*, *"might"*), emphatics ("*it is clear*"), relational markers ("*note that*"), attitude markers (*"surprisingly"*) and person markers (*"I"*).

Hyland's findings are that scientific meta-discourse is ubiquitous: on average, a meta-discourse phrase occurred after every 15 words in running text, hedges being the most frequent type. Hedges have been mentioned in section 3.1.2; they are a pragmatic construct with which authors distance themselves from a scientific statement (Salager-Meyer, 1994). Hyland (1998a) observes that hedges soften scientific claims and thus help gain communal acceptance for new publications.

Another factor is that meta-discourse often contains indicators of "here"-ness, as observed by Myers (1992). Two of the examples on p. 253 contain such indicators, namely "*in this paper*" and "*here*".

Orasan (2000) investigates meta-discourse phrases containing "*this paper*" and variations thereof. For instance, he finds "*paper*" 473 times in 917 abstracts from different disciplines,[85] "*study*" (used as a noun) 170 times, "*research*" 154 times and "*work*" 111 times. Fig. 92 shows the most frequent n-grams from Orasan's corpus after stemming. One can immediately recognise meaningful indicators such as "*in this paper we*". Apart from a few domain-dependent expressions ("*the world wide web*"), the phrases are general and should apply across disciplines. This is a good property for the kinds of uses I want to put meta-discourse to in this book.

Meta-discourse, which is defined as the exclusion set of statements about the object level, has a natural fit with the KCDM, a model that carefully avoids representing anything about the object level.

The main role of scientific meta-discourse in my approach will be in the automatic recognition phase, but the association of meta-discourse with rhetorical moves is also theoretically interesting: it could potentially be of help in the long-term task of an automatic representation and interpretation of the semantics of the moves.

Out of Hyland's categories, interpersonal meta-discourse is of most interest to me, because it is closely related to entity and action-based meta-discourse. In particular, I will use attitude markers, evidentials, and person markers. For instance, all boldfaced phrases in the examples on p. 253 contain the person marker *we*.

9.1 Actions/States

A point of departure from previous descriptions of meta-discourse is the fact that actions and states play a central role in my definition of scientific meta-discourse.

---

[85] More than half of Orasan's articles came from the area of artificial intelligence. The rest is split between other areas of computer science, biology, medicine, linguistics, chemistry, and anthropology.

3-grams		4-grams	
143	*in this paper*	41	*in this paper we*
115	*be use to*	26	*can be use to*
72	*the use of*	20	*this paper present a*
61	*base on the*	20	*in the context of*
58	*be base on*	17	*the world wide web*
53	*a set of*	17	*it be show that*
50	*show that the*	17	*be one of the*
48	*we show that*	16	*the size of the*
47	*the problem of*	16	*a wide range of*
47	*the development of*	15	*one of the much*
46	*the number of*	15	*be base on a*
44	*this paper present*	14	*this paper we present*
43	*one of the*	14	*on the other hand*
43	*be apply to*	14	*in the form of*
42	*we present a*	14	*be base on the*
42	*this paper we*	13	*this paper describe the*
41	*a number of*	13	*of this paper be*
39	*this paper describe*	13	*in the field of*
39	*can be use*	12	*the performance of the*
37	*a variety of*	12	*on the basis of*
35	*in term of*	12	*in the size of*
35	*be able to*	11	*with respect to the*
34	*of the system*	11	*this paper describe a*
33	*the performance of*	11	*this paper be to*
33	*base on a*	11	*the use of a*
32	*we propose a*	11	*can be apply to*
31	*with respect to*	10	*the development of a*
31	*the result of*	10	*of a set of*

FIGURE 92 Most Frequent N-grams in Abstracts (from Orasan, 2000).

The examples on p. 253, which are instances of the presentational move P-1, contain the verbs *demonstrate*, *report* and *propose*. These form a semantic class which has other obvious members, e.g., *present*, *suggest* and *introduce*. These verbs are a subclass of the class of communication verbs, which have been afforded much attention in the literature. For instance, Myers (1992) performs a pragmatic analysis of communication verbs in combination with knowledge claims; Thomas and Hawes (1994) analyse such verbs in medical texts, and Thompson and Yiyun (1991) study presentation verbs in the context of citations and positive/negative evaluation.

Apart from the presentation-type verb semantics, we have encountered several other natural classes of actions and states during the description of the presentational, rhetorical and hinge moves. I suggest that the following list covers the most important ones:

- **Statements of interest and affect**: Research goals (P-1) can not only be signalled by presentation-verbs, but also by statements of interest in a certain research question (e.g., *aim, attempt*) or statements of involvement or affect towards the solution of a problem (e.g., *seek, want, wish*). This can include expressions of interest in future research, as are necessary for move R-12, via verbs of planning and intention (e.g., *expect, foresee*).

- **Statements about problem-solving and needs:** Scientific writing can be seen as a report of problem-solving processes, as discussed in sections 6.3 and 6.5. The existence of problems plays a special role in moves R-1 and H-13 (where the problem concerned is the one addressed in the new KC), R-11 (where the problem concerned is the limitation of the new KC), H-1 and H-3 (where the problem concerned is associated with an existing KC), and H-18 (where reasons for the problem are given). Solutions to these problems play a special role in moves R-7, H-2, H-4 and H-7. We might therefore distinguish actions which indicate a problematic state (e.g., *fail, degrade, overestimate, waste*), as well as indications that a solution has been found (e.g., *solve, circumvent, mitigate*). A lack or need of something, as signalled by verbs like *require, need, be void of* can also indicate a problem. Needs are also associated with other moves, e.g., the statement that a solution is desirable or missing (R-5 and R-6), or that the authors' solution is necessarily the right one (R-9).
- **Display of awareness**: Verbs such as *know* can be used to weaken the claim of a gap in the literature (R-6), or the claim of the novelty of the authors' solution (R-2), as explicated by the phrase *"we know of no other approach which... "*.
- **Contrast and comparison actions**: Moves H-6 and H-7 state that the authors' solution solves the problem better than somebody else's, as might be signalled by verbs such as *outperform* and *increase.* Moves H-8, H-10, and H-11 are concerned with contrasts and non-compatibility between approaches, as might be signalled by verbs such as *clash, contrast*, and *distinguish.* Contrastive hinges such as H-6 through H-8 and H-11 can contain direct argumentation verbs such as *argue, disagree* and *object* (which might also be contained in goal statement P-1). In H-8, H-9 and H-10, the authors' own and an existing KC are compared, which means that verbs such as "*test against*" are used.
- **Statements of intellectual debt**: There are different ways of stating that an existing knowledge claim is intellectually based on a previous knowledge claim, as expressed by move H-13. This includes *borrow* and *"take as our starting point"*. Intellectual ancestry is expressed by a particularly wide range of lexemes, as we will see.

- **Use and change actions**: Moves H-14 and H-15 are statements of use of an existing knowledge claim, with and without adaptation. We would therefore expect to see indications such as *employ* and *use* on the one hand, and *transform* and *adapt* on the other.
- **Statements of similarity**: The authors' agreement with an existing KC (H-12) or a statement of similarity of KCs (H-16) can be expressed by verbs such as *resemble, be similar*. This can however also be a signal for intellectual ancestry.
- **Structuring actions**: Moves P-2 through P-4 from Level 4 are concerned with presenting and structuring a scientific text. Such actions are often expressed with verbs such as *outline* and *structure*.

It is also clear that negation cannot be ignored: the difference between solving and not solving is obviously important in the KCDM.

Another observation concerns the fact that a KCDM move can be signalled by very different meta-discourse constructions. Consider the following example sentences, which all express intellectual ancestry:

> ***The starting point for this work*** *was Scha and Polanyi's discourse grammar (Scha and Polanyi 1988; Pruest et al. 1994).* (9502018, S-4)
>
> ***We use the framework*** *for the allocation and transfer of control of Whittaker and Stenton (1988).* (9504007, S-36)
>
> ***Following Laur (1993)****, we consider simple prepositions (like in) as well as prepositional phrases (like "in front of").* (9503007, S-48)
>
> *Our lexicon* ***is based on*** *a finite-state transducer lexicon (Karttunen et al. 1992).* (9503004, S-2)
>
> *Instead of feature based syntax trees and first-order logical forms we will adopt a simpler, monostratal representation* ***that is more closely related to those found in*** *dependency grammars (e.g., Hudson (1984)).* (9408014, S-116)
>
> *The centering algorithm as defined by Brennan et al. (BNF algorithm),* ***is derived from*** *a set of rules and constraints put forth by Grosz et al. (Grosz et al. 1983; Grosz et al. 1986).* (9410006, S-56)
>
> ***We employ*** *Suzuki's algorithm to learn case frame patterns as dendroid distributions.* (9605013, S-23)
>
> ***Our method combines*** *similarity-based estimates* ***with*** *Katz's back-off scheme, which is widely used for language modeling in speech recognition.* (9405001, S-151)

These examples display a wide range of linguistic variation. Intellectual ancestry can be expressed with non-verbal constructs, e.g., the adverbial phrase "*Like Laur (1993)*". As far as the verbs used are concerned, their semantics and subcategorisation frames can differ widely.

For instance, the syntactic subject may be a method or authors, and may refer to the originators or the followers of the idea.

Metaphorical use of verbs is frequent in meta-discourse expressing intellectual ancestry, e.g., *adopt, follow, build on*. An ambiguity with the verb's literal meaning is then possible, as the following examples show:

> *For our analysis of gapping, we* ***follow*** *Sag (1976) in hypothesizing...* (9405010, S-38)
>
> *From this or-node we* ***follow*** *an arc labelled Id...* (9405022, S-73)

Follow is part of the meta-discourse in the first sentence, where it is metaphorically interpreted, but not in the second, where it is an object-level action. The first sentence is therefore an H-13 move, whereas the second is rhetorically neutral. In this particular example, an analysis of the direct object would suffice to distinguish between the cases, but in general metaphor is an open problem for the meta-discourse approach. Some comfort, however, comes from the observation that within a discipline, word sense ambiguity (of which it is arguably a special case) is usually less of a problem than in general text understanding.

9.2 Agents/Entities

There is another recurring theme in scientific meta-discourse, and that is *who* performs the actions just described. Consider the following examples:

> EX-KC: *ET(30) is a solvent polarity parameter* ***proposed by Dimroth, Reichardt and coworkers****, based on the transition energy for the longest wavelength solvatochromic absorption band of the pyridinium-N-phenoxide betain dye*$^{28-30}$. (b304951e)
>
> **R-6:** ... *and to my knowledge,* ***no previous work has proposed*** *any principles for when to include optional information ...* (9503018, S-9)

In both cases a "*propose*" action is performed, but in the first example it is performed by a specific existing knowledge claim owner, whereas in the second example, there is a lack of such knowledge claim. It is possible to find groups of agents of this kind in all KCDM moves.

My abstraction is that owners of knowledge claims are always significant for the argumentative structure of scientific discourse, wherever they are mentioned in the article. I define four kinds of meta-discourse agents, corresponding to the knowledge claim owners well-known from Level 2 of the KCDM (section 6.4):

- US: the authors refer to themselves, their artefacts, solutions, etc., in a way which signals that they are talking about their own new KC, e.g., "*our technique*";
- THEM: the authors refer to specific other KC owners, e.g., "*his approach*";
- US_PREVIOUS: the authors are acting in their role of owning an already existing knowledge claim, which they published earlier, e.g., "*the approach given in* SELF-CIT"; they are not acting in their role of defending the new knowledge claim,
- GENERAL: When there is no specific knowledge claim, this is often signalled by reference to inspecific groups of researchers, or to the field as a whole, e.g., "*traditional methods*".

Knowing which type of agent to expect in which type of move helps in the recognition of the moves. For instance, moves R-7 to R-11, which state certain properties of the new knowledge claim, are likely to contain entity-based meta-discourse of type US. Moves H-1 to H-5, which express properties of an existing knowledge claim, can be expected to contain meta-discourse of type THEM. Moves H-6 to H-16 make statements about *two* meta-discourse entities, namely the new and an existing knowledge claim. Such moves should therefore be semantically connected with both knowledge claim owners US and THEM.

This makes the four types of knowledge claim owners privileged entities in my definition of meta-discourse. Note that knowledge claim owners also play a role in Hyland's (1998b) definition of meta-discourse: he reserved three of his meta-discourse classes (attitude markers, evidentials, and person markers) for mentions of other researchers or the authors of the article. The first two of these expressly state who makes scientific claims in an article, the third only expresses that the authors are involved in some event or state described.

There are other, non-personal entities of interest which we would expect to occur in meta-discourse; these are contributed by other levels of the KCDM. For instance, problems, solutions and goals occur in the definition of moves R-1 to R-5 and R-12, whereas a research gap or the absence of a solution occurs in move R-6.

I believe that the following non-personal entities are particularly relevant:

- PROBLEM: any problem mentioned, e.g., "*these drawbacks*";
- SOLUTION: any solution mentioned, e.g., "*a way out of this dilemma*";
- GAP: any research gap or lack of a solution mentioned, e.g., "*none of these papers*";
- OUR_AIM: authors' goal, e.g., "*the point of this study*";

- TEXT_STRUCTURE: various entities from the article presentation micro-world, e.g., "*the concluding chapter*".

Note that the type OUR_AIM only marks the goals of the new KC, i.e., explicitly excludes other researchers' goals. This is because for the argumentation, whatever the other researchers' goals might have been plays a less important role than their actual contribution.

I have now provided a list of actions/states and agents/entities which should be relevant components of scientific meta-discourse. They were mainly motivated by their occurrence in rhetorical moves. Let us now see how this idea fits in with my general approach to text understanding.

9.3 Significance for Text Understanding

My long-term goal for text understanding is to model what is happening in two abstract worlds that are described by the KCDM: the research space, and the article presentation world. These worlds are *micro-worlds* in the sense of early AI comprehension experiments, e.g., Winograd's (1972) BlocksWorld. A micro-world is a smaller model of an aspect of the real world, with a restricted set of entities, actions and properties. The two micro-worlds of the KCDM are described by Levels 0-3 (for the research space) and Level 4 (for the article presentation world).

The aim is to track meta-discourse, to extract all relevant entities, actions and states mentioned in it, and to build a representation of the state of affairs in these two micro-worlds. My working hypothesis is that this can be achieved without having to represent any domain knowledge.

The two micro-worlds should be ideal as a starting point for an intermediate-depth text understander: on the one hand, they cover a wide range of rhetorical moves, the recognition of which would contribute towards understanding scientific argumentation better. On the other, their recognition is not impossible, because they are "small" micro-worlds in that they can be modelled with a small number of entities and actions. Additionally, rhetorical expectations in the text type impose constraints, which can guide the bottom-up recognition of the meta-discourse entities and actions.

The special type of meta-discourse that I described in sections 9.1 and 9.2 is rare. Most of the entities that occur in the text are not part of meta-discourse at all, but are instead object-level entities and actions, i.e., they are associated with the science in the article and are therefore not modelled in my approach. This means that one must somehow distinguish them from meta-discourse entities and actions. Section 9.4 will discuss this task from a practical angle.

There is of course no guarantee that entities and actions in the research space micro-world are any easier to recognise and represent than entities and actions in the object world. Dreyfus (1975) and others have argued that it is impossible to define a micro-world that scales up: as soon as one tries to isolate a subsection of the world that looks like it is a simpler subset, the complexity of the entire world is somehow "imported" into this micro-world.

In the end, it is an empirical question whether or not shallow text understanding based on meta-discourse can be made to work. Much more effort will be needed to settle this question than I am reporting in this book. However, what seems promising in the approach is that non-trivial observations from many different articles are abstracted over, so that something new, interesting and useful is extracted that was not known beforehand.

Application to unseen texts and generalisation across articles is an important aspect of this. Because of the structural and rhetorical similarities that exist across articles, a meta-discourse approach should generalise better to other articles in the same discipline, and possibly even across disciplines. There are of course also similarities in terms of the scientific *facts* from one article to the next, but these are much harder to pin down and describe, even for humans. Generalising over the science from one article to the next would require a level of representation and reasoning which is currently out of reach for automatic systems. The rhetorical and structural similarities, such as the meta-discourse, in contrast, are situated at a much lower level. If the right abstraction level is chosen for the features, we can even address text comprehension at this intermediate depth with machine learning. With this approach, the questions for the future are then how well the set of entities and actions proposed here can be recognised, how much of the state of the micro-worlds is covered, and how well the approach scales up when more texts and more phenomena in the micro-words are covered.

On the technical side, modelling the micro-worlds is a non-trivial task. There are many possible representations of meta-discourse entities, and more or less involved ways in which these could be recognised in actual text. Ideally, one would want to work with a full-coverage semantic representation language and an AI knowledge representation framework, as this would allow for a representation of everything that happens in the research space. (Note that there is no contradiction with my insistence on not modelling domain knowledge, because I would model general entities such as knowledge claim owners, rather than any specific scientific facts contained in the article.)

In my approach, a far simpler solution is implemented. Nothing more complicated than a POS-tagger and pattern matching is used to recognise meta-discourse entities and actions.[86] Meta-discourse that has been recognised is encoded in two main features, one expressing who is performing an action in the research space at a particular point in the article (for this the phrase must also occur in subject position), and the other expressing what actions they are performing (for this the verb's stem must be found in the verb lexicon). The two features taken together can be considered as a very rough abstraction of the state of affairs in the research space. Chapter 12 will confirm that even this simple approach already captures many interesting meta-discourse phrases.

There is nevertheless a large gap between the current simplistic implementation and the ideal of a far fuller semantic representation. But with further development of the meta-discourse features in the future, it should be possible to capture more and more of the semantics of the micro-worlds.

Let us now look at the technical details. The first question is how the individual parts of meta-discourse we are interested in (agents and actions) are to be recognised.

9.4 Practical Issues

I will first discuss, in section 9.4.1, how the meta-discourse information is encoded in two features, one for the agents/entities, the other for the actions/states. It turns out that these two features do not cover all interesting meta-discourse, so that a third feature, the formulaic feature, is introduced.

The next issue concerns ambiguity. Many of the surface signals which mark meta-discourse entities in text are more or less unambiguous. However, ambiguous meta-discourse exists and is troublesome as we shall see in section 9.4.2. I will discuss two solutions to the problem.

My implementation relies heavily on lexical lists; these are described in section 9.4.3.

9.4.1 Formulaic Meta-Discourse

In my approach, agents and entities are separately recognised. Separate recognition is more robust towards partial recognition failure and can somewhat alleviate the problem of syntactic variability which we have

[86]This is the case for the original implementation; the approach in Siddharthan and Teufel (2007) is more sophisticated.

encountered in section 9.1 in conjunction with expressions of intellectual ancestry. In those cases where it is impossible to reliably recognise the entire entity-action structure, its partial recognition is preferable to the alternative, which is total loss of information about the meta-discourse. The separate description of entities and actions also benefits a possible manual construction of meta-discourse patterns, making pattern development less time-consuming and less prone to omission errors. (This is particularly the case if the recognition mechanism also frees the pattern writer from having to deal with syntactic variations such as tenses, auxiliary modification, and negation.)

But not all meta-discourse in a text is necessarily verbal or entity-based. My emphasis on entity-hood in meta-discourse as described up to now is unusual; it is at least in part caused by my interest in knowledge claim segments. Entity-based and action-based meta-discourse may be particularly explanatory when it occurs in a sentence, but one also needs a strategy for dealing with the other kinds of meta-discourse in a sentence, which could take the form of adjectives, adverbial phrases, and more fragmentary parts of the sentence. In my model, all meta-discourse which is not concerned with entity-hood and actions is called *formulaic meta-discourse.* A full list of formulaic meta-discourse will be given in Fig. 98 on pg. 284; but I shall summarise the different groups and their corresponding moves and segments here.

The semantics of CONTINUATION (H-13), SIMILARITY (H-12, H-16), AFFECT (P-1), TEXT-STRUCTURING (P-2), COMPARISON (H-7, H-8, H-9, H-11, H-16) and CONTRAST (H-8, H-10, H-11) are known from the actions; the formulaic feature covers non-verbal indicators of these, e.g., *however* for CONTRAST. Concepts known from the agents are PROBLEMS (H-1, R-1, R-11, H-3, H-18), SOLUTIONS (H-2, H-11, R-5, R-7), AUTHORS' OWN GOAL (P-1) and GAP STATEMENT (R-6); "*to our knowledge*" is an example for the latter. Formulaic indications for knowledge claim owners include phrases such as *previously* for ExO-KC, *traditionally* for No-KC and "*along the lines of*" for Ex-KC.

Several formulaic semantic types are new (i.e., do not occur with agents or actions), e.g., that of DEIXIS ("*in this paper*") and METHOD ("*a novel method for X-ing*"), both of which are important for P-1; DETAIL ("*this paper has also*"), which is useful for excluding non-goal statement material; FUTURE ("*avenue for improvement*"), which is important for R-12; and INTENT ("*in order to*"), which can be important for P-1 and P-2 to P-4.

Some formulaic meta-discourse, e.g., PROBLEM and SOLUTION, is aimed at recognising successful and unsuccessful problem-solving activities. While discipline-independent words for problems such as *draw-*

back, flaw, disadvantage exist, some problems are discipline-dependent: in computational linguistics, a method should neither *over-train* nor *under-generate*, whereas in chemistry, *scattering* is problematic.

Formulaic meta-discourse also includes negative and positive adjectives, e.g., *compelling* and *appealing* vs. *haphazard* and *imprecise*. Positive adjectives are correlated with moves R-10, H-5, H-17, whereas negative ones are correlated with R-1, R-11, H-1, H-3, H-4, H-18. Adjective orientation in scientific text also has a discipline-dependent aspect. For instance, the word *exponential* in and of itself should be neutral, but domain knowledge tells us that in computer science articles, its occurrence typically heralds a problem. In chemistry, on the other hand, negative adjectives are used which a computational linguist would not necessarily expect in a scientific text, such as *capricious* or *sluggish* (both of which are undesirable properties of reactions). Note however that even within one discipline adjective orientation is not always unambiguous. For instance, a solution which is *simple* could be interpreted positively as *elegant*, or negatively as *simplistic*.

The lists of adjectives used in my approach (see the GOOD_ADJ and BAD_ADJ categories in appendix D.1; p. 446) are manually selected and carefully disambiguated. The acquisition of such adjectives in new disciplines is an open problem, which will be discussed in chapter 13.

9.4.2 Ambiguous Mentions of Entities

Writers of scientific text have to create linguistic expressions which refer to the entities in their text. Several of these expressions are ambiguous, i.e., they are only *potentially* meta-discourse.

Let us look at how the meta-discourse entities of interest to us are expressed. For instance, while the best indication for other researchers (THEM-type agents) is a formal citation, they may also be referred to by author names, personal pronouns, and variations of patterns such as *"their approach"*:

> **Ex-KC:** *But in* ***Moortgat****'s mixed system all the different resource management modes of the different systems are left intact in the combination and can be exploited in different parts of the grammar.* (9605016, S-16)

> **Ex-KC:** ***They*** *divided patients with MD into two groups by diastolic endocardial velocity maximum and found that those with abnormally slow diastolic endocardial velocity maximum had longer DT and IVRT and lower E/A ratio.* (C119, S-83)

> **Ex-KC:** *In* ***their*** *system, antibody immobilized on a solid substrate reacts with antigen, which binds with another antibody labelled with peroxidase.* (b313094k)

US-type agents are frequently expressed as personal pronouns in first person, or as noun phrases with a possessive pronoun in first person (*our* or *my*). If a textual segment has a high number of such occurrences, that normally means that it is a NEW-KC segment, unless there is evidence to the contrary.

But first-person pronouns don't always signal US: inside an EX-KC zone, the authors might explain their own presentation of somebody else's idea, or clarify somebody else's notation. For instance, after stating that some other researchers have introduced a particular algorithm, the authors might continue "*We will now explain how the algorithm works by way of example*". In these situations, the use of the first-person pronoun does not imply the staking of a new knowledge claim; on the contrary, the authors are reaffirming the other researchers' knowledge claim.

First-person pronouns are involved in another ambiguity, because they are also associated with US_PREVIOUS.[87] The unambiguous determination of US_PREVIOUS normally requires meta-discourse phrases such as *previously*. Without such meta-discourse, the US_PREVIOUS – US ambiguity can be responsible for the phenomenon of "zone bleeding", as discussed in section 6.4.

Nevertheless, the cases discussed up to now can normally be relatively easily resolved. Let us now turn to the harder cases of systematically ambiguous meta-discourse.

There are two types of ambiguity that concern us here: those between meta-discourse and no meta-discourse, and those between different kinds of meta-discourse. Two ambiguities of the first kind exist:

- Third person pronouns such as *he* could refer to other researchers (THEM), or to any object which is not part of the micro-worlds, e.g., people occurring in linguistic example sentences.
- Demonstrative or definite noun phrases involving a goal noun (e.g., "*the goal of the paper*") may be of type OUR_AIM; they may also refer to the goal in some existing KC, which is not recognised as meta-discourse. (In the worst case, they may even refer to a goal on the object-level of the article.)

The literature has contributed solutions to this problem for individual phrases: Kim and Webber's (2006) disambiguation of the personal pronoun *they* in the vicinity of citations (see section 6.5) is an instance of

[87] In CmpLG, US_PREVIOUS is also frequently signalled by *third* person pronoun; see examples on p. 121. This leads to a different kind of ambiguity, namely with EX-KC zones.

a distinction of meta-discourse (citations) from the object-level of science. Litman (1996) addresses a similar problem in a different text type, namely that the phrase *so* in dialogue can have a literal interpretation, or can function as meta-discourse, indicating a change of topic.

The second type of ambiguity holds between different entity types. For instance, a definite or demonstrative noun phrase whose head is a solution noun (*"the approach"*) or a piece of work (*"this paper"*) is ambiguous between referring to US and THEM, as the following examples show:

> ***This approach*** *parallels the treatment of pronoun resolution espoused by Hobbs (1979), in which pronouns are modeled as free variables that are bound as a by-product of coherence resolution.* (9405002, S-5)
>
> *The starting point for* ***this work*** *was Scha and Polanyi's (1988) discourse grammar.* (9502018, S-4)

The difference is crucial for KCDM analysis, where a hinge must involve the authors' new knowledge claim. If the phrases refer to the authors (US), both sentences are H-13 moves; if they refer to somebody else, they concern a comparison between two THEM meta-discourse phrases and are thus of no special interest to the KCDM;[88] they are rhetorically neutral.

There is empirical evidence that it would be worth disambiguating these entities, if a reliable disambiguator exists. In Teufel (2000), I simulated perfect disambiguation of one particularly frequent ambiguous class in CmpLG-D, definite noun phrases where the head refers to something like an article, or something like a method. Such phrases are ambiguous between US, THEM and GENERAL. I manually disambiguated the 632 occurrences of such phrases in the 80 articles, as automatically detected. 436 (69%) were US, 175 (28%) were THEM, and 20 (3%) were GENERAL. The simulated disambiguation resulted in a marked improvement in AZ classification performance. Statistical disambiguation of such entities in a pre-classification step is indeed the approach taken in our later work (Siddharthan and Teufel, 2007, see section 10.4).

In my PhD work, however, no such classifier was available. Instead, I left the ambiguous phrases unresolved, but clustered them into the following special entity classes:

- THEM_PRONOUN, e.g., *they*;
- REF, e.g., *the paper*;
- REF_US, e.g., *this paper*;

[88]Except in CFC, where such cases might qualify as COCOXY.

- AIM_REF, e.g., *its goal.*

Demonstrative noun phrases (REF_US) were separated from definite noun phrases (REF), because I noticed that the demonstrative noun phrases are more likely than the definite ones to refer to US.

Creating special classes for the ambiguous entity types keeps the non-ambiguous entity classes "clean" from pollution through the ambiguous ones (and thus potentially improves their classification), but it leaves the problem of what to do with the ambiguous items to the machine learning algorithm, which might or might not establish a correlation between the ambiguous items and the most likely target category.

Note that ambiguous linguistic forms occur with actions too, e.g., when metaphor is involved, as in the *follow* example on p. 259. The simple representation used in this book (agents and actions as subject-verb pairs) is clearly not enough in this case; one would need to at least take the semantics of the direct object into account as well ("*follow an arch*" vs. "*follow somebody's approach*").

Another way of referring to knowledge claim owners in text exists which I do not yet treat, and that is the so-called "named approach". In computer science and computational linguistics, systems, theories and other research artefacts are sometimes given names, e.g., in the form of acronyms. This is a very common phenomenon: according to my count, 22 of the 80 article titles in CmpLG-D (see appendix A) contain named approaches. Consider the following example:

> *LHIP provides a processing method which allows selected portions of the input to be ignored or handled differently.* (9408006, S-5)

For our purposes, a named approach is equivalent to a citation or the researchers' names they are associated with. If "*LHIP*" refers to the authors, it is a meta-discourse entity of type US, and S-5 expresses the new KC's successful problem-solving act (R-7). If "*LHIP*" refers to somebody else, S-5 is an H-4 move (praise of another KC).

Named approaches are harder to identify than regular referring expressions, because naming is less conventionalised. The resolution of named approaches should therefore find and make use of the explicit "naming" sentence, which is bound to be somewhere in the article. In the particular case from above, it is crucial that we know which of the following two naming situations applies:

> *This paper describes LHIP (Left-Head Corner Island Parser), a parser designed for broad-coverage handling of unrestricted text.* (9408006, S-0)

> *Gold et al. (1989) introduced LHIP (Left-Head Corner Island Parser), a parser designed for broad-coverage handling of unrestricted text.*
> (9408006, S-0')

The treatment of named approaches would almost certainly help recognition and has therefore been earmarked as future work. Apart from improving KCA, AZ and CFC classification, named approaches are also useful information for other information management applications. As they are often associated with schools of thought, they are valid across time and can provide an abstraction over specific researchers. Such information is particularly valuable for partially-informed users. Knowing what a named approach stands for is also of advantage for re-generative approaches to summarisation (see section 14.3).

The last practical issue in meta-discourse determination I will discuss in this chapter concerns the lexical lists used.

9.4.3 Lexical Equivalence

Entities in meta-discourse can be clustered into equivalence classes with similar semantics. The concept of "*general people in the research space*", which signals agents of type GENERAL, can be expressed in scientific discourse as professions, e.g., *linguists, computer scientists, researchers, workers*. Other typical concept types associated with the GENERAL class include "*previous papers*", "*the literature*", and "*traditional solutions in the field*".

Mapping such types into one class should help the machine learning step to generalise over similar contexts. I therefore created several manually compiled lists of replaceable concepts; Fig. 93 gives some examples from the concept lexicon.

researchers: *colleagues, community, computer scientists, computational linguists, discourse analysts, experts, investigators, linguists, logicians, psycholinguists,...*

method: *account, algorithm, analysis, approach, application,..., methodology, model, module, process, procedure,...*

advantage/success: *benefit, breakthrough, edge, improvement, innovation, success, triumph,...*

FIGURE 93 Equivalence Classes in Meta-Discourse.

The concept lexicon (appendix D.1, p. 445) covers 617 nouns, adjectives, pronouns, and noun phrases grouped into 45 semantic concepts. For instance, the concept `trad_adj` (adjectives expressing traditional approaches) includes 37 entries such as *classic* or *long-standing* and occurs in 29 formulaic patterns. `bad_adj` is the concept with the most entries (119), but there are also 7 concepts with only two entries (e.g., first-person pronoun in nominative).

Not only do concepts contain a different number of lexical entries, but patterns can also contain more than one replaceable concept. According to my calculation, the 168 entity patterns correspond to 19,892 individual expressions, and the 396 formulaic patterns to 32,427 individual expressions. Of course, many of these combinations are implausible and will never be encountered in text.

The patterns can also use POS wildcards which are checked against the POS-tags in running text,[89] and the placeholders `CITE`, `SELFCITE`, and `CREF`, which are checked against citations, self-citations and cross references. An interpreter for this simple regular expression language was implemented.

In section 13.3, I will describe a data-driven approach to compiling such lists. In theory, replaceable concepts could also come from a thesaurus (a dictionary listing synonyms), instead of a hand-compiled or automatically derived list. However, equivalence for meta-discourse is not the same as synonymy; e.g., *theory* and *method* are not true synonyms, although they are exchangeable for our purposes. The use of a thesaurus without the parallel use of automatic word sense disambiguation would also introduce noise through unrelated word senses. For instance, occurrences of the meta-discourse phrase "*this article*" in the wrong sense, i.e., as grammatical determiner, should be excluded.

The recognition of action-based meta-discourse also uses a manually compiled list, the verb lexicon (see appendix D.4). When adapting the recognition mechanism to a different discipline (a question addressed in more detail in chapter 13), one might want to replace the manually created verb classes with automatically clustered ones. There are several approaches for data-driven verb clustering (e.g., Schulte im Walde, 2006, Korhonen et al., 2003), which are based on Levin's (1993) observation that similarities in subcategorisation frames often translate to similar semantics.

One prediction is that verb classes would behave differently when moving across disciplines; for instance, RESEARCH_ACTION models the object world and is thus a lot more discipline-dependent than other classes. One would therefore expect to see more changes in this class than in the PRESENTATION_ACTION class, for instance.

---

[89]The numbers of individual patterns given above do not take this type of variation into account.

9.5 Use of Meta-Discourse in the Literature

My definition of formulaic meta-discourse is similar to the long-standing use of scientific meta-discourse in sentence extraction, which I will review now. The accepted terminology for meta-discourse in this field is *cue phrase*, which is a simple model of meta-discourse mainly based on Hyland's (1998b) categories frame markers, emphatics and hedges.

Edmundson (1969) uses two cue phrase lists which were statistically acquired and manually corrected. One contains positive cue phrases like superlatives or explicit markers of importance or confidence (*important*, *definitely*). A second list of "stigma" words contains belittling expressions, expressions of insignificant detail or speculation/hedging, e.g., *hardly, unclear, perhaps, for example.* Sentences containing such words are discouraged from being extracted, whereas sentences containing the positive cue phrases are likely to be extracted. ADAM, the first commercially used automatic abstracting system (Pollock and Zamora, 1975), used a similar but much more extensive list containing 777 terms, most of which are negative, i.e., designed to detect hedges.

Paice and colleagues (Paice, 1981, Paice and Jones, 1993, Johnson et al., 1993) use syntactically and semantically complex indicator phrases, such as "*the purpose of this research is*" or "*our investigation has shown that*". Paice (1981) reports the first pattern-matching extraction mechanism for longer indicator phrases, which supports a concept lexicon (e.g., *"study", "article", "paper"*). This work is extended by Paice and Jones (1993) to the agriculture domain and used for fact extraction-based summarisation, as mentioned in section 3.2.1. In the spirit of Paice (1981), Orasan (2000) presents an automatic analysis of meta-discourse in computer science articles which is based on POS-tagging, parsing and n-grams.

Meta-discourse is also used for NLP tasks which are more rhetorically or argumentatively oriented. RST recognition usually relies on Hyland's logical connectives, such as conjunctions (Knott, 1994, Marcu, 1997b). Garzone and Mercer's (2000) citation function classifier is also based on cue phrases, in particular on discourse cue phrases (Mercer and Di Marco, 2003) and cue phrases indicating hedging (Mercer et al., 2004). Nanba and Okumura (1999) use 86 keywords indicating discourse coherence for the determination of citation contexts.

My approach is similar in the use of meta-discourse and the modular recognition of concepts to that of Sandor and colleagues (Lisacek et al., 2005, Sandor et al., 2006). They address the problem of identifying "paradigm shifts" in the biomedical literature, i.e., statements of thwarted expectation (my move type H-11). In their system, a sentence only qualifies if several concepts of a particular type are present, and if the right syntactic relationship holds between them. Concepts (e.g., CONTRAST) are associated with fixed, manually compiled lists of strings. In my approach, however, machine learning decides which combinations of concepts are important for a rhetorical move, instead of a fixed combination of concepts.

The positive and negative adjectives used in the formulaic feature are reminiscent of the sentiment lexicons from the field of sentiment detection. Most of the entries in these are adjectives, which are typically automatically acquired by a machine learning technique (e.g., Turney, 2002). Statistical models of word occurrence used include the multinomial Naive Bayes model (Pang et al., 2002, Pang and Lee, 2004). Hatzivassiloglou and McKeown (1997) use different kinds of coordination between two adjectives (*but* vs. *and*) as an additional constraint for propagating sentiment amongst a set of adjectives.

And finally, modern approaches to hedge detection and interpretation exist: Medlock and Briscoe (2007) present a statistical classification of all sentences in a scientific article as hedges or non-hedges. Morante and Daelemans (2009) learn the scope of hedges in a semantic representation from text.

9.6 Cross-Discipline Differences in Meta-Discourse

The meta-discourse concepts expressed above, such as DIFFERENCE and GOAL-HOOD, are an important aspect of my approach to meta-discourse, as their semantics provides part of the model's explanation for the observed discourse structure. The model generalises over surface realisations via concept lists, which contain lexicalisations of the concepts; as far as the argumentation is concerned, these lexicalisations are equivalent. The present section presents some observations about the occurrence of meta-discourse concepts and their lexicalisations across disciplines.

The concepts were defined using a corpus of computational linguistics, but the hope is that the concepts should also be present in other articles, by different authors in the same discipline, and also in articles in other disciplines. To find out whether this is the case, I searched in corpora of five other disciplines (namely genetics, medicine, agriculture, computer science and chemistry) for the meta-discourse concepts known from computational linguistics, and found them generally to be present. However, while the semantics of the meta-discourse seems relatively stable across disciplines, I found that the linguistic realisations of the concepts differed.

Hyland (1998b), whose meta-discourse classification scheme was reproduced as Fig. 91 (page 254), also studies variation in meta-discourse. He reports a remarkable similarity in the *density* of meta-discourse in the four disciplines microbiology, marketing, astrophysics and applied linguistics (a meta-discourse phrase occurs after every 15 words of running text), but also significant differences with respect to the type of meta-discourse used: marketing and applied linguistics articles use far more interpersonal meta-discourse than biology and astrophysics, which tend to prefer textual meta-discourse.

In order to quantify the cross-discipline variability of meta-discourse, I performed an experiment similar to Orasan's (2000), which was reported in section 6.3.[90] Using the scientific web search engine Google Scholar (`http://scholar.google.com`), I searched for five near-synonymous cue phrases, and categorised the top 100 documents of each return set according to which discipline they come from.

The phrases used are *"in this paper/article/study we"*, and variations *"in the current/present paper"*. These phrases were chosen because their status as meta-discourse is unambiguous: mentions of the current article in combination with the pronoun *we* almost always constitute an AIM move.

I categorised the articles returned into the 11 disciplines listed in Fig. 94. The disciplines were chosen based on general intuitions about science; they are defined broadly, e.g., economics includes finance, management and operations research, and medicine includes physiology, health care and pharmacology. Items returned by the search which were not journal or conference articles (e.g., books or PhD theses) were excluded. The categorisation of the remaining articles into disciplines used the title of the journal as the main decision criteria. If this did not provide enough information, the Google Scholar summary was additionally read; next, the first page of the article was considered. Any item still too difficult to classify after this stage was excluded; this happened only three times in the 500 documents classified.

The absolute frequencies are given in Fig. 94. Note that this experiment allows to estimate the conditional probability of a discipline given a cue phrase. The absolute numbers in Fig. 94 are influenced by the discipline priors, i.e., how likely Google Scholar is to index a discipline overall. Medicine is probably the most frequent discipline overall, and life and engineering sciences are more frequently indexed than humanities, but the exact priors are not known.

[90] The numbers reported by Orasan conflate the different disciplines, and so do not allow for statements about discipline difference.

	Me	Bi	Ch	Ph	Ps	En	CS	Ec	Ma	Ne	Oth
I	1	5	9	20	2	1	28	6	11	1	3
II	70	12	-	-	5	-	1	1	-	5	2
III	25	16	1	3	13	2	11	10	7	3	2
IV	11	8	4	9	5	4	26	20	2	6	0
V	1	15	9	45	2	2	6	2	11	3	2

I: *"In this paper we"*
II: *"In this study we"*
III: *"In this article we"*
IV: *"In the current paper we"*
V: *"In the present paper we"*

Me: Medicine
Bi: Biology and Genetics
Ch: Chemistry
Ph: Physics
Ps: Psychology, Psychiatrics
En: Engineering, incl. Speech
CS: Computer Science
Ec: Economics, Finance
Ma: Mathematics
Ne: Neurology, Neuroscience
Oth: Agriculture, Sociology, Linguistics, Geology

FIGURE 94 Frequency of 5 Cue Phrases in Top 100 Google Scholar Results.

Arguably, one may be more interested in the reverse conditional probability (that of a cue phrase given a discipline), but estimating these probabilities empirically would be prohibitively labour intensive, as Google Scholar does not provide the possibility to sort articles by discipline prior to string search.

There are striking differences in the frequency of the cue phrases across disciplines. Some of these differences are to be expected: comparing Phrases I and II (*paper* vs. *study*), we see that Phrase I appears about evenly in physics and computer science, and not at all in medicine, whereas Phrase II appears almost exclusively in medicine (70% of all occurrences). This is because articles in the life sciences are routinely referred to as *studies*, whereas computer science and physics articles are not.

There is no such simple explanation for the differences between Phrases I and III (*paper* vs. *article*). Phrase III, which is generally associated with journal publications, displays a reasonably even distribution between medicine, biology, physics, computer science and economics. As most of the articles indexed by Google Scholar are journal articles, *article* seems to be a discipline-neutral way of referring to one's work. The fact that journals are of less importance in CS than in other disciplines may explain why CS is less prominent in comparison to the other disciplines. However, it does not explain why physicists also seem to prefer *paper* over *article*, although publication in physics is mainly journal-based. In psychology and biology, *article* also seems to be far more common than *study*, but not in medicine. Considering that the phrases are near-synonyms, the differences are surprising.

Similarly marked are the differences between the pre-modifiers of *paper*, namely *this* vs. *the current* vs. *the present*. All these phrases point to the current situation, the "here and now", as predicted by Myers (1992). *This* seems to be a physics and computer science speciality, whereas *current* (Phrase V) is dominated by physics (with some mathematics and biology, but noticeably little CS and no medicine). *Present* (Phrase IV) is probably the pre-modifier which is most evenly-distributed amongst disciplines; it occurs markedly often in the economics domain, but also in CS, and to a certain degree in medicine and biology, but not in physics.

Where could these large differences in the distribution of near-synonymous meta-discourse come from? The explanation provided by Woolgar (1988) and Gilbert and Mulkay (1984) is that much of the specialised terminology in a scientific domain is conventionalised language, which is created by an evolutionary process. Which language to use is to a certain degree "negotiated" between the practitioners in a field, via the publication process. But obviously it is not only terminology that is being conventionalised, but also the "normal" English phrases which make up personal meta-discourse. Newcomers to a field will, after a certain time of exposure to the prose in their new discipline, imitate the style and finally produce text which is "acceptable" to that specific field, at which point they will start propagating the sub-language. Crucially, as meta-discourse is based on random historic events such as the writing style of a field's pioneers, it contains a strong element of unpredictability.

This observation is interesting for my work in several respects. It implies the necessity to construct new lexical resources for the AZ, CFC or KCA recognisers for each new discipline, or to adapt the existing ones. This will be discussed in section 13.3.

The unpredictability of meta-discourse also provides a justification for writing support tools for novices, which should be discipline-specific for the reasons given above. In section 14.1, I will describe such a tool for computer science. By suggesting appropriate meta-discourse from authentic writing samples, it helps newcomers simulate the prevalent writing style in the field.

Chapter Summary

This chapter has introduced meta-discourse, a phenomenon that plays an important role in my approach to partial text understanding and discourse structure modelling. Meta-discourse, according to my definition in this chapter, is the set of statements about the micro-worlds of the research space and article presentation. By recognising the moves and segments defined in the KCDM, the meta-discourse features aim to abstract away from much of the contents of the article. This approach is motivated by my belief that it is both impossible and unnecessary to fully represent the article's scientific contents.

I have discussed some of the practical issues with the recognition of meta-discourse. Actions and agents are recognised separately, and combined only at the machine learning stage. A third feature, called the formulaic feature, captures non-agent/action related meta-discourse. One problem concerns linguistically ambiguous meta-discourse expressions. To deal with these, one can either define ambiguous entity classes or perform pre-classification disambiguation. Another practical issue concerns how one should derive the lists of lexically equivalent items that are used in my approach.

Apart from the actual implementation, the theoretical motivations behind the meta-discourse approach are independently important: which type of meta-discourse one is aiming for, and what kinds of representations could result from it. This, rather than the details of my current solution, is the core message of this chapter.

Like Hyland (1998b), I also found that meta-discourse changes across disciplines. This is potentially a problem for a discourse analysis such as mine which aims to be discipline-inspecific and relies on meta-discourse. I will return to this issue in chapter 13.

The next chapter will now describe the implementation of all features used in my approach, including the non-meta-discourse ones.

10

Features

Our main goal at this point is still the automatic recognition of KCDM status. The previous chapter has explored one of the most relevant phenomena for this task, meta-discourse, but I will use others as well. The current chapter will describe how one can bring various phenomena into a format which allows for their exploitation for this task.

How can the rhetorical status of a sentence or citation be determined in principle? It cannot possibly be done via the scientific knowledge embodied in the text; this would require text understanding and knowledge representation far beyond current NLP and AI technology. In a situation where one cannot exactly "calculate" (or reason about) some phenomenon, supervised machine learning is a popular choice. This approach has been successfully applied to similar tasks such as sentiment detection and emotion classification.

Two types of data are needed for supervised machine learning: the *target category*, i.e., a definition of the desired outcome, and the *features*, i.e., a set of automatically determinable properties of the text. The target categories, in the form of KCA, CFC and AZ labels, have been provided by human annotation, as discussed in chapter 8. The current chapter discusses which automatic features are suitable for an automatic analysis according to the KCDM. I see the definition of the features as the main intellectual effort behind automatic AZ, KCA and CFC. The classification itself is then performed by standard supervised machine learning algorithms, as described in chapter 11.

Several of the features in this chapter are borrowed from the sentence extraction literature (see section 3.2.2). Although sentence extraction features aim for general sentence importance and not rhetorical status, they can still be used to provide a starting point for our enterprise. This is because several of the KCDM moves express importance or summary function (e.g., R-2 and P-1 to P-4), and because descriptions of existing

Paragraph (Struct-2)	AIM	BAS	BKG	CTR	OTH	OWN	TXT	**Total**
Initial	117	92	267	135	601	2532	73	**3817**
Medial	56	87	306	289	971	3779	68	**5556**
Final	34	47	147	172	442	2125	82	**3049**
Total	**207**	**226**	**720**	**596**	**2014**	**8436**	**223**	**12422**

FIGURE 95 Contingency Table for Paragraph Feature (Struct-2).

KCs tend to use high-level statements, which are comparable to those in summaries.

The aim of the feature definition step is to find features which perform well in the automatic classification. There is often an interaction between the choice of machine learning algorithm and the definition of the features. Naive Bayes, my initial choice of machine learning (ML) algorithm, has influenced my feature definition in at least two ways:

- It assumes that the features are *statistically independent* of each other. (Two features are independent if the probability of their joint occurrence $P(A, B)$ is equal to the product of the individual probabilities $P(A)P(B)$.) Classification performance can decrease if features are used which are by accident statistically dependent. Naive Bayes does not perform any feature selection; instead, it is the feature designer's responsibility do make sure that this assumption holds.
- The Naive Bayes classifier also restricts the number of allowable values per feature per classified item to one, unlike other classifiers such as Maximum Entropy, where any number of values can be assigned to a classified item.

When defining features for statistical classification, one aims to make them maximally *distinctive*, i.e., each feature value's distribution over the target categories should be as different as possible from each other value and from the marginal distribution. This can be tested using a contingency table.

A contingency table for a feature, such as the one in Fig. 95, is a two-dimensional table, one dimension being the values of the feature, the other the values of the target feature (here: the AZ categories). The cells of the table are filled with co-occurrence counts for the two joint events. Statistical measures exist which test how different the two distributions are, e.g., χ^2 or the log-likelihood score (Dunning, 1993). One of the things Fig. 95 shows is that AIM occurs more frequently in initial paragraph position than is statistically expected.

Another desirable property for a feature is *non-skewedness*. Features which are skewed assign the same value to most item, and only show a different value in rare cases. An example of such a feature is the occurrence of the phrase "*in this paper*" in a sentence. An example of a non-skewed feature is verb tense, which is much more evenly distributed, but typically does not give a strong indication for either target category. Many independent, non-skewed features in combination, however, can influence the statistical classification in the right direction.

Feature design should also aim for *generalisable* features. It is important not to encode idiosyncrasies of the training data which are accidental to the data, as such information will not help in the classification of unseen, but similar data. This is known as the *overfitting* problem. Radically skewed features are prone to overfitting, and are of little help for most items during classification, but when a rare value occurs, they can be very accurate. My feature pool contains a mixture of skewed and non-skewed features.

There is another aspect to this: some features are theoretically more interesting than others because they are more *explanatory* within the framework of the KCDM. Explanatory features are factors which are more basic and easier to understand than the target phenomenon, and which are causally (or otherwise) connected to it. Examples of such features are "this sentence is part of a detailed description of an algorithm" or "this sentence contains a description of somebody else's research". These factors can provide some of the explanation for a sentence's rhetorical status: descriptions of algorithms are part of the zones which describe a knowledge claim; and the mention of other researchers is logically connected to EX-KC zones and to the semantics of hinge moves.

Explanatory features should be easier to detect than the target categories (that is their *raison d'être*), but they are often much harder to detect than non-explanatory features, which are simply read off the text. In fact, they might sometimes be themselves the outcome of a classification task. This is an approach we take in section 10.4, where a pre-classifier determines a feature we called *scientific attribution* – a referential property of noun phrases in text (Siddharthan and Teufel, 2007). This property is then used in the form of several features in the main classification, which leads to the target category. Features which are themselves the outcome of a prior classification process are called *secondary* features. Explanatory features can be expected to generalise better to unseen scientific text,[91] and are often useful information by

[91]A similar claim has been made by Sillince (1992), who argues that rhetorical

themselves for subsequent downstream applications. For instance, information about ownership of KCs (as captured by one of the meta-discourse features) is necessary for the regenerative summarisation step suggested in section 14.3.

Contrast this to non-explanatory features such as "all words occurring in the sentence", which is typically used in text classification and in word sense disambiguation, or sentence length, which is often used in sentence extraction. Such features do not tell us anything about the underlying structure of the document, and they do not generalise to new texts in an interesting way. My implementation uses some non-explanatory features in an opportunistic manner, but because of my general approach to text understanding they are of little theoretical interest to me.

The rest of this chapter describes all features in the feature pool used in chapter 11.

10.1 Entity-Based Meta-Discourse (`Ent`)

The `Ent` feature describes whether a given sentence contains any recognised meta-discourse entities: people or other entities which belong to the two micro-worlds described by the KCDM. The 13 feature values are listed in Fig. 96; they consist of knowledge claim owners, non-personal entities, and ambiguous entities, as explained in section 9.4. If no meta-discourse entity is recognised in a sentence, the sentence receives the value `NIL`.

The entity lexicon used for recognition contains 168 entity patterns, which are listed in appendix D.3 (p. 452). These are found by pattern matching. My implementation contains 45 different groups of replaceable concepts (containing 617 words), which may form part of entity patterns, as listed in appendix D.1 (p. 445).

The subject normally introduces the main focus in the sentence; I therefore assume that if a potential meta-discourse entity occurs in a different syntactic position in the sentence, it is less likely to be part of the meta-discourse. Therefore, in order for an entity to receive a non-`NIL` value for `Ent`, it must be in subject position (or equivalent[92]).

If a potential meta-discourse entity is detected which is not in subject position it will receive the `Ent` value `NIL`. However, its presence in the sentence might nevertheless be meaningful. It is therefore recorded by a different mechanism, namely the `Formu` feature (see section 10.3).

---

indexing should provide more discipline-independence than semantic indexing, i.e., indexing by keywords.

[92]In active sentences the entity must be the grammatical subject; in passive sentences, the object of a prepositional phrase headed by *by*, if such a phrase exists.

Entity Type	Example
Knowledge Claim Owners:	
US_ENTITY	*we*
THEM_ENTITY	*his approach*
US_PREVIOUS_ENTITY	*the approach given in* SELF-CIT
GENERAL_ENTITY	*traditional methods*
Non-personal Entities:	
PROBLEM_ENTITY	*these drawbacks*
SOLUTION_ENTITY	*a way out of this dilemma*
GAP_ENTITY	*none of these papers*
OUR_AIM_ENTITY	*the point of this study*
TEXT_STRUCTURE_ENTITY	*the concluding chapter*
Ambiguous Entities:	
REF_ENTITY	*the paper*
THEM_PRONOUN_ENTITY	*they*
REF_US_ENTITY	*this paper*
AIM_REF_ENTITY	*its goal*

FIGURE 96 Types of Entities.

In earlier versions of the implementation, where Naive Bayes was used, e.g., in Teufel (2000), exactly one `Ent` feature had to be chosen per sentence. The decision depended on the `Act` (action) feature, which will be described in section 10.2. The following algorithm was used: if at least one verb with non-`NIL` `Ent` value and non-`NIL` `Act` value exists in the sentence, then the first of these verbs is chosen. (Verbs in the beginning of the sentence are preferred, for two reasons: in the case of clause coordination, I assume that the more important material might have been presented first; in the case of clause subordination, I assume that matrix verbs carry more information with respect to meta-discourse.) If no such verb exists, then the first verb with a non-`NIL` `Ent` value is chosen. If none exists, the first verb associated with a non-`NIL` `Act` value is chosen. Failing this `NIL` is returned for both `Ent` and `Act`.

In Siddharthan and Teufel (2007), the version which is mainly described in chapter 11, we still use a Naive-Bayes-style representation (one value per item), but we reserve three `Ent` and three `Act` features per sentence. These are called `1stEnt`, `2ndEnt`, `3rdEnt`, `1stAct`, `2ndAct`, and `3rdAct`.

A variant implementation of the `Ent` feature, `S-Ent` ("sequential entity"), introduced in Teufel and Moens (2002), explicitly models the segmental nature of knowledge claim segments. KCA status, once signalled at the beginning of a segment, extends logically through an entire segment, even if no more signals occur in the rest of the segment. `S-Ent` models this by remembering the last-seen explicit entity-hood signal, and associating it with each sentence until a new explicit entity-hood signal occurs.[93] `S-Ent` consistently outperformed `Ent`, in Teufel and Moens (2002) and in several subsequent experiments. The final results in chapter 12 therefore use `S-Ent` instead of `Ent`. (Note however that this feature is nevertheless called `Ent` in chapter 12, not `S-Ent`.)

10.2 Action-Based Meta-Discourse (`Act`)

Action Type	Example
PRESENTATION_ACTION	*we* ***present*** *here a method for...*
INTEREST_ACTION	*we* ***are concerned with*** *...*
FUTURE_INTEREST_ACTION	*we* ***intend*** *to improve ...*
AFFECT_ACTION	*we* ***hope*** *to improve our results*
PROBLEM_ACTION	*this approach* ***fails****...*
SOLUTION_ACTION	*we* ***solve*** *this problem by...*
BETTER_SOLUTION_ACTION	*our system* ***outperforms*** *...*
NEED_ACTION	*this approach, however,* ***lacks****...*
AWARENESS_ACTION	*we* ***are not aware of*** *attempts*
CONTRAST_ACTION	*our approach* ***differs from*** *...*
COMPARISON_ACTION	*we* ***tested*** *our system against...*
ARGUMENTATION_ACTION	*we* ***argue*** *against a model of...*
SIMILAR_ACTION	*our approach* ***resembles*** *that of...*
CONTINUATION_ACTION	*we* ***follow*** *Sag (1976) ...*
USE_ACTION	*we* ***employ*** *Suzuki's method...*
CHANGE_ACTION	*we* ***extend*** CITE *'s algorithm*
TEXT_STRUCTURE_ACTION	*the paper* ***is organized****...*
RESEARCH_ACTION	*we* ***collected*** *our data from...*
COPULA_ACTION	*our goal* ***is*** *to...*
POSSESSION_ACTION	*we* ***have*** *three goals...*

FIGURE 97 Types of Actions.

Fig. 97 lists the actions I distinguish for the feature `Act`. They were introduced and explained in section 9.1. Here is a short summary: The first group of actions is concerned with the presentation of current or future research goals, namely PRESENTATION_ACTION, INTEREST_ACTION, FUTURE-INTEREST_ACTION, and AFFECT_ACTION.

[93] Sequence-based machine learning techniques such as Conditional Random Fields should be able to detect such dependencies automatically, without requiring special encoding for them.

The next group concerns problem-solving: PROBLEM_ACTION, SOLUTION_ACTION and BETTER-SOLUTION_ACTION. Lack of something is often expressed as a NEED_ACTION. If what is missing is a particular method, we often observe a simultaneous occurrence of an AWARENESS_ACTION, which authors can use to soften their own novelty claims. This group, together with negation, serves to recognise successful and unsuccessful problem-solving activities. There is a group for CONTRAST_ACTION, COMPARISON_ACTION and ARGUMENTATION_ACTION, and another for SIMILAR_ACTION, CONTINUATION_ACTION, USE_ACTION and CHANGE_ACTION. TEXT_STRUCTURE_ACTION is required for the presentation micro-world and concerns explicit statements about how the authors structure their article.

I also include a value for typical research actions (RESEARCH_ACTION), which has not yet been discussed. This group includes general, domain-independent verbs such as *analyse, observe, collect* and *classify.* Other members of this class are discipline-dependent (e.g., *parse* for CL and *rinse* and *immerse* for chemistry). All describe researchers' actions in the object world of science. This is actually in conflict with my general philosophy to model nothing outside the micro-worlds, but this class may improve classification by indicating the *absence* of meta-discourse. Research-type verbs also have the advantage that they are frequent and can easily be listed, which increases the coverage of the `Act` feature.

Two semantically rather vacuous values are added as well, namely COPULA_ACTION and POSSESSION_ACTION. They are assigned when a form of *be* and *have* are used as main verbs. One could easily have assigned the value `NIL` to such occurrences, as they are unlikely to carry much meaning that should matter for the KCDM (other than for instance the fact that statements of goals are often done using a copula construction) but I decided to distinguish them nevertheless, in order to establish whether a (possibly very weak) association with a target category exists.

The verb lexicon contains a total of 365 verbs; it is reproduced in appendix D.4 (p. 454). It also contains phrasal verbs and longer idiomatic expressions (e.g., *have to* is a NEED_ACTION; *be inspired by* is a CONTINUE_ACTION). Negation is treated with a simple window-based mechanism.

10.3 Formulaic Meta-Discourse (`Formu`, `F-Strength`, `Formu-XXX`)

Formulaic meta-discourse is modelled by the feature `Formu`, which assigns the 20 values given in Fig. 98. As discussed in chapter 9, the formulaic meta-discourse feature contains a sentiment aspect and also models hedging.[94] Whereas entity-based meta-discourse concentrates on noun phrases, formulaic meta-discourse is less syntactically restrictive. Its phrases include prepositional phrases (*"in the following section"*), adverbials (e.g., *however*) and entire clauses (e.g., *"as far as we know..."*). Additionally, all strings which qualify as entities but which do not appear as grammatical subject (or as object of a *by*-phrase, if the clause is in passive voice) are automatically labelled as formulaic expressions. Therefore, `Formu` generally has far more non-`NIL` values than `Ent`.

Formulaic Type	**Example**
GAP_INTRODUCTION	*to our knowledge*
OUR_AIM	*main contribution of this paper*
TEXT_STRUCTURE	*then we describe*
DEIXIS	*in this paper*
CONTINUATION	*following the argument in*
SIMILARITY	*similar to*
COMPARISON	*when compared to our*
CONTRAST	*however*
DETAIL	*this paper has also*
METHOD	*a novel method for X-ing*
PREVIOUS_CONTEXT	*elsewhere, we have*
FUTURE	*avenue for improvement*
AFFECT	*hopefully*
PROBLEM	*drawback*
SOLUTION	*insight*
IN_ORDER_TO	*in order to*
POSITIVE_ADJECTIVE	*appealing*
NEGATIVE_ADJECTIVE	*unsatisfactory*
THEM_FORMULAIC	*along the lines of*
GENERAL_FORMULAIC	*in traditional approaches*

FIGURE 98 Types of Formulaic Expressions.

Other `Formu`-related features were added in later work. In the CFC implementation described in Teufel et al. (2006a), the `Formu` cue phrase list is complemented by 892 meta-discourse phrases which the annotators found in the development corpus during annotation (and typed into the annotation tool). This models the fact that certain formulaic cue phrases are strongly associated with one feature. These phrases

[94]In my implementation, hedging is also expressed in terms of other features, e.g., the presence of a modal auxiliary in feature `Syn-3` and certain verbs in feature `Act` (*"indicate"* rather than *"show"*).

were turned into 12 binary features, the names of which are derived by appending the target category to `Formu` (e.g., `Formu-WEAK`).

In Siddharthan and Teufel (2007), each formulaic expression has a manually assigned "strength" value, which is encoded in the feature `Formu-Strength`. This feature can take the value of -1, if a cue phrase is known to mark a sentence as non-meta-discourse. An example of such a phrase is "*we then*", which is likely to describe detail. I assigned these values manually, according to my intuitions about how likely this phrase is to mark a sentence as meta-discourse.

In that work, we also added three features, `Formu-AIM`, `Formu-CTR` and `Formu-TXT`, which contain those cue phrases from the 2006 CFC list that have a particularly high statistical association with three target features (AIM, CONTRAST, and TEXTUAL).

10.4 Scientific Attribution (`SciAtt-X`)

In Siddharthan and Teufel (2007), entity-related meta-discourse is not only modelled via the `Ent` feature, but also via the feature group `SciAtt-X`. The property reported in this feature group, which we call *scientific attribution*, concerns the referential behaviour of a special set of referring expressions in text. The only possible referents in this task are articles; we distinguish between the current article (US) and the articles cited in it (THEM); noun phrases that refer to anything other than an article are considered non-referring. The referring expressions treated are all demonstrative noun phrases in the article, all pronouns and all noun phrases headed by a "work noun" such as "*article*", "*study*" (the list of work nouns is given in appendix D.1). The specific definition of reference used here includes anaphoric identity and the subpart relation. Human agreement on the task was measured at $\kappa > 0.8$.

The values of the feature group `SciAtt-X` are themselves determined by an automatic classification step. The features used for this step are the distance between an NP and its nearest citation, whether the NP or the citation appears first in text, whether the citation is a self-citation, whether the citation is authorial or parenthetical, the distance between the citation and nearest first person pronoun or "*this paper*" in text, morpho-syntactic agreement (in number of authors and in person), the section heading, relative importance measures for the citation (e.g., how often it is cited in the article), and whether or not the citation was chosen by Hobbs' (1986) anaphora resolution algorithm.

Rather than feeding the outcome of the scientific attribution classifier into the feature `Ent`, it is encoded in the binary features `SciAtt-Us`,

SciAtt-Them, SciAtt-0 and SciAtt-Subj in the following way:

- SciAtt-Us = 1 if there is any reference to current work in the sentence, else 0;
- SciAtt-Them = 1 if there is any reference to any specific citation in the sentence, else 0;
- SciAtt-0 = 1 if there is any reference in the sentence to work that is in neither the current article nor any specific citation, else 0;
- SciAtt-Subj = 1 if the respective NP with scientific attribution, if any, is in subject position, else 0.

Scientific attribution is a non-standard definition of anaphora resolution, and only one of many possible ways by which anaphora resolution could be employed to help in the final discourse classification problem.

While the meta-discourse features are the ones that are most central to my approach, my feature pool also contains 16 other features, which record citation status, position of a sentence, verb syntax, context in terms of rhetorical status, headline of the current section, bag-of-words content of the sentence, and sentence length. I will discuss them here and describe the history of the features along the way.

10.5 Citations (Cit)

Citations and phrases such as "*Hindle's work*" are called "evidentials" in Hyland's categorisation of meta-discourse. They are important in my approach: the guidelines for KCA, for example, mention citations specifically as one of the signals of knowledge claim discourse structure. Citations signal THEM-type meta-discourse and are also represented in the set of patterns that make up the entity-based meta-discourse feature. By defining citations as a separate feature we can additionally observe how much they, on their own, contribute to the recognition of discourse structure.

In particular, four properties of citations are modelled: Citation Presence/Type (Cit-1), Self-Citation (Cit-2), Citation Location (Cit-3) and Citation Number (Cit-4).

Cit-1 records the presence or non-presence of a formal citation or a cited author in the sentence. Possible values are REF, REFAUTHOR and 0. If a citation or author name is recognised, its further properties are reported in Cit-2 to Cit-4: only in those cases will these features have a non-zero value. Cited author names are a useful feature for recognising KCA because they typically indicate the continuation or the reprisal of an Ex-KC segment, and rarely the start of a first mention Ex-KC segment.

Feature Cit-2 encodes for each citation whether at least one of the authors of the current article is also an author in the given citation. In that case, the citation is called a *self-citation*, and Cit-2 takes the value Self-Cit; in all other cases, it takes the value No-Self-Cit. Cit-2 should help differentiating ExO-KC zones from Ex-KC zones.

There are interactions of self-citations with other features: One would also expect self-citations to be described with a more positive attitude, as in moves H-4 or H-5, e.g., using positive adjectives. It is also more likely that such KCs are used as a basis for the current work, i.e., that they are connected with moves H-13, H-14 or H-15.

In Harvard-type citation styles, two types of citations are possible in running text: citations which form a syntactically integral part of the sentence are called *authorial* (sometimes *syntactic*), those that do not are called *parenthetical* (Swales, 1990). Authorial citations play a stronger part in the focus structure of the text, and might therefore signal particular argumentative moves. As an approximation of the authorial/parenthetical distinction, Cit-3 records the relative location of a citation in a sentence as one of the values Front, Mid or End.

The number of citations in a sentence (Cit-4) is the final citation feature. Consider the following examples:

> *Similar advances have been made in machine translation (Frederking and Nirenburg, 1994), speech recognition (Fiscus, 1997) and named entity recognition (Borthwick et al., 1998).* (0006003, S-6)

> *These studies have shown that the charge on the DNA molecule, for example, can inhibit diffusion of redox entities to the electrode surface, thereby modifying the resistance across the interface.*[10,13,14,15,16] (b307591e)

If authors plan to hinge their new KC to an existing KC, they do not normally introduce the existing KC in combination with others. It is therefore possible that there is an inverse relationship between the number of citations in a clause or sentence and their importance.

10.6 Tense, Voice and Aspect (Syn)

Three verb-syntactic features are covered in my feature pool: voice, tense and modification by a modal auxiliary. Such features are not typically used for sentence extraction, but have been used for the detection of text structure by tense (Hitzeman et al., 1999) and for genre classification (Kessler et al., 1997). Biber and Finegan (1994), Biber et al. (1998) and Milas-Bracovic (1987) found them to be indicators of the IMRD section structure (see chapter 5). This makes it plausible that they are also correlated with KCDM phenomena.

With respect to the first verb-syntactic feature, grammatical voice (`Syn-1`), Riley (1991) found a correlation between passive voice and rhetorical role, which she explained by the connection between voice and the phenomenon of authors' perspective. In turn, author's perspective depends crucially on whether an idea is the authors' own work or somebody else's work, which is immediately KCDM-relevant. There is likely to be a strong discipline-dependent element in this: the passive voice is far more common in the life sciences to describe the own work than it is in computational linguistics.

Tense, the second verb-syntactic feature (`Syn-2`), should also be related to a sentence's argumentative status. Many prescriptive guidelines recommend the past tense for descriptions of previous work, including own previous work, and present tense for current work. However, we will have to see experimentally how systematically tense is used in CmpLG, whose articles are not edited and often written by non-native speakers.

The general connection of tense and rhetorical status is confirmed by various studies: Biber and Finegan (1994) and Milas-Bracovic (1987) find that authors use different tenses for different rhetorical segments or for certain argumentative tasks. Myers (1992) lists the following linguistic features of goal statements (my move P-1): the verb is *present, report* or similar; first-person pronouns are used, and the tense is present perfect. Experimentally, in Grover et al.'s (2003) AZ-like classification of legal texts, tense (of the main verb group of a sentence) was one of the features which improved the rhetorical classification. Aspect and tense have also been shown to correlate with various other discourse structures (Salager-Meyer, 1992, Hwang and Schubert, 1992, Malcolm, 1987).

Tense should also be relevant because of its connection to the aspect system in English, which signals the state of an activity. Pending problems, like other unfinished states, are often associated with the present perfect. The use of past tense, on the other hand, signals that some kind of end state or accomplishment has been reached. This is of interest to us because the distinction between solved and open problems is one of the central concepts in the KCDM.

The `Syn-2` feature distinguishes 9 simple and complex tenses: present tense, present continuous, past tense, past continuous, past perfect, present perfect, future, future continuous and future perfect.

The third verb-syntactic feature (`Syn-3`) records the presence or absence of a modal auxiliary in a clause. This is one of the markers of hedging. Wiebe (1994) also uses the occurrence of a modal auxiliary (other than *will*) for the distinction between subjective and objective language (see section 6.5).

10.7 Category History (`Hist`)

My discourse model does not impose a fixed ordering on the moves and zones it recognises, although there are observed and predicted regularities in the sequence of moves in argumentation, e.g., the moves and segments to be expected in the vicinity of citations (see section 6.5).

The simplest method of modelling the argumentative and rhetorical neighbourhood of a sentence is to record the categories of the last sentence, as the `Hist` feature does. One can also record more than one sentence going back. But this feature has a problem which is not shared by the other features discussed so far: it cannot be determined in a first-pass feature detection step, because at feature detection time, the system's classification of a sentence is not known yet. In fact, interdependencies between neighbouring categories are likely to be bi-directional, i.e., the sentence's category influences that of the previous sentence as well. We call such features, which cannot be determined in isolation, *non-static*.

This technical dilemma has several possible solutions, as we will see in chapter 11. Whichever solution is chosen, the predicted target category of the sentence itself must somehow be derived in a first pass,[95] and this means that the history feature needs to be treated separately from the static features.

Context could alternatively be modelled by using the n previous *categories* encountered in text, rather than the category of the n last sentences. This would model the sequence of target categories independently of their characteristic lengths. Given enough training material, more complex sequential models such as Conditional Random Fields (CRFs) could capture sequential dependencies between features, e.g., the relative location (with respect to other features) at which the first AIM sentence occurs in a text.

10.8 Structural Indicators (`Loc`, `Struct`)

In previous experiments on sentence extraction, location has been found to be strongly correlated with importance (e.g., Lin and Hovy, 1997). The typical assumption is that more relevant sentences can be found in the periphery of the document (Edmundson, 1969). Location can be defined absolutely, i.e., from article beginning, or relatively, i.e., with respect to smaller structures such as the physical section, the rhetorical section or the paragraph.

[95] In Siddharthan and Teufel (2007), we additionally use the First-pass target category prediction for the sentence itself as a feature, which is called `Curr`.

Absolute location has been shown to be the single most important feature for text extraction in the news domain (Brandow et al., 1995, Lin and Hovy, 1997). It should also be a good correlate for AZ, KCA and CFC, because certain moves and segments can be expected in certain areas of the article. For instance, the first KCA segment in almost all articles is No-KC, and Textual moves are likely to begin or end intermediate sections.

My definition of absolute location, modelled by feature `Loc`, has 10 values, corresponding to 10 differently-sized segments, as shown in Fig. 99. Segments consist of one or more pieces, which were created by cutting the text into 20 equal parts. The segments mimic the structure of ideal documents: segment size is smaller towards the beginning and the end of the document, where documents are often written more densely, and where the rhetorical units can therefore be expected to be smaller. Segments in the middle are large; e.g., Segment F, the sixth segment, covers 40% of the text. I found empirically that differently-sized segment length leads to an improvement over uniform segment length.

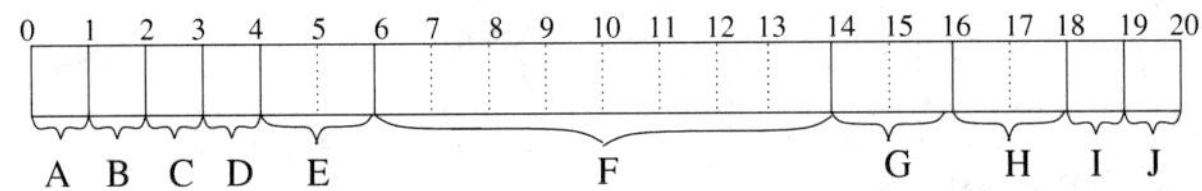

FIGURE 99 Values for Location Feature.

Another location-style organising principle is defined relatively to the physical division structure in the article, and is covered by the feature `Struct-1`. P-1 and P-2 moves, for instance, often occur towards the end of introduction sections, whereas P-3 and P-4 moves (e.g., *"in this section we will"*) often occur as the first or last sentence in a section.

The feature `Struct-1` divides the section into three equally sized segments, and additionally reserves special values for the first and the last sentence of each section. The sixth value records if a sentence is in either the second or the third sentence in a section; the second-last plus third-last sentence count as a seventh value.

Paragraph structure is another general principle of text organisation. My feature `Struct-2` reports whether a sentence is initial, medial or final to a paragraph.

A common assumption in the text extraction literature is that well-written research articles are hierarchically structured, and that sentences at the beginning and end of the paragraph are thus more likely to be relevant. However, there is some contention over to which degree paragraph structure is indeed associated with logical writing units. For instance, Longacre (1979) claims that the function of many paragraph breaks is purely aesthetic. I observed informally in CmpLG-D that the number and placement of paragraph breaks seems to be affected by whether or not an article was typeset in "two-column" style, which would confirm this to a certain degree.

Both human and automatic paragraph-reintroduction experiments have been conducted for various text types, where the task is to insert paragraphs back into a text from which they have been removed. Starck (1988) reports poor results for fiction: only nine of the 17 paragraph breaks in a text were correctly identified by more than 50% of the subjects. She concluded from this that paragraph length plays a minor role in higher-level interpretive tasks. Sporleder and Lapata (2006) ask humans to reintroduce paragraph boundaries into English, Greek and German text from different text types, with far better results, e.g., $\kappa = 0.47$; $P(A) = 0.70$ for English news text, $\kappa = 0.72$; $P(A) = 0.82$ for English fiction, and $\kappa = 0.76$; $P(A) = 0.82$ for English parliamentary reports.

For scientific articles, Baxendale (1958) reports strong evidence in favour of paragraph structure. In 85% of paragraphs, the relevant sentence ("topic sentence" in her parlance) is indeed the initial sentence, and in 7% the final.

Some higher-level rhetorical tasks also use paragraph boundaries as a feature. Marcu (1997c) and Wiebe (1994) find paragraph structure useful for their respective tasks (determination of the most important textual units in a text for RST, and determination of private-state sentences in narrative), whereas Hearst (1997) reports that thematic shifts often do not coincide with paragraph boundaries.

The headline feature (`Struct-3`) estimates which rhetorical section of the IMRD structure a sentence is contained in. A correlation between AZ, CFC and KCA categories and the IMRD structure can be expected, in as far as the IMRD structure is present. For instance, many hinges in method sections will be of a use type, whereas hinges in the motivation section tend to be either contrastive, critical, or of type BASIS. Nanba and Okumura (1999) also assume a correlation between rhetorical section and type of citation – they expect CONTRAST-type citations to occur more often in the introduction, discussion and related work sections, and BASIS-type citations to occur more often in the introduction and method sections.

In my implementation, headlines are classified into 15 equivalence classes: *Introduction, Problem Statement, Method, Discussion, Conclusion, Result, Related Work, Limitations, Further Work, Problems, Im-*

plementation, Example, Experiment, Evaluation, Data and *Solution*. If a sentence appears under one of these headlines, it receives the name of the headline as a value. Semantic and morphological variants are also included; for instance, in the absence of an *Introduction* section with that name, the same function can be fulfilled by sections titled "*Motivation*" or "*Background*", or by the first paragraphs of the first section. If the headline does not match any of the headline strings, the value `Other` is assigned.

10.9 Content and Sentence Length (`Cont`, `Len`)

The next two features model the sentential content of the sentence; they are directly borrowed from the sentence extraction literature. The assumption behind the content features is that certain concepts (or terms, i.e., strings representing particular domain knowledge relevant in the article) are particularly important in a given document, and that these concepts somehow transfer their importance to the sentences in which they occur.

The importance of concepts is often statistically determined by frequency and association metrics (Luhn, 1958, Church and Hanks, 1990), but can include more complicated methods, from relational models such as lexical chains (Barzilay and Elhadad, 1997), to vector-space methods, e.g., Latent Semantic Analysis (Deerwester et al., 1990) and random walk models (Mihalcea and Tarau, 2004, Erkan and Radev, 2004).

The first of the two content features is called `Cont-1`. It uses term frequency, via *TF*IDF* (term frequency times inverse-document-frequency) weighting, to determine concepts that are characteristic for the contents of the document. The *TF*IDF* method stems from information retrieval (Salton and McGill, 1983).

Concepts with a high *TF*IDF* value are those which are frequent in a given document but rare in the overall collection. Such concepts should characterise this particular document well. In contrast, concepts which occur too frequently overall in the document collection represent concepts which are common in the domain. They have a low discriminating power and are penalised by a low *IDF* score. On the other hand, concepts which appear only once in a corpus may be over-specific or noise (e.g., misspelled words); such words are penalised by their low *TF* score.

Concepts can be realised as single (stemmed or unstemmed) words, lemmas (words normalised to their lexicon entries), word pairs or even syntactic phrases. The *TF*IDF* value of a concept is calculated by multiplying the relative frequency weights (the *TF* element) with an inverse function of the number of documents in the document collection D which contain the concept at least once (the *IDF* element):

$$TF^*IDF(w,d,D) = TF(w,d) * log(\frac{100*N}{DF(w,D)})$$

N:	number of documents in document collection D
$TF(w,d)$:	term frequency of w in document d
$DF(w,D)$:	number of documents in document collection D which contain w at least once
$TF^*IDF(w,d,D)$:	*TF*IDF* weight for concept w in document d, with respect to document collection D

There are variations of the formula in the literature. The first text extraction experiments (Luhn, 1958, Baxendale, 1958) used a predecessor of today's *TD*IDF* formula which omits the *IDF* part. The logarithm is often used for the *TF* part (Brandow et al., 1995). One of the most successful incarnations of this formula is the BM25 algorithm (Robertson, 1977).

*TD*IDF* weighting can be converted to a sentence-based feature by selecting a number of high scoring *TF*IDF* concepts in a first step, and weighting sentences according to the presence, frequency or *TF*IDF* weight of those concepts in the sentence. The relative length of the sentence may also be taken into account.

However, there has been doubt about whether this application of *TF*IDF* measures from document retrieval to text extraction is sensible. Hearst (1997) argues that concepts with high *TF*IDF* values, which distinguish *between* documents, might not be the concepts which distinguish between smaller segments *within* a document.

Feature `Cont-2` draws its definition of what an important concept is from the co-occurrence of a word in a sentence with a word in the title and/or headline of the article.

This feature goes back to Edmundson (1969). Titles in the life sciences are often so informative that they can be considered as a document surrogate in their own right (e.g., "*Low Dose Dobutamine Echocardiography Is More Predictive of Reversible Dysfunction After Acute Myocardial Infarction Than Resting Single Photon Emission Computed Tomographic Thallium-201 Scintigraphy*".[96]) Titles could thus be a good search ground for terms which are globally important for the given document. Along the same lines, section titles within the

[96] American Heart Journal, 134(5): 822-834, 1997.

document can be considered summaries of the major content of the section. This of course only holds for those headlines which are not markers of the IMRD structure, as those headlines (e.g., *Introduction* or *Results*) are content-free.

One reason against using titles as a source of important concepts is the fashion for "jokey" titles in some disciplines, e.g., *"Four out of five ain't bad"*.[97] Such titles have only a vague connection to the article's topic.

Sentences can also be classified simply by the unigrams and bigrams of tokens they contain. Such features are used in combination with a unigram multinomial Naive Bayes event model (McCallum and Nigam, 1998). This means that all words in the sentence are used for classification, and word frequency is implicitly taken into account. Text classification relies on the distribution of "content-bearing" words and phrases occurring in the sentences. Such models are standardly used in document classification, e.g., by topic (Lewis, 1992, Doan and Horiguchi, 2004, Colas et al., 2007) and sentiment (Pang et al., 2002), and therefore present a sensible baseline to compare against (and I will do so in chapter 12). Hachey and Grover (2006) are the first to use n-gram features for an AZ-like classification; Merity et al. (2009) demonstrate their good performance for AZ on the CmpLG-D corpus.

Content features are non-explanatory features: there is not much reason to believe that the argumentative category of a sentence would be related to whether or not it contains important key words. My main interest in this book remains with the features which are close in spirit to the KCDM and which are explanatory (such as the structural and meta-discourse features) and how they are connected to the argumentation. While it is moderately interesting to see how content features perform in comparison to more explanatory features, I do not set out to prove that they are *not* useful for determining rhetorical status.[98] Overall, I am quite agnostic about content features.

Similarly, there is even less of an obvious connection between sentence length and relevance or argumentation. Nevertheless, sentence length has in the past been successfully used as a feature for text extraction. Several authors state that longer sentences are preferable for extraction; Earl (1970) argues that short sentences in her material are more likely to contain trivial material, and sentence length improved

[97] Archives of General Psychiatry, 55(10): 865-866, 1998.

[98] In addition, the `Cont` features implemented here are the simplest kind of frequency-based and overlap-based content features, so it would be hard to construe a possible negative performance as a strong argument against content-based features in discourse processing.

results in Kupiec et al.'s (1995) experiment.[99] Robin and McKeown (1996) also find that complex sentences are advantageous in a summary, as they convey a maximal number of facts. Others prefer shorter sentences for summarisation (e.g., Marcu, 1997a).

Sentence length is also an indicator of sentence complexity, a feature which has been used in extraction experiments before. Sentence complexity might be a useful feature for determining AZ, KCA and CFC status, because many of those NEW-KC or EX-KC sentences which describe details of the solution can be expected to be less complex (e.g., because they contain less meta-discourse) and thus shorter.

There are several ways in which sentence length can be turned into a feature. Instead of recording the raw number of tokens per sentence, in my feature `Len`, which is binary, a threshold of 12 tokens is used to distinguish short and long sentences.

Chapter Summary

This chapter has presented many surface features which I expect to be correlated with the rhetorical and argumentative phenomena recognised by the discourse model described in chapter 6. An overview of these features is given in Fig. 100 (for static features) and Fig. 101 (for secondary features).

Of the static features, the first subgroup (meta-discourse, see chapter 9) is the most explanatory one, and the one which is most idiosyncratic to my approach. The meta-discourse features aim to recognise and classify mentions of particular entities (feature `Ent`, e.g., the authors of the current article), particular actions (feature `Act`, e.g., to use some other researcher's knowledge claim), and general cue phrases (feature `Formu`, e.g., the expression "*to my knowledge*"). This is done with a set of specialised concepts, which are correlated with the semantics of the rhetorical moves from chapter 6.

Citations (`Cit-1` to `Cit-4`) are a special form of meta-discourse: My features model whether these are present in a sentence, whether they are self-citations, which syntactic form they take, and how many of them there are in a sentence. Another important set of features is concerned with the location of a sentence in the article (`Loc`). Background material, for instance, is far more likely to occur at the beginning of a scientific text than anywhere else. There are also features which

[99] This is however quite likely to be a side-effect of their text encoding: the feature successfully filters out short non-sentences such as captions, titles and headings which are wrongly encoded as sentences. A cleaner native encoding such as SciXML would have already distinguished such strings from sentences, which means that the sentence length feature might be redundant in my experiments.

Feature	Description	Possible Values
Meta-Discourse:		
(S-)Ent	Type of entity; sequential or non-sequential	13 entity types, NIL
Act	Type of action	20 action types×neg., NIL
Formu	Type of scientific meta-discourse	20 formu types + 13 entity types, NIL
Formu-WEAK etc.	Scientific meta-discourse associated with target category	0, 1
F-Strength	"strength" of meta-discourse	-1, 0, 1, 2, 3
Citations:		
Cit-1	Presence of citation or cit. author	Cit, CitAuthor, 0
Cit-2	Self-citation	Self-Cit, No-Self-Cit, 0
Cit-3	Citation location	Front, Mid, End, 0
Cit-4	Number of citations in sentence	integer
Verb Syntax:		
Syn-1	Voice	Active, Passive, 0
Syn-2	Tense	9 tenses, 0
Syn-3	Auxiliary modification	Modal, nonModal, 0
Location:		
Loc	Absolute position of sentence	10 segments (A-J)
Struct-1	Position of sentence in section	7 values
Struct-2	Position of sentence in paragraph	Initial, Medial, Final
Struct-3	Section type/headline	15 types, Other
Content and Length:		
Cont-1	Presence of terms with high *TF*IDF* value	0, 1
Cont-2	Presence of title/headline words	0, 1
Length	Sentence length above threshold?	0, 1

FIGURE 100 Overview of Simple Features Used in Chapter 11.

Feature	Description	Possible Values
History:		
Hist	Category of previous sentence	Target categories
Curr	Category of current sentence (according to first-pass estimate)	Target categories
Scientific Attribution:		
SciAtt-US	An NP in sentence refers to current article	0,1
SciAtt-THEM	An NP in sentence refers to some cited article	0,1
SciAtt-0	No NP in sentence refers to any particular article	0,1
SciAtt-SUB	The ambiguous NP in sentence is in subject position	0,1

FIGURE 101 Overview of Sequential/Secondary Features Used in Chapter 11.

cover location relative to paragraph boundaries or section boundaries (Struct-1 and Struct-2), and which record the headline a sentence occurs under (Struct-3).

Verb syntax is treated with another set of features (Syn-1 to Syn-3). Grammatical voice is an important aspect of scientific writing style. The tense of each verb group is also determined, and whether or not it is modified by a modal auxiliary. Another set of features is borrowed from the text extraction literature. These model sentential content, e.g., via occurrence statistics (features Cont-1 and Cont-2).

As far as the secondary features (Fig. 101) are concerned, the rhetorical status of a sentence is also likely to be influenced by the status of the previous sentence, as we have observed in connection with hinge moves in section 8.6. This phenomenon is modelled by the history feature Hist.

Another secondary group of features concerns scientific attribution (features SciAtt-X). This records for each sentence containing an ambiguous noun phrase, whether it is more likely to refer to the authors of the current article, or to any of the cited articles in the text.

The exact implementation of the features is discussed in the following chapter 11. There, the features are used for the simulation of the human annotation experiment, i.e., for the automatic recognition of the three schemes.

11

Automatic AZ, KCA and CFC

Chapter 10 described features (algorithmically determinable properties) of the sentence, which should plausibly be correlated with the phenomena described in the annotation schemes from chapter 7. For each sentence or citation in unseen text, an automatic recogniser for Argumentative Zoning (AZ), Knowledge Claim Attribution (KCA) and Citation Function Classification (CFC) should decide what the most appropriate target category is, given the sentence's or citation's features. This requires some sort of combination of the information contained in the features. The prototype systems presented here[100] all use supervised machine learning, but other ways of utilising the features are equally possible. A rule-based system, for instance, which combines the features symbolically, is described in Teufel (2000).

The AZ, KCA and CFC implementations are based on a Unix pipeline, originally with support from the LTG's Text Tokenisation Toolkit (TTT, Grover et al., 1999). The AZ system can be parameterised to work with KCA data, and the CFC implementation, while being its own system, is very similar to the AZ implementation and its features are either identical to or an adaptation of the AZ features.

The first two processes in both systems are performed as a one-time offline effort:

- SciXML-**conversion and citation parsing**: Each document in the training corpus is preprocessed from their source (LaTeX , PDF, XML or HTML) into SciXML (as described in section 5.4).
- **Human annotation**: A gold standard in the form of manual AZ, KCA or CFC annotation is needed for supervised machine learning. The creation of this material has been described in chapter 8.

[100]The AZ systems were published in Teufel (2000), Teufel and Moens (2002) and Siddharthan and Teufel (2007); the CFC system was published in Teufel et al. (2006a).

The next step, which is the workhorse in this implementation, is the determination of the features discussed in chapter 10:

- **Feature determination**: Values for each of the features and for each annotation unit are derived. This step will be described in section 11.1.

The classification, which will be described in section 11.2, is done by a statistical classifier, which consists of a training and a testing phase:

- **Statistical training**: Several statistical classifiers are used to derive a statistical model. This model records the correlation between the features and the target categories.
- **Statistical testing**: In the testing phase, unseen annotation units are classified, on the basis of the features in the annotation unit, and the statistical model acquired in the training phase. In contrast to the training phase, no knowledge of the correct target categories is available in this step, as the data is unseen.

The system output is evaluated in two ways:

- **Intrinsic evaluation**: The output of the statistical AZ, KCA and CFC systems is compared to the corresponding human annotation, as will be reported in section 12.1.
- **Extrinsic evaluation**: The system output is presented to humans, who are asked to perform a task with it. Their performance on this task is measured and serves as an indirect indication of the quality of the system output. Such an experiment is reported in section 12.2.

The rest of the chapter will describe the feature determination and the statistical classification in detail.

11.1 Feature Determination

Fig. 102 gives details about the processes involved in feature determination; it also shows which feature values are derived at which stage in the processing.[101] Different phases of the pipeline add information in the form of XML elements and attributes to an intermediate SciXML representation of the document. Citation parsing is followed by tokenisation and sentence boundary detection, *TF*IDF* calculation, headline matching, POS tagging, formulaic matching, syntactic processing, action matching, agent matching and scientific attribution. The history feature is determined by a second classification step. Whenever the correctness of a given feature determination step cannot be trivially

[101] Note that in project SciBorg a different infrastructure is used, which is based on RMRS (Copestake, 2003, 2009).

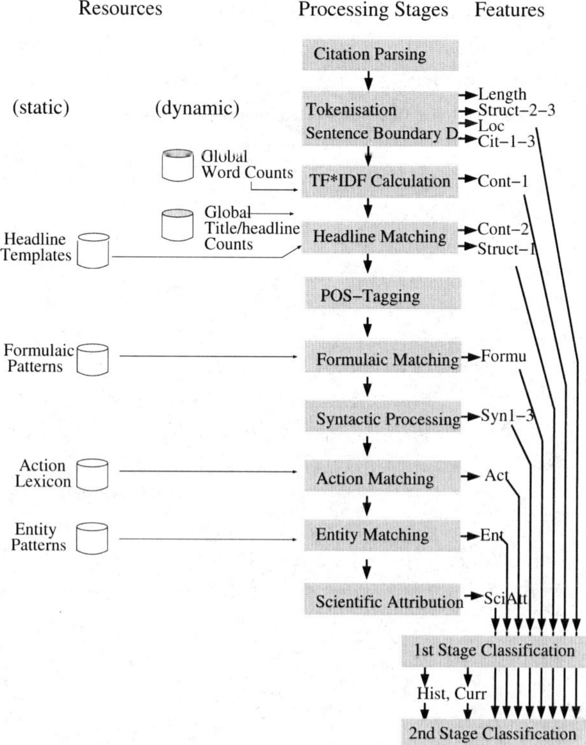

FIGURE 102 Feature Determination Steps.

assumed, I will in the following perform an evaluation of it. Contingency tables, as introduced in chapter 10, are given in the electronic appendix to this book.

The input to the feature determination pipeline is basic SciXML as described in chapter 5; this means that the text is contained in paragraphs (P elements), and that sentences and citations are not yet marked up.

Preprocessing and Citation Parsing

Text contained in paragraphs is first citation parsed, then tokenisation and sentence boundary detection take place in a combined step. Also, surface alignment between abstract and document sentences is performed, using the length of the longest common substring between the sentences as a heuristic, as described in section 5.1.2. Alignments are encoded using the attributes `DOCUMENTC` and `ABSTRACTC` in abstract and document sentences, respectively.

In some cases, citation recognition may already have happened during the transformation step into SciXML. For instance, if the source text was in LaTeX, and if the command `\cite` was used systematically, all citation instances may already been identified in the transformation step. In the publisher-specific XML we worked with later, parenthetical citations were already marked. However, even in those cases some form of citation processing is still necessary if one wants to detect all mentions of author names (`REFAUTHOR`) in running text.

In the pipeline used for the CmpLG corpus, I adapted a grammar written in the specific syntax of the program `fsgmatch`, which is provided with TTT (Grover et al., 1999), and which was originally written by Colin Mattheson. The reference list at the end of an article is parsed according to a grammar for bibliographic entries which encodes typical citation styles. Author names and dates are marked up as such, and a `REFLABEL` element is constructed for each bibliographic entry, based on this information. A second pass searches for occurrences of the surnames of all cited authors in the text. If they appear with dates, they are wrapped as XML-elements `REF`; if they occur on their own, they are marked as `REFAUTHOR`. In the next step, each reference is checked for overlap of the cited authors with the authors of the article (by comparison of all cited authors with the `CURRENT_SURNAME` field). Citations with author overlap are marked as self-citations.

A more modern version of this citation parser, written by Anna Ritchie, was used on the ACL Anthology. Ritchie et al. (2006) report high accuracy on the task: 94% of citations are recognised, provided the reference list is error-free.

The next step is sentence boundary disambiguation, which is performed with the TTT tool `ltstop`. `ltstop` is trained on newspaper text; if it is applied to scientific text, it is faced with abbreviations and naming conventions which it would not have come across in news text. Consider for instance the following unrecognised sentence boundary after the name *h*:

> <S> [...] *we make use of parameters ("dependency parameters")* `EQN` *for the probability, given a node h and a relation r, that w is an r-dependent of* ***h. Under*** *the assumption that the dependents of a head are chosen independently from each other, the probability of deriving c is:*</S> (9408014, S-190)

Code was added to repair such common errors.

Every single feature in the pool requires knowledge about sentence boundaries. For AZ and KCA, this is obvious, as sentences are the units of classification. For CFC, the units of classification are **REF** and **REFAUTHOR** items rather than sentences, but correct sentence boundaries are still important as sentences provide the window in which features are determined and then associated with the citations that are contained in them.

Some feature values can be determined directly after the sentence boundary detection step, namely the features `Struct-1` (Position in Section), `Struct-2` (Position in Paragraph), `Length` (Sentence Length), `Loc` (Absolute Location), the citation features `Cit-1` to `Cit-4` and feature `Cont-1`:

- For feature `Struct-1`, the section is divided into three equally sized portions (measured in sentences). In those cases where a sentence is in a specific position within the section as described in section 10.8, the resulting values "overwrite" the tri-section values, which are applied in all other cases.
- For feature `Struct-2`, sentences are marked as paragraph-initial, paragraph-final or paragraph-medial. If a paragraph contains only one sentence, that sentence receives the value `Initial`. If a paragraph contains only two sentences, the first sentence receives the value `Initial` and the second the value `Final`.
- Values of the feature `Loc` are determined by dividing the sentence number of the document by 20, and assigning values according to the diagram in Fig. 99. Document areas corresponding to A, B, C, D, I, J are one twentieth of the document in length, E, G, H one tenth, and value F two fifths.
- For feature `Length`, the value 0 is assigned if the sentence is shorter than a fixed threshold (here: 12 tokens including punctuation), 1 otherwise.
- Feature `Cit-1` reports the existence of a **REF** or a **REFAUTHOR** in a sentence (if a sentence contains both, **REF** is chosen).
- Feature `Cit-2` reports whether or not a citation is a self-citation. In cases where a self-citation and a non-self-citation appear in one sentence, the self-citation takes precedence.
- Feature `Cit-3` gives the location of a citation in sentence. If more than one citation is contained in a sentence, **Front** is given preference over both other features, and **End** is given preference over **Mid**.
- For feature `Cont-1`, the *TF*IDF* score of each word contained in a document is calculated by the formula given on p. 293. The n top-scoring words are chosen, and the sentence score is the number

of top-scoring words, meaned by sentence length. The m top-rated sentences obtain score 1, all others 0. I received best results with $n = 10$ and $m = 40$. This feature requires a second pass through the document.

Headline Matching

Headlines are used for two features, `Struct-3` and `Cont-2`:

- For feature `Struct-3`, the headlines are matched against 89 patterns which correspond to 15 prototypical headlines (*Introduction, Problem Statement, Method, Discussion, Conclusion, Result, Related Work, Limitations, Further Work, Problems, Implementation, Example, Experiment, Evaluation, Data* and *Solution*). If no pattern matches, the value `Other` is assigned. If divisions are hierarchically nested, the headlines of the deeper embedded sections are considered first for any value assignment. In the absence of a section titled *Introduction*, the same function can be fulfilled by sections titled *Motivation* or *Background*, or by the first paragraphs of the first section.
- Feature `Cont-2` checks for overlap of words between headlines and titles and individual sentences. In my implementation, values for this feature are determined as the mean frequency of n (or less) title word occurrences (excluding stop-list words). If the title contains more than n non-stoplist words, the n top-scoring words according to the *TF*IDF* method are chosen. Again, the m top-scoring sentences receive the value 1, all others 0. I use empirically determined thresholds n=10 and m=18. I tested using words from all headlines as well as the title, but better results were achieved using only title words.

More than 45% of all sentences in CmpLG-D (5576/12422) are not covered by prototypical section headings, i.e., they cannot be associated with a rhetorical section. This supports the argument in section 5.1.2 that IMRD structuring in CmpLG is weak.

POS-Tagging

The next process in the pipeline is Part-of-Speech (POS) tagging. It provides information for the meta-discourse matching algorithms further downstream. I originally used the TTT program `ltpos` (Mikheev, 1998), which assigns one of the tags of the BROWN tagset (Francis and Kucera, 1982) to each token in text.

As later processing heuristics depend on the correct determination of finite verbs, it makes sense to establish the error rate of the POS-tagging step. I manually checked the POS-labels assigned to finite verbs, i.e., VBP, VBZ and VBD, on a random sample of 100 sentences containing finite verbs. The 100 sentences contained 184 finite verbs, 174 of which the system recognised (recall of 95%). Most of the false negatives were verbs in present tense which the system erroneously tagged as singular or plural nouns. Precision was 93%; the POS-Tagger erroneously tagged 14 tokens of other classes as finite verbs. These words were mostly past participles in reduced relative constructions.

According to the POS tagging, 23% (2829/12422) of the sentences in CmpLG-D do not contain a finite verb. This surprisingly high number might be a side-effect of my treatment of paragraph-style equations (see section 5.4), which produces many incomplete sentences.

Formulaic Matching

For feature `Formu`, formulaic patterns are matched against the text without any syntactic restrictions, using 396 formulaic patterns (see appendix D.2), which correspond to 32,427 individual expressions (disregarding POS-variations).

An additional set of formulaic patterns is made up of the 168 entity patterns from feature `Ent`, whenever these do not occur as the grammatical agent of a sentence, as was explained in section 10.3.

Pattern matching against thousands of patterns is slow, but a trigger mechanism can reduce the number of comparisons necessary. A trigger concept is chosen for each pattern, and only those sentences which contain a trigger concept are subsequently searched for the full formulaic patterns. Better still, they are searched only for those patterns which contain the trigger that just matched.[102] Trigger concepts should have the following properties:

- They should be rare words in the corpus, so that the trigger mechanism is not unnecessarily invoked; and
- each of them should cover as many patterns as possible, so that only a few trigger words have to be matched against every sentence.

The choice of a minimal set of triggers for a pattern set is an interesting constraint satisfaction problem, but in my implementation, the triggers are manually chosen.

The Naive Bayes classifier allows one value per feature of each classified entity. If a sentence contains more than one formulaic pattern, I choose the first.

[102] In the pattern lists in appendices D.2 and D.3, triggers are marked with the character $\uparrow$.

Syntactic Processing and Action Matching

Syntactic processing determines the verb-syntactic features voice, tense, modality (`Syn-1, Syn-2, Syn-3`) and negation. It also determines the base form of the semantic verb, information which is needed for feature `Act`. Verb-syntactic features can only receive a non-zero value if a finite verb is present.

The algorithm starts from the first finite verbs in the sentence; this is known after POS-tagging. A finite state-based recogniser written in perl checks the left and right context of the finite verb, searching for verb forms of interest which are part of more complex tenses. Whether the semantic and finite verb are two different tokens or the same depends on the tense. Copular *be* and possessive uses of *have* are recognised and counted as semantic verbs. The search is performed within the assumed clause boundaries (i.e., commas or other finite verbs), and additionally within a fixed window of 6 tokens to the right of the finite verb. The base form of the semantic verb is passed to the action matching step.

Negation is determined by a simple heuristic that searches for a list of 32 negation items in the surrounding window of 5 tokens. The list of negation items can be found in appendix D.1 (p. 445).

Action matching consists of a look-up of the base form of the semantic verb in the action lexicon (appendix D.4, p. 454). If the base form is found, the value of feature `Act` is the associated action type (with negation encoded into the value), otherwise `NIL`. The base form of the semantic verb itself is also returned and used in some experiments as feature `Act-Lex`. In the sample of 100 sentences containing finite verbs, action type determination was error-free.

As discussed before, if the sentence contains more than one finite verb and if one is using Naive Bayes or a similar ML algorithm, a resolution strategy is needed. In Teufel (2000), the choice is made in combination with entity matching. Repeating the algorithm from earlier, the first finite verb for which both `Act` and `Ent` are non-`NIL` is chosen. If no such finite verb exists, the value of `Act` is the first non-`NIL` value in the sentence, or else `NIL`. In Siddharthan and Teufel (2007), we instead provide three `Act` and three `Ent` slots.

As exemplified by the following corpus example, the processing is able to detect complicated combinations of voice, complex tenses and modal auxiliaries:[103]

> *The actor* ***is*** *always* <u>*running*</u> (present continuous, active, NIL) *and* <u>***decides***</u> (present, active, AFFECT_ACTION) *at each iteration whether to*

[103] Syntactic information about clausal units is attached to the respective semantic verb, which is underlined, whereas the finite verb is boldfaced.

> *speak or not (according to turn-taking conventions); the system **does** not need* (present, active, NEED_ACTION, negated) *to wait until a user utterance **is** observed* (present, passive, RESEARCH_ACTION) *to invoke the actor, and **need** not respond* (present, active, NIL, modal, negated) *to user utterances in an utterance by utterance fashion.* (9407011, S-137)

In this example, three prototypical actions were recognised: an AFFECT_ACTION – *"the actor decides"*, a (negated) NEED_ACTION – *"the system does not need to wait"* and a (passive) RESEARCH_ACTION – *"a user utterance is observed"*. *Run* and *respond* were not contained in the action lexicon and received an `Act` value of `NIL`. The overall value for `Ent` and `Act` given to this sentence by the Teufel (2000) system is "*the system*" (REF_ENTITY) – "*need*" (NEED_ACTION), because this is the first agent–action combination where both values are non-`NIL`.

An error analysis on the aforementioned 100 sentences with their 174 finite verbs correctly determined by POS-tagging found no errors in the heuristics for negation and modality (100% accuracy), 2 errors in the tense heuristics (99% accuracy) and 7 errors in the voice heuristics, 2 of which are due to POS-tagging errors (a past participle was not recognised in a passive context). The remaining 5 voice errors correspond to a 98% accuracy. Voice errors are undesirable, as they have follow-on effects for entity matching. The following sentence is an example of such a voice error; the error is underlined:[104]

> *At the point where John **knows*** (present, active, NIL) *the truth **has** been processed* (present perfect, passive, NIL) *a complete clause **will** have been built* (future perfect, active, NIL). (9502035, S-15)

This error was caused by the fact that this particular combination of voice and tense is not treated by the threading of auxiliaries in my algorithm.

Entity Matching

Entity matching determines the value of feature `Ent` and takes place after action matching. It uses the entity lexicon given in appendix D.3 (p. 452), which contains 168 entity patterns.

The algorithm is as follows:

1. Start from the first finite verb in the sentence;
2. Search for potential entities: either in the subject-NP to the left, or in a by-PP to the right if such a by-PP exists, depending on

[104] In this example, non-modal and non-negated features are omitted for clarity.

the voice associated with the finite verb. Do not cross assumed clause boundaries, i.e., commas or other finite verbs.

3. If one of the entity patterns matches within that area in the sentence, return the entity pattern and its type. Else return `NIL`.
4. Repeat steps 1, 2, 3 for all further finite verbs in the sentence.

The precision of the algorithm was evaluated using a (new) random sample of 100 sentences which contain entity patterns. Apart from erroneous voice determination through the mechanism described above, errors could also potentially be introduced by my heuristic for clauses, which never steps over commas and is thus stopped by appositions, for example. These 100 sentences contained 111 entities; no entity pattern that should have been identified in those sentences was missed (recall 100%).

The match was fully correct in 105 out of 111 cases, i.e., the matched string entity covered the entire subject or by-PP of the sentence. In 5 cases, the pattern was only *part* of a subject NP, typically the NP in a post-modifying PP (accuracy 95%), as in the following examples, where the recognised patterns are underlined:

the relations in <u>the models</u>	(9408014, S-131)
the problem with <u>these approaches</u>	(9504017, S-12)

The remaining error was caused by a POS-mistagging.

As already mentioned, if only one `Ent` value per sentence had to be chosen, it was the first one which is non-`NIL` and appears in the same clause as a non-`NIL` `Act`, otherwise the first non-`NIL` `Ent` feature, otherwise `NIL`.

To give the reader a better impression of how action and entity matching works, Fig. 103 displays the output of the algorithms on the first page of *Pereira et al. (1993)*. Recognised actions are shown in white boxes; recognised entities in grey boxes. Note that the two THEM_PRONOUN_ENTITIES marked with an asterisks have the wrong interpretation due to ambiguity problems.

Scientific Attribution Features

For features `SciAtt-X`, each noun phrase of a certain kind is classified as referring to an approach cited in the article, to the article itself or to no citation. The values are the outcome of an independent classification step. The noun phrases classified are demonstrative noun phrases and definite noun phrases whose head is of category WORK_NOUN (e.g., "*method, technique, machinery...*"; p. 446) in the concept lexicon

Distributional Clustering of English Words

Fernando Pereira Naftali Tishby Lillian Lee

Abstract

We describe and experimentally evaluate a method for automatically clustering words according to their distribution in particular syntactic contexts. Deterministic annealing is used to find lowest distortion sets of clusters. As the annealing parameter increases, existing clusters become unstable and subdivide, yielding a hierarchical "soft" clustering of the data. Clusters are used as the basis for class models of word occurrence, and the models evaluated with respect to held-out data.

Introduction

Methods for automatically classifying words according to their contexts of use have both scientific and practial interest. The scientific questions arise in connection to distributional views of linguistic (particularly lexical) structure and also in relation to the question of lexical acquisition both from psychological and computational learning perspectives. From the practical point of view, word classification addresses questions of data sparseness and generalization in statistical language models, particularly models for deciding among alternative analyses proposed by a grammar.

It is well known that a simple tabulation of frequencies of certain words participating in certain configurations, for example the frequencies of pairs of transitive main verb and the head of its direct object, cannot be reliably used for comparing the likelihoods of different alternative configurations. The problem is that in large enough corpora, the number of possible joint events is much larger than the number of event occurrences in the corpus, so many events are seen rarely or never, making their frequency counts unreliable estimates of their probabilities.

Hindle (1990) proposed dealing with the sparseness problem by estimating the likelihood of unseen events from that of "similar" events that have been seen. For instance, one may estimate the likelihood of a particular direct object for a verb from the likelihoods of that direct object for similar verbs. This requires a reasonable definition of verb similarity and a similarity estimation method. In Hindle's proposal, words are similar if we have strong statistical evidence that they tend to participate in the same events. His notion of similarity seems to agree with our intuitions in many cases, but it is not clear how it can be used directly to construct classes and corresponding models of association.

Our research addresses some of the same questions and uses similar raw data, but we investigate how to factor word association tendencies into associations of words to certain hidden senses classes and associations between the classes themselves. While it may be worthwhile to base such a model on preexisting sense classes (Resnik, 1992), in the work described here we look at how to derive the classes directly from distributional data. More specifically, we model senses as probabilistic concepts or clusters c with corresponding cluster membership probabilities <EQN/> for each word w. Most other class-based modeling techniques for natural language rely instead on "hard" Boolean classes (Brown et al., 1990). Class construction is then combinatorically very demanding and depends on frequency counts for joint events involving particular words, a potentially unreliable source of information, as we noted above. Our approach avoids both problems.

Problem Setting

In what follows, we will consider two major word classes, <EQN/> and <EQN/>, for the verbs and nouns in our experiments, and a single relation between a transitive main verb and the head noun of its direct object. Our raw knowledge about the relation consists of the frequencies <EQN/> of occurrence of particular pairs <EQN/> in the required configuration in a training corpus. Some form of text analysis is required to collect such a collection of pairs. The corpus used in our first experiment was derived from newswire text automatically parsed by Hindle's parser Fidditch (Hindle, 1993). More recently, we have constructed similar tables with the help of a statistical part-of-speech tagger (Church, 1988) and of tools for regular expression pattern matching on tagged corpora (Yarowsky, p.c.). We have not yet compared the accuracy and coverage of the two methods, or what systematic biases they might introduce, although we took care to filter out certain systematic errors, for instance the misparsing of the subject of a complement clause as the direct object of a main verb for report verbs like "say".

We will consider here only the problem of classifying nouns according to their distribution as direct objects of verbs; the converse problem is formally similar. More generally, the theoretical basis for our method supports the use of clustering to build models for any n-ary relation in terms of associations between elements in each coordinate and appropriate hidden units (cluster controids) and associations between these hidden units.

P Problem_Agent   T Them_Agent   U Us_Agent   TP Them_Pronoun_Agent   R Ref_Agent

Ps Presentation_Action   C Copula   Pb Problem_Action   S Solution_Action   U Use_Action
Po Possession_Action   R Research_Action   N Need_Action   Cn Continue_Action   I Interest_Action

☛ POS-Error   – Negation   % Passive   * Anaphora Disambiguation Problem

FIGURE 103 Entities and Actions in First Page of *Pereira et al. (1993)*.

in appendix D.1. The output of this classifier is converted into the four `SciAtt-X` features as described in chapter 10, namely by considering whether any NP in a sentence refers to anybody else (any specific cited entity), the current article, or nobody in particular.

In order to determine the scientific attribution features, the basic features needed for this classification must be determined first. Most of these are related to citations or the headline type, which have already been determined at this stage in the processing. New features concern the ordering and the distance between an NP and its nearest citation, and between the citation and its nearest first-person pronoun or *"this paper"* in text. Hobbs' (1986) anaphora resolution algorithm was also implemented, which searches left to right starting from the current sentence and then considers previous sentences. We also check for number agreement between authors of a citation and "*he/she*" or "*they*" in text, and determine the number of citation instances in a paragraph and in the entire article.

In Siddharthan and Teufel (2007), we achieved the following results for this pre-classifier:[105] $P(A)$ of 85% (as compared to the humans' performance of 91%), Krippendorff's (1980) α of 0.673 (as opposed to humans' 0.809) and a MUC-F (the co-reference metric of the MUC conferences, Vilain et al., 1995) of 0.913 (as compared to humans' 0.965).[106] Hobbs' prediction, which was used as a baseline, achieved $P(A) = 72\%$, $\alpha = 0.399$, and MUC-F = 0.910.

History Feature

The history feature has a problem which the other features do not share: it requires information which is unknown during testing, namely the most likely category of the preceding sentence.[107] Both forward and backward dependencies exist.

There are several ways in which this problem can be addressed:

- **Unigram Estimate**: The simplest solution to the problem is to classify the previous sentence according to all other features except the history feature in a first step, and to use the most likely category as the sentence's value of the history feature. This is an oversimplification, also because only forward dependencies can possibly be

[105]These results were achieved using the IBk algorithm (see section 11.2), which performed best out of several machine learning algorithms we tested.

[106]The distance metric for α chosen here was Dice.

[107]Whether the category of the previous sentence is really unknown depends on the experimental setting. If one classifies unseen documents (as the final system eventually will), the category of the preceding sentence is really unknown, whereas in a cross-validation setup, one has to *pretend* that the true category is unknown.

considered. It is nevertheless the approach we took in Siddharthan and Teufel (2007), for operational reasons.

- **Unigram Estimate with Search**: An improvement over the unigram estimate of the history feature uses an n-gram model trained on the training corpus, whereby the n-gram model records how likely each category is to follow each other category. Fig. 104 shows a bigram model trained on CmpLG-D. After the first pass, when all unigram probabilities of all sentence/category pairs are available, a search for the most likely previous category can be performed, e.g., by beam search (a beam width of three was used in Teufel and Moens (2002)), or by Viterbi, as in Teufel (2000).

	AIM	BAS	BKG	CTR	OWN	OTH	TXT	END
BEGIN	5	1	57	1	2	14		
AIM	13	15	8	5	86	16	10	2
BAS	2	18	6	9	130	46	9	2
BKG	19	4	544	25	53	75	8	
CTR	32	13	21	215	147	110	13	1
OWN	61	122	57	97	7351	138	88	71
OTH	21	38	23	196	137	1492	18	4
TXT	2	11	12	4	79	38	66	

FIGURE 104 Bigram Model for CmpLG-D (AZ).

In any case, the use of the history feature requires a second classification step. After its value is determined, it is handed to the machine learner for reclassification, together with the static features.

11.2 Statistical Classification

Supervised machine learning methods rely on training examples with externally given "right answers", whereas unsupervised techniques learn associations between data and target categories without such external provision of the correct answer.

Supervised methods such as Kupiec et al.'s (1995) are the logical choice for a new and complicated task such as the ones addressed here. Such classifiers have been shown to achieve good results for similar tasks, e.g., in determining sentiment or sentence relevance, if enough training material is available. Supervised learning also provides a built-in intrinsic evaluation, because one can compare the system output to its annotated training material.

A Naive Bayes classifier was applied to AZ (Teufel, 2000, Teufel and Moens, 2002), as well as an n-gram-based method.[108] This second method estimates the prior probability using n-grams over target categories. The training material was 80 singly-annotated CmpLG-D articles. The system in Siddharthan and Teufel (2007) improves on these results by using a cascade of machine learners, including decision trees and Naive Bayes, as implemented in WEKA (Witten and Frank, 2005).

For CFC, we also use WEKA machine learning. The training material was 116 singly-annotated articles with 2829 citation instances.

Naive Bayes

I adapt Kupiec et al.'s Naive Bayes formula (Fig. 14) for non-binary classification in the obvious way, resulting in the formula given in Fig. 105. As far as the notation is concerned, let us assume there are n features F_0 to F_{n-1}; a feature is then known as F_j, with $0 \leq j < n$. Each of the features F_j has k_j different values V_{jr}, with $0 \leq r < k_j$.

$$P(C^i|V_{0,x},...,V_{n-1,y}) = P(C^i)\frac{P(V_{0,x},...,V_{n-1,y}|C^i)}{P(V_{0,x},...,V_{n-1,y})} \approx P(C^i)\frac{\prod_{j=0}^{n-1} P(V_{j,r}|C^i)}{\prod_{j=0}^{n-1} P(V_{j,r})}$$

$P(C^i\|V_{0,x},\ldots,V_{n-1,y})$:	Probability that a sentence has target category C^i, given its feature values $V_{0,x}$, ..., $V_{n-1,y}$, with $0 \leq x < k_0$ and $0 \leq y < k_{n-1}$;
$P(V_{j,r})$:	Probability of feature value $V_{j,r}$ (rth value of Feature F_j);
$P(C^i)$:	Probability that a sentence has target category C^i;
$P(V_{j,r}\|C^i)$:	Probability of feature-value pair $V_{j,r}$ occurring with target category C^i;

FIGURE 105 My Adaptation of Kupiec et al.'s (1995) Naive Bayes Classifier.

There are m target categories C^0 to C^{m-1}; a target category is then known as C^i, with $0 \leq i < m$. For AZ, m is 7 (whereas Kupiec et al. perform binary classification; $m = 2$), n is 16, and the k_j vary from 2 for j= 0,1,6 (`Cont-1, Cont-2, Length`) to 40 for $j = 15$ (`Act`).

[108] I used my own implementation of the Naive Bayes (NB) classifier. This allowed me easier manipulation of the posterior probabilities, which is needed for the n-gram-based adaptation.

$P(C^i)$, is called the *prior* probability, and $\frac{P(V_{0,x},\ldots,V_{n-1,y}|C^i)}{P(V_{0,x},\ldots,V_{n-1,y})}$ is called the *posterior* probability. In Naive Bayes, the prior probability $P(C^i)$ is estimated by unigram frequency $P(C^i) = \frac{|n^i|}{|N|}$, and the posterior is simply the product of all conditional probabilities. Individual components of the posteriors are estimated directly from the contingency table.

The first derivation in Fig. 105 is due to Bayes' Theorem; the second is specific to the Naive Bayes formula and only legal under the independence assumption, i.e., the assumption that all features are statistically independent $(P(V_{1,x}, V_{2,y}) = P(V_{1,x}) \cdot P(V_{2,y}))$.

The accuracy of the Naive Bayes method may suffer if some features are not statistically independent of each other. In practice, however, it is agreed that Naive Bayes is surprisingly effective despite its simplicity (Kononenko, 1990, Langley et al., 1992, Domingos and Pazzani, 1997).

Fig. 106 shows the output of the Naive Bayes model on the example article.

Other ML algorithms

In joint work with Advaith Siddharthan and Dan Tidhar on automatic CFC (Teufel et al., 2006a), we used various other ML algorithms, as implemented in WEKA (Witten and Frank, 2005), including:

- Decision-Tree based learning (J48). The algorithm J48 is WEKA's version of Quinlan's (1993) Q4.5 Decision Tree learner, which uses information gain as its main mechanism. A training set is recursively split, using the feature which currently has the highest information gain.[109] This results in a tree such that each example ends up in exactly one branch.
- k-Nearest Neighbour (kNN) classifier (which is called IBk in WEKA). An object is assigned to the class most common amongst its k nearest neighbours. Distance is by default the Euclidean distance of the feature values.
- Hidden Naive Bayes (HNB, Zhang et al., 2005). This algorithm is a generalisation of Naive Bayes, which seeks to address Naive Bayes' problem of possible statistical dependence between the attributes. In this model, attributes can be conditioned on other attributes, as well as on the target class (in this, it is similar to other Tree Augmented Naive Bayes algorithms). In particular, in HNB there is a hidden attribute which represents the contribution of all other attributes on the attribute.

[109] The information gain for a given split can be calculated as $G = S(\text{before split}) - S(\text{after split})$. S is the entropy $S = -\sum_i p_i log p_i$, where p_i is the fraction of examples reaching a branch with an attribute value i.

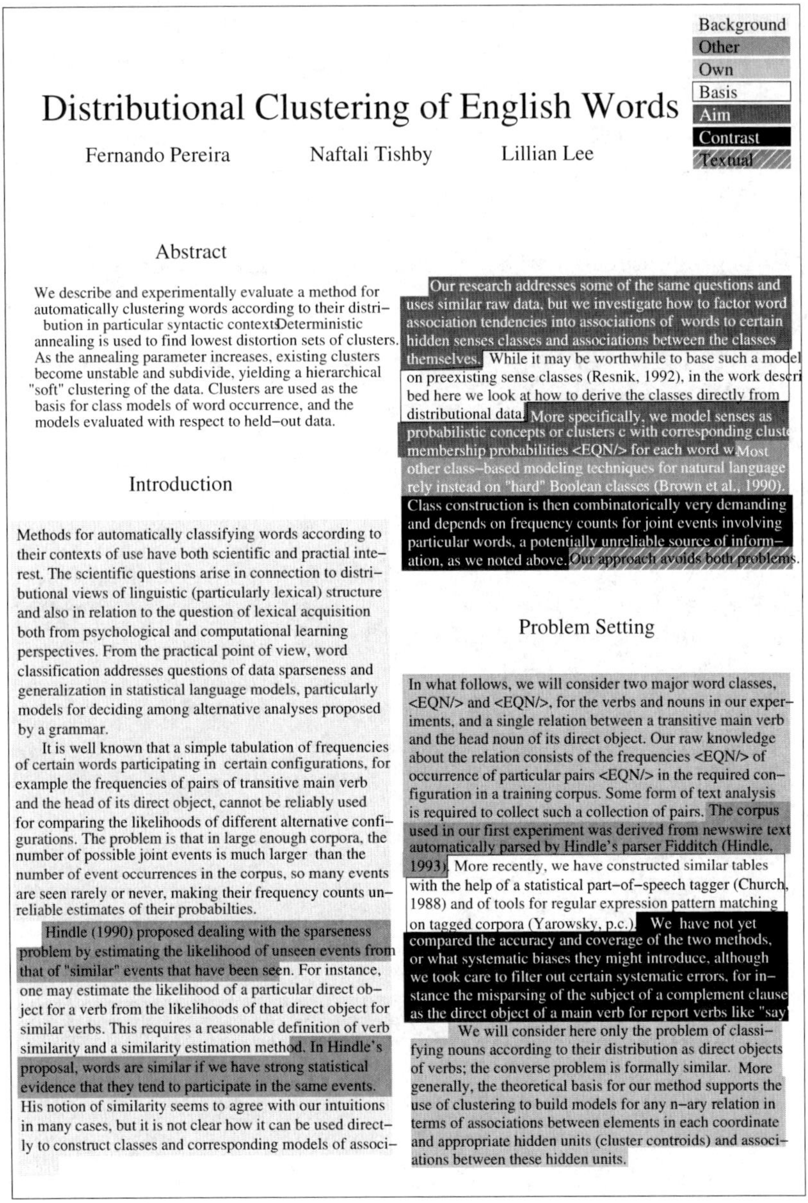

Background
Other
Own
Basis
Aim
Contrast
Textual

Distributional Clustering of English Words

Fernando Pereira Naftali Tishby Lillian Lee

Abstract

We describe and experimentally evaluate a method for automatically clustering words according to their distribution in particular syntactic contexts. Deterministic annealing is used to find lowest distortion sets of clusters. As the annealing parameter increases, existing clusters become unstable and subdivide, yielding a hierarchical "soft" clustering of the data. Clusters are used as the basis for class models of word occurrence, and the models evaluated with respect to held–out data.

Introduction

Methods for automatically classifying words according to their contexts of use have both scientific and practial interest. The scientific questions arise in connection to distributional views of linguistic (particularly lexical) structure and also in relation to the question of lexical acquisition both from psychological and computational learning perspectives. From the practical point of view, word classification addresses questions of data sparseness and generalization in statistical language models, particularly models for deciding among alternative analyses proposed by a grammar.

It is well known that a simple tabulation of frequencies of certain words participating in certain configurations, for example the frequencies of pairs of transitive main verb and the head of its direct object, cannot be reliably used for comparing the likelihoods of different alternative configurations. The problem is that in large enough corpora, the number of possible joint events is much larger than the number of event occurrences in the corpus, so many events are seen rarely or never, making their frequency counts unreliable estimates of their probabilties.

Hindle (1990) proposed dealing with the sparseness problem by estimating the likelihood of unseen events from that of "similar" events that have been seen. For instance, one may estimate the likelihood of a particular direct object for a verb from the likelihoods of that direct object for similar verbs. This requires a reasonable definition of verb similarity and a similarity estimation method. In Hindle's proposal, words are similar if we have strong statistical evidence that they tend to participate in the same events. His notion of similarity seems to agree with our intuitions in many cases, but it is not clear how it can be used directly to construct classes and corresponding models of associ-

Our research addresses some of the same questions and uses similar raw data, but we investigate how to factor word association tendencies into associations of words to certain hidden senses classes and associations between the classes themselves. While it may be worthwhile to base such a model on preexisting sense classes (Resnik, 1992), in the work described here we look at how to derive the classes directly from distributional data. More specifically, we model senses as probabilistic concepts or clusters c with corresponding cluster membership probabilities <EQN/> for each word w. Most other class–based modeling techniques for natural language rely instead on "hard" Boolean classes (Brown et al., 1990). Class construction is then combinatorically very demanding and depends on frequency counts for joint events involving particular words, a potentially unreliable source of information, as we noted above. Our approach avoids both problems.

Problem Setting

In what follows, we will consider two major word classes, <EQN/> and <EQN/>, for the verbs and nouns in our experiments, and a single relation between a transitive main verb and the head noun of its direct object. Our raw knowledge about the relation consists of the frequencies <EQN/> of occurrence of particular pairs <EQN/> in the required configuration in a training corpus. Some form of text analysis is required to collect such a collection of pairs. The corpus used in our first experiment was derived from newswire text automatically parsed by Hindle's parser Fidditch (Hindle, 1993). More recently, we have constructed similar tables with the help of a statistical part–of–speech tagger (Church, 1988) and of tools for regular expression pattern matching on tagged corpora (Yarowsky, p.c.). We have not yet compared the accuracy and coverage of the two methods, or what systematic biases they might introduce, although we took care to filter out certain systematic errors, for instance the misparsing of the subject of a complement clause as the direct object of a main verb for report verbs like "say".

We will consider here only the problem of classifying nouns according to their distribution as direct objects of verbs; the converse problem is formally similar. More generally, the theoretical basis for our method supports the use of clustering to build models for any n–ary relation in terms of associations between elements in each coordinate and appropriate hidden units (cluster controids) and associations between these hidden units.

FIGURE 106 Annotation of First Page of *Pereira et al. (1993)* by Naive Bayes Model.

Out of these, the k-Nearest Neighbour classifier, the IBk algorithm, achieved the highest performance for CFC. In Teufel (2000), I applied RIPPER (Cohen, 1995, 1996) and the classifier described in Mikheev (1998) to the problem, but according to some initial tests, this did not improve results over Naive Bayes. Siddharthan and Teufel (2007) use stacked classifiers: all static features (all features except `Curr` and `Hist`) are first classified by Naive Bayes stacked on a J48 Decision Tree, with Naive Bayes as the meta-classifier. In a second classification, the first-stage results for `Curr` and `Hist` are added to the static feature set, and a Hidden Naive Bayes classification is performed.

More sophisticated machine learning methods could be applied to AZ. For instance, KCA, as the most fundamental distinction, could be classified first, feeding the KCA status as features into subsequent AZ classification. Alternatively, one could apply the most reliable features first, and take other, less obvious decisions later.

Another approach is global optimisation. The minimal-cut algorithm (Nagamochi and Ibaraki, 1992) aims to minimise the number of changes in the sequence of target categories, in balance with the classification confidence of the target categories.

The features can also be used directly in manual rules, sidelining all machine learning. In Teufel (2000), I present a set of symbolic rules based on the features (mostly the meta-discourse features), which is aimed at the determination of the move-based categories AIM, TEXTUAL, BASIS and CONTRAST. The confidence score produced by the rules can be used for high-precision extraction; for instance, AIM sentences can be determined with $P = 0.96$ and $R = 0.23$. The fact that the meta-discourse features `Ent`, `Act` and `Formu` directly useful for this task provides an independent justification for these features.

Chapter Summary

In this chapter I have described my prototype implementation of an automatic system for Argumentative Zoning (AZ) and Citation Function Classification (CFC). The processing is shallow in that the most complicated pre-processing required is POS-tagging. The system does not require a parser, but would probably benefit from the use of one.

Once the features are determined, different machine learning algorithms can be applied to learn correlations between these features and the human annotation, i.e., the target features. I have used Naive Bayes as the main model, but other machine learning algorithms such as kNN and Hidden Naive Bayes have also been applied to the problem over the years. The next chapter formally evaluates the different systems.

12

Evaluation

The last chapter has described how one can build a system that automatically performs AZ, KCA and CFC; this chapter will now judge the quality of such a system.

Generally, there are three main methods for evaluating the output of NLP systems:

- *Evaluation by subjective judgement*: a human judge directly scores certain properties of the system output, often on a fixed scale. For instance, they may be asked how grammatical they find a certain system output, on a scale from 1 to 5.
- *Evaluation by gold standard comparison*: a gold standard is defined by a human judge, which the system output is then compared to.
- *Task-based evaluation*: a human subject is asked to perform some secondary task on the basis of the system output: i.e., a task different from that of the NLP system being evaluated. Depending on the original task, many secondary tasks are possible, e.g., relevance decision, map navigation or answering of comprehension questions. In this setup, the human's performance on the secondary task provides an estimate for the quality of the system output.

Different metrics are used in the three evaluation types. In evaluation by subjective judgement, system performance is reported in terms of points on a quality scale. In gold standard evaluation, where the system output is compared to what it should have been, performance is reported in terms of agreement metrics such as the ones introduced in section 8.1. In task-based evaluation, system performance is reported in terms of the natural performance metric of the secondary task; often, the time used to perform the secondary task is also reported.

In section 12.1 of this chapter, various AZ systems (Teufel, 2000, Teufel and Moens, 2002, Siddharthan and Teufel, 2007) and the CFC system (Teufel et al., 2006a) will be evaluated by gold standard comparison. In section 12.2, the AZ output will be additionally evaluated by extrinsic evaluation and by subjective judgement.

Task-based evaluations do not look at the system output per se. System output is not compared to what it "should" look like, and users are not asked what they think about it. Therefore, task-based evaluations are called *extrinsic* (Spärck Jones and Galliers, 1996): properties of the summary are never measured in isolation, but only in terms of an external secondary task. In contrast, evaluation by subjective judgement and by comparison to a gold standard are called *intrinsic*, because the evaluated entity is considered in isolation.

There is some contention about which kind of evaluation is best, in terms of how convincing the evidence produced is, and how much effort is involved. Evaluation by subjective judgement is normally cheapest, particularly if a system need only be evaluated once. Task-based evaluation is the most expensive type of evaluation, because apart from requiring human judges for each evaluation instance, the secondary task also needs to be carefully set up. For instance, one has to control for the fact that some subjects might be inherently better at performing the secondary task, irrespective of which input they are exposed to.

Gold standard comparisons can rival subjective evaluations in terms of effort, particularly when the evaluation needs to be carried out more than once in time. The production of the gold standard is a one-time effort: once it is created, it can be reused for as many evaluation runs as required. In contrast, both subjective and task-based evaluations have the big disadvantage that the evaluation of each new system version requires new human judgement effort, because the judges have to inspect the new output, which they have never seen before. Particularly if one needs to measure system improvement on a day-to-day basis, gold standard comparison is therefore unbeatable. Additionally, in supervised machine learning, a "free" gold standard is already available in the form of the training material, which is necessary anyway. Gold standard evaluation was therefore a natural choice in my experiments.

However, there are arguments against gold standard evaluation. The most fundamental is that many tasks have no "right" answer. Judgements particularly affected by this problem are high-level ones, such as those involved in discourse structure. In the field of summarisation, comparison against one single summary is therefore nowadays considered with suspicion or entirely avoided, as in the large-scale competition DUC (Document Understanding Conference; now TAC).

Related to this is that we do not know whether human judges would have *accepted* somebody else's AZ-annotation which is similar but not identical to their own. The reliability studies in chapter 8 cannot answer this; they only show that there are some differences in how humans annotate AZ, KCA and CFC from scratch.

Gold standards are based on somebody's thoughts of what the output *should* look like, but the value of a document surrogate, which is a functional text, lies in how well it serves a function in the real world. Only an extrinsic evaluation of summary quality can tell us whether a system output would be practically usable in a real application.

It is also extremely hard to "cheat" in an extrinsic evaluation. In subjective evaluations, if subjects can guess which output is produced by the system to be evaluated, they often (subconsciously or consciously) try to "please" the experimenter by giving higher scores to that system.

Task-based evaluations are therefore considered by many as the best form of evaluation, but there is something to be said for subjective evaluations too: the user's satisfaction does constitute an important aspect of system quality – the best summarisation system is the one whose summaries many users want to use.

I will extrinsically evaluate rhetorical extracts built from the output of the 2002 AZ system, using a relation-based search application as the secondary task. As a side-experiment, subjective evaluation will also be performed. This will be reported in section 12.2.

12.1 Intrinsic Evaluation

This section reports the results of the intrinsic evaluation of various AZ systems and the CFC system described in the previous chapter. The systems used for AZ are:

- Naive Bayes (no History) (Teufel, 2000)
- Naive Bayes + Bigram (Teufel, 2000)
- Naive Bayes (with History as a feature) (Teufel and Moens, 2002), and with some generally improved implementation of the features
- Cascaded, Hidden Naive Bayes (Siddharthan and Teufel, 2007)

The system used for KCA is the Siddharthan and Teufel (2007) system. The system used for CFC is the one described in Teufel et al. (2006a).

Performance is measured by comparison to the full human gold standard annotation. For AZ, the annotated material consists of the 80 CmpLG-D articles (annotated by myself); for KCA, it consists of the same 80 articles (annotated by myself); for CFC, it consists of 116 articles (a third each annotated by Advaith Siddharthan, Dan Tidhar and myself).

I will use the baselines and metrics discussed in chapter 7: baselines by random, most frequent category, text classification via a multinomial

Naive Bayes classifier (LIBBOW; McCallum, 1996); and κ, Macro-F, and $P(A)$. The comparison against a bag-of-words text classification baseline tests my hypothesis in chapter 10 that the other features defined there should be better at generalising over the data, which should translate into better performance.

If a system is based on observation of a large amount of data (either by a machine learning algorithm, or by a human during rule writing), then it is essential to evaluate this system on data which is different to the one used during observation. This is a general methodological principle, resulting from the fact that we want systems which generalise over similarities in the data, rather than just "remembering" the data they have seen during training. Using unseen data is the only way to make sure that that the evaluation can make predictions about how well the system generalises to similar data.

If annotation is cheap, test and training data can be kept apart by setting aside a designated set of annotated articles as a test corpus for evaluation, which are not used for training or development. There is however a certain reluctance in the field to do that, because machine learning (ML) algorithms generally perform better with more data, so there is almost always a drive to use as much of the data as possible for training purposes.

A trick commonly used is *cross-validation*: the data is split into equal parts, and several sub-experiments with different combinations of the parts are performed. In each of these, a large proportion of the material is used for training and only a small section for testing. All along, the design makes sure that the system is never tested on material it has been trained on.

It works by splitting the corpus into n equal-sized parts, and by running n batches. Each batch uses a different part of the entire data for evaluation ($\frac{1}{n}$ of the data), and the other $\frac{n-1}{n}$ of the data for training. Evaluation compares the system's output with the gold standard annotation; the average performance on the n batches is reported the final result. This means that every item in the entire data set is used exactly once for evaluation, and that if an item is currently being evaluated, there is a guarantee that it has not been part of the training data for that particular batch.

12.1.1 Automatic AZ

Fig 107 shows the performance of different AZ implementations. The 2007 system, which was the outcome of joint work with Advaith Siddharthan and which uses a Hidden Naive Bayes model and a two-pass classification for estimating the `Hist` feature, achieves the best results

Method	κ	$P(A)$	Macro-F
System (against 1 Human):			
Siddharthan and Teufel (2007) HNB	0.48	0.76	0.54
Teufel and Moens (2002) NB w. `Hist`	0.45	0.73	0.50
Teufel (2000) NB + Bigram	0.41	0.70	0.46
Teufel (2000) NB	0.39	0.71	0.46
Human:			
Task-trained (3 Humans)	0.71	0.87	0.69
Non task-trained (3 Groups of 6, avg.)	0.51	0.76	0.49
Baseline (against 1 Human):			
Most frequent category	-0.12	0.68	0.11
Random, uniform distribution	-0.10	0.14	0.09
Random, observed distribution	0.00	0.48	0.14
Text Classification	0.30	0.72	0.30

FIGURE 107 Automatic and Human AZ: Summary of Results.

at $\kappa = 0.482 \pm 0.0141$[110] (k=2, n=7, N=12464) and Macro-F of 0.54. In the rest of the chapter, most analysis is performed using this system.

In comparison, the 2002 system reaches $\kappa = 0.45$ (k=2, n=7, N=12188). This system uses the category history feature `Hist` (2nd pass classification) for Naive Bayes learning. The NB system in Teufel (2000) does not take category history into account at all ($\kappa = 0.39$; k=2, n=7, N=12471). In contrast to this, the 2000 system with a bigram prior (NB + Bigram), which exploits category history, results in an improvement to $\kappa = 0.41$, but no improvement in Macro-F (indeed, a slightly lowered Macro-F). In contrast to the 2000 NB system, the NB+Bigram system shows better F-measures for the categories AIM, OTHER and OWN, and lower ones for CONTRAST, TEXTUAL, BASIS and BACKGROUND.

All four systems perform substantially better than the baselines. As predicted, text classification (TC) is the most difficult baseline to beat at $\kappa = 0.30$, but even the 2000 simple NB system easily defeats it. This shows that the features from chapter 10 are providing information above and beyond the simple words contained in the sentence. As we already know from chapter 8, baselines by random agreement and by most frequent category baseline perform badly.

Fig. 108 shows the performance of the 2007 system per AZ category, in comparison to the text categorisation baseline (LIBBOW) and the average of the pairwise agreement between humans from Study II

[110]This means that the 95% confidence interval is [0.467511 .. 0.495725]. As described in section 8.1, variance is calculated according to Fleiss et al. (1969).

2007 System							
	Aim	Ctr	Txt	Own	Bkg	Bas	Oth
P	0.59	0.46	0.60	0.83	0.48	0.50	0.59
R	0.63	0.31	0.66	0.92	0.46	0.30	0.40
F	0.61	0.37	0.63	0.87	0.47	0.38	0.48
Baseline (LIBBOW)							
	Aim	Ctr	Txt	Own	Bkg	Bas	Oth
P	0.30	0.31	0.56	0.78	0.32	0.15	0.47
R	0.07	0.12	0.15	0.90	0.17	0.05	0.42
F	0.11	0.17	0.23	0.83	0.22	0.07	0.44
Humans (avg.)							
	Aim	Ctr	Txt	Own	Bkg	Bas	Oth
P	0.72	0.50	0.79	0.94	0.68	0.82	0.74
R	0.56	0.55	0.79	0.92	0.75	0.34	0.83
F	0.63	0.52	0.79	0.93	0.71	0.48	0.78

FIGURE 108 Automatic AZ: P, R and F per Category.

(section 8.3). The F-measures reached by the system range from 0.63 (Textual) and 0.61 (Aim) to 0.47 (Background), 0.38 (Basis) and 0.37 (Contrast). For categories Contrast and Basis, recall at around 0.3 is much lower than precision at around 0.5. That the classifier recognises Aim and Textual more robustly than Basis and Contrast is in line with the human results from chapter 8; in particular, there is a low human ceiling for the categories Contrast and Basis at F-measures of around 0.5.

LIBBOW classification does not constitute an acceptable solution to the AZ problem. It nearly almost chooses Own and Other segments; the move-based categories Background, Aim, Contrast and Basis are retrieved with low precision and recall.

There is still a big performance gap between humans and system. If the system is put into a pool of annotators for the 25 articles for which 3-way human judgement exists, agreement drops from $\kappa = 0.71$ to $\kappa = 0.61$, which is a clear indication that the system's annotation is still very definitely different from human annotation.

If we consider the AZ system as a sentence extractor, then the high compression achieved (0.02 for Aim, Basis and Textual sentences, 0.05 for Contrast sentences and 0.06 for Background sentences) is already a positive result. Directly comparison is difficult, because relevance and rhetorical status are orthogonal, but if we assume that Aim is similar to relevant sentences (as we did in chapter 8), then the F-measure of 0.61 compares favourably to Kupiec et al.'s (1995) of 0.42.

We can also compare these results to a simpler task, namely the detection of rhetorical sections in medical structured abstracts (see section 3.1.2). For this task, Hirohata et al. (2008) achieve $P(A) = 0.96$,[111] using a CRF and the features location, category history, and n-grams over words contained in the sentence. The $P(A)$ of the Siddharthan and Teufel (2007) system is 0.78.

Let us now look at the system's misclassifications in some more detail. Fig. 109 shows the confusion matrix of the 2007 system.

Automatic AZ

		AIM	CTR	TXT	OWN	BKG	BAS	OTH	**Total**
	AIM	**133**	4	12	47	14	2	10	**212**
	CTR	8	**177**	4	227	56	6	91	**569**
	TXT	6	2	**150**	60	3	1	5	**227**
H	OWN	56	93	63	**7789**	116	23	321	**8461**
	BKG	8	29	2	265	**348**	6	101	**759**
	BAS	11	6	8	95	12	**72**	35	**239**
	OTH	3	72	9	923	163	34	**793**	**1997**
	Total	**225**	**383**	**248**	**9406**	**712**	**144**	**1346**	**12464**

FIGURE 109 Automatic AZ: Confusion Matrix.

AIM and OWN sentences are likely to get confused (100 out of 172 sentences incorrectly classified as AIM by the system turned out to be OWN sentences). The system also shows a tendency to confuse OTHER and OWN sentences, and it sometimes fails to distinguish categories involving other people's work, e.g., OTHER, BASIS and CONTRAST.

[111] This is a per-sentence result; their per-abstract $P(A)$ is 0.69.

Overall, these tendencies mirror human errors, as a comparison with Fig. 70 shows.

We can perform various analyses to find out how useful the individual features are for the classification. This is essential for Naive Bayes, which does not perform any feature selection and which might show decreased performance when features are used which are strongly dependent on each other. Whether this is the case cannot be assessed by looking at the feature's isolated performance, but must be considered in combination with other features.

Recall that the 2007 system is a complicated 2-stage system, where the first stage is stacked and uses Naive Bayes and J48, and the second stage is a Hidden Naive Bayes (HNB) classification. A semi-exhaustive search in the space of feature combinations of that final HNB classification found the optimal feature combination to be the use of all features except from `Cit-1`, `Cit-2`, `Cit-3`, `Cit-4` and `Cont-1`. The final numbers presented in Figs. 107 and 108 are derived with this feature combination.

The performance of each feature can be tested on its own, and I have done so in Fig. 110. However, a feature might be too weak to break the prior. In this case, it will classify every item with the most frequent category (and therefore achieve κ = -0.12 here). In the given feature set, this is the case for `Cont-1`, `SciAtt-0`, `SciAtt-THEM`, `Syn-2`, `2ndAct`, `Syn-1`, `Cont-2`, `Formu-AIM`, `Formu-TXT`, `Syn-3`, `Struct-2`, `SciAtt-US`, `Struct-1`, and `Formu-CTR`. This does however not mean that these features do not help in the classification, if combined with other features. The NB classifier derives the posterior probability by multiplying evidence from each feature, so even slight evidence coming from one feature can influence the decision in the right direction. Subtractive feature analysis is therefore often more informative.

Fig. 110 lists the performance of each feature which performs differently from the prior. Out of these, `SciAtt-SUB` is the only one which actively *decreases* results. The best-performing features other than `Curr` (which performs at κ = 0.464), are `Hist` at $kappa$ = 0.299, and also the header feature `Struct-3`, the citation features `Cit-1`, `Cit-2`, `Cit-3`, `Cit-4`, `Loc` and `Formu`.

In the subtractive analysis (Fig. 111), each feature is omitted from the feature pool and performance is measured without it. Combinations of features which form a logical unit and are best interpreted together, such as the `SciAtt-X` features, are treated like single features in Fig. 111. The analysis confirms that the strongest features are `Curr`, the headline feature `Struct-3`, the combination of attribution features and entity features, the formulaic feature `Formu` and the history fea-

Feature	κ	Feature	κ	Feature	κ
Curr	0.464	Cit-4	0.182	SciAtt-X	-0.115
Hist	0.299	Loc	0.174	1stAct	-0.116
Struct-3	0.206	Formu	0.130	3rdAct	-0.116
Cit-1	0.182	1stEnt	-0.082	3rdEnt	-0.116
Cit-2	0.182	F-Strength	-0.098	Cit-1--4	-0.116
Cit-3	0.182	2ndEnt	-0.101	SciAtt-SUB	-0.478

FIGURE 110 Automatic AZ: Performance of Individual Features.

ture Hist. All these features are significantly better than the average classification, according to a 95% confidence interval after Fleiss et al. (1969) (shown in bold face in Fig. 111). Other good performances came from the section feature (Struct-1), the scientific attribution features on their own (SCIATT), the target category-specific meta-discourse features Formu-TXT, Formu-CTR and Formu-AIM, location (Loc), the verb-syntactic features taken together (Syn-1, Syn-2, Syn-3), the first scientific attribution feature (SciAtt-Us), the first action in the sentence (1stAct) and the strength of the formulaic expression (F-Strength). The following features lowered performance: 3rdEnt, Cont-1 (the *TF*IDF* feature), Cit-1, Cit-2, Cit-3, Cit-4, and out of these, Cit-4 in particular, and SciAtt-O.

In Siddharthan and Teufel (2007), we omit the SciAtt features from the entire classification (at both stages; this is different from how Fig. 111 was compiled, where features are omitted only from the second stage). This decreased performance from $\kappa = 0.48$ to $\kappa = 0.45$, showing that even imperfect resolution of ambiguous anaphora in scientific text can improve the performance of an AZ classifier.

In Teufel and Moens (2002), where a subset of these features are tested in a more straightforward statistical classification, Loc was the single most distinctive feature, followed by 1stEnt ($\kappa = 0.19$), Cit-1 ($\kappa = 0.18$), Struct-3 (headlines, $\kappa = 0.17$), Ent[112] ($\kappa = 0.08$) and Formu ($\kappa = 0.07$). The following features are too weak to break the prior: Loc, Struct-2, Cont-1, Length, Syn-1, Syn-2, and Syn-3. 1stAct at $\kappa = -0.11$ performs slightly better than the baseline by most frequent category, but worse than random by observed distribution (which is zero by definition). The feature Hist, which is optimised by beam-search, performs very badly on its own at $\kappa = -0.51$; it classifies almost all sentences as BACKGROUND. This is because the probability of the first sentence being a BACKGROUND sentence is almost 1,

[112]This is the segmental version of the feature (S-Ent); it outperformed the non-segmental version in all situations.

and, if no other information is available, it is it very likely that a BACKGROUND sentence is followed by another BACKGROUND sentence.

Feature	κ	$\delta\kappa$
`Curr`	**0.446**	**-0.31**
`Struct-3`	**0.462**	**-0.15**
`Ag-1, Ag-2, Ag-2, SciAtt-X`	**0.462**	**-0.15**
`Formu`	**0.464**	**-0.13**
`Hist`	**0.465**	**-0.10**
`Struct-1`	0.467	-0.10
`SciAtt-X`	0.467	-0.10
`Formu-TXT, Formu-CTR, Formu-AIM`	0.469	-0.08
`Loc`	0.470	-0.07
`Syn-1, Syn-2, Syn-3`	0.471	-0.06
`CTR`	0.471	-0.06
`1stAct, 2ndAct, 3rdAct`	0.472	-0.05
`SciAtt-US`	0.472	-0.05
`1stAct`	0.473	-0.04
`F-Strength`	0.473	-0.04
`1stEnt, 2ndEnt, 3rdEnt`	0.474	-0.03
`Struct-2`	0.475	-0.03
`Syn-3`	0.475	-0.02
`Formu-TXT`	0.475	-0.02
`Formu-AIM`	0.476	-0.01
`1stEnt`	0.476	-0.01
`2ndEnt`	0.476	-0.01
`3rdAct`	0.476	-0.01
`Cont-2`	0.476	-0.01
`Cit-3`	0.476	-0.01
`Syn-1`	0.476	-0.01
`2ndAct`	0.477	0
`Cit-1`	0.477	0
`Cit-2`	0.477	0
`Syn-2`	0.477	0
`SciAtt-THEM`	0.477	0
`SciAtt-SUB`	0.477	0
`3rdEnt`	0.478	+0.01
`Cont-1`	0.478	+0.01
`Cit-4`	0.478	+0.01
`Cit-1, Cit-2, Cit-3, Cit-4`	0.478	+0.01
`SciAtt-0`	0.480	+0.03

FIGURE 111 Automatic AZ: Subtractive Feature Analysis.

The WEKA machine learning toolkit (Witten and Frank, 2005) allows for experimentation with different classifiers. Our best results was achieved with the Hidden Markov Model; Fig. 112 gives the corresponding best results with other WEKA ML algorithms we tried.

Fig. 113 shows all AIM, BASIS and CONTRAST sentences that the 2002

Method	κ	Method	κ
Hidden Naive Bayes	0.480	J48 (decision trees)	0.423
WAODE	0.477	JRip	0.378
Naive Bayes	0.460	IBk(1)	0.359
Decision Table	0.423	IBk(3)	0.355
Bayes Net	0.410		

FIGURE 112 Automatic AZ: Different Machine Learning Methods.

system found in *Pereira et al. (1993)*. Ticks after a sentence number indicate that the human judge agrees with the system's decision, as is the case in 15 out of the 20 extracted sentences. In the case of disagreement, the human's preferred category is given in brackets after the sentence.

Whereas the first system-proposed AIM sentence (S-8) is clearly wrong, all other "incorrect" AIM sentences (S-41, S-12, S-150) do carry important information about the authors' research goal. Similarly, in S-21 the `Ent` and `Act` features detected that the first part of the sentence has something to do with comparisons, which resulted in the (plausible but incorrect) classification as CONTRAST.

This example again illustrates that evaluation by gold standard comparison may be too strict. The gold standard results for CONTRAST and BASIS are quite low (R around 0.3 and P around 0.5), but in a real task the low recall might not matter much. Citation function is often redundantly expressed in a document, and downstream applications such as citation maps need only recognise it once. I will investigate empirically, with the extrinsic evaluation in section 12.2, whether the information provided by the AZ system is useful in information management.

Aim:

× **S-8** *In Hindle's proposal, words are similar if we have strong statistical evidence that they tend to participate in the same events.* (Other)

√ **S-10** *Our research addresses some of the same questions and uses similar raw data, but we investigate how to factor word association tendencies into associations of words to certain hidden senses classes and associations between the classes themselves.*

√ **S-11** *While it may be worthwhile to base such a model on preexisting sense classes (Resnik, 1992), in the work described here we look at how to derive the classes directly from distributional data.*

× **S-12** *More specifically, we model senses as probabilistic concepts or clusters c with corresponding cluster membership probabilities* ***EQN*** *for each word w.* (Own)

√ **S-22** *We will consider here only the problem of classifying nouns according to their distribution as direct objects of verbs; the converse problem is formally similar.*

× **S-41** *However, this is not very satisfactory because one of the goals of our work is precisely to avoid the problems of data sparseness by grouping words into classes.* (Contrast)

× **S-150** *We also evaluated asymmetric cluster models on a verb decision task closer to possible applications to disambiguation in language analysis.* (Own)

√ **S-162** *We have demonstrated that a general divisive clustering procedure for probability distributions can be used to group words according to their participation in particular grammatical relations with other words.*

Basis:

√ **S-19** *The corpus used in our first experiment was derived from newswire text automatically parsed by Hindle's parser Fidditch (Hindle, 1993).*

√ **S-20** *More recently, we have constructed similar tables with the help of a statistical part-of-speech tagger (Church, 1988) and of tools for regular expression pattern matching on tagged corpora (Yarowsky, 1992).*

√ **S-113** *The analogy with statistical mechanics suggests a deterministic annealing procedure for clustering (Rose et al., 1990), in which the number of clusters is determined through a sequence of phase transitions by continuously increasing the parameter* ***EQN*** *following an annealing schedule.*

Contrast:

√ **S-9** *His notion of similarity seems to agree with our intuitions in many cases, but it is not clear how it can be used directly to construct word classes and corresponding models of association.*

√ **S-14** *Class construction is then combinatorially very demanding and depends on frequency counts for joint events involving particular words, a potentially unreliable source of information as we noted above.*

× **S-21** *We have not yet compared the accuracy and coverage of the two methods, or what systematic biases they might introduce, although we took care to filter out certain systematic errors, for instance the misparsing of the subject of a complement clause as the direct object of a main verb for report verbs like "say".* (Own)

√ **S-43** *This is a useful advantage of our method compared with agglomerative clustering techniques that need to compare individual objects being considered for grouping.*

FIGURE 113 Automatic AZ: Aim, Basis and Contrast Sentences from *Pereira et al. (1993).*

12.1.2 Automatic KCA

The agreement between the Siddharthan and Teufel (2007) system and production mode KCA annotation (80 articles) is $\kappa = 0.50 \pm 0.0155$. This means that the 95% confidence κ interval is [0.484593 .. 0.515693]. $P(A) = 0.80$, and Macro-F = 0.64. These results are measured using all features excluding `Cont-1`, `Cit-1`, `Cit-2`, `Cit-3`, `Cit-4` and `SciAtt-3`. This compares to a human ceiling of $\kappa = 0.78$, and a text classification baseline of $\kappa = 0.34$. Fig. 114 shows precision and recall per category whereas Fig. 115 gives the confusion matrix.

Fig. 116 presents a subtractive feature analysis, i.e., answers the question of which features are most useful for classification. In order to be significantly different from the κ achieved with all features (0.484), the 95% confidence interval is [0.471936 .. 0.503428]. No feature other that `Curr` (which is not a regular feature) achieves this.

	NO-KC	EX-KC	NEW-KC
P	0.52	0.64	0.85
R	0.42	0.53	0.91
F	0.46	0.58	0.88

FIGURE 114 Automatic KCA: P, R and F per Category.

	NO-KC	EX-KC	NEW-KC	**Total**
NO-KC	315	178	266	759
EX-KC	179	1479	1147	2805
NEW-KC	113	664	8123	8900
Total	607	2321	9536	12464

FIGURE 115 Automatic KCA: Confusion Matrix.

The picture that emerges is similar to the one for AZ in section 12.1.1 above. Again, the scientific attribution features are doing better than the `Ent` features, and seem to be replacing both them and the citation features, which in this feature pool are now the worst features. The only feature whose omission significantly decreases results is the preclassified first-pass result (`Curr`), but other well-performing features include headlines (`Struct-3`), formulaic expressions (`Formu`), the scientific attribution features (`SciAtt-X`) and the verb-syntactic features (`Syn-1` to `Syn-3`), particularly if taken together. Surprisingly, the first-pass guess of the previous sentence's category (`Prev`) lowered results in this task.

Feature	κ	$\delta\kappa$
`Curr`	**0.445**	**-0.39**
`Struct-3`	0.473	-0.11
`Formu`	0.474	-0.10
`SciAtt-X`	0.477	-0.07
`Struct-1`	0.479	-0.05
`Syn-1, Syn-2, Syn-3`	0.479	-0.05
`TXT,AIM,CTR`	0.480	-0.04
`Loc`	0.481	-0.03
`Syn-3`	0.482	-0.02
`Syn-1`	0.483	-0.01
`Syn-3`	0.484	0
`Cont-2`	0.485	+0.01
`1stAct, 2ndAct, 3rdAct`	0.485	+0.01
`Hist`	0.486	+0.02
`Cont-1`	0.486	+0.02
`1stEnt, 2ndEnt, 3rdEnt`	0.486	+0.02
`Struct-2`	0.487	+0.03
`Cit-1, Cit-2, Cit-3, Cit-4`	0.494	+0.10

FIGURE 116 Automatic KCA: Subtractive Feature Analysis.

12.1.3 Automatic CFC

Work on automatic CFC as reported in Teufel et al. (2006a) was done jointly with Advaith Siddharthan and Dan Tidhar.

The features used for CFC are: `Formu`, `Ent`, `Act`, `Formu-TXT`, `Formu-CTR`, `Formu-AIM`, `Cit-1` to `Cit-4`, `Syn-1`, `Syn-2`, `Syn-3`, `Loc`, `Struct-1`, `Struct-2` and `Struct-3`. We find memory-based learning (IBk) to outperform other models in WEKA (Witten and Frank, 2005). The best results ($\kappa = 0.57$ (n=12, N=2829, k=2); $P(A) = 0.77$; Macro-F = 0.57) are measured with 10-fold cross-validation and k=3.

Fig. 117 gives individual precision, recall and F-measure results per category. PMot is the best non-neutral category with an F-measure of 0.69. Features Weak, CoCoGM, CoCoR0, CoCoXY, PBas and PUse have F-measures of around 0.60, whereas PSim and PSup are just below 0.50. The two lower outliers are PModi ($F = 0.37$) and CoCo- ($F = 0.28$).

If we compare this to the human classification in Fig. 81 (p. 236), we see many similarities. Both humans and machine found PMot, CoCoGM, and PUse easiest to distinguish, in this order. In both cases, PSup and CoCo- are at the lower end. However, humans had

Category	P	R	F	Category	P	R	F
NEUT	0.80	0.92	0.86	PBAS	0.76	0.46	0.58
PMOT	0.75	0.64	0.69	COCORO	0.77	0.46	0.57
COCOGM	0.81	0.52	0.64	PSIM	0.68	0.38	0.48
PUSE	0.66	0.61	0.63	PSUP	0.83	0.32	0.47
COCOXY	0.72	0.54	0.62	PMODI	0.60	0.27	0.37
WEAK	0.78	0.49	0.60	COCO-	0.56	0.19	0.28

FIGURE 117 Automatic CFC: P, R and F per Category.

particular difficulties with PSUP,[113] and the system with COCO-. What might make COCO- hard for the system to recognise is that it requires the interpretation of the directionality of a numerical comparison of two results.

The other categories split into two sets: First, those that the system found relatively hard and humans found relatively easy, namely COCORO, PSIM and PMODI. PMODI and PSIM are expressed with a wide range of lexical realisations, which is challenging for the system. Second, those that the humans have difficulty with, but which the system finds relatively easy, are COCOXY, WEAK and BASIS. A factor that might make WEAK and BASIS appear less well-defined to humans is that they are to a certain degree subject to sociological interpretation.

We next experimented with collapsing the obvious similar categories (all P categories into one category, and all COCO categories into another) to give four top level categories WEAK, POSITIVE, CONTRAST, NEUTRAL.[114] This increases agreement with the human gold standard to $\kappa = 0.59$ (n=4; N=2829; k=2). For comparison, the human agreement for this situation is $\kappa = 0.76$ (n=4; N=548; k=3), corresponding to a $P(A)$ of 0.79, and a Macro-F of 0.68. Fig. 118 gives results for the four collapsed categories. Precision for all the categories is now at 0.75 or higher.

Fig. 119 shows the confusion matrix between two annotators for categories which are collapsed yet further, to simulate more standard sentiment classification. What is surprising is that there is only one case of confusion between clearly positive and negative references to cited work. The vast majority of disagreements reflects genuine ambiguity as to whether the authors were trying to stay neutral or express a

[113]The comparison between system and human performance made here is relative and not absolute; in absolute terms, the humans performed almost universally better than the system.

[114]Note that this is slightly different from the top distinction in Fig. 53, where COCO- is clustered with WEAK.

	Weak	Positive	Contrast	Neutral
P	0.80	0.75	0.77	0.81
R	0.49	0.65	0.52	0.90
F	0.61	0.70	0.62	0.86

FIGURE 118 Automatic CFC, Collapsed Categories: P, R and F.

sentiment, an effect also found in the area of sentiment classification (see section 6.5).

	Weak	Positive	Neutral
Weak	**9**	1	12
Positive		**140**	13
Neutral	4	30	**339**

FIGURE 119 Human CFC, Collapsed Categories: Confusion Matrix.

As an illustration of correct cases and possible sources of misclassification, Fig. 120 shows some of the system's PUse decisions from one CmpLG article; the human's decision for the given citation is given in the second row.

The first example is a straightforward (and correct) case of PUse. The second one, also correct, shows that the system can deal even with weak cues ("*for... task... presented in*"). In the third example, the human decided that the citation was for a detail in the used software package, not for the software package itself – a semantic distinction which the machine cannot replicate. In the next example, the human applied expert knowledge (they knew that the F-measure was not attributable to that citation). In the last two examples, the machine is mislead by the strong PUse-cues in the respective preceding sentences.

This concludes the description of the gold standard based evaluation of the AZ, KCA and CFC systems. Let us now turn to the question of how we can measure whether the system output is useful in a real information management task.

12.2 Extrinsic Evaluation (AZ)

The output of the AZ system can be evaluated by building rhetorical extracts on the basis of an AZ classification of an article, and then testing the extracts in a user-based evaluation. The experiment reported here and in Teufel (2001) uses rhetorical extracts which are designed to describe the contribution of a scientific article in relation to other work, like the difference-and-similarity extracts discussed in section 4.1. They

Citation and Context	Human
S-52 *We have used the baseNP data presented in* **Ramshaw and Marcus (1995)** (PUSE).	PUSE
S-20 *We have compared four complete and three partial data representation formats for the baseNP recognition task presented in* **Ramshaw and Marcus (1995)** (PUSE).	PUSE
S-34 *In the version of the algorithm that we have used, IB1-IG, the distances between feature representations are computed as the weighted sum of distances between individual features* **(Bosch 1998)** (PUSE).	NEUT
S-60 *We will follow* **Argamon et al. (1998)** (PUSE) *and use a combination of the precision and recall rates: F=(2*precision*recall)/(precision+recall).*	PSIM
S-90 *This algorithm standardly uses the single training item closest to the test i.e., However* **Daelemans et al. (1999)** (PUSE) *report that for baseNP recognition better results can be obtained by making the algorithm consider the classification values of the three closest training items.*	NEUT
S-98 *They are better than the results for section 15 because more training data was used in these experiments. Again the best result was obtained with IOB1 (F=92.37) which is an improvement of the best reported F-rate for this data set* **(Ramshaw and Marcus 1995)** (PUSE) *(F=92.03).* (9907006)	COCO-

FIGURE 120 Automatic CFC: Examples of PUSE Classifications by System.

consist of up to three AIM, CONTRAST and BASIS sentences each. A rhetorical extract for CmpLG-D article 9405001 is given in Fig. 121. The figure shows the correct answer in parentheses for those sentences which are misclassified.[115]

When setting up an extrinsic evaluation, the secondary task has to be chosen carefully. I use a citation-based extraction task here: users are asked to list approaches which are positively or negatively cited in the text. This will be compared against their performance under other conditions: namely, when they have either the full text or other document surrogates available instead. One of these is the "gold standard" rhetorical extract, which is generated on the basis of the human gold standard annotation. The condition we are most interested in is of course the "real" system extract, for which the 2002 AZ system is used.[116]

[115]Note that this information does not appear in the actual experimental materials.

[116]This is not an anachronism – the 2002 system was already fully implemented in 2001, when this experiment was performed.

Aim

S-22 *We now give a similarity-based method for estimating the probabilities of cooccurrences unseen in training.*

S-151 *Our method combines similarity-based estimates with Katz's back-off scheme, which is widely used for language modeling in speech recognition.* (Basis)

Contrast

S-20 *Their model, however, is not probabilistic, that is, it does not provide a probability estimate for unobserved cooccurrences.*

S-28 *We applied our method to estimate unseen bigram probabilities for Wall Street Journal text and compared it to the standard back-off model.* (Own)

S-115 *We will outline here the main parallels and differences between our method and cooccurrence smoothing.*

Basis

S-23 *Similarity-based estimation was first used for language modeling in the cooccurrence smoothing method of Essen and Steinbiss (1992), derived from work on acoustic model smoothing by Sugawara et al. (1985).* (Other)

S-87 *The baseline back-off model follows closely the Katz design, except that for compactness all frequency one bigrams are ignored.*

122 *Notice that this formula has the same form as our similarity model CREF, except that it uses confusion probabilities where we use normalized weights.* (Contrast) (9405001)

FIGURE 121 Sample System-Generated Rhetorical Extract (Condition **S**).

The task normally used in extrinsic summary evaluation is *relevance decision* in a document retrieval context: subjects have to decide on the basis of a summary whether or not a document is relevant to a given query (e.g., Mani et al., 2002). The two variables measured are task completion time and task performance, i.e., recall and precision of correct relevance decisions. The perfect summary is one which allows a user to predict the relevance of a document to a query as well as the full article would have, while saving reading time. Extrinsic evaluations of this kind often compare summaries to the full texts. An alternative is a baseline of the same length as the summary.

Previous extrinsic evaluations of extracts show that extracts are useful for relevance decisions: Tombros et al. (1998) found that their query-based sentence extracts improved recall on 50 TREC queries from 0.50 to 0.66 when compared to typical IR output (namely title and first few sentences) and precision from 0.44 to 0.55. Their sentence extracts also increased speed: users were able to examine 22.6 documents in 5 minutes, compared with 20 documents. Mani et al. (1999a), evaluating 16 sentence-extraction-based systems contrastively in the large-scale TIPSTER SUMMAC evaluation exercise, found that summaries as short as 17% of the full text length can speed up decision making by a factor of 2, without degrading F-measure. More recent task-based extrinsic evaluations measure the advantage of real headlines versus ultra-short summaries for relevance decision task (Zajic et al., 2004), with similar results.

However, there is some doubt whether relevance decision is the right task to measure summary quality in the first place. All that is required to perform relevance decision is knowledge about the *topic* of a document, and there are simpler document surrogates that can provide this. For example, experts in a field often decide on the basis of title and author alone if they need to read an article or not (Bazerman, 1985); this is particularly the case in medicine where the titles tend to be long and informative. Keywords (automatically chosen index terms) often accurately portray the topic of a text, and one can speculate that they would also work well for relevance decision. Another example of a simple baseline are randomly chosen sentences from the document. However, previous task-based summary evaluations do not normally compare performance against these kinds of simpler baselines, probably due to the extensive effort required to prepare and run relevance decision evaluations.

In comparison to these simpler document surrogates, summaries are coherent texts. Their added value lies in their ability to convey more complex information about concepts and events and how they relate to the overall message of the document. If we want to show the advantage of summaries over simpler document surrogates, then a task is needed that is harder than relevance decision. Also, we need to show that simpler document surrogates cannot perform this task equally well.

My proposal for such a secondary task is to ask subjects in which respect a scientific article relates to the previous work it describes and cites. After seeing an article in one particular condition, they have to sort the articles from the reference list into those that are criticised and those that are used in a supportive fashion; their answers are then scored. What counts as correct is defined in each instance by the experimental group which has access to the entire document.

As a side-experiment, I also elicit subjective judgements about the rhetorical extracts, namely whether subjects find them useful (on a scale from 1 to 10) for performing the task.

12.2.1 Experimental Design

In an experimental setting, each of the main alternatives we want to test (here: the document surrogates) are called *conditions*. The only thing that changes between experiments should be the conditions; all other factors which might influence the outcome should be controlled for across conditions, i.e., kept constant. An example for such a factor is the length of a document surrogate in a relevance decision task: is is experimentally known that there is a direct link between the amount of information in an extract and task performance.

Each individual piece of material used in an experiment is called an *item*. An item will occur in different conditions, e.g., as a rhetorical extract or a full document. Here, the items are scientific articles.

A methodologically sound evaluation should follow several principles from experimental psychology. For instance, each experimental group should be sampled randomly from the same subject population, and should be large enough to factor out possible intrinsic individual performance differences between the groups. When subjects are shown an item, they must not know which condition it is in; ideally, they should not even be able to guess how many conditions there are.[117] This makes sure that subjects cannot guess and thus consciously influence the outcome. Items are to be randomised, so that attention deficits towards the end of the experiment, and training effects in the beginning, are distributed evenly over the conditions.

It is also crucial that a subject should see each item only once, due to an interference phenomenon called *experimental bias*. The subject is in a fresh state of mind about an item the first time they encounter it, and only then. When they are shown the same item a second time (in a different condition), there is an interference with the knowledge about this item which they have just gained from the first exposure.

For instance, if one asks subjects to perform a task with a summary of a text they have already seen in another condition, (i.e., a different summary of the same text), their task performance with the second summary will invariably be influenced by their knowledge of the first summary. Experimental psychologists have found this a strong factor for all kinds of experiments, including linguistic ones. This bias is subconscious – subjects can demonstrably not be asked to "switch it off". Therefore, it is generally agreed in experimental psychology that each item should only be shown to a subject in one single condition only.

[117]Some experimental setups use so-called *filler* items to confuse the subjects as to the real purpose of the experiment. Filler items are unrelated material that looks superficially similar to the real items, and will not be used for the analysis.

In terms of statistical significance tests, non-parametric tests such as the sign test are to be preferred to parametric tests such as Student's t-test because parametric tests make assumptions about how the data is distributed (e.g., normally). In natural language, we typically do not know *a priori* how the values we measure are going to be distributed. Paired tests are in general preferable, as they can show effects with less data. In paired tests, comparable data points are measured from the same subject, which means that each subject is his or her own control with respect to other conditions. This is useful, because subjects may have individual tendencies (one subject may always give low scores, for instance). The use of paired tests is however in conflict with the requirement of showing each item to each subject only once.

The Latin Square design offers a solution to this dilemma. It distributes materials in different conditions to the subject groups in such a way that each subject sees several items in different conditions, but no item in more than one condition. The number of conditions determines how many subject groups are required. Fig. 122 shows how subjects are assigned to items and conditions in my experiment. There are six conditions (**F, A, G, S, R** and **K**, to be explained below), which means that subjects had to be recruited in multiples of six (I ended up with 24 subjects in 6 groups of 4 people each). The design also dictated that the number of articles used had to be multiples of six. I decided to restrict this to six articles. This was because the effort involved per subject was not to exceed one hour (partially because subjects were unpaid).

	Articles					
	1	2	3	4	5	6
Group 1	F	A	G	R	K	S
Group 2	A	G	R	K	S	F
Group 3	G	R	K	S	F	A
Group 4	R	K	S	F	A	G
Group 5	K	S	F	A	G	R
Group 6	S	F	A	G	R	K

FIGURE 122 Experimental Design (Latin Square).

Unfortunately, we know from chapter 8 that there is a high degree of variation between scientific articles. The normal remedy would be to raise the number of items a subject sees, but this was not an option because of limitations on subjects' time. The use of the Latin Square Design is an alternative which allowed me to collect data points for many different baselines in a time-efficient way, and to use a paired test, thus factoring out the differences between subjects and items.

The following six conditions are considered:

- **F**: The full article, presented in printed form
- **A**: The author-written abstract
- **K**: A list of keywords, as derived by the *TF*IDF* measure
- **R**: A random selection of sentences from the document
- **S**: A rhetorical extract, generated by the 2002 system
- **G**: A rhetorical extract, generated from the gold standard

Condition **S** is the main condition: rhetorical extracts are generated on the basis of the system's AZ annotation. The target length of an extract is 9 sentences: three Aim, plus three Contrast, plus three Basis sentences. If the system output contains more than three sentences of a type, three were chosen at random. If it contains fewer than three sentences, a shorter rhetorical extract is created, and all other conditions for that item are shortened to the same degree. For an article to qualify as experimental material, at least one sentence for each type must be present.

For condition **G** (gold standard rhetorical extracts), the production mode gold standard annotation (section 8.6) is used instead of the system's annotation; otherwise, the same algorithm for the construction of extracts is used. This condition allows us to evaluate whether (perfect) AZ-extracts are *in principle* useful document surrogates for this task – condition **G** is perfect in comparison to the "imperfect" condition **S**. The difference between conditions **S** and **G** therefore tells us how well the system output approximates the gold standard.

Condition **F** is the ceiling. Subjects with access to the entire article should in principle be in the best position to perform the task. For time reasons, skim-reading time of the full text condition is restricted to 10 minutes.

Conditions **A**, **K** and **R** are the baselines. Abstracts (condition **A**) are human-written artefacts and thus of high quality. However, we know from section 3.1.2 that they are not written to express relations between articles. For condition **K** (keywords), the n highest *TF*IDF* scoring single words are selected (IDFs calculated from CmpLG-D). For condition **R**, sentences are chosen at random from the document.

The length I am standardising to is the minimum of sentences in the three conditions **A**, **G** and **S**. If either type of sentence (Aim, Basis, or Contrast) in conditions **S** and **G** contains fewer than three sentences, the other document surrogates for that item have to be reduced to mirror the shorter length. If an article's abstract contains more than nine sentences or fewer than three, the article is discarded. For abstracts of between three and nine sentences, conditions G and S are shortened, by removing sentences in a round-robin fashion per sentence type, so that overall a balance between sentence types is reached.

Condition **R** is length-controlled against condition **G** by approximately balancing the number of words in both conditions. Condition **K** presents as many keywords as there are noun phrases in Condition **G**. As a result, the amount of information presented in conditions **S**, **G**, **R** and **K** should be approximately the same. As a result, difference in performance across conditions should be due to the type and quality, rather than to the amount of information presented.

The one condition which cannot be length-controlled is **F**, the full article. This condition is to test the subjects' performance, given the maximal information about an article, so truncating the information they are exposed to is not sensible.

Six articles were randomly chosen from CmpLG-D, re-sampling if the above conditions were not met. Document representations in all six conditions were created for these six items.

24 subjects participated. 21 were graduate students and faculty members working in computational linguistics (Columbia University and Edinburgh University), 3 were graduate students in other fields of computer science from Columbia University. Subjects were unpaid. Each experimental group consisted of 4 randomly selected subjects. Not all subjects were native speakers of English, but all are familiar with the field of computational linguistics, and accustomed to extracting information from scientific articles.

Each experimental group sees each of the six items in a different condition, but in the same order of items. Subjects are also given the title of the article. In condition **F**, they are allowed 10 minutes to skim-read the full text. After seeing each item, the subject is asked to answer the five questions in Fig. 123. Answers are collected on a tabular answer sheet. While filling in the answer sheet, the subjects also have access to the citation list of the article. Task completion time, though not formally measured, was much lower in the document surrogate conditions **A, K, R, S, T** than it was in the full article condition (**F**). Total task completion time was on average around 40–50 minutes for all six items.

Questions 1, 2, and 3 elicit text or lists from the subjects. These answers are then manually scored and reported as *Task Scores* (TS), namely Task Score C for question 2, and Task Score B for question 3. Questions 2 and 3 provide the main data in this experiment; Ques-

1. What is the goal/contribution of the article?

2. Contrastive approaches
   (a) Which approaches are mentioned? Identify them by citation or informal name.
   (b) What is the criticism/ difference/ contrast?

3. Prior approaches which are supportive or part of the solution:
   (a) Which other approaches are mentioned?
   (b) In which respect is their solution included?

4. How useful did you find the information you were given to solve the task? Indicate on a scale from 10 to 1, with 10 being extremely useful and 1 being useless.

5. Did you know this article beforehand? Is this article closely connected to your own research or field of expertise?

FIGURE 123 Questions Asked in Task-Based Evaluation.

tion 4 measures task adequacy in a subjective way on a scale from 1 (useless) to 10 (very useful). It produces the so-called *Utility Score*, which is interpreted as a measure of the subjects' confidence in their task performance. Question 5 was added because subjects were at different levels of expertise. A potential post-hoc analysis could filter out subjects who already knew the articles beforehand; but in the analysis reported here, this information is not used.

I decided not to use Question 1 because there is no objective way to judge the quality of the answers. Most subjects, having read the title, could guess the goal of the article fairly well. Only in four out of the $24 \times 6 = 144$ data points was a subject unable to guess the aim of the article. Instead, the answers differ in depth of understanding and specificity.

Fig. 124 shows the answers that one subject gave after they had read the rhetorical extract in Fig. 121. This is a generally well-informed answer, but note that the subject is unable to tell *who* is criticised as being non-probabilistic, because sentence S-20 does not provide that information, as the grammatical subject of that sentence is anaphoric (*"their model"*).

The gold standard against which subjects' answers to Questions 2 and 3 are scored is created in the experiment itself: it is defined as the union of the answers of the four subjects in the group that saw the full articles (Condition **F**). These subjects arguably had access to the "maximum" available information. Due to the Latin Square design, each item is seen by a different set of subjects in condition **F**, so gold

1. Aim: *Extending co-occurrence probabilites of unseen events using similarity measures and a corpus*	
2. Contrastive Approaches:	
(a) Approach	**(b) Relation**
?	*not probabilistic*
cooccurrence smoothing (Essen, Steinbiss, 92)	*differences*
Katz (1987) standard back-off model	*differences*
3. Supported Approaches:	
(a) Approach	**(b) Relation**
Katz (1987) back-off model	*further development*
Essen & Steinbiss 92	*idea and formula*
4. Usefulness: *6*	
5. Known Article? *No*	

FIGURE 124 An Example of an Answer Sheet.

standard creation is distributed over the entire subject pool. Fig. 125 shows the gold standard for article 9405001.

Contrastive	**Weight**	**Supported**	**Weight**
Essen and Steinbiss (1992)	3	*Katz (1987)*	3
Brown et al. (1992); class	2	*Pereira et al. (1993)*	3
-based models	1	*Paul (1991)*	1
Dagan et al. (1993)	1	*Dagan et. al (1993)*	1
Grishman and Sterling (1993)	1	*Essen and Steinbiss (1992)*	1
Katz (1987)	1	*Baseline bigram model (MIT)*	1
	8		10

FIGURE 125 Gold Standard Answers for Fig. 124.

Each approach in the combined gold standard is assigned a weight, which is the number of judges who listed the given approach. Thus, the weight ranges between 1 and 4. It should reflect the relevance of the approach in the article; judges are under time pressure, and approaches which are more prominent should be noticed by more judges.

When scoring the sheets, I found hardly any *wrong* answers: subjects seem to only have listed approaches if they felt sure that they were correct. This means that in almost all cases, precision is 100%. I therefore only report recall.

With respect to the string describing the relation between the current article and the cited approach (right-hand side of Fig. 124), the same subjectivity problem as for Question 1 applied. I therefore decided to use the existence of a plausible right-hand side as a precondition to assigning *any* score for the left-hand side. If no right-hand side description is present at all, the corresponding approach receives a score of 0.

Each answer sheet is scored by assigning the corresponding weight from the gold standards. This resulted in Task Scores B and C. In rare cases, it is not obvious if two descriptions match: a description of an approach might have been generally correct, but very vague. In these cases, half the score is assigned. The final score is normalised to 1 by dividing by the sum of all weights for this question and item.[118]

The Combined Task Score is the micro-averaged score of Task Scores C and B. For instance, the answer sheet in Fig. 124 scored $\frac{0.5+3+1=4.5}{8} = 0.563$ for Task Score C (the half-score is assigned for the underspecified reference to *Dagan et al.*), $\frac{1+3}{10} = 0.4$ for Task Score B, and $\frac{8.5}{18} = 0.477$ for the Combined Task Score.

12.2.2 Results

Fig. 126 gives the average task scores (recall) for the six conditions.

Conditions	**Task Scores**			**Utility**
	C	B	Combined	**Score**
F Full text	0.59	0.56	0.59	8.8
G Gold standard	0.31	0.34	0.34	6.6
S System output	0.32	0.32	0.33	7.0
A Abstracts	0.06	0.20	0.16	3.5
R Random	0.07	0.07	0.06	2.6
K Keywords	0.01	0.11	0.07	1.4

FIGURE 126 Mean Task Scores and Utility Score for the Six Conditions.

A Wilcoxon matched-pairs signed-rank test (Siegel and Castellan, 1988) found all differences to be statistically significant at $p < 0.01$, except the following:

[118] This way of scoring has the positive effect that each item (article) contributes the same amount to the final score, but the negative effect that individual citations contribute differently across items, i.e., approaches in articles with fewer citations count more.

G and **S**	not signif. for TS C, B and Combined
K and **R**	not signif. for TS C, B and Combined
A and **R**	not signif. for TS C and B, signif. at $p<0.05$ for TS Combined
A and **K**	not signif. for TS C and B, signif. at $p<0.05$ for TS Combined
A and **S**	signif. at $p<0.05$ for TS B
A and **G**	signif. at $p<0.02$ for TS B
A and **R**	signif. at $p<0.02$ for TS B

The task scores, as the main quality measurement, show that rhetorical extracts, both in the gold standard version (**G**) and as actual system output (**S**), improve users' performance significantly over the baseline document surrogates (Combined TS of 0.34 and 0.33 respectively), as opposed to abstracts (Combined TS of 0.16), keywords (Combined TS of 0.07) and random sentences (Combined TS of 0.06). Thus rhetorical extracts are better-suited to the task of listing contrastive and supportive approaches cited in an article than obvious document surrogates.

Another important result is that there is no statistically significant difference in performance between rhetorical extracts gained from human and automatic evaluation – humans could solve the same task equally well with either.

With respect to the baselines, both types of task scores confirm that keywords and random sentences are not at all useful for the task. In general, one would assume that random sentences should do better than keywords because sentences are coherent whereas keywords only indicate topical information. This is so for Task Score C, but the Combined Task Score and Task Score B show the reverse effect.[119] With hindsight, there are harder baselines one could have considered, for instance randomly sampled sentences containing citations, or sentences sampled from the *related work* section.

Human-written generic abstracts are high-quality document extracts. For the task in this experimental setup, they are however at a disadvantage because they were not designed for it, whereas rhetorical extracts are. This is mirrored in the relatively low task scores, particularly for Task Score C (Question 2); however, abstracts prove more adequate for Task B (Question 3).

[119]The good performance of keywords for Task B is likely to be noise. Three particularly well-read subjects happened to be assigned to the same group, and they recognised the article which they saw in condition **K**. They were able to guess which work the article was based on, but not which particular work it criticised. Such noise could be eliminated by a larger experiment with more subjects and more items.

Subjects' performance with rhetorical extracts remains significantly under their performance when they had 10-minute access to the the full articles (Condition **F**; combined TS of 0.59). In any case, it is unclear if a direct comparison is methodologically valid, as the scores of the other five conditions depend on the answers defined by condition **F**. Several other things about condition **F** are also problematic, e.g., the fact that the subjects agree only 59% of the 100% cases that are theoretically possible, that majority decisions generally overestimate scores, and that the other conditions are unfairly punished when correct relations have been overlooked by the **F** subjects in the 10 minute skim-read. An independent source of gold standards would therefore be a better solution, e.g., annotators who decide for each citation if it is mentioned in contrastive or supportive context, and who are not operating under a time limit.

Overall, Task Scores B tend to be higher than Task Scores C; it seems easier to guess from restricted information which school of thought an approach belongs to than which other approaches are criticised in it. One possible reason for this is that intellectual ancestry is often described in one single sentence, but contrastive connections can be more complex and might stretch over several sentences (see section 8.6).

The right-hand column of Fig. 126 shows that the subjective Utility Scores generally mirror the task performance scores. A Wilcoxon matched-pairs signed-rank test found all differences to be statistically significant at $p < 0.01$, except differences between **G** and **S** and between **R** and **K**. Differences between **A** and **K**, and differences between **A** and **R**, were significant only at the $p < 0.05$ level.

That means that subjects were aware of the suitability of different document surrogates for the task. In general, they were satisfied with the rhetorical extracts produced by the AZ system. Indeed, some subjects informally remarked how much work it was to extract the approaches from the full text, and how convenient conditions **G** and **S** were (provided that the information in them was reliable).

The similar performance of conditions **G** and **S** is surprising given that the intrinsic evaluation results from section 12.1 showed relatively low agreement of the system's output with the "ideal" annotation ($\kappa = 0.48$). This raises questions about the status of intrinsic versus extrinsic evaluation. I believe that many equally "good" summaries are possible, and a comparison of a system with only one such summary will invariably give distorted results. For day-to-day system tuning, however, there is no alternative to gold standard evaluations.

What I have proposed here is a new task for the extrinsic evaluation of summary-like document surrogates, where subjects list and qualify two types of relations between scientific approaches. This task is "harder" in comparison to relevance decision, in that it seems to require more information about an article than just its topic.

However, tasks used in extrinsic evaluations should also be realistic, i.e., the kind of task that people perform naturally anyway. One of the reasons why relevance decision is accepted as a standard task for extrinsic summary evaluation is that it is performed daily in a professional setting by real users (namely information analysts).

Affect-based classification of citations is not an established task yet. On the one hand, citation relations are very likely to be of practical interest for researchers, and the task of assessing relations between articles is a recurrent task in a researcher's work day. On the other, such tasks are less externally observable and thus less straightforward to define than relevance decision. One way of making progress in such a situation is to conduct large-scale user studies. Another way is to build a practical system that allows researchers to search rhetorical citation relations. My work with Min-Yen Kan on Robust AZ (see section 14.4) is a step in this direction. The extrinsic results reported in this chapter, and preliminary results with Robust AZ, seem to imply that the quality difference between human and automatic annotation might not matter for actual search performance.

A point of concern in this experiment is the level of expertise of the subjects. Subjects who are too well-informed might have prior knowledge of a high proportion of the material, even though it is randomly chosen. In this case they are likely to perform reasonably well even in the less informative conditions. On the other end of the spectrum, subjects who are not well-informed enough might decrease the quality of the gold standard. Ideally, as the final system is aimed at semi-experts in the field, all subjects should be semi-experts at the same level of expertise, and all articles should be unknown to them (which is very hard to control).

From a practical viewpoint, the experimental setup presented here is very time-efficient. The preparation of the materials only requires the generation of the different document surrogates, the compilation of the gold standard from the scoring sheets and the final scoring of the answers. The scoring itself can be done in a rather objective fashion. In the actual experiment, each subject produces several task-scores for the six conditions he or she sees within 40–50 minutes. The number of data points collected this way makes it feasible to test against multiple baselines in one experiment. In contrast, material preparation for relevance decision tasks is notoriously time-consuming. Using an IR system, queries need to be found which are of the right level of specificity. All returned documents must be judged by a human as relevant or irrelevant in order to be able to calculate precision and recall, a task that can take many hours even if techniques such as pooling are used to cut down the size of the judged document set. During the experiment, each query requires considerable time and only provides one data point.

Chapter Summary

This chapter has presented the results of two evaluations: in the intrinsic evaluation, the CFC, KSC and AZ systems' annotation from chapter 11 is compared to the gold standard evaluation; in the extrinsic evaluation, subjects' performance on a search task is measured, when they are given extracts based on the AZ system's output.

The intrinsic evaluation shows that the similarity between system and gold standard classification is far from perfect: $\kappa = 0.48$ for the AZ implementation, and $\kappa = 0.57$ for the CFC implementation. However, the AZ system beats a reasonably sophisticated baseline (by Naive Bayes text classification; $\kappa = 0.30$). Nevertheless the human ceiling is high at $\kappa = 0.71$ for AZ and $\kappa = 0.72$ for CFC, with a lot of room for improvement.

I also presented an extrinsic evaluation of rhetorical extracts, which are based on the 2002 AZ system's output. The task is to list which of the cited articles in an article's reference list are presented critically, and which supportively. The results show that rhetorical extracts produced by the AZ system provide the right kind of information to perform this task, as do full articles, which act as ceiling condition in this experiment. Abstracts were found to provide adequate information for the task of describing supportive approaches, but other baselines performed badly. The experiment also reveals that the output of the AZ system is not statistically significantly different from the human gold standard. These positive results were corroborated by subjective judgements about the usefulness of the document surrogates.

All in all, we have so far seen that the Knowledge Claim Discourse Model from chapter 6 can be annotated both by humans and automatically, with reasonable results. The experiments up to now were performed using a corpus of conference articles in computational linguistics.

The model's remit however is not restricted to computational linguistics, or to any one discipline – it aims to model all scientific and experimental disciplines. The following chapter will therefore consider to which degree the model can be applied across scientific disciplines.

13

Applying the KCDM to Other Disciplines

The experimental part of this book (chapters 8 through 12) demonstrated the intuitiveness and automatic learnability of the discourse model presented in chapter 6: humans can understand the model well enough to annotate several aspects of it consistently, using the annotation schemes defined in chapter 7, and human performance can be simulated automatically to a satisfactory degree. These results were achieved with a corpus of computational linguistics articles. The model, however, is meant to go beyond the description of the argumentative structure of a single discipline: its remit is all scientific and experimental disciplines.

On a rhetorical level, all scientific articles are biased descriptions of their authors' research. Whether they are astrophysicists or geneticists, the authors are forced to justify the existence of the new publication. My model is a formalisation of the universal, discipline-independent expectations which all such justifications have to fulfil.[120] For instance, one of the reasons why academic discourse generally contains explicit comparisons to existing research is that authors are forced to point out to the peer reviewers what is novel about their article. What these differences look like in detail, of course, is highly discipline-dependent – but this is of no concern to an intermediate text understanding approach such as mine. The phenomena described by the KCDM are not affected by individual differences in scientific research from one article to the next.

The claim of applicability I have just made explicitly excludes the humanities. Although I believe that several aspects of the KCDM hold

[120] I am using the term "discipline-independent" loosely in this book, to mean "independent of discipline – within the experimental sciences".

universally, i.e., for all academic discourse, it was not designed with the humanities in mind. In particular where automatic recognition is concerned, the humanities present difficulties which appear orders of magnitude greater than those in the sciences. The structure of a humanities article is intrinsically linked to the academic argument being made; while human recognition of KCDM-like argumentative structure seems just about feasible for humanities articles, its automatic recognition would necessitate deep text comprehension. In the experimental sciences however, the scientific (object-level) and non-scientific (rhetorical) content can be separated in a far more superficial manner – a fact that is exploited by my approach. (Note at this point that several CmpLG-D articles do come from theoretical linguistics, a humanities subject, and that the reliability studies in chapter 8 and in the evaluation results in chapter 12 include these articles.)

One could argue that the successful application of the KCDM to computational linguistics already constitutes a partial demonstration of the model's discipline-neutrality. CL is an interdisciplinary subject area, which covers a wide field of research and presentation traditions;[121] this was one of the original reasons for choosing CL for this research. Stronger evidence yet is provided by experiments with entirely different disciplines, like the ones presented in this chapter.

Various sources have confirmed that the phenomena described in the KCDM intuitively "exist" in other experimental disciplines as well: I have performed informal corpus studies in genetics, chemistry, agriculture, cardiology and computer science (using the corpora described in chapter 5, plus another corpus in computer science not described there) and asked informants from various disciplines. But what would constitute hard evidence for this claim?

The main questions this chapter asks are as follows:

- Do the annotation schemes from chapter 7 capture any truth about discourse structure beyond the discipline of computational linguistics, on which they were tested?
- Do the features from chapter 10 signal the model's phenomena beyond the discipline of computational linguistics, for which they were developed?

As far as the first question is concerned, it is certainly clear that differences in the argumentation style across disciplines do exist. Chemistry, for instance, contains far less overt argumentation than computational linguistics (the reader may have already concluded this from previous

[121] This can for instance be seen from the diversity of the titles of CmpLG-D articles (appendix A; p. 407).

chemistry example sentences), and the range of different citation functions appears to be narrower, but more clearly defined than in CL.

Scientific discourse in CL is rife with explicit argumentation and expressions of intellectual ancestry or contrast with other researchers. This is possibly so because in young, fast-moving disciplines such as CL, standards in terms of methodology and evaluation are not yet set in stone, and new tasks and new methods are constantly being invented. Evaluation is a special case in question: for a new task, there are often several competing evaluation methodologies which could be applied. The negotiation about which of those is most appropriate is thus often played out in print.

In contrast, the methods and tasks in a more established discipline such as chemistry are likely to be well-known and agreed on amongst its practitioners. In this situation, a researcher does not have to argue for their appropriateness or compare them to existing work quite as much; it is often enough to simply mention existing methods, and identify them by name or by citation. I also found few cases of overt criticism in chemistry as articles are written in a detached, "objective" style.[122] As a result, argumentation is often more stylised and far less overt than it is in CL.

There cannot be any doubt that chemistry articles do contain argumentation: there is no getting around the requirement that the existence of each article must be justified somehow. Even the least confrontational article will convey to its readers that the research started out from an unsatisfactory situation in the research space. The point in question is therefore not the existence of argumentation, but its realisation on the surface: is it explicit enough for humans to recognise it reliably, or is it too "hidden"? This is an empirical question which can be resolved by annotation experiments.

Section 13.1 studies whether humans can annotate aspects of the model in chemistry articles, using the Argumentative Zoning II (AZ-II) scheme, which comes from the family of KCDM schemes. In section 13.2, I will then take a look at recent AZ-inspired approaches by other researchers, who have applied their schemes to other disciplines and even another text types.

If there are categories that are not found at all in a new discipline, or if reliable annotation is only possible after drastic changes to the scheme, the discourse model would be discredited. How much damage the model takes depends on how central the categories concerned are.

[122]The example from article b030100 on p. 129 is an exception in this respect.

For instance, if KCA-annotation of chemistry articles resulted in a complete lack of one of the KCA zones, that would cast serious doubt on the truth of knowledge claim attribution as a general phenomenon, and thus on the truth of the entire KCDM. In contrast, if AZ-annotation of chemistry articles resulted in a complete lack of Textual moves, this would be far less severe, as the model makes no claims about the discipline-independence of Level 4 (linearisation and presentation), from which Textual stems.

As to the second of the questions above, namely how the features would change, even a superficial comparison of a chemistry article with a computer science article immediately shows many differences in the language, structure and meta-discourse used. Hyland's (1998b) quantitative study of meta-discourse in several disciplines confirms this (see chapter 9). It thus seems inevitable that the features from chapter 10 will have to be adapted to be applicable across disciplines. From the viewpoint of the discourse model, the adaptation of features is a practical rather than a theoretical problem. The research question here is how to predict (and automate) which features should be changed. Section 13.3 describes a method for adapting some of the meta-discourse features from chapter 9 to unseen texts in an unsupervised way.

13.1 Application to Chemistry

The discourse model was ported to chemistry in the framework of the EPSRC-funded project SciBorg (EP/C010035/1; Copestake et al., 2006). The aim of this project is to provide a deep recognition framework for natural language in an e-science setting, based on a semantic representation language. The application following from this is a search-and-interpretation workbench for chemists, which provides new forms of access to a variety of chemical information in a large set of scientific articles. Part of the system's functionality is the robust identification of chemical compound names in text (Townsend et al., 2005, Corbett and Copestake, 2008). The core area of chemistry covered in the project is organic synthesis, where new compounds are constructed according to specifications.

Sentences are parsed and represented in a semantic representation language called Robust Minimal Recursion Semantics (RMRS; Copestake, 2003, 2009). Discourse processing is used to support fine-grained literature searches. Some of the search and extraction functionalities are "general", i.e., not restricted to chemistry (e.g., the ability to list classified citation links for a particular article), but we also consider search scenarios which are specific to the core application area.

Organic chemistry articles often contain helpful mentions of certain processing steps which were found *not* to work. Such mentions, like the following ones, are typically embedded in a description of a procedure:

> *Initial attempts to improve the dehydration of* **4** *via chemical or thermal means were unsuccessful; similarly, attempts to couple the chlorosilane (Me3Si)2(Me2ClSi)CH with Ag2O failed.* (b510692c)
>
> *Unfortunately, we were unable to obtain the optical absorption spectrum of this intermediate species.* (b513898a)
>
> *We tried to unsuccessfully crystallize brucine and brucinium salts, for example, from tetrachloromethane.* (b515365d)
>
> *Although purification of 8b to a de of 95% has been reported elsewhere*[31] *in our hands it was always obtained as a mixture of the two s-diastereomers.* (b310767a)

This type of information does not get promoted and published like positive results, but it can be very valuable to a chemist, e.g., during the planning of a new synthesis route. Another usage situation is when a synthesis already ran into a particular problem; the relevant question is then whether the same problem has been observed by others before. That such hints are of high value to the chemistry community is demonstrated by the existence of a commercial database called "Database of Failed Reactions" (owned and maintained by Accelrys, `http://www.accelrys.com`).

Partial failure reports are normally followed by a *recovery statement*, which explains how the problem can be avoided. In the following, problem statements are underlined, and recovery statements boldfaced:

> *Subsequent chain extension proceeded as previously described for the synthesis of the macrocycle* **3a** *affording the dicarboxylic acid* **13**. *Nevertheless, several attempts to promote the cyclization under high dilution conditions between the corresponding acid chloride of* **13** *with diamide* **10** *only led to trace amounts of the desired macrocycle* **14**. ***Reversing the roles of the acylating agent, however proved more rewarding. Hence, treatment of the diamide 10 with phosgene and triethylamine followed by the slow addition of the diol 12 at room temperature resulted in a 15% yield of the macrocyclic dicarbamate 6.*** *Encouraged by this result we could likewise extend this cyclization approach to the synthesis of the smaller macrocycle* **5** *in 12% yield in one step from methyl deoxycholate.* ***In this latter case, it was necessary to slowly add the methyl deoxycholate to a refluxing solution of the phosgene-pretreated diamine in order to obtain the desired macrocycle.*** *In contrast, fast addition of the steroid only led to a product composed of the diamine* **10** *coupled to two deoxycholate units according to ES-MS, whereas attempted ring*

> *formation at room temperature afforded no cyclic products signalling a high ring tension in this small macrocyclic structure. Effort was also made to prepare* **5** *by the direct coupling of the diamine* **10** *with the crystalline bis(imidazolylcarbonyl) functionalized deoxycholate*[18]*, although in vain.* *(b110865b)*

The first local failure is that compound **14** could not be produced with the initial method. This can be recovered by reversing the roles of the agents. The second failure description demonstrates that the recovery statement can also textually *precede* the local failure it belongs to.

Argumentatively, recovery statements are important, as they cancel out the local failure and so make sure that the local failure does not run counter to the high-level goal HLG-1 (significance). Indeed, I found few cases of unrecovered local failure; the last sentence in the above example context is one of these.

What makes descriptions of local failures interesting from a theoretical view point is that they are another instance of scientific meta-discourse about problem-solving. Unsuccessful problem-solving processes associated with the authors' new knowledge claim are overall rare in scientific discourse; limitations of and future work following from the new knowledge claim are the only other example of this kind.

The discovery of local failure requires text understanding and discourse processing, because it is often only the existence of the recovery statement which confirms that a statement is a local failure.

A second sentence type of potential use to chemists are descriptions of differences between the compound in question and similar compounds in the literature. These differences may be stated in terms of properties, chemical structure, preparation or applications:

> *The reactions of all of the complexes with an excess (ca. 300 equivalents) of dihydrogen peroxide generated purple solutions with spectroscopic characteristics similar to those we reported*[3] *for the parent [Fe(metpen)(n1-OOH)]2+ in hydroxylic solvents.* (b103844n)

> *The present coordination net has the same topology as that found in Mn[N(CN)2]2(pyz) (pyz = pyrazine)*[9] *and in [M(tp)(bpy)] (tp = terephthalate and M = Co, Cd, Zn).* (b110015g)

> *It shows large Stokes' shifts and its fluorescence quantum yield (f) is greater than that of other known probe dienes (e.g., the nitro diphenyldienes)*[18]*, particularly in biologically significant aqueous medium.* (b304951e)

Local failures and differences between compounds are chemistry-specific rhetorical constructs, which will receive their own categories in AZ-II (section 13.1.2).[123] But before AZ-II is discussed in more detail I will turn to an important change in the annotation procedure, which was necessitated by the move to the new scientific discipline.

13.1.1 Domain-Knowledge-Free Annotation

A defining principle of the KCDM is that one should be able to decide whether its phenomena are present without having to reason about the scientific facts in the text. Instead, which category applies should be derived by nothing but the text itself, and its interpretation should use only general, rhetorical, and logical aspects of the text. This principle is motivated by the technical impossibility to robustly recognise, represent and reason with domain knowledge.

The exact definition of the gold standard, i.e., the description of the theoretically best performance of a system, becomes a crucial issue in all this, as supervised machine-learning systems use the gold standard directly to optimise their behaviour. But where does the ground truth come from in the first place? When expert annotators decide on a category, they use a mixture of information: firstly, there are processes such as reasoning with domain knowledge, which no current automatic process can replicate; and secondly, there are processes such as the recognition of a rhetorical act or a textual parallelism, which could in principle be automated now. The second kind of process is available to a non-expert, whereas the first kind is not.

Let us now consider a system that does not have the technical wherewithal to represent and generalise over domain knowledge. If such a system aims for a gold standard that is impossibly high (because it is influenced by domain knowledge), systematic error analysis and error reduction becomes impossible, because the gold standard hides the error source. An error may be caused because the system does not understand the science in the article, in which case nothing can be done to improve system performance. The error may also be caused by a misclassification of the rhetorical status or knowledge claim status, which should and possibly could be rectified in subsequent system versions; but the two cases cannot be told apart.

A domain-knowledge-free gold standard lowers the goal post to what a non-expert would understand, but this can lead to an overall better situation. The two sources of error can be kept apart if the system only attempts to model the second type of process, and if we do not allow the first kind of process to enter the definition of the gold standard.

[123] Local failures will be called OWN_FAIL; differences between compounds CODI.

In this situation, intermediate system errors can be analysed and fixed because the system should in principle be capable of solving *all* cases covered in the gold standard.

What follows from this is that we must not allow the annotators to use reasoning and domain knowledge when they decide on categories, otherwise the gold standard they produce is tainted. They must be forced to act like non-experts would. The guidelines therefore explicitly instruct annotators to use only general, rhetorical or linguistic knowledge. For instance, lexical and syntactic parallelism in a text can be used to infer that the authors intended to make a comparison between the authors' new KC and some existing KC. In contrast, the use of domain knowledge and reasoning to arrive at a category is strictly forbidden.

It is however unrealistic to expect annotators to be able to disregard their domain knowledge simply because they are *instructed* to do so. Domain experts use scientific knowledge and inference routinely and naturally when they make annotation decisions, and do not even realise when they do.[124] More has to be done to force annotators to comply with the "no-domain-knowledge" principle. Our solution to the expertise problem is to force all annotators to behave like "expert-trained non-experts" via the following rules:

- **Justification:** Annotators have to justify all annotation decisions by pointing to textual evidence in the article, and/or stating the section heading in the guidelines that gives the reason for assigning the category. Justifications have to be typed into the annotation tool and are open to challenge during the training phase. Discipline-specific knowledge an annotator may happen to have is explicitly not allowable as justification. Much of the valid justification comes in the form of general and linguistic principles, e.g., explicit cue phrases, information in the title, or structural similarity of textual strings. An example of an allowable inference is that verb phrases which occur in progressive form in the title are likely to express the article's contribution.[125]
- **Discipline-specific generics:** The guidelines contain a section with high-level facts about general research practices in each discipline covered. The generics constitute the only type of *scientific* knowledge which is acceptable as justification. They aim to help

[124] This problem does not become apparent until one works in a discipline where at least one of the annotators or guideline developers is not a domain expert; in my case, the work with AZ-II was the first such situation.

[125] This is relevant because the indirect moves require knowledge of the contribution of an article.

non-expert annotators recognise how an article might relate to already established scientific knowledge, so that they will be able to avoid common mistakes about the knowledge claim status associated with a particular piece of text. The better they are able to distinguish what is commonly known from what is newly claimed by the authors, the more consistent their annotation will be. Another example of information given in the generics concerns the case where an article states that the authors could not replicate a published result. The guidelines give criteria for distinguishing the cases when this is the authors' fault (and thus a local failure), from the cases where this is an indirect accusation of the previous experiment (and thus a contrastive statement).

Annotation with expert-trained non-experts has the advantage that it makes experts behave more like non-experts (by forcing them to justify their decisions), and non-experts behave more like experts (by providing them with carefully controlled discipline-specific knowledge).

The guidelines are split into a general and a discipline-specific part. A domain expert must be available during the development of the annotation scheme and the guidelines. Their job is to describe scientific knowledge in a general way, in as far as it is necessary for the scheme's distinctions, and to write the domain-specific rules for the individual categories, including the choice of example sentences. Descriptions of individual categories can have discipline-specific as well as general subsections.

These principles were first put into practice in the AZ-II experiments (see section 13.1.2).[126] The annotators were the co-developers of the scheme, who are at very different levels of chemistry expertise, namely Colin Batchelor (Annotator A), Advaith Siddharthan (Annotator B), and myself (Annotator C). Annotators B and C are computational linguists, but Annotator B also has a physics degree and two years' of undergraduate training in chemistry and can therefore be considered a semi-expert. Annotator A is a PhD-level chemist with good background knowledge in computational linguistics, who adapted the guidelines.

The chemistry-specific generics in the guidelines come in the form of a 7-page collection of high-level scientific domain knowledge, which contains:

- a glossary of chemical terminology that a non-chemist would not

[126]Strictly speaking, the CFC guidelines, which were written in 2005/2006, are the first guidelines to formalise the no-domain-knowledge requirement to a certain degree, by prescribing certain linguistic phenomena which allow for restricted inference.

have heard about or would not necessarily recognise as terminology;

- a list of possible types of experiments performed in chemistry;
- a list of possible types of knowledge claims;
- a list of commonly used (types of) machinery;
- a list of phenomena and measurements which can be read off this machinery (e.g., "*Stokes shift*", the fact that a reaction is exothermic)
- and a list of non-obvious positive and negative characterisations of experiments and compounds (e.g., *facile, sluggish, inert*).

For instance, the following is a small subset of the statements about knowledge claims in chemistry: for each chemical substance mentioned, there is in principle a knowledge claim which is associated with its discovery or invention – with the exception of water, rock, salt, the metals known in prehistory and a few others. If however a compound or process has become so common that its name incorporates the inventor's name (*eponyms*, e.g., "*the Stern–Volmer equation*" or "*the Grignard reaction*"), the guidelines decree that it is no longer associated with the inventor's knowledge claim; instead, it is considered to be in the "general domain".

The chemistry generics are not an attempt to summarise all methods and experimentation types in chemistry; this would be an impossible task, certainly in a few pages. Rather, it tries to answer many of the high-level, AZ-specific questions that a non-expert might ask of an expert.

This methodology should be relatively easily expandable to other disciplines, e.g., genetics, experimental physics and cell biology. While the domain-dependent part of the guidelines (in the form of generics) has to be written by a domain expert who understands the AZ principles, the far larger domain-independent part could be reused from discipline to discipline.

Overall, the human annotation experiment for AZ-II shows high agreement between the three annotators (expert, semi-expert, and non-expert), which we take as an indication of the success of the two principles above for providing consistent, domain-knowledge-free annotation. From a practical view point, it also means that both expert and non-expert annotators can be hired for annotation and brought in line with each other. However, the agreements involving the semi-expert are higher than the agreement between expert and non-expert. This probably means that the chemistry generics are not yet fully adequate to enable the non-expert to annotate as well as theoretically possible.

13.1.2 Argumentative Zoning II

Argumentative Zoning II (AZ-II) is a new annotation scheme from the AZ family. The decision tree defining the AZ-II semantics of the categories is given in Fig. 127. The questions in the decision tree are as follows:

- **Q1:** Is this sentence a hinge or part of a KC description?
- **Q2:** Which hinge function is described?
- **Q3:** Which KC type is described?
- **Q4:** Does the sentence describe the research goal?
- **Q5:** Does the sentence describe an advantage of the new KC?
- **Q6:** Which stage in the authors' problem-solving process is described – methods, results, conclusion or local failure?
- **Q7:** Who owns the existing KC – somebody else or the authors themselves?
- **Q8:** Why does this segment have no KC associated with it – is the KC hypothetical, or are the facts described in it too well-known?

A comparison of Fig. 56 (AZ) and Fig.127 (AZ-II) shows that questions **Q1**, **Q2**, **Q3** and **Q4** are identical in the two schemes, although **Q2** has far more possible answers in AZ-II than in AZ, where the choice was only between BASIS and CONTRAST. The other differences are as follows: the rhetorical moves R-10 and R-2 have been given their own category in AZ-II (NOV_ADV; via **Q5**). Unlike KCA and AZ, AZ-II also makes the distinction between EXO-KC and EX-KC (via **Q7**), a distinction which is described in section 6.4.

For several reasons, the TEXTUAL category was discontinued in AZ-II: explicit linearisation (moves P-2 to P-4) is not of central theoretical interest in the KCDM, and no application is implemented yet that uses the TEXTUAL information. TEXTUAL zones were also found to be infrequent in the chemistry texts.

Q8 concerns rhetorical moves R-11 and R-12 (future work), which have a somewhat ambiguous KCA status (see discussion in section 6.4, p. 105). In the AZ-II tree, the category for these moves (FUT) is located next to CO_GRO (which is another name for BACKGROUND). Both categories describe a situation where there is no KC, but for different reasons: in the case of FUT, the KC has yet to be staked (i.e., it is hypothetical), whereas in the case of CO_GRO, the KC has been staked so long ago that it has become generally accepted knowledge.

The one new distinction in AZ-II, and the biggest departure from AZ, is **Q6**: "Which stage in the authors' problem-solving process is

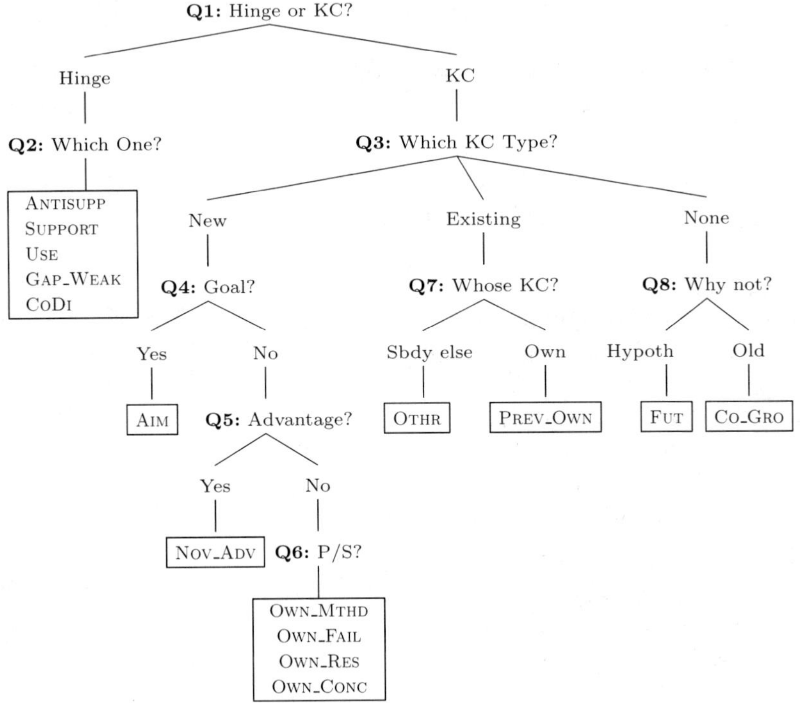

FIGURE 127 Decision Tree for AZ-II.

described – methods, results, conclusion or local failure?" This distinction, which breaks the New-KC segment into smaller segments, is not directly motivated by the KCDM, but it is intuitively a strong phenomenon in many life sciences (cf. the discussion in chapter 7).

The original AZ- and KCA-schemes do not make the distinction expressed in **Q6**, and instead define an undivided New-KC zone (KCA) or Own zone (AZ), as explained on p. 124. There are reasons that speak against a subdivision, although the problem-solving patterns in computational linguistics are not dissimilar to those in chemistry. First, the subdivision does not add any explanatory power to the discourse model, the main goal of which is to describe how scientific argumentation relates to descriptions of own and other work. Second, at the time when I developed AZ, I did not foresee any practical application of the subdivided categories, neither in rhetorical extracts nor in citation maps.

However, several possible tasks exist which call for this subdivision, particularly in the life sciences. One of these is the niche application of failure-and-recovery search in chemistry described earlier. Another possible application for the subdivision is Feltrim et al.'s (2005) rhetorical writing tool for novice writers, which provides training in writing rhetorically well-formed abstracts (see section 14.1). The tool therefore needs a way of distinguishing between methods and results.

Three AZ-like schemes for scientific discourse developed after the publication of Teufel (2000) subdivide OWN in this or a very similar way, namely Mizuta et al.'s (Mizuta and Collier, 2004, Mizuta et al., 2006), Feltrim et al.'s (2005) and Merity et al.'s (2009).[127] However, our work in Teufel et al. (2009) is the first experimental proof that a problem status distinction can be reliably made by humans judges.

To give an example about one problem-solving stage distinction, the difference between results (OWN_RES) and conclusions (OWN_CONC) is defined on the basis of how much reasoning on the authors' part is necessary in order to be able to make the statement concerned. If what is reported is a measurement, i.e., something which is simply read off an instrument, then the label OWN_RES applies. Possible OWN_RES statements, according to the chemistry generics, include: statements of simple numerical result; descriptions of graphs; descriptions of atoms' positions in three-dimensional space; statements of trends (unless a reason for these results is given); and comparisons of results of more than one experiment (unless a reason for these results is given).

Non-expert annotators need to estimate how likely it is that a certain statement was the result of a simple measurement by the authors. The chemistry generics therefore list phenomena which can be read off chemical machinery (e.g., "*Stark effect*"). The list of "read-off-able" phenomena was compiled from the first 30 articles in the development corpus, and generalised well to the next 40 articles.

On the other hand, category OWN_CONC applies if the authors used "cognition" in the widest sense before making the statement. This can be linguistically marked ("*therefore*", "*this means that*"), but in some cases, it is hard to decide without domain knowledge whether a statement is an observation or a claim which required reasoning.

Let us now look at some examples of **Q6**-style problem-structuring in chemistry, where problem-solving processes come in different sizes and can be hierarchically nested. For instance, the start compound for the main synthesis in the article may first have to be synthesised itself, e.g., because it is not commercially available. In that case, the synthesis of the compound is an intermediate, smaller problem-solving

[127] An early annotation scheme of mine also splits NEW-KC into PURPOSE/PROBLEM, SOLUTION/METHOD, RESULT and CONCLUSION/CLAIM (Teufel and Moens, 1998); however, this scheme was rejected in favour of the original AZ scheme.

process, which precedes and enables the main synthesis. (It is of course the main synthesis which constitutes the new KC of the article.) Compounds can also be successively refined, as the following example shows:

> *Preparation of the diacid* **8a** *started with the diallylation of (R)-BINOL*[1]*3 with allyl bromide in the presence of potassium carbonate (Scheme 2). Subsequent hydroboration with 9-BBN and accompanying oxidation afforded the diol* **7** *in 88% overall yield for the two steps. Conversion of the diol to the dicarboxylic acid* **8a** *was achieved by oxidation to the dialdehyde using the Dess-Martin periodinane*[(14)] *and then finally to the diacid with sodium chlorite.* (b110865b)

The description of the embedded problem-solving process often ends with a proof that what has been produced is indeed the desired compound.

The categories and correspondences to AZ are summarised in Figure 128. Again, there is a distinction into move-based and segment-based categories. Annotation examples for each category are given in Fig. 129.

Category	Description	KCA Segment	Move
Segment-Based Categories			
CO_GRO	No knowledge claim is raised (or knowledge claim not significant for the article).	NO-KC	
OTHR	Knowledge claim (significant for article) held by somebody else. Neutral description.	EX-KC	
PREV_OWN	Knowledge claim (significant) held by authors in a previous article. Neutral description.	EXO-KC	
OWN_MTHD	New knowledge claim, own work: methods.	(NEW-KC)	
OWN_FAIL	A solution/method/experiment in the article that did not work.	(NEW-KC)	
OWN_RES	Measurable/objective outcome of own work.	(NEW-KC)	
OWN_CONC	Findings, conclusions (non-measurable) of own work.	(NEW-KC)	
Move-Based Categories			
AIM	Statement of specific research goal, or hypothesis of current article.		P-1, (R-7)
NOV_ADV	Novelty or advantage of own approach.		R-2, R-10
GAP_WEAK	Lack of solution in field, problem with other solution.		H-1, H-2, H-3, R-6
CODI	Comparison, contrast, difference to other solution (neutral).		H-8, H-10
ANTISUPP	Clash with somebody else's results or theory; superiority of own work.		H-6, H-7, H-9, H-11
SUPPORT	Other work supports current work or is supported by current work.		H-12
USE	Other work is used in own work.		H-13, H-14, H-15
FUT	Statements/suggestions about future work (own or general).		R-11, R-12

FIGURE 128 AZ-II Annotation Scheme.

AIM *We now describe in this paper a synthetic route for the functionalisation of the framework of mesoporous organosilica by free phosphine oxide ligands, which can act as a template for the introduction of lanthanide ions.* (b514878b)

NOV_ADV *Moreover, the simplicity and ease of application of the electrochemical method ... should also be emphasised and makes it an interesting and valuable synthetic tool.* (b513402a)

CO_GRO *A wide range of organosulfur compounds are biologically active and some find commercial application as fungicides and bactericides*[1–4]. (b514441h)

OTHR *In their system, antibody immobilized on a solid substrate reacts with antigen, which binds with another antibody labelled with peroxidase.* (b313094k)

PREV_OWN *As a program aimed at the applications of imines*[(2a,g,5)] *we have studied the formation of carbanions from imines and their subsequent reactions.* (b200198e)

OWN_MTHD *On the other hand, a tertiary amide can be an excellent linking functional group.* (b201987f)

OWN_FAIL *Initial attempts to improve the dehydration of* **4** *via chemical or thermal means were unsuccessful; similarly, attempts to couple the chlorosilane (Me3Si)2 (Me2ClSi)CH with Ag2O failed.* (b510692c)

OWN_RES *While the acid 1a readily coupled to the olefin, the corresponding boronic ester was surprisingly inert under the reaction conditions.* (b311492a)

OWN_CONC *It is unlikely that every VOC emitted by plants serves an ecological or physiological role ...* (b507589k)

GAP_WEAK *Various methods of preparation have been developed, but they often suffer from low yield and tedious separation.*[16,17,28,31] (b200888m)

CODI *However, the measured values of the dielectric constant (ϵ = 310) are lower than the values reported by Ganguli and coworkers*[(21)] *for BSTO pellets sintered at 1100* deg*C ...* (b506578j)

ANTISUPP *Although purification of 8b to a de of 95% has been reported elsewhere*[[31]], *in our hands it was always obtained as a mixture of the two [EQN]-diastereomers.* (b310767a)

SUPPORT *This is in line with the findings of Martin and Illas for inorganic solids* [(84,85)]. (b515732c)

USE *The diamine* **10** *was prepared following a previously published procedure*[(4d)]. (b110865b)

FUT *Our further efforts are directed towards the above goal,... and overcoming limitations pertaining to the electron-poor arylboronic acids.* (b311492a)

FIGURE 129 AZ-II: Annotation Examples (Chemistry).

Human Agreement

30 random-sampled articles from journals published by the Royal Society of Chemistry were used for annotation, as listed in Fig. 130.[128] The articles cover all areas of chemistry and some areas close to chemistry, such as climate modelling, process engineering, and a double-blind medical trial. They were automatically sentence-split, and errors were manually corrected. This resulted in a total of 3745 sentences (92,705 words).

Type of Material	Articles				
Development	b110865b	b200198e	b200888m	b200921h	b201987f
	b203544h	b307457a	b307591a	b307591e	b308237b
	b309215a	b310125h	b310655a	b311197k	b311254c
	b311492a	b311589c	b311589e	b311804e	b312245j
	b312769a	b313316h	b316168b	b404735b	b503169a
	b503623b	b506211j	b506219a	b506219e	b506578j
	b506644a	b506974b	b507589k	b507599h	b508332j
	b508438e	b508655h	b508769d	b508772b	b509038e
	b509119e	b509380e	b509586g	b510156e	b510302a
	b510373h	b510432g	b510649d	b510669a	b510692c
	b510742c	b510831d	b510875f	b510999j	b511153f
	b511229j	b511330j	b511337g	b511350d	b511398a
	b511496a	b511512d	b511832h	b512086a	b512182e
	b512236h	b703835f	b704599a	b705100j	b709062e
Annotation	b103844n	b105514n	b107078a	b108236c	b109309f
	b110015g	b303244b	b303587p	b304951e	b305738k
	b306564b	b308032n	b308699b	b309235f	b309237b
	b309893a	b310238f	b310495h	b310767a	b310806f
	b311304c	b311934c	b312329d	b312407j	b313094k
	b313584e	b314140c	b314176d	b314686c	b314955b

FIGURE 130 AZ-II: Materials (Chemistry).

The AZ-II guidelines were further developed from the AZ guidelines, using a development corpus of 70 chemistry articles, which are distinct from the ones used for annotation. The guidelines are 102 pages long and contain the following parts:

- a general section;
- a decision tree;
- a description of each category, with sub-section headings for subcases, and 200+ example sentences from chemistry and CL (about

[128] 100 articles across a spread of disciplines from the January 2004 issues of the RSC were chosen randomly from a selection of journals covering most areas of chemistry. 30 out of these were selected for annotation; the rest were used for development.

20% of the rules defining individual categories are chemistry-specific);

- 75 pairwise rules between easily confusable categories, which are indexed in both category sections and also listed in a global index.

A variant of the annotation tool from the CFC experiment (section 8.5) was used for guideline development and annotation.

The inter-annotator agreement was $\kappa = 0.71$ ($N = 3745, n = 15, k = 3$). The Fleiss (1971) estimate of the standard error $se(\kappa)$ is 0.0044, making the 95% interval [0.697–0.715]. Given the subjective nature of the task and the number of categories, this agreement seems acceptable. Reliability is numerically identical to the AZ results, although the AZ-II categories are more fine-grained and informative. The new experiment also uses a non-expert annotator, who had no chemistry knowledge apart from the chemistry generics in the guidelines.

In order to determine whether Annotator A was influenced during annotation by domain knowledge which Annotator C did not have, and Annotator B had to a lower degree, pairwise agreement was calculated, which was $\kappa = 0.75 \pm 0.022$ (A–B), $\kappa = 0.68 \pm 0.019$ (A–C), and $\kappa = 0.75 \pm 0.022$ (B–C); all: $N = 3745, n = 15, k = 2$. That means that the non-expert (C) and the expert (A) disagree most, and the difference in their result is statistically significant at 95% from that of the two other pairs, but not from the overall result.[129] This points to the fact that Annotators A and B might have used domain knowledge they are not allowed to use, i.e., which is not part of the chemistry generics in the guidelines. It might also mean that the chemistry generics do not fully capture the high-level knowledge necessary to annotate consistently, and should be expanded.

The relative frequencies of the categories are given in Fig. 131. The large discrepancy in frequency between the rare move-based categories and the more frequent segment-based categories OWN_MTHD, OWN_RES, OWN_CONC, OTHR and CO_GRO is in line with the observations from AZ and CFC.

In an attempt to determine how well categories are defined, we first consider the binary distinction between hinge/move-type categories and KCA-type categories (corresponding to question **Q1** in Fig. 127). This distinction shows an inter-annotator agreement of $\kappa = 0.78 \pm 0.047$ (N=3745, n=2, k=3). Pairwise agreement was $\kappa = 0.80 \pm 0.09$ (A–B); $\kappa = 0.74 \pm 0.08$ (B–C) and $\kappa = 0.79 \pm 0.1$ (A–C). This indicates that annotators find it relatively easy to distinguish hinges/moves from KCA segments.

[129]The other two pairs are statistically indistinguishable from each other, and are significantly better than the overall result.

Category	%	Category	%	Category	%
OWN_MTHD	25.4	CO_GRO	6.7	FUT	1.0
OWN_RES	24.0	PREV_OWN	3.4	NOV_ADV	1.0
OWN_CONC	15.1	AIM	2.3	CODI	0.8
OTHR	8.3	SUPPORT	1.5	OWN_FAIL	0.8
USE	7.9	GAP_WEAK	1.1	ANTISUPP	0.5

FIGURE 131 AZ-II: Frequency of Categories (Chemistry).

Krippendorff's (1980) category distinctions, which use artificial binary splits of the data, are given in Fig. 132 (all are κ measured with N=3745, n=2, k=3). Higher numbers point to categories that the annotators could distinguish well. Values where the 95% interval indicates significant difference from overall reliability ($\kappa = 0.71 \pm 0.01$) are shown in bold face.

Fig. 132 shows that categories USE, AIM, OWN_MTHD, OWN_RES and FUT are particularly well distinguished (significant at 95% for USE and OWN_MTHD). This is a positive result, as these categories are important for several types of searches. The guidelines seem to fully suffice for the description of these categories.

However there are four categories with particularly low distinguishability: CODI, ANTISUPP, OWN_FAIL, PREV_OWN and OWN_FAIL (although the sample size is too small to show significance for OWN_FAIL). As these categories are crucial for the envisaged downstream tasks (apart from PREV_OWN, possibly), the problems with their definition should be identified and solved. We have since performed a systematic troubleshooting exercise for these categories, and amended the guidelines, bringing them up to 111 pages.

AZ-II annotation can be more directly compared with the original AZ scheme described in chapter 7. To do so, one can collapse the distinctions which are not made in AZ, namely the following:

- USE and SUPPORT map to BASIS;
- CODI, GAP_WEAK, and ANTISUPP map to CONTRAST;
- CO_GRO maps to BACKGROUND;
- OTHRand PREV_OWN map to OTHER;
- OWN_FAIL, OWN_MTHD, OWN_RES, OWN_CONC, FUTand NOV_ADV map to OWN.

As TEXTUAL is not marked up in AZ-II, the original AZ annotation was also collapsed, by incorporating TEXTUAL examples into OWN. Both collapsed AZ and AZ-II now have the same six categories and are in principle comparable to each other. However, one has to keep in

Category	κ	**95% Interval**
Use	**0.82 ± 0.06**	[0.769–0.888]
Aim	0.80 ± 0.12	[0.681–0.919]
Own_Mthd	**0.76 ± 0.03**	[0.734–0.790]
Own_Res	0.73 ± 0.03	[0.699–0.757]
Fut	0.72 ± 0.18	[0.544–0.903]
Co_Gro	0.69 ± 0.07	[0.626–0.795]
Support	0.67 ± 0.15	[0.518–0.814]
Othr	0.65 ± 0.06	[0.595–0.713]
Nov_Adv	0.64 ± 0.18	[0.459–0.821]
Gap_Weak	0.63 ± 0.17	[0.455–0.805]
Own_Conc	**0.63 ± 0.04**	[0.593–0.674]
Prev_Own	**0.60 ± 0.10**	[0.503–0.697]
Own_Fail	0.52 ± 0.20	[0.320–0.727]
Antisupp	**0.36 ± 0.26**	[0.160–0.549]
CoDi	**0.35 ± 0.19**	[0.103–0.615]

FIGURE 132 AZ-II: Krippendorff's Diagnostics for Category Distinction (Chemistry).

mind that such a comparison can of course only ever approximate the smallest common denominator between two schemes.

Reliability of the collapsed AZ-II is $\kappa = 0.75 \pm 0.02$ (N=3745, n=6, k=3), which compares favourably to the collapsed AZ's agreement of $\kappa = 0.70 \pm 0.03$ (N=3420, n=6, k=3). The increase could be due to the changes in annotation scheme and guidelines, to the difference in discipline (chemistry in AZ-II, CL in AZ), or to both.

Overall, the outcome of the AZ-II annotation experiment is positive. The high reliability measured demonstrates the discipline-independence of the phenomena described by the annotation scheme, and thus the discourse model. Additionally, annotation was performed with a mixture of experts and non-experts in the field; the fact that they agreed to a high degree bodes well for the method of using expert-trained non-experts as annotators.

The distinctions made by AZ and AZ-II are very similar. Even though AZ-II has more categories than AZ, a similar reliability was achieved. This probably means that the quality and the informativeness of the annotation has increased (which is not unlikely as much additional work went into the guidelines since the original AZ annotation). It could however also mean that discourse annotation of chemistry is intrinsically easier than discourse annotation of CL (although I have argued at the beginning of this section why the opposite might be true).

We are currently performing an AZ-II annotation exercise with computational linguistics articles. This work aims to demonstrate cross-discipline annotation with a single scheme, rather than with two similar ones (AZ and AZ-II). As the core ideas behind AZ-II came from initial work with CL, and as porting the annotation from AZ to AZ-II worked so well for chemistry, we do not foresee any principled problems with reapplying the scheme to CL. The only real question is how well the subdivision of NEW-KC segments will play out in a discipline that we know not to comply to the IMRD structure. Most of the practical work goes into the development of CL generics. Initial results are reported in Teufel et al. (2009); some annotation examples for CL with AZ-II are given in Fig. 133. AZ-II annotation of other disciplines, e.g., genetics, is also planned.

I will now present some initial automatic AZ-II results. Currently, only a third of the annotated training material used for AZ is available for AZ-II; more is being created. Therefore, what follows is very preliminary.

Automatic Annotation Results

In this experiment, the following features were used: `Ag`, `Ent`, `Formu`, `Cont-1-2`, `Syn-1-3`, `Cit-1-3`, `Loc`, and `Hist` (with a 2-pass estimation). The statistical classifier used was WEKA's Naive Bayes (Witten and Frank, 2005) with 30-fold cross-validation, achieving Cohen's $\kappa = 0.41$; Macro-F $= 0.34$; $P(A) = 0.51$. P, R and F per category are given in Fig. 134. CODI and ANTISUPP are not listed, because the system did not assign any sentences to these categories. When the scheme is collapsed as described above, Cohen's κ rises to 0.51 (Macro-F=0.51, $P(A) = 0.76$, and P, R and F per category as in Fig. 135).

The results are not directly comparable to the numbers reported in Teufel and Moens (2002) ($\kappa = 0.45$, Macro-F=0.50, P(A) = 0.73), because of the different scheme, discipline and data used. However, this experiment nevertheless shows that even without fine-tuning any of the lexical features, and with less training material, the recognition for AZ-II is roughly in the ballpark of the earlier results.

However, CODI and ANTISUPP were not recognised at all, and the rare categories NOV_ADV, OWN_FAIL, FUT, GAP_WEAK resulted in low F-measures. Even in the collapsed categories, it is still the conglomerate of contrastive sentiment (CONTRAST, with its F-measure of 0.20) which is clearly problematic. Probable reasons for this are the small number of examples of these classes, and the fact that negative sentiment is often hedged. More effort is needed, in analysis, feature selection, and choice of machine learner, to improve these results.

AIM *The aim of this paper is to examine the role that training plays in the tagging process ...* (9410012)

NOV_ADV *Other than the economic factor, an important advantage of combining morphological analysis and error detection/correction is the way the lexical tree associated with the analysis can be used to determine correction possibilities.* (9504024)

CO_GRO *It has often been stated that discourse is an inherently collaborative process ...* (9504007)

OTHR *But in Moortgat's mixed system all the different resource management modes of the different systems are left intact in the combination and can be exploited in different parts of the grammar.* (9605016)

PREV_OWN *Earlier work of the author (Feldweg 1993; Feldweg 1995a) within the framework of a project on corpus based development of lexical knowledge bases (ELWIS) has produced LIKELY ...* (9502038)

OWN_MTHD *In order for it to be useful for our purposes, the following extensions must be made:* (0102021)

OWN_FAIL *When the ABL algorithms try to learn with two completely distinct sentences, nothing can be learned.* (0104006)

OWN_RES *All the curves have a generally upward trend but always lie far below backoff (51% error rate).* (0001012)

OWN_CONC *Unless grammar size takes on proportionately much more significance for such longer inputs, which seems implausible, it appears that in fact the major problems do not lie in the area of grammar size, but in input length.* (9405033)

GAP_WEAK *Here, we will produce experimental evidence suggesting that this simple model leads to serious overestimates of system error rates...* (9407009)

CODI *Unlike most research in pragmatics that focuses on certain types of presuppositions or implicatures, we provide a global framework in which one can express all these types of pragmatic inferences.* (9504017)

ANTISUPP *This result challenges the claims of recent discourse theories (Grosz and Sidner 1986, Reichman 1985) which argue for a the close relation between cue words and discourse structure.* (9504006)

SUPPORT *Work similar to that described here has been carried out by Merialdo (1994), with broadly similar conclusions.* (9410012)

USE *We use the framework for the allocation and transfer of control of Whittaker and Stenton (1988).* (9504007)

FUT *An important area for future research is to develop principled methods for identifying distinct speaker strategies pertaining to how they signal segments.* (9505025)

FIGURE 133 AZ-II: Annotation Examples (Computational Linguistics).

	AIM	NOV_ADV	OTHR	CO_GRO	PREV_OWN	OWN_FAIL	OWN_MTHD
P	0.45	0.21	0.51	0.50	0.47	0.25	0.56
R	0.77	0.09	0.47	0.50	0.28	0.18	0.67
F	0.57	0.13	0.49	0.50	0.35	0.21	0.61
	FUT	OWN_CONC	USE	SUPPORT	OWN_RES	GAP_WEAK	
P	0.14	0.45	0.63	0.36	0.53	0.27	
R	0.05	0.43	0.29	0.43	0.61	0.23	
F	0.07	0.44	0.39	0.39	0.57	0.25	

FIGURE 134 Automatic AZ-II. *P*, *R* and *F* per Category (Chemistry)

	AIM	BASIS	CONTRAST	OWN	OTHER	BACKGROUND
P	0.43	0.64	0.21	0.85	0.54	0.51
R	0.77	0.34	0.19	0.93	0.45	0.46
F	0.55	0.44	0.20	0.89	0.49	0.49

FIGURE 135 Automatic AZ-II, Collapsed Categories: *P*, *R* and *F* per Category (Chemistry).

13.2 Variant AZ-Schemes

Other AZ-inspired annotation schemes for different disciplines and even for a different text type have been presented by other researchers over the years. I will give an overview of these here.

13.2.1 For Computer Science (Feltrim et al.)

In Feltrim et al. (2005), we introduce the modified AZ scheme in Fig. 136, which describes abstracts and introductions of computer science (CS) theses. The aim of this scheme is to support a writing tool for novice writers in CS in Portuguese (the tool will be further discussed in section 14.1).

In comparison to the original AZ scheme, the categories OTHER and BASIS were dropped, partly because they are rare in CS abstracts and introductions. (Recall from section 8.6 that these categories are also quite rare in CL abstracts, which was one of the reasons against an annotation shortcut involving abstracts and introductions.) However, this means that the scheme does not follow the KCDM (even if it is inspired by it), as the treatment of existing knowledge claims with separate categories is a prerequisite to KCDM-compliance.

The OWN category was split into METHODOLOGY, RESULTS and CONCLUSION, similar to the distinction between OWN_MTHD, OWN_RES, OWN_CONC and OWN_FAIL in AZ-II. Sentences describing a need for the current application or the gap in the literature receive the category GAP. This category is a subset of AZ-II's category GAP_WEAK(which

Category	Description	Original AZ Category	Freq.
BACKGROUND	Background	BACKGROUND; OTHER	21%
GAP	Gap Statement	CONTRAST	10%
PURPOSE	Problem statement	AIM	18%
METHODOLOGY	Methodology used	OWN	12%
RESULT	Experimental results	OWN	32%
CONCLUSION	Claims, conclusions, speculation	OWN	5%
OUTLINE	Textual outline of article sections	TEXTUAL	2%

FIGURE 136 Feltrim et al.'s (2005) Scheme for Computer Science.

also includes criticism), and a subset of AZ's category CONTRAST(which also includes comparisons, criticism and contrast statements). BACKGROUND, AIM and TEXTUAL are retained, but the latter two categories are renamed as PURPOSE and OUTLINE. These modifications result in a more uniform distribution than in the original AZ scheme, with the largest category (RESULT) covering 32% of sentences.

The reliability of the scheme was measured roughly as described in chapter 8, but on a much smaller data set. Three judges (first, third and fourth authors of Feltrim et al. (2005), all Portuguese native speakers) independently annotated 46 abstracts (320 sentences) on the basis of written guidelines. Annotator training used 6 abstracts (46 sentences) in 3 rounds of an "explanation, annotation, discussion" cycle; the observed category frequencies are given in Fig. 136. Reliability was measured at $\kappa = 0.69$ (n=7, N=320, k=3) for the full scheme, and at $\kappa = 0.82$ (n=5, N=320, k=3) for a scheme where METHODOLOGY, RESULTS and CONCLUSION were collapsed back into the OWN category. This is more comparable with AZ, albeit full comparability is not given: BASIS and OTHER are still missing, and AZ annotates full articles and not only abstracts (recall from section 8.6 that abstracts were found to be overall easier to annotate than full articles).

A Naive Bayes classifier, as implemented by the WEKA system (Witten and Frank, 2005) was trained on a development corpus of 52 abstracts. Features are as in Teufel and Moens (2002), with the exception of the meta-discourse features and the verb-syntactic features, which had to be ported to Portuguese. [130] For this system, 13-fold cross-

[130] A new meta-discourse feature was created by collapsing `Formu`, `Ent` and `Act` into a flat list of regular expressions, translated into Portuguese, and manu-

validation results reached $\kappa = 0.65$ ($P(A)$ of 0.74), beating both the random baseline by observed distribution ($\kappa = 0$) and Most Frequent Category baseline ($\kappa = 0.26$). The classifier did not find any of the OUTLINE sentences, but performed well for the other categories (PURPOSE has an F-measure of 0.84, followed by RESULT at 0.77). Like the human annotators, the classifier also was rather bad at distinguishing METHODOLOGY, RESULT and CONCLUSION. In terms of single features, the collapsed meta-discourse feature was the strongest, followed by the `Hist` feature. Syntactic features and citations were the weakest.

13.2.2 For Biology (Mizuta and Collier)

Mizuta and Collier (2004) present another adaptation of the AZ annotation scheme, this time for full genetics articles. Two major differences are made in terms of categories:

- the OWN class is subdivided into different stages of the experimental procedure (as just discussed);
- the classes CNN (which is like BASIS) and DFF (which is like CONTRAST) are defined to cover relations between data/findings, rather than relations between entire knowledge claims (articles) as in AZ.

This results in the scheme with the 11 categories listed in Fig. 137. Neither this scheme nor Feltrim et al.'s (2005) consider the attribution of knowledge claims (OTHER and BACKGROUND in original AZ); the fact that these categories are classed together shows that the main analytic interest of both schemes are indeed the problem-solving phases, rather than knowledge claim status. There is therefore only a weak link between these schemes and the KCDM. Also note the category ELS, which collects all sentences which do not fit into any of the other OWN subdivisions; I have called such categories *garbage categories* in section 7.1.

Mizuta and Collier's (2004) scheme also allows nested annotation, i.e., a piece of text can belong to multiple zones, whereas in the KCDM, annotation within one level is always non-overlapping. Also, Mizuta and Collier's annotation span is variable: while the sentence remains the basic annotation unit, zones may cover strings as short as syntactic phrases. This makes the space of observations larger and might pose a

---

ally expanded on the basis of a corpus study. This resulted in a set of 377 regular expressions, which are estimated to generate around 80,000 strings (the large multiplication factor, in comparison to English, is due to the inflectional variation in Portuguese). The port also required re-definitions of `Syn-1` (voice), where passive includes occurrences of indeterminate subjects (particle *"se"*), and `Syn-2`, which has 14 different tenses in the Portuguese version.

Category	Description	Original AZ Category
BCK	Background (previous work or generally accepted facts)	BACKGROUND, OTHER
PBM	Problem setting; problem to be solved; goal of article	AIM, CONTRAST
OTL	Outline; characterization/ summary of article	AIM
TXT	Section organisation	TEXTUAL
OWN	Author's own work	
MTH	Method, experimental procedure	OWN
RSL	Results of the experiment	OWN
INS	Author's insights and findings obtained from experimental results (including interpretation) or from previous work	OWN, (OTHER)
IMP	Implications of experimental results (e.g., conjectures, assessment, applications, future work) or those of previous work	OWN
ELS	Anything else within OWN	OWN, (OTHER)
CNN	Connection, correlation or consistency between data and/or findings	BASIS
DFF	Difference, contrast or inconsistency between data and/or findings	CONTRAST

FIGURE 137 Mizuta and Collier's (2004) Scheme for Genetics.

problem for automatic classification. At the time of writing, agreement studies and automatic classification results with the scheme were not published.

13.2.3 For Astrophysics (Merity et al.)

Merity et al. (2009) present an AZ-like annotation scheme for the astrophysics discipline, as shown in Fig. 138. The categories are similar to the KCA scheme in that they model existing knowledge claims, new knowledge claims and background material. The categories for existing and new KCs (called OTH and OWN) are however both subdivided according to problem-solving status, similar to several of the above-mentioned AZ-schemes, including AZ-II, namely into data (DAT), observations (OBS) and techniques (TEC). For material which belongs to a description of existing or new KCs but which is neither data nor observation nor techniques, the categories OWN and OTH are used. A corpus in astrophysics is annotated by one of the authors with this scheme to provide the data for machine-learning experiments, but no reliability studies are presented. The implementation uses a maximum entropy model and Viterbi search for the history feature.

Category	**Description**	**Orig. AZ Cat.**
BACKGROUND	Background material	BACKGROUND
OTH-DAT	Existing KC – data	OTHER
OTH-OBS	Existing KC – observations	OTHER
OTH-TEC	Existing KC – techniques	OTHER
OTH	Existing KC – anything else	OTHER
OWN-DAT	New KC – data	OWN
OWN-OBS	New KC – observation	OWN
OWN-OBS	New KC – techniques	OWN
OWN-OBS	New KC – anything else	OWN

FIGURE 138 Merity et al.'s (2009) Scheme for Astrophysics.

13.2.4 For Legal Texts (Hachey and Grover)

The knowledge claim discourse model cannot be applied outside the text type of scientific research articles. Core aspects of the model (e.g., the high-level goals) are closely connected to rhetorical expectations in scientific writing. However, some of the general principles of the KCDM approach to text understanding and discourse can be transferred to other text types, if the following conditions hold:

- A set of rhetorical acts can be identified, which correspond to author intentions, which are *a priori* known, which are textually expressed, and which logically structure the entire text.
- Textual features can be determined, which correspond to the rhetorical acts and which allow for an automatic identification.
- A real-world application is identified or invented which could profit from knowledge about the rhetorical acts.

While such a scheme for a text type other than scientific articles might outwardly look radically different from AZ and its kin, there are still similarities in spirit. Such a scheme could be strengthened if a phenomenon equivalent to knowledge claim attribution could be found, as KCA is unlikely to play a role outside scientific discourse. One should expect that many interesting genres of this kind exist. For instance, Estival and Gayral (1995) analyse the reports of car accidents in insurance claim letters, and describe the constraints in this domain. The argumentative skeleton in these letters is provided by the authors' intention to minimise their responsibility in the incident. I would predict that this text type (and the related type of complaint letters) should lend themselves well to a KCDM-type approach.

Hachey and Grover exemplify how similar general principles can be applied to the legal domain (Grover et al., 2003, Hachey and Grover, 2005a,c,b, 2004, 2006). They use a corpus of 188 House of Lords Judgements (the HOLJ corpus, Grover et al., 2004), which consists of 98,000 sentences, out of which 10,169 are manually annotated. Their scheme is based on the rhetorical structure of legal judgements: on the one hand, such texts are *performative* texts centred around decisions, on the other hand, the judges must convince their professional and academic peers of the soundness of their argument. The communicative purpose of a judgement is to legitimise a decision, by showing that it derives, by a legitimate process, from authoritative sources of law. This is modelled with the six categories given in Fig. 139, e.g., Fact and Framing, plus a garbage category. Interestingly enough, the linearisation of the text plays an important enough role in this text type too that the category Textual was included.

Manual annotation between two annotators was found to be reliable at $\kappa = 0.83$ (N=1955, k=2, n=7). In terms of automatic classification, Hachey and Grover's best result from amongst a large number of classifiers tested (including Maximum Entropy, Winnow, SVM, and Naive Bayes) was $F = 0.65$, which was achieved with C4.5. Naive Bayes at $F = 0.52$ was outperformed by Maximum Entropy ($F = 0.58$) and SVM ($F = 0.61$). Their feature set does not include manually determined cues such as ours, which may account for the relative difference in performance with respect to our Naive Bayes performance.

This concludes the discussion of whether AZ and the KCDM can be applied to other scientific disciplines and text types. Let us now turn to the practical problem of how the *features* would change during such a porting exercise.

Category	Description	Example	Freq.
FACT	A recounting of the events or circumstances which gave rise to legal proceedings	*On analysis the package was found to contain 152 milligrams of heroin at 100% purity.*	8.5%
PROCEEDINGS	A description of legal proceedings taken in the lower courts	*After hearing much evidence, Her Honour Judge Sander, sitting at Plymouth County Court, made findings of fact on 1 November 2000.*	24.0%
BACKGROUND	A direct quotation or citation of source of law material	*Article 5 provides in paragraph 1 that a group of producers may apply for registration ...*	27.5%
FRAMING	Part of the law lord's argumentation	*In my opinion, however, the present case cannot be brought within the principle applied by the majority in ...*	23.0%
DISPOSAL	Either credits or discredits a claim or previous ruling	*I would allow the appeal and restore the order of the Divisional Court.*	9.0%
TEXTUAL	A sentence which has to do with the structure of the document or with things unrelated to a case	*First, I should refer to the facts that have given rise to this litigation.*	7.5%
OTHER	A sentence which does not fit any of the above categories	*Here, as a matter of legal policy, the position seems to me straightforward.*	0.5%

FIGURE 139 Hachey and Grover's (2005a) Scheme for Legal Judgements.

13.3 Automatic Meta-Discourse Discovery

When porting a supervised machine learning system to another type of text, the implementation of many features, such as sentence length, grammatical voice and paragraph structure, does not require any adaptation. Things are different with the meta-discourse features, the workhorse behind CFC, AZ and KCA recognition: they contain much hand-crafted description of meta-discourse, and both Hyland's (1998b) experiment and my own in section 9.6 found that meta-discourse differed markedly between the disciplines studied, so adaptation is very likely to be necessary.

For computational linguistics, the first discipline I worked on, the lexical resources were created manually and in parallel with the development of the KCDM. If further disciplines are to be covered, automatic meta-discourse discovery is attractive, where recently-unseen meta-discourse is found by its similarity to the known meta-discourse phrases. The situation, incidentally, is very similar if one attempts to adapt the features to unseen articles in the same discipline, because differences in personal style can result in considerable variation in the meta-discourse even within the same discipline.

Automatic methods for the detection of meta-discourse have advantages over manual ones, even if one has the resources to perform manual detection on a large amount of data. Firstly, finding new meta-discourse is extremely time-consuming, because an article typically contains only a few meta-discourse phrases, the most frequent of which are repeated many times in the corpus. This means that one may have to read many articles in order to find a single new phrase. Also, it is hard to know whether some newly found meta-discourse is general use or discipline-specific, or even idiosyncratic to a single author. Thus, each port to a new scientific discipline implies a repetition of the same expensive manual process.

The longer and the more linguistically flexible a piece of meta-discourse is, the harder it is to robustly recognise it in unseen text. Methods for automatic meta-discourse discovery include Paice's (1981) use of a pattern matching grammar and a lexicon of manually collected equivalence classes, Hovy and Lin's (1998) use of the ratio of word frequency counts in summaries and their corresponding texts, my own use of most frequent n-grams (Teufel, 1998), and Yang's (2002) use of association measures for frequent n-grams. The main issue with pattern matching techniques and with n-grams is that they cannot capture syntactic generalisations such as active/passive construction, coordination, different tenses and modification by adverbial, adjectival or prepositional phrases, appositions and other parenthetical material. Finite string-based grammars over cue phrases (such as Paice's (1981) and the ones used in this book) are better in this respect, but intervening words in the phrase are still a problem, which can only be dealt with by the pattern writer anticipating all possible combinations and expressing them with placeholders. This limits the number of syntactic variations of a phrase that can be recognised.

While syntactic variants are an important aspect of meta-discourse discovery, the real difficulty is in finding the *lexical* variants. Lexical variation in meta-discourse is the phenomenon that certain words can be replaced by others without changing the meaning of the phrase. Examples for this are *current* and *present* in the Google Scholar experiment in section 9.6, or the lists of exchangable words from the concept lexicon in appendix D.1 (p. 445). The task of finding such variants in meta-discourse is a special case of paraphrasing, i.e., the detection of linguistic formulations with the same meaning in unseen text (respectively, the generation of such formulations).

Bootstrapping methods for paraphrase acquisition methods assume that there are mutual constraints between the paraphrase and the linguistic context in which it occurs. Starting from a set of initial paraphrases or other anchor points, the method learns which contexts they are associated with. The contexts are used in the next iteration to find new paraphrases, which in turn serve to find new contexts.

The acquisition of new contexts and the generalisation over them relies on a model of what a similar context is. Similarity could be defined as vector space similarity (Agichtein and Gravano, 2000), similar lexical sequences and parts-of-speech sequences (Barzilay and McKeown, 2001), or similar distributions of the arguments in a dependency graph (Lin and Pantel, 2001).

In parallel or comparable corpora, it is possible to align different occurrences of the paraphrases or of other anchors, so that the meaning of the contexts is guaranteed to be the same. There are different ways to define the anchors; Barzilay and McKeown (2001) use identical words; Shinyama et al. (2002) identical named entities, Ibrahim et al. (2003) identical nouns and pronouns, and Bannard and Callison-Burch (2005) known translations.

In non-aligned texts something else is needed. Lin and Pantel (2001) use similarity of arguments of dependency paths with two elements, whereas Ravichandran and Hovy (2002) use a paraphrase-based bootstrapping algorithm to find patterns for a question answering (QA) task. Based on training in the form of question and answer term pairs, e.g., {*Mozart, 1756*}, they learn the most likely strings which express the semantics holding between these terms, in this case `was-born-in`. String patterns occurring frequently in the context, such as "*A was born in the year B*", are combined in an n-gram representation of sub-strings from all answer sentences.

Similar bootstrapping approaches have been used in information extraction (IE). Riloff's (1993) system, one of the first of these, learns domain-specific patterns for MUC-style templates, using a parser and substantial hand-crafted knowledge (1500 filled templates as training material and a lexicon of semantic features for roughly 5000 nouns).

Unsupervised bootstrapping is an attractive method for finding related contexts because it does not need a human to inspect intermediate results between iterations. Agichtein and Gravano's (2000) unsupervised system, which uses clustering of vector-space-based patterns, detects information extraction relationships which are far more specific (companies and their headquarters).

In the three IE/QA approaches just mentioned (Ravichandran and Hovy, 2002, Riloff, 1993, Agichtein and Gravano, 2000), the application domain supplies the constraints required for bootstrapping, in this case in the form of uniqueness constraints. For instance, as Mozart can only be born in one year, and as each company has only one headquarter, we know that all contexts involving Mozart and any other year (or a company and a place that we know not to be the headquarter) must be wrong. This knowledge can be used to discredit the contexts where wrong answers came from, so that only good contexts go into the next bootstrapping iteration.

In the meta-discourse case, it is not obvious what the invariants should be. Whereas the semantics of the meta-discourse stays the same across articles (e.g., "*our goal is*"), the context surrounding the meta-discourse, which contains the scientific content in the article, *changes* from article to article. What remains invariant about meta-discourse expressions across articles is only the semantics of the concepts contained in them, the rhetorical status of the phrase, and some other constraints imposed by the rhetorical status, e.g., the fact that meta-discourse associated with P-1 moves requires that it is the authors themselves who present or do something.

In Abdalla and Teufel (2006), we investigate the unsupervised detection of semi-fixed meta-discourse phrases such as "*This paper proposes a novel approach...*" from unseen text, using a handful of seed meta-discourse phrases, a corpus and some general, hard-wired constraints. The output of the algorithm is a list of syntactic and lexical variants of the seed phrase that were found in running text. Syntactic variation dealt with includes passivisation, auxiliary modification, adverbial and prepositional modification of the verb, and coordination, as far as recognised by the RASP parser (Briscoe and Carroll, 2002).

To find the lexical variants, we use the lexical and syntactic constraints holding between two concepts in a meta-discourse phrase. Bootstrapping operates between the two concepts: given the seed phrases "*we introduce a method*" and "*we propose a model*", the algorithm starts by finding all direct objects of "*introduce*" in a corpus and, using an appropriate similarity measure, ranks them according to their distributional similarity to the nouns "*method*" and "*model*". Subsequently, the noun "*method*" is used to find transitive verbs and rank them according to their association with "*introduce*" and "*propose*". This means that new instances of either of the two concepts are found in each iteration, which subsequently constrain the acquisition of the other.

We demonstrate the bootstrapping method with two types of meta-discourse, both of which are transitive verb–direct object pairs. The first are phrases introducing a new methodology, e.g., "*In this paper, we propose a novel algorithm...*".[131]; these are AIM-type meta-discourse; the seeds used were {*analyse, present*}, {*architecture, method*}. The second are phrases indicating continuation of previous research, e.g., "*we adopt the approach presented in [1]...*"; these are BASIS-type meta-discourse. BASIS-type seeds were {*improve, adopt*}, {*model, method*}.

The best distributional similarity metric in our experiments was the Jensen-Shannon (JS) divergence (Lin, 1991), which outperformed a set of commonly used similarity measures for the syntactic vector space. We also found that candidates found via Google Scholar (where more data is analysed, but only with POS-patterns) were better than candidates found via the scientific part of the British National Corpus (where less data is analysed, but with a parser). Our method outperforms Ravichandran and Hovy's (2002) on the task of finding AIM sentences in CmpLG-D. We think this is because the definition of internal anchors is more suited to our task than the external anchors used in IE-type bootstrapping.

Our mechanism requires semantic filters; these encode constraints which apply to all meta-discourse phrases of that rhetorical category. Examples of constraints are: if some work is referred to as being done in previous own work, it is probably not a goal statement; the work in an AIM statement must be presented *here* or *in the current paper*; and the goals must be attributed to the authors, not to other people. These filters are manually defined, but they are modular, encode general principles, and can be combined to be applied to other meta-discourse equivalence classes. We estimate that around 20 semantic constraints will be enough to cover all meta-discourse from chapter 10; future work is necessary to substantiate this estimate.

Fig. 140 shows AIM and BASIS meta-discourse occurrences in sentences which were correctly selected by our algorithm and others which were correctly rejected. The system is capable of identifying syntactically complex patterns such as long distance relationships, and of rejecting some incorrect variants which appear superficially similar to

[131] Note that the nouns we are looking for are the ones of type `WORKNOUN` (see p. 446 in the concept lexicon), and the verbs of type `PRESENTATION_ACTION` (see p. 454).

Correctly found:	
Aim:	*What we aim in this paper is to propose a paradigm that enables partial / local generation through decompositions and reorganizations of tentative local structures.* (9411021, S-5)
Basis:	*In this paper we have discussed how the lexicographical concept of lexical functions, introduced by Melcuk to describe collocations, can be used as an interlingual device in the machine translation of such structures.* (9410009, S-126)
Correctly rejected:	
Aim:	*Perhaps the method proposed by Pereira et al. (1993) is the most relevant in our context.* (9605014, S-76)
Basis:	*Neither Kamp nor Kehler extend their copying / substitution mechanism to anything besides pronouns, as we have done.* (9502014, S-174)

FIGURE 140 Examples of Correct Meta-Discourse Discoveries.

the seed phrases. Fig. 141 gives examples of incorrect system decisions; e.g., the system wrongly ranked "*we derive a set*" above the correct phrase "*we compare a model*".

System's choice:	**Correct choice:**
derive set	*compare model*
illustrate algorithm	*present formalisation*
discuss measures	*present variations*
describe modifications	*propose measures*
accommodate material	*describe approach*
examine material	*present study*

FIGURE 141 Examples of Incorrect Meta-Discourse Discoveries.

Meta-discourse discovery is a new task, and work in this area has just begun. The system just described has limitations; for instance, it requires hard-wired semantic constraints and can only find transitive verb–direct object phrases. Alternatively or additionally, one could exploit the fact that meta-discourse, like terminological phrases, consists of syntactic parts which co-occur more often than expected by chance. Methods from terminology extraction (Church and Hanks, 1990, Dunning, 1993, Daille, 2003, Drouin, 2003) rely on word association measures to distinguish terminology from the rest of the text. These might be adapted and combined with IE bootstrapping and paraphrasing methodology for better meta-discourse discovery.

Chapter Summary

In this chapter, I raised the question whether the KCDM is explanatory of the structure of scientific articles in disciplines other than computational linguistics, and how one could practically port a system to a different discipline (or even a different text type or language). The first part of the chapter describes an annotation experiment with AZ-II, a new version of the AZ scheme from chapter 7, which is joint work with Advaith Siddharthan and Colin Batchelor. High inter-annotator agreement is achieved for chemistry texts, even though the annotator pool contained annotators with very different levels of domain expertise. To make this work, an annotation principle called "expert-trained non-experts" was developed, which forces annotators to use no other high-level domain knowledge during annotation but that which has been explicitly sanctioned in the guidelines.

The chapter also summarises other researchers' annotation schemes based on Argumentative Zoning. These cover different disciplines, including computer science, biology, astrophysics, and even another text type, namely legal judgements.

The last section looked at the acquisition of previously unseen meta-discourse when the system is applied to new text, and presented a system which uses semantic similarity between the components of meta-discourse phrases in a bootstrapping fashion (Abdalla and Teufel, 2006). This concludes the evidence for the Knowledge Claim Discourse Model in this book.

Chapter 14 will now provide an outlook for the future of the KCDM, by discussing potential applications of the model beyond those in chapter 4, and by describing current related research projects.

14

Outlook

The past chapters have shown the KCDM at work: how it is defined, how it can be turned into annotation schemes, how it is annotated by humans and machines, and how it is ported to new disciplines. This chapter will now return to the applications that are made possible by the KCDM. Search-based applications were the focus of chapter 4: one was designed for summarisation (rhetorical extracts) and the other for citation indexing (citation maps). Here, I will describe other possible applications.

The first of these is scientific authoring support (section 14.1): such tools could help novice scientists write better-structured articles and cite in a clearer way. Another possible application is the automatic generation of reviews (section 14.2) and of more sophisticated summaries than the extractive ones introduced in chapters 3 and 4. Apart from an abstractive version of rhetorical extracts, I will also propose rhetorically-inspired scientific multi-document summaries (section 14.3).

I will then turn to real-world digital libraries with tens or hundreds of thousands of articles, and explore the role that AZ and CFC could play in them. Currently, AZ as described in this book requires its input texts to be encoded in SciXML format, but the texts in many digital libraries are still only in PDF. There are two solutions to this dilemma: one could put further work into the noisy PDF to SciXML transformation, or one could make AZ more robust to the quality of its input, so that it can be applied to texts which are not in SciXML, and even to only partially recognised text. I am pursuing both these solutions in parallel, as I will describe in section 14.4.

14.1 Support Tools for Scientific Writing

Writing scientific articles well, i.e., in such a way that they pass the peer review, is a crucial skill for researchers. Young researchers have to learn the writing style and lexis accepted in their field (Sharples and Pemberton, 1992). It has evolved over time and is thus unpredictable, as we have seen in section 9.6. In most cases, they acquire this knowledge as part of a research group, i.e., at a relatively late stage in their career. Undergraduate training rarely acquaints students well enough with the requirements of the academic genre for them to write good articles. Even though writing guides exist and are sometimes consulted, it can be difficult for students to apply such rules to a real text, even if the basic guidelines on scientific writing are explicit and known.

This makes automatic writing tools attractive (e.g., Sharples et al., 1994, Broady and Shurville, 2000, Narita, 2000, Aluisio et al., 2001). Better writing tools could take some of the burden off senior researchers, who spend a considerable amount of their time training novices in the art of article writing.

Some support systems focus specifically on discourse phenomena in the user-produced texts (Burstein et al., 2003, Anthony and Lashkia, 2003). The project SCIPO ("Scientific Portuguese") at the University of São Paolo aims at analysing the rhetorical structure of Portuguese academic texts, in terms of schematic structure, rhetorical strategies and lexical patterns (Feltrim et al., 2003, 2004, 2005, Schuster et al., 2005). In Feltrim et al. (2003), we argue for the benefits of corpus-driven authoring tools: students should be provided with authentic writing examples extracted from articles in their field, including good and bad examples of use.

SCIPO supports novices in writing abstracts and introductions of PhD theses in Computer Science.[132] Users can build a rhetorical structure for their abstracts and introductions, and SCIPO identifies rhetorically similar cases to the current building plan, using a nearest neighbour search on its corpus. The corpus contains 52 abstracts and 48 introductions of theses which are manually annotated with the scheme in Aluisio and Oliveira Jr. (1996) and the AZ-like scheme in Fig. 136 (p. 370). Relevant lexical patterns (meta-discourse) in the example articles are highlighted, and the user can automatically integrate them into the building plan.

In order to determine the rhetorical status of each sentence in the user's text, SCIPO uses the Portuguese version of Argumentative Zon-

[132]These have to be written in Portuguese in the Brazilian education system, unlike research articles, which are preferably written in English.

ing described in section 13.3. It then identifies rhetorically problematic structures in the user's text and suggests how these can be rectified. Apart from the AZ-analysis, this automatic critique also requires a manually created rule base, which was informed by prescriptive writing guidelines and by a corpus analysis of PhD theses with Swales's (1990) and Weissberg and Buker's (1990) models.

The text-critiquing component of SciPo was evaluated in a user study reported in Feltrim et al. (2005). Four subjects (recently finished Masters students) were asked to use SciPo to rewrite the abstracts of their dissertations and subsequently fill in a questionnaire about the system. An expert assessed the quality of their abstracts before and after the use of SciPo. The expert considered the rewritten abstracts to be better structured and more informative, i.e., to contain more factual information than the original ones. However, they could not clearly be classified as being of "higher quality": the rewritten abstracts still contained writing problems concerning grammar, lexical choice, and register, which are not addressed by the tool.

The subjective evaluation of SciPo by questionnaire was mostly positive. All subjects found SciPo useful and intended to use it again in a real situation. All perceived the classifier's results as reliable, and three subjects considered the critiques and suggestions relevant. (In the case of the subject who didn't, it was later found that this was due to a grave classification error by AZ.) Obviously, overall classification quality is a major issue for the usability of SciPo, but considering the large impact in the quality of teaching that scientific writing tools could potentially have, these results are encouraging.

Another aspect of scientific writing is the art of citing. Specialised style guides for scientific text by applied linguists (e.g., Swales and Feak, 2000) exist, which give advice on how to cite, but these rules necessarily remain non-specific.

I am not talking about citing correctly in a syntactic sense, i.e., using the right typography and producing a correct reference list in the right form – such functionality is already provided by bibliography tools, such as BibTex. What I mean is that citations should be included in scientific text in such a way that natural-sounding, non-redundant text is created: the citations should be supportive of the authors' argument, informative and unambiguous.

In order to cite well in this sense, one needs to make the following decisions:

1. whether a statement should be supported at all by a citation;
2. which citation out of a set of equivalent citations (e.g., by the

same researcher) one should use;
3. which citation out of a set of citations by different researchers one should use;
4. how to make clear how a certain citation relates to one's own work;
5. how to make clear which particular statement in one's text is associated with a citation;
6. which referring expressions to use when discussing a citation (the formal citation, the authors' names, a pronoun, or some other linguistic expression describing the approach).

Item 1 concerns the question of whether there exists a knowledge claim in the literature for a fact one wants to include in an article. Item 2 concerns the choice of one publication out of several equivalent ones by the same author; possibilities include the most well-known, the oldest, or the latest citation. Which one of these is most appropriate depends on what the author's intention is for including the citation. The earliest citation can support claims of a long tradition of a certain research area, or acknowledge the time of invention of an idea, whereas the latest citation best supports the claim that the work concerned belongs to a vibrant, active research area. Automation of either decision (items 1 and 2) is daunting.

In contrast, item 3 expresses connections between the new KC and similar work in a field – the kind of connections that an experienced scientist's internalised Bazermanian research map (see chapter 2) encodes. The automatic provision of such suggestions would be of great use even to experts, as it would make it less likely for them to overlook relevant new articles in the field. Current tools providing such suggestions (e.g., Babaian et al., 2002) typically use content-based metrics of document similarity borrowed from the field of information retrieval. Citation Function Classification (CFC; section 7.3) should provide a valuable addition to such techniques.

Item 4 is about how clearly expressed the citation's function in the argumentation is. This question could also be quite naturally addressed with CFC. If an unclear function is detected, the user could be presented with the system's classification (e.g., "*Did you mean this statement as a criticism, motivating your own research?*").

I will propose something else, namely the automated detection of citation-related writing problems which are closer to the text, such as items 5 and 6. Such problems are in my opinion particularly suited to be investigated by a combination of discourse analysis, linguistic analysis and citation content analysis.

Item 5 concerns the string in the text that best characterises the knowledge claim that is acknowledged by a citation,[133] and item 6 concerns how one should linguistically refer to the owner of the knowledge claim.

Any unclarity in the description of knowledge claims is undesirable (for the author as well as for readers); a citation-oriented authoring tool should therefore flag cases where more than one knowledge claim could be associated with a citation. KCDM analysis, which is based on the notions of knowledge claim structure, hinging, citation blocks, and meta-discourse, should be of use in the detection of such cases.

Let us consider a few examples of associations between citations and knowledge claims. If the citation is authorial, the attribution is mostly to the entire clause (and possibly to much longer segments), as in the following case:

> *Chomsky (1981) observes that annotated surface structures may be simply defined with respect to certain admissibility conditions...*
> (J84-3005)

If a sentence which expresses a fact or finding contains a parenthetic citation, but no meta-discourse, the entire sentence is commonly associated with the citation:

> *For example, rainfall runoff from urban roadways often contains appreciable concentrations of metals that have adverse effects on ecological systems and human health*$^{(1-4)}$. (b310125h)

But parenthetical citations are also often associated with the noun phrase directly to their left, as in the following enumerations of KCs:

> *By applying this strategy, a best-first behavior is achieved instead of pure breadth-first (Reiter, Dale, 1992), depth-first (Dale, Haddock, 1991), and iterative deepening (Horacek, 1995, Horacek, 1996) strategies.* (P97-1027)
>
> *Similar advances have been made in machine translation (Frederking and Nirenburg 1994, speech recognition (Fiscus 1997) and named entity recognition (Borthwick et al. 1998).* (W05-1518)

Meta-discourse can disambiguate what a parenthetical citation refers to, and thus achieve clearer attribution of knowledge claims:

[133] In Ritchie et al. (2006) we discuss the same question from an IR indexing perspective, namely how to identify indexing terms in the citing sentence which describe the citation best.

One approach to the QA task consists of applying the IR methods to retrieve documents relevant to a user's question, and then using the shallow NLP to extract features from both the user's question and the most promising retrieved documents. These features are then used to identify an answer within each document which best matches the user's question. This approach was adopted in (Kupiec 1993; Abney et al. 2000; Cardie et al. 2000; Moldovan et al. 2000). (P01-1070)

The approach described in the segment is clearly attributed to the citations via meta-discourse ("*This approach was adopted in...* "). Additionally, the start and end point of the citation block are signalled by co-referring strings ("*One approach*", "*this approach*").

Complications arise when citations are ambiguously placed. For instance, the following example could be wrongly interpreted as Hobbs and Baldwin stating that relatively little work has been done, when in fact what is probably meant is that Hobbs and Baldwin are the exceptions to this statement:

Relatively little work has been done on alternate approaches to pronoun resolution (Hobbs, 1976; Baldwin, 1995). (P02-1012)

Scopal phenomena such as negation and comparatives can have an effect on the interpretation of citations, e.g., when the scope includes a part of the sentence that might or might not be attributed to a citation:

The results of disambiguation strategies reported for pseudo-words and the like are consistently above 95% overall accuracy, far higher than those reported for disambiguating three or more senses of polysemous words (Wilks et al. 1993; Leacock, Towell, and Voorhees 1993). (J98-1006)

Another logical possibility would be trie encodings which compact the grammar states by common suffix rather than common prefix, as in (Leermakers, 1992). (P01-1044)

In both cases, it is unclear whether the citations are associated with the approach directly to their left, which is under negative or comparative scope ("*disambiguating three or more senses of polysemous words*"; "*common prefix*"), or with the other approach, which is not under scope. In the first sentence, a third possibility exists, namely that the citation supports the observation expressed in the entire sentence.

Whether something is ambiguous often depends on how many syntactically possible distractors there are to the left of the citation, and exactly how the citation is syntactically connected to the rest of the sentence. Often, the sentence can be disambiguated by inserting phrases such as "*e.g.*" and "*as suggested in*".

Experienced authors as well as novices would be well-served by a syntactically- and semantically-minded citation support tool which checks their citations for them. The tool's task would be to identify ambiguous citations, list possible interpretations, and suggest potential reformulations for each of the interpretations.

14.2 Automatic Review Generation

Human-written review articles are of high value: they quickly give readers a grasp of an entire research area and of the interconnections between related strands of research in it. However, they come with their own disadvantages: they take effort to write, they can only include material known to the authors, and they only have space to refer to a fraction of the primary literature. They also soon become outdated. Therefore, any type of automation which enables the dynamic creation of more up-to-date reviews is desirable.

Research on review generation ranges from the automatic identification of human-written reviews in a digital library (Nanba and Okumura, 2005) to the identification of the most useful input material for extraction-based reviews (Mohamma et al., 2009). A more ambitious idea is the task of automatically updating an outdated human-written review article. The old review would then be used to seed traditional searches in a digital library, and the articles returned by the search must then somehow be included in the updated review in the right places.

A task which is more straightforward is the provision of support to a human review writer. This was one of the motivations behind the design of citation maps in section 4.2. A list of all incoming hinge functions for an article of interest should provide added value to a review writer, in comparison to the more traditional approach of listing the citation sentences. The hinges express how an article was received in its field, both now and at the time it was published, whereas the citation sentences often only give a neutral summary of the high-level goals of the article.

But an entire scientific area can be very large, and there may be several interesting dimensions a review writer could explore. The job of a specialised review support tool is to tease these dimensions out and present them to the user. Citation maps, in contrast, are general search tools at a high level of granularity, which are most suitable once one has already narrowed down an area of interest.

The review tool's first step would be to determine a group of similar articles, either by keyword-based query, by following citation links, by lexical similarity, by co-citation or by bibliographic coupling. Differentiating between the similar approaches, and portraying the differences to the user, is the more exciting part of the task of review generation.

Chronology is one obvious aspect of review writing. As a scientific field develops, new work builds on old and older approaches are abandoned. A tool that supports time-line search would allow review writers to explore chronological trends, follow up new developments and compare similar approaches published at the same time.

Additionally, new definitions of article similarity are possible on the basis of a KCDM analysis; for instance, by comparing like with like AZ-zones from different articles, it should be possible to cluster articles which contain similar criticisms of other approaches.

An even more fine-grained distinction could be based on the articles' individual statements of methods and goals. If two approaches share the same goal and data set but use a different methodology then they are direct rivals, which is likely to be of interest to the review writer. Aim sentences are the preferable input sentences for extraction of such material, because the goal and method phrases contained in them are guaranteed to be at a high level of abstraction, whereas sentences extracted from Own zones might contain low-level sub-goals.

The Aim sentences in Fig. 142 were extracted from a set of articles on topic segmentation: *Hearst (1997), Reynar (1998), Choi (2000)* and *Beeferman et al (1997)*. The meta-discourse in these sentences (which is marked by underlining) points us to several descriptions of goals and methods. The meta-discourse phrase "*approach uses*", for instance, is always followed by description of a method, whereas the meta-discourse phrases "*method for*" and "*has the goal of*" are always followed by a goal. In the examples above, this information is marked by bracketing and by the subscript identifiers at the beginning of the associated syntactic phrase, which starts with a "G" (for goal) or "M" (for method).

An automation of this type of extraction would require additional syntactic and rhetorical information about each meta-discourse phrase. Even if this is available, the correct start and end points of the goal or method phrase must be found in the syntactic parse. This is not a trivial task, but it may be machine-learnable from annotated examples.

A simple tabulation of the method and goal phrases thus extracted already produces a highly informative list, particularly if the phrases are grouped by similarity, as is shown in Fig. 143. At one glance, we can

Hearst (1997):
This article has described an algorithm that uses [M1 changes in patterns of lexical repetition] as the cue for [G1 the segmentation of expository texts into multi-paragraph subtopic structure].
In contrast, TextTiling has the goal of [G2 identifying major subtopic boundaries], attempting [G3 only a linear segmentation].
This paper presents fully-implemented algorithms that use [M2 lexical cohesion relations] to [G4 partition expository texts into multi-paragraph segments that reflect their subtopic structure].

Reynar (1998):
This article outlines a new method of [G5 locating discourse boundaries] based on [M3 lexical cohesion] and [M4 a graphical technique called dotplotting].
This paper is about an automatic method of [G6 finding discourse boundaries] based on [M5 the repetition of lexical items].

Choi (2000):
The aim of [G7 linear text segmentation] is to [G8 discover the topic boundaries].

The primary distinction of our method is [M6 the use of a ranking scheme and the cosine similarity measure (van Rijsbergen 1979) in formulating the similarity matrix.]

Beeferman et al. (1997):
This paper introduces a new statistical approach to [G9 partitioning text automatically into coherent segments].
Our attack on the [G10 segmentation] problem is based on [M7 a statistical framework that we call feature induction for random fields and exponential models (Berger 1996a, DellaPietra 96a)].
Central to our approach to [G11 segmenting] is [M8 a pair of tools: a short- and long-range model of language].

FIGURE 142 AIM Sentences from Four Articles on Text Segmentation.

see that the articles concerned have rather similar goals, but different methods. Three goal clusters are identified – "*partitioning text*", "*segmenting text*" and "*finding topic/discourse boundaries*". These goals are paraphrases of each other, but without access to knowledge representation and reasoning, a clustering method will probably not be able to make this decision. However, the system output is useful to a human even if it does not (as in Fig. 143).

Such lists could be made even more informative by including the concept of novelty into the overviews, as modelled by the AZ-II category NOV_ADV. Novelty is particularly important for the decision of which articles to include in a review, as it can help distinguish incre-

Goal 1 (Hearst, Reynar, Choi):	
G2:	*identifying major subtopic boundaries*
G5:	*locating discourse boundaries*
G6:	*finding discourse boundaries*
G8:	*discover the topic boundaries*
Goal 2 (Hearst, Choi, Beeferman):	
G1:	*the segmentation of expository texts into multi-paragraph subtopic structure*
G3:	*only a linear segmentation*
G7:	*linear text segmentation*
G10:	*segmentation*
G11:	*segmenting*
Goal 3 (Hearst, Beeferman):	
G4:	*partition expository texts into multi-paragraph segments that reflect their subtopic structure*
G9:	*partitioning text automatically into coherent segments*

Method 1 (Hearst, Reynar):	
M2:	*lexical cohesion relations*
M3:	*lexical cohesion*
Method 2 (Hearst, Reynar):	
M1:	*changes in patterns of lexical repetition*
M5:	*the repetition of lexical items*
Method 3 (Raynar):	
M4:	*a graphical technique called dotplotting*
Method 4 (Choi):	
M6:	*the use of a ranking scheme and the cosine similarity measure (van Rijsbergen 1979) in formulating the similarity matrix*
Method 5 (Beeferman):	
M7:	*a statistical framework that we call feature induction for random fields and exponential models (Berger 1996a)*
Method 6 (Beeferman):	
M8:	*a pair of tools: a short- and long-range model of language*

FIGURE 143 Similar Research Goals and Methods in Sentences from Fig. 142.

mental articles from those that shape a field. Other than supporting experienced authors in the task of writing review articles, such support would also be of great use to reviewers of articles or grant proposals.

Instead of using a tabular presentation, the differences between approaches could also be presented visually: articles could be positioned within their scientific field and chronological time-line. Visual tools have long been used to organise articles and to display similarities between them e.g., Info-PubMed (`https://www-tsujii.is.s.u-tokyo.`

ac.jp/info-pubmed/cite), Olsen et al. (1993), Hearst and Pedersen (1996), Spangler et al. (2002), Karamanis et al. (2007), and the visually stunning "maps of science" (Nature 444, 985-991; http://www.didi.com/brad/). These approaches use topical similarity between articles, typically as distance in term-based vector space, which is the main distinction from the discourse-aware kind of similarity I am suggesting here.

14.3 Scientific Summaries Beyond Extraction

The rhetorical extracts presented in chapter 4 and evaluated in chapter 12 are guided by rhetorical information, but they rely on extractive summarisation, which is suboptimal for the reasons detailed in section 3.2.2. The use of *abstractive*, and in particular *re-generative* methods, is far more attractive.

The task of *re-generation* is that of creating new sentences out of sub-sentential material extracted from source sentences. The research area of summary re-generation includes the shortening and fusing of sentences and other forms of sentence revision (Grefenstette, 1998, Mani et al., 1999b, Barzilay et al., 1999, Jing and McKeown, 2000, Knight and Marcu, 2000, Clarke and Lapata, 2008). Sentence condensation, for instance as modelled in the DUC task of headline generation, is one aspect of this task (Knight and Marcu, 2000, Dorr et al., 2003, Jing, 2000).

In contrast to deeper text generation methods (such as McKeown, 1985, Hovy, 1993, Robin and McKeown, 1996, Moore and Paris, 1993, Dale et al., 1998), re-generation is more robust, as it does not rely on specialised, often domain-dependent semantic representations.

Fig. 144 and Fig. 145 demonstrate the output of an ideal re-generation system. The summaries simulated here use textual snippets from *Pereira et al. (1993)*, and rely on AZ-annotation. The text is manipulated in various ways: first-person personal pronouns are changed into impersonal constructions, citations are added to their respective hinge sentence, and comparisons are reformulated. The resulting summaries are grammatically well-formed and maximally concise. How feasible is their automatic construction?

Template-based generation is a well-established method in generation. A special kind of template, which applies syntactic and rhetorical constraints on its filler material, could be employed to generate the abstracts in Fig. 144 and 145. For instance, a template such as *"This paper's topic is to"* (Fig. 144) requires a verb phrase in base form, with the rhetorical type "goal".

*This paper's topic is to automatically classify words according to their context of use (**S-1**; Background). The problem is that for large enough corpora the number of possible joint events is much larger than the number of event occurrences in the corpus, so many events are seen rarely or never, making their frequency counts unreliable estimates of their probabilities (**S-4**; Background). The paper's specific goal is to group words according to their participation in particular grammatical relations with other words (**S-164**; Aim), more specifically to classify nouns according to their distribution as direct objects of verbs (**S-22**; Aim). The authors' classification method will construct a set EQN of clusters and cluster membership probabilities EQN.* (**S-26**; Own_Mthd)

FIGURE 144 Short General Purpose Abstract for Uninformed Reader (Corresponding Rhetorical Extract: Fig. 16).

The input to the templates would be a high-precision list of goals and methods like the one in Fig. 143. The previous section 14.2 has described how such lists could be created: by performing Argumentative Zoning, parsing Aim sentences and excising rhetorically-tagged syntactic material from the vicinity of meta-discourse. For instance, a rhetorically appropriate verb phrase of type "goal" for the template described above can be found in the following sentence:

> *Methods for **automatically classifying words according to their contexts of use** have both scientific and practical interest.*(9408011, S-1)

The bold-faced material now needs to be adapted in order to fit into the template; the result is the first sentence of Fig. 144. A change in inflectional morphology is enough in this particular case, but a more sophisticated system could also use derivational morphology, i.e., it could turn "*classifying*" into the deverbal noun phrase "*classification*". In many cases, this will also require a syntactic manipulation of the arguments of the nominalisation, which is not a trivial task. However, the more syntactic contexts are covered, the wider the choice of possible filler material will be available, which will in turn lead to more varied output text.

The summaries shown are overly optimistic in at least one respect. Consider, for example, the following sentence from Fig. 145, which was constructed from the original sentences S-5 and S-9:

> *Hindle's approach differs from the authors' in that he does not directly construct word classes and corresponding models of association.*

To produce this sentence, on would have to make the two pragmatic

This paper investigates how to factor word association tendencies into associations of words to certain hidden senses classes and associations between the classes (**S-10**; AIM). *The authors consider here only the problem of classifying nouns according to their distribution as direct objects of verbs; the converse problem is formally similar* (**S-22**; AIM).
Hindle's approach differs from the authors' in that he does not directly construct word classes and corresponding models of association (**S-5** and **S-9**; CONTRAST). *Brown et al.'s (1992) approach has the problem that class construction is combinatorially very demanding and depends on frequency counts for joint events involving particular words, a potentially unreliable source of information* (**S-13** and **S-14**; CONTRAST).
The paper uses a deterministic annealing procedure for clustering (Rose et al. 1990), in which the number of clusters is determined through a sequence of phase transitions by continuously increasing the parameter EQN following an annealing schedule (**S-113**; BASIS). *The combined entropy maximization entropy and distortion minimization is carried out by a two-stage iterative process similar to the EM method (Dempster et al. 1977)* (**S-65**; BASIS).

FIGURE 145 Short Similarity-and-Difference Abstract for Informed Reader (Corresponding Rhetorical Extract: Fig. 17).

inferences that Hindle does not construct these word classes, but that the authors do, from the following text:

> *His notion of similarity seems to agree with our intuitions in many cases, but it is not clear how it can be used directly to construct word classes and corresponding models of association. Our research addresses some of the same questions and uses similar raw data, but we investigate how to factor word association tendencies into associations of words to certain hidden senses classes and associations between the classes themselves.* (9408011, S-9/S-10)

Any attempt to automate such inference involving comparisons and negation at the current state of the art in NLP, i.e., without accurate deep semantic representation, scope identification and pragmatic inference, risks creating text which is not truth-preserving.

Let us now consider the creation of scientific *multi-document* summaries. The list of goals and methods in Fig. 143 could be used without changes as input material; it provides (almost) all the information we need for this task.

The four articles display much overlap in the descriptions of research goals, but there are clear differences in methods. While some methods are shared between approaches, e.g., the use of lexical cohesion by both Hearst and Raynar, several other methods are unique to one approach. This information needs to be expressed in a linguistically coherent form.

There are goals which are common between these four papers: Hearst and Reynar are interested in finding discourse/topic boundaries; Hearst and Beeferman et al. share two aims: text segmentation and the partitioning of text into coherent segments.
Hearst and Reynar share some methodology, namely the use of lexical repetition and lexical cohesion. Beeferman et al.'s methods include the use of a statistical framework that they call feature induction for random fields and exponential models, and of a pair of tools: a short and long-range model of language. Reynar uses a graphical tool called dotplotting, whereas Choi uses a ranking scheme and the cosine similarity measure in formulating the similarity matrix.

FIGURE 146 Multi-Document Summary of the Four Articles.

In analogy to the single-document case, a similarity-and-difference multi-document summary such as the one in Fig. 146 could be re-generated by a technique based on flexible templates.

While the clusters of goals and methods are already available in Fig. 143, what is missing is a high-level description of each cluster. Without going into the details here, the task of creating the description (e.g., the most redundant string shared between sentences in each cluster) requires a semantically and syntactically sophisticated similarity metric, which is also needed to cluster the snippets in the first place.

This brings us to the end of the description of new applications based on the KCDM. Between them, chapter 4 and the current chapter have suggested many such applications, from citation indexing and summarisation, via navigation within an article, to authoring/training and review support. This wide range of tasks is another confirmation of the level of generalisation chosen in the KCDM, as it is unlikely that such different tasks would be able to draw information from a model whose distinctions are unintuitive to human searchers and information users.

14.4 Digital Libraries and Robust AZ

Another focus of my current research is the integration of automatic Argumentative Zoning into a large-scale digital library. The automatic processing described in chapter 11 is not restricted to the corpora in chapter 5; any corpus in SciXML can in principle be AZ-processed. More and more articles are published in formats for which SciXML conversion is straightforward or already available, such as the texts in the Cambridge-based projects SciBorg (where texts are imported from publisher-specific XML) and FLYSLIP (which contributed a SCIXML converter from the PLoS format (Public Library of Science, `www.plos.org`)).

It would of course be advantageous to enable AZ-processing for random scientific articles on the web, many of which are in PDF. As described in chapter 5, the difficulty is that SCIXML is a highly informative and precise text format which encodes complex document semantics, much of which is not readily retrievable from PDF. There are two ways to attack the problem: One could work on better PDF-to-SCIXML converters, or one could try to make AZ less dependent on the high-level information contained in SCIXML. With different colleagues and collaborators, I am exploring both routes.

The ACL Anthology (ACL Anthology Project, 2002, `http://aclweb.org/anthology-new/`) is a real-world test-case for PDF-to-SCIXML conversion. It is a project by the Linguistic Data Consortium (LDC) and the Association for Computational Linguistics (ACL) which provides PDF versions of all high quality publications in the field of computational linguistics (nine conferences, several workshops and one journal) from 1962 to now. It currently contains around 16,000 articles, but is constantly growing as new conference proceedings and journal articles are added to the site.

It is unusual for a discipline that its entire literature since the beginnings of the field is contained in a single, compact collection; of course this is only possible for relatively young disciplines. A related observation is that the ACL Anthology has a high proportion of internal references.[134] If many articles in a corpus cite articles in the same corpus, it is easier to construct citation networks where the full text of both the citing and the cited article are available.

These properties make the ACL Anthology a particularly valuable resource for modern citation-based research such as citation indexing (Nanba and Okumura, 1999, Garzone and Mercer, 2000, Teufel et al., 2006a), automatic review generation (Qazvinian and Radev, 2008, Nakov et al., 2004), and citation-based information retrieval (Bradshaw, 2003, Ritchie, 2008). The only problem is that all its texts are in PDF.

Work is currently underway in my group to compile the ACL Anthology into SCIXML format, which will extend the processing described in this book to tens of thousands of articles. The ACL Anthology presents

[134] Ritchie (2008) found an average of 33% internal references in Hollingsworth's (2008) ACL Anthology snapshot, far higher than that of a comparable corpus of genetics articles. The numbers range from 42% for the conference COLING to 18% for the *Computational Linguistics* journal.

many PDF-specific problems: due to the long time frame considered, it contains PDFs which were produced by several production routes and in many different publication styles and layouts. The conversion is due to Bill Hollingsworth; Anna Ritchie wrote the code which identifies reference items and citation instances.

The statistics of the ACL Anthology snapshot (Hollingsworth, 2008), which was compiled in 2005, are listed in Fig. 147. It contains a total of 44 million words in over 10,000 articles, after non-articles such as letters to the editor were automatically removed. However, at the current stage the SciXML is still far noisier than that of the manually edited CmpLG corpus, which is near-perfect. The ACL Anthology conversion is therefore an ongoing project.

ID	**Publication**	**Date**	**Articles**	**Words**
A	ANLP Proceedings	83-00	334	2,639,646
C	COLING Proceedings	65-06	2195	8,745,090
E	EACL Proceedings	83-06	490	2,044,573
H	HLT Proceedings	86-06	703	1,915,735
I	IJCNLP Proceedings	05	130	416,744
J	Comp. Linguistics Journal	74-04	545	4,812,524
M	MUC Proceedings	91-95	167	710,052
N	NAACL Proceedings	00-06	237	886,016
P	ACL Proceedings	79-06	1,647	7,379,254
W	ACL Workshop Proceedings	90-06	3344	14,504,933
T	TINLAP Proceedings	75,78,87	124	480,066
X	Tipster Proceedings	93,96,98	113	462,852
Total			10,029	44,997,287

FIGURE 147 Statistics of Hollingsworth's (2008) ACL Anthology Snapshot.

But there is another way to make sure that AZ can run on arbitrary texts: by making it less dependent on the high-level information contained in SciXML. Another recent development is the Robust AZ (RAZ) project, a collaboration with Min-Yen Kan from the National University of Singapore (NUS). This research is supported and exemplified by a large digital library in computer science and computational linguistics, which was built and maintained by Kan's group. It contains 2 million full-text documents from three sources (CiteSeerX, DBLP, dAnth). This is one of the largest repositories of scientific text outside the medical field, and unlike many of the entries in MEDLINE, it includes full text rather than only abstracts. dAnth is a text version of the ACL Anthology without structure (Bird et al., 2008).

Robust AZ is one of a number of applications which are implemented to access this digital library. For Robust AZ, the assumptions in terms of input text quality are minimal. Part of the input text may be ungrammatical, therefore the syntactic features are not used. Features which rely on SCIXML marking, such as the title and headline features, are also excluded. Instead, we use robust reimplementations of the citation, location and *TF*IDF* features, and combine them with a maximum entropy classifier. Lexical features include unigrams and bigrams of tokens and POS-sequences, and keywords extracted from the meta-discourse resources from appendix D. Whether the robust core of AZ still provides enough information to power real applications is a question we are currently investigating with a use study.

It is also possible to create parallel corpora of SCIXML-perfect and two versions of PDF-to-SCIXML imperfect texts from CmpLG, dAnth and Hollingsworth's (2008) ACL Anthology snapshot. I can therefore measure how much of the deterioration in performance we observe is due to the lower text quality of the PDF-inputs, as opposed to the absence of SCIXML information. This concludes the outlook on current and future research on AZ and CFC.

Chapter Summary

I have discussed current efforts to include AZ in a large digital library, and suggested new applications beyond those from chapter 4. Two of these require the syntactic and semantic manipulation of sub-sentential material (re-generation and citation support); in my opinion, this is a particularly promising prospect of this work for the future.

We have now almost reached the end of this book; what remains is to reconsider the original goals of the research in the light of what has actually been achieved.

15

Conclusions

The core message of this book is that knowledge claims provide a meaningful structuring principle in scientific discourse, and that keeping track of the scientific argumentation around knowledge claims is a useful enterprise. On the theoretical side, such an analysis can give us an explanatory structure of the discourse; on the practical side, information access applications can benefit from it.

The motivation for this book was the provision of better search technology for scientists, but the research presented here was also driven by a fascination with discourse theory and artificial intelligence. This double motivation resulted in a corpus linguistics exercise with an interdisciplinary outlook. The project spanned corpus collection and encoding (chapter 5), theory development (chapter 6), human annotation (chapters 7 and 8), feature detection and machine learning (chapters 10–12) and the design of several information management applications (chapters 2–4 and 14). Amongst the disciplines encountered on the way were citation content analysis, rhetoric of science, library science, information retrieval, content analysis, and some psycholinguistic methodology.

In particular, this book has brought together discourse linguistics, a notoriously subjective area of study, with information retrieval (IR) and search, a field that prides itself on its practicality and objectivity. I believe that these two opposed disciplines can greatly benefit from each other. Discourse theory can provide IR with the analysis necessary for scientific niche searches, which neither keyword search nor citation indexing addresses well. What IR can bring to discourse studies, in turn, is the "real-world" appeal: if a subjective theory improves performance on a real-world task, as objectively measured by the sophisticated IR evaluation methods on a large amount of unadulterated text, then its usefulness is hard to dispute.

15.1 An Interdisciplinary Project

Let us now look at each of the disciplines the research has touched upon, and summarise what has been achieved.

As far as discourse linguistics is concerned, I presented a rhetorically-based model of the nature of discourse structure in scientific text, which is influenced by insights from the philosophy of science. The *Knowledge Claim Discourse Model*, described in chapter 6, is a computationally-minded theory of rhetorical structure, which is based on the manifestations of knowledge claims in scientific discourse.

A core question for a model of discourse structure is at which abstraction level its units and relations should be defined, so that the description generalises to other texts. In my work, an important element of abstraction is provided by the connections between the central contribution in the article (the new knowledge claim) and existing scientific work.

According to the KCDM, there are several important aspects to the structure of a scientific article: who the knowledge claims described in the article are attributed to, which role other people's knowledge claims play for the main argument in the article, and which rhetorical statements in defense of the new knowledge claim are made. These factors correspond to different levels in the KCDM. The result of the analysis encodes, for instance, what the contribution of the article is, how it relates to other articles, and where in the text those other approaches are described.

This analysis has not been defined in a vacuum, but with a view to supporting information access applications in the areas of information retrieval and library science. I have argued in chapters 2 and 3 that there is a need for relation-based information in scientific information management which the current keyword- and citation-based search technology cannot fulfil. For fine-grained scientific search, an article often needs to be considered in contrast to similar research. The Knowledge Claim Discourse Model is ideal for such tasks because of its interest in the functional connection between two articles, and the idea that this connection forms an important aspect of both articles' characterisations.

I designed two new document surrogates for scientific information management, *rhetorical extracts* and *citation maps*, which demonstrate the added value of discourse analysis for summarisation and citation indexing. Chapter 14 added designs for other text understanding tasks such as authoring tools, multi-document summarisation and review generation, which could also profit from a KCDM analysis.

Evidence for the theory is collected in the practical part of the book, which is based on manual and automatic annotation of a corpus of scientific articles. If there is agreement between human subjects' annotation which was independently arrived at, this is generally accepted as objective evidence for a theory. Chapter 7 defines three annotation schemes based on the KCDM, and in the course reviews the methodology of annotation studies. One of the schemes, *Argumentative Zoning* (AZ), assigns argumentative status to each sentence in the text. The others concern the attribution of knowledge claims (KCA) and the rhetorical function of citations (CFC). The reliability studies for the schemes are described in chapter 8.

The automatic evidence is presented in chapters 10–12. Supervised machine learning is used to simulate the annotation. This requires the implementation of automatically detectable features, such that they are correlated with the hidden rhetorical structure (i.e., the target features, which are defined by the human annotation). The set of features I propose are described in chapter 10; in terms of computational linguistics and artificial intelligence, their definition is probably the biggest contribution of this book.

The meta-discourse features are the most explanatory features, as chapter 9 explains. They keep track of what is going on in the micro-world of the research space: who is acting (the authors or other researchers), and which kinds of actions they are performing. Meta-discourse is closely related to the rhetoric of science, and to how problem-solving processes are described in scientific discourse. It is also a general phenomenon, which remains invariant when we move from one article to the next, in contrast to the scientific content, which radically changes when we turn to a new article.

A comparison of the system output with the gold standard (section 12.1) shows that AZ, CFC and KCA can be performed automatically and robustly. The system easily beats baselines of random choice or bag-of-word classification, although there is still a large performance gap to the human ceiling. However, the extrinsic evaluation in section 12.2 shows that even a crude implementation of rhetorical extracts can improve a user's performance in a relation-based search task.

It is an important principle of the Knowledge Claim Discourse Model and the meta-discourse features that they are not defined on the basis of specific scientific knowledge, but only by generic linguistic knowledge. This is why the model should be applicable across scientific disciplines. Evidence from section 13.1 confirms this, where a successful KCDM analysis of chemistry articles is reported (the rest of the book uses computational linguistics articles).

I consider the implementation a step towards robust text understanding, for two reasons: Firstly, the features that are being produced carry some meaning in themselves. They are independently interpretable, and are explanatory of some discourse effects (e.g., "the authors just made their first appearance in the text, and they performed a change-type action"), rather than being low-level features with no intrinsic meaning, such as bags-of-words or POS-patterns. Secondly, the task is purposefully defined in such a way that scientific knowledge cannot tarnish the definition of the truth. In my opinion, the best way to define a gold standard for a robust text understanding task is by what a non-expert sees in a text, not by what an expert sees in it. Such a gold standard will direct automatic efforts towards generalisable, representable effects. Admittedly, the level of understanding in the current implementation is only skin-deep; for instance, the meta-discourse features encode only subject–verb information. But as the truth is defined without recourse to world knowledge, better representations of generalisable discourse phenomena can lead to a steady and systematic increase in the level of understanding performed, as and when they become available.

15.2 Limitations

The discourse model has the following limitations:

- **Scope**: It only describes discourse structure in research articles in the experimental sciences – not in the humanities, and not in any other text type. While it has been shown to work well for computational linguistics and chemistry, adaption of the schemes to other disciplines, e.g., genetics, is currently ongoing.
- **Depth**: The depth of the analysis is limited by the currently relatively simple modelling of meta-discourse, and by the fact that the author intentions recognised come from a predefined list.
- **Units**: The practical annotation is limited by the fact that only full sentences can be used as annotation units, although it is known that this is suboptimal in some cases.

The automatic recognisers for AZ, KCA and CFC suffer from limitations too:

- **Structure of Recognisers**: The current implementation, with its one-time classification of all phenomena at once, is simplistic. It does not take into account the interplay between the separate levels of the model. For instance, a cascading system could perform an analysis of the KCA structure in parallel with a recognition of moves and hinges, although it is unclear how these types of information should best be combined.

- **Statistical Classifiers**: It is also likely that even within the one-time statistical classification framework, there is room for improvement. A thorough investigation of supervised classifiers (both generative and discriminative ones, e.g. SVMs, CRFs and perceptrons) should be performed, which would likely improve performance; this is what Hachey and Grover (2005a) find when they optimised their system for the AZ-style classification of legal texts.
- **Complexity of Meta-Discourse**: The current meta-discourse features only use subject and verb information, which results in a blurred picture of what is going on in the research space. A syntactically and semantically more precise representation, particularly of comparisons and their direction, would be advantageous from an AI knowledge representation as well as from a practical viewpoint.
- **Use of Parser**: The current feature detection step does not use a parser; the most complicated linguistic processing used is a POS-tagger. While this can be seen as an advantage in terms of robustness, a parser is likely to improve the recognition of the meta-discourse features `Ent`, `Act` and `Formu`, and the verb-syntactic features `Syn-1`, `Syn-2`, `Syn-3`.
- **Polysemy**: The feature recognition step currently avoids dealing with polysemous meta-discourse, which introduces noise.
- **Use vs. Mention Problem**: Concepts such as "*goal*", "*topic*" and "*similarity*", which play a special role in meta-discourse, can also be part of the object level, i.e., refer to the scientific content in the article. The areas of logic programming, discourse modelling and statistical NLP are the most likely ones where this can happen.[135] It is possible that measures of the relative local importance of concepts in a document, such as the *TF*IDF* measure, might detect meta-discourse features which occur too frequently in a document to really be meta-discourse.
- **Meta-Discourse Discovery**: Porting the recognisers to new domains currently still involves manual work, because the meta-discourse discovery procedure described in section 13.3 is still in its infancy and has only been tested on one syntactic frame. This approach should also be compared against methods for clustering verb semantics by their argument structure, as in Levin (1993), Schulte im Walde (2006), Korhonen et al. (2003).

[135] My own publications, which talk about such concepts a lot, are of course another prime example of this effect.

The IR applications could also be improved:

- **Scope of Experiment**: The experiment in section 12.2 proposed one particular task in information management and measured which document surrogates can help in it, but it is only a first step in a yet under-explored research area. Not much is known about scientists' relation-seeking searches. One should investigate what exactly they look for, and to which degree different system outputs help them find it.
- **Linking of Hinges with Citations**: The creation of citation maps requires that each Contrast or Basis sentence is associated with its citation in text, which is not a trivial task. In order to achieve higher-quality citation maps than the ones that can currently be built, what is required is a thorough investigation of the structure of citation blocks and the linguistic phenomena at work inside them.

A

CmpLG-D Articles

No.	Title/Authors/Conference	W/S/A
0 9405001	Similarity-Based Estimation of Word Cooccurrence Probabilities/Dagan, Pereira, Lee (ACL94)	4400/160/7
1 9405002	Temporal Relations: Reference or Discourse Coherence?/Kehler (ACL94S)	2340/ 79/5
2 9405004	Syntactic-Head-Driven Generation/Koenig (COLI94)	3490/116/4
3 9405010	Common Topics and Coherent Situations: Interpreting Ellipsis in the Context of Discourse Inference/Kehler (ACL94)	5369/156/5
4 9405013	Collaboration on Reference to Objects that are not Mutually Known/Edmonds (COLI94)	4030/135/5
5 9405022	Grammar Specialization through Entropy Thresholds/Samuelsson (ACL94)	4660/170/4
6 9405023	An Integrated Heuristic Scheme for Partial Parse Evaluation/Lavie (ACL94S)	2470/102/5
7 9405028	Semantics of Complex Sentences in Japanese/Nakagawa, Nishizawa (COLI94)	4715/200/5
8 9405033	Relating Complexity to Practical Performance in Parsing with Wide-Coverage Unification Grammars/Carroll (ACL94)	5460/121/2
9 9405035	Dual-Coding Theory and Connectionist Lexical Selection/Wang (ACL94S)	1931/ 90/2
10 9407011	Discourse Obligations in Dialogue Processing/Traum, Allen (ACL94)	6578/233/2
11 9408003	Typed Feature Structures as Descriptions/King (COLI94)	2509/167/2
12 9408004	Parsing with Principles and Probabilities/Fordham, Crocker (ACL94W)	3689/ 97/3
13 9408006	LHIP: Extended DCGs for Configurable Robust Parsing/Ballim, Russell (COLI94)	4498/184/2
14 9408011	**EXAMPLE PAPER: Distributional Clustering of English Words/Pereira, Tishby, Lee (ACL93)**	**4825/170/4**
15 9408014	Qualitative and Quantitative Models of Speech Translation/Alshawi (ACL94W)	7726/296/4
16 9409004	An Experiment on Learning Appropriate Selectional Restrictions from a Parsed Corpus/Ribas (COLI94)	4095/179/3

No.		Title/Authors/Conference	W/S/A
17	9410001	Improving Language Models by Clustering Training Sentences/Carter (ANLP94)	5435/150/6
18	9410005	A Centering Approach to Pronouns/Brennan, Friedman, Pollard (ACL87)	2536/ 98/4
19	9410006	Evaluating Discourse Processing Algorithms/Walker (ACL89)	7381/258/8
20	9410008	Recognizing Text Genres with Simple Metrics Using Discriminant Analysis/Karlgren, Cutting (COLI94)	1986/ 66/3
21	9410009	Lexical Functions and Machine Translation (Reserve)/Heylen, Maxwell, Verhagen (COLI94)	3840/135/2
22	9410012	Does Baum-Welch Re-estimation Help Taggers?/Elworthy (ANLP94)	4201/141/10
23	9410022	Automated Tone Transcription/Bird (ACL94W)	7184/322/8
24	9410032	Planning Argumentative Texts/Huang (COLI94)	3861/183/4
25	9410033	Default Handling in Incremental Generation/Harbusch, Kikui, Kilger (COLI94)	4258/176/5
26	9411019	Focus on "only" and "not"/Ramsay (COLI94)	2842/ 99/2
27	9411021	Free-ordered CUG on Chemical Abstract Machine/Tojo (COLI94)	2088/ 86/5
28	9411023	Abstract Generation Based on Rhetorical Structure Extraction/Ono, Sumita, Miike (COLI94)	2860/112/4
29	9412005	Segmenting Speech without a Lexicon: the Roles of Phonotactics and Speech Source/Cartwright, Brent (ACL94W)	5537/166/6
30	9412008	Analysis of Japanese Compound Nouns using Collocational Information/Kobayasi, Tokunaga, Tanaka (COLI94)	3499/172/4
31	9502004	Bottom-Up Earley Deduction/Erbach (COLI94)	3637/126/3
32	9502005	Off-line Optimization for Earley-style HPSG Processing/Minnen, Gerdemann, Goetz (EACL95)	4197/129/3
33	9502006	Rapid Development of Morphological Descriptions for Full Language Processing Systems/Carter (EACL95)	5346/162/4
34	9502009	On Learning More Appropriate Selectional Restrictions/Ribas (EACL95)	3811/166/4
35	9502014	Ellipsis and Quantification: A Substitutional Approach/Crouch (EACL95)	5352/230/2
36	9502015	The Semantics of Resource Sharing in Lexical-Functional Grammar/Kehler, Dalrymple, Lamping, Saraswat (EACL95)	4304/155/3
37	9502018	Algorithms for Analysing the Temporal Structure of Discourse/Hitzeman, Moens, Grover (EACL95)	4033/137/4
38	9502021	A Tractable Extension of Linear Indexed Grammars/Keller, Weir (EACL95)	4013/140/3
39	9502022	Stochastic HPSG/Brew (EACL95)	3408/129/3
40	9502023	Splitting the Reference Time: Temporal Anaphora and Quantification in DRT/Nelken, Francez (EACL95)	4326/149/5
41	9502024	A Robust Parser Based on Syntactic Information/Lee, Kweon, Seo, Kim (EACL95)	3317/159/7
42	9502031	Cooperative Error Handling and Shallow Processing/Bowden (EACL95S)	2485/ 88/6

No.		Title/Authors/Conference	W/S/A
43	9502033	An Algorithm to Co-Ordinate Anaphora Resolution and PPS Disambiguation Process/Azzam (EACL95S)	1332/ 45/3
44	9502035	Incorporating " Unconscious Reanalysis " into an Incremental, Monotonic Parser/Sturt (EACL95S)	4416/126/4
45	9502037	A State-Transition Grammar for Data-Oriented Parsing/Tugwell (EACL95S)	3322/116/2
46	9502038	Implementation and evaluation of a German HMM for POS disambiguation/Feldweg (EACL95W)	3670/129/5
47	9502039	Multilingual Sentence Categorization according to Language/Giguet (EACL95W)	2158/ 93/13
48	9503002	Computational Dialectology in Irish Gaelic/Kessler (EACL95)	4618/165/5
49	9503004	Creating a Tagset, Lexicon and Guesser for a French tagger/Chanod, Tapanainen (EACL95W)	4720/170/3
50	9503005	A Specification Language for Lexical Functional Grammars/Blackburn, Gardent (EACL95)	4992/218/4
51	9503007	The Semantics of Motion/Sablayrolles (EACL95)	2392/ 85/3
52	9503009	Distributional Part-of-Speech Tagging/Schuetze (EACL95)	5083/184/3
53	9503013	Incremental Interpretation: Applications, Theory, and Relationship to Dynamic Semantics/Milward, Cooper (COLI94)	5776/186/6
54	9503014	Non-Constituent Coordination: Theory and Practice/Milward (COLI94)	5339/192/3
55	9503015	Incremental Interpretation of Categorial Grammar/Milward (EACL95)	4986/165/4
56	9503017	Redundancy in Colaborative Dialogue/Walker (COLI92)	5305/212/9
57	9503018	Discourse and Deliberation: Testing a Collaborative Strategy/Walker (COLI94)	5406/182/4
58	9503023	A Fast Partial Parse of Natural Language Sentences Using a Connectionist Method/Lyon, Dickerson (EACL95)	5091/230/4
59	9503025	Occurrence Vectors from Corpora vs. Distance Vectors from Dictionaries/Niwa, Nitta (COLI94)	2810/110/3
60	9504002	Tagset Design and Inflected Languages/Elworthy (EACL95W)	3495/130/3
61	9504006	Cues and Control in Expert-Client Dialogues/Whittaker, Stenton (ACL88)	3969/152/4
62	9504007	Mixed Initiative in Dialogue: An Investigation into Discourse Segmentation/Walker, Whittaker (ACL90)	5125/190/9
63	9504017	A Uniform Treatment of Pragmatic Inferences in Simple and Complex Utterances and Sequences of Utterances/Marcu, Hirst (ACL95)	3977/132/4
64	9504024	A Morphographemic Model for Error Correction in Nonconcatenative Strings/Bowden, Kiraz (ACL95)	3207/143/4
65	9504026	The Intersection of Finite State Automata and Definite Clause Grammars/vanNoord (ACL95)	3664/151/8
66	9504027	An Efficient Generation Algorithm for Lexicalist MT/Poznanski, Beaven, Whitelock (ACL95)	4280/175/3
67	9504030	Statistical Decision-Tree Models for Parsing/Magerman (ACL95)	4583/188/8

No.		Title/Authors/Conference	W/S/A
68	9504033	Corpus Statistics Meet the Noun Compound: Some Empirical Results/Lauer (ACL95)	4459/191/4
69	9504034	Bayesian Grammar Induction for Language Modeling/Chen (ACL95)	4661/175/5
70	9505001	Response Generation in Collaborative Negotiation/Chu-Carroll, Carberry (ACL95)	6066/154/5
71	9506004	Using Higher-Order Logic Programming for Semantic Interpretation of Coordinate Constructs/Kulick (ACL95)	3418/130/4
72	9511001	Countability and Number in Japanese-to-English Machine Translation/Bond, Ogura, Ikehara (COLI94)	3463/136/2
73	9511006	Disambiguating Noun Groupings with Respect to WordNet Senses/Resnik (ACL95W)	6040/159/5
74	9601004	Similarity between Words Computed by Spreading Activation on an English Dictionary/Kozima, Furugori (EACL93)	4429/212/4
75	9604019	Magic for Filter Optimization in Dynamic Bottom-up Processing/Minnen (ACL96)	4014/157/3
76	9604022	Unsupervised Learning of Word-Category Guessing Rules/Mikheev (ACL96)	6172/236/4
77	9605013	Learning Dependencies between Case Frame Slots/Li, Abe (COLI96)	4939/170/8
78	9605014	Clustering Words with the MDL Principle/Li, Abe (COLI96)	4533/167/5
79	9605016	Parsing for Semidirectional Lambek Grammar is NP-Complete/Doerre (ACL96)	3090/126/4

B

DTD for SciXML

```
<!ELEMENT PAPER    (METADATA|CURRENT_TITLE|CURRENT_AUTHORLIST|ABSTRACT|
                  BODY|REFERENCELIST|FOOTNOTELIST|FIGURELIST|TABLELIST)*>

<!ELEMENT METADATA (#PCDATA|FILENO|REFLABEL|APPEARED|CLASSIFICATION|
                                                        JOURNAL)*>

<!ELEMENT FILENO (#PCDATA)>

<!ELEMENT APPEARED (#PCDATA|CONFERENCE|YEAR)*>

<!ELEMENT CONFERENCE (#PCDATA)>
<!ATTLIST CONFERENCE
          TYPE     (MAIN|STUDENT|Student|WORKSHOP) "MAIN">
<!ELEMENT YEAR     (#PCDATA)>
<!ELEMENT JOURNAL  (#PCDATA|YEAR|ISSUE)*>
<!ELEMENT ISSUE    (#PCDATA)>
<!ELEMENT NUMBER   (#PCDATA)>

<!ELEMENT CURRENT_TITLE    (#PCDATA|REFAUTHOR|REF|XREF)*>
<!ELEMENT CLASSIFICATION   (#PCDATA)>

<!ELEMENT CURRENT_AUTHORLIST (CURRENT_AUTHOR)*>
<!ELEMENT CURRENT_AUTHOR      (#PCDATA|CURRENT_SURNAME)*>

<!ELEMENT CURRENT_SURNAME (#PCDATA)>

<!ELEMENT BODY (DIV)+>

<!ELEMENT DIV   (HEADER?, (DIV|P|EQN|IMAGE|EXAMPLE)*)>
<!ATTLIST DIV   DEPTH  CDATA  #REQUIRED>

<!ELEMENT HEADER (#PCDATA|REF|EQN|CREF|REFAUTHOR)*>
<!ATTLIST HEADER
          ID  ID  #IMPLIED
          HEADER_MARKER CDATA #IMPLIED>

<!ELEMENT P (#PCDATA|S|IMAGE|EXAMPLE|EQN)*>
<!ATTLIST P TYPE (ITEM|TXT) "TXT">

<!ELEMENT S  (#PCDATA|REF|REFAUTHOR|XREF|CREF|EQN)*>
<!ATTLIST S
          ID            ID          #REQUIRED
          TYPE          (ITEM|TXT)  "TXT"
          ABSTRACTC     CDATA       #IMPLIED>

<!ELEMENT ABSTRACT  (A-S)*>
```

```
<!ELEMENT A-S (#PCDATA|REF|REFAUTHOR|CREF|XREF|EQN)*>
<!ATTLIST A-S
          ID            ID          #REQUIRED
          TYPE          (ITEM|TXT)  "TXT"
          DOCUMENTC     CDATA       #IMPLIED>

<!ELEMENT EQN  #PCDATA>
<!ATTLIST EQN ID ID #IMPLIED>

<!ELEMENT IMAGE (#PCDATA|REF|REFAUTHOR|CREF|EQN)*>
<!ATTLIST IMAGE ID ID #REQUIRED>

<!ELEMENT EXAMPLE (#PCDATA|EQN|REF|CREF|EX-S)*>
<!ATTLIST EXAMPLE ID ID #IMPLIED>

<!ELEMENT EX-S (#PCDATA|REF|REFAUTHOR|CREF|EQN)*>
<!ATTLIST EX-S
          ID            ID          #REQUIRED>

<!ELEMENT REF (#PCDATA)>
<!ATTLIST REF
          ID             CDATA    #IMPLIED
          REFID          CDATA    #REQUIRED
          SELF           (YES|NO) #IMPLIED>

<!ELEMENT REFAUTHOR (#PCDATA)>
<!ATTLIST REFAUTHOR
          ID             ID       #IMPLIED

<!ELEMENT CREF EMPTY>
<!ELEMENT XREF (#PCDATA)>
<!ATTLIST XREF
          ID            CDATA    #IMPLIED
          TYPE          CDATA    #IMPLIED>

<!ELEMENT REFERENCELIST (REFERENCE)*>
<!ELEMENT REFERENCE (#PCDATA|REFLABEL|SURNAME|DATE|EQN|REF|TITLE|
                     CONFERENCE|JOURNAL)*>
<!ATTLIST REFERENCE ID CDATA #IMPLIED>
<!ELEMENT REFLABEL (#PCDATA)>
<!ATTLIST REFLABEL SELF  (YES|NO) #IMPLIED>
<!ELEMENT TITLE  (#PCDATA|REFAUTHOR|REF|XREF)*>
<!ELEMENT SURNAME (#PCDATA)>
<!ELEMENT DATE (#PCDATA)>

<!ELEMENT FOOTNOTELIST (#PCDATA|FOOTNOTE)*>
<!ELEMENT FOOTNOTE (#PCDATA|TITLE|REF|REFAUTHOR|XREF|P)*>
<!ATTLIST FOOTNOTE
          ID  CDATA  #IMPLIED
          MARKER  CDATA  #IMPLIED>

<!ELEMENT FIGURELIST (#PCDATA|FIGURE)*>
<!ELEMENT FIGURE (#PCDATA|TITLE|REF|P)*>
<!ATTLIST FIGURE
          ID  CDATA  #IMPLIED
          SRC  CDATA  #IMPLIED
          SEQ  CDATA  #IMPLIED>

<!ELEMENT TABLELIST (#PCDATA|TABLE)*>
<!ELEMENT TABLE (#PCDATA|TITLE|REF|P)*>
<!ATTLIST TABLE
          ID  CDATA  #IMPLIED
          SRC  CDATA  #IMPLIED
          SEQ  CDATA  #IMPLIED>
```

C

Guidelines

C.1 KCA Guidelines (1998)

These guidelines describe a classification scheme for scientific papers which covers the ownership of ideas. The classification scheme is displayed in Fig. 148.

Each of the classes is associated with a colour, and these colours are matched with marker pens. Please use these to mark your judgement on the printout of the papers.

BACKGROUND	Generally accepted background knowledge (YELLOW)
OTHER	Neutral description of specific previous work (ORANGE)
OWN	Own work: method, results, future work... (BLUE)

FIGURE 148 Overview of KCA Annotation Scheme.

Annotation procedure

Before annotation

Skim-read the paper before annotation. This is important, as in some papers, the interpretation of certain sentences in the context of the overall argumentation only becomes apparent after one has an overview of the whole paper. Don't try to understand the solution in detail—you can jump over the parts of the paper where you think the own solution is described in details. Rather try to understand the structure of the scientific argumentation. Concentrate on those parts of the paper where the connection to the subject field and the connection to other work is described. In particular, skim-read the abstract, the introduction, the conclusions (if it is summary-style), and sections reviewing other research (often after introduction or before conclusions; they could be marked sections with headlines like "Relation to other work", "Prior research", "X in the literature" etc.).

During Annotation

Annotation proceeds sentence by sentence, and is mutually exclusive: Each sentence can have only one category.

When interpreting the role of a sentence, you should treat the sentence in the way in which you think the *author* intended it in their argumentation. Context and location of a sentence are important.

There are two questions you need to answer.

- **Question 1: Does this sentence talk about the authors' own work, as opposed to somebody else's work?**
  If yes, assign OWN, if no, answer question 2.
- **Question 2: If it talks about other people's work, is it concerned with general statements, as opposed to a specific approach?**
  If yes, assign BACKGROUND, if no, assign OTHER.

Consecutive sentences are often marked with the same category if they *together* fulfil the criteria of the category. Please annotate all sentences in the abstract, and all sentences in the document except acknowledgement sentences. Also mark (linguistic) example sentences.

The questions

Question 1: Does this sentence talk about own work?

Own work in the context of this paper means work presented as performed by the authors *in the given paper*, i.e. as new research.

Description of own work should make up a large part of the paper—it includes descriptions of the own solution, method, results, discussion, limitations and future work.

Previous own research, i.e. research done by the authors before and published elsewhere, does *not* count as own work. Sometimes the fact that previous work is discussed is specifically marked ("*we have previously*"), sometimes it can only be inferred because there is a reference indicating the author's name. Check the reference list to make sure that the string "*et al.*" in a citation (cited paper) does not "hide" one of the authors of the current paper. Unfortunately, authors tend to talk about previous own work in much the same way as they do about the current (own) work. This might constitute a problem here. It is your job to decide if certain statements are presented as if they were the contribution of the paper. There is one exception: PhD or MSc theses do not count as published work (otherwise, some entire papers would have to be marked as other work if the paper is a short version of a PhD or MSc thesis). In that case, the sentence first citing the thesis is to be marked as BASIS. In all other contexts, reference to the thesis/research is to be considered as own.

Sometimes, short descriptions of own work (statements of opinion) appear within sections talking about other work (background or specific). For example, an author might describe a general problem, then individualize the present research by setting the scope within the current work ("*We will here only be interested in VP gapping as opposed to NP gapping*"), then continue describing general specific to VP gapping. These scope declarations should be considered as own work because they talk about the given work/opinions. The grammatical subject in a sentence does not always tell you whether it's own work or not. Sometimes the criticism of other work might look like own opinion ("*However, we are convinced that this is wrong* [...]"). Cases like this should *not* be considered as own work, but as weaknesses of other work, i.e., CONTRAST.

In particular, watch out for the first mention of the own work, typically two thirds down in the introduction. Most of the information under the Summary or Conclusion section is normally own work. Sometimes, individual sentences in the conclusion section make direct comparisons with other work, e.g., detailing advantages of the approach. Only mark these as OTHER if the other work is described again, using more than one sentence of description, else mark as OWN.

Question 2: Does this sentence describe background?

BACKGROUND marks sentences which are presented as uncontroversial in the field. In such sentences, the research context is established. This includes statements of general capacity of the field, general problems, research goals, methodologies and general solutions ("*In recent years, there has been a growing interest in the field of X in the subject of Y*"). The most prototypical use of BACKGROUND is in the beginning of the paper.

Examples for general problems:

- *One of the difficult problems in machine translation from Japanese to English or other European languages is the treatment of articles and numbers.*
- *Complications arise in spelling rule application from the fact that, at compile time, neither the lexical nor the surface form of the root, nor even its length, is known.*

- *Collocations present specific problems in translation, both in human and automatic contexts.*

Examples for generally accepted/old solutions or claims:

- *Tagging by means of a Hidden Markov Model (HMM) is widely recognised as an effective technique for assigning parts of speech to a corpus in a robust and efficient manner.*
- *Current research in lexical aquisition is eminently knowledge-based.*
- *Literature in psychology has amply demonstrated that children do not acquire* [...]

In linguistics papers, mark the description of the linguistic phenomena being covered as BACKGROUND.PS. This includes example sentences. In contrast, the *analysis* of the phenomena are typically either own or other work.

It may be that there is a BACKGROUND segment somewhere in the middle of the paper. It may then not be easy to decide if it is BACKGROUND or OWN. Use the following test: if you think that this segment could have been used as an introductory text at the beginning of the paper, and if it does not contain material that is individualized to the authors themselves, then it should be marked as BACKGROUND.

References to "pioneers" in the field are also BACKGROUND material—sentences which describe other work in an introductory way without any criticism. These are usually older references.

Sometimes there is no BACKGROUND segment, namely if the authors start directly by describing one specific individualized approach.

The difference between BACKGROUND and OTHER is only in degree of *specificity.*

OTHER are descriptions of other work which is described *specifically* enough to contrast the own work to it, to criticize it or to mention that it provides support for own idea. For some work to be considered specific other work, it must be clearly attributable to some other researchers, otherwise it might be too general to count as specific other work. Often such segments are started by markers of specific work, citations:

- *<REF> argues that children don't acquire grammar frames until they have a lexicon* [...]
- *<REF> 's solution solves the problem of data-sparseness.*
- *<REF> 's formalism allows the treatment of coordinated structures.*
- *The bilingual dual-coding theory <REF> partially answers the above questions.*
- *<REF> introduced the notion of temporal anaphora, to account for ways in which temporal expressions depend on surrounding elements*

in the discourse for their semantic contribution to the discourse.

Named solutions can also count as specificity markers for other work:

- *Similarity-based models suggest an appealing approach for dealing with data sparseness.*

The distinction between BACKGROUND and OTHER might be difficult to make. Stop marking as BACKGROUND at the point where ideas, solutions, or tasks are clearly being individualized, i.e., attributed to researchers in such a way that they can get criticized, and required for the paper's own argumentation. At this point, mark existing approaches as OTHER. Often the breaking point looks like this: "<*General problem description*> *Recently, some researchers have tried to tackle this by doing* <*More specific description with references*>" In that case, the border is before *"Recently"*.

When authors give specific information about research, but express no stance towards that work, particularly if it happens in the beginning, they seem to imply the statements are generally accepted in the field. You might in this case decide to mark it as BACKGROUND.

When it gets difficult

There are several reasons why the annotation scheme might not work well for a given paper. The writing style in some papers might make it difficult to see who the intellectual ownership is ascribed to. In some papers however, the scheme's assumptions that research with different ownership (own/other/background) is indeed presented in separate segments in the paper are violated:

- Our model assumes that the author perceives a clear separation between own work and work outside the scope of the paper, and presents work according to that separation. However, if the paper describes some minute detail of a previous, larger work of the author, then this separation might not be given.
- A specialized case of this, and another example of a potential breakdown of the simple model is for evaluation papers, especially where the authors compare several of their own solutions with each other, or if they compare their solution to somebody else's.
- The scheme is only created for research papers; there must be some new, practical contribution described in the paper. If you are given a paper to annotate which looks like a position or review articles, do not annotate it.

Please keep a note of all difficulties that you encounter with determining individualized segments, and write down your reasons for finding it difficult (i.e. in which way the given paper made it hard for our model to describe what was going on).

C.2 AZ Guidelines (1998)

These guidelines describe a classification scheme for scientific papers for ownership of ideas, relation to other work and internal paper structure. The classification scheme is displayed in Fig. 149.

Each of the classes is associated with a colour, and these colours are matched with marker pens. Please use these to mark your judgement on the printout of the papers.

BACKGROUND	Generally accepted background knowledge (YELLOW)
OTHER	Neutral description of specific previous work (ORANGE)
OWN	Own work: method, results, future work... (BLUE)
AIM	Specific research goal (PINK)
TEXTUAL	Textual section structure (RED)
CONTRAST	Contrast, comparison, weakness of other solution (GREEN)
BASIS	Other work provides basis for own work (PURPLE)

FIGURE 149 Overview of AZ Annotation Scheme.

Annotation procedure

Before annotation

Skim-read the paper before annotation. This is important, as in some papers, the interpretation of certain sentences in the context of the overall argumentation only becomes apparent after one has an overview of the whole paper. Don't try to understand the solution in detail—you can jump over the parts of the paper where you think the own solution is described in details. Rather try to understand the structure of the scientific argumentation. Concentrate on those parts of the paper where the connection to the subject field and the connection to other work is described. In particular, skim-read the abstract, the introduction, the conclusions (if it is summary-style), and sections reviewing other research (often after introduction or before conclusions; they could be marked sections with headlines like "Relation to other work", "Prior research", "X in the literature" etc.).

During Annotation

Annotation proceeds sentence by sentence, and is mutually exclusive: Each sentence can have only one category. The main decision procedure is given in Fig. 150. For each sentence, the following questions have to be answered.

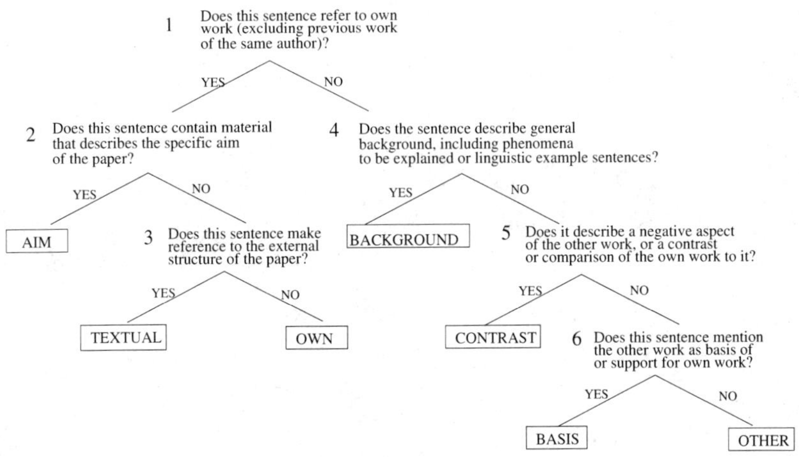

FIGURE 150 AZ Decision Process.

Therefore, if there is a conflict, the "higher" classes in the decision tree (the ones that you reach first) will win over the "lower" classes. These guidelines will give details about the questions.

When interpreting the role of a sentence, you should treat the sentence in the way in which you think the *author* intended it in their argumentation. Context and location of a sentence are important.

- **Question 1: Does this sentence talk about own work?**
  If your answer is 'yes', proceed to Question 2.
  If your answer is 'no', proceed to Question 4.
- **Question 2: Does it contain a goal statement?**
  If your answer is 'yes', assign class Aim and move to next sentence.
  If your answer is 'no', proceed to Question 3.
- **Question 3: Does it contain a textual overview?**
  If your answer is 'yes', assign tag Textual and move to the next sentence.
  If your answer is 'no', assign tag Own and move to the next sentence.
- **Question 4: Does it describe background?**

If your answer is 'yes', assign tag BACKGROUND and move to the next sentence.
If your answer is 'no', proceed to Question 6.

- **Question 5: Is the other work described in a contrastive way?**
If your answer is 'yes', assign tag CONTRAST and move to next sentence.
If your answer is 'no', proceed to Question 5.
- **Question 6: Is the own work based on other work?**
If your answer is 'yes', assign tag BASIS.
If your answer is 'no', assign tag OTHER.

You can mark consecutive sentences with the same category if they *together* fulfil the criteria of the category. E.g. you could mark two sentences as AIM if they together describe the specific goal of a paper well. If you cannot assign a category, please mark the sentence and take a note describing the difficulties.

As soon as you have reached a leaf, assign the corresponding category to the sentence. Please annotate all sentences in the abstract, and all sentences in the document except acknowledgement sentences. Also mark (linguistic) example sentences.

After annotation

Check a few things, and rectify your annotation if necessary:

- There must be at least one AIM sentence in the paper. If this is not the case, reclassify some other candidate sentences, until you have found at least one sentence that represents the specific aim of the given paper.
- There must not be more than 5 AIM sentences per paper. The only exception is if each of them is a straight hit, i.e. they are indisputably goal statements, particularly if the sentences are paraphrases of each other.

  If you have to eliminate AIM sentences, do the following:

  - Prefer explicit AIM statements (prefer 'direct' goal statements and 'functionality-provided' to 'solved' and other types).
  - Prefer AIM sentences towards the periphery (e.g., at the beginning of summarizing conclusions), and in the border area with OTHER or BACKGROUND segments;
  - If all fails, pick the ones you think are most relevant in the context of distinguishing this piece of research from others.

The questions

Question 1: Does this sentence talk about own work?

Own work in the context of this paper means work presented as performed by the authors *in the given paper*, i.e. as new research.

Description of own work should make up a large part of the paper—it includes descriptions of the own solution, method, results, discussion, limitations and future work.

Previous own research, i.e. research done by the authors before and published elsewhere, does *not* count as own work. Sometimes the fact that previous work is discussed is specifically marked ("*we have previously*"), sometimes it can only be inferred because there is a reference indicating the author's name. Check the reference list to make sure that the string "*et al.*" in a citation (cited paper) does not "hide" one of the authors of the current paper. Unfortunately, authors tend to talk about previous own work in much the same way as they do about the current (own) work. This might constitute a problem here. It is your job to decide if certain statements are presented as if they were the contribution of the paper. There is one exception: PhD or MSc theses do not count as published work (otherwise, some entire papers would have to be marked as other work if the paper is a short version of a PhD or MSc thesis). In that case, the sentence first citing the thesis is to be marked as Basis. In all other contexts, reference to the thesis/research is to be considered as own.

Sometimes, short descriptions of own work (statements of opinion) appear within sections talking about other work (background or specific). For example, an author might describe a general problem, then individualize the present research by setting the scope within the current work ("*We will here only be interested in VP gapping as opposed to NP gapping*"), then continue describing general specific to VP gapping. These scope declarations should be considered as own work because they talk about the given work/opinions. The grammatical subject in a sentence does not always tell you whether it's own work or not. Sometimes the criticism of other work might look like own opinion ("*However, we are convinced that this is wrong* [...]"). Cases like this should *not* be considered as own work, but as weaknesses of other work, i.e., Contrast.

In particular, watch out for the first mention of the own work, typically two thirds down in the introduction. Most of the information under the Summary or Conclusion section is normally own work. Sometimes, individual sentences in the conclusion section make direct comparisons with other work, e.g., detailing advantages of the approach.

Only mark these as OTHER if the other work is described again, using more than one sentence of description, else mark as OWN.

Question 2: Does this sentence contain a goal statement?

Two kinds of sentences count as goal statements:

- Goal statements (i.e. description of research goal)
- Scope statement (i.e. delimitation of research goal: what the goal is not)

If the sentence describes a general goal in the field, e.g., *"machine translation"*, it should not be marked as AIM. AIM sentences describe *particular* goals of the paper. There are different ways of expressing the particular goal of the paper.

A prime location of AIM sentences is around the first 2/3 of the introduction, when the authors are mentioned for the first time.

Direct aim/goal description:

- *Our aim in this paper is to* [...]
- *We, in contrast, aim at defining categories that help us* [...]

Also descriptions of phenomena plus the statement that current work tries to explain them, e.g.:

- *We aim to find a method of inducing grammar rules.*
- *Our goal, however, is to develop a mechanism for* [...]
- *We will introduce PHENOMENON X that we seek to explain*
- *I show how grammar rules can be induced.*

Functionality provided: Another way of expressing the research goal is to say that one has accomplished doing a certain task.

- *This paper gives a syntactic-head-driven generation algorithm which includes a well-defined treatment of moved constituents.*
- *We have presented an analysis of the data sparseness problem*
- *I have presented an analysis of PHENOMENON X*
- *We have presented an analysis of why children cannot* [...] (PHENOMENON)

Hypothesis: In experimental papers the goal might be expressed as a hypothesis:

- *The hypothesis investigated in this paper is that children can acquire* [...]

Goal as focus: The declaration of a research interest can count as an Aim:

- *This paper focuses on inducing grammar rules.*
- *This paper concerns the formal definitions underlying synchronous tree-adjoining grammars.*
- *In this paper, we focus on the application of the developed techniques in the context of the comparatively neglected area of HPSG generation.*
- *This paper will focus on* [...] *our analysis of narrative progression, rhetorical structure, perfects and temporal expressions.*

Solutionhood: Sometimes a sentence states that the own solution works, i.e. solves a particular research task. Such sentences can under certain circumstances be Aims, but they are Aims of a lower quality. You must be sure that the announcement of the successful problem-solving process is indeed important enough to cover the goal of the whole paper, and you must be sure that the sentence refers to the *highest* level of problem solving. If it talks about a *sub*problem, don't consider the sentence an Aim. Often such statements are dressed as a claim.

Examples:

- *[we present an analysis] which automatically gives the right results for quantifier scope ambiguities and interactions with bound anaphora.*
- *In this paper we presented a new model that implements the similarity-based approach to provide estimates for the conditional probabilities of unseen word cooccurrences*
- *Our technique segments continuous speech into words using only distributional and phonotactic information*
- *The Spoken Language Translator (SLT) is a prototype system that translates air travel (ATIS) queries from spoken English to spoken Swedish and to French.*

Definition of a desired property or as necessity: The goal can be given by describing a hypothetical, desired mechanism or a desired outcome. This is not a typical way to describe the paper's Aim, but the context can still make this the "best Aim around".

Examples:

- *A robust Natural Language Processing (NLP) system must be able to process sentences that contain words unknown to its lexicon.*
- *The importance of a method for SPECIFIC-TASK grows as the coverage of* [...] *improves.*

- *and I demonstrate the importance of having a Y tool which allows for X.*

Advantage of a solution: Sometimes the description of an advantage of a solution can provide an acceptable AIM:

- *Our method yields polynomial complexity in an elegant way.*
- *Our method avoids problems of non-determinacy.*
- *First, it is in certain respects simpler, in that it requires no postulation of otherwise unmotivated ambiguities in the source clause.*
- *The traditional problems of training times do not arise.*

Scope statement: These sentences define the goal as *part* of previous goal, e.g., *"here we will look only at relative pronouns"*, excluding some other, similar goals.

Indirect aim/goal description: In some cases, if you find nothing better, you can also look for more indirect ways of expressing what the goal might have been.

- *In this paper we address two issues relating to the application of preference functions.*
- [...] *and make a specific proposal concerning the interface between these and the syntactic and semantic representations they utilize.*
- *In addition, we have taken a few steps towards determining the relative importance of different factors to the successful operation of discourse modules.*

Question 3: Does this sentence contain a textual overview?

All statements whose primary function it is to give us an overview of the section structure (*"in the next section we will* [...]"). Several such sentences often occur at the end of the introduction.

Mark also backward looking pointers at the beginning of a section (first sentence) (*"In the previous section we have implemented a model"*) or before the end of the section (*"in the next section, we will turn our attention to* [...] ". Some authors give an overview of the section at the beginning of the section (*"in this section I will [dots]"*), or summarize after each section (*"in this section I have [dots]"* or *"this concludes my discussion of X"*.

Caveat: Sentences referring to figures or tables are not meant here (*"figure 3 shows* [...]")!

Sentences summing up main conclusions from *previous* sections are also not meant here:

- *"In chapter 3, we have seen that children cannot reliably form generalizations about* [...]".

Question 4: Does this sentence describe background?

Background marks sentences which are presented as uncontroversial in the field. In such sentences, the research context is established. This includes statements of general capacity of the field, general problems, research goals, methodologies and general solutions ("*In recent years, there has been a growing interest in the field of X in the subject of Y*"). The most prototypical use of Background is in the beginning of the paper.

Examples for general problems:

- *One of the difficult problems in machine translation from Japanese to English or other European languages is the treatment of articles and numbers.*
- *Complications arise in spelling rule application from the fact that, at compile time, neither the lexical nor the surface form of the root, nor even its length, is known.*
- *Collocations present specific problems in translation, both in human and automatic contexts.*

Examples for generally accepted/old solutions or claims:

- *Tagging by means of a Hidden Markov Model (HMM) is widely recognised as an effective technique for assigning parts of speech to a corpus in a robust and efficient manner.*
- *Current research in lexical aquisition is eminently knowledge-based.*
- *Literature in psychology has amply demonstrated that children do not acquire* [...]

In linguistics papers, mark the description of the linguistic phenomena being covered as Background.ps. This includes example sentences. In contrast, the *analysis* of the phenomena are typically either own or other work.

It may be that there is a Background segment somewhere in the middle of the paper. It may then not be easy to decide if it is Background or Own. Use the following test: if you think that this segment could have been used as an introductory text at the beginning of the paper, and if it does not contain material that is individualized to the authors themselves, then it should be marked as Background.

References to "pioneers" in the field are also Background material—sentences which describe other work in an introductory way without any criticism. These are usually older references.

Sometimes there is no Background segment, namely if the authors start directly by describing one specific individualized approach.

The difference between BACKGROUND and OTHER is only in degree of *specificity*.

OTHER are descriptions of other work which is described *specifically* enough to contrast the own work to it, to criticize it or to mention that it provides support for own idea. For some work to be considered specific other work, it must be clearly attributable to some other researchers, otherwise it might be too general to count as specific other work. Often such segments are started by markers of specific work, citations:

- *<REF> argues that children don't acquire grammar frames until they have a lexicon* [...]
- *<REF> 's solution solves the problem of data-sparseness.*
- *<REF> 's formalism allows the treatment of coordinated structures.*
- *The bilingual dual-coding theory <REF> partially answers the above questions.*
- *<REF> introduced the notion of temporal anaphora, to account for ways in which temporal expressions depend on surrounding elements in the discourse for their semantic contribution to the discourse.*

Named solutions can also count as specificity markers for other work:

- *Similarity-based models suggest an appealing approach for dealing with data sparseness.*

The distinction between BACKGROUND and OTHER might be difficult to make. Stop marking as BACKGROUND at the point where ideas, solutions, or tasks are clearly being individualized, i.e., attributed to researchers in such a way that they can get criticized, and required for the paper's own argumentation. At this point, mark existing approaches as OTHER. Often the breaking point looks like this: "*<General problem description> Recently, some researchers have tried to tackle this by doing <More specific description with references>*" In that case, the border is before *"Recently"*.

When authors give specific information about research, but express no stance towards that work, particularly if it happens in the beginning, they seem to imply the statements are generally accepted in the field. You might in this case decide to mark it as BACKGROUND.

Question 5: Is the other work described in a contrastive way?

These sentences make one type of connection between specific other work and own work. Comparative sentences might occur within segments describing other work or own work (e.g. in conclusions).

Mark sentences which contain mentions of:

- Weaknesses of other people's solutions
- The absence of a solution for a given problem
- Difference in approach/solution
- Superiority of own solution
- Statements of direct comparisons with other work or between several other approaches (these appear mostly in evaluation papers)
- Incompatibility between own and other claims or results

Weaknesses of other solutions:

- *<REF>'s solution is problematic for several reasons.*
- *The results suggest that a completely unconstrained initial model does not produce good quality results.*
- *Here, we will produce experimental evidence suggesting that this simple model leads to serious overestimates of system error rates.*
- *The analysis of sentences such as <CREF> in <REF>, within the framework of Discourse Representation Theory (DRT) <REF> gives the wrong truth-conditions, when the temporal connective in the sentence is "before" or "after".*
- *A limiting factor of this method is the potentially large number of distinct parse trees.*

Absence of a solution:

- *While we know of previous work which associates scores with feature structures <REF> we are not aware of any previous treatment which makes explicit the link to classical probability theory.*
- *First, although much work has been done on how agents request clarifications, or respond to such requests, little attention has been paid to the collaborative aspects of clarification discourse.*

Difference in approach/solution:

- *In contrast to standard approaches, we use a statistical model.*
- *In this paper, we propose an alternative approach in which a performance-oriented (behaviour-based) perspective is taken instead of a competence-oriented (knowledge-based) one.*
- *Namely, since we use semantic/pragmatic roles instead of grammatical roles in constraints* [...]

Superiority of own solution:

- *Our model outperforms simple pattern-matching models by 25%.*
- *Our results indicate that our full integrated heuristic scheme for selecting the best parse out-performs the simple heuristic* [...]

- *We have also argued that an architecture that uses obligations provides a much simpler implementation than the strong plan-based approaches.*

Direct comparisons with other work:

- *In this paper, we will compare two tagging algorithms, one based on classifying word types, and one based on classifying words-plus-context.*
- *[...] and a comparison with manual scaling in section <CREF>.*
- *The performance of both implementations is evaluated and compared on a range of artificial and real data.*

Incompatibility between own and other claims or results:

- *This result challenges the claims of recent discourse theories (<REF>, <REF>) which argue for a the close relation between cue words and discourse structure.*
- *It is implausible that children learn grammar on the fly.*

There can be a conflict between AIM and CONTRAST when goals are introduced contrastively in a single sentence, as in the following examples. These sentences would normally be tagged AIM (because AIM is more important than CONTRAST, unless there are many (better) AIM sentences around.

- *Until now, research has focused on demonstrations of infants' sensitivity to various sources; we have begun to provide quantitative measures of the usefulness of those sources.*
- *However our objective is not to propose a faster algorithm, but is to show the possibility of distributed processing of natural languages.*
- *This article proposes a method for automatically finding the appropriate tree-cutting criteria in the EBG scheme, rather than having to hand-code them.*

If the sentence expresses no sentential content other than the fact that there is a contrast ("*however, our approach is quite different*") mark this sentence only as CONTRAST if you cannot find a better one.

If authors compare their own work contrastively to somebody else's (e.g. a linguistic analysis) to explain in which aspects their own work is superior, you might be undecided as to whether to mark it as CONTRAST or OWN (or even AIM, in some cases!). Assign AIM only if the authors specifically say that they did something differently in order to achieve a (different?) goal. Assign CONTRAST if you believe that the main function of the sentence is to mention a negative aspect of the other work. Assign OWN if the focus is on their own work rather than on the other work.

Question 6: Is the own work based on other work?

There are 5 different classes of how work could be based or positively related:

- Direct Based
- Adaptation
- Consistency
- Similarity
- Quality

Consistency, Similarity and Quality cases should be marked only if the approaches are important to the paper, i.e. if some more discussion about that work is given in the paper.

Direct Based: It is explicitly stated that the own solution builds on another solution (intellectual ancestry).

- *We base our model on <REF>'s backup model.*
- *Our approach is in the spirit of <REF> 's approach*
- *We choose to use Link Grammar <REF>*

The last example describes a BASIS describing intellectual ancestry with more than one other approach.

Adaptation: The authors have adapted a solution, contributed by somebody else. As the solution was not initially invented for the current research task, and needs to be adapted.

- *The main aim is to show how existing text planning techniques can be adapted for this particular application.*
- *We extend the model for doing X by allowing it to do Y, too.*
- *We have suggested some ways in which LFs can be enriched with lexical semantic information to improve translation quality.*
- *This model draws upon <REF>, but adapts it to the collaborative situation.*
- *In our work, we have taken <REF>'s descriptive model and recast it into a computational one* [...]

Consistency: Statements about consistency with another theoretical framework or other people's results can be BASIS, even if the own solution is not directly based on it:

- *Our account* [...] *fits within a general framework for* [...]

Similarity: Statements about similarities between the own and other approaches can be a BASIS, if these similarities are not "cancelled" later by mentioning a contrasting property.

- *The analysis presented here has strong similarities to analyses of the same phenomena discussed by <REF> and <REF>.*
- *The method, which is related to that of <REF>,*
- *In this section we define a grammar similar to <REF>'s first grammar.*

Quality of other approach: If you think that an approach provides a basis, and is important enough to be marked up as a BASIS, but you can find no explicit sentence expressing it, you can mark up statements about the quality of the approach.

- *We discuss the advantages of <REF>'s model.*
- [...] *the success of an abstract model such as <REF>'s* [...]
- [...] *thus demonstrating the computational feasibility of their work and its compatibility with current practices in artificial intelligence.*
- *Earley deduction is a very attractive framework for natural language processing because it has the following properties and applications.*

(The original guidelines showed here the first pages of 9502024 and 9502023 with sample AZ annotation, which are not reproduced here.)

When it gets difficult

There are several reasons why the annotation scheme might not work well for a given paper. The writing style in some papers might make it difficult to see the trisection according to intellectual ownership. In some papers however, the scheme's assumptions that research with different ownership (own/other/background) is indeed presented in separate segments in the paper are violated:

- Our model assumes that the author perceives a clear separation between own work and work outside the scope of the paper, and presents work according to that separation. However, if the paper describes some minute detail of a previous, larger work of the author, then this separation might not be given.
- A specialized case of this, and another example of a potential breakdown of the simple model is for evaluation papers, especially where the authors compare several of their own solutions with each other, or if they compare their solution to somebody else's.
- The scheme is only created for research papers; there must be some new, practical contribution described in the paper. If you are given

a paper to annotate which looks like a position or review articles, do not annotate it.

Please keep a note of all difficulties that you encounter with determining individualized segments, and write down your reasons for finding it difficult (i.e. in which way the given paper made it hard for our model to describe what was going on).

C.3 CFC Guidelines; Excerpt (2005)

The following shows a section of the CFC guidelines, namely rules 22–60, which are concerned with contrasts and comparisons, i.e., categories CoCoXY, CoCoGM, CoCo- and CoCoR0.

Contrast and Comparisons:CoCoXY, CoCoGM, CoCoR-, CoCoR0

You have detected a contrast or comparison between the current paper and the cited work (CoCoG/M/R) or between two cited works (CoCoXY). You now have to take up to three decisions:

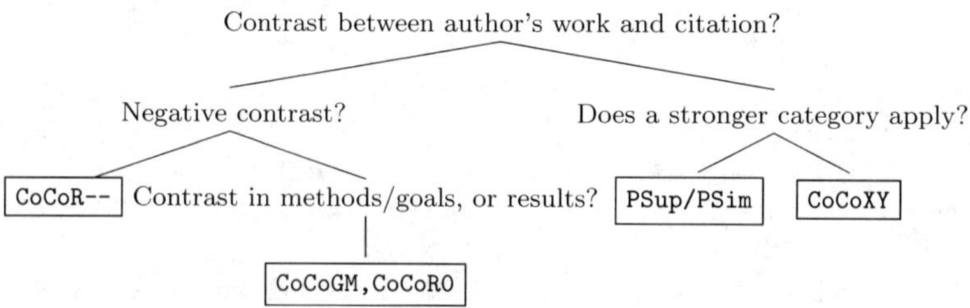

General rules for Contrast/Comparisons

General Rule 22 (CoCo): What counts as "contrast"? The contrast must be expressed explicitly. By this we mean that a phrase such as "in contrast", or "however, their method works differently" must be present. "Alternative" counts, "other" not. "Range" implies large differences between approaches and counts. Simple lists of methods (which you may know are different) are not enough, the difference must be pointed out. The general rule is that the contrast must be clear to somebody who has no world knowledge. "X does something, while Y does something else", where you need to understand what the "somethings" are, is not enough (too much inference required). Contrasts in results between two other approaches are obvious and need less explicit signalling.

General Rule 23 (CoCo): Parallel structures. If you detect a parallel structure, such as "we do xxx, while CitX does XXX", and you perceive 'xxx' and 'XXX' to be parallel (e.g., large parts of the string/arguments copied, but a contrast in one part of the sentence, or a negation in one part), then that is superficially marked enough to count as a contrast ("general principles", cf. Page 1).

General Rule 24 (CoCo): Span of contrast/cue phrases.

The contrast can span sentence boundaries. You should be more inclined towards marking a contrast if there additionally is a contrast marker, such as "whereas", "however", "in contrast", "while", "alternative/different".

General Rule 25 (CoCo): Aspect of contrast. The contrast can be in results, general methods or large parts of methods, and goals, but should be substantial enough to count as a "real" difference.

- *Unlike previous approaches [Ellison 1994] (CoCoXY), [Walther 1996] (CoCoXY), [Karttunen] (CoCoXY) ' s approach is encoded entirely in the finite state calculus, with no extra-logical procedures for counting constraint violations.*

General Rule 26 (CoCo): Non-applicability. The impossibility to apply a method to the paper's goal or exclusion of a cited method from experimentation in the paper is not enough to qualify for a contrast between the cited method and the paper.

General Rule 27 (CoCo): Meta-statements and context. If within the paragraph there is a meta-statement that a comparison to other work is being made, then all cited works, even if they are by themselves expressed neutrally (ie., without signalling of direct contrast) can by virtue of this statement be considered `CoCo` (unless overruled). This *can* be enough, even in cases where it is unclear to you what exactly the comprison exists in, because it is still in the scope of the meta-statement.

- *We will outline here the main parallels and differences between our method and previous work. In cooccurrence smoothing [Brown et al. 1993] (CoCoGM), as in our method, a baseline model is combined with a similarity-based model that refines some of its probability estimates. In Brown et al's work, given a baseline probability model P, which is taken to be the MLE, the confusion probability EQN between conditioning words EQN and EQN is defined as EQN and the probability that EQN is followed by the same context words as EQN. S-121 Then the bigram estimate derived by cooccurrence smoothing is given by EQN. S-123 In addition, the cooccurrence smoothing method sums over all words in the lexicon. [Miller et al] (CoCoGM) suggest a similar method... They do...*

Brown et al do *something*. We don't need to understand in which way their method differs from the authors (there may even have been a statement that "X use method Y", and you think that Method Y is different from the author's approach). Because of the meta-statement ("we will outline..."), Brown and Miller are tagged as `CoCoGM` (even though, on its own without the meta-statement, Brown would probably have been tagged as `PSim`, and Miller as `Neut`.

General Rule 28 (CoCo): Sequences Sim–Contrast or Contrast–Sim. If in a sequence of sentences, the first sentence states similarities with a cited approach, and the next a contrast, or the other way round, there is a possible conflict with `PSim`. Always tag the citation with the *second* type (stronger in rhetorical context) – even if the formal citation is in the first sentence. Sim-Contrast is the more typical pattern.

- *There are similarities between our approach and with estimation using MDL R-14 [Rissanen 1989] (CoCoGM). S-108 However, our implementation does not explicitly attempt to minimise code lengths.*
- *Our notation is somewhat different, but equivalent to Cit1 (PSim).*

General Rule 29 (CoCo-, CoCoGM, CoCoR0): Specificity to current paper. You should be able to identify a phrase that demonstrates that specific work from the current paper is being compared. This could include first person pronouns; demonstrative pronouns ("this work"); deictic expressions ("work presented here") or named system or theory names which clearly refer to the author's specific contribution (including names explicitly given in the paper). Contrasts with families of approaches presented in the paper with a citation does not qualify (apart from one rare subcase of CoCoGM, contrast in goals). By "families of approaches" we mean general methods, such as "maximum entropy", which are too general to be associated with just one citation.

General Rule 30: Hypothetical/negated contrast. The contrast or comparison must really take place. Statements like "we do not attempt a comparison with X (Neut) because..." is not enough.

CoCoXY

Rule 31: Two other works. Contrast must be between two cited works (or aspects thereof), neither of which is the current paper. The reference to this work or approach does not have to be a formal citation but can be a string identifying the approach as long as the citation is associated with that approach somewhere in the paper. Previous work by the same authors is considered different from the current paper.

Rule 32: What counts as "other work"? Normally, both works are cited. But sometimes, only one of the methods is cited, and the other is mentioned by name (e.g., "whereas the boosting framework"). The name mentions can count as other work, if they are specific enough to be associated with a citation somewhere in the paper.

Rule 33: What counts as Contrast/Comparison? You have found two citations that the author relates to each other. Mark `CoCoXY` only if you would have marked a `CoCoR/GM` category had one of the objects of comparison been the current work. So exclude `PModi/PBas` etc relationships between two citations.

Rule 34: Who gets annotated? Both X and Y can receive the `CoCoXY` tag, but more likely, only one will. Having identified the cue phrase for CoCoXY, mark up the closer of X and Y to the identified cue phrase (distance is measure in sentences). Thus, in the following example (1), the identified cue is "slightly better than"; [Ramshaw and Marcus] get tagged as they are the closer citation (same sentence as cue), and [Tjong et al. 1999] is not marked `CoCoXY`. If X and Y are in the same sentence, mark both (2). If the contrast is equidistant from both citatations (eg. in example (3), the rule is to tag the second citation with `CoCoXY`.

- (1) *[Tjong et al. 1999] (Neut) compare different data representations for this task. S-135 Their baseNP results are slightly better than those of [Ramshaw and Marcus] (CoCoXY) (F EQN =92.37).*
- (2) *Unlike previous approaches [Ellison 1994] (CoCoXY) [Walther 1996] (CoCoXY), [Karttunen] (CoCoXY) ' s approach is encoded entirely in the finite state calculus, with no extra-logical procedures for counting constraint violations.*
- (3) *[Ellison 1994] (Neut) proposes a method for phonological segmentation based on morphological cues. This is in sharp contrast to approaches based on prosody. The best-known of these approaches is [Hirschberg and Passonneau 1991] (CoCoXY).*

Rule 35: Comparative evaluation (amongst cited work, no own work). Some papers/sections evaluate other approaches against each other. The citations associated with the evaluated approaches should be marked `CoCoXY`, if you are sure that the author's own work does not participate in the evaluation.

- *We evaluate Cit1 (CoCoXY) and Cit2 (CoCoXY) against each other.*

Rule 36: Statement of method competing. `CoCoXY` is also assigned if there is a statement that the cited method is one of the competing methods in an evaluation performed by the authors – if you are sure that the author's own method does not participate in the evaluation.

- *We perform an evaluation of parsers. ... Cit1 (CoCoXY) is tested by running it against...*

Rule 37: Comparison to own work overrules. If X and Y are compared to the author's work (and thus indirectly to each other), you should mark the direct comparison with own work, using one of the other CoCo categories, and *not* consider CoCoXY. In other words, CoCoXY-comparisons must be direct comparisons of the two othe approaches to each other.

Rule 38: Object of comparison. Citations must be the *object* of comparison to qualify as CoCoXY. In a context like:

- *We compared Cit1 (CoCoXY) and Cit2 (CoCoXY)*
- *Cit0 (Neut) evaluates Cit1 (CoCoXY) and Citation2 (CoCoXY).*

Cit1 and Cit2 are directly compared so they are marked as CoCoXY, but Cit0 is not CoCoXY because it is not the object of a comparison (but the agent of it).

Rule 39: X and Y in one citation. X and Y can be associated with the same single citation, if that citation covers more than one approach or if the approaches are different versions of an algorithm discussed there:

- *For this purpose we have evaluated different voting mechanisms, effectively the voting methods as described in R-17 [van Halteren et al. 1998] (CoCoXY)*

Rule 40: Lists of approaches. Do not infer differences between cited work just from the different names of methods mentioned in an enumeration/list (even though those differences undoubtedly exist) – only differences explicitly stated count. In other words, if you *judge* that there is a difference between two approaches (particularly in methods and goals, as results are more obvious), this in itself is not enough if not lexically signalled.

Three illustrations of this case (counterexamples):

- (1) *Two state-of-the-art technologies are R-2 Katz 1987 (Neut) 's backoff method and R-3 Jelinek and Mercer (Neut)' s interpolation method.*
- (2) *The line data was revisited by Cit1 (Neut) Cit2 (Neut). The former do (MethodX), ... the latter do (MethodY).*
- (3) MethodX (Cit1)... and MethodY (Cit2) ... are introduced. *S-102 The former take an ensemble approach where the output from two neural networks is combined; one network is based on a representation of local context while the other represents topical context. S-103 The latter utilize a Naive Bayesian classifier.*

(1) is not a contrast because it is not explicit enough; just listing of approaches. In (2), no difference was stated, even if MethodX and

MethodY are different to your knowledge. In (3), you might judge a contrast between "neural networks" and "Bayesian classifiers" or between "local" and "topical context" but the formulation (former/latter) is not explicit enough a difference to warrant a `CoCoXY` label.

CoCoGM

Rule 41: Own work and cited work. There must be a contrast in methods or goals between cited and current work. In the case of contrast in goals (Rules 42-43), an approach differs in application area or goal, but uses the same approach or same class of approaches as the current work. In the case of contrast in methods (Rules 36-), a different method from the authors is described or named (and cited), and a contrast between these methods is explicitly stated.

- *Our algorithms solve the lexical choice problem by learning the words (via features in the maximum entropy probability model) that correlate with a given attribute and local context, whereas [Elhadad et al. 1997] (CoCoGM) uses a rule-based a pproach to decide the word choice.* (contrast in methods)
- *The goals of the two papers are slightly different : [Moore] (CoCoGM) 's approach is designed to reduce the total grammar size (i.e., the sum of the lengths of the productions), while our appro ach minimizes the number of productions.* (contrast in goals)

Rule 42: What counts as "own work"? Reminder: **This is an addendum to the General Rule 29**: For contrast in goals, the requirement on specific reference to the author's current work is relaxed, as contrasts in goals are normally expressed in a more general way, e.g., as reference to names of techniques used (even if the authors don't claim originality of that technique).

- (1) *X has been done in IR, but Cit1 (CoCoGM) does it in NLP*
- (2) *This approach was used by [Palmer 1997] (CoCoGM) for word segmentation, whereas we use it for syllabification here.*

where X is the author's goal. The connection between the authors and X need not be stated as explicitly as it would need to be stated for a contrast in methods; it can be inferred by the annotator (e.g., from reading the abstract), but must be marked (cf. section 4).

Rule 43: What counts as "goal"? The following, non-exhaustive, list contains potential goals: to provide an explanation for a linguistic phenomenon, to give a theory, to provide a practical application that does a certain task. Notice that a contrast in goals can also be a contrast in the use of a method by different fields of study (cf. example sentence (1) above).

Rule 44: Contrast between own work and other method. The most common case of contrast in methods is where a different method from the authors is described or named (and cited), and a contrast between these methods is explicitly stated.

- *Our approach contrasts with the merely heuristic and empirical justification of similarity-based approaches to clustering [Dagan et al. 1998] (CoCoGM) for which so far no clear probabilistic interpretation has been given.*
- *The probability model we use can be found earlier in R-5 [Pereira et al. 1993] (CoCoGM). S-19 However, in contrast to this approach, our statistical inference method for clustering is formalized clearly as an EM - algorithm.*

Rule 45: Non-identical but similar methods. When the contrast is in goals, the method which is jointly used (for different goals) does not need to be exactly the same (it can be stated as being similar):

- *Watson (CoCoGM) does something similar, but applies it to WSD.*
- *S-41 Boosting has been used in a few NLP systems. S-42 R-21 [Haruno et al. 1998] (CoCoGM) used boosting to produce more accurate classifiers which were embedded as control mechanisms of a parser for Japanese. In contrast, we...*

where "boosting" can be associated with the author's goals. "Something similar" is in context something similar to the author's goals or methods. Note that there is a theoretical conflict with `PSim`, but `CoCoGM` is to be annotated as it is more informative.

Rule 46: Neutrality. `CoCoGM` is a neutral description of methods. If you detect descriptions of advantages or other positive bias towards the curent method, choose `CoCoR-`.

Rule 47: Statement of other method competing (against authors). `CoCoGM` gets assigned if there is a statement that the cited method is one of the competing methods in an evaluation performed by the authors, where the authors' own method *must* be one of the other competing methods compared. The only difference between Rule 31 and Rule 43 is in whether or not the author's own method participates in the evaluation.

- *S-98 We compare our approach to three versions of the TextTiling algorithm R-64 [Hearst 1994] (CoCoGM).*

Rule 48: Method competing overruled by results. Rule 43 only holds if that citation does nothing but state the fact that the method is a participant. If there are explicit results in that sentence/context associated with the citation, then you should use `CoCoR`.

(Rule 31, the parallel to Rule 43 for CoCoXY is not overruled by this rule as CoCoXY already includes results.)

Rule 49: Baselines. If the paper's approach is directly compared to a baseline established by somebody else's system, this counts as a CoCoGM. However, baselines not associated with particular approaches (such as random) do not qualify as a contrast.[136]

- *As a baseline, we use [Raynar 1998] (CoCoGM).*

Rule 50: Nonaddressing of a problem. This can be a CoCoGM, if there is an explicit statement that the authors do address this problem.

- (1) *R-16 [Moore 2000] (CoCoGM) does not address left-corner tree-transforms, or questions of sparse data and parsing accuracy that are covered in section CREF.*
- (2) *[Tesar and Smolensky] (Neut) proposed an algorithm for this problem, RIP/CD, but left its efficiency and correctness for future research.* (no explicit statement that authors address it)
- (3) *R-6 [Nakatani and Hirschberg 1993] (Neut) suggest a acoustic/prosodic detector to identify IPs but don't discuss the problem of finding the correct segmentation in depth.* (authors don't address it either)

Rule 51: Fallback for all contrasts. If you are unsure whether something is a contrast in results or in methods, use CoCoGM; CoCoGM is the most neutral way of annotating a clearly stated contrast (in something).

- *They show how large models (two orders of magnitude larger than those reported by R-12 [Johnson et al] (CoCoGM)) can be estimated using the parsed Wall Street Journal corpus.*

Here, we don't know whether "larger models" are good or bad (an advantage or not), so we choose the (neutral) CoCoGM tag.

CoCoR-

Reminder: **General Rule 29** concerns what counts as "own work".

Rule 52: negativeness/value. CoCoR- is assigned to situations where the other approach (its results or its properties/advantages) are presented as different, and of a lower value. If you cannot decide something is clearly negative, mark it as CoCoRO.

Rule 53: Numerical results or result statements. You should mark numerical results where the authors work is better as CoCoR-.

- *Cit1 (CoCoR-) achieves 78%, we achieve 54%.*

[136] This may be irrelevant, as they are mostly not associated with a citation.

- *However, the gain achieved by [Beil et al. 1999] (CoCoR-), due to grammar lexicalizaton is only 2%, compared to about 10% in our case.*

Rule 54: Go by raw numbers. You should go by the raw numbers if the unit and metric of comparison is well-known and clear. You are not expected to make significance judgements; unless the authors say that differences are not significant, you should assume significance, ie. directly compare numbers (ie, 86.9% is worse than 87.1%).

Rule 55: Polarity/meaning of metrics. You need to understand the metric when making the comparison (error rate or accuracy, recall, precision, f-measure etc). If the metric is described in terms of a ratio or formula, and you cannot understand its polarity, do not force the comparison either way; instead back off to `CoCoR0`. But you are allowed to use a bit of knowledge to try and understand the metric reported.

Rule 56: Statements of superiority in worth/results. Linguistic expressions of superiority count as well as numerical results.

- *Compared to the F-score with using [Carroll et al. 1999] (CoCoR-) (IaC), the IaU F-score is " borderline " statistically significantly better (11% significance level).* (with IaU being the authors' method).
- *According to a comparsion of the results presented here with those in R-24 [Ratnaparkhi 1996] (CoCoR0), the Maximum Entropy framework seems to be the only other approach yielding comparable results to the one presented here.*

Rule 57: Advantages/improvements Advantages of one method against another are marked as `CoCoR-`. This is because `CoCoGM` is by definition neutral. Advantages can be in terms of efficiency, elegance,...

- *At the same time, we believe our method has advantages over the approach developed initially at IBM R-21 [Brown 1990] (CoCoR-) R-22 [Brown 1993] (CoCoR-) for training translation systems automatically. S-187 One advantage is...*
- *Our experiments on a frequency-controlled pseudoword disambiguation task showed that using any of the three in a distance-weighted averaging scheme yielded large improvements over R-8 [Katz] (CoCoR-)' s backoff smoothing method in predicting unseen coocurrences.*
- *A new finite-state treatment of gradient constraints is presented which improves upon the approximation of R-2 [Karttunen 1998] (CoCoR-).*

Careful: it is sometimes difficult to distinguish "improvements" from `PUse` cases:

- *We use this related system/small training set combination to improve the performance of the transformation-based error-driven learner described in [Ferro et al. 1999] (PUse).*

This is a `PUse`, because they do not "improve upon" (i.e., take their own and make it better than somebody elses), but "improve" something made by somebody else, which they take and use.

Rule 58: Existence vs. nonexistence of a problem. Direct comparisons where the other piece of work has a problem which the current paper does not have also counts as `CoCoR-`.

- *Intuitively, such usage is infelicitous because of a dependency on a contextually salient time which has not been previously introduced. S-70 This is not captured by the R-27 [Lascarides and Asher] (Weak) account because sentences containing the past perfect are treated as sententially equivalent to those containing the simple past ... S-72 All of these facts are explained by the account given here.*

This is different from the case covered under Rule 13 (if a cited approach does not solve a problem when the authors do, then it is a weakness of that approach).

- *Finally, it happens that our proposal solves a problem encountered by R-42 [Johnson] (Weak).*

Rule 59: Author's work object of comparison. There must be a comparison of the author's work with some other work. In the following example, this is not the case:

- *S-175 According to current tagger comparisons R-22 [Halteren et al. 1998] (PSup), R-23 [Zavrel and Daelemans 1999] (PSup), the Maximum Entropy framework seems to be the only other approach yielding comparable results to the one presented here.*

Even though R-22 and R-23 describe a comparison/evaluation experiment, this experiment does not concern a comparison of the author's work with some other work. It is left unspecified which work is compared in those citations, thus it cannot be `CoCoR`. (In this case, it turns out that the experiments are used to support the author's own claim, namely that ME and the own results are comparable, and thus this context should be tagged `PSup`).

CoCoR0

Reminder: **General Rule 28** concerns what counts as "own work".

Rule 60: neutrality, both+-, or better. `CoCoR0` is assigned if the value/result of the compared approaches is seen as different but no explicit value statement is made. Alternatively, there could be comparisons along several axes, some of which are positive and some of which are negative, such that the overall comparison direction is ambiguous. If the other approach is actually *better* than the own one this also counts as `CoCoR0`.

- *According to a comparison of the results presented here with those in [Ratnaparkhi 1996] (CoCoR0), the Maxiumum Entropy framework seems to be the only other approach yielding comparable results to the one presented here.*
- *Being 10 - 12% better than SCFGs, comparable with the Minimal model and [Magerman 1995] (CoCoR-) and about 7.0% worse than the best system, it is fair to say that (depth 5) T-grams perform more like bilexicalized dependency systems than bare SCFGs.* (with T-grams being the authors' approach)
- *Our system is better than Cit1 if measured in accuracy, but in recall it's worse.*
- *Our approach is more elegant than Cit2, but slower.*

D

Lexical Resources

D.1 Concept Lexicon

NEGATION:

no, not, nor, non, neither, none, never, aren't, can't, cannot, hadn't, hasn't, haven't, isn't, didn't, don't, doesn't, n't, wasn't, weren't, nothing, nobody, less, least, little, scant, scarcely, rarely, hardly, few, rare, unlikely

3RD PERSON PRONOUN (NOM): *they, he, she, theirs, hers, his*
3RD PERSON PRONOUN (ACC): *her, him, them*
3RD POSS PRONOUN: *their, his, her*
3RD PERSON REFLEXIVE: *themselves, himself, herself*
1ST PERSON PRONOUN (NOM): *we, i, ours, mine*
1ST PERSON PRONOUN (ACC): *us, me*
1ST POSS PRONOUN:*my, our*
1ST PERSON REFLEXIVE: *ourselves, myself*
REFERENTIAL: *this, that, those, these*
REFLEXIVE: *itself, ourselves, myself, themselves, himself, herself*
QUESTION: *?, how, why, whether, wonder*
GIVEN:

noted, mentioned, addressed, illustrated, described, discussed, given, outlined, presented, proposed, reported, shown, taken

PROFESSIONALS:

collegues, community, computer scientists, computational linguists, discourse analysts, expert, investigators, linguists, logicians, philosophers, psycholinguists, psychologists, researchers, scholars, semanticists, scientists

DISCIPLINE:

computer science, computer linguistics, computational linguistics, discourse analysis, logics, linguistics, psychology, psycholinguistics, philosophy, semantics, several disciplines, various disciplines

TEXT_NOUN: *paragraph, section, subsection, chapter*
SIMILAR_NOUN: *analogy, similarity*
COMPARISON_NOUN:

accuracy, baseline, comparison, competition, evaluation, inferiority, measure, measurement, performance, precision, optimum, recall, superiority

CONTRAST_NOUN: *contrast, conflict, clash, clashes, difference, point of departure*
AIM_NOUN: *aim, goal, intention, objective, purpose, task, theme, topic*
ARGU_NOUN:

assumption, belief, hypothesis, hypotheses, claim, conclusion, confirmation, opinion, recommendation, stipulation, view

PROBLEM_NOUN:

Achilles heel, caveat, challenge, complication, contradiction, damage, danger, deadlock, defect, detriment, difficulty, dilemma, disadvantage, disregard, doubt, downside, drawback, error, failure, fault, foil, flaw, handicap, hindrance, hurdle, ill, inflexibility, impediment, imperfection, intractability, inefficiency, inadequacy, inability, lapse, limitation, malheur, mishap, mischance, mistake, obstacle, oversight, pitfall, problem, shortcoming, threat, trouble, vulnerability, absence, dearth, deprivation, lack, loss, fraught, proliferation, spate

QUESTION_NOUN:
question, conundrum, enigma, paradox, phenomena, phenomenon, puzzle, riddle

SOLUTION_NOUN:
answer, accomplishment, achievement, advantage, benefit, breakthrough, contribution, explanation, idea, improvement, innovation, insight, justification, proposal, proof, remedy, solution, success, triumph, verification, victory

INTEREST_NOUN: *attention, quest*

RESULT_NOUN: *evidence, experiment, finding, progress, observation, outcome, result*

CHANGE_NOUN:
alternative, adaptation, extension, development, modification, refinement, version, variant, variation

PRES_NOUN: *article, draft, paper, project, report, study*

NEED_NOUN: *necessity, motivation*

WORK_NOUN:
account, algorithm, analysis, analyses, approach, approaches, application, architecture, characterization, characterisation, component, design, extension, formalism, formalization, formalisation, framework, implementation, investigation, machinery, method, methodology, model, module, moduls, process, procedure, program, prototype, research, researches, strategy, system, technique, theory, tool, treatment, work

TRAD_NOUN:
acceptance, community, convention, disciples, disciplines, folklore, literature, mainstream, school, tradition, textbook

CHANGE_ADJ: *alternate, alternative*

GOOD_ADJ:
adequate, advantageous, appealing, appropriate, attractive, automatic, beneficial, capable, cheerful, clean, clear, compact, compelling, competitive, comprehensive, consistent, convenient, convincing, constructive, correct, desirable, distinctive, efficient, elegant, encouraging, exact, faultless, favourable, feasible, flawless, good, helpful, impeccable, innovative, insightful, intensive, meaningful, neat, perfect, plausible, positive, polynomial, powerful, practical, preferable, precise, principled, promising, pure, realistic, reasonable, reliable, right, robust, satisfactory, simple, sound, successful, sufficient, systematic, tractable, usable, useful, valid, unlimited, well worked out, well, enough

BAD_ADJ:
absent, ad-hoc, adhoc, ad hoc, annoying, ambiguous, arbitrary, awkward, bad, brittle, brute-force, brute force, careless, confounding, contradictory, defect, defunct, disturbing, elusive, erraneous, expensive, exponential, false, fallacious, frustrating, haphazard, ill-defined, imperfect, impossible, impractical, imprecise, inaccurate, inadequate, inappropriate, incomplete, incomprehensible, inconclusive, incorrect, inelegant, inefficient, inexact, infeasible, infelicitous, inflexible, implausible, inpracticable, improper, insufficient, intractable, invalid, irrelevant, labour-intensive, labor-intensive, labour intensive, labor intensive, limited-coverage, limited coverage, limited, limiting, meaningless, modest, misguided, misleading, non-existent, NP-hard, NP-complete, NP hard, NP complete, questionable, pathological, poor, prone, protracted, restricted, scarce, simplistic, suspect, time-consuming, time consuming, toy, unacceptable, unaccounted for, unaccounted-for, unaccounted, unattractive, unavailable, unavoidable, unclear, uncomfortable, unexplained, undecidable, undesirable, unfortunate, uninnovative, uninterpretable, unjustified, unmotivated, unnatural, unnecessary, unorthodox, unpleasant, unpractical, unprincipled, unreliable, unsatisfactory, unsound, unsuccessful, unsuited, unsystematic, untractable, unwanted, unwelcome, useless, vulnerable, weak, wrong, too, overly, only

BEFORE_ADJ: *earlier, past, previous, prior*

CONTRAST_ADJ: *different, distinguishing, contrary, competing, rival*

TRAD_ADJ:
better known, better-known, cited, classic, common, conventional, current, customary, established, existing, extant, available, favourite, fashionable, general, obvious, long-standing, mainstream, modern, naive, orthodox, popular, prevailing, prevalent, published, quoted, seminal, standard, textbook, traditional, trivial, typical, well-established, well-known, widely-assumed, unanimous, usual

MANY:
a number of, a body of, a substantial number of, a substantial body of, most, many, several, various

COMPARISON_ADJ:
evaluative, superior, inferior, optimal, better, best, worse, worst, greater, larger, faster, weaker, stronger

PROBLEM_ADJ:
demanding, difficult, hard, non-trivial, nontrivial

RESEARCH_ADJ:
empirical, experimental, exploratory, ongoing, quantitative, qualitative, preliminary, statistical, underway

AWARE_ADJ: *unnoticed, understood, unexplored*

NEW_ADJ:
new, novel,state-of-the-art, state of the art, leading-edge, leading edge, enhanced

FUTURE_ADJ: *further, future*

MAIN_ADJ:
main, key, basic, central, crucial, essential, eventual, fundamental, great, important, key, largest, main, major, overall, primary, principle, serious, substantial, ultimate

D.2 Formulaic Patterns

GENERAL_FORMULAIC
in @TRAD_ADJ JJ ↑@WORK_NOUN
in @TRAD_ADJ used ↑@WORK_NOUN
in @TRAD_ADJ ↑@WORK_NOUN
in @MANY JJ ↑@WORK_NOUN
in @MANY ↑@WORK_NOUN
in @BEFORE_ADJ JJ ↑@WORK_NOUN
in @BEFORE_ADJ ↑@WORK_NOUN
in other JJ ↑@WORK_NOUN
in other ↑@WORK_NOUN
in such ↑@WORK_NOUN

THEM_FORMULAIC
↑according to CITE
along the ↑lines of CITE
↑like CITE
CITE ↑style
a la ↑CITE
CITE - ↑style

US_PREVIOUS_FORMULAIC
@SELF_NOM have ↑previously
@SELF_NOM have ↑earlier
@SELF_NOM have ↑elsewhere
@SELF_NOM ↑elsewhere
@SELF_NOM ↑previously
@SELF_NOM ↑earlier
↑elsewhere @SELF_NOM
↑elswhere @SELF_NOM
↑elsewhere , @SELF_NOM
↑elswhere , @SELF_NOM
presented ↑elswhere
presented ↑elsewhere
@SELF_NOM have shown ↑elsewhere
@SELF_NOM have argued ↑elsewhere
@SELF_NOM have shown ↑elswhere
@SELF_NOM have argued ↑elswhere
@SELF_NOM will show ↑elsewhere
@SELF_NOM will show ↑elswhere
@SELF_NOM will argue ↑elsewhere
@SELF_NOM will argue ↑elswhere
↑elsewhere SELFCITE
↑elswhere SELFCITE
in a @BEFORE_ADJ ↑@PRES_NOUN
in an earlier ↑@PRES_NOUN
another ↑@PRES_NOUN

TEXTSTRUCTURE_FORMULAIC
↑then @SELF_NOM describe
↑then , @SELF_NOM describe
↑next @SELF_NOM describe
↑next , @SELF_NOM describe
↑finally @SELF_NOM describe
↑finally , @SELF_NOM describe
↑then @SELF_NOM present
↑then , @SELF_NOM present
↑next @SELF_NOM present
↑next , @SELF_NOM present
↑finally @SELF_NOM present
↑finally , @SELF_NOM present
↑briefly describe
↑briefly introduce
↑briefly present
↑briefly discuss

METHOD_FORMULAIC
a new ↑@WORK_NOUN
a novel ↑@WORK_NOUN
a ↑@WORK_NOUN of
an ↑@WORK_NOUN of
a JJ ↑@WORK_NOUN of
an JJ ↑@WORK_NOUN of
a NN ↑@WORK_NOUN of
an NN ↑@WORK_NOUN of
a JJ NN ↑@WORK_NOUN of
an JJ NN ↑@WORK_NOUN of
a ↑@WORK_NOUN for
an ↑@WORK_NOUN for
a JJ ↑@WORK_NOUN for
an JJ ↑@WORK_NOUN for
a NN ↑@WORK_NOUN for
an NN ↑@WORK_NOUN for
a JJ NN ↑@WORK_NOUN for
an JJ NN ↑@WORK_NOUN for
↑@WORK_NOUN designed to VV
↑@WORK_NOUN intended for
↑@WORK_NOUN for VV_ING
↑@WORK_NOUN for the NN
↑@WORK_NOUN designed to VV
↑@WORK_NOUN to the NN
↑@WORK_NOUN to NN
↑@WORK_NOUN to VV_ING
↑@WORK_NOUN for JJ VV_ING
↑@WORK_NOUN for the JJ NN
↑@WORK_NOUN to the JJ NN
↑@WORK_NOUN to JJ VV_ING
the ↑problem of RB VV_ING
the ↑problem of VV_ING
the ↑problem of how to

CONTINUE_FORMULAIC
↑following CITE
↑following the @WORK_NOUN of CITE
↑following the @WORK_NOUN given in CITE
↑following the @WORK_NOUN presented in CITE
↑following the @WORK_NOUN proposed in CITE
↑following the @WORK_NOUN discussed in CITE
↑adopt CITE 's
↑starting point for @REFERENTIAL @WORK_NOUN
↑starting point for @SELF_POSS @WORK_NOUN
as a ↑starting point
as ↑starting point
↑use CITE 's
↑base @SELF_POSS

↑supports @SELF_POSS
↑supports @OTHERS_POSS
↑support @OTHERS_POSS
↑support @SELF_POSS
lends ↑support to @SELF_POSS
lends ↑support to @OTHERS_POSS

CONTRAST_FORMULAIC
however, nevertheless, nonetheless, unfortunately, yet, although

GAP_FORMULAIC
as far as @SELF_NOM ↑know
to @SELF_POSS ↑knowledge
to the best of @SELF_POSS ↑knowledge

COMPARISON_FORMULAIC
↑against CITE
↑against @SELF_ACC
↑against @SELF_POSS
↑against @OTHERS_ACC
↑against @OTHERS_POSS
↑against @BEFORE_ADJ @WORK_NOUN
↑against @MANY @WORK_NOUN
↑against @TRAD_ADJ @WORK_NOUN
↑than CITE
↑than @SELF_ACC
↑than @SELF_POSS
↑than @OTHERS_ACC
↑than @OTHERS_POSS
↑than @TRAD_ADJ @WORK_NOUN
↑than @BEFORE_ADJ @WORK_NOUN
↑than @MANY @WORK_NOUN
point of ↑departure from @SELF_POSS
points of ↑departure from @OTHERS_POSS
↑advantage over @OTHERS_ACC
↑advantage over @TRAD_ADJ
↑advantage over @MANY @WORK_NOUN
↑advantage over @BEFORE_ADJ @WORK_NOUN
↑advantage over @OTHERS_POSS
↑advantage over CITE
↑advantage to @OTHERS_ACC
↑advantage to @OTHERS_POSS
↑advantage to CITE
↑advantage to @TRAD_ADJ
↑advantage to @MANY @WORK_NOUN
↑advantage to @BEFORE_ADJ @WORK_NOUN
↑advantages over @OTHERS_ACC
↑advantages over @TRAD_ADJ
↑advantages over @MANY @WORK_NOUN
↑advantages over @BEFORE_ADJ @WORK_NOUN
↑advantages over @OTHERS_POSS
↑advantages over CITE
↑advantages to @OTHERS_ACC
↑advantages to @OTHERS_POSS
↑advantages to CITE
↑advantages to @TRAD_ADJ
↑advantages to @MANY @WORK_NOUN
↑advantages to @BEFORE_ADJ @WORK_NOUN
↑benefit over @OTHERS_ACC
↑benefit over @OTHERS_POSS
↑benefit over CITE
↑benefit over @TRAD_ADJ
↑benefit over @MANY @WORK_NOUN
↑benefit over @BEFORE_ADJ @WORK_NOUN
↑difference to CITE
↑difference to @TRAD_ADJ
↑difference to CITE
↑difference to @TRAD_ADJ
↑difference to @MANY @WORK_NOUN
↑difference to @BEFORE_ADJ @WORK_NOUN
↑difference to @OTHERS_ACC
↑difference to @OTHERS_POSS
↑difference to @SELF_ACC
↑difference to @SELF_POSS
↑differences to CITE
↑differences to @TRAD_ADJ
↑differences to @MANY @WORK_NOUN
↑differences to @BEFORE_ADJ @WORK_NOUN
↑differences to @OTHERS_ACC
↑differences to @OTHERS_POSS
↑differences to @SELF_ACC
↑differences to @SELF_POSS
↑difference between CITE
↑difference between @TRAD_ADJ
↑difference between @MANY @WORK_NOUN
↑difference between @BEFORE_ADJ @WORK_NOUN
↑difference between @OTHERS_ACC
↑difference between @OTHERS_POSS
↑difference between @SELF_ACC
↑difference between @SELF_POSS
↑differences between CITE
↑differences between @TRAD_ADJ
↑differences between @MANY @WORK_NOUN
↑differences between @BEFORE_ADJ @WORK_NOUN
↑differences between @OTHERS_ACC
↑differences between @OTHERS_POSS
↑differences between @SELF_ACC
↑differences between @SELF_POSS
↑contrast with CITE
↑contrast with @TRAD_ADJ
↑contrast with @MANY @WORK_NOUN

↑contrast with @BEFORE_ADJ
@WORK_NOUN
↑contrast with @OTHERS_ACC
↑contrast with @OTHERS_POSS
↑contrast with @SELF_ACC
↑contrast with @SELF_POSS
↑unlike @SELF_ACC
↑unlike @SELF_POSS
↑unlike CITE
↑unlike @TRAD_ADJ
↑unlike @BEFORE_ADJ
@WORK_NOUN
↑unlike @MANY @WORK_NOUN
↑unlike @OTHERS_ACC
↑unlike @OTHERS_POSS
in ↑contrast to @SELF_ACC
in ↑contrast to @SELF_POSS
in ↑contrast to CITE
in ↑contrast to @TRAD_ADJ
in ↑contrast to @MANY
@WORK_NOUN
in ↑contrast to @BEFORE_ADJ
@WORK_NOUN
in ↑contrast to @OTHERS_ACC
in ↑contrast to @OTHERS_POSS
as ↑opposed to @SELF_ACC
as ↑opposed to @SELF_POSS
as ↑opposed to CITE
as ↑opposed to @TRAD_ADJ
as ↑opposed to @MANY
@WORK_NOUN
as ↑opposed to @BEFORE_ADJ
@WORK_NOUN
as ↑opposed to @OTHERS_ACC
as ↑opposed to @OTHERS_POSS
↑contrary to @SELF_ACC
↑contrary to @SELF_POSS
↑contrary to CITE
↑contrary to @TRAD_ADJ
↑contrary to @MANY
@WORK_NOUN
↑contrary to @BEFORE_ADJ
@WORK_NOUN
↑contrary to @OTHERS_ACC
↑contrary to @OTHERS_POSS
↑whereas @SELF_ACC
↑whereas @SELF_POSS
↑whereas CITE
↑whereas @TRAD_ADJ
↑whereas @BEFORE_ADJ
@WORK_NOUN
↑whereas @MANY @WORK_NOUN
↑whereas @OTHERS_ACC
↑whereas @OTHERS_POSS
↑compared to @SELF_ACC
↑compared to @SELF_POSS
↑compared to CITE
↑compared to @TRAD_ADJ
↑compared to @BEFORE_ADJ
@WORK_NOUN
↑compared to @MANY
@WORK_NOUN
↑compared to @OTHERS_ACC
↑compared to @OTHERS_POSS
in ↑comparison to @SELF_ACC
in ↑comparison to @SELF_POSS
in ↑comparison to CITE
in ↑comparison to @TRAD_ADJ
in ↑comparison to @MANY
@WORK_NOUN
in ↑comparison to @BEFORE_ADJ
@WORK_NOUN
in ↑comparison to @OTHERS_ACC
in ↑comparison to @OTHERS_POSS
↑while @SELF_NOM
↑while @SELF_POSS
↑while CITE
↑while @TRAD_ADJ
↑while @BEFORE_ADJ
@WORK_NOUN
↑while @MANY @WORK_NOUN
↑while @OTHERS_NOM
↑while @OTHERS_POSS

NO_TEXTSTRUCTURE_FORMULAIC

(↑TXT_NOUN CREF)
as explained in ↑@TXT_NOUN CREF
as explained in the @BEFORE_ADJ
↑@TXT_NOUN
as ↑@GIVEN earlier in this
@TXT_NOUN
as ↑@GIVEN below
as @GIVEN in ↑@TXT_NOUN CREF
as @GIVEN in the @BEFORE_ADJ
↑@TXT_NOUN
as @GIVEN in the next
↑@TXT_NOUN
NN @GIVEN in ↑@TXT_NOUN
CREF
NN @GIVEN in the @BEFORE_ADJ
↑@TXT_NOUN
NN @GIVEN in the next
↑@TXT_NOUN
NN @GIVEN ↑below
cf. ↑@TXT_NOUN CREF
cf. ↑@TXT_NOUN below
cf. the ↑@TXT_NOUN below
cf. the @BEFORE_ADJ
↑@TXT_NOUN
cf. ↑@TXT_NOUN above
cf. the ↑@TXT_NOUN above
e. g. , ↑@TXT_NOUN CREF
e. g , ↑@TXT_NOUN CREF
e. g. ↑@TXT_NOUN CREF
e. g ↑@TXT_NOUN CREF
compare ↑@TXT_NOUN CREF
compare ↑@TXT_NOUN below
compare the ↑@TXT_NOUN below
compare the @BEFORE_ADJ
↑@TXT_NOUN
compare ↑@TXT_NOUN above
compare the ↑@TXT_NOUN above
see ↑@TXT_NOUN CREF
see the @BEFORE_ADJ
↑@TXT_NOUN

recall from the @BEFORE_ADJ ↑@TXT_NOUN
recall from the ↑@TXT_NOUN above
recall from ↑@TXT_NOUN CREF
@SELF_NOM shall see ↑below
@SELF_NOM will see ↑below
@SELF_NOM shall see in the ↑next @TXT_NOUN
@SELF_NOM will see in the ↑next @TXT_NOUN
@SELF_NOM shall see in ↑@TXT_NOUN CREF
@SELF_NOM will see in ↑@TXT_NOUN CREF
example in ↑@TXT_NOUN CREF
example CREF in ↑@TXT_NOUN CREF
examples CREF and CREF in ↑@TXT_NOUN CREF
examples in ↑@TXT_NOUN CREF

SIMILARITY_FORMULAIC
along the same ↑lines
in a ↑similar vein
as in ↑@SELF_POSS
as in ↑CITE
as ↑did CITE
like in ↑CITE
↑like CITE 's
similarity with ↑CITE
similarity with ↑@SELF_POSS
similarity with ↑@OTHERS_POSS
↑similarity with @TRAD_ADJ
↑similarity with @MANY
↑similarity with @BEFORE_ADJ
in analogy to ↑CITE
in analogy to ↑@SELF_POSS
in analogy to ↑@OTHERS_POSS
in ↑analogy to @TRAD_ADJ
in ↑analogy to @MANY
in ↑analogy to @BEFORE_ADJ
↑similar to that described here
↑similar to that of
↑similar to those of
↑similar to CITE
↑similar to @SELF_ACC
↑similar to @SELF_POSS
↑similar to @OTHERS_ACC
↑similar to @TRAD_ADJ
↑similar to @MANY
↑similar to @BEFORE_ADJ
↑similar to @OTHERS_POSS
↑similar to CITE
a ↑similar NN to @SELF_POSS
a ↑similar NN to @OTHERS_POSS
a ↑similar NN to CITE
↑analogous to that described here
↑analogous to CITE
↑analogous to @SELF_ACC
↑analogous to @SELF_POSS
↑analogous to @OTHERS_ACC
↑analogous to @TRAD_ADJ
↑analogous to @MANY
↑analogous to @BEFORE_ADJ
↑analogous to @OTHERS_POSS
↑analogous to CITE
the ↑same NN as @SELF_POSS
the ↑same NN as @OTHERS_POSS
the ↑same NN as CITE
the ↑same as @SELF_POSS
the ↑same as @OTHERS_POSS
the ↑same as CITE
in ↑common with @OTHERS_POSS
in ↑common with @SELF_POSS
in ↑common with @TRAD_ADJ
in ↑common with @MANY
in ↑common with @BEFORE_ADJ
most ↑relevant to @SELF_POSS

HERE_FORMULAIC
in this ↑@PRES_NOUN
the present ↑@PRES_NOUN
@SELF_NOM ↑here
↑here @SELF_NOM
↑here , @SELF_NOM
@GIVEN ↑here
@SELF_NOM ↑now
↑now @SELF_NOM
↑now , @SELF_NOM
@GIVEN ↑now
herein

FUTURE_FORMULAIC
in the ↑future
in the near ↑future
promising ↑avenues
↑@FUTURE_ADJ @WORK_NOUN
↑@FUTURE_ADJ @AIM_NOUN
↑@FUTURE_ADJ development
needs ↑further
requires ↑further
beyond the ↑scope
↑avenue for improvement
↑avenues for improvement
↑avenues for @FUTURE_ADJ improvement
↑areas for @FUTURE_ADJ improvement
↑areas for improvement
↑avenues of @FUTURE_ADJ research
promising ↑avenue

AFFECT_FORMULAIC
hopefully
thankfully
fortunately
unfortunately

GOOD_FORMULAIC
@POS_ADJ

BAD_FORMULAIC
@NEG_ADJ

TRADITION_FORMULAIC
@TRAD_ADJ

IN_ORDER_TO_FORMULAIC
in ↑order to

DETAIL_FORMULAIC
@SELF_NOM have ↑also
@SELF_NOM ↑also
this @PRES_NOUN ↑also
this @PRES_NOUN has ↑also

D.3 Entity Patterns

US_ENTITY
@SELF_NOM
@SELF_POSS JJ ↑@WORK_NOUN
@SELF_POSS JJ ↑@PRES_NOUN
@SELF_POSS JJ ↑@ARGU_NOUN
@SELF_POSS JJ ↑@SOLUTION_NOUN
@SELF_POSS JJ ↑@RESULT_NOUN
@SELF_POSS ↑@WORK_NOUN
@SELF_POSS ↑@PRES_NOUN
@SELF_POSS ↑@ARGU_NOUN
@SELF_POSS ↑@SOLUTION_NOUN
@SELF_POSS ↑@RESULT_NOUN
↑@WORK_NOUN @GIVEN here
↑@WORK_NOUN @GIVEN below
↑@WORK_NOUN @GIVEN in this @PRES_NOUN
↑@WORK_NOUN @GIVEN in @SELF_POSS @PRES_NOUN
the ↑@SOLUTION_NOUN @GIVEN here
the ↑@SOLUTION_NOUN @GIVEN in this @PRES_NOUN
the first ↑author
the second ↑author
the third ↑author
one of the ↑authors
one of ↑us

REF_US_ENTITY
this ↑@PRES_NOUN
the present ↑@PRES_NOUN
the current ↑@PRES_NOUN
the present JJ ↑@PRES_NOUN
the current JJ ↑@PRES_NOUN
the ↑@WORK_NOUN @GIVEN

OUR_AIM_ENTITY
@SELF_POSS ↑@AIM_NOUN
the point of this ↑@PRES_NOUN
the ↑@AIM_NOUN of this @PRES_NOUN
the ↑@AIM_NOUN of the @GIVEN @WORK_NOUN
the ↑@AIM_NOUN of @SELF_POSS @WORK_NOUN
the ↑@AIM_NOUN of @SELF_POSS @PRES_NOUN
the most important feature of ↑@SELF_POSS @WORK_NOUN
contribution of this ↑@PRES_NOUN
contribution of the @GIVEN ↑@WORK_NOUN
contribution of ↑@SELF_POSS @WORK_NOUN
the question @GIVEN in this ↑PRES_NOUN
the question @GIVEN ↑here
@SELF_POSS @MAIN ↑@AIM_NOUN
@SELF_POSS ↑@AIM_NOUN in this @PRES_NOUN
@SELF_POSS ↑@AIM_NOUN here
the JJ point of this ↑@PRES_NOUN
the JJ purpose of this ↑@PRES_NOUN
the JJ ↑@AIM_NOUN of this @PRES_NOUN
the JJ ↑@AIM_NOUN of the @GIVEN @WORK_NOUN
the JJ ↑@AIM_NOUN of @SELF_POSS @WORK_NOUN
the JJ ↑@AIM_NOUN of @SELF_POSS @PRES_NOUN
the JJ question @GIVEN in this ↑PRES_NOUN
the JJ question @GIVEN ↑here

AIM_REF_ENTITY
its ↑@AIM_NOUN
its JJ ↑@AIM_NOUN
@REFERENTIAL JJ ↑@AIM_NOUN
contribution of this ↑@WORK_NOUN
the most important feature of this ↑@WORK_NOUN
feature of this ↑@WORK_NOUN
the ↑@AIM_NOUN
the JJ ↑@AIM_NOUN

US_PREVIOUS_ENTITY
SELFCITE
this @BEFORE_ADJ ↑@PRES_NOUN
@SELF_POSS @BEFORE_ADJ ↑@PRES_NOUN
@SELF_POSS @BEFORE_ADJ ↑@WORK_NOUN
in ↑SELFCITE , @SELF_NOM
in ↑SELFCITE @SELF_NOM
the ↑@WORK_NOUN @GIVEN in SELFCITE

REF_ENTITY
@REFERENTIAL JJ ↑@WORK_NOUN
@REFERENTIAL ↑@WORK_NOUN
this sort of ↑@WORK_NOUN
this kind of ↑@WORK_NOUN
this type of ↑@WORK_NOUN
the current JJ ↑@WORK_NOUN
the current ↑@WORK_NOUN
the ↑@WORK_NOUN
the ↑@PRES_NOUN
the ↑author
the ↑authors

THEM_PRONOUN_ENTITY
@OTHERS_NOM

THEM_ENTITY
CITE
CITE 's NN
CITE 's ↑@PRES_NOUN
CITE 's ↑@WORK_NOUN
CITE 's ↑@ARGU_NOUN
CITE 's JJ ↑@PRES_NOUN
CITE 's JJ ↑@WORK_NOUN
CITE 's JJ ↑@ARGU_NOUN

the CITE ↑@WORK_NOUN
the ↑@WORK_NOUN @GIVEN in CITE
the ↑@WORK_NOUN of CITE
@OTHERS_POSS ↑@PRES_NOUN
@OTHERS_POSS ↑@WORK_NOUN
@OTHERS_POSS ↑@RESULT_NOUN
@OTHERS_POSS ↑@ARGU_NOUN
@OTHERS_POSS ↑@SOLUTION_NOUN
@OTHERS_POSS JJ ↑@PRES_NOUN
@OTHERS_POSS JJ ↑@WORK_NOUN
@OTHERS_POSS JJ ↑@RESULT_NOUN
@OTHERS_POSS JJ ↑@ARGU_NOUN
@OTHERS_POSS JJ ↑@SOLUTION_NOUN

GAP_ENTITY
none of these ↑@WORK_NOUN
none of those ↑@WORK_NOUN
no ↑@WORK_NOUN
no JJ ↑@WORK_NOUN
none of these ↑@PRES_NOUN
none of those ↑@PRES_NOUN
no ↑@PRES_NOUN
no JJ ↑@PRES_NOUN

GENERAL_ENTITY
@TRAD_ADJ JJ ↑@WORK_NOUN
@TRAD_ADJ used ↑@WORK_NOUN
@TRAD_ADJ ↑@WORK_NOUN
@MANY JJ ↑@WORK_NOUN
@MANY ↑@WORK_NOUN
@BEFORE_ADJ JJ ↑@WORK_NOUN
@BEFORE_ADJ ↑@WORK_NOUN
@BEFORE_ADJ JJ ↑@PRES_NOUN
@BEFORE_ADJ ↑@PRES_NOUN
other JJ ↑@WORK_NOUN
other ↑@WORK_NOUN
such ↑@WORK_NOUN
these JJ ↑@PRES_NOUN
these ↑@PRES_NOUN
those JJ ↑@PRES_NOUN
those ↑@PRES_NOUN
@REFERENTIAL ↑authors
@MANY ↑authors
↑researchers in @DISCIPLINE
@PROFESSIONAL_NOUN

PROBLEM_ENTITY
@REFERENTIAL JJ ↑@PROBLEM_NOUN
@REFERENTIAL ↑@PROBLEM_NOUN
the ↑@PROBLEM_NOUN

SOLUTION_ENTITY
@REFERENTIAL JJ ↑@SOLUTION_NOUN
@REFERENTIAL ↑@SOLUTION_NOUN
the ↑@SOLUTION_NOUN
the JJ ↑@SOLUTION_NOUN

TEXTSTRUCTURE_ENTITY
↑@TXT_NOUN CREF
↑@TXT_NOUN CREF and CREF
this ↑@TXT_NOUN
next ↑@TXT_NOUN
next CD ↑@TXT_NOUN
concluding ↑@TXT_NOUN
@BEFORE_ADJ ↑@TXT_NOUN
↑@TXT_NOUN above
following ↑@TXT_NOUN
remaining ↑@TXT_NOUN
subsequent ↑@TXT_NOUN
following CD ↑@TXT_NOUN
remaining CD ↑@TXT_NOUN
subsequent CD ↑@TXT_NOUN
↑@TXT_NOUN that follow
rest of this ↑@PRES_NOUN
remainder of this ↑@PRES_NOUN
in ↑@TXT_NOUN CREF , @SELF_NOM
in this ↑@TXT_NOUN , @SELF_NOM
in the next ↑@TXT_NOUN , @SELF_NOM
in @BEFORE_ADJ ↑@TXT_NOUN , @SELF_NOM
in the @BEFORE_ADJ ↑@TXT_NOUN , @SELF_NOM
in the ↑@TXT_NOUN above , @SELF_NOM
in the ↑@TXT_NOUN below , @SELF_NOM
in the following ↑@TXT_NOUN , @SELF_NOM
in the remaining ↑@TXT_NOUN , @SELF_NOM
in the subsequent ↑@TXT_NOUN , @SELF_NOM
in the ↑@TXT_NOUN that follow , @SELF_NOM
in the rest of this ↑@PRES_NOUN , @SELF_NOM
in the remainder of this ↑@PRES_NOUN , @SELF_NOM
↑below , @SELF_NOM
the ↑@AIM_NOUN of this @TXT_NOUN
↑@TXT_NOUN below

D.4 Action Lexicon

AFFECT_ACTION
afford, believe, decide, feel, hope, imagine, regard, trust, think

ARGUMENTATION_ACTION
agree, accept, advocate, argue, claim, conclude, comment, defend, embrace, hypothesize, imply, insist, posit, postulate, reason, recommend, speculate, stipulate, suspect

AWARE_ACTION
be unaware, be familiar with, be aware, be not aware, know of

BETTER_SOLUTION_ACTION
boost, enhance, defeat, improve, go beyond, perform better, outperform, outweigh, surpass

CHANGE_ACTION
adapt, adjust, augment, combine, change, decrease, elaborate, expand, extend, derive, incorporate, increase, manipulate, modify, optimize, optimise, refine, render, replace, revise, substitute, tailor, upgrade

COMPARISON_ACTION
compare, compete, evaluate, test

CONTINUE_ACTION
adopt, agree with CITE, base, be based on, be derived from, be originated in, be inspired by, borrow, build on, follow CITE, originate from, originate in, side with

CONTRAST_ACTION
be different from, be distinct from, conflict, contrast, clash, differ from, distinguish @RFX, differentiate, disagree, disagreeing, dissent, oppose

FUTURE_INTEREST_ACTION
plan on, plan to, expect to, intend to

INTEREST_ACTION
aim, ask @SELF_RFX, ask @OTHERS_RFX, address, attempt, be concerned, be interested, be motivated, concern, concern @SELF_ACC, concern @OTHERS_ACC, consider, concentrate on, explore, focus, intend to, like to, look at how, motivate @SELF_ACC, motivate @OTHERS_ACC, pursue, seek, study, try, target, want, wish, wonder

NEED_ACTION
be dependent on, be reliant on, depend on, lack, need, necessitate, require, rely on

PRESENTATION_ACTION
describe, discuss, give, introduce, note, notice, point out, present, propose, put forward, recapitulate, remark, report, say, show, sketch, state, suggest, talk about

PROBLEM_ACTION
abound, aggravate, arise, be cursed, be incapable of, be forced to, be limited to, be problematic, be restricted to, be troubled, be unable to, contradict, damage, degrade, degenerate, fail, fall prey, fall short, force @SELF_ACC, force @OTHERS_ACC, hinder, impair, impede, inhibit, misclassify, misjudge, mistake, misuse, neglect, obscure, overestimate, over-estimate, overfit, over-fit, overgeneralize, over-generalize, overgeneralise, over-generalise, overgenerate, over-generate, overlook, pose, plague, preclude, prevent, remain, resort to, restrain, run into, settle for, spoil, suffer from, threaten, thwart, underestimate, under-estimate, undergenerate, under-generate, violate, waste, worsen

RESEARCH_ACTION
apply, analyze, analyse, build, calculate, categorize, categorise, characterize, characterise, choose, check, classify, collect, compose, compute, conduct, confirm, construct, count, define, delineate, detect, determine, equate, estimate, examine, expect, formalize, formalise, formulate, gather, identify, implement, indicate, inspect, integrate, interpret, investigate, isolate, maximize, maximise, measure, minimize, minimise, observe, predict, realize, realise, reconfirm, simulate, select, specify, test, verify

SIMILAR_ACTION
bear comparison, be analogous to, be alike, be related to, be closely related to, be reminiscent of, be the same as, be similar to, be in a similar vein to, have much in common with, have a lot in common with, pattern with, resemble

SOLUTION_ACTION
accomplish, account for, achieve, apply to, answer, alleviate, allow for, allow @SELF_ACC, allow @OTHERS_ACC, avoid, benefit, capture, clarify, circumvent, contribute, cope with, cover, cure, deal with, demonstrate, develop, devise, discover, elucidate, escape, explain, fix, gain, go a long way, guarantee, handle, help, implement, justify, lend itself, make progress, manage, mend, mitigate, model, obtain, offer, overcome, perform, preserve, prove, provide, realize, realise, rectify, refrain from, remedy, resolve, reveal, scale up, sidestep, solve, succeed, tackle, take care of, take into account, treat, warrant, work well, yield

TEXTSTRUCTURE_ACTION
begin by, illustrate, conclude by, organize, organise, outline, return to, review, start by, structure, summarize, summarise, turn to

USE_ACTION
apply, employ, use, make use, utilize

References

Abdalla, Rashid M. and Simone Teufel. 2006. A bootstrapping approach to unsupervised detection of cue phrase variants. In *Proceedings of 44th Annual Meeting of the Association for Computational Linguistics and the 21st International Conference on Computational Linguistics (ACL/COLING-06)*. Sydney, Australia.

Abracos, Jose and Gabriel Pereira Lopes. 1997. Statistical methods for retrieving most significant paragraphs in newspaper articles. In I. Mani and M. T. Maybury, eds., *Proceedings of the ACL/EACL-97 Workshop on Intelligent Scalable Text Summarization*, pages 51–57.

ACL Anthology Project. 2002. `http://acl.ldc.upenn.edu/`.

Adhoc. 1987. Ad hoc working group for critical appraisal of the medical literature. A proposal for more informative abstracts of clinical articles. *Annals of Internal Medicine* 106:508–604.

Adler, Annette, Anuj Gujar, Beverly L. Harrison, Kenton O'Hara, and Abigail Sellen. 1998. A diary study of work-related reading: Design implications for digital reading devices. In *Proceedings of CHI-98, ACM*, pages 241–248.

Adler, Robert, John Ewing, and Peter Taylor. 2008. Joint committee on quantitative assessment of research citation statistics. `http://www.mathunion.org/fileadmin/IMU/Report/CitationStatistics.pdf`.

Agichtein, Eugene and Luis Gravano. 2000. Snowball: Extracting relations from large plain-text collections. In *Proceedings of the 5th ACM International Conference on Digital Libraries*.

Alexandersson, Jan, Elisabeth Maier, and Norbert Reithinger. 1995. A robust and efficient three-layered dialogue component for a speech-to-speech translation system. In *Proceedings of the Seventh Meeting of the European Chapter of the Association for Computational Linguistics*, pages 188–193.

Alley, Michael. 1996. *The Craft of Scientific Writing*. Springer.

Alterman, Richard. 1985. A dictionary based on concept coherence. *Artificial Intelligence* 25(2):153–186.

Aluisio, Sanda M., Iris Barcelos, Jander Sampaio, and Osvaldo Oliveira Jr. 2001. How to learn the many unwritten "rules of the game" of the academic discourse: A hybrid approach based on critiques and cases. In *In Proceedings of the IEEE International Conference on Advanced Learning Technologies*, pages 257–260. Madison, WI.

Aluisio, Sandra M. and Osvaldo N. Oliveira Jr. 1996. A detailed schematic structure of research papers introductions: An application in support-writing tools. *Revista de la Sociedad Espanyola para el Procesamiento del Lenguaje Natural* 19:141–147.

Andreevskaia, Alina and Sabine Bergler. 2006. Semantic tagging at the sense level. In *Proceedings of the Twenty-first National Conference on Artificial Intelligence (AAAI-06)*. Boston, MA.

ANSI. 1979. American National Standard for Writing Abstracts. Tech. rep., American National Standards Institute, Inc., New York, NY. ANSI Z39.14.1979.

Anthony, Laurence and George Lashkia. 2003. Mover: A machine learning tool to assist in the reading and writing of technical papers. *IEEE Transactions on Professional Communication* 46(3):185–193.

Aone, Chinatsu, Mary Ellen Okurowski, James Gorlinsky, and Bjornar Larsen. 1999. A trainable summarizer with knowledge acquired from robust nlp techniques. In I. Mani and M. T. Maybury, eds., *Advances in Automatic Text Summarization*, pages 71–80. Cambridge, MA: MIT Press.

Arndt, Kenneth A. 1992. The informative abstract. *Archives of Dermatology* 128(1):101.

Artstein, Ron and Massimo Poesio. 2005. Kappa^3 = alpha (or beta). Tech. Rep. CSM-437, University of Essex.

Artstein, Ron and Massimo Poesio. 2008. Inter-coder agreement for computational linguistics. *Computational Linguistics* 34(4):555–596.

Babaian, Tamara, Barbara J. Grosz, and Stuart M. Shieber. 2002. A writer's collaborative assistant. In *Proceedings of the 7th International Conference on Intelligent User Interfaces*.

Baldi, Susan. 1998. Normative versus social constructivist processes in the allocation of citations: A network-analytic model. *American Sociological Review* 63(6):829–846.

Baldwin, Breck and Tom Morton. 1998. Dynamic coreference-based summarization. In *Proceedings of the Third Conference on Empirical Methods in Natural Language Processing (EMNLP-3)*.

Bannard, Colin and Christopher Callison-Burch. 2005. Paraphrasing with bilingual parallel corpora. In *Proceedings of the 43rd Annual Meeting of the Association for Computational Linguistics (ACL-05)*, pages 597–604. Ann Arbor.

Barzilay, Regina and Michael Elhadad. 1997. Using lexical chains for text summarization. In I. Mani and M. T. Maybury, eds., *Proceedings of the ACL/EACL-97 Workshop on Intelligent Scalable Text Summarization*.

Barzilay, Regina and Mirella Lapata. 2004. Modeling local coherence: An entity-based approach. *Computational Linguistics* 34(1):1–34.

Barzilay, Regina and Kathleen R. McKeown. 2001. Extracting paraphrases from a parallel corpus. In *Proceedings of the 39th Annual Meeting of the Association for Computational Linguistics (ACL-01)*, pages 50–57. Toulouse, France.

Barzilay, Regina and Kathleen R. McKeown. 2005. Sentence fusion for multi-document news summarization. *Computational Linguistics* 31(3):297–328.

Barzilay, Regina, Kathleen R. McKeown, and Michael Elhadad. 1999. Information fusion in the context of multi-document summarization. In *Proceedings of the 37th Annual Meeting of the Association for Computational Linguistics (ACL-99)*, pages 550–557. College Park, Maryland.

Bates, Marcia J. 1998. Indexing and access for digital libraries and the internet: Human, database and domain factors. *Journal of the American Society for Information Science* 49:1185–1205.

Baxendale, Phyllis B. 1958. Man-made index for technical literature—an experiment. *IBM Journal of Research and Development* 2(4):354–361.

Bayerl, Petra Saskia and Karsten Ingmar Paul. 2007. Identifying sources of disagreement: Generalizability theory in manual annotation studies. *Computational Linguistics* 33(1):3–8.

Bazerman, Charles. 1985. Physicists reading physics, schema-laden purposes and purpose-laden schema. *Written Communication* 2(1):3–23.

Bazerman, Charles. 1988. *Shaping Written Knowledge: The Genre and Activity of the Experimental Article in Science*. Madison, WI: University of Wisconsin Press.

Beeferman, D., A. Berger, and J. Lafferty. 1999. Statistical models for text segmentation. *Machine Learning* .

Biber, Douglas, S Conrad, and Rippen R. 1998. *Corpus Linguistics: Investigating Language Structure and Use*. Cambridge University Press.

Biber, Douglas and E. Finegan. 1994. Intra-textual variation within medical research articles. In Oostdijk and de Haan, eds., *Corpus-Based Research into Language*, chap. 13, pages 201–221. Amsterdam: Rodoph.

Bird, Steven, Robert Dale, Bonnie Dorr, Bryan Gibson, Mark T. Joseph, Min-Yen Kan, Dongwon Lee, Brett Powley, Dragomir R. Radev, and Yee Fan Tan. 2008. The ACL anthology reference corpus: a reference dataset for bibliographic research. In *Proceedings of LREC*. Marrakesh, Morocco.

Blitzer, John, Mark Dredze, and Fernando Pereira. 2007. Biographies, bollywood, boom-boxes and blenders: Domain adaptation for sentiment classification. In *Proceedings of 45th Annual Meeting of the Association for Computational Linguistics (ACL-07)*, pages 440–447.

Boguraev, Branimir and Christopher Kennedy. 1999. Salience-based content characterization of text documents. In I. Mani and M. T. Maybury, eds., *Advances in Automatic Text Summarization*, pages 99–110. Cambridge, MA: MIT Press.

Boguraev, Branimir, Christopher Kennedy, Rachel Bellamy, Sascha Brawer, Yin Yin Wong, and Jason Swartz. 1998. Dynamic presentation of document content for rapid on-line skimming. In D. R. Radev and E. H. Hovy, eds., *Working Notes of the AAAI Spring Symposium on Intelligent Text Summarization*.

Bonzi, Susan. 1982. Characteristics of a literature as predictors of relatedness between cited and citing works. *Journal of the American Society for Information Science* 33(4):208–216.

Borgman, Christine L. 1996. Why are online catalogs still hard to use? *Journal of the American Society for Information Science* 47:493–503.

Borko, Harold and C. L. Bernier. 1975. *Abstracting Concepts and Methods*. San Diego, CA: Academic Press.

Borko, Harold and Seymour Chatman. 1963. Criteria for acceptable abstracts: A survey of abstractors' instructions. *American Documentation* 14(2):149–160.

Boulton, Christina. 2002. Sexism in publishing: Citation patterns in sex research journals. *?* .

Bradshaw, Shannon. 2003. Reference directed indexing: Redeeming relevance for subject search in citation indexes. In *Proceedings of ECDL*, pages 499–510.

Bradshaw, Shannon and Marc Light. 2007. Annotation consensus: implications for passage recommendation in scientific literature. In *Proceedings of the eighteenth Conference on Hypertext and Hypermedia*. Manchester, UK.

Brandow, Ronald, Karl Mitze, and Lisa F. Rau. 1995. Automatic condensation of electronic publications by sentence selection. *Information Processing and Management* 31(5):675–685.

Brin, Sergey and Lawrence Page. 1998. The anatomy of a large-scale hypertextual web search engine. In *Proceedings of the 7th International World Wide Web Conference*.

Briscoe, Ted and John Carroll. 2002. Robust accurate statistical annotation of general text. In *Proc. of LREC*, pages 1499–1504. Las Palmas, Gran Canaria.

Broady, E. and S. Shurville. 2000. Developing Academic Writer: Designing a writing environment for novice academic writers. In E. Broady, ed., *Second Language Writing in a Computer Environment*, pages 131–151. London: CILT.

Brooks, Terrence A. 1986. Evidence of complex citer motivations. *Journal of the American Society for Information Science* 37:34–36.

Brown, Ann L. and Jeanne D. Day. 1983. Macrorules for summarizing text: The developments of expertise. *Journal of Verbal Learning and Verbal Behaviour* 22:1–14.

Burstein, Jill, Daniel Marcu, and Kevin Knight. 2003. Finding the write stuff: Automatic identification of discourse structure in student essays. *IEEE Intelligent Systems: Special Issue on Natural Language Processing* 18(1):32–39.

Busch-Lauer, Ines A. 1995. Abstracts in German medical journals: A linguistic analysis. *Information Processing and Management* 31(5):769–776.

Buxton, A. B. and A. J. Meadows. 1978. Categorization of the information in experimental papers and their author abstracts. *Journal of Research in Communication Studies* 1:161–182.

Caraballo, Sharon A. and Eugene Charniak. 1999. Determining the specificity of nouns from text. In *Proceedings of SIGDAT-99*.

Carbonell, Jaime and Jade Goldstein. 1998. The use of MMR, diversity-based reranking for reordering documents and producing summaries. In *Proceedings of the 21th Annual International Conference on Research and Development in Information Retrieval (SIGIR-98)*, pages 335–336. Melbourne, Australia.

Carletta, Jean. 1996. Assessing agreement on classification tasks: The kappa statistic. *Computational Linguistics* 22(2):249–254.

Carletta, Jean, Amy Isard, Stephen Isard, Jacqueline C. Kowtko, Gwyneth Doherty-Sneddon, and Anne H. Anderson. 1997. The reliability of a dialogue structure coding scheme. *Computational Linguistics* 23(1):13–31.

Carlson, Lynn, Daniel Marcu, and Mary-Ellen Okurowski. 2003. Building a discourse-tagged corpus in the framework of Rhetorical Structure Theory. In J. C. van Kuppevelt and R. W. Smith, eds., *Current and New Directions in Discourse and Dialogue*, pages 85–112. Dordrecht, The Netherlands: Kluwer.

Charney, Davida. 1993. A study in rhetorical reading—how evolutionists read "The Spandrels of San Marco". In J. Selzer, ed., *Understanding Scientific Prose*. Madison, WI: The University of Wisconsin Press.

Chubin, Daryl E. and S. D. Moitra. 1975. Content analysis of references: Adjunct or alternative to citation counting? *Social Studies of Science* 5(4):423–441.

Church, Kenneth W. and P. Hanks. 1990. Word association norms, mutual information, and lexicography. *Computational Linguistics* 16(1):22–29.

Clarke, James and Mirella Lapata. 2008. Global inference for sentence compression: An integer linear programming approach. *Journal of Artificial Intelligence Research* 31:399–429.

Clove, J. F. and B. C. Walsh. 1988. Online text retrieval via browsing. *Information Processing and Management* 24(1):31–37.

CMP_LG. 1994. The Computation and Language E-Print Archive, `http://xxx.lanl.gov/cmp-lg`.

Cohen, Jacob. 1960. A coefficient of agreement for nominal scales. *Educational and Psychological Measurement* 20:37–46.

Cohen, Jacob. 1968. Weighted kappa: Nominal scale agreement with provision for scaled disagreement or partial credit. *Psychological Bulletin* 70(4):213–220.

Cohen, Robin. 1987. Analyzing the structure of argumentative discourse. *Computational Linguistics* 13:11–24.

Cohen, William W. 1995. Fast effective rule induction. In *Proceedings of the Twelfth International Conference on Machine Learning*, pages 115–123.

Cohen, William W. 1996. Learning trees and rules with set-valued features. In *Proceedings of AAAI-96*.

Colas, Fabrice, Pavel Paclík, Joost N. Kok, and Pavel Brazdil. 2007. Does SVM really scale up to large bag of words feature spaces? In *Proceedings of the International Symposium of Intelligent Data Analysis (IDA) 2007*.

Copestake, Ann. 2003. Report on the design of RMRS. DeepThought project deliverable.

Copestake, Ann. 2009. Slacker Semantics: Why superficiality, dependency and avoidance of commitment can be the right way to go. In *Proceedings of the 12th Meeting of the European Chapter of the Association for Computational Linguistics (EACL 2009)*, pages 1–9. Athens, Greece.

Copestake, Ann, Peter Corbett, Peter Murray-Rust, CJ Rupp, Advaith Siddharthan, Simone Teufel, and Ben Waldron. 2006. An architecture for language processing for scientific texts. In *Proceedings of the UK e-Science Programme All Hands Meeting 2006 (AHM2006)*. Nottingham, UK.

Corbett, Peter and Ann Copestake. 2008. Cascaded classifiers for confidence-based chemical named entity recognition. *BMC Bioinformatics* 9(Suppl 11):S4.

Core, Mark G. and James F. Allen. 1997. Coding dialogs with the DAMSL annotation scheme. In *Working Notes of the AAAI Fall Symposium on Communicative Action in Humans and Machines*. Cambridge, MA. `www.cs.umd.edu/~traum/CA/fpapers.html`.

Couto, Javier and Jean-Luc Minel. 2006. Sextant, un language de modelisation des connaissances pour la navigation textuelle. In P. Enjalbert, ed., *Proceedings of the International Symposium Discourse and Document*. Prepublications de l'Universite de Caen Basse-Normandie.

Craggs, Richard and Mary McGee Wood. 2005. Evaluating discourse and dialogue coding schemes. *Computational Linguistics* 31(3):289–295.

Cremmins, Edward T. 1996. *The Art of Abstracting*. Arlington, VA: Information Resources Press, 2nd edn.

Crookes, Graham. 1986. Towards a validated analysis of scientific text structure. *Applied Linguistics* 7(1):57–70.

Culotta, Aron and Jeffrey Sorensen. 2004. Dependency tree kernels for relation extraction. In *Proceedings of 42nd Annual Meeting of the Association for Computational Linguistics and the 12th Annual Meeting of the Association for Computational Linguistics (ACL/EACL-04)*. Barcelona, Spain.

CWTS. 2007. Scoping study on the use of bibliometric analysis to measure the quality of research in UK higher education institutions. `http://www.hefce.ac.uk/pubs/rdreports/2007/rd18_07/`.

Daelemans, Walter and Miles Osbourne, eds. 2003. *Proceedings of The Seventh Conference on Natural Language Learning (CoNLL-2003)*. `http://www.cnts.ua.ac.be/conll2003/proceedings.html`.

Dagan, Ido, Oren Glickman, and Bernardo Magnini. 2006. The PASCAL recognising textual entailment challenge. *Lecture Notes in Computer Science* 3944:177–190.

Daille, Beatrice. 2003. Conceptual structuring through term variation. In *Proceedings of ACL-WS on Multiword Expressions*. Sapporo, Japan.

Dale, Robert, Jon Oberlander, Maria Milosavljevic, and Ali Knott. 1998. Integrating natural language generation and hypertext to produce dynamic documents. *Interacting with Computers* 11(2):109–135.

Day, Robert A. and Barbara Gastell. 2006. *How to Write and Publish a Scientific Paper*. Cambridge, England: Cambridge University Press, 6th edn.

Deerwester, S., Susan Dumais, G. W. Furnas, T. K. Landauer, and R. Harshman. 1990. Indexing by Latent Semantic Analysis. *Journal of the American Society for Information Science* 41(6):391–407.

DeJong, Gerald F. 1982. An Overview of the FRUMP System. In W. G. Lehner and Ringle, eds., *Strategies for Natural Language Processing*, chap. 5. Hillsdale NJ: Lawrence Erlbaum.

Di Eugenio, Barbara, Pamela W. Jordan, Johanna D. Moore, and Richmond H. Thomason. 1998. An empirical investigation of proposals in collaborative dialogues. In *Proceedings of 36th Annual Meeting of the Association for Computational Linguistics and the 17th International Conference on Computational Linguistics (ACL/COLING-98)*, pages 325–329. Montreal, Canada.

DiEugenio, Barbara and Michael Glass. 2004. The kappa statistic: a second look. *Computational Linguistics* 30(1):95–101.

Dillon, Andrew. 1992. Reading from paper versus from screens: A critical review of the empirical literature. *Ergonomics* 35(10):1297–1326.

Dillon, Andrew, Lisa Kleinman, Gil Ok Choi, and Randolph Bias. 2006. Visual search and reading tasks using cleartype and regular displays: two experiments. In *Proceedings of the SIGCHI conference on Human Factors in computing systems*. Montreal, Quebec, Canada.

Dillon, Andrew, John Richardson, and Cliff McKnight. 1989. Human factors of journal usage and the design of electronic text. *Interacting with Computers* 1(2):183–189.

Doan, S. and S. Horiguchi. 2004. An efficient feature selection using multi-criteria in text categorization. In *Proceedings of Fourth International Conference on Hybrid Intelligent Systems, 2004. (HIS '04)*, pages 86– 91.

Domingos, P. and M. Pazzani. 1997. Beyond independence: Conditions for the optimality of the simple Bayesian classifier. *Machine Learning* 29:462–467.

Doran, Christine, John Aberdeen, Laurie Domianos, and Lynette Hirschman. 2001. Comparing several aspects of human-computer and human-human dialogues. In *Proceedings of the 2rd SIGDIAL Workshop on Discourse and Dialogue*. Aalborg, Denmark.

Dorr, Bonnie J., Christof Monz, Stacy President, Richard Schwartz, and David Zajic. 2005. A methodology for extrinsic evaluation of text summarization: Does ROUGE correlate? In *Proceedings of ACL-WS "Intrinsic and Extrinsic Evaluation Measures for Machine Translation and/or Summarization"*.

Dorr, Bonnie J., David Zajic, and Richard Schwartz. 2003. Hedge: A parse-and-trim approach to headline generation. In *Proceedings of the HLT-NAACL Text Summarization Workshop and Document Understanding Conference (DUC 2003)*, pages 1–8. Edmonton, Canada.

Drakos, Nikos. 1994. From text to hypertext: A post-hoc rationalisation of latex2html. In *The Proceedings of the First WorldWide Web Conference*.

Dreyfus, Hubert L. 1975. From micro-worlds to knowledge representation: AI at an impasse. In J. Haugeland, ed., *Mind Design—What Computers Can't Do*. New York, NY: Harper and Row.

Drouin, Patrick. 2003. Term extraction using non-technical corpora as a point of leverage. *Terminology* 9(1):99–115.

DUC. 2001. *Document Understanding Conference (DUC-2001)*. Electronic proceedings, `http://www-nlpir.nist.gov/projects/duc/pubs.html`.

Dunning, Ted. 1993. Accurate methods for the statistics of surprise and coincidence. *Computational Linguistics* 19(1):61–74.

Duszak, Anna. 1994. Academic discourse and intellectual styles. *Journal of Pragmatics* 21:291–313.

Earl, Lois L. 1970. Experiments in automatic extracting and indexing. *Information Storage and Retrieval* 6(6):313–334.

Edmundson, H. P. 1969. New methods in automatic extracting. *Journal of the Association for Computing Machinery* 16(2):264–285.

Edmundson, H. P. et al. 1961. *Final Report on the Study for Automatic Abstracting*. Canoga Park, CA: Thompson Ramo Wooldridge.

Elkiss, Aaron, Siwei Shen, Anthony Fader, Gunecs Erkan, David States, and Dragomir R. Radev. 2008. Blind men and elephants: What do citation summaries tell us about a research article? *Journal of the American Society for Information Science* 59(1):51–62.

Ellis, D. 1989a. A behavioural approach to information system design. *Journal of Documentation* 45(3):171–212.

Ellis, D. 1989b. A behavioural model for information system design. *Journal of Information Science* 15(4):237–247.

Ellis, David. 1992. The physical and cognitive paradigms in information retrieval research. *Journal of Documentation* 48:45–64.

Endres-Niggemeyer, Brigitte. 1998. *Summarizing Information.* New York, NY: Springer-Verlag.

Endres-Niggemeyer, Brigitte, Elisabeth Maier, and Alexander Sigel. 1995. How to implement a naturalistic model of abstracting: Four core working steps of an expert abstractor. *Information Processing and Management* 31(5):631–674.

Erkan, Gunes and Dragomir Radev. 2004. Lexrank: Graph-based lexical centrality as salience in text summarization. *Journal of Artificial Intelligence Research* 22:457–479.

Estival, Dominique and Francoise Gayral. 1995. An NLP approach to a specific type of texts: Car accident reports. cmp-lg/9502032.

Farr, A. D. 1985. *Science Writing for Beginners.* Oxford: Blackwell Scientific Publications.

Feltrim, Valéria, Jorge Marques Pelizzoni, Simone Teufel, Maria das Graças Volpe Nunes, and Sandra Aluísio. 2004. Applying argumentative zoning in an automatic critiquer of academic writing. In *Proceedings of the Seventeenth Symposium of Brazilian Artificial Intelligence (SBIA).*

Feltrim, V., Simone Teufel, Graças Nunes, and S. Alusio. 2005. Argumentative zoning applied to critiquing novices' scientific abstracts. In J. G. Shanahan, Y. Qu, and J. Wiebe, eds., *Computing Attitude and Affect in Text: Theory and Applications*, pages 233–245. Dordrecht, The Netherlands: Springer.

Feltrim, Valeria D., Sandra M. Aluisio, and Maria das Graças V. Nunes. 2003. Analysis of the rhetorical structure of computer science abstracts in Portuguese. In *Proceedings of the Corpus Linguistics Conference.* Lancaster, UK.

Ferber, Marianne A. 1988. Citations and networking. *Gender and Society* 2(1):82–89.

Fidel, R. 1985. Moves in online searching. *Online Review* 9(1):61–74.

Fidel, R. 1991. Searchers' selection of search keys. *Journal of the American Society for Information Science* 42(7):490–527.

Fleiss, Joesph L. 1971. Measuring nominal scale agreement among many raters. *Psychological Bulletin* 76:378–381.

Fleiss, Joseph L., Jacob Cohen, and B.S. Everitt. 1969. Large sample standard errors of kappa and weighted kappa. *Psychological Bulletin* 72(5):323–327.

Francis, W. Nelson and Henry Kucera. 1982. *Frequency Analysis of English Usage: Lexicon and Grammar.* Boston, MA: Houghton Mifflin.

Froom, P. and J. Froom. 1993. Deficiencies in structured medical abstracts. *Journal of Clinical Epidemiology* 46:591–594.

Frost, Carolyn O. 1979. The use of citations in literary research: A preliminary classification of citation functions. *Library Quarterly* 49:405.

Galley, Michael, Kathleen McKeown, Eric Fosler-Lussier, and Hongyan Jing. 2003. Discourse segmentation of multi-party conversation. In *Proceedings of the 41st Annual Meeting of the Association for Computational Linguistics (ACL-03)*, pages 562–569. Sapporo, Japan.

Garfield, Eugene. 1979. *Citation Indexing: Its Theory and Application in Science, Technology and Humanities*. New York, NY: J. Wiley.

Garfield, Eugene. 1996. The significant scientific literature appears in a small group of journals. *The Scientist* 10(17):13–16.

Garvey, W. and B. Griffith. 1971. Scientific communication: Its role in the conduct of research and creation of knowledge. *American Psychologist* 26:349–362.

Garzone, Mark and Robert E. Mercer. 2000. Towards an automated citation classifier. In *Proceedings of the 13th Biennial Conference of the CSCI/SCEIO (AI-2000)*, pages 337–346.

Geertzen, Jeroen and Harry Bunt. 2006. Measuring inter-annotator agreement in a complex hierarchical dialogue act annotation scheme. In *Proceedings of the 7th SIGdial Workshop on Discourse and Dialogue*, pages 126–133. Sydney, Australia.

Gilbert, G. N. and M. Mulkay. 1984. *Opening Pandora's Box; A Sociological Analysis of Scientists' Discourse*. Cambridge: Cambridge University Press.

Giles, C. Lee, Kurt D. Bollacker, and Steve Lawrence. 1998. Citeseer: An automatic citation indexing system. In *Proceedings of the Third ACM Conference on Digital Libraries*, pages 89–98.

Giles, C. Lee and Isaac G. Councill. 2004. Who gets acknowledged: measuring scientific contributions through automatic acknowledgement indexing. *PNAS (Proceedings of the National Academy of Sciences of the United States of America)* 101(51):17599–17604.

Girju, Roxana, Dan Moldovan, Marta Tatu, and Daniel Antohe. 2005. On the semantics of noun compounds. *Computer, Speech and Language* 19(4):479–496.

Goodrum, Abby A., Katherine W. McCain, Steve Lawrence, and C. Lee Giles. 2001. Scholarly publishing in the internet age: a citation analysis of computer science literature. *Information Processing and Management* 37:661–675.

Gopnik, M. 1972. *Linguistic Structures in Scientific Texts*. The Hague: Mouton.

Graetz, N. 1985. Teaching EFL students to extract information from abstracts. In J. M. Ulijn and A. K. Pugh, eds., *Reading for Professional Purposes: Methods and Materials in Teaching Languages*, pages 123–135. Leuven, Belgium: Acco.

Grefenstette, Gregory. 1998. Producing intelligent telegraphic text reduction to provide an audio scanning service for the blind. In D. R. Radev and E. H. Hovy, eds., *Working Notes of the AAAI Spring Symposium on Intelligent Text Summarization*, pages 111–117.

Grishman, Ralph and Beth Sundheim. 1995. Design of the MUC-6 evaluation. In *Proceedings of the Sixth Message Understanding Conference*, pages 1–11.

Grosz, Barbara J. and Candace L. Sidner. 1986. Attention, intentions and the structure of discourse. *Computational Linguistics* 12(3):175–204.

Grover, Claire, Ben Hachey, and Ian Hughson. 2004. The HOLJ corpus: supporting summarisation of legal texts. In *Proceedings of the 5th International Workshop on Linguistically Interpreted Corpora (LINC-04)*. Geneva, Switzerland.

Grover, Claire, Ben Hachey, Ian Hughson, and Chris Korycinski. 2003. Automatic summarisation of legal documents. In *Proceedings of the 9th International Conference on Artificial Intelligence and Law (ICAIL 2003)*. Edinburgh, Scotland.

Grover, Claire, Andrei Mikheev, and Colin Matheson. 1999. LT TTT version 1.0: Text tokenisation software. Tech. rep., Human Communication Research Centre, University of Edinburgh. `http://www.ltg.ed.ac.uk/software/ttt/`.

Hachey, Ben and Claire Grover. 2004. Sentence classification experiments for legal text summarisation. In *Proceedings of the 17th Annual Conference on Legal Knowledge and Information Systems (Jurix 2004)*. Berlin, Germany.

Hachey, Ben and Claire Grover. 2005a. Automatic legal text summarisation: Experiments with summary structuring. In *Proceedings of the 10th International Conference on Artificial Intelligence and Law (ICAIL 2005)*. Bologna, Italy.

Hachey, Ben and Claire Grover. 2005b. Sentence extraction for legal text summarisation. In *Proceedings of 19th International Joint Conference on Artificial Intelligence (IJCAI-05)*. Edinburgh, Scotland.

Hachey, Ben and Claire Grover. 2005c. Sequence modelling for sentence classification in a legal summarisation system. In *Proceedings of the 2005 ACM Symposium on Applied Computing (SAC 2005)*. Santa Fe, New Mexico USA.

Hachey, Ben and Claire Grover. 2006. Extractive summarisation of legal texts. *Artificial Intelligence and Law: Special Issue on E-government.* 14(4):305–345.

Hahn, Udo, Manfred Klenner, and Klemens Schnattinger. 1995. Learning from texts - a terminological metareasoning perspective. *Learning for Natural Language Processing* pages 453–468.

Hartley, James and Matthew Sydes. 1997. Are structured abstracts easier to read than traditional ones? *Journal of Research in Reading* 20(2):122–136.

Hartley, James, Matthew Sydes, and Antony Blurton. 1996. Obtaining information accurately and quickly: are structured abstracts more efficient? *Journal of Information Science* 22(5):349–356.

Hatzivassiloglou, Vasileios and Kathleen R. McKeown. 1997. Predicting the semantic orientation of adjectives. In *Proceedings of the 35th Annual Meeting of the Association for Computational Linguistics and the 8th Meeting of the European Chapter of the Association for Computational Linguistics (ACL/EACL-97)*.

Haynes, R. B. 1990. More informative abstracts revisited. *Annals of Internal Medicine* 113:69–76.

Hearst, Marti A. 1994. Multi-paragraph segmentation of expository text. In *Proceedings of 32nd Annual Meeting of the Association for Computational Linguistics (ACL-94)*. Las Cruces, New Mexico.

Hearst, Marti A. 1997. Texttiling: Segmenting text into multi-paragraph subtopic passages. *Computational Linguistics* 23(1):33–64.

Hearst, Marti A. and Jan O. Pedersen. 1996. Reexamining the cluster hypothesis: Scatter/gather on retrieval results. In *Proceedings of the 19th Annual International Conference on Research and Development in Information Retrieval (SIGIR-96)*, pages 76–84. Zürich, CH.

Herner, Saul. 1959. Subject slanting in scientific abstracting publications. In *Proceedings on the International Conference on Scientific Information*, vol. 1, pages 407–427.

Hersh, William R., Ravi T. Bhuptiraju, Laura Ross, Phoebe Johnson, Aaron M. Cohen, and Dale F. Kraemer. 2004. TREC 2004 Genomics Track Overview. In *Proceedings of TREC*.

Hirohata, Kenji, Naoaki Okazaki, Sophia Ananiadou, and Mitsuru Ishizuka. 2008. Identifying sections in scientific abstracts using conditional random fields. In *Proceedings of the Third International Joint Conference on Natural Language Processing (IJCNLP 2008)*, pages 381–388. Hyderabad, India. ACL Anthology Ref. I08-1050.

Hirsch, Jorge E. 2005. An index to quantify an individual's scientific research output. *Proceedings of the National Academy of Sciences of the United Stated of America (PNAS)* 102(46).

Hirschberg, D. S. 1975. A linear space algorithm for computing maximal common subsequences. *Communications of the ACM* 18(6):341–343.

Hitzeman, Janet, Marc Moens, and Claire Grover. 1999. Algorithms for analysing the temporal structure of discourse. In *Proceedings of the 7th Meeting of the European Chapter of the Association for Computational Linguistics (EACL-99)*.

Hobbs, Jerry R. 1986. Resolving pronoun references. In B. J. Grosz, K. Spärck Jones, and B. L. Webber, eds., *Readings in Natural Language Processing*, pages 627–649. Morgan Kaufman.

Hoey, Michael. 1979. *Signalling in Discourse*. No. 6 in Discourse Analysis Monograph. Birmingham, UK: University of Birmingham.

Hoey, Michael. 1991. *Patterns of Lexis in Text*. Oxford University Press.

Hollingsworth, Bill, Ian Lewin, and Dan Tidhar. 2005. Retrieving hierarchical text structure from typeset scientific articles - a prerequisite for e-science text mining. In *Proc. 5th E-Science All Hands Meeting (AHM2005)*, pages 267–273. Nottingham.

Hollingsworth, William. 2008. *Using Lexical Chains to Characterise Scientific Text*. Ph.D. thesis, University of Cambridge Computer Laboratory.

Hornbaek, Kasper and Erik Frokjaer. 2003. Reading patterns and usability in visualizations of electronic documents. *ACM Transactions on Computer-Human Interaction (TOCHI)* 10(2):119–149.

Horsella, Maria and Gerda Sindermann. 1992. Aspects of scientific discourse: Conditional argumentation. *English for Specific Purposes* 11:129–139.

Houp, Kenneth W., T. E. Pearsall, Elizabeth Tebeaux, and Sam Dragga. 2001. *Reporting Technical Information*. Oxford, UK: Oxford University Press.

Hovy, Eduard and Chin-Yew Lin. 1998. Automated text summarization and the SUMMARIST system. In *Proc. of the TIPSTER Text Program*, pages 197–214.

Hovy, Eduard H. 1993. Automated discourse generation using discourse structure relations. *Artificial Intelligence* 63:341–385.

Hsueh, Pei-Yun, Johanna Moore, and Steve Renals. 2006. Automatic segmentation of multiparty dialogue. In *Proceedings of the 11th Meeting of the European Chapter of the Association for Computational Linguistics (EACL-06)*, pages 273–280. Trento, Italy.

Hutchins, J. W. 1977. On the structure of scientific texts. *UEA Papers in Linguistics* 5(3):18–39.

Hwang, Chung Hee and Lenhart K. Schubert. 1992. Tense trees as the "fine structure" of discourse. In *Proceedings of 30th Annual Meeting of the Association for Computational Linguistics (ACL-92)*, pages 232–240. Newark, Delaware.

Hyland, Ken. 1998a. *Hedging in scientific research articles*. John Benjamins Publishing Company.

Hyland, Ken. 1998b. Persuasion and context: The pragmatics of academic metadiscourse. *Journal of Pragmatics* 30(4):437–455.

Ibrahim, Ali, Boris Katz, and Jimmy Lin. 2003. Extracting structural paraphrases from aligned monolingual corpora. In *Proceedings of the Second International Workshop on Paraphrasing*, page 57–64. Sapporo, Japan.

Ingwersen, Peter. 1996. Cognitive perspectives of information retrieval interaction: Elements of a cognitive IR theory. *Journal of Documentation* 52:3–50.

ISO. 1976. Documentation—Abstracts for publication and documentation. ISO 214-1976. Tech. rep., International Organisation for Standardisation.

Iwanska, L. 1985. Discourse structure in factual reports. Tech. rep., GE Artificial Intelligence Laboratory, NY. unpublished.

Jing, Hongyan. 2000. Sentence reduction for automatic text summarization. In *Proceedings of the 6th Applied Natural Language Conference(ANLP-00) and the 1st Meeting of the North American Chapter of the Association for Computational Linguistics (NAACL-00)*, page 310. Seattle, WA.

Jing, Hongyan, Regina Barzilay, Kathleen R. McKeown, and Michael Elhadad. 1998. Summarization evaluation methods: Experiments and analysis. In D. R. Radev and E. H. Hovy, eds., *Working Notes of the AAAI Spring Symposium on Intelligent Text Summarization*, pages 60–68.

Jing, Hongyan and Kathleen R. McKeown. 2000. Cut and paste based summarization. In *Proceedings of the 6th Applied Natural Language Conference(ANLP-00) and the 1st Meeting of the North American Chapter of the Association for Computational Linguistics (NAACL-00)*, pages 178–185. Seattle, WA.

Johnson, Frances C., Chris D. Paice, William J. Black, and A. P. Neal. 1993. The application of linguistic processing to automatic abstract generation. *Journal of Document and Text Management* 1(3):215–241.

Jordan, Michael P. 1984. *Rhetoric of Everyday English Texts*. London, UK: George Allen and Unwin.

Josselson, Ruthellen and Amia Lieblich. 1996. Fettering the mind in the name of "science". *American Psychologist* 51(6):651–652.

Jurafsky, Daniel, Elizabeth Shriberg, and Debra Biasca. 1997. Switchboard SWBD-DAMSL Shallow-Discourse-Function Annotation Coders Manual. TR–97-02. Tech. rep., Institute of Cognitive Science, University of Colorado at Boulder, Boulder, CO.

Kando, Noriko. 1997. Text-level structure of research papers: Implications for text-based information processing systems. In *Proceedings of BCS-IRSG Colloquium*, pages 68–81.

Kaplan, Dain, Tyu Iida, and Takenobu Tokunaga. 2009. Automatic extraction of citation contexts for research paper summarization: A coreference-chain based approach. In *Proceedings of the ACL-IJCNLP-09 Workshop on Text and Citation Analysis for Scholarly Digital Libraries*, pages 88–95. Singapore.

Karamanis, Nikiforos, Ian Lewin, Ruth Seal, Rachel Drysdale, and Ted Briscoe. 2007. Integrating natural language processing with FlyBase curation. In *Proceedings of the Pacific Symposium on Biocomputing (PSB-2007)*, pages 245–256. Maui, Hawaii.

Kessler, Brett, Geoffrey Nunberg, and Hinrich Schütze. 1997. Automatic detection of text genre. In *Proceedings of the 35th Annual Meeting of the Association for Computational Linguistics and 8th Meeting of the European Chapter of the Association for Computational Linguistics (ACL/EACL-97)*, pages 32–38. Madrid, Spain.

Kessler, Myer Mike. 1963. Bibliographic coupling between scientific papers. *American Documentation* 14(1):10–25.

Kilgarriff, Adam. 1999. 95% replicability for manual word sense tagging. In *Proceedings of the 9th Meeting of the European Chapter of the Association for Computational Linguistics (EACL-99), Poster Session*, page 277. Bergen, Norway.

Kim, Jin-Dong, Tomoko Ohta, Sampo Pyysalo, Yoshinobu Kano, and Junichi Tsujii. 2009. Overview of BioNLP-09 Shared Task on Event Extraction. In *Proceedings of NAACL Workshop "BioNLP-09, Shared Task"*, pages 1–9. Bolder, Colorado.

Kim, Jin-Dong, Tomoko Ohta, Yoshimasa Tsuruoka, Yuka Tateisi, and Nigel Collier. 2004. Introduction to the bio-entity recognition task at JNLPBA. In N. Collier, P. Ruch, and A. Nazarenko, eds., *COLING 2004 International Joint workshop on Natural Language Processing in Biomedicine and its Applications (NLPBA/BioNLP) 2004*, pages 73–78. Geneva, Switzerland: COLING.

Kim, Yunhyong and Bonnie Webber. 2006. Automatic reference resolution in astronomy articles. In *Proceedings of 20th CODATA conference*. Berlin, Germany.

King, Rosemary A. 1967. A comparison of the readability of abstracts with their source documents. *Journal of the American Society for Information Science* 27(2):118–121.

Kintsch, Walter and Teun A. van Dijk. 1978. Toward a model of text comprehension and production. *Psychological Review* 85(5):363–394.

Kircz, Joost G. 1991. The rhetorical structure of scientific articles: The case for argumentational analysis in information retrieval. *Journal of Documentation* 47(4):354–372.

Kircz, Joost G. 2001. New practices for electronic publishing 1: Will the scientific paper keep its form? *Learned Publishing* 14(4):265–272. See: www.learned-publishing.org.

Knight, Kevin and Daniel Marcu. 2000. Statistics-based summarization — step one: Sentence compression. In *Proceeding of The 17th National Conference of the American Association for Artificial Intelligence (AAAI-2000)*, pages 703–710.

Knott, Alistair. 1994. Defining a set of coherence relations using a taxonomy of cue phrases. In *Proceedings of 32nd Annual Meeting of the Association for Computational Linguistics (ACL-94)*. Las Cruces, New Mexico.

Knott, Alistair. 1996. *A Data-Driven Methodology for Motivating a Set of Discourse Relations*. Ph.D. thesis, Centre for Cognitive Science, University of Edinburgh, Edinburgh, UK.

Kononenko, I. 1990. Comparison of inductive and Naive Bayesian learning approaches to automatic knowledge acquisition. In B. Wielinga, ed., *Current Trends in Knowledge Acquisition*. IOS Press.

Korhonen, Anna, Yuval Krymolowski, and Zvika Marx. 2003. Clustering polysemic subcategorization frame distributions semantically. In *Proceedings of the 41st Annual Meeting of the Association for Computational Linguistics (ACL-03)*.

Kowkto, Jacqueline C., Stephen D. Isard, and Gwyneth M. Doherty. 1992. Conversational games within dialogue. Tech. rep., Human Communication Research Centre, University of Edinburgh.

Krenn, Brigitte, Stefan Evert, and Heike Zinsmeister. 2004. Determining intercoder agreement for a collocation identification task. In *Proceedings of Konvens-04*.

Krippendorff, Klaus. 1980. *Content Analysis: An Introduction to its Methodology*. Beverly Hills, CA: Sage Publications.

Krippendorff, Klaus. 2004. *Content Analysis: An Introduction to its Methodology*. Beverly Hills, CA: Sage Publications, 2nd edn.

Kupiec, Julian, Jan O. Pedersen, and Francine Chen. 1995. A trainable document summarizer. In *Proceedings of the 18th Annual International Conference on Research and Development in Information Retrieval (SIGIR-95)*, pages 68–73.

Lancaster, Frederick Wilfrid. 1998. *Indexing and Abstracting in Theory and Practice*. London, UK: Library Association.

Lancaster, Frederick Wilfrid. 2003. *Indexing and Abstracting in Theory and Practice*. Champaign, IL: University of Illinois, Graduate School of Library and Information Science.

Landis, J. Richard and Gary G. Koch. 1977. The measurement of observer agreement for categorical data. *Biometrics* 33:159–174.

Langley, P., W. Iba, and Thomas K. 1992. An analysis of Bayesian classifiers. In *Proceedings of the Tenth National conference on Artificial Intelligence*, pages 223–228. AAAI Press.

Lannon, John M. 2008. *The Writing Process: A Concise Rhetoric, Reader and Handbook*. New York, NY: Longman, 10th edn.

Latex2Html. 1999. `http://cbl.leeds.ac.uk/nikos/tex2html/doc/latex2html/latex2html.html`.

Latour, Bruno and Steven Woolgar. 1986. *Laboratory Life: The Social Construction of Scientific Facts*. Beverley Hills, CA: Sage Publications.

Leech, Geoffrey. 1992. Corpora and theories of linguistic performance. In J. Svartvik, ed., *Directions in Corpus Linguistics*, pages 105–122. Berlin: Mouton de Gruyter.

Lehnert, Wendy G. 1981. Plot units and narrative summarization. *Cognitive Science* 4:293–331.

Levin, Beth. 1993. *English Verb Classes and Alternations*. Chicago, IL: University of Chicago Press.

Levy, D. M. 1997. I read the news today, oh boy: Reading and attention in digital libraries. In *Proceedings of Digital Libraries T97, ACM*, pages 228–235.

Lewin, Ian. 2007. Using hand-crafted rules and machine learning to infer SciXML document structure. In *Proceedings of the 7th E-Science All Hands Meeting (AHM2007)*.

Lewis, David D. 1991. Evaluating text categorisation. In *Speech and Natural Language: Proceedings of the ARPA Workshop of Human Language Technology*.

Lewis, David D. 1992. Text representation for intelligent text retrieval: A classification-oriented view. In P. S. Jacobs, ed., *Text-Based Intelligent Systems: Current Research and Practice in Information Extraction and Retrieval*. Hillsdale, NJ: Lawrence Erlbaum.

Li, Gangmin, Victoria Uren, Enrico Motta, Simon Buckingham Shum, and John Domingue. 2002. Claimaker: Weaving a semantic web of research papers. In *ISWC2002, the 1st International Semantic Web Conference*. Sardinia, Italia.

Liddy, Elizabeth DuRoss. 1991. The discourse-level structure of empirical abstracts: An exploratory study. *Information Processing and Management* 27(1):55–81.

Lin, Chin-Yew. 2004. Rouge: A package for automatic evaluation of summaries. In *Proceedings of Workshop "Text Summarization Branches Out" at ACL-04*. Barcelona, Spain.

Lin, Chin-Yew and Eduard H. Hovy. 1997. Identifying topics by position. In *Proceedings of the 5th Applied Natural Language Conference (ANLP-97)*, pages 283–290.

Lin, Dekang and P. Pantel. 2001. Discovery of inference rules for question-answering. *Natural Language Engineering* 7(4):343–360.

Lin, Jianhua. 1991. Divergence measures based on the Shannon entropy. *IEEE transactions on Information Theory* 37(1):145–151.

Lin, Jimmy, Damianos Karakos, Dina Demner-Fushman, and Sanjeev Khudanpur. 2006. Generative content models for structural analysis of medical abstracts. In *Proceedings of the HLT/NAACL 2006 Workshop on Biomedical Natural Language Processing (BIONLP-06)*, pages 65–72. New York City, USA.

Lisacek, Frederique, Christine Chichester, Aaron Kaplan, and Agnes Sandor. 2005. Discovering paradigm shift patterns in biomedical abstracts: Application to neurodegenerative diseases. In *Proc. of the SMBM*. European Bioinformatics Institute, Hinxton, UK.

Litman, Diane J. 1996. Cue phrase classification using machine learning. *Journal of Artificial Intelligence Research* 5:53–94.

Longacre, Robert E. 1979. The paragraph as a grammatical unit. In T. Givon, ed., *Syntax and Semantics: Discourse and Syntax*, pages 115–134. Academic Press.

Luhn, Hans Peter. 1958. The automatic creation of literature abstracts. *IBM Journal of Research and Development* 2(2):159–165.

Luukkonen, Terttu. 1992. Is scientists' publishing behaviour reward-seeking? *Scientometrics* 24:297–319.

Macinino, Clara and Donia Scott. 2006. Hyper-document structure: Maintaining discourse coherence in non-linear documents. In P. Enjalbert, ed., *Proceedings of the International Symposium Discourse and Document*. Prepublications de l'Universite de Caen Basse-Normandie.

MacRoberts, Michael H. and Barbara R. MacRoberts. 1984. The negational reference: Or the art of dissembling. *Social Studies of Science* 14:91–94.

Maizell, R. E., J. F. Smith, and T. E. R. Singer. 1971. *Abstracting Scientific and Technical Literature: An Introductory Guide and Texts for Scientists, Abstractors and Management*. New York, NY: Wiley-Interscience.

Malcolm, L. 1987. What rules govern tense usage in scientific articles? *English for Specific Purposes* 6:31–43.

Mani, Inderjeet. 2001. *Automatic Summarization*. John Benjamins.

Mani, Inderjeet and Eric Bloedorn. 1998. Machine learning of generic and user-focused summarization. In *Proceedings of the Fifteenth National Conference on AI (AAAI-98)*, pages 821–826.

Mani, Inderjeet, Therese Firmin, David House, Gary Klein, Beth Sundheim, and Lynette Hirschman. 1999a. The TIPSTER Summac Text Summarization Evaluation. In *Proceedings of the 9th Meeting of the European Chapter of the Association for Computational Linguistics (EACL-99)*, pages 77–85. Bergen, Norway.

Mani, Inderjeet, Barbara Gates, and Eric Bloedorn. 1999b. Improving summaries by revising them. In *Proceedings of the 37th Annual Meeting of the Association for Computational Linguistics (ACL-99)*, pages 558–565. College Park, Maryland.

Mani, Inderjeet, Gary Klein, David House, Lynette Hirschman, Therese Firmin, and Beth Sundheim. 2002. Summac: a text summarization evaluation. *Natural Language Engineering* 8(1):43 – 68.

Mann, William C. and Sandra A. Thompson. 1987. Rhetorical Structure Theory: A theory of text organisation. ISI/RS-87-190. Tech. rep., Information Sciences Institute, University of Southern California, Marina del Rey, CA.

Mann, William C. and Sandra A. Thompson. 1988. Rhetorical structure theory: Toward a functional theory of text organisation. *Text* 8(3):243–281.

Manning, Alan D. 1990. Abstracts in relation to larger and smaller discourse structures. *Journal of Technical Writing and Communication* 20(4):369–390.

Manning, Christopher D. and Hinrich Schütze. 1999. *Foundations of Statistical Natural Language Processing*. Cambridge, MA: MIT Press.

Marcu, Daniel. 1997a. From discourse structures to text summaries. In I. Mani and M. T. Maybury, eds., *Proceedings of the ACL/EACL-97 Workshop on Intelligent Scalable Text Summarization*, pages 82–88.

Marcu, Daniel. 1997b. The rhetorical parsing of natural language texts. In *Proceedings of the 35th Annual Meeting of the Association for Computational Linguistics and the 8th Meeting of the European Chapter of the Association for Computational Linguistics (ACL/EACL-97)*. Madrid, Spain.

Marcu, Daniel. 1997c. *The Rhetorical Parsing, Summarization, and Generation of Natural Language Texts*. Ph.D. thesis, University of Toronto, Ont., Canada.

Marcu, Daniel. 1999a. The automatic construction of large-scale corpora for summarization research. In *Proceedings of the 22nd Annual International Conference on Research and Development in Information Retrieval (SIGIR-99)*, pages 137–144. Berkeley, CA.

Marcu, Daniel. 1999b. A decision-based approach to rhetorical parsing. In *Proceedings of the 37th Annual Meeting of the Association for Computational Linguistics (ACL-99)*, pages 365–372. College Park, Maryland.

Marcu, Daniel. 1999c. Discourse trees are good indicators of importance in text. In I. Mani and M. T. Maybury, eds., *Advances in Automatic Text Summarization*, pages 123–136. Cambridge, MA: MIT Press.

Markert, Katja and Malvina Nissim. 2005. Comparing knowledge sources for nominal anaphora resolution. *Computational Linguistics* 31(3):367–402.

Matthews, Janyce R. and Robert W. Matthews. 2007. *Successful Scientific Writing: A Step-by-Step Guide for the Biological and Medical Sciences*. Cambridge University Press, 3rd edn.

McCallum, Andrew and K Nigam. 1998. A comparison of event models for Naive Bayes text classification. In *Procedings of AAAI-98 workshop on learning for text categorization*.

McCallum, Andrew Kachites. 1996. Bow: A toolkit for statistical language modeling, text retrieval, classification and clustering. http://www.cs.cmu.edu/ mccallum/bow.

McGirr, Clinton J. 1973. Guidelines for abstracting. *Technical Communication* 25(2):2–5.

McKeown, Kathleen R. 1985. *Text Generation: Using Discourse Strategies and Focus Constraints to Generate Natural Language Text*. Studies in Natural Language Processing. Cambridge: Cambridge University Press.

McKeown, Kathleen R., Shifu Chang, James Cimino, Steve Feiner, Carol Friedman, Luis Gravano, Vasileios Hatzivassiloglou, Steve Johnson, Desmond Jordan, Judith Klavans, Andre Kushniruk, Vimla Patel, and Simone Teufel. 2001. Persival, a system for personalized search and summarization over multimedia healthcare information. In *Proceedings of JCDL-2001*.

McKeown, Kathleen R. and Dragomir R. Radev. 1995. Generating summaries of multiple news articles. In *Proceedings of the 18th Annual International Conference on Research and Development in Information Retrieval (SIGIR-95)*, pages 74–82.

McKnight, Larry and Padmini Arinivasan. 2003. Categorization of sentence types in medical abstracts. In *In AMIA-03 Symposium Proceedings*, page 440–444.

Medawar, P. 1963. Is the scientific paper a fraud? *The Listener and BBC Television Review* 70(1798):377–378.

Medlock, Benjamin and Ted Briscoe. 2007. Weakly supervised learning for hedge classification in scientific literature. In *Proceedings of ACL-07*.

Mercer, Robert E. and Chrysanne Di Marco. 2003. The importance of fine-grained cue phrases in scientific citations. In *Proceedings of the 16th Conference of the CSCSI/SCEIO (AI-2003)*.

Mercer, Robert E., Chrysanne Di Marco, and Frederick W. Kroon. 2004. The frequency of hedging cues in citation contexts in scientific writing. In *Proceedings of the 17th Conference of the CSCI/SCEIO (AI-2004)*.

Merity, Stephen, Tara Murphy, and James R. Curran. 2009. Accurate argumentative zoning with maximum entropy models. In *Proceedings of ACL-IJCNLP-09 Workshop on text and citation analysis for scholarly digital libraries (NLPIR4DL)*, pages 19–26. Singapore.

Michaelson, Herbert B. 1990. *How to Write and Publish Engineering Papers and Reports*. Greenwood Press, 3rd edn.

Microsoft. 1997. Office-97. `http://www.microsoft.com/Office/`.

Midgley, T. Daniel. 2009. Dialogue segmentation with large numbers of volunteer internet annotators. In *Proceedings of 47th Annual Meeting of the Association for Computational Linguistics and the 4th International Joint Conference on Natural Language Processing (ACL/IJCNLP-09)*.

Mihalcea, Rada and Paul Tarau. 2004. Textrank: Bringing order into texts. In *Proceedings of EMNLP-04*, page 404–411. barcelona, Spain.

Mikheev, Andrei. 1998. Feature lattices and maximum entropy models. In *Proceedings of 36th Annual Meeting of the Association for Computational Linguistics and the 17th International Conference on Computational Linguistics (ACL/COLING-98)*. Montreal, Canada.

Milas-Bracovic, Milica. 1987. The structure of scientific papers and their author abstracts. *Informatologia Yugoslavica* 19(1–2):51–67.

Miltsakaki, Eleni, Rashmi Prasad, Aravind Joshi, and Bonnie Webber. 2004. The Penn Discourse TreeBank. In *Proceedings of the Language Resources and Evaluation Conference*. Lisbon, Portugal.

Minsky, M. 1975. A framework for representing knowledge. In P. Winston, ed., *The Psychology of Computer Vision*. New York, NY: McGraw-Hill.

Mizuta, Yoko and Nigel Collier. 2004. An annotation scheme for rhetorical analysis of biology articles. In *Proceedings of LREC'2004*.

Mizuta, Yoko, Anna Korhonen, Tony Mullen, and Nigel Collier. 2006. Zone analysis in biology articles as a basis for information extraction. *International Journal of Medical Informatics* 75(6):468–487.

Mohamma, Saif, Bonnie Dorr, Melissa Egan, Ahmed Hassan, Pradeep Muthukrishan, Vahed Qazvinian, Dragomir R. Radev, and David Zajic. 2009. Generating surveys of scientific paradigms. In *Proceedings of HLT-NAACL 2009*. Boulder, CO.

Moore, Johanna D. and Cecile L. Paris. 1993. Planning text for advisory dialogues: Capturing intentional and rhetorical information. *Computational Linguistics* 19:651–694.

Morante, Roser and Walter Daelemans. 2009. Learning the scope of hedge cues in biomedical texts. In *Proceedings of BioNLP-09*.

Moravcsik, Michael J. and Poovanalingan Murugesan. 1975. Some results on the function and quality of citations. *Social Studies of Science* 5:88–91.

Morris, Andrew H., George M. Kasper, and Dennis A. Adams. 1992. The effects and limitations of automated text condensing on reading comprehension performance. *Information Systems Research* 3(1):17–35.

Morris, Jane and Graeme Hirst. 1991. Lexical cohesion computed by thesaural relations as an indicator of the structure of text. *Computational Linguistics* 17:21–48.

Moser, Megan G. and Johanna D. Moore. 1996. Toward a synthesis of two accounts of discourse structure. *Computational Linguistics* 22(3):409–420.

Mulkay, M. 1984. The scientist talks back: A one-act play, with a moral about replication in science and reflexivity in sociology. *Social Studies of Science* 14:265–282.

Mullins, Nicholas C., William E. Snizek, and Kay Oehler. 1988. The structural analysis of a scientific paper. In A. F. J. van Raan, ed., *Handbook of Quantitative Studies of Science and Technology*, pages 81–106. Amsterdam, NL: North-Holland.

Myers, Greg. 1992. In this paper we report...—speech acts and scientific facts. *Journal of Pragmatics* 17(4):295–313.

Nagamochi, H. and T. Ibaraki. 1992. Linear time algorithms for finding a sparse k-connected spanning subgraph of a k-connected graph. *Algorithmica* 7:583–596.

Nakov, Preslav, Ariel Schwarz, and Marti Hearst. 2004. Citances: Citation sentences for semantic analysis of bioscience text. In *SIGIR'04 Workshop on Search and Discovery in Bioinformatics*.

Nanba, H., N Kando, and M. Okumura. 2000. Classification of research papers using citation links and citation types: Towards automatic review article generation. In *American Society for Information Science SIG Classification Research Workshop: Classification for User Support and Learning*.

Nanba, Hidetsugu and Manabu Okumura. 1999. Towards multi-paper summarization using reference information. In *Proceedings of the XXth International Joint Conference on Artificial Intelligence (IJCAI-99)*, pages 926–931.

Nanba, H. and M Okumura. 2005. Automatic detection of survey articles. In *Research and Advanced Technology for Digital Libraries, 9th European Conference, ECDL 2005*, pages 391–401. Vienna, Austria: Springer. Lecture Notes in Computer Science, Vol. 3652.

Narita, Masumi. 2000. Corpus-based English language assistant to Japanese software engineers. In *Proceedings of MT-2000 Machine Translation and Multilingual Applications in the New Millennium*, pages 24–1 - 24–8.

Nedellec, Claire. 2005. Learning language in logic — genetic interaction extraction challenge. In *In Proceedings of the 4th Learning Language in Logic Workshop (LLL05)*. Bonn, Germany.

Nenkova, Ani and Rebecca J. Passonneau. 2004. Evaluating content selection in summarization: The pyramid method. In *Proceedings of NAACL/HLT-04*. Boston, MA.

Obendorf, Hartmut and Harald Weinreich. 2003. Comparing link marker visualization techniques: changes in reading behavior. In *Proceedings of the 12th international conference on World Wide Web*. Budapest, Hungary.

O'Connor, John. 1982. Citing statements: Computer recognition and use to improve retrieval. *Information Processing and Management* 18(3):125–131.

Oddy, Robert Norman, Elizabeth DuRoss Liddy, B. Balakrichnan, A. Bishop, J. Elewononi, and E. Martin. 1992. Towards the use of situational information in information retrieval. *Journal of Documentation* 48:123–171.

O'Hara, Kenton and Abigail Sellen. 1997. A comparison of reading paper and on-line documents. In *Proceedings of CHI-97, ACM*, pages 335–342.

O'Hara, Kenton, F. Smith, W. Newman, and Abigail Sellen. 1998. Student reader's use of library documents: implications for library technologies. In *Proceedings of CHI-98, ACM*, pages 233–240.

Olsen, Kai A., Robert R. Korfhage, Kenneth M. Sochats, Michael B. Spring, and James G. Williams. 1993. Visualizing of a document collection: The VIBE system. *Information Processing and Management* 29(1):69–81.

Ono, Kenji, Kazuo Sumita, and Seijii Miike. 1994. Abstract generation based on rhetorical structure extraction. In *Proceedings of the 15th International Conference on Computational Linguistics(COLING-94)*, pages 344–348.

Oppenheim, Charles and Susan P. Renn. 1978. Highly cited old papers and the reasons why they continue to be cited. *Journal of the American Society for Information Science* 29:226–230.

Orasan, Constantin. 2000. Patterns in scientific abstracts. In *Proceedings of Corpus Linguistics 2001 Conference*, pages 433–443. Lancaster University, Lancaster, UK.

O'Seaghdha, Diarmuid and Ann Copestake. 2008. Using lexical and relational similarity to classify semantic relations. In *Proceedings of the 12th Conference of the European Chapter of the Association for Computational Linguistics (EACL-09)*. Athens, Greece.

Paice, Chris D. 1981. The automatic generation of literary abstracts: an approach based on the identification of self-indicating phrases. In R. N. Oddy, S. E. Robertson, C. J. van Rijsbergen, and P. W. Williams, eds., *Information Retrieval Research*, pages 172–191. London, UK: Butterworth.

Paice, Chris D. 1990. Constructing literature abstracts by computer: Techniques and prospects. *Information Processing and Management* 26:171–186.

Paice, Chris D. and G.D. Husk. 1987. Towards the automatic recognition of anaphoric features in English text: The impersonal pronoun *it*. *Computer, Speech and Language* 2:109–32.

Paice, Chris D. and A. Paul Jones. 1993. The identification of important concepts in highly structured technical papers. In *Proceedings of the 16th Annual International Conference on Research and Development in Information Retrieval (SIGIR-93)*, pages 69–78.

Pang, Bo and Lillian Lee. 2004. A sentimental education: Sentiment analysis using subjectivity summarization based on minimum cuts. In *Proceedings of 42nd Annual Meeting of the Association for Computational Linguistics and the 12th Meeting of the European Chapter of the Association for Computational Linguistics (ACL/EACL-04)*. Barcelona, Spain.

Pang, Bo and Lillian Lee. 2008. *Opinion Mining and Sentiment Analysis*. Now Publishers Incorporated.

Pang, Bo, Lillian Lee, and Skivakumar Vaithyanathan. 2002. Thumbs up? Sentiment classification using machine learning techniques. In *Proceeding of Conference on Empirical Methods in Natural Language Processing (EMNLP-2002)*.

Paris, Cecile L. 1988. Tailoring object descriptions to a user's level of expertise. *Computational Linguistics* 14(3):64–78. Special Issue on User Modelling.

Paris, Cecile L. 1994. User modeling in text generation. *Computational Linguistics* 20(2):318–321.

Passonneau, Rebecca. 2004. Computing reliability for coreference annotation. In *Proceedings of the Language Resources and Evaluation Conference (LREC 2004)*. Lisbon, Portugal.

Passonneau, Rebecca. 2006. Measuring agreement on set-valued items (MASI) for semantic and pragmatic annotation. In *Proceedings of the Language Resources and Evaluation Conference (LREC 2006)*. Genoa, Italy.

Passonneau, Rebecca, Nizar Habash, and Owen Rambow. 2006. Inter-annotator agreement on a multilingual semantic annotation task. In *Proceedings of the Language Resources and Evaluation Conference (LREC 2006)*. Genoa, Italy.

Passonneau, Rebecca J. and Diane J. Litman. 1993. Intention-based segmentation: Human reliability and correlation with linguistic cues. In *Proceedings of the 31st Annual Meeting of the Association for Computational Linguistics (ACL-93)*, pages 148–155. Columbus, Ohio.

Perelman, Chaim and Lucie Olbrechts-Tyteca. 1969. *The New Rhetoric, a Tractise on Argumentation*. Notre Dame, IN: University of Notre Dame Press.

Pevzner, L. and Marti Hearst. 2002. A critique and improvement of an evaluation metric for text segmentation. *Computational Linguistics* 28(1):19–36.

Pinelli, Thomas E., Virginia M. Cordle, and Raymond F. Vondran. 1984. The function of report components in the screening and reading of technical reports. *Journal of Technical Writing and Communication* 14(2):87–94.

Poesio, Massimo. 2004. An empirical investigation of definiteness. In *Proceedings of the International Conference on Linguistic Evidence*. Tubingen.

Poesio, Massimo, Olga Uryupina, Renata Vieira, Mijail Alexandrov-Kabadjov, and Rodrigo Goulart. 2004. Discourse-new detectors for definite description resolution: A survey and a preliminary proposal. In *Proceedings of the ACL-04 Workshop on Reference Resolution*. Barcelona, Spain.

Pollack, Martha E. 1986. A model of plan inference that distinguishes between the beliefs of actors and observers. In *Proceedings of the 24th Annual Meeting of the Association for Computational Linguistics (ACL-86)*, pages 207–214. New York, US.

Pollock, Joseph J. and Antonio Zamora. 1975. Automatic abstracting research at the chemical abstracts service. *Journal of Chemical Information and Computer Sciences* 15(4):226–232.

Ponte, Jay M. and W. Bruce Croft. 1998. A language modeling approach to information retrieval. In *Proceedings of the 21st Annual International Conference on Research and Development in Information Retrieval (SIGIR-98)*.

Purver, Matthew, Konrad P. Kording, Thomas L. Griffiths, and Joshua B. Tenenbaum. 2006. Unsupervised topic modelling for multi-party spoken discourse. In *Proceedings of 44th Annual Meeting of the Association for Computational Linguistics and the 21st International Conference on Computational Linguistics (ACL/COLING-06)*, pages 17–24. Sydney, Australia.

Qayyum, Muhammad Asim. 2008. Capturing the online academic reading process. *Information Processing and Management* 44(2):581–595.

Qazvinian, Vahed and Dragomir R. Radev. 2008. Scientific paper summarization using citation summary networks. In *Proceedings of COLING 2008*. Manchester, UK.

Quinlan, J. R. 1993. *Q4.5: Programs for Machine Learning*. Morgan. Kaufmann.

Radev, Dragomir, Hongyan Jing, Magorzata Stys, and Daniel Tam. 2004. Centroid-based summarization of multiple documents. *Information Processing and Management* 40(6):919–938.

Radev, Dragomir, Simone Teufel, Horacio Saggion, Wai Lam, John Blitzer, Hong Qi, Arda Celebi, Danyu Liu, and Elliot Drabek. 2003. Evaluation challenges in large-scale multi-document summarization. In *Proceedings of the 41st Annual Meeting of the Association for Computational Linguistics (ACL-03)*. Sapporo, Japan.

Radev, Dragomir R. and Kathleen R. McKeown. 1998. Generating natural language summaries from multiple on-line sources. *Computational Linguistics* 24(3):469–500.

Rath, G.J, A. Resnick, and T. R. Savage. 1961. The formation of abstracts by the selection of sentences. *American Documentation* 12(2):139–143.

Ravichandran, Deepak and Eduard Hovy. 2002. Learning surface text patterns for a question answering system. In *Proceedings of the 40th Annual Meeting of the Association for Computational Linguistics (ACL-02)*. Philadelphia, PA.

Reed, Chris and Floriana Grasso. 2007. Recent advances in computational models of natural argument. *International Journal of Intelligent Systems* 22(1):1–15.

Rees, Alan M. 1966. The relevance of relevance to the testing and evaluation of document retrieval systems. *Aslib Proceedings* 18:316–324.

Reidsma, D. and J. Carletta. 2008. Reliability measurement without limits. *Computational Linguistics* 34(3):319–326.

Rennie, D. and R. M. Glass. 1991. Structuring abstracts to make them more informative. *Journal of the American Medical Association* 266(1):116–117.

Riley, Kathryn. 1991. Passive voice and rhetorical role in scientific writing. *Journal of Technical Writing and Communication* 21(3):239–257.

Riloff, Ellen. 1993. Automatically constructing a dictionary for information extraction tasks. In *Proceedings 11th National Conference on Artificial Intelligence (AAAI-93)*, pages 811–816.

Ritchie, Anna. 2008. *Citation context analysis for information retrieval*. Ph.D. thesis, Computer Laboratory, Cambridge University.

Ritchie, Anna, Stephen Robertson, and Simone Teufel. 2008. Comparing citation contexts for information retrieval. In *Proceeding of the 17th ACM conference on Information and Knowledge mining (CIKM-08)*.

Ritchie, Anna, Simone Teufel, and Stephen Robertson. 2006. Creating a test collection for citation-based IR experiments. In *Proceedings of NAACL/HLT-06*. New York, US.

Robertson, Stephen E. 1977. The probability ranking principle in IR. *Journal of Documentation* 33(4):294–304.

Robertson, Stephen E. and Karen Spärck-Jones. 1976. Relevance weighting of search terms. *Journal of the American Society for Information Science* 27(3):129–146.

Robin, Jacques and Kathleen R. McKeown. 1996. Empirically designing and evaluating a new revision-based model for summary generation. *Artificial Intelligence* 85:135–179.

Rowley, Jennifer. 1982. *Abstracting and Indexing*. London, UK: Bingley.

Rupp, CJ, Ann Copestake, Peter Corbett, Peter Murray-Rust, Advaith Siddharthan, Simone Teufel, and Benjamin Waldron. 2008. Language resources and chemical informatics. In *Proceedings of 6th International Conference on Language Resources and Evaluation (LREC-2008)*. Marrakech, Morocco.

Rupp, CJ, Ann Copestake, Simone Teufel, and Ben Waldron. 2006. Flexible interfaces in the application of language technology to an eScience corpus. In *Proceedings of the 4th UK E-Science All Hands Meeting*. Nottingham, UK.

Saggion, Horacio. 2000. *Generation Automatique de Resumes par Analyse Selective*. Ph.D. thesis, Departement d'informatique, University of Montreal, Canada.

Salager-Meyer, Francoise. 1990. Discoursal flaws in medical English abstracts: A genre analysis per research- and text type. *Text* 10(4):365–384.

Salager-Meyer, Francoise. 1991. Medical English abstracts: How well structured are they? *Journal of the American Society for Information Science* 42:528–532.

Salager-Meyer, Francoise. 1992. A text-type and move analysis study of verb tense and modality distributions in medical English abstracts. *English for Specific Purposes* 11:93–113.

Salager-Meyer, Francoise. 1994. Hedges and textual communicative function in medical English written discourse. *English for Specific Purposes* 13(2):149–170.

Salton, Gerard. 1971. Cluster search strategies and the optimization of retrieval effectiveness. In G. Salton, ed., *The SMART Retrieval System; Experiments in Automatic Document Processing*, pages 223–242. Englewood Cliffs, NJ: Prentice Hill.

Salton, Gerard, James Allan, Chris Buckley, and Amit Singhal. 1994a. Automatic analysis, theme generation, and summarisation of machine readable texts. *Science* 264:1421–1426.

Salton, Gerard and Michael J. McGill. 1983. *Introduction to Modern Information Retrieval*. Tokyo: McGraw-Hill.

Salton, Gerard, Amit Singhal, Chris Buckley, and Mandar Mitra. 1994b. Automatic text decomposition using text segments and text themes. Tech. rep., Cornell University.

Salton, Gerard, Amit Singhal, Mandar Mitra, and Chris Buckley. 1997. Automatic text structuring and summarization. *Information Processing and Management* 33(2):193–208.

Samuels, S. J., R. Tennyson, L. Sax, P. Mulcahy, N. Schermer, and H. Hajovy. 1987. Adults' use of text structure in the recall of a scientific journal article. *Journal of Education Research* 81:171–174.

Sandor, Agnes, Aaron Kaplan, and Gilbert Rondeau. 2006. Finding contradictions in citations. In P. Enjalbert, ed., *Proceedings of the International Symposium Discourse and Document*. Caen, France: Prepublications de l'Universite de Caen Basse-Normandie.

Saracevic, Tefko. 1975. Relevance: A review of and a framework for the thinking on the notion in information science. *Journal of the American Society for Information Science* 26(6):321–343.

Saracevic, Tefko, Paul B. Kantor, A. Y. Chamis, and D. Trivison. 1988. A study of information seeking and retrieving. I. Background and methodology. *Journal of the American Society for Information Science* 39(3):161–176.

Schamber, Linda, Michael B. Eisenberg, and Michael S. Nilan. 1990. A re-examination of relevance. Toward a dynamic, situational definition. *Information Processing and Management* 26:755–776.

Schank, Roger C. and Robert P. Abelson. 1977. *Scripts, Goals, Plans and Understanding*. Hillsdale, NJ: Lawrence Erlbaum.

Schulte im Walde, Sabine. 2006. Experiments on the automatic induction of German semantic verb classes. *Computational Linguistics* 32(2):159–194.

Schulz, Stefan and Udo Hahn. 2005. Part-whole representation and reasoning in formal biomedical ontologies. *Artificial Intelligence in Medicine* 34(4):179–200.

Schuster, Ethel, Sandra M. Alusio, Valeria D. Feltrim, Adalberto Pessoa Jr, and Osvaldo N Oliviera Jr. 2005. Enhancing the writing of scientific abstracts: a two-phased process using software tools and human evaluation. In *Proceedings of Encontro Nacional de Inteligencia Artificial (ENIA)*, pages 962–971. Sao Lourenco.

Scott, William A. 1955. Reliability of conent analysis: the case of nominal scale coding. *Public Opinion Quarterly* 19(3):321–325.

Sharples, M., J. Goodlet, and A. Clutterbuck. 1994. A comparison of algorithms for hypertext notes network linearization. *International Journal of Human Computer Studies* 40(4):727–752.

Sharples, Mike and Lyn Pemberton. 1992. Representing writing: external representations and the writing process. In P. Holt and N. Williams, eds., *Computers and Writing: State of the Art*, pages 319–336. Oxford: Intellect.

Sherrard, Carol. 1985. The psychology of summary writing. *Journal of Technical Writing and Communication* 15(3):247–258.

Shinyama, Yusuke, Satoshi Sekine, Kiyoshi Sudo, and Ralph Grishman. 2002. Automatic paraphrase acquisition from news articles. In *Proceedings of Human Language Technology Conference (HLT)*, page 40–46. San Diego.

Shriberg, Elizabeth, Raj Dhillon, Sonali Bhagat, Jeremy Ang, and Hannah Carvey. 2004. The icsi meeting recoder dialog act (MRDA) corpus. In *Proceedings of the 5th SIGdial Workshop on Discourse and Dialogue*, pages 97–100. Cambridge, MA.

Shum, Simon Buckingham. 1998. Evolving the web for scientific knowledge: First steps towards an "HCI knowledge web". *Interfaces, British HCI Group Magazine* 39:16–21.

Shum, Simon Buckingham, Enrico Motta, and John Domingue. 1999. Representing scholarly claims in internet digital libraries: A knowledge modelling approach. In *Proceedings of ECDL'99: Third European Conference on Research and Advanced Technology for Digital Libraries*, Lecture Notes in Computer Science. Heidelberg, Germany: Springer Verlag.

Shum, Simon Buckingham, Victoria Uren, Gangmin Li, John Domingue, and Enrico Motta. 2002. Visualizing internetworked argumentation. In P. A. Kirschner, S. J. B. Shum, and C. S. Carr, eds., *Visualizing Argumentation: Software Tools for Collaborative and Educational Sense-Making*. London: Springer-Verlag.

Shum, Simon Buckingham, Victoria Uren, Gangmin Li, Bertrand Sereno, and Clara Mancini. 2004. Modelling naturalistic argumentation in research literatures: Representation and interaction design issues. Tech. Rep. kmi-04-28, Knowledge Media Institute, Open University.

Siddharthan, Advaith. 2003. *Syntactic simplification and Text Cohesion*. Ph.D. thesis, University of Cambridge, UK.

Siddharthan, Advaith and Simone Teufel. 2007. Whose idea was this, and why does it matter? Attributing scientific work to citations. In *Proceedings of the North American chapter of the Association of Computational Linguistics (NAACL-07)*.

Siegel, Sidney and N. John Jr. Castellan. 1988. *Nonparametric Statistics for the Behavioral Sciences*. Berkeley, CA: McGraw-Hill, 2nd edn.

SIGMOD. 1999. `http://www.acm.org/sigs/sigmod/sigmod99`.

Sillince, John Anthony Arthur. 1992. Literature searching with unclear objectives: A new approach using argumentation. *Online Review* 16(6):391–410.

Skorochod'ko, E. F. 1972. Adaptive method of automatic abstracting and indexing. In *Information Processing 71*, vol. 2, pages 1179–1182. North-Holland.

Small, Henry G. 1973. Co-citation in the scientific literature: A new measure of the relationship between two documents. *Journal of the American Society for Information Science* 24:265–269.

Solov'ev, V. I. 1981. Functional characteristics of the author's abstract of a dissertation and the specifics of writing it. *Scientific and Technical Information Processing* 3:80–88. English translation of *Nauchno-Tekhnicheskaya Informatsiya*, Seriya 1, Number 6, 1981, 20–24.

Spangler, W. Scott, J. Kreulen, and J. Lessler. 2002. Mindmap: Utilizing multiple taxonomies and visualization to understand a document collection. In *35th Annual Hawaii International Conference on System Sciences (HICSS'02)*, page 102.

Spärck Jones, Karen. 1988. Tailoring output to the user: What does user modelling in generation mean? tr–158. Tech. rep., Computer Laboratory, University of Cambridge, Cambridge, UK.

Spärck Jones, Karen. 1990. What sort of thing is an AI experiment? In D. Partridge and Y. Wilks, eds., *The Foundations of Artificial Intelligence: A Sourcebook*. Cambridge, UK: Cambridge University Press.

Spärck Jones, Karen. 1994. Discourse modelling for automatic summarising. Tech. Rep. TR-290, Computer Laboratory, University of Cambridge.

Spärck Jones, Karen. 1999. Automatic summarising: Factors and directions. In I. Mani and M. T. Maybury, eds., *Advances in Automatic Text Summarization*, pages 1–12. Cambridge, MA: MIT Press.

Spärck Jones, Karen and Julia Galliers. 1996. *Evaluating Natural Language Systems*. Springer Verlag.

Spärck Jones, Karen and Cornelis Joost van Rijsbergen. 1976. Information retrieval test collections. *Journal of Documentation* 32:59–75.

Spärck Jones, Karen and Peter Willett. 1997. *Readings in Information Retrieval*. San Francisco: Morgan Kauffman.

Spiegel-Rösing, Ina. 1977. Science studies: Bibliometric and content analysis. *Social Studies of Science* 7:97–113.

Sporleder, Caroline and Mirella Lapata. 2006. Broad coverage paragraph segmentation across languages and domains. *ACM Transactions in Speech and Language Processing* 3(2):1–35.

Starck, Heather A. 1988. What do paragraph markings do? *Discourse Processes* 11(3):275–304.

Stolcke, Andreas, Noah Coccaro, Rebecca Bates, Paul Taylor, Carol Van Ess-Dykema, Klaus Ries, Elizabeth Shriberg, Daniel Jurafsky, Rachel Martin, and Marie Meteer. 2000. Dialogue act modeling for automatic tagging and recognition of conversational speech. *Computational Linguistics* 26:339–373.

Strzalkowski, Tomek, Gees Stein, Jin Wang, and Bowden Wise. 1999. A robust practical text summarizer. In I. Mani and M. T. Maybury, eds., *Advances in Automatic Text Summarization*, pages 137–154. Cambridge, MA: MIT Press.

Sumner, Tamara and Simon Buckingham Shum. 1998. From documents to discourse: Shifting conceptions of scholarly publishing. In A. Press, ed., *Proceedings of the CHI-98 ACM*, pages 95–102. New York, NY.

Suppe, Frederick. 1993. Credentialing scientific claims. *Perspectives on Science* 1/2:153–202.

Suppe, Frederick. 1998. The structure of a scientific paper. *Philosophy of Science* 65:381–405.

Swales, John. 1986. Citation analysis and discourse analysis. *Applied Linguistics* 7(1):39–56.

Swales, John. 1990. *Genre Analysis: English in Academic and Research Settings. Chapter 7: Research articles in English*, pages 110–176. Cambridge, UK: Cambridge University Press.

Swales, John and C. B. Feak. 2000. *English in Today's Research World: A Writing Guide*. Ann Arbour, MI: The University of Michigan Press.

Taddio, A., T. Pain, F. F. Fassos, H. Boon, A. L. Ilersich, and Elnarson T. R. 1994. Quality of nonstructured and structured abstracts of original research articles in the *british medical journal*, the *canadian medical association journal* and the *journal of the american medical association*. *Canadian Medical Association Journal* 150(10):1611–1615.

Tbahriti, Imad, Christine Chichester, Frederique Lisacek, and Patrick Ruch. 2006. Using argumentation to retrieve articles with similar citations: An inquiry into improving related articles search in the medline digital library. *International Journal OF Medical Informatics* 75(6):488–495.

Teufel, Simone. 1998. Meta-discourse markers and problem-structuring in scientific articles. In *Proceedings of the ACL-98 Workshop on Discourse Structure and Discourse Markers*, pages 43–49. Montreal, Canada.

Teufel, Simone. 2000. *Argumentative Zoning: Information Extraction from Scientific Text*. Ph.D. thesis, School of Cognitive Science, University of Edinburgh, Edinburgh, UK.

Teufel, Simone. 2001. Task-based evaluation of summary quality: Describing relationships between scientific papers. In *Proceedings of NAACL-01 Workshop "Automatic Text Summarization"*. Pittsburgh, PA.

Teufel, Simone. 2005. Argumentative zoning for improved citation indexing. In J. G. Shanahan, Y. Qu, and J. Wiebe, eds., *Computing Attitude and Affect in Text: Theory and Applications*, pages 159–170. Springer.

Teufel, Simone, Jean Carletta, and Marc Moens. 1999. An annotation scheme for discourse-level argumentation in research articles. In *Proceedings of the 9th Meeting of the European Chapter of the Association for Computational Linguistics (EACL-99)*, pages 110–117. Bergen, Norway.

Teufel, Simone and Noemie Elhadad. 2002. Collection and linguistic processing of a large-scale corpus of medical articles. In *Proceedings of the Third International Conference on Language Resources and Evaluation (LREC 2002)*, pages 1214–1219.

Teufel, Simone and Marc Moens. 1997. Sentence extraction as a classification task. In I. Mani and M. T. Maybury, eds., *Proceedings of the ACL/EACL-97 Workshop on Intelligent Scalable Text Summarization*, pages 58–65.

Teufel, Simone and Marc Moens. 1998. Sentence extraction and rhetorical classification for flexible abstracts. In D. R. Radev and E. H. Hovy, eds., *Working Notes of the AAAI Spring Symposium on Intelligent Text Summarization*, pages 16–25.

Teufel, Simone and Marc Moens. 2002. Summarising scientific articles — experiments with relevance and rhetorical status. *Computational Linguistics* 28(4):409–446.

Teufel, Simone, Advaith Siddharthan, and Colin Batchelor. 2009. Towards discipline-independent argumentative zoning: Evidence from chemistry and computational linguistics. In *Proceedings of EMNLP-09*. Singapore.

Teufel, Simone, Advaith Siddharthan, and Dan Tidhar. 2006a. An annotation scheme for citation function. In *Proceedings of SIGDIAL-06*. Sydney, Australia.

Teufel, Simone, Advaith Siddharthan, and Dan Tidhar. 2006b. Automatic classification of citation function. In *Proceedings of EMNLP-06*.

Thomas, Sarah and Thomas Hawes. 1994. Reporting verbs in medical journal articles. *English for Specific Purposes* 13(4):129–148.

Thompson, Geoff and Ye Yiyun. 1991. Evaluation in the reporting verbs used in academic papers. *Applied Linguistics* 12(4):365–382.

Tibbo, Helen R. 1992. Abstracting across the disciplines: A content analysis of abstracts from the natural sciences, and the humanities with implications for abstracting standards and online information retrieval. *Library and Information Science Research* 14(1):31–56.

Tipster SUMMAC. 1999. `http://www.itl.nist.gov/div894/894.02/related_projects/tipster_summac/index/cmp_lg.html`.

Tombros, Anastasios, Mark Sanderson, and Phil Gray. 1998. Advantages of query biased summaries in information retrieval. In D. R. Radev and E. H. Hovy, eds., *Working Notes of the AAAI Spring Symposium on Intelligent Text Summarization*.

Toulmin, Stephen, ed. 1972. *Human Understanding: The Collective Use and Evolution of Concepts*. Princeton, NJ: Princeton University Press.

Townsend, Joe, Ann Copestake, Peter Murray-Rust, Simone Teufel, and Chris Waudby. 2005. Language technology for processing chemistry publications. In *Proc. UK e-Science All Hands Meeting*. Nottingham, UK.

Trawinski, Bogdan. 1989. A methodology for writing problem-structured abstracts. *Information Processing and Management* 25(6):693–702.

Turney, Peter. 2002. Thumbs up or thumbs down? Semantic orientation applied to unsupervised classification of reviews. In *Proceedings of the 40th Annual Meeting of the Association for Computational Linguistics (ACL-02)*, pages 417–424. Philadelphia, PA.

Uren, Victoria, Simon Buckingham Shum, M. Bachler, and Gangmin Li. 2006. Sensemaking tools for understanding research literatures: Design, implementation and user evaluation. *International Journal of Human Computer Studies* 64(5):420–445.

Uren, Victoria, Simon Buckingham Shum, Gangmin Li, John Domingue, and Enrico Motta. 2003. Scholarly publishing and argument in hyperspace. In *WWW2003*.

van Dijk, Teun A. 1980. *Macrostructures: An Interdisciplinary Study of Global Structures in Discourse, Interaction and Cognition*. Hillsdale, NJ: Lawrence Erlbaum.

van Emden, Joan and Jennifer Easteal. 1996. *Technical Writing and Speaking: An Introduction*. London, UK: McGraw-Hill.

van Halteren, Hans and Simone Teufel. 2003. Examining the consensus between human summaries: initial experiments with factoid analysis. In *Proceedings of the HLT workshop on Automatic Summarization*.

van Rijsbergen, Cornelis Joost. 1979. *Information Retrieval*. London, UK: Butterworth, 2nd edn.

Vaughan, Liwen and Debora Shaw. 2008. A new look at evidence of scholarly citation in citation indexes and from web sources. *Scientometrics* 74(2):317–330.

Vilain, Mark, John Burger, John Aberdeen, Dennis Connolly, and Hirschman Lynette. 1995. A model-theoretic coreference scoring scheme. In *Proceedings of MUC-6*.

Wan, Xiaojun. 2008. Using bilingual knowledge and ensemble techniques for unsupervised chinese sentiment analysis. In *Proceedings of EMNLP-08*.

Webber, Bonnie L. 2004. D-LTAG: Extending lexicalized TAG to discourse. *Cognitive Science* 28(5):751–779.

Weil, B. H., H. Owen, and I. Zarember. 1963. Technical abstracting fundamentals. ii. writing principles and practices. *Journal of Chemical Documentation* 3(2):125–132.

Weinstock, Melvin. 1971. Citation indexes. In *Encyclopedia of Library and Information Science*, vol. 5, pages 16–40. New York, NY: Dekker.

Weissberg, Robert and Susanne Buker. 1990. *Writing up Research: Experimental Research Report Writing for Students of English*. Prentice Hall.

Wellons, M. E. and G. P. Purcell. 1999. Task-specific extracts for using the medical literature. In *Proceedings of the American Medical Informatics Symposium*, pages 1004–1008.

West, Gregory K. 1980. That-nominal constructions in traditional rhetorical divisions of scientific research papers. *TESOL Quarterly* 14(4):483–488.

White, Howard D. 2004. Citation analysis and discourse analysis revisited. *Applied Linguistics* 25(1):89–116.

Wiebe, Janyce. 1994. Tracking point of view in narrative. *Computational Linguistics* 20(2):223–287.

Wiebe, Janyce, Rebecca F. Bruce, and Thomas P. O'Hara. 1999. Development and use of a gold-standard data set for subjectivity classifications. In *Proceedings of 37th Annual Meeting of the Association for Computational Linguistics (ACL-99)*, pages 246–253. College Park, Maryland.

Wiebe, Janyce and Rada Mihalcea. 2006. Word sense and subjectivity. In *Proceedings of 44th Annual Meeting of the Association for Computational Linguistics and the 21st International Conference on Computational Linguistics (ACL/COLING-06)*. Sydney, Australia.

Wilson, Theresa, Janyce Wiebe, and Paul Hoffmann. 2009. Recognizing contextual polarity: an exploration of features for phrase-level sentiment analysis. *Computational Linguistics* .

Winograd, Terry. 1972. Understanding natural language. *Cognitive Psychology* 3:1–191.

Witten, Ian and Eibe Frank. 2005. *Data Mining: Practical Machine Learning Tools and Techniques*. Morgan Kaufmann, 2nd edn.

Woolgar, Steven. 1988. *Science: The very idea*. Ellis Horwood.

Yang, Wanjuan. 2002. *Automatic Identification of Cue Phrases for Summarisation*. Master's thesis, Cambridge University.

Yang, Yiming and Xin Liu. 1999. A re-examination of text categorization methods. In *Proceedings of 22nd Annual International Conference on Research and Development in Information Retrieval (SIGIR-99)*, pages 42–49.

Yu, Hong and Vasileios Hatzivassiloglou. 2003. Towards answering opinion questions: Separating facts from opinions and identifying the polarity of opinion sentences. In *Proceedings of EMNLP-03*.

Zajic, David, Bonnie J. Dorr, Richard Schwartz, and Stacy President. 2004. Headline evaluation experiment results. Tech. rep., University of Maryland, College Park, MD.

Zappen, James P. 1983. A rhetoric for research in sciences and technologies. In P. V. Anderson, R. J. Brockman, and C. R. Miller, eds., *New Essays in Technical and Scientific Communication Research Theory Practice*, pages 123–138. Farmingdale, NY: Baywood Publishing Company, Inc.

Zhang, Harry, Liangxiao Jiang, and Jiang Su. 2005. Hidden Naive Bayes. In *Proceedings of AAAI-05*.

Ziman, John M. 1968. *Public Knowledge: An Essay Concerning the Social Dimensions of Science*. Cambridge, UK: Cambridge University Press.

Ziman, John M. 1969. Information, communication, knowledge. *Nature* 224:318–324.

Zuckerman, Harriet and Robert K. Merton. 1973. Institutionalized patterns of evaluation in science. In R. K. Merton, ed., *The Sociology of Science: Theoretical and Empirical Investigations*, pages 460–496. Chicago, IL: University of Chicago Press.

Author Index

Subject Index